Foundations of Probabilistic Logic Programming
Languages, Semantics, Inference and Learning
Second Edition

RIVER PUBLISHERS SERIES IN SOFTWARE ENGINEERING

The "River Publishers Series in Software Engineering" is a series of comprehensive academic and professional books which focus on the theory and applications of Computer Science in general, and more specifically Programming Languages, Software Development and Software Engineering.

Books published in the series include research monographs, edited volumes, handbooks and textbooks. The books provide professionals, researchers, educators, and advanced students in the field with an invaluable insight into the latest research and developments.

Topics covered in the series include, but are by no means restricted to the following:

- Software Engineering
- Software Development
- Programming Languages
- Computer Science
- Automation Engineering
- Research Informatics
- Information Modelling
- Software Maintenance

For a list of other books in this series, visit www.riverpublishers.com

Foundations of Probabilistic Logic Programming
Languages, Semantics, Inference and Learning
Second Edition

Fabrizio Riguzzi

University of Ferrara, Italy

NEW YORK AND LONDON

Published 2023 by River Publishers

River Publishers

Alsbjergvej 10, 9260 Gistrup, Denmark

www.riverpublishers.com

Distributed exclusively by Routledge

605 Third Avenue, New York, NY 10017, USA

4 Park Square, Milton Park, Abingdon, Oxon OX14 4RN

Foundations of Probabilistic Logic Programming / by Fabrizio Riguzzi.

Routledge is an imprint of the Taylor & Francis Group, an informa business

ISBN 978-87-7022-719-3 (print)

ISBN 978-87-7022-958-6 (paperback)

ISBN 978-10-0092-321-6 (online)

ISBN 978-1-003-42742-1 (ebook master)

While every effort is made to provide dependable information, the publisher, authors, and editors cannot be held responsible for any errors or omissions.

Contents

Foreword

The computational foundations of Artificial Intelligence (AI) are supported by two corner stones: logics and machine learning. Computational logic has found its realization in a number of frameworks for logic-based approaches to knowledge representation and automated reasoning, such as Logic Programming, Answer Set Programming, Constraint Logic Programming, Description Logics, and Temporal Logics. Machine Learning, and its recent evolution to Deep Learning, has a huge number of applications in video surveillance, social media services, big data analysis, weather predictions, spam filtering, online customer support, etc.

Emerging interest in the two communities for finding a bridge connecting them is witnessed, for instance, by the prize *test-of-time, 20 years* assigned by the association for logic programming in 2017 to the paper *Hybrid Probabilistic Programs*. Also in 2017, Holger H. Hoos was invited to give the talk *The best of both worlds: Machine learning meets logical reasoning* at the international conference on logic programming. Here, machine learning is used to tune the search heuristics in solving combinatorial problems (e.g., encoded using SAT or ASP techniques). A couple of months later, in a panel organized by the Italian Association for Artificial Intelligence (AI*IA), the machine learning researcher Marco Gori posed five questions to the communities. Among them: *How can we integrate huge knowledge bases naturally and effectively with learning processes? How to break the barriers of machine learning vs (inductive) logic programming communities? How to derive a computational model capable of dealing with learning and reasoning both in the symbolic and sub-symbolic domains? How to acquire latent semantics?* These are fundamental questions that need to be resolved to allow AI research to make another quantum leap. Logical languages can add structural semantics to statistical inference.

This book, based on 15 years of top-level research in the field by Fabrizio Riguzzi and his co-authors, addresses these questions and fills most of the gaps between the two communities. A mature, uniform retrospective of several proposals of languages for Probabilistic Logic Programming is reported.

The reader can decide whether to explore all the technical details or simply use such languages without the need of installing tools, by simply using the web site maintained by Fabrizio's group in Ferrara.

The book is self-contained: all the prerequisites coming from discrete mathematics (often at the foundation of logical reasoning) and continuous mathematics, probability, and statistics (at the foundation of machine learning) are presented in detail. Although all proposals are summarized, those based on the distribution semantics are dealt with in a greater level of detail. The book explains how a system can reason precisely or approximately when the size of the program (and data) increases, even in the case on non-standard inference (e.g., possibilistic reasoning). The book then moves toward parameter learning and structure learning, thus reducing and possibly removing the distance with respect to machine learning. The book closes with a lovely chapter with several encodings in PLP. A reader with some knowledge of logic programming can start from this chapter, having fun testing the programs (for instance, discovering the best strategy to be applied during a *truel*, namely, a duel involving three gunners shooting sequentially) and then move to the theoretical part.

As the president of the Italian Association for Logic Programming (GULP) I am proud that this significant effort has been made by one of our associates and former member of our Executive Committee. I believe that it will become a reference book for the new generations that have to deal with the new challenges coming from the need of reasoning on Big Data.

Agostino Dovier
University of Udine

Preface to the Second Edition

The field of Probabilistic Logic Programming is rapidly growing and much has happened since the first edition of this book in 2018. This new edition aims at reporting the most exciting novelties since 2018.

The semantics for hybrid programs with function symbols was placed on a sound footing and this is presented in Chapter 5.

Probabilistic Answer Set Programming gained a lot of interest and a whole chapter is now devoted to it (Chapter 6). Several works have started to appear on the complexity of inference in PLP and PASP and they are now surveyed in Chapter 7.

Algorithms specifically devoted to solving the MPE and MAP tasks are described in Section 8.9.

Inference for hybrid programs has changed dramatically with the introduction of Weighted Model Integration (see Section 12.2) so that the whole set of inference approaches for hybrid programs is now collected in their own Chapter 12.

With respect to learning, the first approaches for neuro-symbolic integration have appeared (DeeProbLog, see Section 13.7) together with algorithms for structure learning hybrid programs (DiceML, see Section 14.6).

Moreover, given the cost of learning PLPs, various works proposed language restrictions to speed up learning and improve its scaling: LIFTCOVER, see Section 14.7.1, and SLEAHP, see Section 14.7.2.

Finally, this second edition gave me the opportunity to fix various errors and imprecisions that were unfortunately present in the first edition.

Preface

The field of Probabilistic logic programming (PLP) was started in the early 1990s by seminal works such as those of [Dantsin, 1991], [Ng and Subrahmanian, 1992], [Poole, 1993b], and [Sato, 1995].

However, the problem of combining logic and probability has been studied since the 1950s [Carnap, 1950; Gaifman, 1964]. Then the problem became prominent in the field of Artificial Intelligence in the late 1980s to early 1990s when researchers tried to reconcile the probabilistic and logical approaches to AI [Nilsson, 1986; Halpern, 1990; Fagin and Halpern, 1994; Halpern, 2003].

The integration of logic and probability combines the capability of the first to represent complex relations among entities with the capability of the latter to model uncertainty over attributes and relations. Logic programming provides a Turing complete language based on logic and thus represents an excellent candidate for the integration.

Since its birth, the field of Probabilistic Logic Programming has seen a steady increase of activity, with many proposals for languages and algorithms for inference and learning. The language proposals can be grouped into two classes: those that use a variant of the Distribution semantics (DS) [Sato, 1995] and those that follow a Knowledge Base Model Construction (KBMC) approach [Wellman et al., 1992; Bacchus, 1993].

Under the DS, a probabilistic logic program defines a probability distribution over normal logic programs and the probability of a ground query is then obtained from the joint distribution of the query and the programs. Some of the languages following the DS are: Probabilistic Logic Programs [Dantsin, 1991], Probabilistic Horn Abduction [Poole, 1993b], PRISM [Sato, 1995], Independent Choice Logic [Poole, 1997], pD [Fuhr, 2000], Logic Programs with Annotated Disjunctions [Vennekens et al., 2004], ProbLog [De Raedt et al., 2007], P-log [Baral et al., 2009], and CP-logic [Vennekens et al., 2009].

Instead, in KBMC languages, a program is seen as a template for generating a ground graphical model, be it a Bayesian network or a Markov network. KBMC languages include Relational Bayesian Network [Jaeger, 1998], CLP(BN) [Costa et al., 2003], Bayesian Logic Programs [Kersting and De Raedt, 2001], and the Prolog Factor Language [Gomes and Costa, 2012]. The distinction among DS and KBMC languages is actually non-sharp as programs in languages following the DS can also be translated into graphical models.

This book aims at providing an overview of the field of PLP, with a special emphasis on languages under the DS. The reason is that their approach to logic-probability integration is particularly simple and coherent across languages but nevertheless powerful enough to be useful in a variety of domains. Moreover, they can be given a semantics in purely logical terms, without necessarily resorting to a translation into graphical models.

The book doesn't aim though at being a complete account of the topic, even when restricted to the DS, as the field has grown large, with a dedicated workshop series started in 2014. My objective is to present the main ideas for semantics, inference, and learning and to highlight connections between the methods.

The intended audience of the book are researchers in Computer Science and AI that want to get an overview of PLP. However, it can also be used by students, especially graduate, to get acquainted with the topic, and by practitioners that would like to get more details on the inner workings of methods.

Many examples of the book include a link to a page of the web application `cplint` on SWISH (https://cplint.eu) [Riguzzi et al., 2016a; Alberti et al., 2017], where the code can be run online using `cplint`, a system we developed at the University of Ferrara that includes many algorithms for inference and learning in a variety of languages.

The book starts with Chapter 1 that presents preliminary notions of logic programming and graphical models. Chapter 2 introduces the languages under the DS, discusses the basic form of the semantics, and compares it with alternative approaches in PLP and AI in general. Chapter 3, describes the semantics for languages allowing function symbols. Chapters 4 and 5 present the semantics for languages with continuous random variables, without and with function symbols respectively. Probabilistic Answer Set Programming is discussed in Chapter 6 while Chapter 7 presents complexity results. Chapter 8 illustrates various algorithms for exact inference. Lifted inference is discussed in Chatper 9 and approximate inference in Chapter 10. Non-standard inference problems are illustrated in Chapter 11. Chapter 12 presents inference for programs with continuous random variables. Then Chapters 13 and 14 treat the problem of learning parameters and structure of programs, respectively. Chapter 15 presents some examples of use of the system `cplint`. Chapter 16 concludes the book discussing open problems.

Acknowledgments

I am indebted to many persons for their help and encouragement. Evelina Lamma and Paola Mello taught me to love logical reasoning and always supported me, especially during the bad times. My co-workers at the University of Ferrara Evelina Lamma, Elena Bellodi, Riccardo Zese, Giuseppe Cota, Marco Alberti, Marco Gavanelli, Arnaud Nguembang Fadja and Damiano Azzolini greatly helped me shape my view of PLP through exiting joint work and insightful discussions. I have been lucky enough to collaborate also with Theresa Swift, Nicola Di Mauro, Stefano Bragaglia, Vitor Santos Costa, and Jan Wielemaker and the joint work with them has found its way into the book.

Agostino Dovier, Evelina Lamma, Elena Bellodi, Riccardo Zese, Giuseppe Cota, and Marco Alberti read drafts of the book and gave me very useful comments.

I would also like to thank Michela Milano, Federico Chesani, Paolo Torroni, Luc De Raedt, Angelika Kimmig, Wannes Meert, Joost Vennekens, and Kristian Kersting for many enlightening exchanges of ideas.

This book evolved from a number of articles. In particular, Chapter 2 is based on [Riguzzi and Swift, 2018], Chapter 3 on [Riguzzi, 2016], Chapter 5 on [Azzolini et al., 2021], Section 8.6 on [Riguzzi and Swift, 2010, 2011, 2013], Section 8.10 on [Riguzzi, 2014], Section 10.2 on [Riguzzi, 2013], Chapter 9 on [Riguzzi et al., 2017a], Section 13.4 on [Bellodi and Riguzzi, 2013, 2012], Section 14.2 on [Riguzzi, 2004, 2007b, 2008b], Section 14.5 on [Bellodi and Riguzzi, 2015], Section 14.7.1 on [Nguembang Fadja and Riguzzi, 2019], Section 14.7.2 on [Nguembang Fadja et al., 2021] and Chapter 15 on [Riguzzi et al., 2016a; Alberti et al., 2017; Riguzzi et al., 2017b; Nguembang Fadja and Riguzzi, 2017].

Finally, I would like to thank my wife Cristina for putting up with a husband with the crazy idea of writing a book without taking a sabbatical. Without her love and support, I would not have been able to bring the idea into reality.

List of Figures

List of Tables

List of Examples

List of Definitions

xxxiii

List of Theorems

List of Acronyms

ADD Algebraic decision diagram

AMC Algebraic model counting

ASP Answer set programming

BDD Binary decision diagram

BN Bayesian network

CBDD Complete binary decision diagram

CLP Constraint logic programming

CNF Conjunctive normal form

CPT Conditional probability table

DC Distributional clauses

DCG Definite clause grammar

d-DNNF Deterministic decomposable negation normal form

DLT Distributional logic tree

DP Dirichlet process

DS Distribution semantics

EM Expectation maximization

ESS Expected sufficient statistics

FED Factored explanation diagram

FG Factor graph

GP Gaussian process

HMM Hidden markov model

HPT Hybrid probability tree

ICL Independent choice logic

IHPMC Iterative hybrid probabilistic model counting

IID independent and identically distributed

ILP Inductive logic programming

JMP Joint model program

LDA Latent dirichlet allocation

LL Log likelihood

LPAD Logic program with annotated disjunctions

MCMC Markov chain monte carlo

MDD Multivalued decision diagram

MLN Markov logic network

MN Markov network

NAD Neural annotated disjunction

NLP Natural language processing

NN Neural network

NNF Negation normal form

PASP Probabilistic answer set programming

PCFG Probabilistic context-free grammar

PCLP Probabilistic constraint logic programming

PHA Probabilistic horn abduction

PHPT Partially evaluated hybrid probability tree

PILP Probabilistic inductive logic programming

PLCG Probabilistic left corner grammar

PLP Probabilistic logic programming

POS Part-of-speech

PPDF Product probability density function

PPR Personalized page rank

PRV Parameterized random variable

QSAR Quantitative structure-activity relationship

SAT Satisfiability

SDD Sentential decision diagram

SLP Stochastic logic program

SMT Satisfiability modulo theory

WFF Well-formed formula

WFM Well-founded model

WFOMC Weighted first order model counting

WFS Well-founded semantics

WMC Weighted model counting

WMI Weighted model integration

1

Preliminaries

This chapter provides basic notions of logic programing and graphical models that are needed for the book. After the introduction of a few mathematical concepts, the chapter presents logic programming and the various semantics for negation. Then it provides a brief recall of probability theory and graphical models.

For a more in-depth treatment of logic programming see [Lloyd, 1987; Sterling and Shapiro, 1994] and of graphical models see [Koller and Friedman, 2009].

1.1 Orders, Lattices, Ordinals

A *partial order* $\leqslant$ is a reflexive, antisymmetric, and transitive relation. A *partially ordered set* S is a set with a partial order $\leqslant$. For example, the natural numbers $\mathbb{N}$ (non-negative integers), the positive integers $\mathbb{N}_1$, and the real numbers $\mathbb{R}$ with the standard less-than-or-equal relation $\leqslant$ are partially ordered sets and so is the powerset $\mathbb{P}(S)$ (the set of all subsets) of a set S with the inclusion relation between subsets $\subseteq$. $a \in S$ is an *upper bound* of a subset X of S if $x \leqslant a$ for all $x \in X$ and $b \in S$ is a *lower bound* of X if $b \leqslant x$ for all $x \in X$. If it also holds that $a \in X$ and $b \in X$, then a is called the *largest element* of X and b the *smallest element* of X.

An element $a \in S$ is the *least upper bound* of a subset X of S if a is an upper bound of X and, for all upper bounds a' of X, $a \leqslant a'$. An element $b \in S$ is the *greatest lower bound* of a subset X of S if b is a lower bound of X and, for all lower bounds b' of X, $b' \leqslant b$. The least upper bound of X may not exist. If it does, it is unique and we denote it with $\mathrm{lub}(X)$. Similarly, the greatest lower bound of X may not exist. If it does, it is unique and is denoted by $\mathrm{glb}(X)$. For example, for $\mathbb{P}(S)$ and $X \subseteq \mathbb{P}(S)$, $\mathrm{lub}(X) = \bigcup_{x \in X} x$, and $\mathrm{glb}(X) = \bigcap_{x \in X} x$.

A partially ordered set L is a *complete lattice* if $\text{lub}(X)$ and $\text{glb}(X)$ exist for every subset X of L. We denote with $\top$ the *top element* $\text{lub}(L)$ and with $\bot$ the *bottom element* $\text{glb}(L)$ of the complete lattice L. For example, the powerset is a complete lattice.

A relation $<$, defined by $a < b$ iff $a \leqslant b$ and $a \neq b$, is associated with any partial order $\leqslant$ on S.

A partial order $\leqslant$ on a set S is a *total order* if it is *total*, i.e., for any $a, b \in S$, either $a \leqslant b$ or $b \leqslant a$. A set S with a total order is called a *totally ordered set*. A set S is *well-ordered* if it has a total order $\leqslant$ such that every subset of S has a smallest element. The set $\mathbb{N}$ is well-ordered by its usual order, the real line $\mathbb{R}$ is not.

A function $f : A \rightarrow B$ is *one-to-one* if $f^{-1}(\{b\})$ is a set containing a single element. f is *onto* B if $f(A) = B$. A set A is *equipotent* with a set B iff there is a one-to-one function f from A onto B. Equipotency captures the intuitive notion of having the same number of elements.

A set S is *denumerable* iff S is equipotent with $\mathbb{N}$. A set S is *countable* iff it is finite or denumerable, S is *uncountable* otherwise.

Ordinal numbers are a generalization of natural numbers. The set $\mathbf{\Omega}$ of *ordinal numbers* is well-ordered. We call its elements *ordinals* and we denote them by Greek smallcase letters. Since $\mathbf{\Omega}$ is well-ordered, it has a smallest element, that we denote with 0. If $\alpha < \beta$, we say that α is a *predecessor* of β and β is a *successor* of α. α is the *immediate predecessor* of β and β is the *immediate successor* of α if α is the largest ordinal smaller than β. Every ordinal α has an immediate successor, denoted with $\alpha+1$. Some ordinals have predecessors but no immediate predecessor, which are called *limit ordinals*. The others are called *successor ordinals*. We denote the immediate successor of the least element 0 with 1, the immediate successor of 1 with 2, and so on. So the first elements $0, 1, 2, \ldots$ of $\mathbf{\Omega}$ are the naturals. Since $\mathbf{\Omega}$ is well-ordered, there is a smallest ordinal larger than $0, 1, 2, \ldots$ that we denote with ω. It is the *first infinite ordinal* and is countable. We can form its successors as $\omega + 1, \omega + 2, \ldots$, effectively adding a "copy" of $\mathbb{N}$ to the tail of ω. The smallest ordinal larger than $\omega + 1, \omega + 2, \ldots$ is called 2ω and we can continue in this way building 3ω, 4ω, and so on.

The smallest ordinal larger than these is ω^2. We can repeat the process countably many times obtaining ω^3, ω^4, and so on.

A canonical representation of the ordinals (the so-called *von Neumann ordinals*) sees each ordinal as the set of its predecessors, so $0 = \varnothing, 1 = \{\varnothing\}$, $2 = \{\varnothing, \{\varnothing\}\}, 3 = \{\varnothing, \{\varnothing\}, \{\varnothing, \{\varnothing\}\}\}, \ldots$ In this case, the order is set membership.

The sequence of ordinals is also called *transfinite*. Mathematical induction is extended to the ordinals with the *principle of transfinite induction*. Suppose $P(\alpha)$ is a property defined for all ordinals $\alpha \in \Omega$. To prove that P is true for all ordinals by transfinite induction, we need to assume the fact that $P(\beta)$ is true for all $\beta < \alpha$ and prove that $P(\alpha)$ is true. Proofs by transfinite induction usually consider two cases: that α is a successor ordinal, or a limit ordinal.

See [Srivastava, 2013] for a full formal definition of ordinal numbers and [Willard, 1970; Hitzler and Seda, 2016] for accessible introductions.

1.2 Mappings and Fixpoints

A function $T : L \to L$ from a lattice L to itself is a *mapping*. A mapping T is *monotonic* if $T(x) \leqslant T(y)$, for all x and y such that $x \leqslant y$. $a \in L$ is a *fixpoint* of T if $T(a) = a$. $a \in L$ is the *least fixpoint* of T if a is a fixpoint and, for all fixpoints b of T, it holds that $a \leqslant b$. Similarly, we define the *greatest fixpoint*.

Consider a complete lattice L and a monotonic mapping $T : L \to L$. We define the *increasing ordinal powers* of T as:

- $T \uparrow 0 = \bot$;
- $T \uparrow \alpha = T(T \uparrow (\alpha - 1))$, if α is a successor ordinal;
- $T \uparrow \alpha = \mathrm{lub}(\{T \uparrow \beta | \beta < \alpha\})$, if α is a limit ordinal;

and the *decreasing ordinal powers* of T as:

- $T \downarrow 0 = \top$;
- $T \downarrow \alpha = T(T \downarrow (\alpha - 1))$, if α is a successor ordinal;
- $T \downarrow \alpha = \mathrm{glb}(\{T \downarrow \beta | \beta < \alpha\})$, if α is a limit ordinal.

The Knaster–Tarski theorem [Knaster and Tarski, 1928; Tarski, 1955] states that if L is complete lattice and T a monotonic mapping, then the set of fixpoints of T in L is also a lattice. An important consequence of the theorem is the following proposition.

Proposition 1 (Monotonic Mappings Have a Least and Greatest Fixpoint). *Let L be a complete lattice and $T : L \to L$ be monotonic. Then T has a least fixpoint, $\mathrm{lfp}(T)$ and a greatest fixpoint $\mathrm{gfp}(T)$.*

A sequence $\{x_\alpha | \alpha \in \Omega\}$ is *increasing* if $x_\beta \leqslant x_\alpha$ for all $\beta \leqslant \alpha$ and is *decreasing* if $x_\alpha \leqslant x_\beta$ for all $\beta \leqslant \alpha$.

The increasing and decreasing ordinal powers of a monotonic mapping form an increasing and a decreasing sequence, respectively. Let us prove it for $T \uparrow \alpha$ by transfinite induction. If α is a successor ordinal, $T \uparrow (\alpha - 2)$ $\leqslant T \uparrow (\alpha - 1)$ for the inductive hypothesis. By the monotonicity of T, $T(T \uparrow (\alpha - 2)) \leqslant T(T \uparrow (\alpha - 1))$, so $T \uparrow (\alpha - 1) \leqslant T \uparrow \alpha$. Since $T \uparrow \beta \leqslant T \uparrow (\alpha - 1)$ for all $\beta \leqslant \alpha - 1$, for the transitivity of $\leqslant$, the thesis is proved. If α is a limit ordinal, $T \uparrow \alpha = \mathrm{lub}(\{T \uparrow \beta | \beta < \alpha\})$, so the thesis is proved. It can be proved for $T \downarrow \alpha$ similarly. Note that in general the fact that T is a monotonic mapping does not imply that $x \leqslant T(x)$ for all x.

1.3 Logic Programming

This section provides some basic notions of first-order logic languages and logic programming.

A *first-order logic language* is defined by an alphabet that consists of the following sets of symbols: variables, constants, functions symbols, predicate symbols, logical connectives, quantifiers, and punctuation symbols. The last three are the same for all logic languages. The connectives are $\neg$ (negation), $\wedge$ (conjunction), $\vee$ (disjunction), $\leftarrow$ (implication), and $\leftrightarrow$ (equivalence); the quantifiers are the existential quantifier $\exists$ and the universal quantifier $\forall$, and the punctuation symbols are "(", ")", and ",".

Well-formed formulas (WFFs) of the language are the syntactically correct clauses of the language and are inductively defined by combining elementary formulas, called *atomic formulas*, by means of logical connectives and quantifiers. On their turn, atomic formulas are obtained by applying the predicates symbols to elementary terms.

A *term* is defined recursively as follows: a variable is a term, a constant is a term, if f is a function symbol with *arity* n and $t_1, \ldots, t_n$ are terms, then $f(t_1, \ldots, t_n)$ is a term. An *atomic formula* or *atom* a is the application of a predicate symbol p with arity n to n terms: $p(t_1, \ldots, t_n)$.

The following notation for the symbols will be adopted: predicates, functions, and constants start with a lowercase letter, while variables start with an uppercase letter (as in the Prolog programming language, see below). So $x, y, \ldots$ are constants and $X, Y, \ldots$ are variables. Bold typeface is used throughout the book for vectors, so $\boldsymbol{X}, \boldsymbol{Y}, \ldots$ are vectors of logical variables.

An example of a term is $mary$, a constant, or $father(mary)$, a complex term, where $father$ is a function symbol with arity 1. An example of an atom is $parent(father(mary), mary)$ where $parent$ is a predicate with arity 2. To take into account the arity, function symbols and predicates are usually indicated as *father*/1 and *parent*/2. In this case, the symbols *father* and *parent* are called functors. Atoms are indicated with lowercase letters $a, b, \ldots$

A WFF is defined recursively as follows:

- every atom a is a WFF;
- if A and B are WFFs, then also $\neg A$, $A \wedge B$, $A \vee B$, $A \leftarrow B$, $A \leftrightarrow B$ are WFFs (possibly enclosed in balanced brackets);
- if A is WFF and X is a variable, $\forall X\ A$ and $\exists X\ A$ are WFF.

A *variant* ϕ' of a formula ϕ is obtained by renaming all the variables in ϕ.

The class of formulas called clauses has important properties. A *clause* is a formula of the form

$$\forall X_1 \forall X_2 \ldots \forall X_s (a_1 \vee \ldots \vee a_n \vee \neg b_1 \vee \ldots \vee \neg b_m)$$

where each a_i, b_i are atoms and $X_1, X_2, \ldots, X_s$ are all the variables occurring in $(a_1 \vee \ldots \vee a_n \vee \neg b_1 \vee \ldots \vee \neg b_m)$. The clause above can also be represented as follows:

$$a_1 ; \ldots ; a_n \leftarrow b_1, \ldots, b_m$$

where commas stand for conjunctions and semicolons for disjunctions. The part preceding the symbol $\leftarrow$ is called the *head* of the clause, while the part following it is called the *body*. An atom or the negation of an atom is called a *literal*. A *positive literal* is an atom, and a *negative literal* is the negation of an atom. Sometimes, clauses will be represented by means of a set of literals:

$$\{a_1, \ldots, a_n, \neg b_1, \ldots, \neg b_m\}$$

An example of a clause is

$$male(X) ; female(X) \leftarrow human(X).$$

A clause is a *denial* if it has no positive literal, *definite* if it has one positive literal, and *disjunctive* if it has more than one positive literal. A *Horn clause* is either a definite clause or a denial. A *fact* is a definite clause without negative literals, the $\leftarrow$ symbol is omitted for facts. A clause C is *range restricted* if and only if the variables appearing in the head are a subset of those in the body. A *definite logic program* P is a finite set of definite clauses.

Examples of a definite clause, a denial, and a fact are, respectively:
$$human(X) \leftarrow female(X)$$
$$\leftarrow male(X), female(X)$$
$$female(mary)$$

In this book, I will also present clauses in monospaced font especially when they form programs that can be directly input into a logic programming system (*concrete syntax*). In that case, the implication symbol is represented by :− as in

```
human(X) :- female(X).
```

In logic programming, another type of negation is also taken into account, namely, the so-called *default negation* $\sim$. The formula $\sim a$ where a is an atom is called a *default negative literal*, sometimes abbreviated as simply *negative literal* if the meaning is clear from the context. A *default literal* is either an atom (a *positive literal*) or a default negative literal. Again the word default can be dropped if the meaning is clear from the context.

A *normal clause* is a clause of the form

$$a \leftarrow b_1, \ldots, b_m$$

where each b_i is a default literal. A *normal logic program* is a finite set of normal clauses. Default negation in the concrete syntax is represented either with \+ (Prolog, see page 9) or not (Answer Set Programming, see Section 1.4.3). In this book, we will use the Prolog convention and use \+.

A normal clause is *range restricted* if and only if the variables appearing in the head are a subset of those appearing in positive literals in the body. A normal logic program is *range restricted* if and only if all of its clauses are range restricted.

A *substitution* $\theta = \{X_1/t_1, \ldots, X_k/t_k\}$ is a function mapping variables to terms. $\theta = \{X/father(mary), Y/mary\}$ is an example of a substitution. The *application* $\phi\theta$ of a substitution θ to a formula ϕ means replacing all the occurrences of each variable X_j in ϕ by the same term t_j. So $parent(X, Y)\theta$ is, for example, $parent(father(mary), mary)$.

The composition $\theta\sigma$, of two substitutions $\theta = \{X_1/t_1, \ldots, X_k/t_k\}$ and $\sigma = \{Y_1/s_1, \ldots, Y_m/s_m\}$ is defined as the substitution obtained by removing from the set

$$\{X_1/t_1\sigma, \ldots, X_k/t_k\sigma, Y_1/s_1, \ldots, Y_m/s_m\}$$

the pairs $X_i/t_i\sigma$ such that X_i is equal to $t_i\sigma$ and the pairs Y_i/s_i such that $Y_i \in \{X_1, \ldots, X_k\}$. Composition is associative and $\phi(\theta\sigma) = (\phi\theta)\sigma$.

Given two substitutions, θ and σ, we we say that θ is *at least as general as* σ (and we write $\theta \leqslant \sigma$) if there exists a substitution γ such that $\theta\gamma = \sigma$. The relation $\leqslant$ is a preorder (a binary relation that is reflexive and transitive).

Given two formulas, ϕ and ϕ', a substitution θ such that $\phi\theta = \phi'\theta$ is called a *unifier*. The *most general unifier* of ϕ and ϕ' is a unifier θ that is most general, i.e., such that, for every other unifier σ, $\theta \leqslant \sigma$.

A *ground* clause (term) is a clause (term) without variables. A substitution θ is *grounding* for a formula ϕ if $\phi\theta$ is ground.

The *Herbrand universe* $\mathcal{U}$ of a language or a program is the set of all the ground terms that can be obtained by combining the symbols in the language or program. The *Herbrand base* $\mathcal{B}$ of a language or a program is the set of all possible ground atoms built with the symbols in the language or program. Sometimes they will be indicated with $\mathcal{U}_P$ and $\mathcal{B}_P$ where P is the program. The *grounding $ground(P)$ of a program* P is obtained by replacing the variables of clauses in P with terms from $\mathcal{U}_P$ in all possible ways.

If P does not contain function symbols, then $\mathcal{U}_P$ is equal to the set of constants and is finite; otherwise, it is infinite (e.g., if P contains constant 0 and function symbol $s/1$, then $\mathcal{U}_P = \{0, s(0), s(s(0)), \ldots\}$). Therefore, if P does not contain function symbols, $ground(P)$ is finite and is infinite if P contains function symbols and at least one variable. The language of programs without function symbols is called *Datalog*.

The semantics of a set of formulas can be defined in terms of interpretations and models. We will here consider the special case of *Herbrand interpretations* and *Herbrand models* that are sufficient for giving a semantics to sets of clauses. For a definition of interpretations and models in the general case, see [Lloyd, 1987]. A *Herbrand interpretation* or *two-valued interpretation* I is a subset of the Herbrand base, i.e., $I \subseteq \mathcal{B}$. Given a Herbrand interpretation, it is possible to assign a truth value to formulas according to the following rules. A ground atom $p(t_1, t_2, \ldots, t_n)$ is true under the interpretation I if and only if $p(t_1, t_2, \ldots, t_n) \in I$. A conjunction of atomic formulas $b_1, \ldots, b_m$ is true in I if and only if $\{b_1, \ldots, b_m\} \subseteq I$. A ground clause $a_1 ; \ldots ; a_n \leftarrow b_1, \ldots, b_m$ is true in an interpretation I if and only if at least one of the atoms of the head is true in the case in which the body is true. A clause C is true in an interpretation I if and only if all of its ground instances with terms from $\mathcal{U}$ are true in I. A set of clauses Σ is true in an interpretation I if and only if all the clauses $C \in \Sigma$ are true.

A two-valued interpretation I represents the set of true ground atoms and we say that a is false if $a \notin I$. The set *Int2* of two-valued interpretations for a program P forms a complete lattice where the partial order $\leqslant$ is given by the subset relation $\subseteq$. The least upper bound and greatest lower bound are thus $\text{lub}(X) = \bigcup_{I \in X} I$ and $\text{glb}(X) = \bigcap_{I \in X} I$. The bottom and top element are, respectively, $\emptyset$ and $\mathcal{B}_P$.

An interpretation I *satisfies* a set of clauses Σ, notation $I \models \Sigma$, if Σ is true in I; we also say that I is a *model* of Σ. A set of clauses is *satisfiable* if it is satisfied by some interpretation, *unsatisfiable* otherwise. If all models of a set of clauses Σ are also models of a clause C, we say that Σ *logically entails* C or C is a *logical consequence* of Σ, and we write $\Sigma \models C$. We use the same symbol for the entailment relation and for the satisfaction relation between interpretations and formulas in order to follow the standard logic practice. In cases where this may cause misunderstanding, the intended meaning will be indicated in words.

Herbrand interpretations and models are sufficient for giving a semantics to sets of clauses in the following sense: a set of clauses is unsatisfiable if and only if it does not have a Herbrand model, a consequence of Herbrand's theorem [Herbrand, 1930]. For sets of definite clauses, Herbrand models are particularly important because they have the relevant property that the intersection of a set of Herbrand models for a set of definite clauses P is still a Herbrand model of P. The intersection of all the Herbrand models of P is called the *minimal Herbrand model* of P and is represented with $\mathrm{lhm}(P)$. The least Herbrand model of P always exists and is unique. The *model-theoretic semantics* of a program P is the set of all ground atoms that are logical consequences of P. The least Herbrand model provides the model theoretic semantics for P: $P \models a$ if and only if $a \in \mathrm{lhm}(P)$ where a is a ground atom.

For example, the program P below

$$human(X) \leftarrow female(X)$$
$$female(mary)$$

has the $\mathrm{lhm}(P) = \{female(mary), human(mary)\}$.

A *proof procedure* is an algorithm for checking whether a formula is provable from a theory. If formula ϕ is *provable* from the set of formulas Σ, we write $\Sigma \vdash \phi$. Two important properties of proof procedures are *soundness* and *completeness*. A proof procedure is *sound*, with respect to the model-theoretic semantics, if $\Sigma \vdash \phi$ implies $\Sigma \models \phi$; it is *complete* if $\Sigma \models \phi$ implies $\Sigma \vdash \phi$.

A proof procedure for clausal logic that is particularly suitable to be automated on a computer is *resolution* [Robinson, 1965]. The resolution inference rule allows one to prove, from two clauses $F_1 \vee l_1$ and $F_2 \vee \neg l_2$ where F_1 and F_2 are disjunctions of literals, the clause $(F_1 \vee F_2)\theta$, where θ is the most general unifier of l_1 and l_2. For definite clauses, this consists in matching the head of one clause with a literal in the body of another. To prove a conjunction of literals ϕ (a *query* or *goal*) from a set of clauses Σ,

ϕ is negated obtaining $\leftarrow \phi$ and added to Σ: if the empty denial $\leftarrow$ can be obtained from $\Sigma \cup \{\leftarrow \phi\}$ using a sequence of applications of the resolution inference rule, then ϕ is provable from Σ, $\Sigma \vdash \phi$. For example, if we want to prove that $P \vdash human(mary)$, we need to prove that $\leftarrow$ can be derived from $P \cup \{\leftarrow human(mary)\}$. In this case, from $human(X) \vee \neg female(X)$ and $female(mary)$, we can derive $human(mary)$ by resolution.

Logic programming was originally proposed by considering Horn clauses and adopting a particular version of resolution, *SLD resolution*,[Kowalski, 1974]. SLD resolution builds a sequence of formulas $\phi_1, \phi_2, \ldots, \phi_n$, where $\phi_1 = \leftarrow \phi$, that is called a *derivation*. At each step, the new formula ϕ_{i+1} is obtained by resolving the previous formula ϕ_i with a variant of a clause from the program P. If no resolution can be performed, then $\phi_{i+1} =$ fail and the derivation cannot be further extended. If $\phi_n = \leftarrow$, the derivation is *successful*; if $\phi_n =$ fail, the derivation is *unsuccessful*. The query ϕ is proved (*succeeds*) if there exists a successful derivation for it and *fails* otherwise. SLD resolution was proven to be sound and complete (under certain conditions) for Horn clauses (the proofs can be found in [Lloyd, 1987]).

A particular logic programming language is defined by choosing a rule for the selection of the literal in the current formula to be reduced at each step (*selection rule*) and by choosing a search strategy that can be either depth first or breadth first. In the *Prolog* [Colmerauer et al., 1973] programming language, the selection rule selects the *left-most* literal in the current goal and the search strategy is depth first with chronological backtracking. Prolog builds an *SLD tree* to answer queries: nodes are formulas and each path from the root to a leaf is an SLD derivation; branching occurs when there is more than one clause that can be resolved with the goal of a node. Prolog adopts an extension of SLD resolution called *SLDNF resolution* that is able to deal with normal clauses by *negation as failure* [Clark, 1978]: a negative selected literal $\sim a$ is removed from the current goal if a proof for a fails. An *SLDNF tree* is an SLD tree where the literal $\sim a$ in a node is handled by building a nested tree for a: if the nested tree has no successful derivations, the literal $\sim a$ is removed from the node and derivation proceeds; otherwise; the node has fail as the only child.

If the goal ϕ contains variables, a *solution* to ϕ is a substitution θ obtained by composing the substitutions along a branch of the SLDNF tree that is successful. The *success set* of ϕ is the set of solutions of ϕ. If a normal program is range restricted, every successful SLDNF derivation for goal ϕ completely grounds ϕ [Muggleton, 2000a].

Example 1 (Path – Prolog).   *The following program computes paths in a graph:*

$$path(X, X).$$
$$path(X, Y) \leftarrow edge(X, Z), path(Z, Y).$$
$$edge(a, b).$$
$$edge(b, c).$$
$$edge(a, c).$$

$path(X, Y)$ *is true if there is a path from X to Y in the graph where the edges are represented by facts for the predicate $edge/2$. This program computes the transitive closure of the relation $edge$. This is possible because the program contains an* inductive definition, *that of $path/2$.*

Computing transitive closures is an example of a problem for which first order logic is not sufficient and a Turing-complete language is required. Inductive definitions provide Prolog this expressive power.

The first clause states that there is a path from a node to itself. The second states that there is a path from a node X to a node Y if there exists a node Z such that there is an edge from X to Z and there is a path from Z to Y. Variables appearing in the body only, such as Z above, become existentially quantified when the universal quantifier for them is moved to have the body as scope.

Figure 1.1 shows the SLD tree for the query $path(a, c)$. The labels of the edges indicate the most general unifiers used. The query has two successful derivations, corresponding to the paths from the root to the $\leftarrow$ leaves.

Suppose we add the following clauses to the program

$$ends(X, Y) \leftarrow path(X, Y), \sim source(Y).$$
$$source(X) \leftarrow edge(X, Y).$$

$ends(X, Y)$ *is true if there is a path from X to Y and Y is a terminal node, i.e., it has no outgoing edges.*

The SLDNF tree for the query $ends(b, c)$ is shown in Figure 1.2: to prove $\sim source(c)$, an SLDNF tree is built for $source(c)$, shown in the rectangle. Since the derivation of $source(c)$ fails, then $\sim source(c)$ succeeds and can be removed from the goal.

A ground atom is *relevant* with respect to a query ϕ if it occurs in some proof of an atom from $atoms(\phi)$, where $atoms(\phi)$ returns the set of atoms appearing in the conjunction of literals ϕ. A ground rule is relevant if it contains only relevant atoms. In Example 1, $path(b, c)$, and $path(c, c)$ are relevant for $path(a, c)$, while $path(a, b)$, $path(b, a)$, $path(c, a)$, and $path(c, b)$

aren't. For the query $ends(b, c)$, instead $path(b, c)$, $path(c, c)$, and $source(c)$ are relevant, while $source(b)$ is not.

Proof procedures provide a method for answering queries in a top-down way. We can also proceed bottom-up by computing all possible consequences of the program using the T_P or *immediate consequence operator*.

Definition 1 (T_P operator). *For a definite program P, we define the operator* $T_P : Int2 \rightarrow Int2$ *as*

$$T_P(I) = \{a|\ \text{there is a clause } b \leftarrow l_1, ..., l_n \text{ in } P, \text{ a grounding substitution } \theta$$
$$\text{such that } a = b\theta \text{ and, for every } 1 \leqslant i \leqslant n, l_i\theta \in I\}.$$

The T_P operator is such that its least fixpoint is equal to the least Herbrand model of the program: $\mathrm{lfp}(T_P) = \mathrm{lhm}(P)$.

It can be shown that the least fixpoint of the T_P operator is reached at most at the first infinite ordinal ω [Hitzler and Seda, 2016].

In logic programming, data and code take the same form, so it is easy to write programs that manipulate code. For example, *meta-interpreters* or programs for interpreting other programs are particularly simple to write. A meta-interpreter for pure Prolog is [Sterling and Shapiro, 1994]:

```
solve(true).
solve((A,B))  :-
```

Figure 1.1 SLD tree for the query $path(a, c)$ from the program of Example 1.

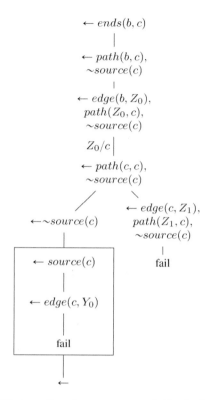

Figure 1.2   SLDNF tree for the query $ends(b, c)$ from the program of Example 1.

```
    solve(A),
    solve(B).
solve(Goal) :-
    clause(Goal,Body),
    solve(Body).
```

where `clause(Goal,Body)` is a predicate that succeeds if `Goal :- Body` is a clause of the program.

Pure Prolog is extended to include primitives for controlling the search process. An example is *cut* which is a predicate `!/0` that always succeeds and cuts choice points. If we have the program

```
p(S1) :- A1.
...
p(Sk) :- B, !, C.
```

```
. . .
p(Sn)  :- An.
```

when the k-th clause is evaluated, if B succeeds, then ! succeeds and the evaluation proceeds with C. In the case of backtracking, all the alternative for B are eliminated, as well as all the alternatives for p(...) provided by the clauses from the k-th to the n-th.

Cut is used in the implementation of an if-then-else construct in Prolog that is represented as

```
(B->C1;C2).
```

The construct evaluates B; it if succeeds, it evaluates C1; if it fails, it evaluates C2.

The construct is implemented as

```
if_then_else(B, C1, C2)  :- B, !, C1.
if_then_else(B, C1, C2)  :- C2.
```

Prolog systems usually include many built-in predicates. The predicate is/2 (usually written in infix notation) evaluates the second argument as an arithmetic expression and unifies the first argument with the result. So for example, A is 3+2 is a goal that, when executed, unifies A with 5.

1.4 Semantics for Normal Logic Programs

In a normal program, the clauses can contain default negative literals in the body, so a general rule has the form

$$C = h \leftarrow b_1, \ldots, b_n, \sim c_1, \ldots, \sim c_m \tag{1.1}$$

where $h, b_1, \ldots, b_n, c_1, \ldots, c_m$ are atoms.

Many semantics have been proposed for normal logic programs; see [Apt and Bol, 1994] for a survey. Of them, the one based on Clark's completion, the Well-founded Semantics (WFS), and the stable model semantics are the most widely used.

1.4.1 Program completion

Program completion or *Clark's completion* [Clark, 1978] assigns a semantics to a normal program by building a first-order logical theory representing the meaning of the program. The idea of the approach is to formally model the fact that atoms not inferable from the rules in the program are to be regarded as false.

The *completion of a clause*

$$p(t_1, \ldots, t_n) \leftarrow b_1, \ldots, b_m, \sim c_1, \ldots, \sim c_l.$$

with variables $Y_1, \ldots, Y_d$ is the clause

$$p(X_1, \ldots, X_n) \leftarrow \exists Y_1, \ldots, \exists Y_d((X_1 = t_1) \wedge \ldots \wedge (X_n = t_n) \wedge$$
$$b_1 \wedge \ldots \wedge b_m \wedge \neg c_1 \wedge \ldots \wedge \neg c_l)$$

where $=$ is a new predicate symbol representing equality. If the program contains $k \geqslant 1$ clauses for predicate p, we obtain k formulas of the form

$$p(X_1, \ldots, X_n) \leftarrow E_1$$
$$\vdots$$
$$p(X_1, \ldots, X_n) \leftarrow E_k.$$

The *competed definition* of p is then

$$\forall X_1, \ldots \forall X_n(p(X_1, \ldots, X_n) \leftrightarrow E_1 \vee \ldots \vee E_k).$$

If a predicate appearing in the program does not appear in the head of any clause, we add

$$\forall X_1, \ldots \forall X_n \neg p(X_1, \ldots, X_n).$$

The predicate $=$ is constrained by the following formulas that form an *equality theory*:

1. $c \neq d$ for all pairs c, d of distinct constants,
2. $\forall(f(X_1, \ldots, X_n) \neq g(Y_1, \ldots, Y_m))$ for all pairs f, g of distinct function symbols,
3. $\forall(t[X] \neq X)$ for each term $t[X]$ containing X and different from X,
4. $\forall((X_1 \neq Y_1) \vee \ldots \vee (X_n \neq Y_n) \rightarrow f(X_1, \ldots, X_n) \neq f(Y_1, \ldots, Y_n))$ for each function symbol f,
5. $\forall(X = X)$,
6. $\forall((X_1 = Y_1) \wedge \ldots \wedge (X_n = Y_n) \rightarrow f(X_1, \ldots, X_n) = f(Y_1, \ldots, Y_n))$ for each function symbol f,
7. $\forall((X_1 = Y_1) \wedge \ldots \wedge (X_n = Y_n) \rightarrow p(X_1, \ldots, X_n) \rightarrow p(Y_1, \ldots, Y_n))$ for each predicate symbol p (including $=$).

Given a normal program P, the completion $comp(P)$ of P is the theory formed by the completed definition of each predicate of P and the equality theory.

Note that the completion of a program may be inconsistent. In this case, the theory has no models and everything is a logical consequence. This is a situation to be avoided so restrictions are imposed on the form of the program.

The idea of the semantics based on Clark's completion is to consider a conjunction of ground literals

$$b_1, \ldots, b_m, \sim c_1, \ldots, \sim c_l$$

true if

$$b_1 \wedge \ldots \wedge b_m \wedge \neg c_1 \wedge \ldots \wedge \neg c_l$$

is a logical consequence of $comp(P)$, i.e., if

$$comp(P) \models b_1 \wedge \ldots \wedge b_m \wedge \neg c_1 \wedge \ldots \wedge \neg c_l.$$

SLDNF resolution was proven sound and complete (under certain conditions) with respect to the Clark's completion semantics [Clark, 1978].

Example 2 (Clark's completion).
Consider the program P_1

$$b \leftarrow \sim a.$$
$$c \leftarrow \sim b.$$
$$c \leftarrow a.$$

Its completion $comp(P_1)$ is

$$b \leftrightarrow \neg a.$$
$$c \leftrightarrow \neg b \vee a.$$
$$\neg a$$

We see that $comp(P_1) \models \neg a, b, \neg c$ so $\sim a, b$ and $\sim c$ can be derived with SLDNF resolution. The SLDNF tree for query c is shown in Figure 1.3 and, as expected, returns false.

Consider the program P_2

$$p \leftarrow p.$$

Its completion $comp(P_2)$ is

$$p \leftrightarrow p.$$

Here $comp(P) \not\models p$ and $comp(P) \not\models \neg p$. SLDNF resolution for query p would loop forever. This shows that SLNDF does not handle well loops, in this case positive *loops.*

Consider the program P_3

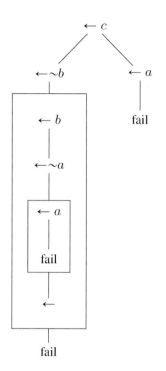

Figure 1.3   SLDNF tree for the query c from the program of Example 2.

    $p \leftarrow \sim p.$
Its completion $comp(P_3)$ *is*
    $p \leftrightarrow \neg p.$
which is inconsistent, so everything is a consequence. SLDNF resolution for query p would loop forever. SLNDF resolution does not handle well also loops through negation or negative loops.

1.4.2 Well-founded semantics

The WFS [Van Gelder et al., 1991] assigns a three-valued model to a program, i.e., it identifies a consistent three-valued interpretation as the meaning of the program.

    A *three-valued interpretation* $\mathcal{I}$ is a pair $\langle I_T, I_F \rangle$ where I_T and I_F are subsets of $\mathcal{B}_P$ and represent, respectively, the set of true and false atoms. So a is true in $\mathcal{I}$ if $a \in I_T$ and is false in $\mathcal{I}$ if $a \in I_F$, and $\sim a$ is true in $\mathcal{I}$ if $a \in I_F$ and is false in $\mathcal{I}$ if $a \in I_T$. If $a \notin I_T$ and $a \notin I_F$, then a assumes the third truth value, *undefined*. We also write $\mathcal{I} \models a$ if $a \in I_T$ and $\mathcal{I} \models \sim a$ if $a \in I_F$. A *consistent* three-valued interpretation $\mathcal{I} = \langle I_T, I_F \rangle$ is such that $I_T \cap I_F = \varnothing$. The union of two three-valued interpretations $\langle I_T, I_F \rangle$ and $\langle J_T, J_F \rangle$ is defined as $\langle I_T, I_F \rangle \cup \langle J_T, J_F \rangle = \langle I_T \cup J_T, I_F \cup J_F \rangle$. The intersection of two three-valued interpretations $\langle I_T, I_F \rangle$ and $\langle J_T, J_F \rangle$ is defined as $\langle I_T, I_F \rangle \cap \langle J_T, J_F \rangle = \langle I_T \cap J_T, I_F \cap J_F \rangle$. Sometimes we represent a three-valued interpretation $\mathcal{I} = \langle I_T, I_F \rangle$ as a single set of literals, i.e.,

$$\mathcal{I} = I_T \cup \{\sim a | a \in I_F\}.$$

The set $Int3$ of three-valued interpretations for a program P forms a complete lattice where the partial order $\leqslant$ is defined as $\langle I_T, I_F \rangle \leqslant \langle J_T, J_F \rangle$ if $I_T \subseteq J_T$ and $I_F \subseteq J_F$. The least upper bound and greatest lower bound are defined as $\mathrm{lub}(X) = \bigcup_{\mathcal{I} \in X} \mathcal{I}$ and $\mathrm{glb}(X) = \bigcap_{\mathcal{I} \in X} \mathcal{I}$. The bottom and top element are, respectively, $\langle \varnothing, \varnothing \rangle$ and $\langle \mathcal{B}_P, \mathcal{B}_P \rangle$.

Given a three-valued interpretation $\mathcal{I} = \langle I_T, I_F \rangle$, we define the functions $true(\mathcal{I}) = I_T$, $false(\mathcal{I}) = I_F$, and $undef(\mathcal{I}) = \mathcal{B}_P \backslash I_T \backslash I_F$ that return the set of true, false and undefined atoms, respectively.

The WFS was given in [Van Gelder et al., 1991] in terms of the least fixpoint of an operator that is composed by two sub-operators, one computing consequences, and the other computing unfounded sets. We give here the alternative definition of the WFS of [Przymusinski, 1989] that is based on an iterated fixpoint.

Definition 2 (*OpTrue$_{\mathcal{I}}^{P}$* and *OpFalse$_{\mathcal{I}}^{P}$* operators). *For a normal program P, sets Tr and Fa of ground atoms, and a three-valued interpretation $\mathcal{I}$, we define the operators* $OpTrue_{\mathcal{I}}^{P} : Int2 \to Int2$ *and* $OpFalse_{\mathcal{I}}^{P} : Int2 \to Int2$ *as*

$OpTrue_{\mathcal{I}}^{P}(Tr) = \{a | a$ *is not true in $\mathcal{I}$; and there is a clause $b \leftarrow l_1, ..., l_n$ in P, a grounding substitution θ such that $a = b\theta$ and for every $1 \leqslant i \leqslant n$ either $l_i\theta$ is true in $\mathcal{I}$, or $l_i\theta \in Tr\}$;*

$OpFalse_{\mathcal{I}}^{P}(Fa) = \{a | a$ *is not false in $\mathcal{I}$; and for every clause $b \leftarrow l_1, ..., l_n$ in P and grounding substitution θ such that $a = b\theta$ there is some i $(1 \leqslant i \leqslant n)$ such that $l_i\theta$ is false in $\mathcal{I}$ or $l_i\theta \in Fa\}$.*

In words, the operator $OpTrue_{\mathcal{I}}^{P}(Tr)$ extends the interpretation $\mathcal{I}$ to add the new true atoms that can be derived from P knowing $\mathcal{I}$ and true atoms Tr, while $OpFalse_{\mathcal{I}}^{P}(Fa)$ computes new false atoms in P by knowing $\mathcal{I}$ and false atoms Fa. $OpTrue_{\mathcal{I}}^{P}$ and $OpFalse_{\mathcal{I}}^{P}$ are both monotonic [Przymusinski,

1989], so they both have least and greatest fixpoints. An iterated fixpoint operator builds up *dynamic strata* by constructing successive three-valued interpretations as follows.

Definition 3 (Iterated fixpoint).   *For a normal program P, let* $IFP^P\!\!: Int3 \to Int3$ *be defined as*

$$IFP^P(\mathcal{I}) = \mathcal{I} \cup \langle \mathrm{lfp}(OpTrue_{\mathcal{I}}^P), \mathrm{gfp}(OpFalse_{\mathcal{I}}^P)\rangle.$$

IFP^P is monotonic [Przymusinski, 1989] and thus has a least fixpoint $\mathrm{lfp}(IFP^P)$. The Well-founded model (WFM) $WFM(P)$ of P is $\mathrm{lfp}(IFP^P)$. Let δ be the smallest ordinal such that $WFM(P) = IFP^P \uparrow \delta$. We refer to δ as the *depth* of P. The *stratum* of atom a is the least ordinal β such that $a \in IFP^P \uparrow \beta$ (where a may be either in the true or false component of $IFP^P \uparrow \beta$). Undefined atoms of the WFM do not belong to any stratum – i.e., they are not added to $IFP^P \uparrow \delta$ for any ordinal δ.

   If $undef(WFM(P)) = \varnothing$, then the WFM is called *total* or *two-valued* and the program *dynamically stratified*.

Example 3 (WFS computation).   *Let us consider program* P_1 *of Example 2:*

$b \leftarrow \sim a.$
$c \leftarrow \sim b.$
$c \leftarrow a.$

Its iterated fixpoint is

$$
\begin{aligned}
IFP^P \uparrow 0 &= \langle \varnothing, \varnothing \rangle; \\
IFP^P \uparrow 1 &= \langle \varnothing, \{a\} \rangle; \\
IFP^P \uparrow 2 &= \langle \{b\}, \{a\} \rangle; \\
IFP^P \uparrow 3 &= \langle \{b\}, \{a,c\} \rangle; \\
IFP^P \uparrow 4 &= IFP^P \uparrow 3 = WFM(P_1).
\end{aligned}
$$

Thus, the depth of P_1 *is 3 and the WFM of* P_1 *is given by*

$$
\begin{aligned}
true(WFM(P_1)) &= \{b\} \\
undef(WFM(P_1)) &= \varnothing \\
false(WFM(P_1)) &= \{a,c\}.
\end{aligned}
$$

So $WFM(P_1)$ *is two-valued and* P_1 *is dynamically stratified.*

   Let us consider program P_4 *from [Przymusinski, 1989]*

$b \leftarrow \sim a.$
$c \leftarrow \sim b.$
$c \leftarrow a, \sim p.$
$p \leftarrow \sim q.$
$q \leftarrow \sim p, b.$

Its iterated fixpoint is

$$
\begin{aligned}
IFP^P \uparrow 0 &= \langle \emptyset, \emptyset \rangle; \\
IFP^P \uparrow 1 &= \langle \emptyset, \{a\} \rangle; \\
IFP^P \uparrow 2 &= \langle \{b\}, \{a\} \rangle; \\
IFP^P \uparrow 3 &= \langle \{b\}, \{a, c\} \rangle; \\
IFP^P \uparrow 4 &= IFP^P \uparrow 3 = WFM(P_4).
\end{aligned}
$$

So the depth of P_4 is 3 and the WFM of P_4 is given by

$$
\begin{aligned}
true(WFM(P_4)) &= \{b\} \\
undef(WFM(P_4)) &= \{p, q\} \\
false(WFM(P_4)) &= \{a, c\}.
\end{aligned}
$$

Consider now the program P_2 of Example 2:

$p \leftarrow p.$

Its iterated fixpoint is

$$
\begin{aligned}
IFP^P \uparrow 0 &= \langle \emptyset, \emptyset \rangle; \\
IFP^P \uparrow 1 &= \langle \emptyset, \{p\} \rangle; \\
IFP^P \uparrow 2 &= IFP^P \uparrow 1 = WFM(P_2).
\end{aligned}
$$

P_2 is dynamically stratified and assigns value false to p. So positive loops are resolved by assigning value false to the atom.

Let us consider the program P_3 of Example 2:

$p \leftarrow \sim p.$

Its iterated fixpoint is

$$
\begin{aligned}
IFP^P \uparrow 0 &= \langle \emptyset, \emptyset \rangle; \\
IFP^P \uparrow 1 &= IFP^P \uparrow 0 = WFM(P_3).
\end{aligned}
$$

P_3 is not dynamically stratified and assigns value undefined to p. So negative loops are resolved by assigning value undefined to the atom.

Let us consider the program P_5:

$p \leftarrow \sim q.$

$q \leftarrow \sim p.$

Its iterated fixpoint is

$$
\begin{aligned}
IFP^P \uparrow 0 &= \langle \emptyset, \emptyset \rangle; \\
IFP^P \uparrow 1 &= IFP^P \uparrow 0 = WFM(P_5).
\end{aligned}
$$

Thus, the depth of P_5 is 0 and the WFM of P_5 is given by

$$
\begin{aligned}
true(WFM(P_5)) &= \emptyset \\
undef(WFM(P_5)) &= \{p, q\} \\
false(WFM(P_5)) &= \emptyset.
\end{aligned}
$$

So $WFM(P_5)$ is three-valued and P_5 is not dynamically stratified.

Given its similarity with the T_P operator, it can be shown that $OpTrue_{\mathcal{I}}^P$ reaches its fixpoint at most at the first infinite ordinal ω. IFP^P instead doesn't satisfy this property, as the next example shows.

Example 4 (Fixpoint of IFP^P beyond ω).   *Consider the following program inspired from [Hitzler and Seda, 2016, Program 2.6.5, page 58]:*

$p(0,0).$
$p(Y, s(X)) \leftarrow r(Y), p(Y, X).$
$q(Y, s(X)) \leftarrow \sim p(Y, X).$
$r(0).$
$r(s(Y)) \leftarrow \sim q(Y, s(X)).$
$t \leftarrow \sim q(Y, s(X)).$

The ordinal powers of IFP^P are shown in Figure 1.4, where $s^n(0)$ is the term where the functor s is applied n times to 0. We need to reach the immediate successor of ω to compute the WFS of this program.

The following properties identify important subsets of programs.

Definition 4 (Acyclic, stratified and locally stratified programs).

- *A* level mapping *for a program P is a function $|\ | : \mathcal{B}_P \to \mathbb{N}$ from ground atoms to natural numbers. For $a \in \mathcal{B}_P$, $|a|$ is the* level *of a. If $l = \neg a$ where $a \in \mathcal{B}_P$, we define $|l| = |a|$.*
- *A program T is called* acyclic *[Apt and Bezem, 1991] if there exists a level mapping such as, for every ground instance $a \leftarrow B$ of a clause of T, the level of a is greater than the level of each literal in B.*
- *A program T is called* locally stratified *if there exists a level mapping such as, for every ground instance $a \leftarrow B$ of a clause of T, the level of a is greater than the level of each negative literal in B and greater or equal than the level of each positive literals.*
- *A program T is called* stratified *if there exists a level mapping according to which the program is locally stratified and such that all the ground atoms for the same predicate can be assigned the same level.*

The WFS for locally stratified programs enjoys the following property.

Theorem 1 (WFS for locally stratified programs [Van Gelder et al., 1991]). *If P is locally stratified, then it has a total WFM.*

Programs P_1 and P_2 of Example 3 are (locally) stratified while programs P_3, P_4, and P_5 are not (locally) stratified. Note that stratification is stronger than local stratification that is stronger than dynamic stratification.

   SLG resolution [Chen and Warren, 1996] is a proof procedure that is sound and complete (under certain conditions) for the WFS. SLG uses *tabling*:

$$IFP^P \uparrow 0 \ = \ \langle \emptyset, \emptyset \rangle;$$
$$IFP^P \uparrow 1 \ = \ \langle \{p(0, s^n(0)| n \in \mathbb{N}\} \cup \{r(0)\},$$
$$\{q(s^m(0), 0)| m \in \mathbb{N}\}\rangle;$$
$$IFP^P \uparrow 2 \ = \ \langle \{p(0, s^n(0))| n \in \mathbb{N}\} \cup \{r(0)\},$$
$$\{q(0, s^n(0))| n \in \mathbb{N}_1\} \cup \{q(s^m(0), 0)| m \in \mathbb{N}\}\rangle;$$
$$IFP^P \uparrow 3 \ = \ \langle \{p(s^m(0), s^n(0))| n \in \mathbb{N}, m \in \{0, 1\}\} \cup$$
$$\{r(0), r(s(0))\},$$
$$\{q(0, s^n(0))| n \in \mathbb{N}_1\} \cup \{q(s^m(0), 0)| m \in \mathbb{N}\}\rangle;$$
$$IFP^P \uparrow 4 \ = \ \langle \{p(s^m(0), s^n(0))| n \in \mathbb{N}, m \in \{0, 1\}\} \cup$$
$$\{r(0), r(s(0)), r(s(s(0)))\},$$
$$\{q(0, s^n(0)), q(s(0), s^n(0))| n \in \mathbb{N}_1\} \cup$$
$$\{q(s^m(0), 0)| m \in \mathbb{N}\}\rangle;$$

$$\ldots$$

$$IFP^P \uparrow 2(i + 1) \ = \ \langle \{p(s^m(0), s^n(0)))| n \in \mathbb{N}, m \in \{0, \ldots, i\}\} \cup$$
$$\{r(s^m(0))| m \in \{0, \ldots, i + 1\}\},$$
$$\{q(s^m(0), s^n(0))| n \in \mathbb{N}_1, m \in \{0, \ldots, i\}\} \cup$$
$$\{q(s^m(0), 0)| m \in \mathbb{N}\}\rangle;$$

$$\ldots$$

$$IFP^P \uparrow \omega \ = \ \langle \{p(s^m(0), s^n(0)))| n, m \in \mathbb{N}\} \cup$$
$$\{r(s^m(0))| m \in \mathbb{N}\},$$
$$\{q(s^m(0), s^n(0))| n, m \in \mathbb{N}\}\rangle;$$
$$IFP^P \uparrow \omega + 1 \ = \ \langle \{t\} \cup \{p(s^m(0), s^n(0)))| n, m \in \mathbb{N}\} \cup$$
$$\{r(s^m(0))| m \in \mathbb{N}\},$$
$$\{q(s^m(0), s^n(0))| n, m \in \mathbb{N}\}\rangle;$$

Figure 1.4 Ordinal powers of IFP^P for the program of Example 4.

it keeps a store of the subgoals encountered in a derivation together with answers to these subgoals. If one of the subgoals is encountered again, its answers are retrieved from the store rather than recomputing them. Besides saving time, tabling ensures termination for programs without function symbols. For a discussion of the termination properties of SLG in the general case, see [Riguzzi and Swift, 2014]. SLG resolution is implemented in the Prolog systems XSB [Swift and Warren, 2012], YAP [Santos Costa et al., 2012], and SWI-prolog [Wielemaker et al., 2012].

1.4.3 Stable model semantics

The stable model semantics [Gelfond and Lifschitz, 1988] associates zero, one, or more two-valued models to a normal program.

A model I of a program P is minimal if there is no other model J such that $J \subseteq I$.

Definition 5 (Reduction).   *Given a normal program P and a two-valued interpretation I, the reduction P^I of P relative to I is obtained from $ground(P)$ by deleting*

> *1. each rule that has a negative literal $\sim a$ such that $a \in I$*
> *2. all negative literals in the body of the remaining rules.*

Definition 6 (Stable model).   *A two-valued interpretation I is a stable model or an* answer set *of a program P if it is a minimal model of P^I.*

Since P^I is a program without negation as failure, it has a unique minimal model that is the least Herbrand model $\mathrm{lhm}(P^I)$.

The *stable model semantics* of a program P is the set of its stable models/answer sets and is denoted by $AS(P)$.

The relationship between the WFS and the stable model semantics is given by the following two theorems [Van Gelder et al., 1991].

Theorem 2 (WFS total model vs stable models).   *If P has a total WFM, then that model is the unique stable model.*

Theorem 3 (WFS vs stable models).   *The WFM of P is a subset of every stable model of P seen as a three-valued interpretation.*

ASP is a problem-solving paradigm based on the computation of the answer sets of a program.

Example 5 (Answer set computation).
> *Let us consider program P_1 of Example 2:*
> $b \leftarrow \sim a.$
> $c \leftarrow \sim b.$
> $c \leftarrow a.$

Its only answer set is $\{b\}$ so $AS(P_1))\{\{b\}\}$.

> *Let us consider program P_4 from [Przymusinski, 1989]*
> $b \leftarrow \sim a.$
> $c \leftarrow \sim b.$
> $c \leftarrow a, \sim p.$
> $p \leftarrow \sim q.$
> $q \leftarrow \sim p, b.$

The program has two answer sets: $AS(P_4) = \{\{b, p\}, \{b, q\}\}$. $WFM(P_4) = \langle \{b\}, \{a, c\} \rangle$ is a subset of both seen as the three-valued interpretations $\langle \{b, p\}, \{a, c, q\} \rangle$ and $\langle \{b, q\}, \{a, c, p\} \rangle$

Let us consider program P_2 of Example 2:

   $p \leftarrow p.$

Its only answer set is $\emptyset$.

   Program P_3 of Example 2

   $p \leftarrow \sim p.$

has no answer sets.

   Program P_5:

   $p \leftarrow \sim q.$

   $q \leftarrow \sim p.$

has the answer sets $\{p\}$ and $\{q\}$ and $WFM(P_5) = \langle \emptyset, \emptyset \rangle$ is a subset of both seen as the three-valued interpretations $\langle \{p\}, \{q\} \rangle$ and $\langle \{q\}, \{p\} \rangle$.

In general, loops through an odd number of negations may cause the program to have no answer set, while loops through an even number of negations may cause the program to have multiple answer sets. In this sense, the stable model semantics differs from the WFS that makes the atoms involved in the loops undefined in both cases.

We can also define brave and cautious consequences.

Definition 7 (Cautious and brave consequences). *A ground atom q is a brave consequence of a program P if $\exists A \in AS(P)$ such that $q \in A$. We denote the set containing all the brave consequences with $BC(P)$. Similarly, q is a cautious consequence if $\forall A \in AS(P)$, $q \in A$, and we denote the set containing all the cautious consequences with $CC(P)$.*

Example 6 (Cautious and brave consequences). *For the program P_4 from Example 5 we have*

$$BC(P_4) = \{b, p, q\}$$
$$CC(P_4) = \{b\}$$

For the program P_5 from Example 5 we have

$$BC(P_4) = \{p, q\}$$
$$CC(P_4) = \emptyset$$

DLV [Leone et al., 2006; Alviano et al., 2017], Smodels [Syrjänen and Niemelä, 2001], and Potassco [Gebser et al., 2011] are examples of systems for ASP.

1.5 Probability Theory

Probability theory provides a formal mathematical framework for dealing with uncertainty. The notions used in the book are briefly reviewed here; for a more complete treatment, please refer to textbooks such as [Ash and Doléans-Dade, 2000; Chow and Teicher, 2012].

Let W be a set called the *sample space*, whose elements are the *outcomes* of the random process we would like to model. For example, if the process is that of throwing a coin, the sample space can be $W^{coin} = \{h, t\}$ with h standing for heads and t for tails. If the process is that of throwing a die, $W^{die} = \{1, 2, 3, 4, 5, 6\}$. If we throw two coins, the sample space is $W^{2\_coins} = \{(h, h), (h, t), (t, h), (t, t)\}$. If we throw an infinite sequence of coins, $W^{coins} = \{(o_1, o_2, \ldots) | o_i \in \{h, t\}\}$. If we measure the position of an object along a single axis, $W^{pos\_x} = \mathbb{R}$, on a plane $W^{pos\_x\_y} = \mathbb{R}^2$ and in the space $W^{pos\_x\_y\_z} = \mathbb{R}^3$. If the object is limited to the unit interval, square, and cube, then $W^{unit\_x} = [0, 1]$, $W^{unit\_x\_y} = [0, 1]^2$, and $W^{unit\_x\_y\_z} = [0, 1]^3$.

Definition 8 (Algebra).   *The set Ω of subsets of W is an* algebra *on the set W iff*

- $W \in \Omega$;
- Ω *is closed under complementation, i.e.,* $\omega \in \Omega \rightarrow \omega^c = (\Omega \backslash \omega) \in \Omega$;
- Ω *is closed under finite union, i.e.,* $\omega_1 \in \Omega, \omega_2 \in \Omega \rightarrow (\omega_1 \cup \omega_2) \in \Omega$

Definition 9 (σ-algebra).   *The set Ω of subsets of W is a σ-algebra on the set W iff it is an algebra and*

- Ω *is closed under countable union, i.e., if $\omega_i \in \Omega$ for $i = 1, 2, \ldots$ then* $\bigcup_i \omega_i \in \Omega$.

Definition 10 (Minimal σ-algebra).   *Let $\mathcal{A}$ be an arbitrary collection of subsets of W. The intersection of all σ-algebras containing all elements of $\mathcal{A}$ is called the σ-algebra generated by $\mathcal{A}$, or the minimal σ-algebra containing $\mathcal{A}$. It is denoted by $\sigma(\mathcal{A})$.*

$\sigma(\mathcal{A})$ is such that $\Sigma \supseteq \sigma(\mathcal{A})$ whenever $\Sigma \supseteq \mathcal{A}$ and Σ is a σ-algebra. $\sigma(\mathcal{A})$ always exists and is unique [Chow and Teicher, 2012, page 7].

The elements of a σ-algebra Ω on W are called *measurable sets* or *events* and (W, Ω) is called a *measurable space*. When W is finite, Ω is usually the powerset of W. In general, however, not every subset of W need be present in Ω.

When throwing a coin, the set of events may be $\Omega^{coin} = \mathbb{P}(W^{coin})$ and $\{h\}$ is an event corresponding to the coin landing heads. When throwing a die, an example of the set of events is $\Omega^{die} = \mathbb{P}(W^{die})$ and $\{1,3,5\}$ is an event, corresponding to obtaining an odd result. When throwing two coins, $(W^{2\_coin}, \Omega^{2\_coins})$ with $\Omega^{2\_coins} = \mathbb{P}(W^{2\_coins})$ is a measurable space.

When throwing an infinite sequence of coins, $\{(h, t, o_3, \ldots) | o_i \in \{h, t\}\}$ may be an event, corresponding to obtaining head and tails in the first two throws. When measuring the position of an object on an axis and $W^{pos\_x} = \mathbb{R}$, Ω^{pos_x} may be the *Borel σ-algebra $\mathcal{B}$ on the set of real numbers*, the one generated, for example, by closed intervals $\{[a, b] : a, b \in \mathbb{R}\}$. Then $[-1, 1]$ may be an event, corresponding to observing the object in the $[-1, 1]$ interval. If the object is constrained to the unit interval W^{uit_x}, Ω^{unit_x} may be $\sigma(\{[a, b] : a, b \in [0, 1]\})$.

Definition 11 (Probability measure). *Given a measurable space (W, Ω) of subsets of W, a probability measure is a function $\mu : \Omega \to \mathbb{R}$ that satisfies the following axioms:*

μ-**1** $\mu(\omega) \geqslant 0$ *for all $\omega \in \Omega$;*

μ-**2** $\mu(W) = 1$;

μ-**3** *μ is countably additive, i.e., if $O = \{\omega_1, \omega_2, \ldots\} \subseteq \Omega$ is a countable collection of pairwise disjoint sets, then $\mu(\bigcup_{\omega \in O}) = \sum_i \mu(\omega_i)$.*

(W, Ω, μ) *is called a* probability space.

We also consider finitely additive probability measures.

Definition 12 (Finitely additive probability measure). *Given a sample space W and an algebra Ω of subsets of W, a finitely additive probability measure is a function $\mu : \Omega \to \mathbb{R}$ that satisfies axioms (μ-1) and (μ-2) of Definition 11 and axiom*

m-3 *μ is finitely additive, i.e., $\omega_1 \cap \omega_2 = \varnothing \to \mu(\omega_1 \cup \omega_2) = \mu(\omega_1) + \mu(\omega_2)$ for all $\omega_1, \omega_2 \in \Omega$.*

(W, Ω, μ) *is called a* finitely additive probability space.

Example 7 (Probability spaces). *When throwing a coin, $(W^{coin}, \Omega^{coin}, \mu^{coin})$ with $\mu^{coin}(\varnothing) = 0$ $\mu^{coin}(\{h\}) = 0.5$, $\mu^{coin}(\{t\}) = 0.5$, and $\mu^{coin}(\{h, t\}) = 1$ is a (finitely additive) probability space. When throwing a die, $(W^{die}, \Omega^{die}, \mu^{die})$ with $\mu^{coin}(\omega) = |\omega| \cdot \frac{1}{6}$ is a (finitely additive) probability space.*

When throwing two coins, $(W^{2\_coins}, \Omega^{2\_coins}, \mu^{2\_coins})$ with μ^{2_coins} $(\omega)=|\omega| \cdot \frac{1}{36}$ is a (finitely additive) probability space. For the position of an object on an axis, $(W^{unit\_x}, \Omega^{unit\_x}, \mu^{unit\_x})$ with $\mu^{unit\_x}(I)=\int_I dx$ is a probability space. $(W^{pos\_x}, \Omega^{pos\_x}, \mu^{pos\_x})$ with $\mu^{pos\_x}(I)=\int_{I \cap [0,1]} dx$ is also a probability space.

Let (W, Ω, μ) be a probability space and (S, Σ) a measurable space. A function $X : W \to S$ is said to be *measurable* if the preimage of σ under X is in Ω for every $\sigma \in \Sigma$, i.e.,

$$X^{-1}(\sigma) = \{w \in W \mid X(w) \in \sigma\} \in \Omega, \quad \forall \sigma \in \Sigma.$$

Definition 13 (Random variable). *Let (W, Ω, μ) be a probability space and let (S, Σ) be a measurable space. A measurable function $X : W \to S$ is a* random variable. *We call the elements of S the* values *of X. With $P(X \in \sigma)$ for $\sigma \in \Sigma$, we indicate the* probability that random variable X has value in σ, *defined as $\mu(X^{-1}(\sigma))$.*

If Σ is finite or countable, X is a discrete *random variable. If Σ is uncountable, then X is a* continuous *random variable.*

We indicate random variables with Roman uppercase letters $X, Y, \ldots$ and the values with Roman lowercase letters $x, y, \ldots$.

When $(W, \Omega) = (S, \Sigma)$, X is often the identity function and $P(X \in \omega) = \mu(\omega)$.

In the discrete case, the values of $P(X \in \{x\})$ for all $x \in S$ define the *probability distribution* of random variable X, often abbreviated as $P(X=x)$ and $P(x)$. We indicate the probability distribution for random variable X with $P(X)$.

Example 8 (Discrete random variables). *An example of a discrete random variable X for the probability space $(W^{coin}, \Omega^{coin}, \mu^{coin})$ is the identity function and the probability distribution is $P(X=h) = 0.5$, $P(X=t) = 0.5$. When throwing a die, a discrete random variable X can be the identity and $P(X=n)=\frac{1}{6}$ for all $n \in \{1, 2, 3, 4, 5, 6\}$. Another discrete random variable E for a die can represent whether the outcome was even or odd with $(S, \Sigma) = (\{e, o\}, \mathbb{P}(S))$ and E: $W^{die} \to S$ defined as E=$\{1 \to o, 2 \to e, 3 \to o, 4 \to e, 5 \to o, 6 \to e\}$. The probability distribution is then $P(E = e) = \mu^{die}(\{2, 4, 6\}) = \frac{1}{6} \times 3 = \frac{1}{2}$ and $P(E = o) = \mu^{die}(\{1, 3, 5\}) = \frac{1}{6} \times 3 = \frac{1}{2}$.*

For the probability space $(W^{2\_coins}, \Omega^{2\_coins}, \mu^{2\_coins})$, *a discrete random variable may be the function* $X : W^{2\_coins} \to W^{coin}$ *defined as*

$$X(\{c_1, c_2\}) = c_1,$$

i.e., the function returning the outcome of the first coin. For value $h \in W^{coin}$, *we have*

$$X^{-1}(\{h\}) = \{(h, h), (h, t)\}$$

and

$$P(X = h) = \mu^{2\_coins}(\{(h, h), (h, t)\}) = 0.5.$$

In the continuous case, we define the cumulative distribution and the probability density.

Definition 14 (Cumulative distribution and probability density). *The cumulative distribution of a random variable* $X : (W, \Omega) \to (\mathbb{R}, \mathcal{B})$ *is the function* $F(x) : \mathbb{R} \to [0, 1]$ *defined as*

$$F(x) = P(X \in \{t | t \leqslant x\}).$$

We write $P(X \in \{t | t \leqslant x\})$ *also as* $P(X \leqslant x)$. *The probability density of* X *is a function* $p(x)$ *such that*

$$P(X \in A) = \int_A p(x) dx$$

for any measurable set $A \in \mathcal{B}$.

It holds that:

$$F(x) = \int_{-\infty}^{x} p(t) dt$$

$$p(x) = \frac{dF(x)}{dx}$$

$$P(X \in [a, b]) = F(b) - F(a) = \int_a^b p(x) dx$$

A discrete random variable is described by giving its probability distribution $P(X)$ while a continuous random variable is described by giving its cumulative distribution $F(x)$ or probability density $p(x)$.

Example 9 (Continuous random variables). *For the probability space of an object in the unit interval* $(W^{unit\_x}, \Omega^{unit\_x}, \mu^{unit\_x})$*, the identity* X *is a continuous random variable with cumulative distribution and density*

$$F(\mathrm{x}) \; = \; \int_0^{\mathrm{x}} d\mathsf{t} = \mathrm{x}$$

$$p(\mathrm{x}) \; = \; 1$$

for $\mathrm{x} \in [0,1]$*. For probability space* $(W^{pos\_x}, \Omega^{pos\_x}, \mu^{pos\_x})$*, the identity* X *is a continuous random variable with cumulative distribution and density*

$$F(\mathrm{x}) \; = \; \begin{cases} 0 & \text{if } \mathrm{x} < 0 \\ \mathrm{x} & \text{if } \mathrm{x} \in [0,1] \\ 1 & \text{if } \mathrm{x} > 1 \end{cases}$$

$$p(\mathrm{x}) \; = \; \begin{cases} 1 & \text{if } \mathrm{x} \in [0,1] \\ 0 & \text{otherwise} \end{cases}$$

This is an example of an uniform density. In general, the uniform density *in the interval* $[\mathrm{a}, \mathrm{b}]$ *is*

$$p(\mathrm{x}) \; = \; \begin{cases} \frac{1}{\mathrm{b}-\mathrm{a}} & \text{if } \mathrm{x} \in [\mathrm{a}, \mathrm{b}] \\ 0 & \text{otherwise} \end{cases}$$

Another notable density is the normal or Gaussian density, *with*

$$p(\mathrm{x}) \; = \; \frac{1}{\sqrt{2\pi\sigma^2}} e^{-\frac{(\mathrm{x}-\mu)^2}{2\sigma^2}}$$

where μ *and* σ *are parameters denoting the mean and the standard deviation* (σ^2 *is the variance). We use* $\mathcal{N}(\mu, \sigma)$ *to indicate a normal density. Examples of Gaussian densities for various values of the parameters are shown in Figure 1.5.*

When the values of a random variable are numeric, we can compute its *expected value* or *expectation*, which intuitively is the average of the values obtained by repeating infinitely often the experiment it represents. The expectation of a discrete variable X is

$$\mathbf{E}(X) = \sum_{\mathrm{x}} \mathrm{x} P(\mathrm{x})$$

while the expectation of a continuous variable X with domain $\mathbb{R}$ is

$$\mathbf{E}(X) = \int_{-\infty}^{+\infty} \mathrm{x} p(\mathrm{x}) d\mathrm{x}.$$

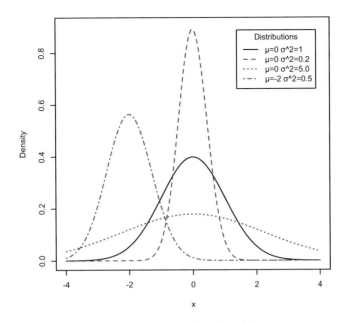

Figure 1.5   Gaussian densities.

Multiple random variables can be defined on the same space (W, Ω, μ), especially when $(W, \Omega) \neq (S, \Sigma)$. Suppose two random variables X and Y are defined on the probability space (W, Ω, μ) and measurable spaces (S_1, Σ_1) and (S_2, Σ_2), respectively. We can define the *joint probability* $P(X \in \sigma_1, Y \in \sigma_2)$ as $\mu(X^{-1}(\sigma_1) \cap Y^{-1}(\sigma_2))$ for $\sigma_1 \in \Sigma_1$ and $\sigma_2 \in \Sigma_2$. Since X and Y are random variables and Ω is a σ-algebra, then $X^{-1}(\sigma_1) \cap Y^{-1}(\sigma_2) \in \Omega$ and the joint probability is well defined. If X and Y are discrete, the values of $P(X=\{x\}, Y=\{y\})$ for all $x \in S_1$ and $y \in S_2$ define the *joint probability distribution* of X and Y often abbreviated as $P(X=x, Y=y)$ and $P(x, y)$. We call $P(X, Y)$ the joint probability distribution of X and Y. If X and Y are continuous, we can define the *joint cumulative distribution* $F(x, y)$ as $P(X \in \{t | t \leqslant x\}, Y \in \{t | t \leqslant y\})$ and *joint probability density* as the function $p(x, y)$ such that $P(X \in A, Y \in B) = \int_A \int_B p(x, y) dx dy$.

If X is discrete and Y continuous, we can still define the joint cumulative distribution $F(x, y)$ as $P(X=x, Y \in \{t | t \leqslant y\})$ and the joint probability density as the function $p(x, y)$ such that $P(X=x, Y \in B) = \int_B p(x, y) dy$.

Example 10 (Joint distributions). *When throwing two coins, we can define two random variables X_1 and X_2 as $X_1((c_1, c_2)) = c_1$ and $X_2((c_1, c_2)) =$*

c_2: *the first indicates the outcome of the first coin and the second of the second. The joint probability distribution is* $P(X_1 = x_1, X_2 = x_2) = \frac{1}{4}$ *for all* $x_1, x_2 \in \{h, t\}$.

For the position of an object on a plane, we can have random variable X *for its position on the X-axis and* Y *on the Y-axis. An example of joint probability density is the bivariate normal or Gaussian density*

$$p(\mathbf{x}) = \frac{\exp\left(-\frac{1}{2}(\mathbf{x} - \boldsymbol{\mu})^{\mathrm{T}}\boldsymbol{\Sigma}^{-1}(\mathbf{x} - \boldsymbol{\mu})\right)}{\sqrt{(2\pi)^2 \det \boldsymbol{\Sigma}}} \tag{1.2}$$

where $\mathbf{x}$ *is a real two-dimensional column vector,* $\boldsymbol{\mu}$ *is a real two-dimensional column vector, the* mean, $\boldsymbol{\Sigma}$ *is a* 2×2 *symmetric positive-definite[1] matrix called* covariance matrix, *and* $\det \boldsymbol{\Sigma}$ *is the determinant of* $\boldsymbol{\Sigma}$.

A bivariate Gaussian density with parameters $\mu = [0, 0]^T$ *and*

$$\boldsymbol{\Sigma} = \begin{bmatrix} 1 & 0 \\ 0 & 1 \end{bmatrix} = \mathbf{I}$$

is shown in Figure 1.6.

Definition 15 (Product σ-algebra and product space).   *Given two measurable spaces* (W_1, Ω_1) *and* (W_2, Ω_2), *define the* product σ-algebra $\Omega_1 \otimes \Omega_2$ *as*

$$\Omega_1 \otimes \Omega_2 = \sigma\left(\{\omega_1 \times \omega_2 | \omega_1 \in \Omega_1, \omega_2 \in \Omega_2\}\right).$$

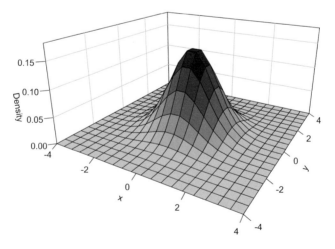

Figure 1.6   Bivariate Gaussian density.

---

[1] All its eigenvalues are positive.

Note that $\Omega_1 \otimes \Omega_2$ differs from the Cartesian product $\Omega_1 \times \Omega_2$ because it is the minimal σ-algebra generated by all possible Cartesian products of pairs of elements from Ω_1 and Ω_2.

Then define the product space $(W_1, \Omega_1) \times (W_2, \Omega_2)$ *as*

$$(W_1, \Omega_1) \times (W_2, \Omega_2) = (W_1 \times W_2, \Omega_1 \otimes \Omega_2).$$

Given two random variables X and Y that are defined on the probability space (W, Ω, μ) and measurable spaces (S_1, Σ_1) and (S_2, Σ_2), respectively, we can define the function XY such that $XY(w) = (X(w), Y(w))$. Such a function is a random variable defined on the same probability space and the product measurable space $(S_1, \Sigma_1) \times (S_2, \Sigma_2)$ [Chow and Teicher, 2012, Theorem 1, page 13]. So, for example, two discrete random variables X and Y with values x_i and y_j with their joint distribution $P(X, Y)$ can be interpreted as a random variable XY with values (x_i, y_j) and distribution $P((X, Y))$. The results in the following thus apply also by replacing a random variable with a vector (or set) of random variables. We usually denote vectors of random variables with boldface capital letters such as $\mathbf{X}, \mathbf{Y}, \ldots$ and vectors of values with boldface lowercase letters such as $\mathbf{x}, \mathbf{y}, \ldots$.

Definition 16 (Conditional probability). *Given two discrete random variables X and Y and two values x and y for them, if $P(y) > 0$, we can define the* conditional probability $P(x|y)$ *as*

$$P(x|y) = \frac{P(x, y)}{P(y)}$$

If $P(y) = 0$, then $P(x|y)$ is not defined.

$P(x|y)$ provides the probability distribution of variable X given that random variable Y was observed having value y.

From this, we get the important *product rule*

$$P(x, y) = P(x|y)P(y)$$

expressing a joint distribution in terms of a conditional distribution.

Moreover, x and y can be exchanged obtaining $P(x, y) = P(y|x)P(x)$, so by equating the two expressions, we find *Bayes' theorem*

$$P(x|y) = \frac{P(y|x)P(x)}{P(y)}.$$

Now consider two discrete random variables X and Y, with X having a finite set of values $\{x_1, \ldots, x_n\}$, and let y be a value of Y. The sets

$$X^{-1}(\{x_1\}) \cap Y^{-1}(\{y\}), \ldots, X^{-1}(\{x_n\}) \cap Y^{-1}(\{y\})$$

are mutually exclusive because X is a function and

$$Y^{-1}(y) = X^{-1}(\{x_1\}) \cap Y^{-1}(\{y\}) \cup \ldots \cup X^{-1}(\{x_n\}) \cap Y^{-1}(\{y\}).$$

Given the fact that probability measures are additive, then

$$P(X \in \{x_1, \ldots, x_n\}, y) = P(y) = \sum_{i=1}^{n} P(x_i, y)$$

This is the *sum rule* of probability theory, often expressed as

$$P(y) = \sum_{x} P(x, y)$$

The sum rule eliminates a variable from a joint distribution and we also say that we *sum out* the variable and that we *marginalize* the joint distribution.

For continuous random variables, we can similarly define the *conditional density* $p(X|y)$ as

$$p(x|y) = \frac{p(x, y)}{p(y)}$$

when $p(y) > 0$, and get the following versions of the product and sum rules

$$p(x, y) = p(x|y)p(y)$$
$$p(y) = \int_{-\infty}^{\infty} p(x, y)dx$$

We can also define *conditional expectations* as

$$\mathbf{E}(X|y) = \sum_{x} xP(x|y)$$
$$\mathbf{E}(X|y) = \int_{-\infty}^{+\infty} xp(x|y)dx.$$

for X a discrete or continuous variable, respectively.

For continuous random variables, we may have evidence on Y in the form of the measurement of a value y for it. In many practical cases, such as the Gaussian distribution, $P(y) = 0$ for all values y of Y, so the conditional probability $P(X \in \omega_1|y)$ is not defined. This is known as the *Borel–Kolmogorov paradox* [Gyenis et al., 2017].

In some cases, it can be solved by defining the conditional probability as

$$P(X \in \omega_1|y) = \lim_{dv \to 0} \frac{P(X \in \omega_1, Y \in [y - dv/2, y + dv/2])}{P(Y \in [y - dv/2, y + dv/2])}.$$

However, the limit is not always defined.

Definition 17 (Independence and conditional indepedence). *Two random variables* X *and* Y *are* independent, *indicated with* $I(X, Y, \varnothing)$ *iff*

$$P(x|y) = P(x) \text{ whenever } P(y) > 0$$

Two random variables X *and* Y *are* conditionally independent given Z, *indicated with* $I(X, Y, Z)$ *iff*

$$P(x|y, z) = P(x|z) \text{ whenever } P(y, z) > 0$$

1.6 Probabilistic Graphical Models

It is often convenient to describe a domain using a set of random variables. For example, a home intrusion detection system can be described with the random variables

- Earthquake E, which assumes value true (t) if an earthquake occurred and false (f) otherwise;
- Burglary B, which assumes value true (t) if a burglary occurred and false (f) otherwise;
- Alarm A, which assumes value true (t) if the alarm went off and false (f) otherwise;
- Neighbor call N, which assumes value true (t) if the neighbor called and false (f) otherwise.

These variables may describe the situation of the system at a particular point in time, such as last night. We would like to answer the questions such as

- What is the probability of a burglary? (compute $P(B{=}t)$, belief computation)
- What is the probability of a burglary given that the neighbor called? (compute $P(B{=}t|N{=}t)$, belief updating)
- What is the probability of a burglary given that there was an earthquake and the neighbor called? (compute $P(B{=}t|N{=}t, E{=}t)$, belief updating)
- What is the probability of a burglary and of the alarm ringing given that there was an earthquake and the neighbor called? (compute $P(A{=}t, B{=}t|N{=}t, E{=}t)$, belief updating)

- What is the most likely value for burglary given that the neighbor called? ($\arg\max_b P(b|N{=}t)$, belief revision).

When assigning a causal meaning to the variables, the problems are also called

- Diagnosis: computing $P(cause|symptom)$.
- Prediction: computing $P(symptom|cause)$.

Moreover, another inference problem is

- Classification: computing $\arg\max_{class} P(class|data)$.

In general, we want to compute the probability $P(\mathbf{q}|\mathbf{e})$ of a *query* $\mathbf{q}$ (assignment of values to a set of variables $\mathbf{Q}$) given the evidence $\mathbf{e}$ (assignment of values to a set of variables $\mathbf{E}$). This problem is called *inference*. If $\mathbf{X}$ denotes the set of all variables describing the domain and we know the joint probability distribution $P(\mathbf{X})$, i.e., we know $P(\mathbf{x})$ for all $\mathbf{x}$, we can answer all types of queries using the definition of conditional probability and the sum rule:

$$
P(\mathbf{q}|\mathbf{e}) = \frac{P(\mathbf{q}, \mathbf{e})}{P(\mathbf{e})} = \frac{\sum_{\mathbf{y}, \mathbf{Y}=\mathbf{X}\backslash\mathbf{Q}\backslash\mathbf{E}} P(\mathbf{y}, \mathbf{q}, \mathbf{e})}{\sum_{\mathbf{z}, \mathbf{Z}=\mathbf{X}\backslash\mathbf{E}} P(\mathbf{z}, \mathbf{e})}
$$

However, if we have n binary variables ($|\mathbf{X}| = n$), knowing the joint probability distribution requires storing $O(2^n)$ different values. Even if we had the space to store all the 2^n different values, computing $P(\mathbf{q}|\mathbf{e})$ would require $O(2^n)$ operations. Therefore, this approach is impractical for real-world problems and a different solution must be adopted.

First note that if $\mathbf{X} = \{X_1, \ldots, X_n\}$, a value of $\mathbf{X}$ is a tuple $(x_1, \ldots, x_n)$ also called a *joint event* and we can write

$$P(\mathbf{x}) = P(x_1, \ldots, x_n) =$$
$$P(x_n|x_{n-1}, \ldots, x_1)P(x_{n-1}, \ldots, x_1) =$$
$$\ldots$$
$$P(x_n|x_{n-1}, \ldots, x_1) \ldots P(x_2|x_1)P(x_1) = \quad (1.3)$$
$$\prod_{i=1}^{n} P(x_i|x_{i-1}, \ldots, x_1)$$

where Equation (1.3) is obtained by repeated application of the product rule. This formula expresses the so-called *chain rule*.

Now if we knew, for each variable X_i, a subset $\mathbf{Pa}_i$ of $\{X_{i-1}, \ldots, X_1\}$ such that X_i is conditionally independent of $\{X_{i-1}, \ldots, X_1\} \backslash \mathbf{Pa}_i$ given $\mathbf{Pa}_i$, i.e.,

$$P(x_i|x_{i-1}, \ldots, x_1) = P(x_i|\mathbf{pa}_i) \text{ whenever } P(x_{i-1}, \ldots, x_1) > 0,$$

then we could write

$$P(\mathbf{x}) = P(x_1, \ldots, x_n) =$$
$$P(x_n|x_{n-1}, \ldots, x_1) \ldots P(x_2|x_1)P(x_1) =$$
$$P(x_n|\mathbf{pa}_n) \ldots P(x_2|\mathbf{pa}_1)P(x_1|\mathbf{pa}_1) =$$
$$\prod_{i=1}^{n} P(x_i|\mathbf{pa}_i)$$

Therefore, in order to compute $P(\mathbf{x})$, we have to store $P(x_i|\mathbf{pa}_i)$ for all values x_i and $\mathbf{pa}_i$. The set of values $P(x_i|\mathbf{pa}_i)$ is called the Conditional probability table (CPT) of variable X_i. If $\mathbf{Pa}_i$ is much smaller than $\{X_{i-1}, \ldots, X_1\}$, then we have huge savings. For example, if k is the maximum size of $\mathbf{Pa}_i$, then the storage requirements are $O(n2^k)$ instead of $O(2^n)$. So it is important to take into account independencies among the variables as they enable much faster inference. One way to do this is by means of *graphical models* that are graph structures that represent independencies.

An example of a graphical model is a BN [Pearl, 1988] that represents a set of variables with a directed graph with a node per variable and an edge from X_j to X_i only if $X_j \in \mathbf{Pa}_i$. The variables in $\mathbf{Pa}_i$ are in fact also called the *parents* of X_i and X_i is called a *child* of every node in $\mathbf{Pa}_i$. Given that $\mathbf{Pa}_i \subseteq \{X_{i-1}, \ldots, X_1\}$, the parents of X_i will always have an index lower than i and the ordering $\langle X_1, \ldots, X_n \rangle$ is a topological sort of the graph that is therefore acyclic. A BN together with the set of CPTs $P(x_i|\mathbf{pa}_i)$ defines a joint probability distribution.

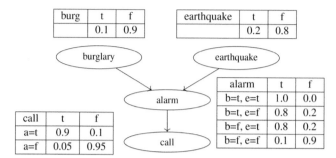

Figure 1.7   Example of a Bayesian network.

Example 11 (Alarm – BN).   *For our intrusion detection system and the variable order* $\langle E, B, A, N \rangle$, *we can identify the following independencies*

$$P(e) = P(e)$$
$$P(b|e) = P(b)$$
$$P(a|b, e) = P(a|b, e)$$
$$P(n|a, b, e) = P(n|a)$$

which result in the BN of Figure 1.7 that also shows the CPTs.

When a CPT contains only the values 0.0 and 1.0, the dependency of the child from its parents is *deterministic* and the CPT encodes a function: given the values of the parents, the value of the child is completely determined. For example, if the variables are Boolean, a *deterministic CPT* can encode the AND or the OR Boolean function.

The concepts of ancestors of a node and of descendants of a node are defined as the transitive closure of the parent and child relationships: if there is a directed path from X_i to X_j, then X_i is an *ancestor* of X_j and X_j is a *descendant* of X_i. Let $ANC(X)$ $(DESC(X))$ be the set of ancestors (descendants) of X.

From the definition of BN, we know that, given its parents, a variable is independent of its other ancestors. However, BNs allow reading other independence relationship using the notion of d-separation.

Definition 18 (d-separation [Murphy, 2012]).   *An undirected path P in a BN is a path connecting two nodes not considering edge directions.*

An undirected path P is d-separated *by a set of nodes* **C** *iff at least one of the following conditions hold:*

- *P contains a chain,* S → M → T *or* S ← M ← T; *where* M ∈ **C**;
- *P contains a fork,* S ← M → T, *where* M ∈ **C**
- *P contains a collider* S → M ← T, *where* M ∉ **C** *and* ∀X ∈ DESC(M) : X ∉ **C**.

Two sets of random variables **A** *and* **B** *are* d-separated *given a set* **C** *if and only if each undirected path from every node* A ∈ **A** *to every node* B ∈ **B** *is d-separated by* **C**.

It is possible to prove that **A** is independent from **B** given **C** iff **A** is d-separated from **B** given **C**, so d-separation and conditional independence are equivalent.

The set of parents, children, and other children of the parents of a variable d-separates it from the other variables, so it forms a sufficient set of nodes to make the variable independent from all the others. Such a set is called a *Markov blanket* and is shown in Figure 1.8.

Graphical models are a way to represent a factorization of a joint probability distribution. BNs represent a factorization in terms of conditional probabilities. In general, a *factorized model* takes the form

$$P(\mathbf{x}) = \frac{\prod_{i=1}^{m} \phi_i(\mathbf{x}_i)}{Z}$$

where each $\phi_i(\mathbf{x}_i)$ for $i = 1, \ldots, m$ is a *potential* or *factor*, a function taking non-negative values on a subset $\mathbf{X}_i$ of $\mathbf{X}$. Factors are indicated with $\phi, \psi, \ldots$

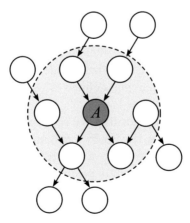

Figure 1.8 Markov blanket. Figure from https://commons.wikimedia.org/wiki/File:Diagram_of_a_Markov_blanket.svg.

Since the numerator of the fraction may not lead to a probability distribution (the sum of all possible values at the numerator may not be one), the denominator Z is added that makes the expression a probability distribution since it is defined as

$$Z = \sum_{\mathbf{x}} \prod_i \phi_i(\mathbf{x}_i)$$

i.e., it is exactly the sum of all possible values of the numerator. Z is thus a *normalizing constant* and is also called *partition function*.

A potential $\phi_i(\mathbf{x}_i)$ can be seen as a table that, for each possible combination of values of the variables in $\mathbf{X}_i$, returns a non-negative number. Since all potentials are non-negative, $P(\mathbf{x}) \geqslant 0$ for all $\mathbf{x}$. Potentials influence the distribution in this way: all other things being equal, a larger value of a potential for a combination of values of the variables in its domain corresponds to a larger probability value of the instantiation of $\mathbf{X}$.

An example of a potential for a university domain is a function defined over the random variables Intelligent and GoodMarks expressing the fact that a student is intelligent and that he gets good marks, respectively. The potential may be represented by the table

Intelligent	GoodMarks	$\phi_i(\mathrm{I}, \mathrm{G})$
false	false	4.5
false	true	4.5
true	false	1.0
true	true	4.5

where the configuration where the student is intelligent but he does not get good marks has a lower value than the other configurations.

A BN can be seen as defining a factorized model with a potential for each *family* of nodes (a node and its parents) defined as $\phi_i(\mathrm{x}_i, \mathbf{pa}_i) = P(\mathrm{x}_i | \mathbf{pa}_i)$. It is easy to see that in this case $Z = 1$.

If all the potentials are strictly positive, we can replace each factor $\phi_i(\mathbf{x}_i)$ with the exponential $\exp(w_i f_i(\mathbf{x}_i))$ with w_i a real number called *weight* and $f_i(\mathbf{x}_i)$ a function from the values of $\mathbf{X}_i$ to the reals (often only to $\{0, 1\}$) called *feature*. If the potentials are strictly positive, this reparameterization is always possible. In this case, the factorized model becomes:

$$P(\mathbf{x}) = \frac{\exp(\sum_i w_i f_i(\mathbf{x_i}))}{Z}$$
$$Z = \sum_{\mathbf{x}} \exp(\sum_i w_i f_i(\mathbf{x_i}))$$

This is also called a *log-linear model* because the logarithm of the joint is a linear function of the features. An example of a feature corresponding to the example potential above is

$$f_i(\text{Intelligent, GoodMarks}) = \begin{cases} 1 & \text{if } \neg\text{Intelligent} \vee \text{GoodMarks} \\ 0 & \text{otherwise} \end{cases}$$

If $w_i = 1.5$, then $\phi_i(i, g) = \exp(w_i f_i(i, g))$ for all values i, g for random variables I, G in our university example.

A Markov network (MN) or Markov random field [Pearl, 1988] is an undirected graph that represents a factorized model. An MN has a node for each variable and each pair of nodes that appear together in the domain of a potential are connected by an edge. In other words, the nodes in the domain of each potential form a *clique*, a fully-connected subset of the nodes.

Example 12 (University – MN). *An MN for a university domain is shown in Figure 1.9. The network contains the example potential above plus a potential involving the three variables GoodMarks, CouDifficulty, and TeachAbility.*

As BNs, MNs also allow reading off independencies from the graph. In an MN where $P(\mathbf{x}) > 0$ for all $\mathbf{x}$ (a strictly positive distribution), two sets of random variables $\mathbf{A}$ and $\mathbf{B}$ are independent given a set $\mathbf{C}$ if and only if each path from every node $A \in \mathbf{A}$ to every node $B \in \mathbf{B}$ passes through an element of $\mathbf{C}$ [Pearl, 1988]. Then the Markov blanket of a variable is the set of its neighbors. So reading independencies from the graph is much easier than for BNs.

MNs and BNs can each represent independencies that the other cannot represent [Pearl, 1988], so their expressive power is not comparable. MNs have the advantage that the potentials/features can be defined more freely, because they do not have to respect the normalization that conditional probabilities must respect. On the other hand, parameters in an MN are diffi-

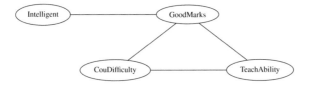

Figure 1.9 Example of a Markov network.

cult to interpret, because their influence on the joint distribution depends on the whole set of potentials, while in a BN, the parameters are conditional probabilities, so they are easier to interpret and to estimate.

Given a BN, an MN representing the same joint distribution can be obtained by *moralizing* the graph: adding edges between all pairs of nodes that have a common child (marrying the parents), and then making all edges in the graph undirected. In this way, each family $\{X_i, \mathbf{Pa}_i\}$ of the BN forms a clique associated with the potential $\phi_i(x_i, \mathbf{pa}_i) = P(x_i|\mathbf{pa}_i)$.

Given an MN, an equivalent BN can be obtained containing a node for each variable plus a Boolean node F_i for each potential ϕ_i. Edges are then added so that a potential node has all the nodes in its scope as parents. The BN equivalent to the MN of Figure 1.9 is shown in Figure 1.10.

The CPT for node F_i is

$$P(F_i = 1|\mathbf{x}_i) = \frac{\phi_i(\mathbf{x}_i)}{C_i}$$

where C_i is a constant depending on the potential that ensures that the values are probabilities, i.e., that they are in $[0, 1]$. It can be chosen freely provided that $C_i \geqslant \max_{\mathbf{x}_i} \phi(\mathbf{x}_i)$, for example, it can be chosen as $C_i = \max_{\mathbf{x}_i} \phi(\mathbf{x}_i)$ or $C_i = \sum_{\mathbf{x}_i} \phi_i(\mathbf{x}_i)$. The CPT for each variable node assigns uniform probability to its values, i.e., $P(x_j) = \frac{1}{k_j}$ where k_j is the number of values of X_j.

Then the joint conditional distribution $P(\mathbf{x}|\mathbf{F} = 1)$ of the BN is equal to the joint of the MN. In fact

$$P(\mathbf{x}, \mathbf{F} = 1) = \prod_i P(F_i = 1|\mathbf{x}_i) \prod_j P(x_j) = \prod_i \frac{\phi_i(\mathbf{x}_i)}{C_i} \prod_j \frac{1}{k_j} =$$

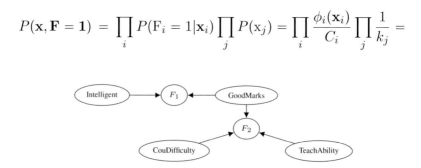

Figure 1.10 Bayesian network equivalent to the Markov network of Figure 1.9.

Figure 1.11 Example of a factor graph.

$$\frac{\prod_i \phi_i(\mathbf{x}_i)}{\prod_i C_i} \prod_j \frac{1}{k_j}$$

and

$$P(\mathbf{x}|\mathbf{F} = 1) = \frac{P(\mathbf{x}, \mathbf{F} = 1)}{P(\mathbf{F} = 1)} = \frac{P(\mathbf{x}, \mathbf{F} = 1)}{\sum_{\mathbf{x}'} P(\mathbf{x}', \mathbf{F} = 1)} =$$

$$\frac{\frac{\prod_i \phi_i(\mathbf{x}_i)}{\prod_i C_i} \prod_j \frac{1}{k_j}}{\sum_{\mathbf{x}'} \frac{\prod_i \phi_i(\mathbf{x}'_i)}{\prod_i C_i} \prod_j \frac{1}{k_j}} =$$

$$\frac{\frac{1}{\prod_i C_i} \prod_j \frac{1}{k_j} \prod_i \phi_i(\mathbf{x}_i)}{\frac{1}{\prod_i C_i} \prod_j \frac{1}{k_j} \sum_{\mathbf{x}'} \prod_i \phi_i(\mathbf{x}'_i)} = \frac{\prod_i \phi_i(\mathbf{x}_i)}{Z}$$

So, a query **q** given evidence **e** to the MN can be answered using the equivalent BN by computing $P(\mathbf{q}|\mathbf{e}, \mathbf{F} = 1)$.

The equivalent BN encodes the same conditional independencies as the MN provided that the set of condition nodes is extended with the set of factor nodes, so an independence $I(\mathbf{A}, \mathbf{B}, \mathbf{C})$ holding in the MN will hold in the equivalent BN in the form $I(\mathbf{A}, \mathbf{B}, \mathbf{C} \cup \mathbf{F})$. For example, a pair of nodes from the scope $\mathbf{X}_i$ of a factor given the factor node F_i cannot be made independent no matter what other nodes are added to the condition set because of d-separation, just as in the MN where they are neighbors.

A third type of graphical model is the Factor graph (FG) which can represent general factorized models. An FG is undirected and bipartite, i.e., its nodes are divided into two disjoint sets, the set of variables and the set of factors, and the edges always have an endpoint in a set and the other in the other set. A factor corresponds to a potential in the model. An FG contains an edge connecting each factor with all the variables in its domain. So from an FG, one can immediately read the factorization of the model. An FG representing the factorized model of Figure 1.9 is shown in Figure 1.11.

FGs are specially useful for expressing inference algorithms, in particular the formulas for belief propagation are simpler to express for FGs than for BNs and MNs.

2

Probabilistic Logic Programming Languages

Various approaches have been proposed for combining logic programming with probability theory. They can be broadly classified into two categories: those based on the *Distribution Semantics* (DS) [Sato, 1995] and those that follow a *Knowledge Base Model Construction* (KBMC) approach.

For languages in the first category, a probabilistic logic program without function symbols defines a probability distribution over normal logic programs (termed *worlds*). To define the probability of a query, this distribution is extended to a joint distribution of the query and the worlds and the probability of the query is obtained from the joint distribution by marginalization, i.e., by summing out the worlds. For probabilistic logic programs with function symbols, the definition is more complex, see Chapter 3.

The distribution over programs is defined by encoding random choices for clauses. Each choice generates an alternative version of the clause and the set of choices is associated with a probability distribution. The various languages that follow the DS differ in how the choices are encoded. In all languages, however, choices are independent from each other.

In the KBMC approach, instead, a probabilistic logic program is a compact way of encoding a large graphical model, either a BN or MN. In the KBMC approach, the semantics of a program is defined by the method for building the graphical model from the program.

2.1 Languages with the Distribution Semantics

The languages following the DS differ in how they encode choices for clauses, and how the probabilities for these choices are stated. As will be shown in Section 2.4, they all have the same expressive power. This fact shows that the differences in the languages are syntactic, and also justifies speaking of *the* DS.

2.1.1 Logic programs with annotated disjunctions

In Logic Programs with Annotated Disjunctions (LPADs) [Vennekens et al., 2004], the alternatives are expressed by means of annotated disjunctive heads of clauses. An *annotated disjunctive clause* C_i has the form

$$h_{i1} : \Pi_{i1} ; \ldots ; h_{in_i} : \Pi_{in_i} \leftarrow b_{i1}, \ldots, b_{im_i}$$

where $h_{i1}, \ldots, h_{in_i}$ are logical atoms, $b_{i1}, \ldots, b_{im_i}$ are logical literals, and $\Pi_{i1}, \ldots, \Pi_{in_i}$ are real numbers in the interval $[0, 1]$ such that $\sum_{k=1}^{n_i} \Pi_{ik} = 1$. An LPAD is a finite set of annotated disjunctive clauses.

Each world is obtained by selecting one atom from the head of each grounding of each annotated disjunctive clause.

Example 13 (Medical symptoms – LPAD).   *The following LPAD models the appearance of medical symptoms as a consequence of disease. A person may sneeze if she has the flu or if she has hay fever:*

$$sneezing(X) : 0.7 ; null : 0.3 \leftarrow flu(X).$$
$$sneezing(X) : 0.8 ; null : 0.2 \leftarrow hay\_fever(X).$$
$$flu(bob).$$
$$hay\_fever(bob).$$

The first clause can be read as: if X has the flu, then X sneezes with probability 0.7 and nothing happens with probability 0.3. Similarly, the second clause can be read as: if X has hay fever, then X sneezes with probability 0.8 and nothing happens with probability 0.2. Here, and for the other languages based on the distribution semantics, the atom null does not appear in the body of any clause and is used to represent an alternative in which no atom is selected. It can also be omitted obtaining

$$sneezing(X) : 0.7 \leftarrow flu(X).$$
$$sneezing(X) : 0.8 \leftarrow hay\_fever(X).$$
$$flu(bob).$$
$$hay\_fever(bob).$$

As can be seen from the example, LPADs encode in a natural way programs representing causal mechanisms: flu and hay fever are causes for sneezing, which, however, is probabilistic, in the sense that it may or may not happen even when the causes are present. The relationship between the DS, and LPADs in particular, and causal reasoning is discussed in Section 2.8.

2.1.2 ProbLog

The design of ProbLog [De Raedt et al., 2007] was motivated by the desire to make the simplest probabilistic extension of Prolog. In ProbLog, alternatives are expressed by *probabilistic facts* of the form

$$\Pi_i :: f_i$$

where $\Pi_i \in [0, 1]$ and f_i is an atom, meaning that each ground instantiation $f_i\theta$ of f_i is true with probability Π_i and false with probability $1 - \Pi_i$. Each world is obtained by selecting or rejecting each grounding of each probabilistic fact.

Example 14 (Medical symptoms – ProbLog). *Example 13 can be expressed in ProbLog as:*

$$sneezing(X) \leftarrow flu(X), flu\_sneezing(X).$$
$$sneezing(X) \leftarrow hay\_fever(X), hay\_fever\_sneezing(X).$$
$$flu(bob).$$
$$hay\_fever(bob).$$
$$0.7 :: flu\_sneezing(X).$$
$$0.8 :: hay\_fever\_sneezing(X).$$

2.1.3 Probabilistic horn abduction

Probabilistic horn abduction (PHA) [Poole, 1993b] and Independent choice logic (ICL) [Poole, 1997] express alternatives by facts, called *disjoint statements*, having the form

$$disjoint([a_{i1} : \Pi_{i1}, \ldots, a_{in} : \Pi_{in_i}]).$$

where each a_{ik} is a logical atom and each Π_{ik} a number in $[0, 1]$ such that $\sum_{k=1}^{n_i} \Pi_{ik} = 1$. Such a statement can be interpreted in terms of its ground instantiations: for each substitution θ grounding the atoms of the statement, the $a_{ik}\theta$s are random alternatives and $a_{ik}\theta$ is true with probability Π_{ik}. Each world is obtained by selecting one atom from each grounding of each disjoint statement in the program. In practice, each ground instantiation of a disjoint statement corresponds to a random variable with as many values as the alternatives in the statement.

Example 15 (Medical symptoms – ICL). *Example 13 can be expressed in ICL as:*

$$sneezing(X) \leftarrow flu(X), flu\_sneezing(X).$$
$$sneezing(X) \leftarrow hay\_fever(X), hay\_fever\_sneezing(X).$$
$$flu(bob).$$
$$hay\_fever(bob).$$

$$disjoint([flu\_sneezing(X) : 0.7, null : 0.3]).$$
$$disjoint([hay\_fever\_sneezing(X) : 0.8, null : 0.2]).$$

In ICL, LPADs, and ProbLog, each grounding of a probabilistic clause is associated with a random variable with as many values as alternatives/head disjuncts for ICL and LPADs and with two values for ProbLog. The random variables corresponding to different instantiations of a probabilistic clause are independent and identically distributed (IID).

2.1.4 PRISM

The language PRISM [Sato and Kameya, 1997] is similar to PHA/ICL but introduces random facts via the predicate $msw/3$ (*multi-switch*):

$$msw(SwitchName, TrialId, Value).$$

The first argument of this predicate is a *random switch name*, a term representing a set of discrete random variables; the second argument is an integer, the *trial id*; and the third argument represents a value for that variable. The set of possible values for a switch is defined by a fact of the form

$$values(SwitchName, [v_1, \ldots, v_n]).$$

where $SwitchName$ is again a term representing a switch name and each v_i is a term. Each ground pair $(SwitchName, TrialId)$ represents a distinct random variable and the set of random variables associated with the same switch are IID.

The probability distribution over the values of the random variables associated with $SwitchName$ is defined by a directive of the form

$$\leftarrow set\_sw(SwitchName, [\Pi_1, \ldots, \Pi_n]).$$

where Π_i is the probability that variable $SwitchName$ takes value v_i. Each world is obtained by selecting one value for each trial id of each random switch.

Example 16 (Coin tosses – PRISM). *The modeling of coin tosses shows differences in how the various PLP languages represent IID random variables. Suppose that coin c_1 is known not to be fair, but that all tosses of c_1 have the same probabilities of outcomes – in other words, each toss of c_1 is taken from a family of IID random variables. This can be represented in PRISM as*

$$values(c_1, [head, tail]).$$
$$\leftarrow set\_sw(c_1, [0.4, 0.6])$$

Different tosses of c_1 can then be identified *using the* trial id *argument of* $msw/3$.

In PHA/ICL and many other PLP languages, each ground instantiation of a disjoint/1 *statement represents a distinct random variable, so that IID random variables need to be represented through the statement's instantiation patterns: e.g.,*

$$disjoint([coin(c_1, TossNumber, head) : 0.4,$$
$$coin(c_1, TossNumber, tail) : 0.6]).$$

In practice, the PRISM system accepts an $msw/2$ predicate whose atoms do not contain the trial id and for which each occurrence in a program is considered as being associated with a different new variable.

Example 17 (Medical symptoms – PRISM). *Example 15 can be encoded in PRISM as:*

$sneezing(X) \leftarrow flu(X), msw(flu\_sneezing(X), 1).$
$sneezing(X) \leftarrow hay\_fever(X), msw(hay\_fever\_sneezing(X), 1).$
$flu(bob).$
$hay\_fever(bob).$

$values(flu\_sneezing(X), [1, 0]).$
$values(hay\_fever\_sneezing(X), [1, 0]).$
$\leftarrow set\_sw(flu\_sneezing(X), [0.7, 0.3]).$
$\leftarrow set\_sw(hay\_fever\_sneezing(X), [0.8, 0.2]).$

2.2 The Distribution Semantics for Programs Without Function Symbols

We present first the DS for the case of ProbLog as it is the language with the simplest syntax. A ProbLog program $\mathcal{P}$ is composed by a set of normal rules $\mathcal{R}$ and a set $\mathcal{F}$ of probabilistic facts. Each *probabilistic fact* is of the form $\Pi_i :: f_i$ where $\Pi_i \in [0, 1]$ and f_i is an atom[1], meaning that each ground instantiation $f_i\theta$ of f_i is true with probability Π_i and false with probability $1 - \Pi_i$. Each world is obtained by selecting or rejecting each grounding of each probabilistic fact.

An *atomic choice* indicates whether grounding $f\theta$ of a probabilistic fact $F = \Pi :: f$ is selected or not. It is represented with the triple (f, θ, k) where $k \in \{0, 1\}$ and $k = 1$ means that the fact is selected, $k = 0$ that it is not. A set κ of atomic choices is *consistent* if it does not contain two atomic choices (f, θ, k) and (f, θ, j) with $k \neq j$ (only one alternative is selected for a ground probabilistic fact). The function $consistent(\kappa)$ returns true if κ is consistent. A *composite choice* κ is a consistent set of atomic choices. The probability of composite choice κ is

$$P(\kappa) = \prod_{(f_i,\theta,1)\in\kappa} \Pi_i \prod_{(f_i,\theta,0)\in\kappa} 1 - \Pi_i.$$

A *selection* σ is a total composite choice, i.e., it contains one atomic choice for every grounding of every probabilistic fact. A *world* w_σ is a logic program that is identified by a selection σ. The world w_σ is formed by adding f for each atomic choice $(f, \theta, 1)$ of σ to $\mathcal{R}$.

The probability of a world w_σ is $P(w_\sigma) = P(\sigma)$. Since in this section we are assuming programs without function symbols, the set of groundings of each probabilistic fact is finite, and so is the set of worlds $W_\mathcal{P}$. Accordingly, for a ProbLog program $\mathcal{P}$, $W_\mathcal{P} = \{w_1, \ldots, w_m\}$. Moreover, $P(w_\sigma)$ is a distribution over worlds: $\sum_{w\in W_\mathcal{P}} P(w) = 1$. We call *sound* a program for which every world has a two-valued WFM. We consider here sound programs, for non-sound ones, see Chapter 6.

Let q be a query in the form of a ground atom. We define the conditional probability of q given a world w as: $P(q|w) = 1$ if q is true in w and 0 otherwise. Since the program is sound, q can be only true or false in a world. The probability of q can thus be computed by summing out the worlds from the joint distribution of the query and the worlds:

$$P(q) = \sum_w P(q, w) = \sum_w P(q|w)P(w) = \sum_{w\models q} P(w). \qquad (2.1)$$

So the probability of q is the sum of the probabilities of the worlds where q is true. This formula can also be used for computing the probability of a

---

[1] With an abuse of notation, sometimes we use $\mathcal{F}$ to indicate the set containing the atoms f_is. The meaning of $\mathcal{F}$ will be clear from the context.

conjunction $q_1, \ldots, q_n$ of ground atoms since the truth of a conjunction of ground atoms in a world is well defined. So we can compute the conditional probability of a query q given evidence e in the form of a conjunction of ground atoms $e_1, \ldots, e_m$ as

$$P(q|e) = \frac{P(q, e)}{P(e)} \qquad (2.2)$$

We can also assign a probability to a query q by defining a probability space. Since W_P is finite, then $(W_P, \mathbb{P}(W_P))$ is a measurable space. For an element $\omega \in \mathbb{P}(W_P)$, define $\mu(\omega)$ as

$$\mu(\omega) = \sum_{w \in \omega} P(w)$$

with the probability of a world $P(w)$ defined as above. Then it's easy to see that $(W_P, \mathbb{P}(W_P), \mu)$ is a finitely additive probability space.

Given a ground atom q, define the function $Q : W_P \to \{0, 1\}$ as

$$Q(w) = \begin{cases} 1 & \text{if } w \models q \\ 0 & \text{otherwise} \end{cases} \qquad (2.3)$$

Since the set of events is the powerset, then $Q^{-1}(\gamma) \in \mathbb{P}(W_P)$ for all $\gamma \subseteq \{0, 1\}$ and Q is a random variable. The distribution of Q is defined by $P(Q=1)$ $(P(Q=0)$ is given by $1 - P(Q=1))$ and we indicate $P(Q=1)$ with $P(q)$.

We can now compute $P(q)$ as

$$P(q) = \mu(Q^{-1}(\{1\})) = \mu(\{w|w \in W_P, w \models q\}) = \sum_{w \models q} P(w)$$

obtaining the same formula as Equation (2.1).

The distribution over worlds also induces a distribution over interpretations: given an interpretation I, we can define the conditional probability of I given a world w as: $P(I|w) = 1$ is I is the model of w ($I \models w$) and 0 otherwise. The distribution over interpretations is then given by a formula similar to Equation (2.1):

$$P(I) = \sum_w P(I, w) = \sum_w P(I|w)P(w) = \sum_{I \models w} P(w) \qquad (2.4)$$

We call the interpretations I for which $P(I) > 0$ *possible models* because they are models for at least one world.

Now define the function $\mathbf{I} : W_{\mathcal{P}} \to \{0, 1\}$ as

$$\mathbf{I}(I) = \begin{cases} 1 & \text{if } I \models w \\ 0 & \text{otherwise} \end{cases} \tag{2.5}$$

$\mathbf{I}^{-1}(\gamma) \in \mathbb{P}(W_{\mathcal{P}})$ for all $\gamma \subseteq \{0, 1\}$ so $\mathbf{I}$ is a random variable for probability space $(W_{\mathcal{P}}, \mathbb{P}(W_{\mathcal{P}}), \mu)$. The distribution of $\mathbf{I}$ is defined by $P(\mathbf{I}{=}1)$ and we indicate $P(\mathbf{I}{=}1)$ with $P(I)$.

We can now compute $P(I)$ as

$$P(I) = \mu(\mathbf{I}^{-1}(\{1\})) = \mu(\{w | w \in W_{\mathcal{P}}, I \models w\}) = \sum_{I \models w} P(w)$$

obtaining the same formula as Equation (2.4).

The probability of a query q can be obtained from the distribution over interpretations by defining the conditional probability of q given an interpretation I as $P(q|I) = 1$ if $I \models q$ and 0 otherwise and by marginalizing the interpretations obtaining

$$P(q) = \sum_I P(q, I) = \sum_I P(q|I)P(I) = \sum_{I \models q} P(I) = \sum_{I \models q, I \models w} P(w) \tag{2.6}$$

So the probability of a query can be obtained by summing the probability of the possible models where the query is true.

Example 18 (Medical symptoms – worlds – ProbLog). *Consider the program of Example 14. The program has four worlds*

$w_1 = \{$
    flu_sneezing(bob).
    hay_fever_sneezing(bob).
$\}$
$P(w_1) = \quad 0.7 \times 0.8$

$w_2 = \{$

    hay_fever_sneezing(bob).
$\}$
$P(w_2) = \quad 0.3 \times 0.8$

$w_3 = \{$

    flu_sneezing(bob).
$\}$
$P(w_3) = \quad 0.7 \times 0.2$

$w_4 = \{$

$\}$
$P(w_4) = \quad 0.3 \times 0.2$

The query sneezing(bob) is true in three worlds and its probability

$$P(sneezing(bob)) = 0.7 \times 0.8 + 0.3 \times 0.8 + 0.7 \times 0.2 = 0.94.$$

Note that the contributions from the two clauses are combined disjunctively. The probability of the query is thus computed using the rule giving the probability of the disjunction of two independent Boolean random variables:

$$P(a \vee b) = P(a) + P(b) - P(a)P(b) = 1 - (1 - P(a))(1 - P(b)).$$

In our case, $P(sneezing(bob)) = 0.7 + 0.8 - 0.7 \cdot 0.8 = 0.94.$

We now give the semantics for LPADs. A clause

$$C_i = h_{i1} : \Pi_{i1} ; \ldots ; h_{in_i} : \Pi_{in_i} \leftarrow b_{i1}, \ldots, b_{im_i}$$

stands for a set of probabilistic clauses, one for each ground instantiation $C_i\theta$ of C_i. Each ground probabilistic clause represents a choice among n_i normal clauses, each of the form

$$h_{ik} \leftarrow b_{i1}, \ldots, b_{im_i}$$

for $k = 1 \ldots, n_i$. Moreover, another clause

$$null \leftarrow b_{i1}, \ldots, b_{im_i}$$

is implicitly encoded which is associated with probability $\Pi_0 = 1 - \sum_{k=1}^{n_i} \Pi_k$. So, for the LPAD $\mathcal{P}$, an *atomic choice* is the selection of a head atom for a grounding $C_i\theta_j$ of a probabilistic clause C_i, including the atom *null*. An atomic choice is represented in this case by the triple (C_i, θ_j, k), where θ_j is a grounding substitution and $k \in \{0, 1, \ldots, n_i\}$. An atomic choice represents an equation of the form $X_{ij} = k$ where X_{ij} is a random variable associated with $C_i\theta_j$. The definition of consistent set of atomic choices, of composite choices, and of the probability of a composite choice is the same as for ProbLog. Again, a *selection* σ is a total composite choice (one atomic choice for each grounding of each probabilistic clause). A selection σ identifies a logic program w_σ (a *world*) that contains the normal clauses obtained by selecting head atom $h_{ik}\theta$ for each atomic choice (C_i, θ, k):

$$w_\sigma = \{ \ (h_{ik} \leftarrow b_{i1}, \ldots, b_{im_i})\theta | (C_i, \theta, k) \in \sigma,$$
$$C_i = h_{i1} : \Pi_{i1} ; \ldots ; h_{in_i} : \Pi_{in_i} \leftarrow b_{i1}, \ldots, b_{im_i}, C_i \in \mathcal{P}\}$$

As for ProbLog, the probability of w_σ is $P(w_\sigma) = P(\sigma) = \prod_{(C_i, \theta_j, k) \in \sigma} \Pi_{ik}$, the set of worlds $W_P = \{w_1, \ldots, w_m\}$ is finite, and $P(w_\sigma)$ is a distribution over worlds.

If q is a query, we can define $P(q|w)$ as for ProbLog and again the probability of q is given by Equation (2.1)

Example 19 (Medical symptoms – worlds – LPAD). *The LPAD of Example 13 has four worlds:*

$$w_1 = \{$$

$$sneezing(bob) \leftarrow flu(bob).$$
$$sneezing(bob) \leftarrow hay\_fever(bob).$$
$$flu(bob). \quad hay\_fever(bob).$$

$$\}$$
$$P(w_1) = \quad 0.7 \times 0.8$$

$$w_2 = \{$$

$$null \leftarrow flu(bob).$$
$$sneezing(bob) \leftarrow hay\_fever(bob).$$
$$flu(bob). \quad hay\_fever(bob).$$

$$\}$$
$$P(w_2) = \quad 0.3 \times 0.8$$

$$w_3 = \{$$

$$sneezing(bob) \leftarrow flu(bob).$$
$$null \leftarrow hay\_fever(bob).$$
$$flu(bob). \quad hay\_fever(bob).$$

$$\}$$
$$P(w_3) = \quad 0.7 \times 0.2$$

$$w_4 = \{$$

$$null \leftarrow flu(bob).$$
$$null \leftarrow hay\_fever(bob).$$
$$flu(bob). \quad hay\_fever(bob).$$

$$\}$$
$$P(w_4) = \quad 0.3 \times 0.2$$

sneezing(bob) is true in three worlds and its probability is

$$P(sneezing(bob)) = 0.7 \times 0.8 + 0.3 \times 0.8 + 0.7 \times 0.2 = 0.94$$

2.3 Examples of Programs

In this section, we provide some examples of programs to better illustrate the syntax and the semantics.

Example 20 (Detailed medical symptoms – LPAD). *The following LPAD[2] models a program that describe medical symptoms in a way that is slightly more elaborated than Example 13:*

$strong\_sneezing(X) : 0.3 ; moderate\_sneezing(X) : 0.5 \leftarrow$
  $flu(X).$
$strong\_sneezing(X) : 0.2 ; moderate\_sneezing(X) : 0.6 \leftarrow$
  $hay\_fever(X).$
$flu(bob).$
$hay\_fever(bob).$

Here the clauses have three alternatives in the head of which the one associated with atom null *is left implicit. This program has nine worlds, the query* $strong\_sneezing(bob)$ *is true in five of them, and* $P(strong\_sneezing$ $(bob)) = 0.44.$

Example 21 (Coin – LPAD). *The coin example of [Vennekens et al., 2004] is represented as[3]:*

$heads(Coin) : 1/2 ; tails(Coin) : 1/2 \leftarrow$
  $toss(Coin), \sim biased(Coin).$
$heads(Coin) : 0.6 ; tails(Coin) : 0.4 \leftarrow$
  $toss(Coin), biased(Coin).$
$fair(Coin) : 0.9 ; biased(Coin) : 0.1.$
$toss(coin).$

The first clause states that, if we toss a coin that is not biased, it has equal probability of landing heads and tails. The second states that, if the coin is biased, it has a slightly higher probability of landing heads. The third states that the coin is fair with probability 0.9 and biased with probability 0.1 and the last clause states that we toss the coin with certainty. This program has eight worlds, the query $heads(coin)$ *is true in four of them, and its probability is 0.51.*

Example 22 (Eruption – LPAD). *Consider this LPAD[4] from [Riguzzi and Di Mauro, 2012] that is inspired by the morphological characteristics of the Italian island of Stromboli:*

---

[2] https://cplint.eu/e/sneezing.pl
[3] https://cplint.eu/e/coin.pl
[4] https://cplint.eu/e/eruption.pl

$$C_1 = \quad eruption : 0.6 \; ; \; earthquake : 0.3 :\text{-} \; sudden\_energy\_release,$$
$$\quad\quad fault\_rupture(X).$$
$$C_2 = \quad sudden\_energy\_release : 0.7.$$
$$C_3 = \quad fault\_rupture(southwest\_northeast).$$
$$C_4 = \quad fault\_rupture(east\_west).$$

The island of Stromboli is located at the intersection of two geological faults, one in the southwest–northeast direction, the other in the east–west direction, and contains one of the three volcanoes that are active in Italy. This program models the possibility that an eruption or an earthquake occurs at Stromboli. If there is a sudden energy release under the island and there is a fault rupture, then there can be an eruption of the volcano on the island with probability 0.6 or an earthquake in the area with probability 0.3. The energy release occurs with probability 0.7 and we are sure that ruptures occur in both faults.

Clause C_1 has two groundings, $C_1\theta_1$ with

$$\theta_1 = \{X/southwest\_northeast\}$$

and $C_1\theta_2$ with

$$\theta_2 = \{X/east\_west\},$$

while clause C_2 has a single grounding $C_2\varnothing$. Since C_1 has three head atoms and C_2 two, the program has $3 \times 3 \times 2$ worlds. The query $eruption$ is true in five of them and its probability is $P(eruption) = 0.6 \cdot 0.6 \cdot 0.7 + 0.6 \cdot 0.3 \cdot 0.7 + 0.6 \cdot 0.1 \cdot 0.7 + 0.3 \cdot 0.6 \cdot 0.7 + 0.1 \cdot 0.6 \cdot 0.7 = 0.588.$

Example 23 (Monty Hall puzzle – LPAD). *The Monty Hall puzzle [Baral et al., 2009] refers to the TV game show hosted by Monty Hall in which a player has to choose which of three closed doors to open. Behind one door there is a prize, while behind the other two there is nothing. Once the player has selected the door, Monty Hall opens one of the remaining closed doors which does not contain the prize, and then he asks the player if he would like to change his door with the other closed door or not. The problem of this game is to determine whether the player should switch. The following program provides a solution[5]. The prize is behind one of the three doors with the same probability:*

$$prize(1) : 1/3 \; ; \; prize(2) : 1/3 \; ; \; prize(3) : 1/3.$$

The player has selected door 1:

$$selected(1).$$

---

[5] https://cplint.eu/e/monty.swinb

Monty opens door 2 with probability 0.5 and door 3 with probability 0.5 if the prize is behind door 1:

$open\_door(2) : 0.5 \; ; \; open\_door(3) : 0.5 \leftarrow prize(1).$

Monty opens door 2 if the prize is behind door 3:

$open\_door(2) \leftarrow prize(3).$

Monty opens door 3 if the prize is behind door 2:

$open\_door(3) \leftarrow prize(2).$

The player keeps his choice and wins if he has selected a door with the prize:

$win\_keep \leftarrow prize(1).$

The player switches and wins if the prize is behind the door that he has not selected and that Monty did not open:

$win\_switch \leftarrow prize(2), open\_door(3).$

$win\_switch \leftarrow prize(3), open\_door(2).$

Querying win_keep and win_switch we obtain probability 1/3 and 2/3 respectively, so the player should switch. Note that if you change the probability distribution of Monty selecting a door to open when the prize is behind the door selected by the player, then the probability of winning by switching remains the same.

Example 24 (Three-prisoner puzzle – LPAD). *The following program[6] from [Riguzzi et al., 2016a] encodes the three-prisoner puzzle. In [Grünwald and Halpern, 2003], the problem is described as:*

> *Of three prisoners a, b, and c, two are to be executed, but a does not know which. Thus, a thinks that the probability that i will be executed is 2/3 for i ∈ {a, b, c}. He says to the jailer, "Since either b or c is certainly going to be executed, you will give me no information about my own chances if you give me the name of one man, either b or c, who is going to be executed." But then, no matter what the jailer says, naive conditioning leads a to believe that his chance of execution went down from 2/3 to 1/2.*

Each prisoner is safe with probability 1/3:

$safe(a) : 1/3 \; ; \; safe(b) : 1/3 \; ; \; safe(c) : 1/3.$

If a is safe, the jailer tells that one of the other prisoners will be executed uniformly at random:

$tell\_executed(b) : 1/2 \; ; \; tell\_executed(c) : 1/2 \leftarrow safe(a).$

Otherwise, he tells that the only unsafe prisoner will be executed:

---

[6] https://cplint.eu/e/jail.swinb

$tell\_executed(b) \leftarrow safe(c).$
$tell\_executed(c) \leftarrow safe(b).$

The jailer speaks if he tells that somebody will be executed:

$tell \leftarrow tell\_executed(\_).$

where _ indicates a distinct anonymous variable, *i.e., a variable that is there as a placeholder and for which we don't care about its value.*

    a is safe after the jailer utterance if he is safe and the jailer speaks:

$safe\_after\_tell : -safe(a), tell.$

By computing the probability of safe(a) and safe_after_tell, we get the same probability of 1/3, so the jailer utterance does not change the probability of a of being safe.

    We can see this also by considering conditional probabilities: the probability of safe(a) given the jailer utterance tell is

$$P(safe(a)|tell) = \frac{P(safe(a), tell)}{P(tell)} = \frac{P(safe\_after\_tell)}{P(tell)} = \frac{1/3}{1} = 1/3$$

because the probability of tell is 1.

Example 25 (Russian roulette with two guns – LPAD). *The following example[7] models a Russian roulette game with two guns [Baral et al., 2009]. The death of the player is caused with probability 1/6 by triggering the left gun and similarly for the right gun:*

$death : 1/6 \leftarrow pull\_trigger(left\_gun).$
$death : 1/6 \leftarrow pull\_trigger(right\_gun).$
$pull\_trigger(left\_gun).$
$pull\_trigger(right\_gun).$

Querying the probability of death we get the probability of the player of dying.

Example 26 (Mendelian rules of inheritance – LPAD). *Blockeel [2004] presents a program[8] that encodes the Mendelian rules of inheritance of the color of pea plants. The color of a pea plant is determined by a gene that exists in two forms (alleles), purple, p, and white, w. Each plant has two alleles for the color gene that reside on a pair of chromosomes. cg(X, N, A) indicates that plant X has allele A on chromosome N. The program is:*

$color(X, white) \leftarrow cg(X, 1, w), cg(X, 2, w).$
$color(X, purple) \leftarrow cg(X, \_A, p).$

---

[7] https://cplint.eu/e/trigger.pl
[8] https://cplint.eu/e/mendel.pl

$cg(X, 1, A) : 0.5 \; ; \; cg(X, 1, B) : 0.5 \leftarrow$
$\quad mother(Y, X), cg(Y, 1, A), cg(Y, 2, B).$
$cg(X, 2, A) : 0.5 \; ; \; cg(X, 2, B) : 0.5 \leftarrow$
$\quad father(Y, X), cg(Y, 1, A), cg(Y, 2, B).$
$mother(m, c). \quad father(f, c).$
$cg(m, 1, w). \quad cg(m, 2, w). \quad cg(f, 1, p). \quad cg(f, 2, w).$

The facts of the program express that c is the offspring of m and f and that the alleles of m are ww and of f are pw. The disjunctive rules encode the fact that an offspring inherits the allele on chromosome 1 from the mother and the allele on chromosome 2 from the father. In particular, each allele of the parent has a probability of 50% of being transmitted. The definite clauses for color express the fact that the color of a plant is purple if at least one of the alleles is p, i.e., that the p allele is dominant. In the second definite clause, _A indicates an anonymous variable. In a similar way, the rules of blood type inheritance can be written in an LPAD[9].

Example 27 (Path probability – LPAD). *An interesting application of PLP under the DS is the computation of the probability of a path between two nodes in a graph in which the presence of each edge is probabilistic[10]:*

$path(X, X).$
$path(X, Y) \leftarrow path(X, Z), edge(Z, Y).$
$edge(a, b) : 0.3. \quad edge(b, c) : 0.2. \quad edge(a, c) : 0.6.$

This program, coded in ProbLog, was used in [De Raedt et al., 2007] for computing the probability that two biological concepts are related in the BIOMINE network [Sevon et al., 2006].

PLP under the DS can encode BNs [Vennekens et al., 2004]: each value of each random variable is encoded by a ground atom, each row of each CPT is encoded by a rule with the value of parents in the body and the probability distribution of values of the child in the head.

Example 28 (Alarm BN – LPAD). *The BN of Example 10, that we repeat in Figure 2.1 for readability, can be encoded with the program[11]*

---

[9] https://cplint.eu/e/bloodtype.pl
[10] https://cplint.eu/e/path.swinb
[11] https://cplint.eu/e/alarm.pl

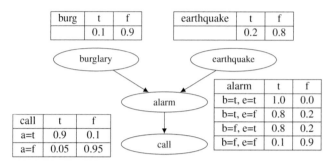

Figure 2.1　Example of a BN.

$burg(t) : 0.1 ; burg(f) : 0.9.$
$earthquake(t) : 0.2 ; earthquake(f) : 0.8.$
$alarm(t) \leftarrow burg(t), earthq(t).$
$alarm(t) : 0.8 ; alarm(f) : 0.2 \leftarrow burg(t), earthq(f).$
$alarm(t) : 0.8 ; alarm(f) : 0.2 \leftarrow burg(f), earthq(t).$
$alarm(t) : 0.1 ; alarm(f) : 0.9 \leftarrow burg(f), earthq(f).$
$call(t) : 0.9 ; call(f) : 0.1 \leftarrow alarm(t).$
$call(t) : 0.05 ; call(f) : 0.95 \leftarrow alarm(f).$

2.4 Equivalence of Expressive Power

To show that all these languages have the same expressive power, we discuss transformations among probabilistic constructs from the various languages.

The mapping between PHA/ICL and PRISM translates each PHA/ICL disjoint statement to a multi-switch declaration and vice versa in the obvious way. The mapping from PHA/ICL and PRISM to LPADs translates each disjoint statement/multi-switch declaration to a disjunctive LPAD fact.

The translation from an LPAD into PHA/ICL (first shown in [Vennekens and Verbaeten, 2003]) rewrites each clause C_i with v variables $\boldsymbol{X}$

$$h_1 : \Pi_1 ; \ldots ; h_n : \Pi_n \leftarrow B.$$

into PHA/ICL by adding n new predicates $\{choice_{i1}/v, \ldots, choice_{in}/v\}$ and a disjoint statement:

$h_1 \leftarrow B, choice_{i1}(\boldsymbol{X}).$

$\vdots$

$h_n \leftarrow B, choice_{in}(\boldsymbol{X}).$

$disjoint([choice_{i1}(\boldsymbol{X}) : \Pi_1, \ldots, choice_{in}(\boldsymbol{X}) : \Pi_n]).$

For instance, the first clause of the medical symptoms LPAD of Example 20 is translated to

$strong\_sneezing(X) \leftarrow flu(X), choice_{11}(X).$
$moderate\_sneezing(X) \leftarrow flu(X), choice_{12}(X).$
$disjoint([choice_{11}(X) : 0.3, choice_{12}(X) : 0.5, choice_{13} : 0.2]).$

where the clause $null \leftarrow flu(X), choice_{13}.$ is omitted since $null$ does not appear in the body of any clause.

Finally, as shown in [De Raedt et al., 2008], to convert LPADs into ProbLog, each clause C_i with v variables $\boldsymbol{X}$

$$h_1 : \Pi_1 ; \ldots ; h_n : \Pi_n \leftarrow B.$$

is translated into ProbLog by adding $n - 1$ probabilistic facts for predicates $\{f_{i1}/v, \ldots, f_{in}/v\}$:

$h_1 \leftarrow B, f_{i1}(\boldsymbol{X}).$
$h_2 \leftarrow B, \sim f_{i1}(\boldsymbol{X}), f_{i2}(\boldsymbol{X}).$

$\vdots$

$h_n \leftarrow B, \sim f_{i1}(\boldsymbol{X}), \ldots, \sim f_{in-1}(\boldsymbol{X}).$

$\pi_1 :: f_{i1}(\boldsymbol{X}).$

$\vdots$

$\pi_{n-1} :: f_{in-1}(\boldsymbol{X}).$

where

$$\pi_1 = \Pi_1$$
$$\pi_2 = \frac{\Pi_2}{1-\pi_1}$$
$$\pi_3 = \frac{\Pi_3}{(1-\pi_1)(1-\pi_2)}$$
$$\ldots$$

In general

$$\pi_i = \frac{\Pi_i}{\prod_{j=1}^{i-1}(1 - \pi_j)}.$$

Note that while the translation into ProbLog introduces negation, the introduced negation involves only probabilistic facts, and so the transformed program will have a two-valued model whenever the original program does.

For instance, the first clause of the medical symptoms LPAD of Example 20 is translated to

$$strong\_sneezing(X) \leftarrow flu(X), f_{11}(X).$$
$$moderate\_sneezing(X) \leftarrow flu(X), {\sim}f_{11}(X), f_{12}(X).$$
$$0.3 :: f_{11}(X).$$
$$0.714285 :: f_{12}(X).$$

2.5 Translation into Bayesian Networks

We discuss here how an acyclic ground LPAD can be translated to a BN. Let us first define the acyclic property for LPADs, extending Definition 4. An LPAD is *acyclic* if an integer level can be assigned to each ground atom so that the level of each atom in the head of each ground rule is the same and is higher than the level of each atom in the body.

An acyclic ground LPAD $\mathcal{P}$ can be translated to a BN $\beta(\mathcal{P})$ [Vennekens et al., 2004]. $\beta(\mathcal{P})$ is built by associating each atom a in $\mathcal{B}_{\mathcal{P}}$ with a binary variable a with values true (1) and false (0). Moreover, for each rule C_i of the following form

$$h_1 : \Pi_1 ; \ldots ; h_n : \Pi_n \leftarrow b_1, \ldots b_m, {\sim}c_1, \ldots, {\sim}c_l$$

in $ground(\mathcal{P})$, we add a new variable ch_i (for "choice for rule C_i") to $\beta(\mathcal{P})$. ch_i has $b_1, \ldots, b_m, c_1, \ldots, c_l$ as parents. The values for ch_i are $h_1, \ldots, h_n$ and $null$, corresponding to the head atoms. The CPT of ch_i is

	$\ldots$	$b_1 = 1, \ldots, b_m = 1, c_1 = 0, \ldots, c_l = 0$	$\ldots$
$\mathrm{ch}_i = h_1$	0.0	Π_1	0.0
$\ldots$			
$\mathrm{ch}_n = h_n$	0.0	Π_n	0.0
$\mathrm{ch}_i = null$	1.0	$1 - \sum_{i=1}^{n} \Pi_i$	1.0

that can be expressed as

$$P(\mathrm{ch}_i | b_1, \ldots, c_l) = \begin{cases} \Pi_k & \text{if } \mathrm{ch}_i = h_k, b_1 = 1, \ldots, c_l = 0 \\ 1 - \sum_{j=1}^{n} \Pi_j & \text{if } \mathrm{ch}_i = null, b_1 = 1, \ldots, c_l = 0 \\ 1 & \text{if } \mathrm{ch}_i = null, \neg(b_1 = 1, \ldots, c_l = 0) \\ 0 & \text{otherwise} \end{cases} \quad (2.7)$$

If the body is empty, the CPT for ch_i is

$\text{ch}_i = h_1$	Π_1
$\ldots$	
$\text{ch}_n = h_n$	Π_n
$\text{ch}_i = null$	$1 - \sum_{i=1}^{n} \Pi_i$

Moreover, for each variable a corresponding to atom $a \in \mathcal{B}_P$, the parents are all the variables ch_i of rules C_i that have a in the head. The CPT for a is the following deterministic table:

	At least one parent equal to a	Remaining columns
$a = 1$	1.0	0.0
$a = 0$	0.0	1.0

encoding the function

$$a = f(\mathbf{ch}_a) = \begin{cases} 1 & \text{if } \exists \text{ch}_i \in \mathbf{ch}_a : \text{ch}_i = a \\ 0 & \text{otherwise} \end{cases}$$

where $\mathbf{ch}_a$ are the parents of a. Note that in order to convert an LPAD containing variables to a BN, its grounding must be generated.

Example 29 (LPAD to BN). *Consider the following LPAD $\mathcal{P}$:*

$$
\begin{aligned}
C_1 &= a_1 : 0.4 \,;\, a_2 : 0.3. \\
C_2 &= a_2 : 0.1 \,;\, a_3 : 0.2. \\
C_3 &= a_4 : 0.6 \,;\, a_5 : 0.4 \leftarrow a_1. \\
C_4 &= a_5 : 0.4 \leftarrow a_2, a_3. \\
C_5 &= a_6 : 0.3 \,;\, a_7 : 0.2 \leftarrow a_2, a_5.
\end{aligned}
$$

Its corresponding network $\beta(\mathcal{P})$ is shown in Figure 1.7, where the CPT for a_2 and ch_5 are shown in Tables 2.1 and 2.2 respectively.

Table 2.1 Conditional probability table for a_2, n stands for *null*

ch_1, ch_2	a_1, a_2	a_1, a_3	$a_1, n,$	a_2, a_2	a_2, a_3	a_2, n	n, a_2	n, a_3	n, n
$a_2 = 1$	1.0	0.0	0.0	1.0	1.0	1.0	1.0	0.0	0.0
$a_2 = 0$	0.0	1.0	1.0	0.0	0.0	0.0	0.0	1.0	1.0

An alternative translation $\gamma(\mathcal{P})$ for a ground program P is built by including random variables a for each atom a in $\mathcal{B}_P$ and ch_i for each clause C_i as for $\beta(\mathcal{P})$. Moreover, $\gamma(\mathcal{P})$ includes the Boolean random variable body_i and the random variable X_i with values $h_1, \ldots, h_n$ and *null* for each clause C_i.

The parents of body_i are $b_1, \ldots, b_m$, and $c_1, \ldots, c_l$ and its CPT encodes the deterministic AND Boolean function:

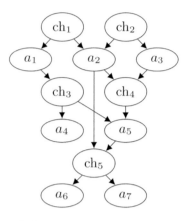

Figure 2.2   BN $\beta(\mathcal{P})$ equivalent to the program of Example 29.

Table 2.2   Conditional probability table for ch_5

a_2, a_5	1,1	1,0	0,1	0,0
$ch_5 = x6$	0.3	0.0	0.0	0.0
$ch_5 = x7$	0.2	0.0	0.0	0.0
$ch_5 = null$	0.5	1.0	1.0	1.0

	$\ldots$	$b_1 = 1, \ldots, b_m = 1, c_1 = 0, \ldots, c_l = 0$	$\ldots$
$body_i = 0$	1.0	0.0	1.0
$body_i = 1$	0.0	1.0	0.0

If the body is empty, the CPT makes $body_i$ surely true

$body_i = 0$	0.0
$body_i = 1$	1.0

X_i has no parents and has the CPT

$ch_i = h_1$	Π_1
$\ldots$	
$ch_i = h_n$	Π_n
$ch_i = null$	$1 - \sum_{i=1}^{n} \Pi_i$

ch_i has X_i and $body_i$ as parents with the deterministic CPT

$body_i, X_i$	$0, h_1$	$\ldots$	$0, h_n$	$0, null$	$1, h_1$	$\ldots$	$1, h_n$	$1, null$
$ch_i = h_1$	0.0	$\ldots$	0.0	0.0	1.0	$\ldots$	0.0	0.0
$\ldots$								
$ch_i = h_n$	0.0	$\ldots$	0.0	0.0	0.0	$\ldots$	1.0	0.0
$ch_i = null$	1.0	$\ldots$	1.0	1.0	0.0	$\ldots$	0.0	1.0

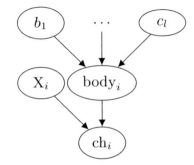

Figure 2.3 Portion of $\gamma(\mathcal{P})$ relative to a clause C_i.

encoding the function

$$\text{ch}_i = f(\text{body}_i, X_i) = \begin{cases} X_i & \text{if body}_i = 1 \\ null & \text{if body}_i = 0 \end{cases}$$

The parents of each variable a in $\gamma(\mathcal{P})$ are the variables ch_i of rules C_i that have a in the head as for $\beta(\mathcal{P})$, with the same CPT as in $\beta(\mathcal{P})$.

The portion of $\gamma(\mathcal{P})$ relative to a clause C_i is shown in Figure 2.3.

If we compute $P(\text{ch}_i|b_1, \ldots, b_m, c_1, \ldots, c_l)$ by marginalizing

$$P(\text{ch}_i, \text{body}_i, X_i|b_1, \ldots, b_m, c_1, \ldots, c_l)$$

we can see that we obtain the same dependency as in $\beta(\mathcal{P})$:

$$P(\text{ch}_i|b_1, \ldots, c_l) =$$

$$= \sum_{X_i} \sum_{\text{body}_i} P(\text{ch}_i, \text{body}_i, X_i|b_1, \ldots, c_l)$$

$$= \sum_{X_i} \sum_{\text{body}_i} P(\text{ch}_i|\text{body}_i, X_i)P(X_i)P(\text{body}_i|b_1, \ldots, c_l)$$

$$= \sum_{X_i} P(X_i) \sum_{\text{body}_i} P(\text{ch}_i|\text{body}_i, X_i)P(\text{body}_i|b_1, \ldots, c_l)$$

$$= \sum_{X_i} P(X_i) \sum_{\text{body}_i} P(\text{ch}_i|\text{body}_i, X_i) \begin{cases} 1 & \text{if body}_i = 1, b_1 = 1, \ldots, c_l = 0 \\ 1 & \text{if body}_i = 0, \neg(b_1 = 1, \ldots, c_l = 0) \\ 0 & \text{otherwise} \end{cases}$$

$$= \sum_{X_i} P(X_i) \sum_{\text{body}_i} \begin{cases} 1 & \text{if ch}_i = x_i, \text{body}_i = 1, b_1 = 1, \ldots, c_l = 0 \\ 1 & \text{if ch}_i = null, \text{body}_i = 0, \neg(b_1 = 1, \ldots, c_l = 0) \\ 0 & \text{otherwise} \end{cases}$$

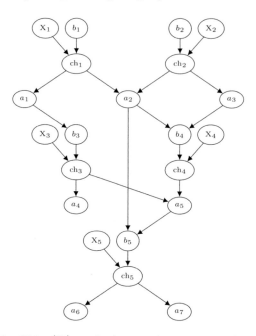

Figure 2.4   BN $\gamma(\mathcal{P})$ equivalent to the program of Example 29.

$$= \sum_{\mathbf{x}_i} P(\mathbf{x}_i) \begin{cases} 1 & \text{if } ch_i = \mathbf{x}_i, b_1 = 1, \dots, c_l = 0 \\ 1 & \text{if } ch_i = null, \neg(b_1 = 1, \dots, c_l = 0) \\ 0 & \text{otherwise} \end{cases}$$

$$= \begin{cases} \Pi_k & \text{if } ch_i = h_k, b_1 = 1, \dots, c_l = 0 \\ 1 - \sum_{j=1}^n \Pi_j & \text{if } ch_i = null, b_1 = 1, \dots, c_l = 0 \\ 1 & \text{if } ch_i = null, \neg(b_1 = 1, \dots, c_l = 0) \\ 0 & \text{otherwise} \end{cases}$$

which is the same as Equation (2.7).

From Figure 2.3 and using d-separation (see Definition 17), we can see that the X_i variables are all pairwise unconditionally independent as between every pair there is the collider $X_i \rightarrow ch_i \leftarrow body_i$.

Figure 2.4 shows $\gamma(\mathcal{P})$ for Example 29.

2.6 Generality of the Distribution Semantics

The assumption of independence of the random variables associated with ground clauses may seem restrictive. However, any probabilistic relationship

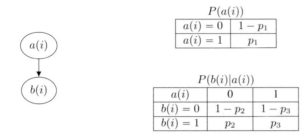

$P(a(i))$	
$a(i) = 0$	$1 - p_1$
$a(i) = 1$	p_1

$P(b(i)|a(i))$		
$a(i)$	0	1
$b(i) = 0$	$1 - p_2$	$1 - p_3$
$b(i) = 1$	p_2	p_3

Figure 2.5 BN representing the dependency between $a(i)$ and $b(i)$.

between Boolean random variables that can be represented with a BN can be modeled in this way. For example, suppose you want to model a general dependency between the ground atoms $a(i)$ and $b(i)$ regarding predicates $a/1$ and $b/1$ and constant i. This dependency can be represented with the BN of Figure 2.5.

The joint probability distribution $P(a(i), b(i))$ over the two Boolean random variables $a(i)$ and $b(i)$ is

$$
\begin{aligned}
P(0,0) &= (1 - p_1)(1 - p_2) \\
P(0,1) &= (1 - p_1)p_2 \\
P(1,0) &= p_1(1 - p_3) \\
P(1,1) &= p_1 p_3
\end{aligned}
$$

This dependency can be modeled with the following LPAD $\mathcal{P}$:

$$
\begin{aligned}
C_1 &= a(i) : p_1 \\
C_2 &= b(X) : p_2 \leftarrow a(X) \\
C_3 &= b(X) : p_3 \leftarrow \sim a(X)
\end{aligned}
$$

We can associate Boolean random variables X_1 with C_1, X_2, with $C_2\{X/i\}$, and X_3 with $C_3\{X/i\}$, where X_1, X_2, and X_3 are mutually independent. These three random variables generate eight worlds. $\neg a(i) \wedge \neg b(i)$ for example is true in the worlds

$$
w_1 = \varnothing, \ w_2 = \{b(i) \leftarrow a(i)\}
$$

whose probabilities are

$$
\begin{aligned}
P'(w_1) &= (1 - p_1)(1 - p_2)(1 - p_3) \\
P'(w_2) &= (1 - p_1)(1 - p_2)p_3
\end{aligned}
$$

so

$$
P'(\neg a(i), \neg b(i)) = (1 - p_1)(1 - p_2)(1 - p_3) + (1 - p_1)(1 - p_2)p_3 = P(0,0).
$$

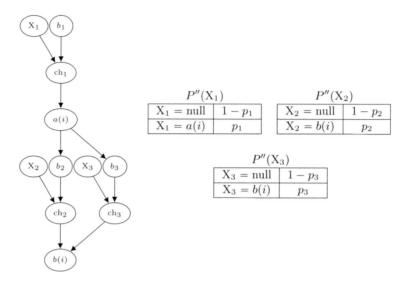

Figure 2.6   BN modeling the distribution over $a(i)$, $b(i)$, X_1, X_2, X_3.

We can prove similarly that the distributions P and P' coincide for all joint states of $a(i)$ and $b(i)$.

Modeling the dependency between $a(i)$ and $b(i)$ with the program above is equivalent to represent the BN of Figure 2.5 with the network $\gamma(\mathcal{P})$ of Figure 2.6.

Since $\gamma(\mathcal{P})$ defines the same distribution as $\mathcal{P}$, the distributions P and P'', the one defined by $\gamma(\mathcal{P})$, agree on the variables $a(i)$ and $b(i)$, i.e.,

$$P(a(i), b(i)) = P''(a(i), b(i))$$

for any value of $a(i)$ and $b(i)$. From Figure 2.6, it is also clear that X_1, X_2, and X_3 are mutually unconditionally independent, thus showing that it is possible to represent any dependency with independent random variables. So we can model general dependencies among ground atoms with the DS.

This confirms the results of Sections 2.3 and 2.5 that graphical models can be translated into probabilistic logic programs under the DS and vice versa. Therefore, the two formalisms are equally expressive.

2.7 Extensions of the Distribution Semantics

Programs under the DS may contain *flexible probabilities* [De Raedt and Kimmig, 2015] or probabilities that depend on values computed during program execution. In this case, the probabilistic annotations are variables, as in the program[12] from [De Raedt and Kimmig, 2015]

```
red(Prob):Prob.

draw_red(R, G):-
  Prob is R/(R + G),
  red(Prob).
```

The query `draw_red(r,g)`, where `r` and `g` are the number of green and red balls in an urn, succeeds with the same probability as that of drawing a red ball from the urn.

Flexible probabilities allow the computation of probabilities on the fly during inference. However, flexible probabilities must be ground when their value is evaluated during inference. Many inference systems support them by imposing constraints on the form of programs.

The body of rules may also contain literals for a meta-predicate such as `prob/2` that computes the probability of an atom, thus allowing nested or meta-probability computations [De Raedt and Kimmig, 2015]. Among the possible uses of such a feature De Raedt and Kimmig [2015] mention: filtering proofs on the basis of the probability of subqueries, or implementing simple forms of combining rules.

An example of the first use is[13]

```
a:0.2:-
  prob(b,P),
  P>0.1.
```

where `a` succeeds with probability 0.2 only if the probability of `b` is larger than 0.1.

An example of the latter is[14]

```
p(P):P.

max_true(G1, G2) :-
  prob(G1, P1),
  prob(G2, P2),
  max(P1, P2, P), p(P).
```

where `max_true(G1,G2)` succeeds with the success probability of its more likely argument.

---

[12] https://cplint.eu/e/flexprob.pl
[13] https://cplint.eu/e/meta.pl
[14] https://cplint.eu/e/metacomb.pl

2.8 CP-logic

CP-logic [Vennekens et al., 2009] is a language for representing causal laws. It shares many similarities with LPADs but specifically aims at modeling probabilistic causality. Syntactically, *CP-logic programs*, or *CP-theories*, are identical to LPADs[15]: they are composed of annotated disjunctive clauses. For each grounding

$$h_1 : \Pi_1 ; \ldots ; h_m : \Pi_n \leftarrow B$$

of a clause of the program, B represents an event whose effect is to cause at most one of the h_i atoms to become true and the probability of h_i of being caused is Π_i. Consider the following medical example.

Example 30 (CP-logic program – infection [Vennekens et al., 2009]). *A patient is infected by a bacterium. Infection can cause either pneumonia or angina. In turn, angina can cause pneumonia and pneumonia can cause angina. This can be represented by the CP-logic program:*

$$angina : 0.2 \leftarrow pneumonia. \tag{2.8}$$

$$pneumonia : 0.3 \leftarrow angina. \tag{2.9}$$

$$pneumonia : 0.4 ; angina : 0.1 \leftarrow infection. \tag{2.10}$$

$$infection. \tag{2.11}$$

The semantics of CP-logic programs is given in terms of probability trees that represent the possible courses of the events encoded in the program. We consider first the case where the program is positive, i.e., the bodies of rules do not contain negative literals.

Definition 19 (Probability tree – positive case). *A probability tree[16] T for a program $\mathcal{P}$ is a tree where every node n is labeled with a two-valued interpretation $I(n)$ and a probability $P(n)$. T is constructed as follows:*

- *The root node r has probability $P(r) = 1.0$ and interpretation $I(r) = \emptyset$.*
- *Each inner node n is associated with a ground clause C_i such that*
  - *no ancestor of n is associated with C_i,*
  - *all atoms in $body(C_i)$ are true in $I(n)$,*

---

[15]   There are versions of CP-logic that have a more general syntax but they are not essential for the discussion here

[16]   We follow here the definition of [Shterionov et al., 2015] for its simplicity.

n has one child node for each atom $h_k \in head(C_i)$. The k-th child has interpretation $I(n) \cup \{h_k\}$ and probability $P(n) \cdot \Pi_k$.
- *No leaf can be associated with a clause following the rule above.*

A probability tree defines a probability distribution $P(I)$ over the interpretation of the program $\mathcal{P}$: the probability of an interpretation I is the sum of the probabilities of the leaf nodes n such that $I = I(n)$.

The probability tree for Example 2.11 is shown in Figure 2.7. The probability distribution over the interpretations is

I	$\{inf, pn, ang\}$	$\{inf, pn\}$	$\{inf, ang\}$	$\{inf\}$
$P(I)$	0.11	0.32	0.07	0.5

There can be more than one probability tree for a program but Vennekens et al. [2009] show that all the probability trees for the program define the same probability distribution over interpretations. So we can speak of *the* probability tree for $\mathcal{P}$ and this defines the semantics of the CP-logic program. Moreover, each program has at least one probability tree.

Vennekens et al. [2009] also show that the probability distribution defined by the LPADs semantics is the same as that defined by the CP-logic semantics. So probability trees represent an alternative definition of the DS for LPADs.

If the program contains negation, checking the truth of the body of a clause must be made with care because an atom that is currently absent from $I(n)$ may become true later. Therefore, we must make sure that for each

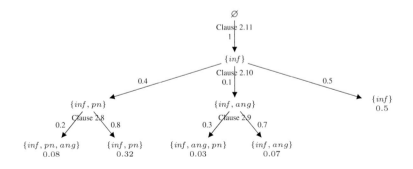

Figure 2.7 Probability tree for Example 2.11. From [Vennekens et al., 2009].

negative literal $\sim a$ in $body(C_i)$, the positive literal a cannot be made true starting from $I(n)$.

Example 31 (CP-logic program – pneumonia [Vennekens et al., 2009]). *A patient has pneumonia. Because of pneumonia, the patient is treated. If the patient has pneumonia and is not treated, he may get fever.*

$$pneumonia. \tag{2.12}$$

$$treatment : 0.95 \leftarrow pneumonia. \tag{2.13}$$

$$fever : 0.7 \leftarrow pneumonia, \sim treatment. \tag{2.14}$$

Two probability trees for this program are shown in Figures 2.8 and 2.9. Both trees satisfy Definition 19 but define two different probability distributions. In the tree of Figure 2.8, Clause 2.14 has negative literal $\sim treatment$ in its body and is applied at a stage where $treatment$ may still become true, as happens in the level below.

In the tree of Figure 2.9, instead Clause 2.14 is applied when the only rule for $treatment$ has already fired, so in the right child of the node at the second level $treatment$ will never become true and Clause 2.14 can safely be applied.

In order to formally define this, we need the following definition that uses three-valued logic. A conjunction in three-valued logic is true or undefined if no literal in it is false.

Definition 20 (Hypothetical derivation sequence). *A hypothetical derivation sequence in a node n is a sequence $(\mathcal{I}_i)_{0 \leq i \leq n}$ of three-valued interpretations that satisfy the following properties. Initially, $\mathcal{I}_0$ assigns false to all atoms*

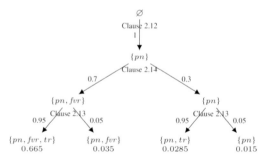

Figure 2.8   An incorrect probability tree for Example 31. From [Vennekens et al., 2009].

not in I(n). For each i > 0, $\mathcal{I}_{i+1} = \langle I_{T,i+1}, I_{F,i+1} \rangle$ is obtained from $\mathcal{I}_i = \langle I_{T,i}, I_{F,i} \rangle$ by considering a rule R with body(R) true or undefined in $\mathcal{I}_i$ and an atom a in its head that is false in $\mathcal{I}$. Then $I_{T,i+1} = I_{T,i+1}$ and $I_{F,i+1} = I_{F,i+1} \backslash \{a\}$.

Every hypothetical derivation sequence reaches the same limit. For a node n in a probabilistic tree, we denote this unique limit as $\mathcal{I}(n)$. It represents the set of atoms that might still become true; in other words, all the atoms in the false part of $\mathcal{I}(n)$ will never become true and so they can be considered as false.

The definition of probability tree of a program with negation becomes the following.

Definition 21 (Probability tree – general case). *A probability tree T for a program $\mathcal{P}$ is a tree*

- *satisfying the conditions of Definition 19, and*
- *for each node n and associated clause C_i, for each negative literal $\sim a$ in body(C_i), $a \in I_F$ with $\mathcal{I}(n) = \langle I_T, I_F \rangle$.*

All the probability trees according for the program according to Definition 21 establish the same probability distribution over interpretations.

It can be shown that the set of false atoms of the limit of the hypothetical derivation sequence is equal to the greatest fixpoint of the operator $OpFalse_{\mathcal{I}}^{P}$ (see Definition 2) with $\mathcal{I} = \langle I(n), \varnothing \rangle$ and P a program that contains, for each rule

$$h_1 : \Pi_1 ; \ldots ; h_m : \Pi_n \leftarrow B$$

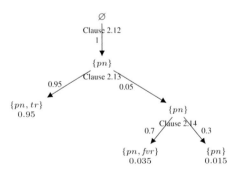

Figure 2.9 A probability tree for Example 31. From [Vennekens et al., 2009].

of $\mathcal{P}$, the rules

$$h_1 \leftarrow B.$$
$$\cdots$$
$$h_m \leftarrow B.$$

In other words, if $\mathcal{I}(n) = \langle I_T, I_F \rangle$ and $\mathrm{gfp}(OpFalse_{\mathcal{I}}^P) = F$, then $I_F = F$.

In fact, for the body of a clause to be true or undefined in $\mathcal{I}_i = \langle I_{T,i}, I_{F,i} \rangle$, each positive literal a must be absent from $I_{F,i}$ and each negative literal $\sim a$ must be such that a is absent from $I_{T,i}$, which are the complementary conditions in the definition of the operator $OpFalse_{\mathcal{I}}^P(Fa)$.

On the other hand, the generation of a child n' of a node n using a rule C_i that adds an atom a to $I(n)$ can be seen as part of an application of $OpTrue_{\mathcal{I}(n)}^P$. So there is a strong connection between CP-logic and the WFS.

In the trees of Figures 2.8 and 2.9, the child $n = \{pn\}$ of the root has $I_F = \varnothing$, so Clause 2.14 cannot be applied as $treatment \notin I_F$ and the only tree allowed by Definition 21 is that of Figure 2.9.

The semantics of CP-logic satisfies these causality principles:

- The *principle of universal causation* states that all changes to the state of the domain must be triggered by a causal law whose precondition is satisfied.
- The *principle of sufficient causation* states that if the precondition to a causal law is satisfied, then the event that it triggers must eventually happen.

and therefore the logic is particularly suitable for representing causation.

Moreover, CP-logic satisfies the *temporal precedence assumption* that states that a rule R will not fire until its precondition is in its final state. In other words, a rule fires only when the causal process that determines whether its precondition holds is fully finished. This is enforced by the treatment of negation of CP-logic.

There are CP-logic programs that do not admit any probability tree, as the following example shows.

Example 32 (Invalid CP-logic program [Vennekens et al., 2009]). *In a two-player game, white wins if black does not win and black wins if white does not win:*

$$win(white) \leftarrow \sim win(black). \tag{2.15}$$
$$win(black) \leftarrow \sim win(white). \tag{2.16}$$

At the root of the probability tree for this program, both Clauses 2.15 and 2.16 have their body true but they cannot fire as I_F for the root is $\emptyset$. So the root is a leaf where however two rules have their body true, thus violating the condition of Definition 19 that requires that leaves cannot be associated with rules.

This theory is problematic from a causal point of view, as it is impossible to define a process that follows the causal laws. Therefore, we want to exclude these cases and consider only *valid* CP-theories.

Definition 22 (Valid CP-theory). *A CP-theory is valid if it has at least one probability tree.*

The equivalence of the LPADs and CP-logic semantics is also carried to the general case of programs with negation: the probability tree of a valid CP-theory defines the same distribution as that defined by interpreting the program as an LPAD.

However, there are sound LPADs that are not valid CP-theories. Recall that a sound LPAD is one where each possible world has a two-valued WFM.

Example 33 (Sound LPAD – invalid CP-theory Vennekens et al. [2009]). *Consider the program*

$$p : 0.5 \,;\, q : 0.5 \leftarrow r.$$
$$r \leftarrow \sim p.$$
$$r \leftarrow \sim q.$$

Such a program has no probability tree, so it is not a valid CP-theory. Its possible worlds are

$$\{p \leftarrow r; r \leftarrow \sim p; r \leftarrow \sim q\}$$

and

$$\{q \leftarrow r; r \leftarrow \sim p; r \leftarrow \sim q\}$$

that both have total WFMs, $\{r, p\}$ and $\{r, q\}$, respectively, so the LPAD is sound.

In fact, it is difficult to imagine a causal process for this program.

Therefore, LPADs and CP-logic have some differences but these arise only in corner cases, so sometimes CP-logic and LPADs are used as a synonyms. This also shows that clauses in LPADs can be assigned in many cases a causal interpretation.

The equivalence of the semantics implies that, for a valid CP-theory, each leaf of the probability tree is associated with the WFM of the possible world obtained by considering all the clauses used in the path from the root to the leaf with the head selected according to the choice of child. If the program is deterministic, the only leaf is associated with the total-well founded model of the program.

2.9 KBMC Probabilistic Logic Programming Languages

In this section, we present three examples of KBMC languages: Bayesian Logic Programs (BLPs), CLP(BN), and the Prolog Factor Language (PFL).

2.9.1 Bayesian logic programs

BLPs [Kersting and De Raedt, 2001] use logic programming to compactly encode a large BN. In BLPs, each ground atom represents a (not necessarily Boolean) random variable and the clauses define the dependencies between ground atoms. A clause of the form

$$a|a_1, \ldots, a_m$$

indicates that, for each of its groundings $(a|a_1, \ldots, a_m)\theta$, $a\theta$ has $a_1\theta$, ..., $a_m\theta$ as parents. The domains and CPTs for the ground atoms/random variables are defined in a separate portion of the model. In the case where a ground atom $a\theta$ appears in the head of more than one clause, a *combining rule* is used to obtain the overall CPT from those given by individual clauses.

For example, in the Mendelian genetics program of Example 26, the dependency that gives the value of the color gene on chromosome 1 of a plant as a function of the color genes of its mother can be expressed as

$$cg(X,1)|mother(Y,X),cg(Y,1),cg(Y,2).$$

where the domain of atoms built on predicate $cg/2$ is *{p,w}* and the domain of *mother(Y,X)* is Boolean. A suitable CPT should then be defined that assigns equal probability to the alleles of the mother to be inherited by the plant.

Various learning systems use BLPs as the representation language: RBLP [Revoredo and Zaverucha, 2002; Paes et al., 2005], PFORTE [Paes et al., 2006], and SCOOBY [Kersting and De Raedt, 2008].

2.9.2 CLP(BN)

In a CLP(BN) program [Costa et al., 2003], logical variables can be random. Their domain, parents, and CPTs are defined by the program. Probabilistic dependencies are expressed by means of constraints as in Constraint logic programming (CLP):

```
{ Var = Function with p(Values, Dist) }
{ Var = Function with p(Values, Dist, Parents) }
```

The first form indicates that the logical variable `Var` is random with domain `Values` and CPT `Dist` but without parents; the second form defines a random variable with parents. In both forms, `Function` is a term over logical variables that is used to parameterize the random variable: a different random variable is defined for each instantiation of the logical variables in the term. For example, the following snippet from a school domain:

```
course_difficulty(CKey, Dif) :-
  { Dif = difficulty(CKey) with p([h,m,l],
    [0.25, 0.50, 0.25]) }.
```

defines the random variable `Dif` with values h, m, and l representing the difficulty of the course identified by `CKey`. There is a different random variable for every instantiation of `CKey`, i.e., for each course. In a similar manner, the intelligence `Int` of a student identified by `SKey` is given by

```
student_intelligence(SKey, Int) :-
  { Int = intelligence(SKey) with p([h, m, l],
    [0.5,0.4,0.1]) }.
```

Using the above predicates, the following snippet predicts the grade received by a student when taking the exam of a course.

```
registration_grade(Key, Grade) :-
  registration(Key, CKey, SKey),
  course_difficulty(CKey, Dif),
  student_intelligence(SKey, Int),
  { Grade = grade(Key) with  p(['A','B','C','D'],
  % h/h   h/m   h/l   m/h   m/m   m/l   l/h   l/m   l/l
  [0.20,0.70,0.85,0.10,0.20,0.50,0.01,0.05,0.10,
    % 'A'
    0.60,0.25,0.12,0.30,0.60,0.35,0.04,0.15,0.40,
    % 'B'
    0.15,0.04,0.02,0.40,0.15,0.12,0.50,0.60,0.40,
    % 'C'
```

```
             0.05,0.01,0.01,0.20,0.05,0.03,0.45,0.20,0.10],
             % 'D'
      [Int,Dif]) }.
```

Here `Grade` indicates a random variable parameterized by the identifier `Key` of a registration of a student to a course. The code states that there is a different random variable `Grade` for each student's registration in a course and each such random variable has possible values `'A'`, `'B'`, `'C'` and `'D'`. The actual value of the random variable depends on the intelligence of the student and on the difficulty of the course, that are thus its parents. Together with facts for `registration/3` such as

```
registration(r0,c16,s0).   registration(r1,c10,s0).
registration(r2,c57,s0).   registration(r3,c22,s1).
....
```

the code defines a BN with a `Grade` random variable for each registration. CLP(BN) is implemented as a library of YAP Prolog. The library performs query answering by constructing the sub-network that is relevant to the query and then applying a BN inference algorithm.

The unconditional probability of a random variable can be computed by simply asking a query to the YAP command line.

The answer will be a probability distribution over the values of the logical variables of the query that represent random variables, as in

```
?- registration_grade(r0,G).
        p(G=a)=0.4115,
        p(G=b)=0.356,
        p(G=c)=0.16575,
        p(G=d)=0.06675 ?
```

Conditional queries can be posed by including in them ground atoms representing the evidence.

For example, the probability distribution of the grades of registration `r0` given that the intelligence of the student is high (`h`) is given by

```
?- registration_grade(r0,G),
        student_intelligence(s0,h).
        p(G=a)=0.6125,
        p(G=b)=0.305,
        p(G=c)=0.0625,
        p(G=d)=0.02 ?
```

As you can see, the probability of the student receiving grade `'A'` is increased.

In general, CLP provides a useful tool for PLP, as is testified by the proposals clp(pdf(Y)) [Angelopoulos, 2003, 2004] and Probabilistic Constraint Logic Programming [Michels et al., 2015], see Section 4.5.

2.9.3 The prolog factor language

The PFL [Gomes and Costa, 2012] is an extension of Prolog for representing first-order probabilistic models.

Most graphical models such as BNs and MNs concisely represent a joint distribution by encoding it as a set of factors. The probability of a set of variables $\mathbf{X}$ taking value x can be expressed as the product of n factors as:

$$P(\mathbf{X} = \mathbf{x}) = \frac{\prod_{i=1,\ldots,n} \phi_i(\mathbf{x}_i)}{Z}$$

where $\mathbf{x}_i$ is a sub-vector of x on which the i-th factor depends and Z is the normalization constant. Often, in a graphical model, the same factors appear repeatedly in the network, and thus we can parameterize these factors in order to simplify the representation.

A Parameterized random variables (PRVs) is a logical atom representing a set of random variables, one for each of its possible ground instantiations. We indicate PRV as $X, Y, \ldots$ and vectors of PRVs as $\mathbf{X}, \mathbf{Y}, \ldots$

A *parametric factor* or *parfactor* [Kisynski and Poole, 2009b] is a triple $\langle \mathcal{C}, \mathbf{V}, F \rangle$ where $\mathcal{C}$ is a set of inequality constraints on parameters (logical variables), $\mathbf{V}$ is a vector of PRVs and F is a factor that is a function from the Cartesian product of ranges of PRVs in $\mathbf{V}$ to real values. A parfactor is also represented as $F(\mathbf{V})|\mathcal{C}$ or $F(\mathbf{V})$ if there are no constraints. A constrained PRV is of the form $V|\mathcal{C}$, where $V = p(X_1, \ldots, X_n)$ is a non-ground atom and $\mathcal{C}$ is a set of constraints on logical variables $\mathbf{X} = \{X_1, \ldots, X_n\}$. Each constrained PRV represents the set of random variables $\{p(\mathbf{x})|\mathbf{x} \in \mathcal{C}\}$, where $\mathbf{x}$ is the tuple of constants $(x_1, \ldots, x_n)$. Given a (constrained) PRV V, we use $RV(V)$ to denote the set of random variables it represents. Each ground atom is associated with one random variable, which can take any value in $range(V)$.

The PFL extends Prolog to support probabilistic reasoning with parametric factors. A PFL factor is a parfactor of the form

$$Type\ \mathbf{F}\ ;\ \phi\ ;\ \mathcal{C},$$

where $Type$ refers to the type of the network over which the parfactor is defined (*bayes* for directed networks or *markov* for undirected ones); **F** is a sequence of Prolog goals each defining a PRV under the constraints in C (the arguments of the factor). If **L** is the set of all logical variables in **F**, then C is a list of Prolog goals that impose bindings on **L** (the successful substitutions for the goals in C are the valid values for the variables in **L**). ϕ is the table defining the factor in the form of a list of real values. By default, all random variables are Boolean but a different domain may be defined. Each parfactor represents the set of its groundings. To ground a parfactor, all variables of **L** are replaced with the values permitted by constraints in C. The set of ground factors defines a factorization of the joint probability distribution over all random variables.

Example 34 (PFL program). *The following PFL program is inspired by the workshop attributes problem of [Milch et al., 2008]. It models the organization of a workshop where a number of people have been invited.* series *indicates whether the workshop is successful enough to start a series of related meetings while* attends(P) *indicates whether person* P *attends the workshop.*

This problem can be modeled by a PFL program such as

```
bayes series, attends(P); [0.51, 0.49, 0.49, 0.51];
    [person(P)].
bayes attends(P), at(P,A); [0.7, 0.3, 0.3, 0.7];
    [person(P),attribute(A)].
```

A workshop becomes a series because people attend. People attend the workshop depending on the workshop's attributes such as location, date, fame of the organizers, etc. The probabilistic atom at(P,A) *represents whether person* P *attends because of attribute* A.

The first PFL factor has the random variables series *and* attends(P) *as arguments (both Boolean),* [0.51,0.49,0.49,0.51] *as table and the list* [person(P)] *as constraint.*

Since KBMC languages are defined on the basis of a translation to graphical models, translations can be built between PLP languages under the DS and KBMC languages. The first have the advantage that they have a semantics that can be understood in logical terms, without necessarily referring to an underlying graphical model.

2.10 Other Semantics for Probabilistic Logic Programming

Here we briefly discuss a few examples of PLP frameworks that don't follow the distribution semantics. Our goal in this section is simply to give the flavor of other possible approaches; a complete account of such frameworks is beyond the scope of this book.

2.10.1 Stochastic logic programs

Stochastic logic programs (SLPs) [Muggleton et al., 1996; Cussens, 2001] are logic programs with parameterized clauses which define a distribution over refutations of goals. The distribution provides, by marginalization, a distribution over variable bindings for the query. SLPs are a generalization of stochastic grammars and hidden Markov models.

An *SLP* S is a definite logic program where some of the clauses are of the form $p : C$ where $p \in \mathbb{R}, p \geqslant 0$, and C is a definite clause. Let $n(S)$ be the definite logic program obtained by removing the probability labels. A *pure* SLP is an SLP where all clauses have probability labels. A *normalized* SLP is one where probability labels for clauses whose heads share the same predicate symbol sum to one.

In pure SLPs, each SLD derivation for a query q is assigned a real label by multiplying the labels of each individual derivation step. The label of a derivation step where the selected atom unifies with the head of clause $p_i : C_i$ is p_i. The probability of a successful derivation from q is the label of the derivation divided by the sum of the labels of all the successful derivations. This forms a distribution over successful derivations from q.

The probability of an instantiation $q\theta$ is the sum of the probabilities of the successful derivations that produce $q\theta$. It can be shown that the probabilities of all the atoms for a predicate q that succeed in $n(S)$ sum to one, i.e., S defines a probability distribution over the success set of q in $n(S)$.

In impure SLPs, the unparameterized clauses are seen as non-probabilistic domain knowledge acting as constraints. Derivations are identified with the set of the parameterized clauses they use. In this way, derivations that differ only on the unparameterized clauses form an equivalence class.

In practice, SLPs define probability distributions over the children of nodes of the SLD tree for a query: a derivation step $u \to v$ that connects node u with child node v is assigned a probability $P(v|u)$. This induces a probability distributions over paths from the root to the leaves of the SLD tree and in turn over answers for the query.

Given their similarity with stochastic grammars and hidden Markov models, SLPs are particularly suitable for representing these kinds of models. They differ from the DS because they define a probability distribution over instantiations of the query, while the DS usually defines a distribution over the truth values of ground atoms.

Example 35 (Probabilistic context-free grammar – SLP). *Consider the probabilistic context free grammar:*

$$0.2 : S \rightarrow aS$$
$$0.2 : S \rightarrow bS$$
$$0.3 : S \rightarrow a$$
$$0.3 : S \rightarrow b$$

The SLP

$$0.2 : s([a|R]) \leftarrow s(R).$$
$$0.2 : s([b|R]) \leftarrow s(R).$$
$$0.3 : s([a]).$$
$$0.3 : s([b]).$$

defines a distribution over the values of S in the success set of $s(S)$ that is the same as the one defined by the probabilistic context-free grammar above. For example, $P(s([a, b])) = 0.2 \cdot 0.3 = 0.6$ according to the program and $P(ab) = 0.2 \cdot 0.3 = 0.6$ according to the grammar.

Various approaches have been proposed for learning SLPs. Muggleton [2000a,b] proposed to use an Inductive logic programming (ILP) system, Progol [Muggleton, 1995], for learning the structure of the programs, and a second phase where the parameters are tuned using a generalization of relative frequency.

Parameters are also learned by means of optimization in failure-adjusted maximization [Cussens, 2001; Angelopoulos, 2016] and by solving algebraic equations [Muggleton, 2003].

2.10.2 ProPPR

ProPPR [Wang et al., 2015] is an extension of SLPs that that is related to Personalized page rank (PPR) [Page et al., 1999].

ProPPR extends SLPs in two ways. The first is the method for computing the labels of the derivation steps. A derivation step $u \rightarrow v$ is not simply assigned the parameter associated with the clause used in the step. Instead, the label of the derivation step, $P(v|u)$ is computed using a log-linear model $P(v|u) \propto \exp(\mathbf{w} \cdot \phi_{u \rightarrow v})$ where $\mathbf{w}$ is a vector of real-valued weights and $\phi_{u \rightarrow v}$ is a 0/1 vector of "features" that depend on the clause being used. The features are user defined and the association between clauses and features is indicated using annotations.

Example 36 (ProPPR program). *The ProPPR program [Wang et al., 2015]*

$$about(X, Z) \leftarrow handLabeled(X, Z). \hspace{2cm} \#base$$
$$about(X, Z) \leftarrow sim(X, Y), about(Y, Z). \hspace{1.5cm} \#prop$$
$$sim(X, Y) \leftarrow link(X, Y). \hspace{2.5cm} \#sim, link$$
$$sim(X, Y) \leftarrow hasWord(X, W), hasWord(Y, W),$$
$$\hspace{1cm} linkedBy(X, Y, W). \hspace{3cm} \#sim, word$$
$$linkedBy(X, Y, W). \hspace{4cm} \#by(W)$$

can be used to compute the topic of web pages on the basis of possible hand labeling or similarity with other web pages. Similarity is defined as well in a probabilistic way depending on the links and words between the two pages.

Clauses are annotated with a list of atoms (indicated after the # symbol) that may contain variables from the head of clauses. In the example, the third clause is annotated with the list of atoms $sim, link$ while the last clause is annotated by the atom $by(W)$. Each grounding of each atom in the list stands for a different feature, so for example $sim, link$, and $by(sprinter)$ stand for three different features. The vector $\phi_{u \to v}$ is obtained by assigning value 1 to the features associated with the atoms in the annotation of the clause used for the derivation step $u \to v$ and value 0 otherwise. If the atoms contain variables, these are shared with the head of the clause and are grounded with the values of the clause instantiation used in $u \to v$.

So a ProPPR program is defined by an annotated program plus values for the weights **w**. This annotation approach considerably increases the flexibility of SLP labels: ProPPR annotations can be shared across clauses and can yield labels that depend on the particular clause grounding that is used in the derivation step. An SLP is a ProPPR program where each clause has a different annotation consisting of an atom without arguments.

The second way in which ProPPR extend SLPs consists in the addition of edges to the SLD tree: an edge is added (a) from every solution leaf to itself; and (b) from every node to the root.

The procedure for assigning probabilities to queries of SLP can then be applied to the resulting graph. The self-loop links heuristically upweight solution nodes and the restart links make SLP's graph traversal a PPR procedure [Page et al., 1999]: a PageRank can be associated with each node, representing the probability that a random walker starting from the root arrives in that node.

The restart links favor the results of short proofs: if the restart probability is α for every node u, then the probability of reaching any node at depth d is bounded by $(1 - \alpha)^d$.

Parameter learning for ProPPR is performed in [Wang et al., 2015] by stochastic gradient descent.

2.11 Other Semantics for Probabilistic Logics

In this section, we discuss semantics for probabilistic logic languages that are not based on logic programming.

2.11.1 Nilsson's probabilistic logic

Nilsson's probabilistic logic [Nilsson, 1986] takes an approach for combining logic and probability that is different from the DS: while the first considers sets of distributions, the latter computes a single distribution over possible worlds. In Nilsson's logic, a *probabilistic interpretation Pr* defines a probability distribution over the set of interpretations *Int2*. The *probability of a logical formula F* according to Pr, denoted $Pr(F)$, is the sum of all $Pr(I)$ such that $I \in Int2$ and $I \models F$. A *probabilistic knowledge base $\mathcal{K}$* is a set of probabilistic formulas of the form $F \geqslant p$ where F is a logical formula and p a number in $[0, 1]$. A probabilistic interpretation Pr *satisfies $F \geqslant p$* iff $Pr(F) \geqslant p$. Pr satisfies $\mathcal{K}$, or Pr is a *model* of $\mathcal{K}$, iff Pr satisfies all $F \geqslant p \in \mathcal{K}$. $Pr(F) \geqslant p$ is a *tight logical consequence* of $\mathcal{K}$ iff p is the infimum of $Pr(F)$ in the set of all models Pr of $\mathcal{K}$. Computing tight logical consequences from probabilistic knowledge bases can be done by solving a linear optimization problem.

With Nilsson's logic, the consequences that can be obtained from logical formulas differ from those of the DS. Consider a ProbLog program (see Section 2.1) composed of the facts $0.4 :: c(a)$ and $0.5 :: c(b)$, and a probabilistic knowledge base composed of $c(a) \geqslant 0.4$ and $c(b) \geqslant 0.5$. For the DS, $P(c(a) \vee c(b)) = 0.7$, while with Nilsson's logic, the lowest p such that $Pr(c(a) \vee c(b)) \geqslant p$ holds is 0.5. This difference is due to the fact that, while Nilsson's logic makes no assumption about the independence of the statements, in the DS, the probabilistic axioms are considered as independent. While independencies can be encoded in Nilsson's logic by carefully choosing the values of the parameters, reading off the independencies from the theories becomes more difficult.

However, the assumption of independence of probabilistic axioms does not restrict expressiveness as shown in Section 2.6.

2.11.2 Markov logic networks

A Markov Logic Network (MLN) is a first-order logical theory in which each sentence is associated with a real-valued weight. An MLN is a template for generating MNs. Given sets of constants defining the domains of the logical variables, an MLN defines an MN that has a Boolean node for each ground atom and edges connecting the atoms appearing together in a grounding of a formula. MLNs follow the KBMC approach for defining a probabilistic model [Wellman et al., 1992; Bacchus, 1993]. The probability distribution encoded by an Markov logic network (MLN) is

$$P(\mathbf{x}) = \frac{1}{Z} \exp\left(\sum_{f_i \in M} w_i n_i(\mathbf{x}) \right)$$

where $\mathbf{x}$ is a joint assignment of truth value to all atoms in the Herbrand base (finite because of no function symbols), M is the MLN, f_i is the i-th formula in M, w_i is its weight, $n_i(\mathbf{x})$ is the number of groundings of formula f_i that are satisfied in $\mathbf{x}$, and Z is a normalization constant.

Example 37 (Markov Logic Network). *The following MLN encodes a theory on the intelligence of friends and on the marks people get:*

```
1.5 Intelligent(x) => GoodMarks(x)
1.1 Friends(x,y) => (Intelligent(x)<=>
                    Intelligent(y))
```

The first formula gives a positive weight to the fact that if someone is intelligent, then he gets good marks in the exams he takes. The second formula gives a positive weight to the fact that friends have similar intelligence: in particular, the formula states that if x and y are friends, then x is intelligent if and only if y is intelligent, so they are either both intelligent or both not intelligent.

If the domain contains two individuals, Anna and Bob, indicated with A and B, we get the ground MN of Figure 2.10.

2.11.2.1 Encoding Markov logic networks with probabilistic logic programming

It is possible to encode MNs and MLNs with LPADs. The encoding is based on the BN that is equivalent to the MN as discussed in Section 1.6: an MN

Figure 2.10   Ground Markov network for the MLN of Example 37.

factor can be represented with an extra node in the equivalent BN that is always observed. In order to model MLN formulas with LPADs, we can add an extra atom $clause_i(\boldsymbol{X})$ for each formula $F_i = w_i\ C_i$ where w_i is the weight associated with C_i and $\boldsymbol{X}$ is the vector of variables appearing in C_i. Then, when we ask for the probability of query q given evidence e, we have to ask for the probability of q given $e \wedge ce$, where ce is the conjunction of the groundings of $clause_i(\boldsymbol{X})$ for all values of i.

Clause C_i must be transformed into a Disjunctive Normal Form (DNF) formula $C_{i1} \vee \ldots \vee C_{in_i}$, where the disjuncts are mutually exclusive and the LPAD should contain the clauses

$$clause_i(\boldsymbol{X}) : e^{w_i}/(1 + e^{w_i}) \leftarrow C_{ij}$$

for all j in $1, \ldots, n_i$, where $1 + e^{w_i} \geq \max_{\mathbf{x_i}} \phi(\mathbf{x_i}) = \max\{1, e^{w_i}\}$. Similarly, $\neg C_i$ must be transformed into a DNF $D_{i1} \vee \ldots \vee D_{im_i}$ and the LPAD should contain the clauses

$$clause_i(\boldsymbol{X}) : 1/(1 + e^{w_i}) \leftarrow D_{il}$$

for all l in $1, \ldots, m_i$.

Moreover, for each predicate p/n, we should add the clause

$$p(\boldsymbol{X}) : 0.5.$$

to the program, assigning *a priori* uniform probability to every ground atom.

Alternatively, if w_i is negative, e^{w_i} will be smaller than 1 and $\max_{\mathbf{x_i}} \phi(\mathbf{x_i}) = 1$. So we can use the two probability values e^{w_i} and 1 with the clauses

$$clause_i(\boldsymbol{X}) : e^{w_i} \leftarrow C_{ij}.$$
$$clause_i(\boldsymbol{X}) \leftarrow D_{il}.$$

This solution has the advantage that some clauses are non-probabilistic, reducing the number of random variables. If w_i is positive in the formula $w_i\ C_i$, we can consider the equivalent formula $-w_i\ \neg C_i$.

The transformation above is illustrated by the following example. Given the MLN

```
1.5 Intelligent(x) => GoodMarks(x)
1.1 Friends(x,y) => (Intelligent(x)<=>Intelligent(y))
```

the first formula is translated to the clauses:

```
clause1(X):0.8175 :- \+intelligent(X).
clause1(X):0.1824 :- intelligent(X),
                     \+good_marks(X).
clause1(X):0.8175 :- intelligent(X),good_marks(X).
```

where $0.8175 = e^{1.5}/(1 + e^{1.5})$ and $0.1824 = 1/(1 + e^{1.5})$.
The second formula is translated to the clauses

```
clause2(X,Y):0.7502 :- \+friends(X,Y).
clause2(X,Y):0.7502 :- friends(X,Y),
                       intelligent(X),
                       intelligent(Y).
clause2(X,Y):0.7502 :- friends(X,Y),
                       \+intelligent(X),
                       \+intelligent(Y).
clause2(X,Y):0.2497 :- friends(X,Y),
                       intelligent(X),
                       \+intelligent(Y).
clause2(X,Y):0.2497 :- friends(X,Y),
                       \+intelligent(X),
                       intelligent(Y).
```

where $0.7502 = e^{1.1}/(1 + e^{1.1})$ and $0.2497 = 1/(1 + e^{1.1})$.
A priori we have a uniform distribution over student intelligence, good marks, and friendship:

```
intelligent(_):0.5.
good_marks(_):0.5.
friends(_,_):0.5.
```

and there are two students:

```
student(anna).
student(bob).
```

We have evidence that Anna is friend with Bob and Bob is intelligent. The evidence must also include the truth of all groundings of the $clause_i$ predicates:

```
evidence_mln :- clause1(anna),clause1(bob),
    clause2(anna,anna),clause2(anna,bob),
    clause2(bob,anna),clause2(bob,bob).
ev_intelligent_bob_friends_anna_bob :-
    intelligent(bob),friends(anna,bob),
    evidence_mln.
```

The probability that Anna gets good marks given the evidence is thus

$$P(\texttt{good\_marks(anna)}|\texttt{ev\_intelligent\_bob\_friends\_anna\_bob})$$

while the prior probability of Anna getting good marks is given by

$$P(\texttt{good\_marks(anna)}).$$

The probability resulting from the first query is higher ($P = 0.733$) than the second query ($P = 0.607$), since it is conditioned to the evidence that Bob is intelligent and Anna is his friend.

In the alternative transformation, the first MLN formula is translated to:

```
clause1(X) :- \+intelligent(X).
clause1(X):0.2231 :- intelligent(X),\+good_marks(X).
clause1(X) :- intelligent(X), good_marks(X).
```

where $0.2231 = e^{-1.5}$.

MLN formulas can also be added to a regular probabilistic logic program. In this case, their effect is equivalent to a soft form of evidence, where certain worlds are weighted more than others. This is the same as soft evidence in Figaro [Pfeffer, 2016]. MLN hard constraints, i.e., formulas with an infinite weight, can instead be used to rule out completely certain worlds, those violating the constraint. For example, given hard constraint C_i equivalent to the disjunction $C_{i1} \vee \ldots \vee C_{in_i}$, the LPAD should contain the clauses

$$clause_i(\boldsymbol{X}) \leftarrow C_{ij}$$

for all j, and the evidence should contain $clause_i(\boldsymbol{x})$ for all groundings $\boldsymbol{x}$ of $\boldsymbol{X}$. In this way, the worlds that violate C_i are ruled out.

2.11.3 Annotated probabilistic logic programs

In Annotated Probabilistic Logic Programming (APLP) [Ng and Subrahmanian, 1992], program atoms are annotated with intervals that can be interpreted probabilistically. An example rule in this approach is:

$$a : [0.75, 0.85] \leftarrow b : [1, 1], c : [0.5, 0.75]$$

that states that the probability of a is between 0.75 and 0.85 if b is certainly true and the probability of c is between 0.5 and 0.75. The probability interval of a conjunction or disjunction of atoms is defined using a *combinator* to construct the tightest bounds for the formula. For instance, if d is annotated with $[l_d, h_d]$ and e with $[l_e, h_e]$, the probability of $e \wedge d$ is annotated with

$$[max(0, l_d + l_e - 1), min(h_d, h_e)].$$

Using these combinators, an inference operator and fixpoint semantics is defined for positive Datalog programs. A model theory is obtained for such programs by considering the annotations as constraints on acceptable probabilistic worlds: an APLP thus describes a family of probabilistic worlds.

APLPs have the advantage that deduction is of low complexity, as the logic is truth-functional, i.e., the probability of a query can be computed directly using combinators. The corresponding disadvantages are that APLPs may be inconsistent if they are not carefully written, and that the use of the above combinators may quickly lead to assigning overly slack probability intervals to certain atoms. These aspects are partially addressed by hybrid APLPs [Dekhtyar and Subrahmanian, 2000], which allow different flavors of combinators based on, e.g., independence or mutual exclusivity of given atoms.

3

Semantics with Function Symbols

When a program contains variables, function symbols, and at least one constant, its grounding is denumerable. In this case, the set of atomic choices in a selection that defines a world is denumerable and there is an uncountable set of worlds.

Theorem 4 (Cardinality of the set of worlds of a ProbLog program). *For a ProbLog program $\mathcal{P}$, the set of all the worlds $W_\mathcal{P}$ is uncountable.*

Proof. The proof uses Cantor's diagonal argument.

If the program contains at least one function symbol and one constant, the Herbrand base $\mathcal{B}_\mathcal{P}$ is denumerable and so is the grounding of the program. In this case, each element of $W_\mathcal{P}$ can be represented as a denumerable sequence of Boolean values. Equivalently, we can represent it with a denumerable sequence of bits $b_1, b_2, b_3, \ldots$

If we suppose that $W_\mathcal{P}$ is denumerable, it is possible to write its element in a list such as

$$b_{1,1}, b_{1,2}, b_{1,3}, \ldots$$
$$b_{2,1}, b_{2,2}, b_{2,3}, \ldots$$
$$b_{3,1}, b_{3,2}, b_{3,3}, \ldots$$
$$\ldots$$

Since $W_\mathcal{P}$ is denumerable, the list should contain all its elements.

If we pick element $\neg b_{1,1}, \neg b_{2,2}, \neg b_{3,3}, \ldots$, this belongs to $W_\mathcal{P}$ because it is a denumerable sequence of Booleans. However, it is not in the list, because it differs from the first element in the first bit, from the second element in the second bit, and so on. In other words, it differs from each element of the list. This is against the hypothesis that the list contains all elements of $W_\mathcal{P}$. Thus, $W_\mathcal{P}$ is not denumerable and so $W_\mathcal{P}$ is uncountable. $\square$

The probability of each individual world is given by an infinite product. We recall the following result from [Knopp, 1951, page 218].

Lemma 1 (Infinite Product). *If $p_i \in [0, b]$ for all $i = 1, 2, \ldots$ with $b \in [0, 1)$, then the infinite product $\prod_{i=1}^{\infty} p_i$ converges to 0.*

Each factor in the infinite product giving the probability of a world is bounded away from one, i.e., it belongs to $[0, b]$ for $b \in [0, 1)$. To see this, it is enough to pick b as the maximum of all the probabilistic parameters that appear in the program. This is possible if the program does not have flexible probabilities or probabilities that depend on values computed during program execution.

So if the program does not contain flexible probabilities, the probability of each individual world is zero and the semantics of Section 2.2 is not well-defined [Riguzzi, 2016].

Example 38 (Program with infinite set of worlds). *Consider the ProbLog program*
$$p(0) \leftarrow u(0).$$
$$p(s(X)) \leftarrow p(X), u(X).$$
$$t \leftarrow \sim s.$$
$$s \leftarrow r, q.$$
$$q \leftarrow u(X).$$
$$F_1 = a :: u(X).$$
$$F_2 = b :: r.$$
This program contains function symbol $s/1$ and constant 0 and a probabilistic fact with a variable, so its set of worlds is uncountable.

Example 39 (Game of dice). *Consider the game of dice proposed in [Vennekens et al., 2004]: the player repeatedly throws a six-sided die. When the outcome is six, the game stops. A ProbLog version of this game where the die has three sides and the game stops when the outcome is 3 is:*
$$F_1 = 1/3 :: one(X).$$
$$F_2 = 1/2 :: two(X).$$
$$on(0, 1) \leftarrow one(0).$$
$$on(0, 2) \leftarrow \sim one(0), two(0).$$
$$on(0, 3) \leftarrow \sim one(0), \sim two(0).$$
$$on(s(X), 1) \leftarrow on(X, \_), \sim on(X, 3), one(s(X)).$$
$$on(s(X), 2) \leftarrow on(X, \_), \sim on(X, 3), \sim one(s(X)), two(s(X)).$$
$$on(s(X), 3) \leftarrow on(X, \_), \sim on(X, 3), \sim one(s(X)), \sim two(s(X)).$$
If we add the clauses
$$at\_least\_once\_1 \leftarrow on(\_, 1).$$
$$never\_1 \leftarrow \sim at\_least\_once\_1.$$

we can ask for the probability that at least once the die landed on face 1 and that the die never landed on face 1. As in Example 38, this program has an infinite and uncountable set of worlds.

3.1 The Distribution Semantics for Programs with Function Symbols

We now present the definition of the DS for ProbLog programs with function symbols following [Poole, 1997]. The semantics for a probabilistic logic program $\mathcal{P}$ with function symbols of [Poole, 1997] is given by defining a finitely additive probability measure μ over an algebra $\Omega_{\mathcal{P}}$ on the set of worlds $W_{\mathcal{P}}$.

We first need some definitions. The *set of worlds ω_κ compatible with a composite choice* κ is $\omega_\kappa = \{w_\sigma \in W_{\mathcal{P}} | \kappa \subseteq \sigma\}$. Thus, a composite choice identifies a set of worlds. For programs without function symbols, $P(\kappa) = \sum_{w \in \omega_\kappa} P(w)$, where

$$P(\kappa) = \prod_{(f_i,\theta,1) \in \kappa} \Pi_i \prod_{(f_i,\theta,0) \in \kappa} 1 - \Pi_i$$

For program with function symbols $\sum_{w \in \omega_\kappa}, P(w)$ may not be defined as ω_κ may be uncountable and $P(w) = 0$. However, $P(\kappa)$ is still well defined. Let us call it μ so $\mu(\kappa) = P(\kappa)$.

Given a *set* of composite choices K, the *set of worlds ω_K compatible with* K is $\omega_K = \bigcup_{\kappa \in K} \omega_\kappa$. Two composite choices κ_1 and κ_2 are *incompatible* if their union is not consistent. A set K of composite choices is *pairwise incompatible* if for all $\kappa_1 \in K, \kappa_2 \in K, \kappa_1 \neq \kappa_2$ implies that κ_1 and κ_2 are incompatible.

Regardless of whether a probabilistic logic program has a finite number of worlds or not, obtaining pairwise incompatible sets of composite choices is an important problem. This is because for program without function symbols, the *probability of a pairwise incompatible set K of composite choices* can be defined as $P(K) = \sum_{\kappa \in K} P(\kappa)$ which is easily computed. Let us call it μ so $\mu(K) = P(K)$. Two sets K_1 and K_2 of composite choices are *equivalent* if they correspond to the same set of worlds: $\omega_{K_1} = \omega_{K_2}$.

One way to assign probabilities to a set K of composite choices is to construct an equivalent set that is pairwise incompatible; such a set can be constructed through the technique of *splitting*. More specifically, if $f\theta$ is an instantiated fact and κ is a composite choice that does not contain an atomic choice (f, θ, k) for any k, the *split of κ on $f\theta$* is the set of composite choices

$S_{\kappa,f\theta} = \{\kappa \cup \{(f,\theta,0)\}, \kappa \cup \{(f,\theta,1)\}\}$. It is easy to see that κ and $S_{\kappa,f\theta}$ identify the same set of possible worlds, i.e., that $\omega_\kappa = \omega_{S_{\kappa,f\theta}}$, and that $S_{\kappa,f\theta}$ is pairwise incompatible. The technique of splitting composite choices on formulas is used for the following result [Poole, 2000].

Theorem 5 (Existence of a pairwise incompatible set of composite choices [Poole, 2000]). *Given a finite set K of composite choices, there exists a finite set K' of pairwise incompatible composite choices such that K and K' are equivalent.*

Proof. Given a finite set of composite choices K, there are two possibilities to form a new set K' of composite choices so that K and K' are equivalent:

1. **Removing dominated elements**: if $\kappa_1, \kappa_2 \in K$ and $\kappa_1 \subset \kappa_2$, let $K' = K \backslash \{\kappa_2\}$.
2. **Splitting elements**: if $\kappa_1, \kappa_2 \in K$ are compatible (and neither is a superset of the other), there is a $(f, \theta, k) \in \kappa_1 \backslash \kappa_2$. We replace κ_2 by the split of κ_2 on $f\theta$. Let $K' = K \backslash \{\kappa_2\} \cup S_{\kappa_2,f\theta}$.

In both cases, $\omega_K = \omega_{K'}$. If we repeat this two operations until neither is applicable, we obtain a splitting algorithm (see Algorithm 1) that terminates because K is a finite set of composite choices. The resulting set K' is pairwise incompatible and is equivalent to the original set. $\square$

Algorithm 1 Function SPLIT: Splitting Algorithm.

```
 1:  function SPLIT(K)
 2:      loop
 3:          if ∃κ₁, κ₂ ∈ K such that κ₁ ⊂ κ₂ then
 4:              K ← K\{κ₂}
 5:          else
 6:              if ∃κ₁, κ₂ ∈ K compatible then
 7:                  choose (f, θ, k) ∈ κ₁\κ₂
 8:                  K ← K\{κ₂} ∪ Sκ₂,Fθ
 9:              else
10:                  return K
11:              end if
12:          end if
13:      end loop
14:  end function
```

Theorem 6 (Equivalence of the probability of two equivalent pairwise incompatible finite sets of finite composite choices [Poole, 1993a]). *If K_1 and*

K_2 are both pairwise incompatible finite sets of finite composite choices such that they are equivalent, then $P(K_1) = P(K_2)$.

Proof. Consider the set D of all instantiated facts $f\theta$ that appear in an atomic choice in either K_1 or K_2. This set is finite. Each composite choice in K_1 and K_2 has atomic choices for a subset of D. For both K_1 and K_2, we repeatedly replace each composite choice κ of K_1 and K_2 with its split $S_{\kappa, f_i \theta_j}$ on an $f_i \theta_j$ from D that does not appear in κ. This procedure does not change the total probability as the probabilities of $(f_i, \theta_j, 0)$ and $(f_i, \theta_j, 1)$ sum to 1.

At the end of this procedure, the two sets of composite choices will be identical. In fact, any difference can be extended into a possible world belonging to ω_{K_1} but not to ω_{K_2} or vice versa. □

For a ProbLog program $\mathcal{P}$, we can thus define a unique finitely additive probability measure $\mu_{\mathcal{P}}^F : \Omega_{\mathcal{P}} \to [0, 1]$ where $\Omega_{\mathcal{P}}$ is defined as the set of sets of worlds identified by finite sets of finite composite choices: $\Omega_{\mathcal{P}} = \{\omega_K | K$ is a finite set of finite composite choices $\}$.

Theorem 7 (Algebra of a program). *$\Omega_{\mathcal{P}}$ is an algebra over $W_{\mathcal{P}}$.*

Proof. We need to prove that $\Omega_{\mathcal{P}}$ respects the three conditions of Definition 8. $W_{\mathcal{P}} = \omega_K$ with $K = \{\varnothing\}$. The complement ω_K^c of ω_K where K is a finite set of finite composite choice is $\omega_{\overline{K}}$ where $\overline{K}$ is a finite set of finite composite choices. In fact, $\overline{K}$ can be obtained with function DUALS(K) of [Poole, 2000] shown in Algorithm 2 for the case of ProbLog. Such a function performs Reiter's hitting set algorithm over K, generating an element κ of $\overline{K}$ by picking an atomic choice (f, θ, k) from each element of K and inserting in κ the atomic choice $(f, \theta, 1-k)$. After this process is performed in all possible ways, inconsistent sets of atom choices are removed obtaining $\overline{K}$. Since the possible choices of atomic choices are finite, so is $\overline{K}$. Finally, closure under finite union holds since the union of ω_{K_1} with ω_{K_2} is equal to $\omega_{K_1 \cup K_2}$ for the definition of ω_K. □

The corresponding measure $\mu_{\mathcal{P}}^F$ is defined by $\mu_{\mathcal{P}}^F(\omega_K) = \mu(K')$ where K' is a pairwise incompatible set of composite choices equivalent to K.

Theorem 8 (Finitely additive probability space of a program). *The triple $\langle W_{\mathcal{P}}, \Omega_{\mathcal{P}}, \mu_{\mathcal{P}}^F \rangle$ with*

$$\mu_{\mathcal{P}}^F(\omega_K) = \mu(K')$$

where K' is a pairwise incompatible set of composite choices equivalent to K, is a finitely additive probability space according to Definition 12.

Algorithm 2 Function DUALS: Duals computation.

1: **function** DUALS(K)
2:      suppose $K = \{\kappa_1, \ldots, \kappa_n\}$
3:      $D_0 \leftarrow \{\emptyset\}$
4:      **for** $i \leftarrow 1 \rightarrow n$ **do**
5:          $D_i \leftarrow \{d \cup \{(f, \theta, 1 - k)\} | d \in D_{i-1}, (f, \theta, k) \in \kappa_i\}$
6:          remove inconsistent elements from D_i
7:          remove any κ from D_i if $\exists \kappa' \in D_i$ such that $\kappa' \subset \kappa$
8:      **end for**
9:      **return** D_n
10: **end function**

Proof. $\mu_{\mathcal{P}}^F(\omega_{\{\emptyset\}})$ is equal to 1. Moreover, $\mu_{\mathcal{P}}^F(\omega_K) \geqslant 0$ for all K and if $\omega_{K_1} \cap \omega_{K_2} = \emptyset$ and K_1' (K_2') is pairwise incompatible and equivalent to K_1 (K_2), then $K_1' \cup K_2'$ is pairwise incompatible and

$$\mu_{\mathcal{P}}^F(\omega_{K_1} \cup \omega_{K_2}) = \sum_{\kappa \in K_1' \cup K_2'} P(\kappa) = \sum_{\kappa_1 \in K_1'} P(\kappa_1) + \sum_{\kappa_2 \in K_2'} P(\kappa_2) =$$
$$\mu_{\mathcal{P}}^F(\omega_{K_1}) + \mu_{\mathcal{P}}^F(\omega_{K_2}).$$

$\square$

Given a query q, a composite choice κ is an *explanation* for q if $\forall w \in \omega_\kappa : \ w \models q$. A set K of composite choices is *covering* with respect to q if every world in which q is true belongs to ω_K.

For a probabilistic logic program $\mathcal{P}$ and a ground atom q, we define the function $Q : W_{\mathcal{P}} \rightarrow \{0, 1\}$ as

$$Q(w) = \begin{cases} 1 & \text{if } w \models q \\ 0 & \text{otherwise} \end{cases} \tag{3.1}$$

If q has a finite set K of finite explanations such that K is covering then $Q^{-1}(\{1\}) = \{w | w \in W_{\mathcal{P}} \wedge w \models q\} = \omega_K \in \Omega_{\mathcal{P}}$ so Q is measurable. Therefore, Q is a random variable whose distribution is defined by $P(Q = 1)$ $(P(Q = 0)$ is given by $1 - P(Q = 1))$. We indicate $P(Q = 1)$ with $P(q)$ and we say that $P(q)$ is *finitely well-defined* for the distribution semantics. A program $\mathcal{P}$ is *finitely well-defined* if the probability of all ground atoms in the grounding of $\mathcal{P}$ is finitely well-defined.

Example 40 (Covering set of explanations for Example 38). *Consider the program of Example 38. The set $K = \{\kappa\}$ with*

$$\kappa = \{(f_1, \{X/0\}, 1), (f_1, \{X/s(0)\}, 1)\}$$

is a pairwise incompatible finite set of finite explanations that are covering for the query $p(s(0))$. *Then* $P(p(s(0)))$ *is finitely well-defined and* $P(p(s(0))) = P(\kappa) = a^2$.

Example 41 (Covering set of explanations for Example 39). *Now consider Example 39. The set* $K = \{\kappa_1, \kappa_2\}$ *with*

$$\kappa_1 = \{(f_1, \{X/0\}, 1), (f_1, \{X/s(0)\}, 1)\}$$
$$\kappa_2 = \{(f_1, \{X/0\}, 0), (f_2, \{X/0\}, 1), (f_1, \{X/s(0)\}, 1)\}$$

is a pairwise incompatible finite set of finite explanations that are covering for the query $on(s(0), 1)$. *Then* $P(on(s(0), 1))$ *is finitely well-and*

$$P(on(s(0), 1)) = P(K) = 1/3 \cdot 1/3 + 2/3 \cdot 1/2 \cdot 1/3 = 2/9.$$

3.2 Infinite Covering Set of Explanations

In this section, we go beyond [Poole, 1997] and we remove the requirement of the finiteness of the covering set of explanations and of each explanation for a query q [Riguzzi, 2016].

Example 42 (Pairwise incompatible covering set of explanations for Example 38). *In Example 38, the query* s *has the pairwise incompatible covering set of explanations*

$$K^s = \{\kappa_0^s, \kappa_1^s, \ldots\}$$

with

$$\kappa_i^s = \{(f_2, \emptyset, 1), (f_1, \{X/0\}, 0), \ldots,$$
$$(f_1, \{X/s^{i-1}(0)\}, 0), (f_1, \{X/s^i(0)\}, 1)\}$$

where $s^i(0)$ *is the term where the functor* s *is applied* i *times to 0. So* K^s *is denumerable. A pairwise incompatible covering set of explanations for* t *is*

$$K^t = \{\{(f_2, \emptyset, 0)\}, \kappa^t\}$$

where κ^t *is the infinite composite choice*

$$\kappa^t = \{(f_2, \emptyset, 1), (f_1, \{X/0\}, 0), (f_1, \{X/s(0)\}, 0), \ldots\}$$

Example 43 (Pairwise incompatible covering set of explanations for Example 39). *In Example 39, the query* $at\_least\_once\_1$ *has the pairwise incompatible covering set of explanations*

$$K^+ = \{\kappa_0^+, \kappa_1^+, \ldots\}$$

with

$$\kappa_0^+ = \{(f_1, \{X/0\}, 1)\}$$
$$\kappa_1^+ = \{(f_1, \{X/0\}, 0), (f_2, \{X/0\}, 1), (f_1, \{X/s(0)\}, 1)\}$$
$$\dots$$
$$\kappa_i^+ = \{(f_1, \{X/0\}, 0), (f_2, \{X/0\}, 1), \dots, (f_1, \{X/s^{i-1}(0)\}, 0),$$
$$(f_2, \{X/s^{i-1}(0)\}, 1), (f_1, \{X/s^i(0)\}, 1)\}$$
$$\dots$$

So K^+ is countable and infinite. The query $never\_1$ has the pairwise incompatible covering set of explanations

$$K^- = \{\kappa_0^-, \kappa_1^-, \dots\}$$

with

$$\kappa_0^- = \{(f_1, \{X/0\}, 0), (f_2, \{X/0\}, 0)\}$$
$$\kappa_1^- = \{(f_1, \{X/0\}, 0), (f_2, \{X/0\}, 1), (f_1, \{X/s(0)\}, 0),$$
$$(f_2, \{X/s(0)\}, 0)\}$$
$$\dots$$
$$\kappa_i^- = \{(f_1, \{X/0\}, 0), (f_2, \{X/0\}, 1), \dots, (f_1, \{X/s^{i-1}(0)\}, 0),$$
$$(f_2, \{X/s^{i-1}(0)\}, 1), (f_1, \{X/s^i(0)\}, 0), (f_2, \{X/s^i(0)\}, 0)\}$$
$$\dots$$

For a probabilistic logic program $\mathcal{P}$, we can define the probability measure $\mu_{\mathcal{P}} : \Omega_{\mathcal{P}} \to [0, 1]$ where $\Omega_{\mathcal{P}}$ is defined as the set of sets of worlds identified by countable sets of countable composite choices: $\Omega_{\mathcal{P}} = \{\omega_K | K$ is a countable set of countable composite choices $\}$.

Before showing that $\Omega_{\mathcal{P}}$ is a σ-algebra, we need some definitions and results regarding sequences of sets. For any sequence of sets $\{A_n | n \geq 1\}$, define [Chow and Teicher, 2012, page 2]

$$\underline{\lim}_{n \to \infty} A_n = \bigcup_{n=1}^{\infty} \bigcap_{k=n}^{\infty} A_k$$

$$\overline{\lim}_{n \to \infty} A_n = \bigcap_{n=1}^{\infty} \bigcup_{k=n}^{\infty} A_k$$

Note that [Chow and Teicher, 2012, page 2]

$$\overline{\lim}_{n\to\infty} A_n = \{a | a \in A_n \text{ i.o.}\}$$
$$\underline{\lim}_{n\to\infty} A_n = \{a | a \in A_n \text{ for all but a finite number of indices } n\}$$

where i.o. denotes infinitely often. The two definitions differ because an element a of $\overline{\lim}_{n\to\infty} A_n$ may be absent from A_n for an infinite number of indices n, provided that there is a disjoint, infinite set of indices n for which $a \in A_n$. For each $a \in \underline{\lim}_{n\to\infty} A_n$, instead, there is a $m \geqslant 1$ such that $\forall n \geqslant m, a \in A_n$.

Then $\underline{\lim}_{n\to\infty} A_n \subseteq \overline{\lim}_{n\to\infty} A_n$. If $\underline{\lim}_{n\to\infty} A_n = \overline{\lim}_{n\to\infty} A_n = A$, then A is called the *limit of the sequence* and we write $A = \lim_{n\to\infty} A_n$.

A sequence $\{A_n | n \geqslant 1\}$ is *increasing* if $A_{n-1} \subseteq A_n$ for all $n = 2, 3, \ldots$. If a sequence $\{A_n | n \geqslant 1\}$ is increasing, the limit $\lim_{n\to\infty} A_n$ exists and is equal to $\bigcup_{n=1}^{\infty} A_n$ [Chow and Teicher, 2012, page 3].

Lemma 2 (σ-algebra of a Program). *$\Omega_\mathcal{P}$ is a σ-algebra over $W_\mathcal{P}$.*

Proof. $W_\mathcal{P} \in \Omega_\mathcal{P}$ is true as in the algebra case. To see that the complement ω_K^c of ω_K is in $\Omega_\mathcal{P}$, let us prove that the dual $\overline{K}$ of K is a countable set of countable composite choices and then that $\omega_K^c = \omega_{\overline{K}}$. Let us consider first the case where K is finite, i.e., let K be $K_n = \{\kappa_1, \ldots, \kappa_n\}$. We will prove the thesis by induction. In the base case, if $K_1 = \{\kappa_1\}$, then we can obtain $\overline{K}_1$ by picking each atomic choice (f, θ, k) of κ_1 and inserting in $\overline{K}_1$ the composite choice $\{(f, \theta, 1 - k)\}$. As there is a countable number of atomic choices in κ_1, $\overline{K}_1$ is a countable set of composite choices each with one atomic choice.

In the inductive case, assume that $K_{n-1} = \{\kappa_1, \ldots, \kappa_{n-1}\}$ and that $\overline{K}_{n-1}$ is a countable set of composite choices. Let $K_n = K_{n-1} \cup \{\kappa_n\}$ and $\overline{K}_{n-1} = \{\kappa_1', \kappa_2', \ldots\}$. We can obtain $\overline{K}_n$ by picking each κ_i' and each atomic choice (f, θ, k) of κ_n. If $(f, \theta, k) \in \kappa_i'$, we discard κ_i', else if $(f, \theta, k') \in \kappa_i'$ with $k' \neq k$, we insert κ_i' in $\overline{K}_n$. Otherwise, we generate the composite choice κ_i'' where $\kappa_i'' = \kappa_i' \cup \{(f, \theta, 1 - k)\}$ and insert it in $\overline{K}_n$. Doing this for all atomic choices (f, θ, k) in κ_n generates a finite set of finite composite choices if κ_n is finite and a denumerable set of finite composite choices if κ_n is denumerable. Doing this for all κ_i', we obtain that $\overline{K}_n$ is a countable union of countable sets which is a countable set [Cohn, 2003, page 3]. $\omega_K^c = \omega_{\overline{K}}$ because all composite choices of $\overline{K}$ are incompatible with each world of ω_K, as they are incompatible with each composite choice of K. So $\omega_K^c \in \Omega_\mathcal{P}$.

If K is denumerable, then let $K = \{\kappa_1, \kappa_2, \ldots\}$. Consider the subsets K_n of the form $K_n = \{\kappa_1, \ldots, \kappa_n\}$. Using the construction above, build

$\overline{K}_n$ for all n and consider the sets $\underline{\lim}_{n\to\infty}\overline{K}_n$ and $\overline{\lim}_{n\to\infty}\overline{K}_n$. Consider a κ' that belongs to $\overline{\lim}_{n\to\infty}\overline{K}_n$. Suppose $\kappa' \in \overline{K}_j$ and $\kappa' \notin \overline{K}_{j+1}$. This means that κ' was removed because $\kappa_{j+1} \subseteq \kappa'$ or because it was replaced by an extension of it. Then κ' will never be re-added to a $\overline{K}_n$ with $n > j+1$ because otherwise ω_{K_n} and $\omega_{\overline{K}_n}$ would have a non-empty intersection. So for a composite choice κ' to appear infinitely often, there must exist an integer $m \geqslant 1$ such that $\kappa' \in \overline{K}_n$ for all $n \geqslant m$. In other words, κ' belongs to $\underline{\lim}_{n\to\infty}\overline{K}_n$. Therefore, $\underline{\lim}_{n\to\infty}\overline{K}_n = \overline{\lim}_{n\to\infty}\overline{K}_n = \lim_{n\to\infty}\overline{K}_n$. Let us call $\overline{K}$ this limit. $\overline{K}$ can thus be expressed as $\bigcup_{n=1}^{\infty}\bigcap_{k=n}^{\infty}\overline{K}_n$.

$\bigcap_{k=n}^{\infty}\overline{K}_n$ is countable as it is a countable intersection of countable sets. So $\overline{K}$ is countable as it is a countable union of countable sets. Moreover, each composite choice of $\overline{K}$ is incompatible with each composite choice of K. In fact, let κ' be an element of $\overline{K}$ and let $m \geqslant 1$ be the smallest integer such that $\kappa' \in \overline{K}_n$ for all $n \geqslant m$. Then κ' is incompatible with all composite choices of K_n for $n \geqslant m$ by construction. Moreover, it was obtained by extending a composite choice κ'' from $\overline{K}_{m-1}$ that was incompatible with all composite choices from K_{m-1}. As κ' is an extension of κ'', it is also incompatible with all elements of K_{m-1}. So $\omega_K^c = \omega_{\overline{K}}$ and $\omega_K^c \in \Omega_{\mathcal{P}}$.

Closure under countable union is true as in the algebra case. □

Given $K = \{\kappa_1, \kappa_2, \ldots\}$ where the κ_is may be infinite, consider the sequence $\{K_n|n \geqslant 1\}$ where $K_n = \{\kappa_1, \ldots, \kappa_n\}$. Since K_n is an increasing sequence, the limit $\lim_{n\to\infty} K_n$ exists and is equal to K. Let us build a sequence $\{K'_n|n \geqslant 1\}$ as follows: $K'_1 = \{\kappa_1\}$ and K'_n is obtained by the union of K'_{n-1} with the splitting of each element of K'_{n-1} with κ_n. By induction, it is possible to prove that K'_n is pairwise incompatible and equivalent to K_n.

For each K'_n, we can compute $\mu(K'_n)$, noting that $\mu(\kappa) = 0$ for infinite composite choices. Let us consider the limit $\lim_{n\to\infty} \mu(K'_n)$.

Lemma 3 (Existence of the limit of the measure of countable union of countable composite choices). $\lim_{n\to\infty} \mu(K'_n)$ *exists*.

Proof. We can see $\mu(K'_n)$ for $n = 1, \ldots$ as the partial sums of a series. A non-decreasing series converges if the partial sums are bounded from above [Brannan, 2006, page 92], so, if we prove that $\mu(K'_n) \geqslant \mu(K'_{n-1})$ and that $\mu(K'_n)$ is bounded by 1, the lemma is proved. Remove from K'_n the infinite composite choices, as they have measure 0. Let $\mathcal{D}_n$ be a ProbLog program containing a fact $\Pi_i :: f_i\theta$ for each instantiated facts $f_i\theta$ that appears in an atomic choice of K'_n. Then $\mathcal{D}_{n-1} \subseteq \mathcal{D}_n$. The triple $(W_{\mathcal{D}_n}, \Omega_{\mathcal{D}_n}, \mu)$ is a finitely additive probability space (see Section 2.2), so $\mu(K'_n) \leqslant 1$. Moreover, since $\omega_{K'_{n-1}} \subseteq \omega_{K'_n}$, then $\mu(K'_n) \geqslant \mu(K'_{n-1})$. □

We can now define the probability space of a program.

Theorem 9 (Probability space of a program). *The triple $\langle W_\mathcal{P}, \Omega_\mathcal{P}, \mu_\mathcal{P} \rangle$ with*

$$\mu_\mathcal{P}(\omega_K) = \lim_{n \to \infty} \mu(K'_n)$$

where $K = \{\kappa_1, \kappa_2, \ldots\}$ and K'_n is a pairwise incompatible set of composite choices equivalent to $\{\kappa_1, \ldots, \kappa_n\}$, is a probability space according to Definition 11.

Proof. (μ-1) and (μ-2) hold as for the finite case. For (μ-3), let

$$O = \{\omega_{L_1}, \omega_{L_2}, \ldots\}$$

be a countable set of subsets of $\Omega_\mathcal{P}$ such that the ω_{L_i}s are the set of worlds compatible with countable sets of countable composite choices L_is and are pairwise disjoint. Let L'_i be the pairwise incompatible set equivalent to L_i and let $\mathcal{L}$ be $\bigcup_{i=1}^{\infty} L'_i$. Since the ω_{L_i}s are pairwise disjoint, then $\mathcal{L}$ is pairwise incompatible. $\mathcal{L}$ is countable as it is a countable union of countable sets. Let $\mathcal{L}$ be $\{\kappa_1, \kappa_2, \ldots\}$ and let K'_n be $\{\kappa_1, \ldots, \kappa_n\}$. Then

$$\mu_\mathcal{P}(O) = \lim_{n \to \infty} \mu(K'_n) = \lim_{n \to \infty} \sum_{\kappa \in K'_n} \mu(\kappa) = \sum_{i=1}^{\infty} \mu(\kappa_i) = \sum_{\kappa \in \mathcal{L}} \mu(\kappa).$$

Since $\sum_{i=1}^{\infty} \mu(\kappa)$ is convergent and a sum of non-negative terms, it is also absolutely convergent and its terms can be rearranged [Knopp, 1951, Theorem 4, page 142]. We thus get

$$\mu_\mathcal{P}(O) = \sum_{\kappa \in \mathcal{L}} \mu(\kappa) = \sum_{n=1}^{\infty} \mu(L'_n) = \sum_{n=1}^{\infty} \mu_\mathcal{P}(\omega_{L_n}).$$

□

For a probabilistic logic program $\mathcal{P}$ and a ground atom q with a countable set K of explanations such that K is covering for q, then $\{w | w \in W_\mathcal{P} \wedge w \models q\} = \omega_K \in \Omega_\mathcal{P}$. So function Q of Equation (3.1) is a random variable.

Again we indicate $P(Q = 1)$ with $P(q)$ and we say that $P(q)$ is *well-defined* for the distribution semantics. A program $\mathcal{P}$ is *well-defined* if the probability of all ground atoms in the grounding of $\mathcal{P}$ is well-defined.

Example 44 (Probability of the query for Example 38). *Consider Example 42. The explanations in K^s are pairwise incompatible, so the probability of s can be computed as*

$$P(s) = ba + ba(1-a) + ba(1-a)^2 + \ldots = \frac{ba}{1-(1-a)} = b.$$

since the sum is a geometric series. K^t is also pairwise incompatible, and $P(\kappa^t) = 0$ so $P(t) = 1 - b + 0 = 1 - b$ which is what we intuitively expect.

Example 45 (Probability of the query for Example 39). *In Example 43, the explanations in K^+ are pairwise incompatible, so the probability of the query at_least_once_1 is given by*

$$
\begin{aligned}
P(at\_least\_once\_1) &= \frac{1}{3} + \frac{2}{3} \cdot \frac{1}{2} \cdot \frac{1}{3} + \left(\frac{2}{3} \cdot \frac{1}{2}\right)^2 \cdot \frac{1}{3} + \ldots \\
&= \frac{1}{3} + \frac{1}{9} + \frac{1}{27} \ldots \\
&= \frac{\frac{1}{3}}{1 - \frac{1}{3}} = \frac{\frac{1}{3}}{\frac{2}{3}} = \frac{1}{2}
\end{aligned}
$$

since the sum is a geometric series.

For the query never_1, the explanations in K^- are pairwise incompatible, so the probability of never_1 can be computed as

$$
\begin{aligned}
P(never\_1) &= \frac{2}{3} \cdot \frac{1}{2} + \frac{2}{3} \cdot \frac{1}{2} \cdot \frac{2}{3} \cdot \frac{1}{2} + \\
&\quad \left(\frac{2}{3} \cdot \frac{1}{2}\right)^2 \cdot \frac{2}{3} \cdot \frac{1}{2} + \ldots = \\
&\quad \frac{1}{3} + \frac{1}{9} + \frac{1}{27} \ldots = \frac{1}{2}.
\end{aligned}
$$

This is expected as never_1 $=\sim$at_least_once_1.

We now want to show that every program is well-defined, i.e., it has a countable set of countable explanations that is covering for each query. In the following, we consider only ground programs that, however, may be denumerable, and thus they can be the result of grounding a program with function symbols.

Given two sets of composite choices K_1 and K_2, define the conjunction $K_1 \otimes K_2$ of K_1 and K_2 as $K_1 \otimes K_2 = \{\kappa_1 \cup \kappa_2 | \kappa_1 \in K_1, \kappa_2 \in K_2, consistent(\kappa_1 \cup \kappa_2)\}$. It is easy to see that $\omega_{K_1 \otimes K_2} = \omega_{K_1} \cap \omega_{K_2}$.

Similarly to [Vlasselaer et al., 2015, 2016], we define parameterized interpretations and an $IFPP^{\mathcal{P}}$ operator that are generalizations of interpretations and the $IFP^{\mathcal{P}}$ operator for normal programs. Differently from [Vlasselaer et al., 2015, 2016], here parameterized interpretations associate each atom with a set of composite choices rather than with a Boolean formula.

Definition 23 (Parameterized two-valued interpretations). *A parameterized positive two-valued interpretation Tr for a ground probabilistic logic program $\mathcal{P}$ with Herbrand base $\mathcal{B}_{\mathcal{P}}$ is a set of pairs (a, K_a) with $a \in \mathcal{B}_{\mathcal{P}}$ and K_a a set of composite choices, such that for each $a \in \mathcal{B}_{\mathcal{P}}$ there is only one such pair (Tr is really a function). A parameterized negative two-valued interpretation Fa for a ground probabilistic logic program $\mathcal{P}$ with Herbrand base $\mathcal{B}_{\mathcal{P}}$ is a set of pairs $(a, K_{\sim a})$ with $a \in \mathcal{B}_{\mathcal{P}}$ and $K_{\sim a}$ a set of composite choices, such that for each $a \in \mathcal{B}_{\mathcal{P}}$ there is only one such pair.*

Parameterized two-valued interpretations form a complete lattice where the partial order is defined as $I \leqslant J$ if $\forall (a, K_a) \in I, (a, L_a) \in J : \omega_{K_a} \subseteq \omega_{L_a}$. The least upper bound and greatest lower bound of a set T always exist and are

$$\mathrm{lub}(T) = \{(a, \bigcup_{I \in T, (a, K_a) \in I} K_a) | a \in \mathcal{B}_{\mathcal{P}}\}$$

and

$$\mathrm{glb}(T) = \{(a, \bigotimes_{I \in T, (a, K_a) \in I} K_a) | a \in \mathcal{B}_{\mathcal{P}}\}.$$

The top element $\top$ is

$$\{(a, \{\varnothing\}) | a \in \mathcal{B}_{\mathcal{P}}\}$$

and the bottom element $\bot$ is

$$\{(a, \varnothing) | a \in \mathcal{B}_{\mathcal{P}}\}.$$

Definition 24 (Parameterized three-valued interpretations). *A parameterized three-valued interpretation $\mathcal{I}$ for a ground probabilistic logic program $\mathcal{P}$ with Herbrand base $\mathcal{B}_{\mathcal{P}}$ is a set of triples $(a, K_a, K_{\sim a})$ with $a \in \mathcal{B}_{\mathcal{P}}$ and K_a and $K_{\sim a}$ sets of composite choices such that for each $a \in \mathcal{B}_{\mathcal{P}}$ there is only one such triple. A consistent parameterized three-valued interpretation $\mathcal{I}$ is such that $\forall (a, K_a, K_{\sim a}) \in \mathcal{I} : \omega_{K_a} \cap \omega_{K_{\sim a}} = \varnothing$.*

Parameterized three-valued interpretations form a complete lattice where the partial order is defined as $\mathcal{I} \leqslant \mathcal{J}$ if $\forall (a, K_a, K_{\sim a}) \in \mathcal{I}, (a, L_a, L_{\sim a}) \in \mathcal{J}$:

$\omega_{K_a} \subseteq \omega_{L_a}$ and $\omega_{K_{\sim a}} \subseteq \omega_{L_{\sim a}}$. The least upper bound and greatest lower bound of a set T always exist and are

$$\text{lub}(T) = \{(a, \bigcup_{\mathcal{I} \in T, (a, K_a, K_{\sim a}) \in \mathcal{I}} K_a, \bigcup_{\mathcal{I} \in T, (a, K_a, K_{\sim a}) \in \mathcal{I}} K_{\sim a}) \mid a \in \mathcal{B}_{\mathcal{P}}\}$$

and

$$\text{glb}(T) = \{(a, \bigotimes_{\mathcal{I} \in T, (a, K_a, K_{\sim a}) \in \mathcal{I}} K_a, \bigotimes_{\mathcal{I} \in T, (a, K_a, K_{\sim a}) \in \mathcal{I}} K_{\sim a}) \mid a \in \mathcal{B}_{\mathcal{P}}\}.$$

The top element $\top$ is

$$\{(a, \{\varnothing\}, \{\varnothing\}) \mid a \in \mathcal{B}_{\mathcal{P}}\}$$

and the bottom element $\bot$ is

$$\{(a, \varnothing, \varnothing) \mid a \in \mathcal{B}_{\mathcal{P}}\}.$$

Definition 25 ($OpTrueP_{\mathcal{I}}^{\mathcal{P}}(Tr)$ and $OpFalseP_{\mathcal{I}}^{\mathcal{P}}(Fa)$). *For a ground program $\mathcal{P}$ with rules $\mathcal{R}$ and facts $\mathcal{F}$, a two-valued parameterized positive interpretation Tr with pairs (a, L_a), a two-valued parameterized negative interpretation Fa with pairs $(a, M_{\sim a})$, and a three-valued parameterized interpretation $\mathcal{I}$ with triples $(a, K_a, K_{\sim a})$, we define $OpTrueP_{\mathcal{I}}^{\mathcal{P}}(Tr) = \{(a, L_a') \mid a \in \mathcal{B}_{\mathcal{P}}\}$ where*

$$L_a' = \begin{cases} \{\{(a, \varnothing, 1)\}\} & \text{if } a \in \mathcal{F} \\ \bigcup_{a \leftarrow b_1, \ldots, b_n, \sim c_1, \ldots, \sim c_m \in \mathcal{R}} ((L_{b_1} \cup K_{b_1}) \otimes \ldots \\ \otimes (L_{b_n} \cup K_{b_n}) \otimes K_{\sim c_1} \otimes \ldots \otimes K_{\sim c_m}) & \text{if } a \in \mathcal{B}_{\mathcal{P}} \backslash \mathcal{F} \end{cases}$$

and $OpFalseP_{\mathcal{I}}^{\mathcal{P}}(Fa) = \{(a, M_a') \mid a \in \mathcal{B}_{\mathcal{P}}\}$ where

$$M_{\sim a}' = \begin{cases} \{\{(a, \varnothing, 0)\}\} & \text{if } a \in \mathcal{F} \\ \bigotimes_{a \leftarrow b_1, \ldots, b_n, \sim c_1, \ldots, \sim c_m \in \mathcal{R}} ((M_{\sim b_1} \otimes K_{\sim b_1}) \cup \ldots \\ \cup (M_{\sim b_n} \otimes K_{\sim b_n}) \cup K_{c_1} \cup \ldots \cup K_{c_m}) & \text{if } a \in \mathcal{B}_{\mathcal{P}} \backslash \mathcal{F} \end{cases}$$

Proposition 2 (Monotonicity of $OpTrueP_{\mathcal{I}}^{\mathcal{P}}$ and $OpFalseP_{\mathcal{I}}^{\mathcal{P}}$). *$OpTrueP_{\mathcal{I}}^{\mathcal{P}}$ and $OpFalseP_{\mathcal{I}}^{\mathcal{P}}$ are monotonic.*

Proof. Let us consider $OpTrueP_{\mathcal{I}}^{\mathcal{P}}$. We have to prove that if $Tr_1 \leqslant Tr_2$, then $OpTrueP_{\mathcal{I}}^{\mathcal{P}}(Tr_1) \leqslant OpTrueP_{\mathcal{I}}^{\mathcal{P}}(Tr_2)$. $Tr_1 \leqslant Tr_2$ means that

$$\forall (a, L_a) \in Tr_1, (a, M_a) \in Tr_2 : \omega_{L_a} \subseteq \omega_{M_a}.$$

Let (a, L'_a) be the elements of $OpTrueP^{\mathcal{P}}_{\mathcal{I}}(Tr_1)$ and (a, M'_a) the elements of $OpTrueP^{\mathcal{P}}_{\mathcal{I}}(Tr_2)$. We have to prove that $\omega_{L'_a} \subseteq \omega_{M'_a}$

If $a \in \mathcal{F}$, then $L'_a = M'_a = \{\{(a, \emptyset, 1)\}\}$. If $a \in \mathcal{B}_{\mathcal{P}} \backslash \mathcal{F}$, then L'_a and M'_a have the same structure. Since $\forall b \in \mathcal{B}_{\mathcal{P}} : \omega_{L_b} \subseteq \omega_{M_b}$, then $\omega_{L'_a} \subseteq \omega_{M'_a}$.

We can prove similarly that $OpFalseP^{\mathcal{P}}_{\mathcal{I}}$ is monotonic. $\qquad\square$

Since $OpTrueP^{\mathcal{P}}_{\mathcal{I}}$ and $OpFalseP^{\mathcal{P}}_{\mathcal{I}}$ are monotonic, they have a least fixpoint and a greatest fixpoint.

Definition 26 (Iterated fixpoint for probabilistic programs). *For a ground program $\mathcal{P}$, let $IFPP^{\mathcal{P}}$ be defined as*

$$IFPP^{\mathcal{P}}(\mathcal{I}) = \{(a, K_a, K_{\sim a})|(a, K_a) \in \text{lfp}(OpTrueP^{\mathcal{P}}_{\mathcal{I}}),$$
$$(a, K_{\sim a}) \in \text{gfp}(OpFalseP^{\mathcal{P}}_{\mathcal{I}})\}.$$

Proposition 3 (Monotonicity of $IFPP^{\mathcal{P}}$). *$IFPP^{\mathcal{P}}$ is monotonic.*

Proof. We have to prove that, if $\mathcal{I}_1 \leqslant \mathcal{I}_2$, then $IFPP^{\mathcal{P}}(\mathcal{I}_1) \leqslant IFPP^{\mathcal{P}}(\mathcal{I}_2)$. $\mathcal{I}_1 \leqslant \mathcal{I}_2$ means that

$$\forall(a, L_a, L_{\sim a}) \in \mathcal{I}_1, (a, M_a, M_{\sim a}) \in \mathcal{I}_2 : \omega_{L_a} \subseteq \omega_{M_a}, \omega_{L_{\sim a}} \subseteq \omega_{M_{\sim a}}.$$

Let $(a, L'_a, L'_{\sim a})$ be the elements of $IFPP^{\mathcal{P}}(\mathcal{I}_1)$ and $(a, M'_a, M'_{\sim a})$ the elements of $IFPP^{\mathcal{P}}(\mathcal{I}_2)$. We have to prove that $\omega_{L'_a} \subseteq \omega_{M'_a}$ and $\omega_{L'_{\sim a}} \subseteq \omega_{M'_{\sim a}}$. This follows from the monotonicity of $OpTrueP^{\mathcal{P}}_{\mathcal{I}}$ and $OpFalseP^{\mathcal{P}}_{\mathcal{I}}$ proved in Proposition 2 and from their monotonicity in $\mathcal{I}$ that can be proved as in Proposition 2. $\qquad\square$

So $IFPP^{\mathcal{P}}$ has a least fixpoint. Let $WFMP(\mathcal{P})$ denote $\text{lfp}(IFPP^{\mathcal{P}})$, and let δ the smallest ordinal such that $IFPP^{\mathcal{P}} \uparrow \delta = WFMP(\mathcal{P})$. We refer to δ as the *depth* of $\mathcal{P}$.

Let us now prove that $OpTrueP^{\mathcal{P}}_{\mathcal{I}}$ and $OpFalseP^{\mathcal{P}}_{\mathcal{I}}$ are sound.

Lemma 4 (Soundness of $OpTrueP^{\mathcal{P}}_{\mathcal{I}}$). *For a ground probabilistic logic program $\mathcal{P}$ with probabilistic facts $\mathcal{F}$ and rules $\mathcal{R}$, and a parameterized three-valued interpretation $\mathcal{I}$, let L^{α}_a be the set associated with atom a in $OpTrueP^{\mathcal{P}}_{\mathcal{I}} \uparrow \alpha$. For every atom a, total choice σ, and iteration α, we have:*

$$w_{\sigma} \in \omega_{L^{\alpha}_a} \rightarrow WFM(w_{\sigma}|\mathcal{I}) \models a$$

where $w_{\sigma}|\mathcal{I}$ is obtained by adding the atoms a for which $(a, K_a, K_{\sim a}) \in \mathcal{I}$ and $w_{\sigma} \in \omega_{K_a}$ to w_{σ}, and by removing all the rules with a in the head for which $(a, K_a, K_{\sim a}) \in \mathcal{I}$ and $w_{\sigma} \in \omega_{K_{\sim a}}$.

Proof. Let us prove the lemma by transfinite induction: let us assume the thesis for all $\beta < \alpha$ and let us prove it for α. If α is a successor ordinal, then it is easily verified for $a \in \mathcal{F}$. Otherwise assume $w_\sigma \in \omega_{L_a^\alpha}$ where

$$L_a^\alpha = \bigcup_{a \leftarrow b_1, \ldots, b_n, \sim c_1, \ldots, \sim c_m \in \mathcal{R}} ((L_{b_1}^{\alpha-1} \cup K_{b_1}) \otimes \ldots \otimes (L_{b_n}^{\alpha-1} \cup K_{b_n}) \otimes$$

$$K_{\sim c_1} \otimes \ldots \otimes K_{\sim c_m})$$

This means that there is rule $a \leftarrow b_1, \ldots, b_n, \sim c_1, \ldots, \sim c_m \in \mathcal{R}$ such that $w_\sigma \in \omega_{L_{b_i}^{\alpha-1} \cup K_{b_i}}$ for $i = 1, \ldots, n$ and $w_\sigma \in \omega_{K_{\sim c_j}}$ for $j = 1 \ldots, m$. By the inductive assumption and because of how $w_\sigma | \mathcal{I}$ is built, then $WFM(w_\sigma | \mathcal{I}) \models b_i$ and $WFM(w_\sigma | \mathcal{I}) \models \sim c_j$ so $WFM(w_\sigma | \mathcal{I}) \models a$.

If α is a limit ordinal, then

$$L_a^\alpha = \mathrm{lub}(\{L_a^\beta | \beta < \alpha\}) = \bigcup_{\beta < \alpha} L_a^\beta$$

If $w_\sigma \in \omega_{L_a^\alpha}$, then there must exist a $\beta < \alpha$ such that $w_\sigma \in \omega_{L_a^\beta}$. By the inductive assumption, the hypothesis holds. □

Lemma 5 (Soundness of $OpFalseP_\mathcal{I}^\mathcal{P}$). *For a ground probabilistic logic program $\mathcal{P}$ with probabilistic facts $\mathcal{F}$ and rules $\mathcal{R}$, and a parameterized three-valued interpretation $\mathcal{I}$, let $M_{\sim a}^\alpha$ be the set associated with atom a in $OpFalseP_\mathcal{I}^\mathcal{P} \downarrow \alpha$. For every atom a, total choice σ, and iteration α, we have:*

$$w_\sigma \in \omega_{M_{\sim a}^\alpha} \rightarrow WFM(w_\sigma | \mathcal{I}) \models \sim a$$

where $w_\sigma | \mathcal{I}$ is built as in Lemma 4.

Proof. As before, we prove the lemma by transfinite induction: we assume that the thesis is true for all ordinals $\beta < \alpha$ and we prove it for α. Consider α a successor ordinal. If $a \in \mathcal{F}$ the statement is easily verified since probabilistic facts do not appear in the head of any rule. If $a \notin \mathcal{F}$ consider $w_\sigma \in \omega_{M_{\sim a}^\alpha}$ where

$$M_{\sim a}^\alpha = \bigotimes_{a \leftarrow b_1, \ldots, b_n, \sim c_1, \ldots, \sim c_m \in \mathcal{R}} ((M_{\sim b_1} \otimes K_{\sim b_1}) \cup \ldots$$

$$\cup (M_{\sim b_n} \otimes K_{\sim b_n}) \cup K_{c_1} \cup \ldots \cup K_{c_m})$$

This means that, for each $a \leftarrow b_1, \ldots, b_n, \sim c_1, \ldots, \sim c_m \in \mathcal{R}$ there exists an index i such that $w_\sigma \in \omega_{M_{\sim b_i}^{\alpha-1} \cap K_{\sim b_i}}$, or there exists an index j such that $w_\sigma \in \omega_{K_{\sim c_j}}$. By the inductive assumption and because of how $w_\sigma \mid \mathcal{I}$ is built, either $WFM(w_\sigma \mid \mathcal{I}) \models \sim b_i$ or $WFM(w_\sigma \mid \mathcal{I}) \models c_j$ hold, so $WFM(w_\sigma \mid \mathcal{I}) \models \sim a$.

Consider now α a limit ordinal. Then,

$$M_{\sim a}^\alpha = \mathrm{glb}(M_{\sim a}^\beta \mid \beta < \alpha\}) = \bigcap_{\beta < \alpha} M_{\sim a}^\beta.$$

If $w_\sigma \in \omega_{M_{\sim a}^\alpha}$, for all $\beta < \alpha$ we have that $w_\sigma \in \omega_{M_{\sim a}^\beta}$. By the inductive assumption, this implies that $WFM(w \mid \mathcal{I}) \models \sim a$. $\qquad\square$

To prove the soundness of $IFPP^{\mathcal{P}}$, we first need a lemma regarding the model of a program obtained by a partial evaluation of the semantics.

Lemma 6 (Partial evaluation). *For a ground normal logic program P and a three-valued interpretation $\mathcal{I} = \langle I_T, I_F \rangle$ such that $\mathcal{I} \leqslant WFM(P)$, let $P \| \mathcal{I}$ be defined as the program obtained from P by adding all atoms $a \in I_T$ and by removing all rules for atoms $a \in I_F$. Then $WFM(P) = WFM(P \| \mathcal{I})$.*

Proof. We first prove that $WFM(P)$ is a fixpoint of $IFP^{P \| \mathcal{I}}$. Pick an atom $a \in OpTrue_{WFM(P)}^{P}(I_T)$. If $a \in I_T$, then a is a fact in $P \| \mathcal{I}$, so it is in $OpTrue_{WFM(P)}^{P \| \mathcal{I}}(I_T)$. Otherwise, there exists a rule $a \leftarrow b_1, \ldots, b_n$ in P such that b_i is true in $WFM(P)$ or $b_i \in I_T$ for $i = 1, \ldots, n$. Such a rule is also in $P \| \mathcal{I}$ so $a \in OpTrue_{WFM(P)}^{P \| \mathcal{I}}(I_T)$.

Now pick an atom $a \in OpFalse_{WFM(P)}^{P}(I_F)$. If $a \in I_F$, then there are no rules for a t in $P \| \mathcal{I}$, so it is in $OpFalse_{WFM(P)}^{P \| \mathcal{I}}(I_F)$. Otherwise, for all rules $a \leftarrow b_1, \ldots, b_n$ in P, there exists a b_i such that it is false in $WFM(P)$ or $b_i \in I_F$. The set of rules for a in $P \| \mathcal{I}$ is the same, so $a \in OpFalse_{WFM(P)}^{P \| \mathcal{I}}(I_F)$.

We can prove similarly that $WFM(P||\mathcal{I})$ is a fixpoint of IFP^P.

Since $WFM(P)$ is a fixpoint of $IFP^{P||\mathcal{I}}$, then $WFM(P||\mathcal{I}) \leqslant WFM(P)$ because $WFM(P||\mathcal{I})$ is the least fixpoint of $IFP^{P||\mathcal{I}}$. Since $WFM(P||\mathcal{I})$ is a fixpoint of IFP^P, then $WFM(P) \leqslant WFM(P||\mathcal{I})$. So $WFM(P) = WFM(P||\mathcal{I})$. $\qquad\square$

The following lemma shows that $IFPP^P$ is sound.

Lemma 7 (Soundness of $IFPP^P$). *For a ground probabilistic logic program $\mathcal{P}$ with probabilistic facts $\mathcal{F}$ and rules $\mathcal{R}$, let K_a^α and $K_{\sim a}^\alpha$ be the sets associated with atom a in $IFPP^P \uparrow \alpha$. For every atom a, total choice σ, and iteration α, we have:*

$$w_\sigma \in \omega_{K_a^\alpha} \;\rightarrow\; WFM(w_\sigma) \vDash a \qquad (3.2)$$

$$w_\sigma \in \omega_{K_{\sim a}^\alpha} \;\rightarrow\; WFM(w_\sigma) \vDash \sim a \qquad (3.3)$$

Proof. We prove the thesis and the formula

$$WFM(w_\sigma \mid IFPP^P \uparrow \alpha) \;=\; WFM(w_\sigma) \qquad (3.4)$$

by transfinite induction. Let us consider a successor ordinal α and let us assume

$$WFM(w_\sigma \mid IFPP^P \uparrow \alpha - 1) \;=\; WFM(w_\sigma) \qquad (3.5)$$

and that

$$w_\sigma \in \omega_{K_a^{\alpha-1}} \;\rightarrow\; WFM(w_\sigma) \vDash a$$

$$w_\sigma \in \omega_{K_{\sim a}^{\alpha-1}} \;\rightarrow\; WFM(w_\sigma) \vDash \sim a$$

From the soundness of $OpTrueP^{\mathcal{P}}_{IFPP^P\uparrow(\alpha-1)}$ and $OpFalseP^{\mathcal{P}}_{IFPP^P\uparrow(\alpha-1)}$ we have that

$$w_\sigma \in \omega_{L_a^\beta} \;\rightarrow\; WFM(w_\sigma|IFPP^P \uparrow (\alpha-1)) \vDash a$$

$$w_\sigma \in \omega_{L_{\sim a}^\beta} \;\rightarrow\; WFM(w_\sigma|IFPP^P \uparrow (\alpha-1)) \vDash \sim a$$

where L_a^β is the formula associated to a in $OpTrueP^{\mathcal{P}}_{IFPP^P\uparrow(\alpha-1)} \uparrow \beta$ and $L_{\sim a}^\beta$ is the formula associated to a in $OpFalseP^{\mathcal{P}}_{IFPP^P\uparrow(\alpha-1)} \uparrow \beta$.

Since this is true for all β, it is also true for the γ and δ such that

$$OpTrueP^{\mathcal{P}}_{IFPP^P\uparrow\alpha-1} \uparrow \gamma = \mathrm{lfp}(OpTrueP^{\mathcal{P}}_{IFPP^P\uparrow\alpha-1})$$

$$OpFalseP^{\mathcal{P}}_{IFPP^P\uparrow\alpha-1} \uparrow \delta = \mathrm{gfp}(OpFalseP^{\mathcal{P}}_{IFPP^P\uparrow\alpha-1})$$

so

$$w_\sigma \in \omega_{K_a^\alpha} \;\to\; WFM(w_\sigma \mid IFPP^{\mathcal{P}} \uparrow (\alpha - 1)) \models a$$
$$w_\sigma \in \omega_{K_{\sim a}^\alpha} \;\to\; WFM(w_\sigma \mid IFPP^{\mathcal{P}} \uparrow (\alpha - 1)) \models \sim a$$

Because of Equation (3.5), then

$$w_\sigma \in \omega_{K_a^\alpha} \;\to\; WFM(w_\sigma) \models a \tag{3.6}$$
$$w_\sigma \in \omega_{K_{\sim a}^\alpha} \;\to\; WFM(w_\sigma) \models \sim a \tag{3.7}$$

Now let us prove that

$$WFM(w_\sigma \mid IFPP^{\mathcal{P}} \uparrow \alpha) \;=\; WFM(w_\sigma) \tag{3.8}$$

Let $\mathcal{I}_\alpha = \langle I_T, I_F \rangle$ be a three-valued interpretation defined as $I_T = \{a \mid w_\sigma \in \omega_{K_a^\alpha}\}$ and $I_F = \{a \mid w_\sigma \in \omega_{K_{\sim a}^\alpha}\}$. Then, for Equation (3.6), $\forall a \in I_T$: $WFM(w_\sigma) \models a$ and, for Equation (3.7), $\forall a \in I_F$: $WFM(w_\sigma) \models \sim a$. So $\mathcal{I}_\alpha \leqslant WFM(w_\sigma)$.

Since $w_\sigma \mid IFPP^{\mathcal{P}} \uparrow \alpha = w_\sigma || \mathcal{I}_\alpha$, by Lemma 6

$$WFM(w_\sigma) \;=\; WFM(w_\sigma || \mathcal{I}_\alpha) \;=\; WFM(w_\sigma \mid IFPP^{\mathcal{P}} \uparrow \alpha).$$

Let us now consider a limit ordinal α and let us assume that

$$w_\sigma \in \omega_{K_a^\beta} \;\to\; WFM(w_\sigma) \models a \tag{3.9}$$
$$w_\sigma \in \omega_{K_{\sim a}^\beta} \;\to\; WFM(w_\sigma) \models \sim a \tag{3.10}$$

for all $\beta < \alpha$ Then $K_a^\alpha = \bigcup_{\beta < \alpha} K_a^\beta$ and $K_{\sim a}^\alpha = \bigcup_{\beta < \alpha} K_{\sim a}^\beta$ so $w_\sigma \in \omega_{K_a^\alpha} \to \exists \beta : w_\sigma \in \omega_{K_a^\beta}$. For Equation (3.9), then $WFM(w_\sigma) \models a$. Moreover $w_\sigma \in \omega_{K_{\sim a}^\alpha} \to \exists \beta : w_\sigma \in \omega_{K_{\sim a}^\beta}$. For Equation (3.10), then $WFM(w_\sigma) \models \sim a$.

The proof of Equation (3.4) for α limit ordinal is the same as for the case of successor ordinal. $\qquad\square$

The following lemma shows that $IFPP^{\mathcal{P}}$ is complete.

Lemma 8 (Completeness of $IFPP^{\mathcal{P}}$). *For a ground probabilistic logic program $\mathcal{P}$ with probabilistic facts $\mathcal{F}$ and rules $\mathcal{R}$, let K_a^α and $K_{\sim a}^\alpha$ be the sets associated with atom a in $IFPP^{\mathcal{P}} \uparrow \alpha$. For every atom a, total choice σ, and iteration α, we have:*

$$a \in IFP^{w_\sigma} \uparrow \alpha \;\to\; w_\sigma \in \omega_{K_a^\alpha}$$
$$\sim a \in IFP^{w_\sigma} \uparrow \alpha \;\to\; w_\sigma \in \omega_{K_{\sim a}^\alpha}$$

Proof. Let us prove it by double transfinite induction. If α is a successor ordinal, assume that

$$a \in IFP^{w_\sigma} \uparrow (\alpha - 1) \rightarrow w_\sigma \in \omega_{K_a^{\alpha-1}}$$
$$\sim a \in IFP^{w_\sigma} \uparrow (\alpha - 1) \rightarrow w_\sigma \in \omega_{K_{\sim a}^{\alpha-1}}$$

Let us perform transfinite induction on the iterations of $OpTrue^{w_\sigma}_{IFP^{w_\sigma}\uparrow(\alpha-1)}$ and $OpFalse^{w_\sigma}_{IFP^{w_\sigma}\uparrow(\alpha-1)}$. Let us consider a successor ordinal δ: assume that

$$a \in OpTrue^{w_\sigma}_{IFP^{w_\sigma}\uparrow(\alpha-1)} \uparrow (\delta - 1) \rightarrow w_\sigma \in \omega_{L_a^{\delta-1}}$$
$$\sim a \in OpFalse^{w_\sigma}_{IFP^{w_\sigma}\uparrow(\alpha-1)} \downarrow (\delta - 1) \rightarrow w_\sigma \in \omega_{M_{\sim a}^{\delta-1}}$$

where $(a, L_a^{\delta-1})$ are the elements of $OpTrue^{P}_{IFPP^{P}\uparrow\alpha-1} \uparrow (\delta - 1)$ and $(a, M_{\sim a}^{\delta-1})$ are the elements of $OpFalse^{P}_{IFPP^{P}\uparrow\alpha-1} \downarrow (\delta - 1)$. We prove that

$$a \in OpTrue^{w_\sigma}_{IFP^{w_\sigma}\uparrow(\alpha-1)} \uparrow \delta \rightarrow w_\sigma \in \omega_{L_a^{\delta}} \qquad (3.11)$$
$$\sim a \in OpFalse^{w_\sigma}_{IFP^{w_\sigma}\uparrow(\alpha-1)} \downarrow \delta \rightarrow w_\sigma \in \omega_{M_{\sim a}^{\delta}} \qquad (3.12)$$

Consider a. If $a \in \mathcal{F}$, it is easily proved.

For the other atoms, $a \in OpTrue^{w_\sigma}_{IFP^{w_\sigma}\uparrow(\alpha-1)} \uparrow \delta$ means that there is a rule $a \leftarrow b_1, \ldots, b_n, \sim c_1, \ldots, \sim c_m$ such that for all $i = 1, \ldots, n$

$$b_i \in OpTrue^{w_\sigma}_{IFP^{w_\sigma}\uparrow(\alpha-1)} \uparrow (\delta - 1) \vee b_i \in IFP^{w_\sigma} \uparrow (\alpha - 1)$$

and for all $j = 1, \ldots, m, \sim c_j \in IFP^{w_\sigma} \uparrow (\alpha - 1)$. For the inductive hypotheses for the inner and outer inductions, $\forall i : w_\sigma \in \omega_{L_{b_i}^{\delta-1}} \vee w_\sigma \in \omega_{K_{b_i}^{\alpha-1}}$ and $\forall j : w_\sigma \in \omega_{K_{\sim c_j}^{\alpha-1}}$ so $w_\sigma \in L_a^{\delta}$. Analogously for $\sim a$.

If δ is a limit ordinal, then $L_a^{\delta} = \bigcup_{\mu<\delta} L_a^{\mu}$ and $M_{\sim a}^{\delta} = \bigotimes_{\mu<\delta} M_{\sim a}^{\mu}$. If $a \in OpTrue^{w_\sigma}_{IFP^{w_\sigma}\uparrow(\alpha-1)} \uparrow \delta$, then there exists a $\mu < \delta$ such that

$$a \in OpTrue^{w_\sigma}_{IFP^{w_\sigma}\uparrow(\alpha-1)} \uparrow \mu.$$

For the inductive hypothesis, $w_\sigma \in \omega_{L_a^{\mu}}$ and so $w_\sigma \in \omega_{L_a^{\delta}}$.

If $\sim a \in OpFalse^{w_\sigma}_{IFP^{w_\sigma}\uparrow(\alpha-1)} \downarrow \delta$, then, for all $\mu < \delta$,

$$\sim a \in OpFalse^{w_\sigma}_{IFP^{w_\sigma}\uparrow(\alpha-1)} \downarrow \mu.$$

For the inductive hypothesis, $w_\sigma \in \omega_{M_{\sim a}^{\mu}}$ and so $w_\sigma \in \omega_{M_{\sim a}^{\delta}}$.

Since $IFP^{w_\sigma} \uparrow \alpha$ is obtained from the fixpoints of $OpTrue^{w_\sigma}_{IFP^{w_\sigma}\uparrow(\alpha-1)}$ and $OpFalse^{w_\sigma}_{IFP^{w_\sigma}\uparrow(\alpha-1)}$, and equations (3.11) and (3.12) hold for all δ, they also hold at the fixpoints and the thesis is proved.

Consider a limit α. Then $K_a^\alpha = \bigcup_{\beta<\alpha} K_a^\beta$ and $K_{\sim a}^\alpha = \bigcup_{\beta<\alpha} K_{\sim a}^\beta$. If $a \in IFP^{w_\sigma} \uparrow \alpha$, then there exists a $\beta < \alpha$ such that $a \in IFP^{w_\sigma} \uparrow \beta$. For the inductive hypothesis, $w_\sigma \in \omega_{K_a^\beta}$ so $w_\sigma \in \omega_{K_a^\alpha}$. Similarly for $\sim a$. □

We can now prove that $IFPP^{\mathcal{P}}$ is sound and complete.

Theorem 10 (Soundness and completeness of $IFPP^{\mathcal{P}}$). *For a ground probabilistic logic program $\mathcal{P}$, let K_a^α and $K_{\sim a}^\alpha$ be the sets associated with atom a in $IFPP^{\mathcal{P}} \uparrow \alpha$. For every atom a and total choice σ, there is an iteration α_0 such that for all $\alpha > \alpha_0$ we have:*

$$w_\sigma \in \omega_{K_a^\alpha} \leftrightarrow WFM(w_\sigma) \models a \tag{3.13}$$

$$w_\sigma \in \omega_{K_{\sim a}^\alpha} \leftrightarrow WFM(w_\sigma) \models \sim a \tag{3.14}$$

Proof. The $\rightarrow$ direction of equations (3.13) and (3.14) is Lemma 7. In the other direction, $WFM(w_\sigma) \models a$ implies $\exists\alpha_0 \forall\alpha : \alpha \geq \alpha_0 \rightarrow IFP_{w_\sigma} \uparrow \alpha \models a$. For Lemma 8, $w_\sigma \in \omega_{K_a^\alpha}$. $WFM(w_\sigma) \models \sim a$ implies $\exists\alpha_0 \forall\alpha : \alpha \geq \alpha_0 \rightarrow IFP^{w_\sigma} \uparrow \alpha \models \sim a$. For Lemma 8, $w_\sigma \in \omega_{K_{\sim a}^\alpha}$. □

We can now prove that every query for every sound program has a countable set of countable explanations that is covering.

Theorem 11 (Well-definedness of the distribution semantics). *For a sound ground probabilistic logic program $\mathcal{P}$, $\mu_{\mathcal{P}}(\{w|w \in W_{\mathcal{P}}, w \models a\})$ for all $a \in B_{\mathcal{P}}$ is well defined.*

Proof. Let K_a^δ and $K_{\sim a}^\delta$ be the formulas associated with atom a in $IFPP^{\mathcal{P}} \uparrow \delta$ where δ is the depth of the program. For the soundness and completeness of $IFPP^{\mathcal{P}}$, then $\{w|w \in W_{\mathcal{P}}, w \models a\} = \omega_{K_a^\delta}$.

Each iteration of $OpTrueP^{\mathcal{P}}_{IFPP^{\mathcal{P}}\uparrow\beta}$ and $OpFalseP^{\mathcal{P}}_{IFPP^{\mathcal{P}}\uparrow\beta}$ for all β generates countable sets of countable explanations since the set of rules is countable. So K_a^δ is a countable set of countable explanations and $\mu_{\mathcal{P}}(\{w|w \in W_{\mathcal{P}}, w \models a\})$ is well defined. □

Moreover, if the program is sound, for all atoms a, $\omega_{K_a^\delta} = \omega^c_{K_{\sim a}^\delta}$ where δ is the depth of the program, as otherwise there would exist a world w_σ such that $w_\sigma \notin \omega_{K_a^\delta}$ and $w_\sigma \notin \omega_{K_{\sim a}^\delta}$. But w_σ has a two-valued WFM so either

$WFM(w_\sigma) \models a$ or $WFM(w_\sigma) \models \sim a$. In the first case, $w_\sigma \in \omega_{K_a^\delta}$ and in the latter, $w_\sigma \in \omega_{K_{\sim a}^\delta}$ against the hypothesis.

To give a semantics to a program with function symbols in the other languages under the DS, we can translate it into ProbLog using the techniques from Section 2.4 and use the above semantics for ProbLog.

3.3 Comparison with Sato and Kameya's Definition

Sato and Kameya [2001] define the distribution semantics for definite programs, i.e., programs without negative literals. They build a probability measure on the set of Herbrand interpretations from a collection of finite distributions. Let the set of ground probabilistic facts $\mathcal{F}$ be $\{f_1, f_2, \ldots\}$ and let X_i be a random variable associated with f_i whose domain $\mathcal{V}_i$ is $\{0, 1\}$.

They define the sample space $\mathcal{V}_\mathcal{F}$ as a topological space with the product topology as the event space such that each $\{0, 1\}$ is equipped with the discrete topology.

In order to clarify this definition, let us introduce some topology terminology. A *topology* on a set $\mathcal{V}$ [Willard, 1970, page 23] is a collection Ψ of subsets of $\mathcal{V}$, called the *open sets*, satisfying: (t-1) any union of elements of Ψ belongs to Ψ, (t-2) any finite intersection of elements of Ψ belongs to Ψ, (t-3) $\varnothing$ and $\mathcal{V}$ belong to Ψ. We say that $(\mathcal{V}, \Psi)$ is a *topological space*. The *discrete topology* of a set $\mathcal{V}$ [Steen and Seebach, 2013, page 41] is the powerset $\mathbb{P}(\mathcal{V})$ of $\mathcal{V}$.

The *infinite Cartesian product* of sets ψ_i for $i = 1, 2, \ldots$ is

$$\underset{i=1}{\overset{\infty}{\times}} \psi_i = \{(s_1, s_2, \ldots) | s_i \in \psi_i, i = 1, 2, \ldots\}$$

A *product topology* [Willard, 1970, page 53] on the infinite Cartesian product $\times_{i=1}^{\infty} \mathcal{V}_i$ is a set containing all possible unions of open sets of the form $\times_{i=1}^{\infty} \nu_i$ where (p-1) ν_i is open $\forall i$ and (p-2) for all but finitely many i, $\nu_i = \mathcal{V}_i$. Sets satisfying (p-1) and (p-2) are called *cylinder sets*. There exists a countable number of them.

So $\mathcal{V}_\mathcal{F} = \times_{i=1}^{\infty} \{0, 1\}$, i.e., it is an infinite Cartesian product with $\mathcal{V}_i = \{0, 1\}$ for all i. Sato and Kameya [2001] define a probability measure $\eta_\mathcal{F}$ over the sample space $\mathcal{V}_\mathcal{F}$ from a collection of finite joint distributions $P_\mathcal{F}^{(n)}(X_1 = k_1, \ldots, X_n = k_n)$ for $n \geq 1$ such that

$$
\begin{cases}
0 \leqslant P_{\mathcal{F}}^{(n)}(X_1 = k_1, \ldots, X_n = k_n) \leqslant 1 \\
\sum_{k_1, \ldots, k_n} P_{\mathcal{F}}^{(n)}(X_1 = k_1, \ldots, X_n = k_n) = 1 \\
\sum_{k_{n+1}} P_{\mathcal{F}}^{(n+1)}(X_1 = k_1, \ldots, X_{n+1} = k_{n+1}) = P_{\mathcal{F}}^{(n)}(X_1 = k_1, \ldots, X_n = k_n)
\end{cases}
$$
$$(3.15)$$

The last equation is called the *consistency condition* or *compatibility condition*. The *Kolmogorov consistency theorem* [Chow and Teicher, 2012, page 194] states that, if the distributions $P_{\mathcal{F}}^{(n)}(X_1 = k_1, \ldots, X_n = k_n)$ satisfy the compatibility condition, there exists a probability space $(\mathcal{V}_{\mathcal{F}}, \Psi_{\mathcal{F}}, \eta_{\mathcal{F}})$ where $\eta_{\mathcal{F}}$ is a unique probability measure on $\Psi_{\mathcal{F}}$, the minimal σ-algebra containing open sets of $\mathcal{V}_{\mathcal{F}}$, such that for any n,

$$\eta_{\mathcal{F}}(X_1 = k_1, \ldots, X_n = k_n) = P_{\mathcal{F}}^{(n)}(X_1 = k_1, \ldots, X_n = k_n). \qquad (3.16)$$

$P_{\mathcal{F}}^{(n)}(X_1 = k_1, \ldots, X_n = k_n)$ is defined by Sato and Kameya [2001] as

$$P_{\mathcal{F}}^{(n)}(X_1 = k_1, \ldots, X_n = k_n) = \pi_1 \cdot \ldots \cdot \pi_n$$

where $\pi_i = \Pi_i$ if $k_i = 1$ and $\pi_i = 1 - \Pi_i$ if $k_i = 0$, with Π_i the annotation of fact f_i. This definition clearly satisfies the properties in Equation (3.15).

The distribution $P_{\mathcal{F}}^{(n)}(X_1 = k_1, \ldots, X_n = k_n)$ is then extended to a probability measure over the set of Herbrand interpretations of the whole program. Let $\mathcal{B}_P$ be $\{a_1, a_2, \ldots\}$ and let Y_i be a random variable associated with a_i whose domain is $\{0, 1\}$. Moreover, let $a^k = a$ if $k = 1$ and $a^k = \sim a$ if $k = 0$. $\mathcal{V}_P$ is the infinite Cartesian product $\mathcal{V}_P = \times_{i=1}^{\infty} \{0, 1\}$.

Measure $\eta_{\mathcal{F}}$ is extended to η_P by introducing a series of finite joint distributions $P_{\mathcal{P}}^{(n)}(Y_1 = k_1, \ldots, Y_n = k_n)$ for $n = 1, 2, \ldots$ by setting

$$[a_1^{k_1} \wedge \ldots \wedge a_n^{k_n}]_{\mathcal{F}} = \{v \in \mathcal{V}_{\mathcal{F}} | \mathrm{lhm}(v) \models a_1^{k_1} \wedge \ldots \wedge a_n^{k_n}\}$$

where $\mathrm{lhm}(v)$ is the least Herbrand model of $\mathcal{R} \cup \mathcal{F}_v$, with $\mathcal{F}_v = \{f_i | v_i = 1\}$.
Then let

$$P_{\mathcal{P}}^{(n)}(Y_1 = k_1, \ldots, Y_n = k_n) = \eta_{\mathcal{F}}([a_1^{k_1} \wedge \ldots \wedge a_n^{k_n}]_{\mathcal{F}})$$

Sato and Kameya state that $[a_1^{k_1} \wedge \ldots \wedge a_n^{k_n}]_{\mathcal{F}}$ is $\eta_{\mathcal{F}}$-measurable and that, by definition, $P_{\mathcal{P}}^{(n)}$ satisfy the compatibility condition

$$\sum_{k_{n+1}} P_{\mathcal{P}}^{(n+1)}(Y_1 = k_1, \ldots, Y_{n+1} = k_{n+1}) = P_{\mathcal{P}}^{(n)}(Y_1 = k_1, \ldots, Y_n = k_n)$$

Hence, there exists a unique probability measure η_P over Ψ_P which is an extension of $\eta_{\mathcal{F}}$.

In order to relate this definition to the one of Section 3.2, we need to introduce some more terminology on σ-algebras.

Definition 27 (Infinite-dimensional product σ-algebra and space). *For any measurable spaces* (W_i, Ω_i), $i = 1, 2, \ldots$, *define*

$$\mathcal{G} = \bigcup_{m=1}^{\infty} \{ \underset{i=1}{\overset{\infty}{\times}} \omega_i | \omega_i \in \Omega_i, 1 \leqslant i \leqslant m \text{ and } \omega_i = W_i, i > m \}$$

$$\bigotimes_{i=1}^{\infty} \Omega_i = \sigma(\mathcal{G})$$

$$\underset{i=1}{\overset{\infty}{\times}} (W_i, \Omega_i) = (\underset{i=1}{\overset{\infty}{\times}} W_i, \bigotimes_{i=1}^{\infty} \Omega_i)$$

Then $\times_{i=1}^{\infty}(W_i, \Omega_i)$ *is the* infinite-dimensional product space *and* $\bigotimes_{i=1}^{\infty} \Omega_i$ *is the* infinite-dimensional product σ-algebra. *This definition generalizes Definition 15 for the case of infinite dimensions.*

It is clear that if $W_i = \{0, 1\}$ and $\Omega_i = \mathbb{P}(\{0, 1\})$ for all i, then $\mathcal{G}$ is the set of all possible unions of cylinder sets, so it is the product topology on $\times_{i=1}^{\infty} W_i$ and

$$\underset{i=1}{\overset{\infty}{\times}} (W_i, \Omega_i) = (\mathcal{V}_{\mathcal{F}}, \Psi_{\mathcal{F}})$$

because, according to [Chow and Teicher, 2012, Exercise 1.3.6], $\Psi_{\mathcal{F}}$ is the minimal σ-algebra generated by cylinder sets. So the infinite-dimensional product space and the topological space $(\mathcal{V}_{\mathcal{F}}, \Psi_{\mathcal{F}})$ coincide.

An infinite Cartesian product $\rho = \times_{i=1}^{\infty} \nu_i$ is *consistent* if it is different from the empty set, i.e., if $\nu_i \neq \varnothing$ for all $i = 1, 2, \ldots$. We can establish a bijective map $\gamma_{\mathcal{F}}$ between infinite consistent Cartesian products $\rho = \times_{i=1}^{\infty} \nu_i$ and composite choices: $\gamma_{\mathcal{F}}(\times_{i=1}^{\infty} \nu_i) = \{(f_i, \varnothing, k_i) | \nu_i = \{k_i\}\}$.

Lemma 9 (Elements of $\Psi_{\mathcal{F}}$ as Countable Unions). *Each element of* $\Psi_{\mathcal{F}}$ *can be written as a countable union of possibly infinite Cartesian products:*

$$\psi = \bigcup_{j=1}^{l} \rho_j \tag{3.17}$$

where $l \in [0, \infty]$, $\rho_j = \times_{i=1}^{\infty} \nu_i$ *and* $\nu_i \in \{\{0\}, \{1\}, \{0, 1\}\}$ *for all* $i = 1, 2, \ldots$.

Proof. We will show that $\Psi_{\mathcal{F}}$ and Φ, the set of all elements of the form of Equation (3.17), coincide. Given a ψ for the form of Equation (3.17), each ρ_j can be written as a countable union of cylinder sets, so it belongs to $\Psi_{\mathcal{F}}$. Since $\Psi_{\mathcal{F}}$ is a σ-algebra and ψ is a countable union, then $\psi \in \Psi_{\mathcal{F}}$ and $\Phi \subseteq \Psi_{\mathcal{F}}$.

We can prove that Φ is a σ-algebra using the same technique of Lemma 2, where Cartesian products replace composite choices. Φ contains cylinder sets: even if each ρ_j must be consistent, l can be 0 so ψ can be the empty set. As $\Psi_{\mathcal{F}}$ is the minimal σ-algebra containing cylinder sets, then $\Psi_{\mathcal{F}} \subseteq \Phi$. □

So each element ψ of $\Psi_{\mathcal{F}}$ can be written as a countable union of consistent possibly infinite Cartesian products.

Lemma 10 ($\Gamma_{\mathcal{F}}$ is Bijective). *Consider the function $\Gamma_{\mathcal{F}} : \Psi_{\mathcal{F}} \to \Omega_{\mathcal{P}}$ defined by $\Gamma_{\mathcal{F}}(\psi) = \omega_K$ where $\psi = \bigcup_{j=1}^{l} \rho_j$ and $K = \bigcup_{j=1}^{l} \{\gamma_{\mathcal{F}}(\rho_j)\}$ with $l \in [0, \infty]$. Then $\Gamma_{\mathcal{F}}$ is bijective.*

Proof. Immediate because $\gamma_{\mathcal{F}}$ is bijective. □

Theorem 12 (Equivalence with Sato and Kameya's definition). *Probability measure $\mu_{\mathcal{P}}$ coincides with $\eta_{\mathcal{P}}$ for definite programs.*

Proof. Consider $(X_1 = k_1, \ldots, X_n = k_n)$ and let K be

$$\{\{(f_1, \emptyset, k_1), \ldots, (f_n, \emptyset, k_n)\}\}.$$

Then $K = \Gamma_{\mathcal{F}}(\{(k_1, \ldots, k_n, v_{n+1}, \ldots) | v_i \in \{0, 1\}, i = n + 1, \ldots\})$ and $\mu_{\mathcal{P}}$ assigns probability $\pi_1 \cdot \ldots \cdot \pi_n$ to K, where $\pi_i = \Pi_i$ if $k_i = 1$ and $\pi_i = 1 - \Pi_i$ otherwise.

So $\mu_{\mathcal{P}}$ is in accordance with $P_{\mathcal{F}}^{(n)}$. But $P_{\mathcal{F}}^{(n)}$ can be extended in only one way to a probability measure $\eta_{\mathcal{F}}$ and there is a bijection between $\Psi_{\mathcal{F}}$ and $\Omega_{\mathcal{P}}$, so $\mu_{\mathcal{P}}$ is in accordance with $\eta_{\mathcal{F}}$ on all $\Psi_{\mathcal{F}}$.

Now consider $C = a_1^{k_1} \wedge \ldots \wedge a_n^{k_n}$. Since $IFPP^{\mathcal{P}} \uparrow \delta$ is such that K_a^{δ} and $K_{\sim a}^{\delta}$ are countable sets of countable composite choices for all atoms a, we can compute a covering set of explanations K for C by taking a finite conjunction of countable sets of countable composite choices, so K is a countable set of countable composite choices.

Clearly, $P_{\mathcal{P}}^{(n)}(Y_1 = k_1, \ldots, Y_n = k_n)$ coincides with $\mu_{\mathcal{P}}(\omega_K)$. But $P_{\mathcal{P}}^{(n)}$ can be extended in only one way to a probability measure $\eta_{\mathcal{P}}$, so $\mu_{\mathcal{P}}$ is in accordance with $\eta_{\mathcal{P}}$ on all $\Psi_{\mathcal{P}}$ when $\mathcal{P}$ is a definite program. □

4

Hybrid Programs

The languages presented in Chapter 2 allow the definition of discrete random variables only. However, some domains naturally include continuous random variables. Probabilistic logic programs including continuous variables are called *hybrid*.

In this chapter, we discuss some languages for hybrid programs together with their semantics.

4.1 Hybrid ProbLog

Hybrid ProbLog [Gutmann et al., 2011a] extends ProbLog with continuous probabilistic facts of the form

$$(X, \phi) :: f$$

where X is a logical variable appearing in the atom f and ϕ is an atom specifying a continuous distribution, such as, for example, $gaussian(0, 1)$ to indicate a Gaussian distribution with mean 0 and standard deviation 1. Variables X of this form are called *continuous variables*.

A Hybrid ProbLog program $\mathcal{P}$ is composed of definite rules $\mathcal{R}$ and facts $\mathcal{F} = \mathcal{F}^d \cup \mathcal{F}^c$ where $\mathcal{F}^d$ are discrete probabilistic facts as in ProbLog and $\mathcal{F}^c$ are continuous probabilistic facts.

Example 46 (Gaussian mixture – Hybrid ProbLog). *A Gaussian mixture model is a way to generate values of a continuous random variable: a discrete random variable is sampled and, depending on the sampled value, a different Gaussian distribution is selected for sampling the value of the continuous variable.*

A Gaussian mixture model with two components can be expressed in Hybrid ProbLog as [Gutmann et al., 2011a]:

115

$0.6 :: heads.$

$tails \leftarrow \sim heads.$

$(X, gaussian(0, 1)) :: g(X).$

$(X, gaussian(5, 2)) :: h(X).$

$mix(X) \leftarrow heads, g(X).$

$mix(X) \leftarrow tails, h(X).$

$pos \leftarrow mix(X), above(X, 0).$

where, for example, $(X, gaussian(0, 1)) :: g(X)$ is a continuous probabilistic facts stating that X follows a Gaussian with mean 0 and standard deviation 1. The values of X in $mix(X)$ are distributed according to a mixture of two Gaussians. The atom pos is true if X is positive.

A number of predicates are defined for manipulating a continuous variable X:

- $below(X, c)$ succeeds if $X < c$ where c is a numeric constant;
- $above(X, c)$ succeeds if $X > c$ where c is a numeric constant;
- $ininterval(X, c_1, c_2)$ succeeds if $X \in [c_1, c_2]$ where c_1 and c_2 are numeric constants.

Continuous variables cannot be unified with terms or used in Prolog comparison and arithmetic operators, so in the example above, it is not possible to use expressions $g(0)$, $(g(X), X > 0)$, $(g(X), 3 * X + 4 > 4)$ in the body of rules. The first two, however, can be expressed as $g(X), ininterval(X, 0, 0)$ and $g(X), above(X, 0)$, respectively.

Hybrid ProbLog assumes a finite set of continuous probabilistic facts and no function symbols, so the set of continuous variables is finite. Let us indicate the set with $\mathbf{X} = \{X_1, \ldots, X_n\}$, defined by the set of atoms for probabilistic facts $F = \{f_1, \ldots, f_n\}$ where each f_i is ground except for variable X_i. An assignment $\mathbf{x} = \{x_1, \ldots, x_n\}$ to $\mathbf{X}$ defines a substitution $\theta_{\mathbf{x}} = \{X_1/x_1, \ldots X_n/x_n\}$ and, in turn, a set of ground facts $F\theta_{\mathbf{x}}$.

Given a selection σ for discrete facts and an assignment $\mathbf{x}$ to continuous variables, a world $w_{\sigma, \mathbf{x}}$ is defined as

$$w_{\sigma, \mathbf{x}} = \mathcal{R} \cup \{f\theta | (f, \theta, 1) \in \sigma\} \cup F\theta_{\mathbf{x}}$$

Each continuous variable X_i is associated with a probability density $p_i(X_i)$. Since all the variables are independent, $p(\mathbf{x}) = \prod_{i=1}^{n} p_i(x_i)$ is a joint probability density over $\mathbf{X}$. $p(\mathbf{X})$ and $P(\sigma)$ then define a joint probability density over the worlds:

$$p(w_{\sigma, \mathbf{x}}) = p(\mathbf{x}) \prod_{(f_i, \theta, 1) \in \sigma} \Pi_i \prod_{(f_i, \theta, 0) \in \sigma} 1 - \Pi_i$$

The probability of a ground atom q different from the atom of a continuous probabilistic fact is then defined as in the DS for discrete programs as

$$P(q) = \int_{\sigma \in S_\mathcal{P}, \mathbf{x} \in \mathbb{R}^n} p(q, w_{\sigma, \mathbf{x}}) d\sigma d\mathbf{x} =$$

$$\int_{\sigma \in S_\mathcal{P}, \mathbf{x} \in \mathbb{R}^n} P(q|w_{\sigma, \mathbf{x}}) p(w_{\sigma, \mathbf{x}}) d\sigma d\mathbf{x} =$$

$$\int_{\sigma \in S_\mathcal{P}, \mathbf{x} \in \mathbb{R}^n : w_{\sigma, \mathbf{x}} \models q} p(w_{\sigma, \mathbf{x}}) d\sigma d\mathbf{x} =$$

$$\sum_{\sigma \in S_\mathcal{P}} \int_{\mathbf{x} \in \mathbb{R}^n : w_{\sigma, \mathbf{x}} \models q} p(w_{\sigma, \mathbf{x}}) d\mathbf{x}$$

where $S_\mathcal{P}$ is the set of all selections over discrete probabilistic facts. If the set $\{(\sigma, \mathbf{x}) | \sigma \in S_\mathcal{P}, \mathbf{x} \in \mathbb{R}^n : w_{\sigma, \mathbf{x}} \models q\}$ is measurable, then the probability is well defined. Gutmann et al. [2011a] prove that, for each selection σ, the set $\{\mathbf{x} | \mathbf{x} \in \mathbb{R}^n : w_{\sigma, \mathbf{x}} \models q\}$ is an n-dimensional interval $I = [a_1, b_1] \times \dots \times [a_n, b_n]$ of $\mathbb{R}^n$ where a_i and b_i can be $-\infty$ and $+\infty$, respectively, for $i = 1, \dots, n$. The probability that $\mathbf{X} \in I$ is then given by

$$P(\mathbf{X} \in I) = \int_{a_1}^{b_1} \dots \int_{a_n}^{b_n} p(\mathbf{x}) d\mathbf{x} \qquad (4.1)$$

The proof is based on considering a *discretized theory* $\mathcal{P}_D$ obtained as

$$\mathcal{P}_D = \mathcal{R} \cup \mathcal{F}^d \cup \{below(X, C), above(X, C), ininterval(X, C1, C2)\} \cup$$
$$\{f\{X/f\} | (X, \phi) :: f \in \mathcal{F}^c\}$$

The discretized program is a regular ProbLog program, so we can consider its worlds. In each world, we can derive the query by SLD resolution and keep track of the instantiations of the facts for the comparison predicates used in each proof. This yields a set of comparison facts that defines an n-dimensional interval. So we can compute the probability of the query in the world with Equation (4.1). By summing these values for all proofs, we get the probability of the query in the world of the ProbLog program. The weighted sum of the probabilities in the worlds over all worlds of $\mathcal{P}_D$ gives the probability of the query, where the weights are the probabilities of the worlds according to the discrete facts.

Example 47 (Query over a Gaussian mixture – Hybrid ProbLog). *For Example 46, the discretized program is*

$0.6 :: heads.$
$tails \leftarrow \sim heads.$
$g(g(X)).$
$h(h(X)).$
$mix(X) \leftarrow heads, g(X).$
$mix(X) \leftarrow tails, h(X).$
$pos \leftarrow mix(X), above(X, 0).$
$below(X, C).$
$above(X, C).$
$ininterval(X, C1, C2).$

which is a ProbLog program with two worlds. In the one containing heads, *the only proof for the query* pos *uses the fact* $above(g(g(X)), 0)$, *so the probability of pos in this world is*

$$P(pos|heads) = \int_0^\infty p(\mathrm{x})d\mathrm{x} = 1 - F(0, 0, 1)$$

where $F(\mathrm{x}, \mu, \sigma)$ *is the Gaussian cumulative distribution with mean* μ *and standard deviation* σ. *Therefore,* $P(pos|heads) = 0.5$.

In the world not containing heads, *the only proof for the query* pos *uses the fact* $above(h(h(X)), 0)$, *so the probability of pos in this world is* $P(pos| \sim heads) = 1 - F(0, 5, 2) \approx 0.994$. *So overall*

$$P(pos) = 0.6 \cdot 0.5 + 0.4 \cdot 0.994 \approx 0.698$$

This approach for defining the semantics also defines a strategy for performing inference. However, Hybrid ProbLog imposes severe restrictions on the programs, not allowing the use of continuous variables in expressions possibly involving other variables.

4.2 Distributional Clauses

Distributional Clauses (DCs) [Gutmann et al., 2011c] are definite clause with an atom $h \sim \mathcal{D}$ in the head, where h is a term, $\sim$ is a binary predicate used in infix notation, and $\mathcal{D}$ is a term specifying a discrete or continuous probability distribution. For each ground instance $(h \sim \mathcal{D} \leftarrow b_1, \ldots, b_n)\theta$, where θ is a substitution over the Herbrand universe of the logic program, a distributional clause defines a random variable $h\theta$ with the distribution indicated by $\mathcal{D}\theta$ whenever all the $b_i\theta$ hold. The term $\mathcal{D}$ can be non-ground, i.e., distribution parameters can be related to conditions in the body, similarly to flexible probabilities, see Section 2.7.

The reserved functor $\simeq/1$ is used to represent the outcome of a random variable: $\simeq d$, for example, indicates the outcome of random variable d. The set of special predicates

$$dist\_rel = \{dist\_eq/2, dist\_lt/2, dist\_leq/2, dist\_gt/2, dist\_geq/2\}$$

can be used to compare the outcome of a random variable with a constant or the outcome of another random variable. These predicates are assumed to be defined by ground facts, one for each true atom for each of the predicates. Terms of the form $\simeq(h)$ can also be used in other predicates with some restrictions, e.g., it does not make sense to unify the outcome of a continuous random variable with a constant or another random variable as the probability that they are equal has measure 0. The predicate $\sim=/2$ is used to unify random variables with terms: $h\sim=v$ means $\simeq(h) = v$, which is true iff the value of the discrete random variable h unifies with v. For continuous random variables, $\sim=/2$ can be used to unify random variables with logical variables.

A DC programs $\mathcal{P}$ is composed by a set of definite clauses $\mathcal{R}$ and a set of DCs $\mathcal{C}$. A *world* of $\mathcal{P}$ is the program $\mathcal{R} \cup \mathcal{F}$ where $\mathcal{F}$ is the set of ground atoms for the predicates in $dist\_rel$ that are true for each random variable $h\theta$ defined by the program.

Let us now see two examples.

Example 48 (Gaussian mixture – DCs). *The Gaussian mixture model of Example 46 can be expressed with DCs as*
  $coin \sim [0.6 : heads, 0.4 : tails].$
  $g \sim gaussian(0, 1).$
  $h \sim gaussian(5, 2).$
  $mix(X) \leftarrow dist\_eq(\simeq coin, heads), g\sim=X.$
  $mix(X) \leftarrow dist\_eq(\simeq coin, tails), h\sim=X.$
  $pos \leftarrow mix(X), dist\_gt(X, 0).$
where, for example, g follows a Gaussian with mean 0 and standard deviation 1.

This example shows that Hybrid ProbLog programs can be expressed in DCs.

Example 49 (Moving people – DCs [Nitti et al., 2016]). *The following program models a set of people moving on a real line:*
  $n \sim poisson(6).$
  $pos(P) \sim uniform(0, M) \leftarrow n\sim=N, between(1, N, P),$
   $M \ is \ 10 * N.$
  $left(A, B) \leftarrow dist\_lt(\simeq pos(A), \simeq pos(B)).$

where $between(1, N, P)$ *is a predicate that, when* P *is not bound, generates all integers between 1 and* N, *and* $is/2$ *is the standard Prolog predicate for the evaluation of expressions.*

The first clause defines the number of people n as a random variable that follows a Poisson distribution with mean 6. The position of each person is modeled with the random variable $pos(P)$ defined in the second clause as a continuous random variable uniformly distributed from 0 to $M = 10n$ (that is, 10 times the number of people), for each integer person identifier P such that $1 \leqslant P \leqslant n$. If the value of n is 2, for example, there will be two independent random variables $pos(1)$ and $pos(2)$ both with distribution $uniform(0, 20)$. The last clause defines relation $left/2$ between people positions.

A DC program must satisfy some conditions to be considered valid.

Definition 28 (Valid program [Gutmann et al., 2011c]). *A DC program* $\mathcal{P}$ *is called* valid *if the following conditions are fulfilled:*

(V1) *In the relation* $h \sim \mathcal{D}$ *that holds in the least fixpoint of a program, there is a functional dependency from* h *to* $\mathcal{D}$, *so there is a unique ground distribution* $\mathcal{D}$ *for each ground random variable* h.

(V2) *The program is distribution-stratified, that is, there exists a function* $rank(\cdot)$ *that maps ground atoms to* $\mathbb{N}$ *and satisfies the following properties: (1) for each ground instance of a clause* $h \sim \mathcal{D} \leftarrow b_1, \ldots b_n$, *it holds that* $rank(h \sim \mathcal{D}) > rank(b_i)$ *for all* i; *(2) for each ground instance of a regular program clause* $h \leftarrow b_1, \ldots b_n$, *it holds* $rank(h) \geqslant rank(b_i)$ *for all* i; *and (3) for each ground atom* b *that contains (the name of) a random variable* h, $rank(b) \geqslant rank(h \sim \mathcal{D})$ *(with* $h \sim \mathcal{D}$ *being the head of the distribution clause defining* h). *The ranking is extended to random variables by setting* $rank(h) = rank(h \sim \mathcal{D})$.

(V3) *The indicator functions (see below) for all ground probabilistic facts are Lebesgue-measurable.*

(V4) *Each atom in the least fixpoint can be derived from a finite number of probabilistic facts (finite support condition [Sato, 1995]).*

We now define the series of distributions $P_{\mathcal{F}}^{(n)}$ as in Sato and Kameya's definition of the DS of Equation (3.15). We consider an enumeration $\{f_1, f_2, \ldots\}$ of atoms for the predicates in $dist\_rel$ such that $i < j \Rightarrow rank(f_i) \leqslant rank(f_j)$ where $rank(\cdot)$ is a ranking function as in Definition 28. We also define, for each predicate $rel/2 \in dist\_rel$, an indicator function:

$$I_{rel}^1(X_1, X_2) = \begin{cases} 1 \text{ if } rel(X_1, X_2) \text{ is true,} \\ 0 \text{ if } rel(X_1, X_2) \text{ is false} \end{cases}$$

$$I_{rel}^0(X_1, X_2) = 1.0 - I_{rel}^1(X_1, X_2)$$

We define the probability distributions $P_{\mathcal{F}}^{(n)}$ over finite sets of ground facts $f_1, \ldots, f_n$ using expectations of indicator functions. Let $x_i \in \{1, 0\}$ for $i = 1, \ldots, n$ be truth values for the facts $f_1, \ldots, f_n$. Let $\{rv_1, \ldots, rv_m\}$ be the set of random variables these n facts depend upon, ordered such that if $rank(rv_i) < rank(rv_j)$, then $i < j$, and let $f_i = rel_i(t_{i1}, t_{i2})$. Let $\theta^{-1} = \{(rv_1)/V_1, \ldots, (rv_m)/V_m\}$ be an antisubstitution that replaces evaluations of the random variables with real variables for integration. Then the probability distributions $P_{\mathcal{F}}^{(n)}$ are given by

$$P_{\mathcal{F}}^{(n)}(f_1 = x_1, \ldots, f_n = x_n) =$$
$$E[I_{rel_1}^{x_1}(t_{11}, t_{12}), \ldots, I_{rel_n}^{x_n}(t_{n1}, t_{n2})] =$$
$$\int \cdots \int I_{rel_1}^{x_1}(t_{11}\theta^{-1}, t_{12}\theta^{-1}) \ldots I_{rel_n}^{x_n}(t_{n1}\theta^{-1}, t_{n2}\theta^{-1})$$
$$d\mathcal{D}_{rv_1}(V_1) \ldots d\mathcal{D}_{rv_m}(V_m) \tag{4.2}$$

For valid DC programs, the following proposition can be proved.

Proposition 4 (Valid DC Program [Gutmann et al., 2011c]). *Let $\mathcal{P}$ be a valid DC program. $\mathcal{P}$ defines a probability measure $P_{\mathcal{P}}$ over the set of fixpoints of operator T_w were w is a world of $\mathcal{P}$. Hence, for an arbitrary formula q over atoms, $\mathcal{P}$ also defines the probability that q is true.*

The semantics of DCs coincides with that of hybrid ProbLog on programs that satisfy the constraints imposed by the latter.

An alternative view of the semantics can be given by means of a stochastic $T_{\mathcal{P}}$ operator, $ST_{\mathcal{P}}$, extending the $T_{\mathcal{P}}$ operator of Definition 1 to deal with probabilistic facts $dist\_rel(t_1, t_2)$. We need a function READTABLE($\cdot$) that evaluates probabilistic facts and stores the sampled values for random variables. READTABLE applied to probabilistic fact $dist\_rel(t_1, t_2)$ returns the truth value of the fact evaluated on the basis of the values of the random variables in the arguments. The values are either retrieved from the table or sampled according to their distribution the first time they are accessed. In the case they are sampled, they are stored for future use.

Definition 29 (*$ST_\mathcal{P}$* operator [Gutmann et al., 2011c]).   *Let $\mathcal{P}$ be a valid DC program. Starting from a set of ground facts I, the $ST_\mathcal{P}$ operator is defined as*

$$ST_\mathcal{P}(I) = \{h | h \leftarrow b_1 \ldots, b_n \in ground(\mathcal{P}) \wedge \forall b_i : b_i \in I \vee \quad (4.3)$$
$$b_i = dist\_rel(t_1, t_2) \wedge$$
$$(t_j = \simeq h \Rightarrow h \sim \mathcal{D} \in I \wedge \text{READTABLE}(b_i) = true)\}$$

Computing the least fixpoint of the $ST_\mathcal{P}$ operator returns a possible model of the program. The $ST_\mathcal{P}$ operator is stochastic, so it defines a sampling process. The distribution over models defined by $ST_\mathcal{P}$ is the same as that defined by Equation (4.2).

Example 50 (*$ST_\mathcal{P}$* for moving people – DC [Nitti et al., 2016]).   *Given the DC program $\mathcal{P}$ defined in Example 49, a possible sequence of application of the ST_P operator is*

$ST_\mathcal{P} \uparrow \alpha$	*Table*
$\varnothing$	$\varnothing$
$\{n \sim poisson(6)\}$	$\{n = 2\}$
$\{n \sim poisson(6), pos(1) \sim uniform(0, 20),$ $pos(2) \sim uniform(0, 20)\}$	$\{n = 2, pos(1) = 3.1,$ $pos(2) = 4.5\}$
$\{n \sim poisson(6), pos(1) \sim uniform(0, 20),$ $pos(2) \sim uniform(0, 20), left(1, 2)\}$	$\{n = 2, pos(1) = 3.1,$ $pos(2) = 4.5\}$

Nitti et al. [2016] proposed a modification of DCs where the relation symbols are replaced with their Prolog versions, the clauses can contain negation, and the $ST_\mathcal{P}$ operator is defined slightly differently.

The new version of the $ST_\mathcal{P}$ operator does not use a separate table for storing the values sampled for random variables and does not store distribution atoms.

Definition 30 (*$ST_\mathcal{P}$* operator [Nitti et al., 2016]).   *Let $\mathcal{P}$ be a valid DC program. Starting from a set of ground facts I, the $ST_\mathcal{P}$ operator is defined as*

$$ST_\mathcal{P}(I) = \{h = v | h \sim \mathcal{D} \leftarrow b_1, \ldots, b_n \in ground(\mathcal{P}) \wedge \forall b_i :$$
$$b_i \in I \vee b_i = dist\_rel(t_1, t_2) \wedge t_1 = v_1 \in I \wedge t_2 = v_2 \in I \wedge$$
$$dist\_rel(v_1, v_2) \wedge v \text{ is sampled from } \mathcal{D}\} \cup$$
$$\{h | h \leftarrow b_1, \ldots, b_n \in ground(\mathcal{P}) \wedge h \neq (r \sim \mathcal{D}) \wedge \forall b_i :$$
$$b_i \in I \vee b_i = dist\_rel(t_1, t_2) \wedge t_1 = v_1 \in I \wedge$$
$$t_2 = v_2 \in I \wedge dist\_rel(v_1, v_2)\}$$

where dist_rel is one of $=, <, \leqslant, >, \geqslant$. *In practice, for each distributional clause* $h \sim \mathcal{D} \leftarrow b_1 \ldots, b_n$, *whenever the body* $b_1 \ldots, b_n$ *is true in I, a value* v *for random variable* h *is sampled from the distribution* $\mathcal{D}$ *and* $h = v$ *is added to the interpretation. Similarly, for deterministic clauses, ground atoms are added whenever the body is true.*

We can provide an alternative definition of world. A world is obtained in a number of steps. First, we must distinguish the logical variables that can hold continuous values from those that can hold values from the logical Herbrand universe. We replace the discrete logical variables with terms from the Herbrand universe in all possible ways. Then we sample, for each distributional clause $h \sim \mathcal{D} \leftarrow b_1 \ldots, b_n$ in the resulting program, a value for h from distribution $\mathcal{D}$ and replace the clause with $h \sim = v \leftarrow b_1 \ldots, b_n$.

If we compute the least fixpoint of T_w for a world w sampled in this way, we get a model that is the same as the one that is the least fixpoint of $ST_{\mathcal{P}}$ if all random variables are sampled in the same way. So the least fixpoint of $ST_{\mathcal{P}}$ is a model of at least one world. The probability measure over models defined by $ST_{\mathcal{P}}$ of Definition 30 coincides with that defined by $ST_{\mathcal{P}}$ of Definition 29 and Equation (4.2). Nitti et al. [2016] call worlds the possible models but we prefer to use the word world for the sampled normal programs.

Example 51 ($ST_{\mathcal{P}}$ *for moving people – DC [Nitti et al., 2016]*).

Given the DC program $\mathcal{P}$ *defined in Example 49 and the sequence of applications of the* $ST_{\mathcal{P}}$ *operator of Definition 29, the corresponding sequence of applications for* $ST_{\mathcal{P}}$ *of Definition 30 is*

$$ST_{\mathcal{P}} \uparrow 0 = \varnothing$$
$$ST_{\mathcal{P}} \uparrow 1 = \{n = 2\}$$
$$ST_{\mathcal{P}} \uparrow 2 = \{n = 2, pos(1) = 3.1, pos(2) = 4.5\}$$
$$ST_{\mathcal{P}} \uparrow 3 = \{n = 2, pos(1) = 3.1, pos(2) = 4.5, left(1, 2)\}$$
$$ST_{\mathcal{P}} \uparrow 4 = ST_P \uparrow 3 = \mathrm{lfp}(ST_P)$$

so $\{n = 2, pos(1) = 3.1, pos(2) = 4.5, left(1, 2)\}$ *is a possible model or a model of a world of the program.*

Regarding negation, since programs need to be stratified to be valid, negation poses no particular problem: the $ST_{\mathcal{P}}$ operator is applied at each rank from lowest to highest, along the same lines as the perfect model semantics [Przymusinski, 1988].

Given a DC program $\mathcal{P}$ and a negative literal $l = \sim a$, to determine its truth in $\mathcal{P}$, we can proceed as follows. Consider the interpretation I obtained by applying the $ST_{\mathcal{P}}$ operator until the least fixpoint for $rank(l)$ is reached (or exceeded). If a is a non-comparison atomic formula, I is true if $a \notin I$ and false otherwise. If a is a comparison atom involving a random variable r such as $l = (r\sim=val)$, then l is true whenever $\exists val' : r = val' \in I$ with $val \neq val'$ or $\nexists val' : r = val' \in I$, i.e., r is not defined in I. Note that I is the least fixpoint for $rank(r \sim \mathcal{D})$ (or higher), thus $\nexists val' : r = val' \in I$ implies that r is not defined also in the following applications of the $ST_{\mathcal{P}}$ operator and so also in the possible model.

Example 52 (Negation in DCs [Nitti et al., 2016]). *Consider an example where we draw nballs balls with replacement from an urn containing an equal number of red, blue, and black balls. nballs follows a Poisson distribution and the color of each ball is a random variable uniformly distributed over the set* $\{red, blue, black\}$*:*
$$nballs \sim poisson(6).$$
$$color(X) \sim uniform([red, blue, black]) \leftarrow$$
$$nballs \simeq N, between(1, N, X).$$
$$not\_red \leftarrow \sim color(2) \simeq red.$$
not_red is true in those possible models where the value of $color(2)$ *is not red or in those in which* $color(2)$ *is not defined, for example, when* $n = 1$.

4.3 Extended PRISM

Islam et al. [2012b] proposed an extension of PRISM that includes continuous random variables with a Gaussian or gamma distribution.

The set_sw directives allow the definition of probability density functions. For instance, $set\_sw(r, norm(Mu, Var))$ specifies that the outcomes of random processes r have Gaussian distribution with mean Mu and variance Var.

Parameterized families of random processes may be specified, as long as the parameters are discrete-valued. For instance,

$$set\_sw(w(M), norm(Mu, Var))$$

specifies a family of random variables, with one for each value of M. As in PRISM, the distribution parameters may be computed as functions of M.

Moreover, PRISM is extended with linear equality constraints over reals. Without loss of generality, we assume that constraints are written as linear equalities of the form $Y = a_1 \cdot X_1 + \ldots + a_n \cdot X_n + b$ where a_i and b are all floating point constants.

Example 53 (Gaussian mixture – Extended PRISM). *The Gaussian mixture model of Example 46 can be expressed with Extended PRISM as*

$mix(X) \leftarrow msw(coin, heads), msw(g, X).$
$mix(X) \leftarrow msw(coin, tails), msw(h, X)$
$values(coin, [heads, tails]).$
$values(g, real).$
$values(h, real),$
$\leftarrow set\_sw(coin, [0.6, 0.4]).$
$\leftarrow set\_sw(g, norm(0, 1)).$
$\leftarrow set\_sw(h, norm(5, 2)).$

Let us now show an example with constraints.

Example 54 (Gaussian mixture and constraints – Extended PRISM). *Consider a factory with two machines a and b. Each machine produces a widget with a continuous feature. A widget is produced by machine a with probability 0.3 and by machine b with probability 0.7. If the widget is produced by machine a, the feature is distributed as a Gaussian with mean 2.0 and variance 1.0. If the widget is produced by machine b, the feature is distributed as a Gaussian with mean 3.0 and variance 1.0. The widget is then processed by a third machine that adds a random quantity to the feature. The quantity is distributed as a Gaussian with mean 0.5 and variance 1.5. This is encoded by the program:*

$widget(X) \leftarrow$
$\quad msw(m, M), msw(st(M), Z), msw(pt, Y), X = Y + Z.$
$values(m, [a, b]).$
$values(st(\_), real).$
$values(pt, real).$
$\leftarrow set\_sw(m, [0.3, 0.7]).$
$\leftarrow set\_sw(st(a), norm(2.0, 1.0)).$
$\leftarrow set\_sw(st(b), norm(3.0, 1.0)).$
$\leftarrow set\_sw(pt, norm(0.5, 0.1)).$

The semantics extends the DS for the discrete case by defining a probability space for the msw switches and then extending it to a probability space for the entire program using the least model semantics of constraint logic programs [Jaffar et al., 1998].

The probability space for the probabilistic facts is constructed from those of discrete and continuous random variables. The probability space for N continuous random variables is the Borel σ-algebra over $\mathbb{R}^N$ and a Lebesgue measure on this set is the probability measure. This is combined with the space for discrete random variables using the Cartesian product. The probability space for facts is extended to the space of the entire program using the least model semantics: a point in this space is an arbitrary interpretation of the program obtained from a point in the space of the facts by means of logical consequence. A probability measure over the space of the program is then defined by using the measure defined for the probabilistic facts alone. The semantics for programs without constraints is essentially equivalent to the one of DC.

The authors propose an exact inference algorithm that extends the one of PRISM by reasoning symbolically over the constraints on the random variables, see Section 12.1. This is permitted by the restrictions on the types of distributions, Gaussian and gamma, and on the form of constraints, linear equations.

4.4 cplint Hybrid Programs

`cplint` handles continuous random variables with its sampling inference module. The user can specify a probability density on an argument Var of an atom a with rules of the form

$$a : Density \leftarrow Body$$

where $Density$ is a special atom identifying a probability density on variable Var and $Body$ (optional) is a regular clause body. $Density$ atoms can be:

- $uniform(Var, L, U)$: Var is uniformly distributed in $[L, U]$.
- $gaussian(Var, Mean, Variance)$: Var follows a Gaussian distribution with parameters $Mean$ and $Variance$. The distribution can be multivariate if $Mean$ is a list and $Variance$ a list of lists representing the mean vector and the covariance matrix, respectively. In this case, the values of Var are lists of real values with the same length as that of $Mean$.
- $dirichlet(Var, Par)$: Var is a list of real numbers following a Dirichlet distribution with parameters α specified by the list Par.
- $gamma(Var, Shape, Scale)$: gamma distribution with parameters $Shape$ and $Scale$.

- $beta(Var, Alpha, Beta)$: beta distribution with parameters $Alpha$ and $Beta$.
- $poisson(Var, Lambda)$: Poisson distribution with parameter $Lambda$.
- $binomial(Var, N, P)$: binomial distribution with parameters N and P.
- $geometric(Var, P)$: geometric distribution with parameter P.

For example

$$g(X) : gaussian(X, 0, 1).$$

states that argument X of $g(X)$ follows a Gaussian distribution with mean 0 and variance 1, while

$$g(X) : gaussian(X, [0, 0], [[1, 0], [0, 1]]).$$

states that argument X of $g(X)$ follows a Gaussian multivariate distribution with mean vector $[0, 0]$ and covariance matrix

$$\begin{bmatrix} 1 & 0 \\ 0 & 1 \end{bmatrix}$$

Example 55 (Gaussian mixture – `cplint`). *Example 46 of a mixture of two Gaussians can be encoded as[1]:*

    $heads : 0.6 ; tails : 0.4.$
    $g(X) : gaussian(X, 0, 1).$
    $h(X) : gaussian(X, 5, 2).$
    $mix(X) \leftarrow heads, g(X).$
    $mix(X) \leftarrow tails, h(X).$

The argument X of $mix(X)$ follows a distribution that is a mixture of two Gaussians, one with mean 0 and variance 1 with probability 0.6 and one with mean 5 and variance 2 with probability 0.4.

The parameters of the distribution atoms can be taken from the probabilistic atom.

Example 56 (Estimation of the mean of a Gaussian – `cplint`). *The program[2]*

    $value(I, X) \leftarrow mean(M), value(I, M, X).$
    $mean(M) : gaussian(M, 1.0, 5.0).$
    $value(\_, M, X) : gaussian(X, M, 2.0).$

---

[1] https://cplint.eu/e/gaussian_mixture.pl
[2] https://cplint.eu/e/gauss_mean_est.pl

states that, for an index I, the continuous variable X is sampled from a Gaussian whose variance is 2 and whose mean M is sampled from a Gaussian with mean 1 and variance 5.

This program can be used to estimate the mean of a Gaussian by querying $mean(M)$ given observations for atom $value(I, X)$ for different values of I.

Any operation is allowed on continuous random variables.

Example 57 (Kalman filter – `cplint`). *A Kalman filter [Harvey, 1990] is a dynamical system, i.e., a system that evolves with time. At every integer time point t, the system is in a state S which is a continuous variable and emits one value $V = S + E$, where E is an error that follows a probability distribution that does not depend on time. The system transitions to a new state $NextS$ at time $t + 1$, with $NextS = S + X$ where X is also an error that follows a probability distribution that does not depend on time. Kalman filters have a wide variety of applications, especially in the estimation of trajectories of physical systems. Kalman filters differ from Hidden markov models (HMMs) because the state and output are continuous instead of discrete.*

The program below[3], adapted from [Islam et al., 2012b], encodes a Kalman filter in `cplint`:

$$kf(N, O) \leftarrow init(S), kf\_part(0, N, S, O).$$
$$kf\_part(I, N, S, [V|RO]) \leftarrow I < N, NextI \text{ is } I + 1,$$
$$\quad trans(S, I, NextS), emit(NextS, I, V),$$
$$\quad kf\_part(NextI, N, NextS, RO).$$
$$kf\_part(N, N, \_S, []).$$
$$trans(S, I, NextS) \leftarrow$$
$$\quad \{NextS =:= E + S\}, trans\_err(I, E).$$
$$emit(S, I, V) \leftarrow \{V =:= S + X\}, obs\_err(I, X).$$
$$init(S) : gaussian(S, 0, 1).$$
$$trans\_err(\_, E) : gaussian(E, 0, 2).$$
$$obs\_err(\_, E) : gaussian(E, 0, 1).$$

$kf(N, O)$ means that the filter run for N time points produced the output sequence O.

Continuous random variables appear in arithmetic expressions (in clauses for $trans/3$ and $emit/3$). It is often convenient, as in this case, to use CLP(R) constraints as in this way the expressions can be used in multiple directions and the same clauses can be used both to sample and to evaluate the weight of the sample on the basis of evidence (see Section 12.3). For example, the

---

[3] https://cplint.eu/e/kalman_filter.pl

expression $\{NextS =:= E + S\}$ *can be used to compute the value of any variable given values for the other two.*

The semantics is given in terms of a stochastic T_P operator as the one of DCs.

Definition 31 (ST_P operator – cplint). *Let $\mathcal{P}$ be a program and $ground(\mathcal{P})$ be the set of all instances of clauses in $\mathcal{P}$ with all variables in the body replaced by constants. Starting from a set of ground facts I, the ST_P operator returns*

$$ST_P(I) = \{h'|h : Density \leftarrow b_1, \ldots, b_n \in ground(\mathcal{P}) \wedge \forall b_i : b_i \in I \wedge$$
$$h' = h\{Var/v\} \text{ with } Var \text{ the continuous variable of } h \text{ and}$$
$$v \text{ sampled from } Density\} \cup$$
$$\{h|Dist \leftarrow b_1, \ldots, b_n \in ground(\mathcal{P}) \wedge \forall b_i : b_i \in I$$
$$\text{with } h \text{ sampled from discrete distribution } Dist\}$$

Differently from ST_P of Definition 30, there is no need for special treatment for the atoms in the body, as they are all logical atoms. For each probabilistic clause $h : Density \leftarrow b_1 \ldots, b_n$ whenever the body $b_1 \ldots, b_n$ is true in I, a value v for the continuous variable Var of h is sampled from the distribution $Density$ and $h\{Var/v\}$ is added to the interpretation. Similarly for discrete and deterministic clauses.

cplint also allows the syntax of DC and Extended PRISM by translating clauses in these languages to cplint clauses.

For DC, this amounts to replacing head atoms of the form

$$p(t_1, \ldots, t_n) \sim density(par_1, \ldots, par_m)$$

with

$$p(t_1, \ldots, t_n, Var) : density(Var, t_1, \ldots, t_n)$$

and body atoms of the form $p(t_1, \ldots, t_n) \sim = X$ with $p(t_1, \ldots, t_n, X)$. On the other hand, terms of the form $\simeq(h)$ for h a random variable are not allowed, and the value of a random variable can be used by unifying it with a logical variable using $h \sim = X$.

For extended PRISM, atoms of the form $msw(p(t_1, \ldots, t_n), val)$ in the body of clauses defined by a directive such as

$$\leftarrow set\_sw(p(t_1, \ldots, t_n), density(par_1, \ldots, par_m)).$$

are replaced by probabilistic facts of the form

$$p(t_1, \ldots, t_n, Var) : density(Var, par_1, \ldots, par_m).$$

The syntax of `cplint` allows a considerable freedom, allowing to express both constraints on random variables and a wide variety of distributions. No syntactic checks are made on the program to ensure validity. In case, for example, random variables are not sufficiently instantiated to exploit expressions for inferring the values of other variables, inference will return an error.

4.5 Probabilistic Constraint Logic Programming

Michels et al. [2013, 2015] and Michels [2016] proposed the language of Probabilistic constraint logic programming (PCLP) that allows continuous random variables and complex constraints on them. PCLP differs from hybrid ProbLog because it allows constraints that are more general than comparing a continuous random variable with a constant. In this sense, it is more similar to DCs. However, DCs allow *generative definitions*, i.e., definition where a parameter of a distribution could depend on the value of another one, while PCLP doesn't. PCLP provides an alternative definition for the semantics of hybrid programs that is not based on a stochastic T_P operator but on an extension of Sato's DS. Moreover, PCLP allows the specification of imprecise probability distributions by means of *credal sets*: instead of specifying exactly the probability distribution from which a variable is sampled, a set of probability distributions (a credal set) is specified that includes the unknown correct distribution.

In PCLP, a program $\mathcal{P}$ is split into a set of rules $\mathcal{R}$ and a set of facts $\mathcal{F}$. The facts define the random variables and the rules define the truth value of the atoms in the Herbrand base of the program given the values of the random variables. The set of random variables is countable $\mathbf{X} = \{X_1, X_2, \ldots\}$ and each has a range $Range_i$ that is not limited to be Boolean but can be a general set, for example, $\mathbb{N}$ or $\mathbb{R}$ or even $\mathbb{R}^n$.

The sample space $W_\mathbf{X}$ is given by

$$W_\mathbf{X} = Range_1 \times Range_2 \times \ldots$$

The event space $\Omega_\mathbf{X}$ is user-defined but it should be a σ-algebra. A probability measure $\mu_\mathbf{X}$ is also given such that $(W_\mathbf{X}, \Omega_\mathbf{X}, \mu_\mathbf{X})$ is a probability space.

A constraint is a predicate φ that takes values of the random variables as arguments, i.e., it is a function from $\{(x_1, x_2, \ldots) | x_1 \in Range_1, x_2 \in$

$Range_2, \ldots \}$ to $\{0, 1\}$. Given a constraint φ, its *constraint solution space* $CSS(\varphi)$ is the set of samples where the constraint holds:

$$CSS(\varphi) = \{\mathbf{x} \in W_{\mathbf{X}} | \varphi(\mathbf{x})\}$$

Definition 32 (Probabilistic Constraint Logic Theory [Michels et al., 2015]). *A Probabilistic Constraint Logic Theory $\mathcal{P}$ is a tuple*

$$(\mathbf{X}, W_{\mathbf{X}}, \Omega_{\mathbf{X}}, \mu_{\mathbf{X}}, Constr, \mathcal{R})$$

where

- *$\mathbf{X}$ is a countable set of random variables $\{X_1, X_2, \ldots\}$ each with range $Range_i$;*
- *$W_{\mathbf{X}} = Range_1 \times Range_2 \times \ldots$ is the sample space;*
- *$\Omega_{\mathbf{X}}$ is the event space, a σ-algebra;*
- *$\mu_{\mathbf{X}}$ is a probability measure such that $(W_{\mathbf{X}}, \Omega_{\mathbf{X}}, \mu_{\mathbf{X}})$ is a probability space;*
- *$Constr$ is a set of constraints closed under conjunction, disjunction, and negation such that the constraint solution space of each constraint is included in $\Omega_{\mathbf{X}}$:*

$$\{CSS(\varphi) | \varphi \in Constr\} \in \Omega_{\mathbf{X}};$$

- *$\mathcal{R}$ is a set of logical rules with constraints:*

$$h \leftarrow l_1, \ldots, l_n, \langle \varphi_1(\mathbf{X}) \rangle, \ldots, \langle \varphi_m(\mathbf{X}) \rangle$$

  where $\varphi_i \in Constr$ and $\langle \varphi_i(\mathbf{X}) \rangle$ is called constraint atom for $1 \leqslant i \leqslant m$.

Random variables are expressed similarly to DC, for example,

  time_comp$_1 \sim exp(1)$

state that time_comp$_1$ is a random variable with an exponential distribution with rate 1.

Example 58 (Fire on a ship [Michels et al., 2015]). *Suppose a fire breaks out in a compartment of a ship. After 0.75 minutes also the next compartment will be on fire. After 1.25 minutes the fire will breach the hull. With this information, we know for sure that if the fire is under control within 0.75 minutes the ship is saved. This can be represented as:*

saved ← ⟨time_comp$_1$ < 0.75⟩

In detail, the previous line says that the value of the continuous random variable time_comp$_1$ *should be less than 0.75 in order for* saved *to be true.*

The second compartment is more fragile than the first one, and the fire must be extinguished within 0.625 minutes. However, for the firemen to reach the second compartment, the fire in the first one must be under control. This means that both fires must be extinguished in 0.75 + 0.625 = 1.375 minutes. In the second compartment four people can work simultaneously, since it is not as isolated as the first one. This means that the fire will be extinguished four times faster. We can encode this situation with:

saved ← ⟨time_comp$_1$ < 1.25⟩,
⟨time_comp$_1$ + 0.25 · time_comp$_2$ < 1.375⟩

We also suppose that both time durations to extinguish the fire are exponentially distributed:

time_comp$_1$ ~ $exp(1)$
time_comp$_2$ ~ $exp(1)$

Given these time constraints and these distributions, we want to know the probability that the ship is saved, i.e., $P(saved)$.

This example is a probabilistic constraint logic theory where

$$\mathbf{X} = \{\text{time\_comp}_1, \text{time\_comp}_2\},$$

$Range_1 = Range_2 = \mathbb{R}$, *the constraint language includes linear inequalities and the probability measure makes the two variables independent and distributed according to an exponential distribution.*

A probability distribution over the logical atoms of the program (the elements of the Herbrand base $\mathcal{B}_\mathcal{P}$) is defined as in PRISM: the logical atoms form a countable set of Boolean random variables $\mathbf{Y} = \{Y_1, Y_2, \ldots\}$ and the sample space is $W_\mathbf{Y} = \{(y_1, y_2, \ldots) | y_i \in \{0, 1\}, i = 1, 2, \ldots\}$.

According to Michels et al. [2015], the sample space $W_\mathbf{Y}$ is countable, and so the event space of the logic part of the program is defined as $\Omega_R = \mathbb{P}(W_\mathbf{Y})$ (the powerset of the sample space). However, Theorem 4 showed that $W_\mathbf{Y}$ is uncountable.

The sample space for the entire theory is $W_\mathcal{P} = W_\mathbf{X} \times W_\mathbf{Y}$ and the event space is the product σ-algebra (see Definition 15), the σ-algebra generated by the products of elements of $\Omega_\mathbf{X}$ and $\Omega_\mathbf{Y}$:

$$\Omega_\mathcal{P} = \Omega_\mathbf{X} \otimes \Omega_\mathbf{Y} = \sigma(\{\omega_\mathbf{X} \times \omega_\mathbf{Y} | \omega_\mathbf{X} \in \Omega_\mathbf{X}, \omega_\mathbf{Y} \in \Omega_\mathbf{Y}\}$$

We now define a probability measure $\mu_\mathcal{P}$ that, together with $W_\mathcal{P}$ and $\Omega_\mathcal{P}$, forms probability space $(W_\mathcal{P}, \Omega_\mathcal{P}, \mu_\mathcal{P})$.

Given $w_{\mathbf{X}} \in W_{\mathbf{X}}$, the set *satisfiable*$(w_{\mathbf{X}})$ contains all the constraints from *Constr* satisfied in sample $w_{\mathbf{X}}$. Thus, $w_{\mathbf{X}}$ determines a logic theory $\mathcal{R} \cup$ *satisfiable*$(w_{\mathbf{X}})$ that must have a unique model denoted with $M_{\mathcal{P}}(w_{\mathbf{X}})$. Then probability measure $\mu_{\mathcal{P}}(\omega_{\mathcal{P}})$ for $\omega_{\mathcal{P}} \in \Omega_{\mathcal{P}}$ is defined by considering the event of $\Omega_{\mathbf{X}}$ identified by $\omega_{\mathcal{P}}$:

$$\mu_{\mathcal{P}}(\omega_{\mathcal{P}}) = \mu_{\mathbf{X}}(\{w_{\mathbf{X}}|(w_{\mathbf{X}}, w_{\mathbf{Y}}) \in \omega_{\mathcal{P}}, M_{\mathcal{P}}(w_{\mathbf{X}}) \models w_{\mathbf{Y}}\}) \qquad (4.4)$$

Michels et al. [2015] state that $\{w_{\mathbf{X}}|(w_{\mathbf{X}}, w_{\mathbf{Y}}) \in \omega_{\mathcal{P}}, M_{\mathcal{P}}(w_{\mathbf{X}}) \models w_{\mathbf{Y}}\}$ is measurable, i.e., that it belongs to $\Omega_{\mathbf{X}}$; however, the statement is not obvious if $\Omega_{\mathbf{X}}$ is not the powerset of $W_{\mathbf{X}}$. In Chapter 5 we provide a proof of this statement, similar to the one of Section 3.2 for ProbLog.

The probability of a query q (a ground atom) is then given by

$$P(q) = \mu_{\mathcal{P}}(\{w_{\mathcal{P}}|w_{\mathcal{P}} \models q\}) \qquad (4.5)$$

If we define the *solution event* $SE(q)$ as

$$SE(q) = \{w_{\mathbf{X}} \in W_{\mathbf{X}}|M_{\mathcal{P}}(w_{\mathbf{X}}) \models q\}$$

then $P(q) = \mu_{\mathbf{X}}(SE(q))$.

Example 59 (Probability of fire on a ship [Michels et al., 2015]). *Continuing Example 58,* $w_{\mathbf{X}} = (\text{time\_comp}_1, \text{time\_comp}_2) = (x_1, x_2)$, $w_{\mathbf{Y}} = saved = y_1$ *with* $Range_1 = Range_1 = [0, +\infty)$, *and* $y_1 \in \{0, 1\}$. *So from Equation (4.5) we get*

$$P(saved) = \mu_{\mathcal{P}}(\{(x_1, x_2, y_1) \in W_{\mathcal{P}}|y_1 = 1\})$$

and from Equation (4.4):

$$P(saved) = \mu_{\mathbf{X}}(\{(x_1, x_2)|(x_1, x_2, y_1) \in W_{\mathcal{P}}, M_{\mathcal{P}}((x_1, x_2)) \models y_1 = 1\})$$

The solution event is

$$SE(saved) = \{(x_1, x_2)|x_1 < 0.75 \vee (x_1 < 1.25 \wedge x_1 + 0.25 \cdot x_2 < 1.375)\}$$

so

$$P(saved) = \mu_{\mathbf{X}}(\{(x_1, x_2)|x_1 < 0.75 \vee (x_1 < 1.25 \wedge x_1 + 0.25 \cdot x_2 < 1.375)\})$$

Since the two constraints $\varphi_1 = x_1 < 0.75$ *and* $\varphi_2 = x_1 < 1.25 \wedge x_1 + 0.25 \cdot x_2 < 1.375$ *are not mutually exclusive, we can use the formula* $\mu_{\mathbf{X}}(\varphi_1 \vee \varphi_2) = \mu_{\mathbf{X}}(\varphi_1) + \mu_{\mathbf{X}}(\neg\varphi_1 \wedge \varphi_2)$ *with*

$$\neg\varphi_1 \wedge \varphi_2 = 0.75 < x_1 < 1.25 \wedge x_1 + 0.25 \cdot x_2 < 1.375 =$$
$$0.75 < x_1 < 1.25 \wedge x_2 < 5.5 - 4x_1$$

Knowing that X_1 *and* X_2 *are distributed according to an exponential distribution with parameter 1 (density* $p(x) = e^{-x}$*), we get*

$$\mu_{\mathbf{X}}(\varphi_1) = \int_0^\infty p(x_1) I_{\varphi_1}^1(x_1) dx_1$$

$$\mu_{\mathbf{X}}(\neg\varphi_1 \wedge \varphi_2) = \int_0^\infty \int_0^\infty p(x_1) p(x_2) I_{\neg\varphi_1 \wedge \varphi_2}^1(x_1, x_2) dx_1 dx_2$$

where $I_{\varphi_1}^1(x_1)$ *and* $I_{\neg\varphi_1 \wedge \varphi_2}^1(x_1, x_2)$ *are indicator functions that take value 1 if the respective constraint is satisfied and 0 otherwise. So*

$$\mu_{\mathbf{X}}(\varphi_1) = \int_0^{0.75} p(x_1) dx_1 = 1 - e^{-0.75} \approx 0.53$$

$$\mu_{\mathbf{X}}(\neg\varphi_1 \wedge \varphi_2) = \int_{0.75}^{1.25} p(x_1) \left(\int_0^{5.5-4x_1} p(x_2) dx_2 \right) dx_1 =$$

$$\int_{0.75}^{1.25} e^{-x_1} (1 - e^{-5.5+4x_1}) dx_1 =$$

$$\int_{0.75}^{1.25} e^{-x_1} - e^{-5.5+3x_1} dx_1 =$$

$$= -e^{-1.25} + e^{-0.75} - \frac{e^{-5.5+3\cdot1.25}}{3} + \frac{e^{-5.5+3\cdot0.75}}{3} \approx$$

$$0.14$$

So

$$P(saved) \approx 0.53 + 0.14 \approx 0.67$$

Proposition 5 (Conditions for exact inference [Michels et al., 2015]).   *The probability of an arbitrary query can be computed exactly if the following conditions hold:*

1. *Finite-relevant-constraints condition: There are only finitely many constraint atoms that are relevant for each query atom (see Section 1.3) and finding them and checking entailment can be done in finite time.*
2. *Finite-dimensional-constraints condition: Each constraint puts a condition only on a finite number of variables.*
3. *Computable-measure condition: It is possible to compute the probability of finite-dimensional events, i.e., finite-dimensional integrals over the probability density of the random variables.*

The example

$$forever\_sun(X) \leftarrow \langle Weather_X = sunny \rangle, forever\_sun(X+1)$$

does not fulfill the finite-relevant-constraints condition as the set of relevant constraints for $forever\_sun(0)$ is $\langle Weather_X = sunny \rangle$ for $X = 0, 1, \ldots$.

4.5.1 Dealing with imprecise probability distributions

In order to relax the conditions for exact inference of Proposition 5, Michels et al. [2015] consider the problem of computing bounds on the probability of queries.

Credal sets, see also Chapter 6, are sets of probability distributions. They can be defined by assigning probability mass to sets of values without specifying exactly how the mass is distributed over those values. For example, for a continuous random variable, we can assign some probability mass to the set of all values between 1 and 3. This mass can be distributed uniformly over the entire set or uniformly over only parts of it or distributed in a more complex manner.

Definition 33 (Credal set specification). *A credal set specification* **C** *is a sequence of finite-dimensional credal set specifications* $C_1, C_2, \ldots$ *Each* C_k *is a finite set of probability-event pairs* $(p_1, \omega_1), (p_2, \omega_2), \ldots, (p_n, \omega_n)$ *such that, for each* C_k,

1. *The events belong to a finite-dimensional event space* $\Omega_{\mathbf{X}}^k$ *over the sample space* $W_{\mathbf{X}} = Range_1 \times Range_2 \times \ldots \times Range_k$.
2. *The sum of the probabilities is 1.0:* $\sum_{(p,\omega) \in C_k} p = 1.0$.
3. *The events must not be the empty set* $\forall (p, \omega) \in C_k : \omega \neq \emptyset$.

Moreover, C_k *must be compatible, i.e., for all* k, $C_k = \pi_k(C_{k+1})$ *where* $\pi_l(C_k)$ *for* $l < k$ *is defined as*

$$\pi_l(C_k) = \left\{ \left(\sum_{(p,\omega) \in C_k, \pi_l(\omega) = \omega'} p, \omega' \right) \middle| \omega' \in \{\pi_l(\omega) | (p,\omega) \in C_k\} \right\}$$

and $\pi_l(\omega)$ *is the* projection *of event* ω *over the first* l *components*

$$\pi_l(\omega) = \{(x_1, \ldots, x_l) | (x_1, \ldots, x_l, \ldots) \in \omega\}$$

Each C_k identifies a set of probability measures $\Upsilon_{\mathbf{X}}^k$ such that, for each measure $\mu_{\mathbf{X}} \in \Upsilon_{\mathbf{X}}^k$ on $\Omega_{\mathbf{X}}^k$ and each event $\omega \in \Omega_{\mathbf{X}}^k$, the following holds:

$$\sum_{(p,\psi) \in C_k, \psi \subseteq \omega} p \leqslant \mu_{\mathbf{X}}(\omega) \leqslant \sum_{(p,\psi) \in C_k, \psi \cap \omega \neq 0} p$$

In fact, the probability mass of events completely included in event ω certainly contributes to the probability of ω, so they are in its lower bound, while the probability of events with a non-empty intersection may fully contribute to the probability, so they are in its upper bound.

Michels et al. [2015] show that, under mild conditions, a credal set specification $\mathbf{C}$ identifies a credal set of probability measures $\Upsilon_{\mathbf{X}}$ over the space $(W_{\mathbf{X}}, \Omega_{\mathbf{X}})$ such that all measures $\mu_{\mathbf{X}}$ of $\Upsilon_{\mathbf{X}}$ agree with each C_i in $\mathbf{C}$. Moreover, this credal set can be extended to credal set $\Upsilon_{\mathcal{P}}$ of probability measures over the whole program $\mathcal{P}$, which in turns originates a set $\mathbf{P}$ of probability distributions over queries.

Given a credal set specification for a program $\mathcal{P}$, we want to compute the lower and upper bounds on the probability of a query q defined as:

$$\underline{P}(q) = \min_{\mu_{\mathcal{P}} \in \Upsilon_{\mathcal{P}}} \mu_{\mathcal{P}}(q)$$

$$\overline{P}(q) = \max_{\mu_{\mathcal{P}} \in \Upsilon_{\mathcal{P}}} \mu_{\mathcal{P}}(q)$$

These bounds can be computed as indicated by the next proposition.

Proposition 6 (Computation of probability bounds). *Given a finite-dimensional credal set specification C_k, the lower and upper probability bounds of a query q fulfilling the finite-dimensional-constraints condition are given by:*

$$\underline{P}(q) = \sum_{(p,\omega) \in C_k, \omega \subseteq SE(q)} p$$

$$\overline{P}(q) = \sum_{(p,\omega) \in C_k, \omega \cap SE(q) \neq \emptyset} p$$

Example 60 (Credal set specification – continuous variables). *Consider example 58 and the following finite-dimensional credal set specification*

$$
\begin{aligned}
C_2 = \{ \ & (0.49, \{(x_1, x_2) | 0 \leqslant x_1 \leqslant 1, 0 \leqslant x_2 \leqslant 1\}), \\
& (0.14, \{(x_1, x_2) | 1 \leqslant x_1 \leqslant 2, 0 \leqslant x_2 \leqslant 1\}), \\
& (0.07, \{(x_1, x_2) | 2 \leqslant x_1 \leqslant 3, 0 \leqslant x_2 \leqslant 1\}), \\
& (0.14, \{(x_1, x_2) | 0 \leqslant x_1 \leqslant 1, 1 \leqslant x_2 \leqslant 2\}), \\
& (0.04, \{(x_1, x_2) | 1 \leqslant x_1 \leqslant 2, 1 \leqslant x_2 \leqslant 2\}), \\
& (0.02, \{(x_1, x_2) | 2 \leqslant x_1 \leqslant 3, 1 \leqslant x_2 \leqslant 2\}), \\
& (0.07, \{(x_1, x_2) | 0 \leqslant x_1 \leqslant 1, 2 \leqslant x_2 \leqslant 3\}),
\end{aligned}
$$

$$(0.02, \{(x_1, x_2) | 1 \leqslant x_1 \leqslant 2, 2 \leqslant x_2 \leqslant 3\}),$$
$$(0.01, \{(x_1, x_2) | 2 \leqslant x_1 \leqslant 3, 2 \leqslant x_2 \leqslant 3\})\}$$

Figure 4.1 shows how the probability mass is distributed over the (x_1, x_2) *plane. The solution event for* $q = saved$ *is*

$$SE(saved) = \{(x_1, x_2) | x_1 < 0.75 \lor (x_1 < 1.25 \land x_1 + 0.25 \cdot x_2 < 1.375)\}$$

and corresponds to the area of Figure 4.1 to the left of the solid line. We can see that the first event, $0 \leqslant x_1 \leqslant 1 \land 0 \leqslant x_2 \leqslant 1$*, is such that* $CSS(0 \leqslant x_1 \leqslant 1 \land 0 \leqslant x_2 \leqslant 1) \subseteq SE(saved)$*, so its probability is part of the lower bound.*

The next event $1 \leqslant x_1 \leqslant 2 \land 0 \leqslant x_2 \leqslant 1$ *instead is not a subset of* $SE(saved)$ *but has a non-empty intersection with* $SE(saved)$*, so the probability of the event is part of the upper bound.*

Event $2 \leqslant x_1 \leqslant 3 \land 0 \leqslant x_2 \leqslant 1$ *instead has an empty intersection with* $SE(saved)$*, so its probability is not part of any bound.*

Of the following events, $0 \leqslant x_1 \leqslant 1 \land 1 \leqslant x_2 \leqslant 2$*,* $1 \leqslant x_1 \leqslant 2 \land 1 \leqslant x_2 \leqslant 2$*, and* $0 \leqslant x_1 \leqslant 1 \land 2 \leqslant x_2 \leqslant 3$ *have a non-empty intersection with* $SE(saved)$ *while the remaining have an empty intersection, so overall*

$$\underline{P}(q) = 0.49$$
$$\overline{P}(q) = 0.49 + 0.14 + 0.14 + 0.04 + 0.07 = 0.88$$

Credal set specifications can also be used for discrete distributions when the information we have on them is imprecise.

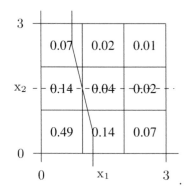

Figure 4.1   Credal set specification for Examples 60 and 62.

Example 61 (Credal set specification – discrete variables).   *Suppose you have a model with a single random variable X_1 with $Range_1 = \{sun, rain\}$ representing the weather tomorrow. A credal set specification may consist of*

$$C_1 = \{(0.2, \{sun, rain\}), (0.8, \{sun\})\}$$

The probability distributions that are included in this credal set are those of the form

$$P(X_1 = sun) = 0.8 + \gamma$$
$$P(X_1 = rain) = 0.2 - \gamma$$

for $\gamma \in [0, 0.2]$. Thus, the probability that tomorrow is sunny is greater than 0.8 but we don't know its precise value.

In the general case of an infinite dimensional credal set specification, the following holds:

$$\underline{P}(q) = \lim_{k \to \infty} \sum_{(p,\omega) \in C_k, \omega \subseteq SE(q)} p$$
$$\overline{P}(q) = \lim_{k \to \infty} \sum_{(p,\omega) \in C_k, \omega \cap SE(q) \neq \emptyset} p$$

A consequence of this is that

$$\underline{P}(q) = 1 - \overline{P}(\sim q)$$
$$\overline{P}(q) = 1 - \underline{P}(\sim q)$$

We can now consider the problem of computing bounds for conditional probabilities. We first define them.

Definition 34 (Conditional probability bounds).   *The lower and upper conditional probability bounds of a query q given evidence e are defined as:*

$$\underline{P}(q|e) = \min_{P \in \mathbf{P}} P(q|e)$$
$$\overline{P}(q|e) = \max_{P \in \mathbf{P}} P(q|e)$$

Bounds for conditional probabilities can be computed using the following proposition.

Proposition 7 (Conditional probability bounds formulas [Michels et al., 2015]).
The lower and upper conditional probability bounds of a query q are determined by:

$$\underline{P}(q|e) = \frac{\underline{P}(q,e)}{\underline{P}(q,e) + \overline{P}(\sim q,e)} \tag{4.6}$$

$$\overline{P}(q|e) = \frac{\overline{P}(q,e)}{\overline{P}(q,e) + \underline{P}(\sim q,e)} \tag{4.7}$$

Example 62 (Conditional probability bounds). *Consider Example 60 and
add the rule $e \leftarrow \langle \text{time\_comp}_2 < 1.5 \rangle$.*
*Suppose the query is $q = saved$ and the evidence is e. To compute the lower
and upper bounds for $P(q|e)$, we need to compute lower and upper bounds
for $q \wedge e$ and $\sim q \wedge e$. The solution event for $SE(e)$ is*

$$SE(e) = \{(x_1, x_2)|x_2 < 1.5\}$$

*and is shown in Figure 4.1 as the area below the dashed line. The solution
event for $q \wedge e$ is*

$$\begin{aligned} SE(q \wedge e) = \ &\{(x_1, x_2)|x_2 < 1.5 \ \wedge \\ &(x_1 < 0.75 \vee (x_1 < 1.25 \wedge x_1 + 0.25 \cdot x_2 < 1.375))\} \end{aligned}$$

and for $\sim q \wedge e$ is

$$\begin{aligned} SE(\sim q \wedge e) = \ &\{(x_1, x_2)|x_2 < 1.5 \ \wedge \\ &\neg(x_1 < 0.75 \vee (x_1 < 1.25 \wedge x_1 + 0.25 \cdot x_2 < 1.375))\} \end{aligned}$$

*We can see that the first event, $0 \leqslant x_1 \leqslant 1 \wedge 0 \leqslant x_2 \leqslant 1$, is such that
$CSS(0 \leqslant x_1 \leqslant 1 \wedge 0 \leqslant x_2 \leqslant 1) \subseteq SE(q \wedge e)$, so its probability contributes
to $\underline{P}(q \wedge e)$ but not to $\underline{P}(\sim q \wedge e)$.*
*The next event $1 \leqslant x_1 \leqslant 2 \wedge 0 \leqslant x_2 \leqslant 1$ has a non-empty intersection with $SE(q)$ and is included in $SE(e)$, so the probability of the event
contributes to $\overline{P}(q \wedge e)$ and $\overline{P}(\sim q \wedge e)$.*
*Event $2 \leqslant x_1 \leqslant 3 \wedge 0 \leqslant x_2 \leqslant 1$ instead has an empty intersection with
$SE(q)$ and is included in $SE(e)$, so it contributes to $\underline{P}(\sim q \wedge e)$ but not to
$\underline{P}(q \wedge e)$.*
*The event $0 \leqslant x_1 \leqslant 1 \wedge 1 \leqslant x_2 \leqslant 2$ has a non-empty intersection with
$SE(q \wedge e)$ and an empty one with $SE(\sim q \wedge e)$, so its probability is part of
$\overline{P}(q \wedge e)$.*

The event $1 \leqslant x_1 \leqslant 2 \wedge 1 \leqslant x_2 \leqslant 2$ *has a non-empty intersection with* $SE(q \wedge e)$ *and* $SE(\sim q \wedge e)$, *so its probability is part of* $\overline{P}(q \wedge e)$ *and* $\overline{P}(\sim q \wedge e)$.

The event $2 \leqslant x_1 \leqslant 3 \wedge 1 \leqslant x_2 \leqslant 2$ *has a non-empty intersection with* $SE(\sim q \wedge e)$, *so it contributes to* $\overline{P}(\sim q \wedge e)$.

The remaining events are included in $SE(\sim e)$, *so they are not part of any bound. Overall, we have*

$$\underline{P}(q \wedge e) = 0.49$$
$$\overline{P}(q \wedge e) = 0.49 + 0.14 + 0.14 + 0.04 = 0.81$$
$$\underline{P}(\sim q \wedge e) = 0.07$$
$$\overline{P}(\sim q \wedge e) = 0.14 + 0.07 + 0.04 + 0.02 = 0.27$$
$$\underline{P}(q|e) = \frac{0.49}{0.49 + 0.27} \approx 0.64$$
$$\overline{P}(q|e) = \frac{0.81}{0.81 + 0.07} \approx 0.92$$

Michels et al. [2015] prove the following theorem that states the conditions under which exact inference of probability bounds is possible.

Theorem 13 (Conditions for exact inference of probability bounds [Michels et al., 2015]).   *The probability bounds of an arbitrary query can be computed in finite time under the following conditions:*

1. *Finite-relevant-constraints condition: as condition 1 of Proposition 5.*
2. *Finite-dimensional-constraints condition: as condition 2 of Proposition 5.*
3. *Disjoint-events-decidability condition: for two finite-dimensional events* ω_1 *and* ω_2 *in the event space* $\Omega_{\mathbf{X}}$, *one can decide whether they are disjoint or not* ($\omega_1 \cap \omega_2 = \varnothing$).

Credal sets can be used to approximate continuous distributions arbitrarily well. One has to provide a credal set specification dividing the domain of the variable X_i in n intervals:

$$\{(P(l_1 < X_i < u_1), l_1 < X_i < u_1), \ldots,$$
$$(P(l_n < X_i < u_n), l_n < X_i < u_n)\}$$

with $l_j \leqslant u_j$, $l_j \in \mathbb{R} \cup \{-\infty\}$ and $u_j \in \mathbb{R} \cup \{+\infty\}$ for $j = 1, \ldots, n$. $P(l_j < X_i < u_j)$ must be such that $P(l_j < X_i < u_j) = \int_{l_j}^{u_j} p(x_i) dx_i = F(u_j) - F(l_j)$ where $p(x_i)$ is the probability density of X_i and $F(x_i)$ is its cumulative distribution. The more intervals we provide, the better we approximate the continuous distribution. The probability bounds of the query provide the maximum error of the approximation.

PCLP fixes a syntax for expressing probability distributions precisely and approximately with credal set specifications.

PCLP allows the definition of random variables as

$$(X_1, \ldots, X_n)(A_1, \ldots, A_m) \sim Density.$$

where $X_1, \ldots, X_n$ are random variables represented by terms, $A_1, \ldots, A_m$ are logical variables appearing in $X_1, \ldots, X_n$, and $Density$ is a probability density, such as *exponential*, *normal*, etc. There is a different multidimensional random variable

$$(X_1, \ldots, X_n)(t_1, \ldots, t_m)$$

for each tuple of ground terms $t_1, \ldots, t_m$ replacing parameters $A_1, \ldots, A_m$. Variables $X_1, \ldots, X_n$ can also be used individually in constraints, the set of them is

$$\{X_i(t_1, \ldots, t_m) | i = 1, \ldots, n, (t_1, \ldots, t_m) \text{ is a tuple of terms}\}.$$

Credal set (approximate) specifications are represented as

$$(X_1, \ldots, X_n)(A_1, \ldots, A_m) \sim \{p_1 : \varphi_1, \ldots, p_l : \varphi_l\}$$

where p_i is a probability, φ_i is a satisfiable constraint, and $\sum_{i=1}^{l} p_i = 1$. The p_is and φ_is can include logical variables.

Examples of specifications are

$$\text{temperature}(Day) \sim \{0.2 : \text{temperature} < 0, 0.8 : \text{temperature} > 0\}.$$
$$\text{temperature}(Day) \sim \{0.2 : \text{temperature} < Day/1000,$$
$$0.8 : \text{temperature} > Day/1000\}.$$

where Day in the second specification must assume numeric values.

In case the program contains multiple definitions for the same random variable, only the first is considered.

PCLP actually defines a family of languages depending on the constraint language $Constr$: a specific language is indicated with PCLP($Constr$). The constraint language must have some properties: infinite dimensional probability measures can be constructed from an infinite number of finite ones with increasing dimensionality and the satisfiability of constraints must be decidable, which is equivalent to decidability of the disjointness of events.

An interesting instance is PCLP(R,D) where the constraints deal with real numbers (R) and discrete domains (D), with the restriction that constraints can include only variables of a single type, either real or discrete.

The constraint theory R is the same as that of CLP over the reals CLP(R): variables can assume real values and the constraints consist of linear equalities and inequalities. The constraint theory D is similar to that of CLP over finite domains CLP(FD): variables can assume discrete values and the constraints consist of set membership ($\in$ and $\notin$) and equality ($=$ and $\neq$). Differently from CLP(FD), the domains can be countably infinite.

A PCLP program with some random variables defined approximately with formulas of the form

$$(X_1, \ldots, X_n)(A_1, \ldots, A_m) \sim \{p_1 : \varphi_1, \ldots, p_l : \varphi_l\}$$

defines a credal set specifications $\mathbf{C} = \{C_1, C_2, \ldots\}$ by combining the specification of the individual variables. We first fix the enumeration of random variables and denote the set of the definitions for the first k random variables as D_k. The credal set specification $\mathbf{C}$ of the program is defined as:

$$C_k = \pi_k \left(\left\{ (p, CSS(\varphi)) | (p, \varphi) \in \hat{\prod}_{d \in D_k} d \right\} \right)$$

where the product of two random variable definitions $d_1 \hat{\times} d_2$ is defined as:

$$d_1 \hat{\times} d_2 = \{(p_1 \cdot p_2, \varphi_1 \wedge \varphi_2) | ((p_1, \varphi_1), (p_2, \varphi_2)) \in d_1 \times d_2\}$$

For example, the following random variable definitions yield the credal set specification of Example 60:

$$\text{time\_comp}_1 \sim \{0.7 : 0 \leqslant \text{time\_comp}_1 \leqslant 1, 0.2 : 1 \leqslant \text{time\_comp}_1 \leqslant 2,$$
$$0.1 : 2 \leqslant \text{time\_comp}_1 \leqslant 3\}$$
$$\text{time\_comp}_2 \sim \{0.7 : 0 \leqslant \text{time\_comp}_2 \leqslant 1, 0.2 : 1 \leqslant \text{time\_comp}_2 \leqslant 2,$$
$$0.1 : 2 \leqslant \text{time\_comp}_2 \leqslant 3\}$$

The *solution constraint* of a query q is defined as:

$$SC(q) = \bigvee_{\phi \subseteq Constr, M_P(\phi) \models q} \bigwedge_{\varphi \in \phi} \varphi$$

where $M_P(\phi)$ is the model of the theory $\mathcal{R} \cup \{\langle\varphi\rangle | \varphi \in \phi\}$.

Function

$$check : Constr \to \{sat, unsat, unknown\}$$

checks satisfiability of constraints and returns

- *sat*: the constraint is certainly satisfiable, i.e., there is a solution.
- *unsat*: the constraint is certainly unsatisfiable, i.e., there is no solution.
- *unknown*: satisfiability could not be decided, i.e., nothing is said about the constraint.

If the constraint theory is decidable, *unknown* is never returned.

Given function *check*, we can compute the lower and upper probability bounds of a query q taking into account only the first n random variables from a PCLP program fulfilling the exact inference conditions, as

$$\underline{P}(q) = \sum_{(p,\varphi)\in C_n, check(\varphi \wedge \neg SC(q))=\text{unsat}} p$$

$$\overline{P}(q) = \sum_{(p,\varphi)\in C_n, check(\varphi \wedge SC(q))=\text{sat}} p$$

If the constraints are partially decidable, we get the following result

$$\underline{P}(q) \geqslant \sum_{(p,\varphi)\in C_n, check(\varphi \wedge \neg SC(q))=\text{unsat}} p$$

$$\overline{P}(q) \leqslant \sum_{(p,\varphi)\in C_n, check(\varphi \wedge SC(q))\neq\text{unsat}} p$$

Inference from a PCLP program can take three forms if *Constr* is decidable:

- exact computation of a point probability, if the random variables are all precisely defined;
- exact computation of lower and upper probabilities, if the information about random variables is imprecise, i.e., it is given as credal sets;
- approximate inference with probability bounds, if information about random variables is precise but credal sets are used to approximate continuous distributions.

If *Constr* is partially decidable, we can perform only approximate inference and obtain bounds in all three cases. In particular, in the second case, we obtain a lower bound on the lower probability and an upper bound on the upper probability.

PCLP, despite the name, is only loosely related to other probabilistic logic formalisms based on CLP such as CLP(BN), see Section 2.9.2, or clp(pdf(y)) [Angelopoulos, 2003] because it uses constraints to denote events and define credal set specifications, while CLP(BN) and clp(pdf(y)) consider probability distributions as constraints.

5

Semantics for Hybrid Programs with Function Symbols

In this chapter we prove that the semantics of PCLP given in Section 4.5 is well-defined also when function symbols are present, i.e., that each query can be assigned a probability. In other words, we prove that the solution event $SE(q)$ is measurable for every query q. These results were presented in [Azzolini et al., 2021].

5.1 Examples of PCLP with Function Symbols

The following two examples use integers, that are representable only by using function symbols (for example, 0 for 0, $s(0)$ for 1, $s(s(0))$ for 2, ...).

Example 63 (Gambling). *Consider a gambling game that repeatedly consists in spinning a roulette wheel and drawing a card from a deck. The card is reinserted in the deck after each play. The player keeps track of the final position of the axis of the wheel (the angle it creates with the geographic east). The game continues until the player draws a red card.*

There are four available prizes that can be won, depending on the position of the wheel and the color of the card: prize a if the card is black and the angle is less than π, prize b if the card is black and the angle is greater than π, prize c if the card is red and the angle is less than π and prize d otherwise. We describe the angle of the wheel with a uniform distribution in $[0, 2\pi)$, and the color of the card with a Bernoulli distribution with $P(red) = P(black) = 0.5$. In this program there is a random variable for every ground instantiation of the (anonymous) logical variable in the random variables card(_) *and* angle(_).

$$\text{card}(\_) \sim \{red : 0.5, \ black : 0.5\}$$
$$\text{angle}(\_) \sim uniform(0, 2\pi)$$

$$prize(0, a) \leftarrow \langle \text{card}(0) = black \rangle, \langle \text{angle}(0) < \pi \rangle$$
$$prize(0, b) \leftarrow \langle \text{card}(0) = black \rangle, \langle \text{angle}(0) \geqslant \pi \rangle$$
$$prize(0, c) \leftarrow \langle \text{card}(0) = red \rangle, \langle \text{angle}(0) < \pi \rangle$$
$$prize(0, d) \leftarrow \langle \text{card}(0) = red \rangle, \langle \text{angle}(0) \geqslant \pi \rangle$$
$$prize(s(X), a) \leftarrow prize(X, \_), \langle \text{card}(X) = black \rangle,$$
$$\langle \text{card}(s(X)) = black \rangle, \langle \text{angle}(s(X)) < \pi \rangle$$
$$prize(s(X), b) \leftarrow prize(X, \_), \langle \text{card}(X) = black \rangle,$$
$$\langle \text{card}(s(X)) = black \rangle, \langle \text{angle}(s(X)) \geqslant \pi \rangle$$
$$prize(s(X), c) \leftarrow prize(X, \_), \langle \text{card}(X) = black \rangle,$$
$$\langle \text{card}(s(X)) = red \rangle, \langle \text{angle}(s(X)) < \pi \rangle$$
$$prize(s(X), d) \leftarrow prize(X, \_), \langle \text{card}(X) = black \rangle,$$
$$\langle \text{card}(s(X)) = red \rangle, \langle \text{angle}(s(X)) \geqslant \pi \rangle$$
$$at\_least\_once\_prize\_a \leftarrow prize(\_X, a)$$
$$never\_prize\_a \leftarrow \sim at\_least\_once\_prize\_a$$

Given this program, $P(at\_least\_once\_prize\_a)$ is the probability that the player wins at least once prize a. Similarly, the probability that the player never wins prize a is $P(never\_prize\_a)$.

Example 64 (Hybrid Hidden Markov Model). *A Hybrid Hidden Markov Model (Hybrid HMM) is the combination of a Hidden Markov Model (HMM, with discrete states) and a Kalman Filter (with continuous states). For every integer time point t the system is in a state $[\text{s}(t), \text{type}(t)]$ described by a discrete random variable $\text{type}(t)$ taking values in $\{a, b\}$, and a continuous variable $\text{s}(t)$ taking values in $\mathbb{R}$. At time t, the model emits one value $\text{v}(t) = \text{s}(t) + \text{obs\_err}(t)$, where $\text{obs\_err}(t)$ is an error that follows a probability distribution depending on $\text{type}(t)$, a or b, and not on time. At time $t' = t + 1$, the system moves to a new state $[\text{s}(t'), \text{type}(t')]$, where $\text{s}(t') = \text{s}(t) + \text{trans\_err}(t)$. Again, $\text{trans\_err}(t)$ is an error that follows a probability distribution that depends on $\text{type}(t)$. Likewise, $\text{type}(t')$ depends on $\text{type}(t)$. We use the random variables init and type_init to describe the state at time 0. All the random variables, except init and type_init, are indexed by an integer value (time step). We want to compute the probability that the value emitted at time step 1 is larger than 2 (predicate $ok/0$). As before, there is a random variable for every ground instantiation of the terms* *indicating the random variables.*

$ok \leftarrow kf(2), \langle v(1) > 2 \rangle$

$kf(N) \leftarrow \langle s(0) = \text{init} \rangle, \langle \text{type}(0) = \text{type\_init} \rangle, kf\_part(0, N)$

$kf\_part(I, N) \leftarrow I < N, NextI \text{ is } I + 1,$
   $trans(I, NextI), emit(I),$
    $kf\_part(NextI, N)$

$kf\_part(N, N) \leftarrow N \neq 0$

$trans(I, NextI) \leftarrow$
   $\langle \text{type}(I) = a \rangle, \langle s(NextI) = s(I) + \text{trans\_err\_a}(I) \rangle,$
   $\langle \text{type}(NextI) = \text{type\_a}(NextI) \rangle$

$trans(I, NextI) \leftarrow$
   $\langle \text{type}(I) = b \rangle, \langle s(NextI) = s(I) + \text{trans\_err\_b}(I) \rangle$
   $\langle \text{type}(NextI) = \text{type\_b}(NextI) \rangle$

$emit(I) \leftarrow$
   $\langle \text{type}(I) = a \rangle, \langle v(I) = s(I) + \text{obs\_err\_a}(I) \rangle$

$emit(I) \leftarrow$
   $\langle \text{type}(I) = b \rangle, \langle v(I) = s(I) + \text{obs\_err\_b}(I) \rangle$

$\text{init} \sim gaussian(0, 1)$

$\text{trans\_err\_a}(\_) \sim gaussian(0, 2)$

$\text{trans\_err\_b}(\_) \sim gaussian(0, 4)$

$\text{obs\_err\_a}(\_) \sim gaussian(0, 1)$

$\text{obs\_err\_b}(\_) \sim gaussian(0, 3)$

$\text{type\_init} \sim \{a : 0.4, b : 0.6\}$

$\text{type\_a}(\_) \sim \{a : 0.3, b : 0.7\}$

$\text{type\_b}(\_) \sim \{a : 0.7, b : 0.3\}$

5.2 Preliminaries

In this section we introduce some preliminaries. We provide a new definition of PCLP that differs from the one of Section 4.5 because we separate
discrete from continuous random variables. The former are encoded using
probabilistic facts as in ProbLog. Recall that with Boolean probabilistic facts
it is possible to encode any discrete random variable (see Section 2.4).

A probabilistic constraint logic program is composed of a set of rules $\mathcal{R}$, a set of Boolean probabilistic facts $\mathcal{F}$, and a countable set of continuous random variables $\mathbf{X} = X_1, X_2, \ldots$ Each X_i has an associated $Range_i$ that can be $\mathbb{R}$ or $\mathbb{R}^n$. The rules in $\mathcal{R}$ define the truth value of the atoms in the Herbrand base of the program given the values of the random variables. We define the sample space of the continuous random variables as $W_{\mathbf{X}} = Range_1 \times Range_2 \times \ldots$ As previously discussed, the probability spaces of individual variables generate an infinite dimensional probability space $(W_{\mathbf{X}}, \Omega_{\mathbf{X}}, \mu_{\mathbf{X}})$. The updated definition of a *probabilistic constraint logic theory* follows.

Definition 35 (Probabilistic Constraint Logic Theory - updated).   *A probabilistic constraint logic theory $\mathcal{P}$ is a tuple $(\mathbf{X}, W_{\mathbf{X}}, \Omega_{\mathbf{X}}, \mu_{\mathbf{X}}, Constr, \mathcal{R}, \mathcal{F})$ where:*

- $\mathbf{X}$ *is a countable set of continuous random variables $\{X_1, X_2, \ldots\}$, where each random variable X_i has a range $Range_i$ equal to $\mathbb{R}$ or $\mathbb{R}^n$.*
- $W_{\mathbf{X}} = Range_1 \times Range_2 \times \ldots$ *is the sample space.*
- $\Omega_{\mathbf{X}}$ *is the event space.*
- $\mu_{\mathbf{X}}$ *is a probability measure, i.e., $(W_{\mathbf{X}}, \Omega_{\mathbf{X}}, \mu_{\mathbf{X}})$ is a probability space.*
- *Constr is a set of constraints closed under conjunction, disjunction, and negation such that $\forall \varphi \in Constr$, $CSS(\varphi) \in \Omega_{\mathbf{X}}$, i.e., such that $CSS(\varphi)$ is measurable for all φ.*
- $\mathcal{R}$ *is a set of rules with logical constraints of the form:* $h \leftarrow l_1, \ldots, l_n, \langle \varphi_1(\mathbf{X}) \rangle, \ldots, \langle \varphi_m(\mathbf{X}) \rangle$ *where l_i is a literal for $i = 1, \ldots, n$, $\varphi_j \in Constr$ and $\langle \varphi_j(\mathbf{X}) \rangle$ is called* constraint atom *for $j = 1, \ldots, m$.*
- $\mathcal{F}$ *is a set of probabilistic facts.*

This definition differs from Definition 32 since we separate discrete and continuous probabilistic facts: $\mathbf{X}$ is the set containing continuous variables only, while $\mathcal{F}$ is a set of discrete probabilistic facts. The probabilistic facts form a countable set of Boolean random variables $\mathbf{Y} = \{Y_1, Y_2, \ldots\}$ with sample space $W_{\mathbf{Y}} = \{(y_1, y_2, \ldots) \mid y_i \in \{0, 1\}, i \in 1, 2, \ldots\}$. The event space is the σ-algebra of set of worlds identified by countable set of countable composite choices: a composite choice $\kappa = \{(f_1, \theta_1, y_1), (f_2, \theta_2, y_2), \ldots\}$ can be interpreted as the assignments $Y_1 = y_1, Y_2 = y_2, \ldots$ if Y_1 is associated to $f_1\theta_1$, Y_2 to $f_2\theta_2$ and so on. Finally, the probability space for the entire program $(W_{\mathcal{P}}, \Omega_{\mathcal{P}}, \mu_{\mathcal{P}})$ is the product of the probability spaces for the continuous

$(W_{\mathbf{X}}, \Omega_{\mathbf{X}}, \mu_{\mathbf{X}})$ and discrete $(W_{\mathbf{Y}}, \Omega_{\mathbf{Y}}, \mu_{\mathbf{Y}})$ random variables, which exists in light of the following theorem.

Theorem 14 (Theorem 6.3.1 from Chow and Teicher [2012]). *Given two probability spaces $(W_{\mathbf{X}}, \Omega_{\mathbf{X}}, \mu_{\mathbf{X}})$ and $(W_{\mathbf{Y}}, \Omega_{\mathbf{Y}}, \mu_{\mathbf{Y}})$, there exists a unique probability space (W, Ω, μ), called the* product space, *such that $W = W_{\mathbf{X}} \times W_{\mathbf{Y}}$, $\Omega = \Omega_{\mathbf{X}} \otimes \Omega_{\mathbf{Y}}$, and*

$$\mu(\omega_{\mathbf{X}} \times \omega_{\mathbf{Y}}) = \mu_{\mathbf{X}}(\omega_{\mathbf{X}}) \cdot \mu_{\mathbf{Y}}(\omega_{\mathbf{Y}})$$

for $\omega_{\mathbf{X}} \in \Omega_{\mathbf{X}}$ and $\omega_{\mathbf{Y}} \in \Omega_{\mathbf{Y}}$. Measure μ is called the product measure *of $\mu_{\mathbf{X}}$ and $\mu_{\mathbf{Y}}$, and it is also denoted by $\mu_{\mathbf{X}} \times \mu_{\mathbf{Y}}$. Moreover, for any $\omega \in \Omega$, we define its* sections *as*

$$\omega^{(\mathbf{X})}(w_{\mathbf{X}}) = \{w_{\mathbf{Y}} \mid (w_{\mathbf{X}}, w_{\mathbf{Y}}) \in \omega\} \quad \omega^{(\mathbf{Y})}(w_{\mathbf{Y}}) = \{w_{\mathbf{X}} \mid (w_{\mathbf{X}}, w_{\mathbf{Y}}) \in \omega\}.$$

Both $\omega^{(\mathbf{X})}(w_{\mathbf{X}})$ and $\omega^{(\mathbf{Y})}(w_{\mathbf{Y}})$ are measurable according to $(W_{\mathbf{Y}}, \Omega_{\mathbf{Y}}, \mu_{\mathbf{Y}})$ and $(W_{\mathbf{X}}, \Omega_{\mathbf{X}}, \mu_{\mathbf{X}})$ respectively, i.e., $\omega^{(\mathbf{X})}(w_{\mathbf{X}}) \in \Omega_{\mathbf{Y}}$ and $\omega^{(\mathbf{Y})}(w_{\mathbf{Y}}) \in \Omega_{\mathbf{X}}$. Consequently, $\mu_{\mathbf{Y}}(\omega^{(\mathbf{X})}(w_{\mathbf{X}}))$ and $\mu_{\mathbf{X}}(\omega^{(\mathbf{Y})}(w_{\mathbf{Y}}))$ are real values.
Measure $\mu = \mu_{\mathbf{X}} \times \mu_{\mathbf{Y}}$ for every $\omega \in \Omega$ also satisfies

$$\mu(\omega) = \int_{W_{\mathbf{Y}}} \mu_{\mathbf{X}}(\omega^{(\mathbf{Y})}(w_{\mathbf{Y}})) d\mu_{\mathbf{Y}} = \int_{W_{\mathbf{X}}} \mu_{\mathbf{Y}}(\omega^{(\mathbf{X})}(w_{\mathbf{X}})) d\mu_{\mathbf{X}}.$$

In our case, $W_{\mathcal{P}} = W_{\mathbf{X}} \times W_{\mathbf{Y}}$, and $\Omega_{\mathcal{P}} = \Omega_{\mathbf{X}} \otimes \Omega_{\mathbf{Y}}$. We indicate with *satisfiable*$(w_{\mathbf{X}})$ the set of constraints that are satisfiable given a valuation $w_{\mathbf{X}}$ of the random variables in $\mathbf{X}$. A *world* is an assignment of values to both the continuous and discrete random variables, i.e., $w = (w_{\mathbf{X}}, w_{\mathbf{Y}})$ with $w_{\mathbf{X}} \in W_{\mathbf{X}}$ and $w_{\mathbf{Y}} \in W_{\mathbf{Y}}$. We say that a world w *satisfies* a constraint φ, and we write $w \models \varphi$, if the values of the continuous random variables in the worlds satisfy the constraint. Starting from a world $w = (w_{\mathbf{X}}, w_{\mathbf{Y}})$ from $W_{\mathcal{P}}$, a ground normal logic program P_w is composed of:

- the groundings of the rules whose constraint are in the set *satisfiable* $(w_{\mathbf{X}})$, with the constraints removed from the body,
- the probabilistic facts associated to random variables Y_i with value 1.

The well-founded model of $w \in W_{\mathcal{P}}$, $WFM(w)$, is defined as the well-founded model of P_w, $WFM(P_w)$, and we require that it is two-valued: if this constraint is satisfied for every sample $w \in W_{\mathcal{P}}$, we call the program *sound*.

The probability of a query q is then given by

$$P(q) = \mu_{\mathcal{P}}(\{w \mid w \in W_{\mathcal{P}}, WFM(w) \models q\}).$$

An *explanation* for a query q of a PCLP is a set of worlds ω_i where the query is true in every element of the set, i.e., $\forall w \in \omega_i$, $WFM(w) \models q$. If every world w such that $WFM(w) \models q$ belongs to the set, the set is termed *covering*. A pairwise incompatible set $\omega = \bigcup_i \omega_i$ is such that $\forall j \neq k$, $\omega_j \cap \omega_k = \varnothing$. We define the probability of a query q as the measure of a covering set of explanations: $P(q) = \mu_P(\{w \mid w \models q\})$. We are now ready to compute the probability the examples previously discussed.

Example 65 (Pairwise incompatible covering set of explanations for Example 63). *Consider Example 63. We represent the extraction of a black card with* $f_1 = black(\_) : 0.5$. $(f_1, \theta, 1)$ *means that the card is black while* $(f_1, \theta, 0)$ *means that the card is not black (red). We associate a random variable* Y_i *to* $black(s^i(0))$: $y_i = 1$ *means that in round* i *a black card was picked. The query* $at\_least\_once\_prize\_a$ *has the pairwise incompatible set of explanations*

$$\omega^+ = \omega_0^+ \cup \omega_1^+ \cup \ldots$$

and ω^+ *is covering for it. The sets* ω_i^+ *are defined as:*

$$\omega_0^+ = \{(w_{\mathbf{X}}, w_{\mathbf{Y}}) \mid w_{\mathbf{X}} = (x_0, x_1, \ldots), w_{\mathbf{Y}} = (y_0, y_1, \ldots),$$
$$x_0 \in [0, \pi], y_0 = 1\}$$
$$\omega_1^+ = \{(w_{\mathbf{X}}, w_{\mathbf{Y}}) \mid w_{\mathbf{X}} = (x_0, x_1, \ldots), w_{\mathbf{Y}} = (y_0, y_1, \ldots),$$
$$x_0 \in [\pi, 2\pi], y_0 = 1, x_1 \in [0, \pi], y_1 = 1\}$$
$$\ldots$$

Similarly, the query $never\_prize\_a$ *has the pairwise incompatible covering set of explanations*

$$\omega^- = \omega_0^- \cup \omega_1^- \cup \omega_2^- \cup \omega_3^- \cup \ldots$$

with

$$\omega_0^- = \{(w_X, w_Y) \mid w_X = (x_0, x_1, \ldots), w_Y = (y_0, y_1, \ldots),$$
$$x_0 \in [0, \pi], y_0 = 0\}$$
$$\omega_1^- = \{(w_X, w_Y) \mid w_X = (x_0, x_1, \ldots), w_Y = (y_0, y_1, \ldots),$$
$$x_0 \in [\pi, 2\pi], y_0 = 0\}$$
$$\omega_2^- = \{(w_X, w_Y) \mid w_X = (x_0, x_1, \ldots), w_Y = (y_0, y_1, \ldots),$$
$$x_0 \in [\pi, 2\pi], y_0 = 1, x_1 \in [0, \pi], y_1 = 0\}$$
$$\omega_3^- = \{\{(w_X, w_Y) \mid w_X = (x_0, x_1, \ldots), w_Y = (y_0, y_1, \ldots),$$
$$x_0 \in [\pi, 2\pi], y_0 = 1, x_1 \in [\pi, 2\pi], y_1 = 0\}$$

$$\ldots$$

Once we have computed the pairwise incompatible covering set of explanations, we can calculate the probability of the query.

Example 66 (Probability of queries for Example 63). *Consider sets* ω^+ *and* ω^- *from Example 65. From Theorem 14,*

$$\mu(\omega_0^+) = \int_{W_X} \mu_Y(\omega^{(X)}(w_X))d\mu_X = \int_{W_X} \mu_Y(\{w_Y \mid (w_X, w_Y) \in \omega_0^+\})d\mu_X$$

and so

$$\mu(\omega_0^+) = \int_0^\pi \mu_Y(\{(y_0, y_1, \ldots) \mid y_0 = 1\})d\mu_X$$
$$= \int_0^\pi \frac{1}{2} \cdot \frac{1}{2\pi}dx_0 = \frac{1}{2} \cdot \frac{1}{2} = \frac{1}{4}$$

since, for the discrete variables, $\mu_Y(\{(y_0, y_1, \ldots) \mid y_0 = 0\}) = \mu_Y(\{(y_0, y_1, \ldots) \mid y_0 = 1\}) = 1/2$, *and* μ_X *is the measure of the uniform density in* $[0, 2\pi]$ *on the set* $[0, \pi]$. *Similarly,*

$$\mu(\omega_1^+) = \int_{W_X} \mu_Y(\{(y_0, y_1, \ldots) \mid y_0 = 1, y_1 = 1\})d\mu_X$$
$$= \int_0^\pi \left(\int_\pi^{2\pi} \frac{1}{4} \cdot \frac{1}{2\pi}dx_0 \right) \cdot \frac{1}{2\pi}dx_1 = \int_0^\pi \frac{1}{8} \cdot \frac{1}{2\pi}dx_1 = \frac{1}{8} \cdot \frac{1}{2} = \frac{1}{16}$$

For ω^-:

$$\mu(\omega_0^-) = \int_{W_{\mathbf{X}}} \mu_{\mathbf{Y}}(\{(y_0, y_1, \ldots) \mid y_0 = 0\}) d\mu_{\mathbf{X}}$$

$$= \int_0^\pi \frac{1}{2} \cdot \frac{1}{2\pi} dx_0 = \frac{1}{2} \cdot \frac{1}{2} = \frac{1}{4}.$$

$$\mu(\omega_1^-) = \int_{W_{\mathbf{X}}} \mu_{\mathbf{Y}}(\{(y_0, y_1, \ldots) \mid y_0 = 0\}) d\mu_{\mathbf{X}}$$

$$= \int_\pi^{2\pi} \frac{1}{2} \cdot \frac{1}{2\pi} dx_0 = \frac{1}{2} \cdot \frac{1}{2} = \frac{1}{4}.$$

$$\mu(\omega_2^-) = \int_{W_{\mathbf{X}}} \mu_{\mathbf{Y}}(\{(y_0, y_1, \ldots) \mid y_0 = 1, y_1 = 0\}) d\mu_{\mathbf{X}}$$

$$= \int_0^\pi \left(\int_\pi^{2\pi} \frac{1}{4} \cdot \frac{1}{2\pi} dx_0 \right) \cdot \frac{1}{2\pi} dx_1 = \int_\pi^{2\pi} \frac{1}{8} \cdot \frac{1}{2\pi} dx_1 = \frac{1}{8} \cdot \frac{1}{2} = \frac{1}{16}$$

$$\mu(\omega_3^-) = \int_{W_{\mathbf{X}}} \mu_{\mathbf{Y}}(\{(y_0, y_1, \ldots) \mid y_0 = 1, y_1 = 0\}) d\mu_{\mathbf{X}}$$

$$= \int_\pi^{2\pi} \left(\int_\pi^{2\pi} \frac{1}{4} \cdot \frac{1}{2\pi} dx_0 \right) \cdot \frac{1}{2\pi} dx_1 = \int_\pi^{2\pi} \frac{1}{8} \cdot \frac{1}{2\pi} dx_1 = \frac{1}{8} \cdot \frac{1}{2} = \frac{1}{16}$$

The sets ω_i^+ from Example 65 are pairwise incompatible, so the measure of ω^+ can be computed by summing the measures of the ω_i^+s. By iteratively applying the previous computations, we can calculate the probability of the query at_least_once_prize_a *as*

$$P(at\_least\_once\_prize\_a) = \frac{1}{4} + \frac{1}{16} + \frac{1}{32} + \ldots$$

$$= \frac{1}{4} + \frac{1}{4} \cdot \left(\frac{1}{4}\right) + \frac{1}{4} \cdot \left(\frac{1}{4}\right)^2 + \ldots$$

$$= \frac{1}{4} \cdot \frac{1}{1 - \frac{1}{4}} = \frac{1}{4} \cdot \frac{4}{3} = \frac{1}{3}$$

since the sum represents a geometric series. Similarly, for query never_ prize_a, *the sets in ω^- are pairwise incompatible, so its probability can be* *computed as*

$$P(never\_prize\_a) = \left(\frac{1}{4} + \frac{1}{4}\right) + \left(\frac{1}{16} + \frac{1}{16}\right) +$$
$$\left(\frac{1}{64} + \frac{1}{64}\right) + \dots$$
$$= \frac{1}{2} + \frac{1}{2} \cdot \left(\frac{1}{4}\right) + \frac{1}{2} \cdot \left(\frac{1}{4}\right)^2 + \dots$$
$$= \frac{1}{2} \cdot \frac{1}{1 - \frac{1}{4}} = \frac{1}{2} \cdot \frac{4}{3} = \frac{2}{3}$$

$P(never\_prize\_a) = 1 - P(at\_least\_once\_prize\_a)$, *as expected.*

Example 67 (Pairwise incompatible covering set of explanations for Example 64). *Consider Example 64. The version of the program with discrete random variables represented using probabilistic facts is*

$ok \leftarrow kf(2), \langle v(1) > 2 \rangle$
$kf(N) \leftarrow \langle s(0) = \text{init} \rangle, type0(T), kf\_part(0, T, N)$
$kf\_part(I, T, N) \leftarrow I < N, NextI \text{ is } I + 1,$
$\quad trans(I, T, NextI, NextT), emit(I, T),$
$\quad kf\_part(NextI, NextT, N)$
$kf\_part(N, \_, N) \leftarrow N \neq 0$
$trans(I, a, NextI, NextT) \leftarrow$
$\quad \langle s(NextI) = s(I) + \text{trans\_err\_a}(I) \rangle,$
$\quad type(NextI, a, NextT)$
$trans(I, b, NextI, NextT) \leftarrow$
$\quad \langle s(NextI) = s(I) + \text{trans\_err\_b}(I) \rangle,$
$\quad type(NextI, b, NextT)$
$emit(I, a) \leftarrow$
$\quad \langle v(I) = s(I) + \text{obs\_err\_a}(I) \rangle$
$emit(I, b) \leftarrow$
$\quad \langle v(I) = s(I) + \text{obs\_err\_b}(I) \rangle$
$type0(a) \leftarrow type\_init\_a.$
$type0(b) \leftarrow {\sim}type\_init\_a.$

$$type(I, a, a) \leftarrow type\_a\_a(I).$$
$$type(I, a, b) \leftarrow \sim type\_a\_a(I).$$
$$type(I, b, a) \leftarrow type\_b\_a(I).$$
$$type(I, b, b) \leftarrow \sim type\_b\_a(I).$$
$$\text{init} \sim gaussian(0, 1)$$
$$\text{trans\_err\_a(\_)} \sim gaussian(0, 2)$$
$$\text{trans\_err\_b(\_)} \sim gaussian(0, 4)$$
$$\text{obs\_err\_a(\_)} \sim gaussian(0, 1)$$
$$\text{obs\_err\_b(\_)} \sim gaussian(0, 3)$$
$$type\_init\_a : 0.4.$$
$$type\_a\_a(\_) : 0.3.$$
$$type\_b\_a(\_) : 0.7.$$

We use the following denotation for discrete random variables: y_0 for type_init_a, y_{1a} for type_a_a(1), y_{1b} for type_b_a(1), y_{2a} for type_a_a(2), y_{2b} for type_b_a(2), ..., with value 1 of the y variables meaning that the corresponding fact is true. A covering set of explanations for the query ok is:

$$\omega = \omega_0 \cup \omega_1 \cup \omega_2 \cup \omega_3$$

with

$$\omega_0 = \{(w_{\mathbf{X}}, w_{\mathbf{Y}}) \mid$$
$$w_{\mathbf{X}} = (\text{init}, \text{trans\_err\_a}(0), \text{trans\_err\_a}(1), \text{obs\_err\_a}(1), \ldots),$$
$$w_{\mathbf{Y}} = (y_0, y_{1a}, y_{1b}, \ldots),$$
$$\text{init} + \text{trans\_err\_a}(0) + \text{trans\_err\_a}(1) + \text{obs\_err\_a}(1) > 2,$$
$$y_0 = 1, y_{1a} = 1\}$$
$$\omega_1 = \{(w_{\mathbf{X}}, w_{\mathbf{Y}}) \mid$$
$$w_{\mathbf{X}} = (\text{init}, \text{trans\_err\_a}(0), \text{trans\_err\_b}(1), \text{obs\_err\_b}(1), \ldots),$$
$$w_{\mathbf{Y}} = (y_0, y_{1a}, y_{1b}, \ldots),$$
$$\text{init} + \text{trans\_err\_a}(0) + \text{trans\_err\_b}(1) + \text{obs\_err\_b}(1) > 2,$$
$$y_0 = 1, y_{1a} = 0\}$$
$$\omega_2 = \{(w_{\mathbf{X}}, w_{\mathbf{Y}}) \mid$$
$$w_{\mathbf{X}} = (\text{init}, \text{trans\_err\_b}(0), \text{trans\_err\_a}(1), \text{obs\_err\_a}(1), \ldots),$$
$$w_{\mathbf{Y}} = (y_0, y_{1a}, y_{1b}, \ldots),$$

$$\text{init} + \text{trans\_err\_b}(0) + \text{trans\_err\_a}(1) + \text{obs\_err\_a}(1) > 2,$$
$$y_0 = 0, y_{1b} = 1\}$$
$$\omega_3 = \{(w_{\mathbf{X}}, w_{\mathbf{Y}}) \mid$$
$$\quad w_{\mathbf{X}} = (\text{init}, \text{trans\_err\_b}(0), \text{trans\_err\_b}(1), \text{obs\_err\_b}(1), \ldots),$$
$$\quad w_{\mathbf{Y}} = (y_0, y_{1a}, y_{1b}, \ldots),$$
$$\quad \text{init} + \text{trans\_err\_b}(0) + \text{trans\_err\_b}(1) + \text{obs\_err\_b}(1) > 2,$$
$$\quad y_0 = 0, y_{1b} = 0\}$$

Example 68 (Probability of queries for Example 64). *Consider the set ω_0 from Example 67. From Theorem 14,*

$$\mu(\omega_0) = \int_{W_{\mathbf{X}}} \mu_{\mathbf{Y}}(\omega^{(\mathbf{X})}(w_{\mathbf{X}})) d\mu_{\mathbf{X}} = \int_{W_{\mathbf{X}}} \mu_{\mathbf{Y}}(\{w_{\mathbf{Y}} \mid (w_{\mathbf{X}}, w_{\mathbf{Y}}) \in \omega_0\}) d\mu_{\mathbf{X}}.$$

Continuous random variables are independent and normally distributed. If $X \sim gaussian(\mu_X, \sigma_X^2)$, $Y \sim gaussian(\mu_Y, \sigma_Y^2)$, and $Z = X + Y$, then $Z \sim gaussian(\mu_X + \mu_Y, \sigma_X^2 + \sigma_Y^2)$. We indicate with $\mathcal{N}(x, \mu, \sigma^2)$ the Gaussian probability density function with mean μ and variance σ^2. The measure for ω_0 can be computed as:

$$\mu(\omega_0) = \int_{W_{\mathbf{X}}} \mu_{\mathbf{X}}(\{(y_0, y_{1a}, y_{1b}, \ldots) \mid y_0 = 1, y_{1a} = 1\}) \, d\mu_{\mathbf{X}}$$
$$= \int_{-\infty}^{2} 0.4 \cdot 0.3 \cdot \mathcal{N}(x, 0 + 0 + 0 + 0, 1 + 2 + 2 + 1) \, dx =$$
$$= 0.12 \cdot 0.207 = 0.0248.$$

The values for ω_1, ω_2, and ω_3 can be similarly computed. The probability of ω is:

$$P(\omega) = \mu(\omega_0) + \mu(\omega_1) + \mu(\omega_2) + \mu(\omega_3) = 0.25.$$

5.3 The Semantics of PCLP is Well-defined

In this section we show that every ground query to every sound program is assigned a probability. Here, we focus only on ground programs, but we allow them to be denumerable. This may seem a restriction, but it is not since the number of groundings of a clause can at most be denumerable if the program has function symbols.

Here we follow the same strategy of Section 3.2 where we proved that every query to a probabilistic logic program with function symbols can be assigned a probability. To do so, we partly reformulate some of the definitions there. In order to avoid introducing new notation, we keep the previous names and notation but here they assume a slightly different meaning.

Definition 36 (Parameterized two-valued interpretations - PCLP). *Given a ground probabilistic constraint logic program $\mathcal{P}$ with Herbrand base $\mathcal{B}_\mathcal{P}$, a parameterized positive two-valued interpretation Tr is a set of pairs (a, ω_a) where $a \in \mathcal{B}_\mathcal{P}$ and $\omega_a \in \Omega_\mathcal{P}$ such that for each $a \in \mathcal{B}_\mathcal{P}$ there is only one such pair (Tr is really a function). Similarly, a* parameterized negative two-valued interpretation *Fa is a set of pairs $(a, \omega_{\sim a})$ where $a \in \mathcal{B}_\mathcal{P}$ and $\omega_{\sim a} \in \Omega_\mathcal{P}$ such that for each $a \in \mathcal{B}_\mathcal{P}$ there is only one such pair.*

Parameterized two-valued interpretations form a complete lattice where the partial order is defined as $I \leqslant J$ if $\forall a \in \mathcal{B}_\mathcal{P}, (a, \omega_a) \in I, (a, \theta_a) \in J, \omega_a \subseteq \theta_a$. For a set T of parameterized two-valued interpretations, the least upper bound and greatest lower bound always exist and are respectively

$$\mathrm{lub}(T) = \{(a, \bigcup_{I \in T, (a, \omega_a) \in I} \omega_a) \mid a \in \mathcal{B}_\mathcal{P}\}$$

and

$$\mathrm{glb}(T) = \{(a, \bigcap_{I \in T, (a, \omega_a) \in I} \omega_a) \mid a \in \mathcal{B}_\mathcal{P}\}.$$

The top element $\top$ is

$$\{(a, W_\mathbf{X} \times W_\mathbf{Y}) \mid a \in \mathcal{B}_\mathcal{P}\}$$

and the bottom element $\bot$ is

$$\{(a, \varnothing) \mid a \in \mathcal{B}_\mathcal{P}\}.$$

Definition 37 (Parameterized three-valued interpretations - PCLP). *Given a ground probabilistic constraint logic program $\mathcal{P}$ with Herbrand base $\mathcal{B}_\mathcal{P}$, a parameterized three-valued interpretation $\mathcal{I}$ is a set of triples $(a, \omega_a, \omega_{\sim a})$ where $a \in \mathcal{B}_\mathcal{P}$, $\omega_a \in \Omega_\mathcal{P}$, and $\omega_{\sim a} \in \Omega_\mathcal{P}$, and such that, for each $a \in \mathcal{B}_\mathcal{P}$, there is one such triple. A parameterized three-valued interpretation $\mathcal{I}$ is consistent if $\forall(a, \omega_a, \omega_{\sim a}) \in \mathcal{I}, \omega_a \cap \omega_{\sim a} = \varnothing$.*

Parameterized three-valued interpretations form a complete lattice where the partial order is defined as $\mathcal{I} \leqslant \mathcal{J}$ if $\forall a \in \mathcal{B}_\mathcal{P}, (a, \omega_a, \omega_{\sim a}) \in \mathcal{I}, (a, \theta_a, \theta_{\sim a}) \in$

$\mathcal{J}$, $\omega_a \subseteq \theta_a$, and $\omega_{\sim a} \subseteq \theta_{\sim a}$. The least upper bound and greatest lower bound for a set T of parameterized three-valued interpretations always exist and are respectively

$$\mathrm{lub}(T) = \{(a, \bigcup_{\mathcal{I} \in T, (a, \omega_a, \omega_{\sim a}) \in \mathcal{I}} \omega_a, \bigcup_{\mathcal{I} \in T, (a, \omega_a, \omega_{\sim a}) \in \mathcal{I},} \omega_{\sim a}) \mid a \in \mathcal{B}_\mathcal{P}\}$$

and

$$\mathrm{glb}(T) = \{(a, \bigcap_{\mathcal{I} \in T, (a, \omega_a, \omega_{\sim a}) \in \mathcal{I}} \omega_a, \bigcap_{\mathcal{I} \in T, (a, \omega_a, \omega_{\sim a}) \in \mathcal{I}} \omega_{\sim a}) \mid a \in \mathcal{B}_\mathcal{P}\}.$$

The top element $\top$ is

$$\{(a, W_\mathbf{X} \times W_\mathbf{Y}, W_\mathbf{X} \times W_\mathbf{Y}) \mid a \in \mathcal{B}_\mathcal{P}\}$$

and the bottom element $\bot$ is

$$\{(a, \varnothing, \varnothing) \mid a \in \mathcal{B}_\mathcal{P}\}.$$

Definition 38 ($OpTrueP_\mathcal{I}^\mathcal{P}(Tr)$ and $OpFalseP_\mathcal{I}^\mathcal{P}(Fa)$ - PCLP). *For a ground probabilistic constraint logic program $\mathcal{P}$ with rules $\mathcal{R}$ and facts $\mathcal{F}$, a parameterized two-valued positive interpretation Tr with pairs (a, θ_a), a parameterized two-valued negative interpretation Fa with pairs $(a, \theta_{\sim a})$, and a parameterized three-valued interpretation $\mathcal{I}$ with triplets $(a, \omega_a, \omega_{\sim a})$, we define $OpTrueP_\mathcal{I}^\mathcal{P}(Tr) = \{(a, \gamma_a) \mid a \in \mathcal{B}_\mathcal{P}\}$ where*

$$\gamma_a = \begin{cases} W_\mathbf{X} \times \omega_{\{\{(a, \varnothing, 1)\}\}} & \text{if } a \in \mathcal{F} \\ \bigcup_{a \leftarrow b_1, \ldots, b_n, \sim c_1, \ldots, \sim c_m, \varphi_1, \ldots, \varphi_l \in \mathcal{R}} ((\theta_{b_1} \cup \omega_{b_1}) \cap \ldots \\ \quad \cap (\theta_{b_n} \cup \omega_{b_n}) \cap \omega_{\sim c_1} \cap \ldots \cap \omega_{\sim c_m} & \text{if } a \in \mathcal{B}_\mathcal{P} \backslash \mathcal{F} \\ \quad \cap CSS(\varphi_1) \times W_\mathbf{Y} \cap \ldots \cap CSS(\varphi_l) \times W_\mathbf{Y}) \end{cases}$$

and $OpFalseP_\mathcal{I}^\mathcal{P}(Fa) = \{(a, \gamma_{\sim a}) \mid a \in \mathcal{B}_\mathcal{P}\}$ where

$$\gamma_{\sim a} = \begin{cases} W_\mathbf{X} \times \omega_{\{\{(a, \varnothing, 0)\}\}} & \text{if } a \in \mathcal{F} \\ \bigcap_{a \leftarrow b_1, \ldots, b_n, \sim c_1, \ldots, \sim c_m, \varphi_1, \ldots, \varphi_l \in \mathcal{R}} ((\theta_{\sim b_1} \cap \omega_{\sim b_1}) \cup \ldots \\ \quad \cup (\theta_{\sim b_n} \cap \omega_{\sim b_n}) \cup \omega_{c_1} \cup \ldots \cup \omega_{c_m} & \text{if } a \in \mathcal{B}_\mathcal{P} \backslash \mathcal{F} \\ \quad \cup (W_\mathbf{X} \backslash CSS(\varphi_1)) \times W_\mathbf{Y} \cup \ldots \\ \quad \cup (W_\mathbf{X} \backslash CSS(\varphi_l)) \times W_\mathbf{Y}) \end{cases}$$

Proposition 8 (Monotonicity of $OpTrueP_\mathcal{I}^\mathcal{P}$ and $OpFalseP_\mathcal{I}^\mathcal{P}$ - PCLP). $OpTrueP_\mathcal{I}^\mathcal{P}$ and $OpFalseP_\mathcal{I}^\mathcal{P}$ are monotonic.

Proof. Here we only consider $OpTruePP_\mathcal{I}^\mathcal{P}$, since the proof for $OpFalsePP_\mathcal{I}^\mathcal{P}$ can be similarly constructed. Essentially, we have to prove that if $Tr_1 \leqslant Tr_2$ then $OpTruePP_\mathcal{I}^\mathcal{P}(Tr_1) \leqslant OpTruePP_\mathcal{I}^\mathcal{P}(Tr_2)$. By definition, $Tr_1 \leqslant Tr_2$ means that

$$\forall a \in \mathcal{B}_\mathcal{P}, (a, \omega_a) \in Tr_1, (a, \theta_a) \in Tr_2 : \omega_a \subseteq \theta_a.$$

Let (a, ω'_a) be the elements of $OpTruePP_\mathcal{I}^\mathcal{P}(Tr_1)$ and (a, θ'_a) the elements of $OpTruePP_\mathcal{I}^\mathcal{P}(Tr_2)$. To prove the monotonicity, we have to prove that $\omega'_a \subseteq \theta'_a$.
   If $a \in \mathcal{F}$, then $\omega'_a = \theta'_a = W_\mathbf{X} \times \omega_{\{\{(a,\varnothing,1)\}\}}$. If $a \in \mathcal{B}_\mathcal{P} \backslash \mathcal{F}$, then ω'_a and θ'_a have the same structure. Since $\forall b \in \mathcal{B}_\mathcal{P}, \omega_b \subseteq \theta_b$, then $\omega'_a \subseteq \theta'_a$.   □

The monotonicity property ensures that both $OpTruePP_\mathcal{I}^\mathcal{P}$ and $OpFalsePP_\mathcal{I}^\mathcal{P}$ have a least fixpoint and a greatest fixpoint. We now define an iterated fixpoint operator and prove its monotonicity.

Definition 39 (Iterated fixpoint for probabilistic constraint logic programs - PCLP). *For a ground probabilistic constraint logic program $\mathcal{P}$ and a parameterized three-valued interpretation $\mathcal{I}$, we define $IFPP^\mathcal{P}(\mathcal{I})$ as*

$$IFPP^\mathcal{P}(\mathcal{I}) = \{(a, \omega_a, \omega_{\sim a}) \mid (a, \omega_a) \in \mathrm{lfp}(OpTruePP_\mathcal{I}^\mathcal{P}),$$
$$(a, \omega_{\sim a}) \in \mathrm{gfp}(OpFalsePP_\mathcal{I}^\mathcal{P})\}.$$

Proposition 9 (Monotonicity of $IFPP^\mathcal{P}$ - PCLP). *$IFPP^\mathcal{P}$ is monotonic.*

Proof. As before, we have to prove that, if $\mathcal{I}_1 \leqslant \mathcal{I}_2$, then $IFPP^\mathcal{P}(\mathcal{I}_1) \leqslant IFPP^\mathcal{P}(\mathcal{I}_2)$. By definition, $\mathcal{I}_1 \leqslant \mathcal{I}_2$ means that

$$\forall a \in \mathcal{B}_\mathcal{P}, (a, \omega_a, \omega_{\sim a}) \in \mathcal{I}_1, (a, \theta_a, \theta_{\sim a}) \in \mathcal{I}_2 : \omega_a \subseteq \theta_a, \omega_{\sim a} \subseteq \theta_{\sim a}.$$

Let $(a, \omega'_a, \omega'_{\sim a})$ be the elements of $IFPP^\mathcal{P}(\mathcal{I}_1)$ and $(a, \theta'_a, \theta'_{\sim a})$ the elements of $IFPP^\mathcal{P}(\mathcal{I}_2)$. We have to prove that $\omega'_a \subseteq \theta'_a$ and $\omega'_{\sim a} \subseteq \theta'_{\sim a}$. This is a direct consequence of the monotonicity of $OpTruePP_\mathcal{I}^\mathcal{P}$ and $OpFalsePP_\mathcal{I}^\mathcal{P}$ proved in Proposition 8 and of their monotonicity in $\mathcal{I}$ that can be proved as in Proposition 8.   □

   $IFPP^\mathcal{P}$ is monotonic and so it has a least fixpoint. We identify $\mathrm{lfp}(IFPP^\mathcal{P})$ with $WFMP(\mathcal{P})$. We call *depth* of $\mathcal{P}$ the smallest ordinal δ such that $IFPP^\mathcal{P} \uparrow \delta = WFMP(\mathcal{P})$. Now we prove that $OpTruePP_\mathcal{I}^\mathcal{P}$ and $OpFalsePP_\mathcal{I}^\mathcal{P}$ are sound.

Lemma 11 (Soundness of $OpTruePP_\mathcal{I}^\mathcal{P}$ - PCLP). *For a ground probabilistic constraint logic program $\mathcal{P}$ with probabilistic facts $\mathcal{F}$, rules $\mathcal{R}$, and a parameterized three-valued interpretation $\mathcal{I}$, denote with θ_a^α the set associated to* atom a in $OpTrueP_{\mathcal{I}}^{\mathcal{P}} \uparrow \alpha$. *For every atom a, world w, and iteration α:*

$$w \in \theta_a^\alpha \to WFM(w \mid \mathcal{I}) \vDash a$$

where $w \mid \mathcal{I}$ is obtained by adding to P_w the atoms a for which $(a, \omega_a, \omega_{\sim a}) \in \mathcal{I}$ and $w \in \omega_a$, and by removing all the rules with a in the head for which $(a, \omega_a, \omega_{\sim a}) \in \mathcal{I}$ and $w \in \omega_{\sim a}$.

Proof. We prove the lemma by transfinite induction: we assume that the thesis is true for all ordinals $\beta < \alpha$ and we prove it for α. There are two cases to cover: α successor ordinal and α limit ordinal. Consider α a successor ordinal. If $a \in \mathcal{F}$, $w \in \theta_a^\alpha$ means that the random variable y_a corresponding to a is set to 1 so a is a fact in P_w and $WFM(w \mid \mathcal{I}) \vDash a$.

If $a \notin \mathcal{F}$, consider $w \in \theta_a^\alpha$ where

$$\theta_a^\alpha = \bigcup_{a \leftarrow b_1,\dots,b_n,\sim c_1,\dots,\sim c_m,\varphi_1,\dots,\varphi_l \in \mathcal{R}} ((\theta_{b_1}^{\alpha-1} \cup \omega_{b_1}) \cap \dots$$
$$\cap (\theta_{b_n}^{\alpha-1} \cup \omega_{b_n}) \cap \omega_{\sim c_1} \cap \dots \cap \omega_{\sim c_m}$$
$$\cap CSS(\varphi_1) \times W_{\mathbf{Y}} \cap \dots \cap CSS(\varphi_l) \times W_{\mathbf{Y}}).$$

This means that there is a rule $a \leftarrow b_1, \dots, b_n, \sim c_1, \dots, \sim c_m, \varphi_1, \dots, \varphi_l \in \mathcal{R}$ such that $w \in \theta_{b_i}^{\alpha-1} \cup \omega_{b_i}$ for $i = 1, \dots, n$, $w \in \omega_{\sim c_j}$ for $j = 1 \dots, m$ and $w \vDash \varphi_k$ for $k = 1, \dots, l$. By the inductive assumption and because of how $w \mid \mathcal{I}$ is built, $WFM(w \mid \mathcal{I}) \vDash b_i$, $WFM(w \mid \mathcal{I}) \vDash \sim c_j$ and $w \vDash \varphi_k$ so $WFM(w \mid \mathcal{I}) \vDash a$.

Consider now α a limit ordinal. Then

$$\theta_a^\alpha = \mathrm{lub}(\{\theta_a^\beta \mid \beta < \alpha\}) = \bigcup_{\beta < \alpha} \theta_a^\beta.$$

If $w \in \theta_a^\alpha$, there must exist a $\beta < \alpha$ such that $w \in \theta_a^\beta$. By the inductive assumption the hypothesis holds. $\qquad\square$

Lemma 12 (Soundness of $OpFalseP_{\mathcal{I}}^{\mathcal{P}}$ - PCLP). *For a ground probabilistic constraint logic program $\mathcal{P}$ with probabilistic facts $\mathcal{F}$, rules $\mathcal{R}$, and a parameterized three-valued interpretation $\mathcal{I}$, denote with $\theta_{\sim a}^\alpha$ the set associated with atom a in $OpFalseP_{\mathcal{I}}^{\mathcal{P}} \downarrow \alpha$. For every atom a, world w and iteration α, the following holds:*

$$w \in \theta_{\sim a}^\alpha \to WFM(w \mid \mathcal{I}) \vDash \sim a$$

where $w \mid \mathcal{I}$ is built as in Lemma 11.

Proof. As before, we prove the lemma by transfinite induction: we assume that the thesis is true for all ordinals $\beta < \alpha$ and we prove it for α. Again, we need to cover two cases: α successor ordinal and α limit ordinal. Consider α a successor ordinal. If $a \in \mathcal{F}$ $w \in \theta^\alpha_{\sim a}$ means that the random variable y_a corresponding to a is set to 0 so a is a not a fact in P_w. Since probabilistic facts do not appear in the head of any rule, then $WFM(w \mid \mathcal{I}) \models \sim a$.

If $a \notin \mathcal{F}$, consider $w \in \theta^\alpha_{\sim a}$ where

$$\theta^\alpha_{\sim a} = \bigcap_{a \leftarrow b_1, \ldots, b_n, \sim c_1, \ldots, \sim c_m, \varphi_1, \ldots, \varphi_l \in \mathcal{R}} ((\theta^{\alpha-1}_{\sim b_1} \cap \omega_{\sim b_1}) \cup \ldots$$

$$\cup (\theta^{\alpha-1}_{\sim b_n} \cap \omega_{\sim b_n}) \cup \omega_{c_1} \cup \ldots \cup \omega_{c_m}$$

$$\cup (W_{\mathbf{X}} \backslash CSS(\varphi_1)) \times W_{\mathbf{Y}} \cup \ldots \cup (W_{\mathbf{X}} \backslash CSS(\varphi_l)) \times W_{\mathbf{Y}}).$$

This means that, for each $a \leftarrow b_1, \ldots, b_n, \sim c_1, \ldots, \sim c_m, \varphi_1, \ldots, \varphi_l \in \mathcal{R}$ there exists an index i such that $w \in \theta^{\alpha-1}_{\sim b_i} \cap \omega_{\sim b_i}$, or there exists an index j such that $w \in \omega_{c_j}$, or there exists an index k such that $w \not\models \varphi_k$. By the inductive assumption and because of how $w \mid \mathcal{I}$ is built, either $WFM(w \mid \mathcal{I}) \models \sim b_i$, $WFM(w \mid \mathcal{I}) \models c_j$, or $w \not\models \varphi_k$ hold, so $WFM(w \mid \mathcal{I}) \models \sim a$.

Consider now α a limit ordinal. Then,

$$\theta^\alpha_{\sim a} = \mathrm{glb}(\{\theta^\beta_{\sim a} \mid \beta < \alpha\}) = \bigcap_{\beta < \alpha} \theta^\beta_{\sim a}.$$

If $w \in \theta^\alpha_{\sim a}$, for all $\beta < \alpha$ we have that $w \in \theta^\beta_{\sim a}$. By the inductive assumption, the hypothesis hold. □

We now prove the soundness and completeness of the operator $IFPP^\mathcal{P}$.

Lemma 13 (Soundness of $IFPP^\mathcal{P}$ - PCLP). *For a ground probabilistic logic program $\mathcal{P}$ with probabilistic facts $\mathcal{F}$ and rules $\mathcal{R}$, denote with ω^α_a and $\omega^\alpha_{\sim a}$ the formulas associated with atom a in $IFPP^\mathcal{P}$. For every atom a, world w and iteration α, the following holds:*

$$w \in \omega^\alpha_a \rightarrow WFM(w) \models a. \tag{5.1}$$

$$w \in \omega^\alpha_{\sim a} \rightarrow WFM(w) \models \sim a. \tag{5.2}$$

Proof. Let us prove it by transfinite induction. Let us consider a successor ordinal α and let us assume

$$WFM(P_w | IFPP^\mathcal{P} \uparrow \alpha - 1) = WFM(w) \tag{5.3}$$

and that

$$w \in \omega_a^{\alpha-1} \rightarrow WFM(w) \models a. \tag{5.4}$$

$$w \in \omega_{\sim a}^{\alpha-1} \rightarrow WFM(w) \models \sim a. \tag{5.5}$$

From the soundness of $OpTruePP^{\mathcal{P}}_{IFPP^{\mathcal{P}}\uparrow(\alpha-1)}$ and $OpFalsePP^{\mathcal{P}}_{IFPP^{\mathcal{P}}\uparrow(\alpha-1)}$ we have that

$$w \in \theta_a^{\beta} \rightarrow WFM(w_\sigma|IFPP^{\mathcal{P}} \uparrow (\alpha - 1)) \models a$$
$$w \in \theta_{\sim a}^{\beta} \rightarrow WFM(w_\sigma|IFPP^{\mathcal{P}} \uparrow (\alpha - 1)) \models \sim a$$

where θ_a^{β} is the formula associated to a in $OpTruePP^{\mathcal{P}}_{IFPP^{\mathcal{P}}\uparrow(\alpha-1)} \uparrow \beta$ and $\theta_{\sim a}^{\beta}$ is the formula associated to a in $OpFalsePP^{\mathcal{P}}_{IFPP^{\mathcal{P}}\uparrow(\alpha-1)} \downarrow \beta$. Since this is true for all β, it is also true for the γ and δ such that

$$OpTruePP^{\mathcal{P}}_{IFPP^{\mathcal{P}}\uparrow\alpha-1} \uparrow \gamma = \mathrm{lfp}(OpTruePP^{\mathcal{P}}_{IFPP^{\mathcal{P}}\uparrow\alpha-1})$$
$$OpFalsePP^{\mathcal{P}}_{IFPP^{\mathcal{P}}\uparrow\alpha-1} \downarrow \delta = \mathrm{gfp}(OpFalsePP^{\mathcal{P}}_{IFPP^{\mathcal{P}}\uparrow\alpha-1})$$

so

$$w \in \omega_a^{\alpha} \rightarrow WFM(w|IFPP^{\mathcal{P}} \uparrow (\alpha - 1)) \models a$$
$$w \in \omega_{\sim a}^{\alpha} \rightarrow WFM(w|IFPP^{\mathcal{P}} \uparrow (\alpha - 1)) \models \sim a$$

Because of Equation (5.3), then

$$w \in \omega_a^{\alpha} \rightarrow WFM(w) \models a \tag{5.6}$$

$$w \in \omega_{\sim a}^{\alpha} \rightarrow WFM(w) \models \sim a \tag{5.7}$$

Now let us prove that

$$WFM(\mathcal{P}_w|IFPP^{\mathcal{P}} \uparrow \alpha) = WFM(w) \tag{5.8}$$

Let $\mathcal{I}_\alpha = \langle I_T, I_F \rangle$ be a three-valued interpretation defined as $I_T = \{a|w \in \omega_a^{\alpha}\}$ and $I_F = \{a|w \in \omega_{\sim a}^{\alpha}\}$. Then, for Equation (5.6), $\forall a \in I_T : WFM(w) \models a$ and, for Equation 5.7, $\forall a \in I_F : WFM(w) \models \sim a$. So $\mathcal{I}_\alpha \leqslant WFM(w)$. Since $P_w|IFPP^{\mathcal{P}} \uparrow \alpha = P_w||\mathcal{I}_\alpha$, by Lemma 6

$$WFM(w) = WFM(P_w||\mathcal{I}_\alpha) = WFM(P_w|IFPP^{\mathcal{P}} \uparrow \alpha).$$

Let us now consider a limit ordinal α and let us assume that

$$w \in \omega_a^{\beta} \rightarrow WFM(w) \models a \tag{5.9}$$

$$w \in \omega_{\sim a}^{\beta} \rightarrow WFM(w) \models \sim a \tag{5.10}$$

for all $\beta < \alpha$ Then $\omega_a^\alpha = \bigcup_{\beta < \alpha} \omega_a^\beta$ and $\omega_{\sim a}^\alpha = \bigcup_{\beta < \alpha} \omega_{\sim a}^\beta$ so $w \in \omega_a^\alpha \to \exists \beta : w \in \omega_a^\beta$. For Equation (5.9), then $WFM(w) \models a$. Moreover $w \in \omega_{\sim a}^\alpha \to \exists \beta : w \in \omega_a^\beta$. For Equation (5.10), then $WFM(w) \models \sim a$. □

Lemma 14 (Completeness of $IFPP^\mathcal{P}$ - PCLP). *For a ground probabilistic constraint logic program $\mathcal{P}$ with probabilistic facts $\mathcal{F}$ and rules $\mathcal{R}$, let ω_a^α and $\omega_{\sim a}^\alpha$ be the sets associated with atom a in $IFPP^\mathcal{P} \uparrow \alpha$. For every atom a, world w and iteration α, we have:*

$$a \in IFP^{P_w} \uparrow \alpha \to w \in \omega_a^\alpha.$$
$$\sim a \in IFP^{P_w} \uparrow \alpha \to w \in \omega_{\sim a}^\alpha.$$

Proof. We prove it by double transfinite induction. If α is a successor ordinal, assume that

$$a \in IFP^{P_w} \uparrow (\alpha - 1) \to w \in \omega_a^{\alpha - 1}$$
$$\sim a \in IFP^{P_w} \uparrow (\alpha - 1) \to w \in \omega_{\sim a}^{\alpha - 1}$$

Let us perform transfinite induction on the iterations of $OpTrue_{IFP^{P_w} \uparrow (\alpha - 1)}^{P_w}$ and $OpFalse_{IFP^{P_w} \uparrow (\alpha - 1)}^{P_w}$. Consider a successor ordinal δ and assume that

$$a \in OpTrue_{IFP^{P_w} \uparrow (\alpha - 1)}^{P_w} \uparrow (\delta - 1) \to w \in \gamma_a^{\delta - 1}.$$
$$a \in OpFalse_{IFP^{P_w} \uparrow (\alpha - 1)}^{P_w} \downarrow (\delta - 1) \to w \in \theta_{\sim a}^{\delta - 1}.$$

where $(a, \gamma_a^{\delta - 1})$ are the elements of $OpTrue_{IFPP^\mathcal{P} \uparrow \alpha - 1}^\mathcal{P} \uparrow (\delta - 1)$ and $(a, \theta_{\sim a}^{\delta - 1})$ are the elements of $OpFalse_{IFPP^\mathcal{P} \uparrow \alpha - 1}^\mathcal{P} \downarrow (\delta - 1)$. We now prove that

$$a \in OpTrue_{IFP^{P_w} \uparrow (\alpha - 1)}^{P_w} \uparrow \delta \to w \in \gamma_a^\delta. \tag{5.11}$$
$$a \in OpFalse_{IFP^{P_w} \uparrow (\alpha - 1)}^{P_w} \downarrow \delta \to w \in \theta_{\sim a}^\delta. \tag{5.12}$$

Consider an atom a. If $a \in \mathcal{F}$, the previous statement can be easily proved. Otherwise, $a \in OpTrue_{IFP^{P_w} \uparrow (\alpha - 1)}^{P_w} \uparrow \delta$ means that there is a rule $a \leftarrow b_1, \ldots, b_n, \sim c_1, \ldots, c_m, \varphi_1, \ldots, \varphi_l$ in $\mathcal{R}$ such that for all $i = 1, \ldots, n$,

$$b_i \in OpTrue_{IFP^{P_w} \uparrow (\alpha - 1)}^{P_w} \uparrow (\delta - 1) \vee b_i \in IFP^{P_w} \uparrow (\alpha - 1),$$

for all $j = 1, \ldots, m$, $\sim c_j \in IFP^{P_w} \uparrow (\alpha - 1)$, and for all $k = 1, \ldots, l$, $w \models \varphi_k$. For the inductive hypothesis, $\forall i : w \in \gamma_{b_i}^{\delta-1} \vee w \in \omega_{b_i}^{\alpha-1}$ and $\forall j : w \in \omega_{\sim c_j}^{\alpha-1}$, so $w \in \gamma_a^{\delta}$. The proof is similar for $a \in OpFalse_{IFP^{P_w} \uparrow (\alpha-1)}^{w} \downarrow \delta$.

Consider now δ a limit ordinal, so $\gamma_a^{\delta} = \bigcup_{\mu<\delta} \gamma_a^{\mu}$, and $\theta_{\sim a}^{\delta} = \bigcap_{\mu<\delta} \theta_{\sim a}^{\mu}$. If $a \in OpTrue_{IFP^{P_w} \uparrow (\alpha-1)}^{P_w} \uparrow \delta$, then there exists a $\mu < \delta$ such that

$$a \in OpTrue_{IFP^{P_w} \uparrow (\alpha-1)}^{P_w} \uparrow \mu.$$

For the inductive hypothesis, $w \in \gamma_a^{\mu}$ and so $w \in \gamma_a^{\delta}$.
If $a \in OpFalse_{IFP^{P_w} \uparrow (\alpha-1)}^{P_w} \downarrow \delta$, then, for all $\mu < \delta$,

$$a \in OpFalse_{IFP^{P_w} \uparrow (\alpha-1)}^{P_w} \downarrow \mu.$$

For the inductive hypothesis, $w \in \theta_a^{\mu}$ and so $w \in \theta_a^{\delta}$.

Since $IFP^{P_w} \uparrow \alpha$ is obtained from the fixpoints of $OpTrue_{IFP^{P_w} \uparrow (\alpha-1)}^{P_w}$ and $OpFalse_{IFP^{P_w} \uparrow (\alpha-1)}^{P_w}$, and equations (5.11) and (5.12) hold for all δ, they also hold at the fixpoints and the thesis is proved.

Consider now α a limit ordinal. Then, $\omega_a^{\alpha} = \bigcup_{\beta<\alpha} \omega_a^{\beta}$ and $\omega_{\sim a}^{\alpha} = \bigcup_{\beta<\alpha} \omega_{\sim a}^{\beta}$.

If $a \in IFP^{P_w} \uparrow \alpha$, there exists a $\beta < \alpha$ such that $a \in IFP^{P_w} \uparrow \beta$. For the inductive hypothesis $w \in \omega_a^{\beta}$, so $w \in \omega_a^{\alpha}$. The proof is similar for $\sim a$. □

Now we can prove that $IFPP^{\mathcal{P}}$ is sound and complete.

Theorem 15 (Soundness and completeness of $IFPP^{\mathcal{P}}$ - PCLP). *For a sound ground probabilistic constraint logic program $\mathcal{P}$, let ω_a^{α} and $\omega_{\sim a}^{\alpha}$ be the sets associated with atom a in $IFPP^{\mathcal{P}} \uparrow \alpha$. For every atom a and world w there is an iteration α_0 such that for all $\alpha > \alpha_0$ we have:*

$$w \in \omega_a^{\alpha} \leftrightarrow WFM(w) \models a. \tag{5.13}$$
$$w \in \omega_{\sim a}^{\alpha} \leftrightarrow WFM(w) \models \sim a. \tag{5.14}$$

Proof. The $\rightarrow$ direction of equations (5.13) and (5.14) is proven in Lemma 13. In the other direction, $WFM(w) \models a$ implies that there exists an α_0 such that $\forall \alpha : \alpha \geqslant \alpha_0$, $IFP^w \uparrow \alpha \models a$. For Lemma 14, $w \in \omega_a^{\alpha}$. Similarly, $WFM(w) \models \sim a$ implies that there exists an α_0 such that $\forall \alpha : \alpha \geqslant \alpha_0 \rightarrow IFP^w \uparrow \alpha \models \sim a$. As before, for Lemma 14, $w \in \omega_{\sim a}^{\alpha}$. □

Finally, we prove that every query for every sound program is well-defined.

Theorem 16 (Well-definedness of the distribution semantics - PCLP).   *For a sound ground probabilistic constraint logic program $\mathcal{P}$, for all ground atoms a, $\mu_\mathcal{P}(\{w \mid w \in W_\mathcal{P},\ WFM(w) \models a\})$ is well-defined.*

Proof. Let ω_a^δ and $\omega_{\sim a}^\delta$ be the sets associated with atom a in $IFPP^\mathcal{P} \uparrow \delta$, where δ denotes the depth of the program. Since $IFPP^\mathcal{P}$ is sound and complete, $\{w \mid w \in W_\mathcal{P},\ WFM(w) \models a\} = \omega_a^\delta$.

Each iteration of $OpTrueP^\mathcal{P}_{IFPP^\mathcal{P}\uparrow\beta}$ and $OpFalseP^\mathcal{P}_{IFPP^\mathcal{P}\uparrow\beta}$ for all β generates sets belonging to $\Omega_\mathcal{P}$, since the set of rules is countable. So $\mu_\mathcal{P}(\{w \mid w \in W_\mathcal{P},\ WFM(w) \models a\})$ is well-defined. $\square$

Moreover, if the program is sound, for all atoms a, $\omega_a^\delta = (\omega_{\sim a}^\delta)^c$ holds, where δ is the depth of the program and the superscript c denotes the complement. Otherwise, there would exist a world w such that $w \notin \omega_a^\delta$ and $w \notin \omega_{\sim a}^\delta$. But w has a two-valued well-founded model, so either $WFM(w) \models a$ or $WFM(w) \models \sim a$. In the first case $w \in \omega_a^\delta$ and in the latter $w \in \omega_{\sim a}^\delta$, against the hypothesis.

6

Probabilistic Answer Set Programming

In Section 2.2 we considered only sound programs, those for which every world has a two-valued WFM. In this way, we avoid non-monotonic aspects of the program and we deal with uncertainty only by means of probability theory.

When a program is not sound in fact, assigning a semantics to probabilistic logic programs is not obvious, as the next section shows.

6.1 A Semantics for Unsound Programs

We start by giving an example of an unsound program.

Example 69 (Insomnia [Cozman and Mauá, 2017]). *Consider the program*
$sleep \leftarrow \sim work, \sim insomnia.$
$work \leftarrow \sim sleep.$
$\alpha :: insomnia.$
This program has two worlds, w_1 containing insomnia and w_2 not containing it. The first has the single stable model (see Section 1.4.3) and total WFM (see Section 1.4.2)

$$I_1 = \{insomnia, \sim sleep, work\}$$

The latter has two stable models

$$I_2 = \{\sim insomnia, \sim sleep, work\}$$
$$I_3 = \{\sim insomnia, sleep, \sim work\}$$

and a WFM $\mathcal{I}_2$ where insomnia is false and the other two atoms are undefined.

If we ask for the probability of sleep, the first world, w_1, with probability α, surely doesn't contribute. We are not sure instead what to do with the second, as sleep is included in only one of the two stable models and it is undefined in the WFM.

165

To handle programs like the above, Hadjichristodoulou and Warren [2012] proposed the WFS for probabilistic logic programs where a program defines a probability distribution over WFMs rather than two-valued models. This induces a probability distribution over random variables associated with atoms that are, however, three-valued instead of Boolean.

An alternative approach, the *credal semantics* [Lukasiewicz, 2005, 2007][1], sees such programs as defining a set of probability measures over the interpretations. The name derives from the fact that sets of probability distributions are often called *credal sets*.

The semantics considers programs syntactically equal to ProbLog (i.e., non-probabilistic rules and probabilistic facts) and generates worlds as in ProbLog. The semantics requires that each world of the program has at least one stable models. Such programs are called *consistent*.

A program then defines a set of probability distributions over the set of all possible two-valued interpretations of the program. Each distribution P in the set is called a *probability model* and must satisfy two conditions:

1. every interpretation I for which $P(I) > 0$ must be a stable model of the world w_σ that agrees with I on the truth value of the probabilistic facts;
2. the sum of the probabilities of the stable models of w_σ must be equal to $P(\sigma)$.

A set of distributions is obtained because we do not fix how the probability mass $P(\sigma)$ of a world w_σ is distributed over its stable models when there is more than one. We indicate with $\mathbf{P}$ the set of probability models and call it the *credal semantics* of the program. Given a probability model, we can compute the probability of a query q as for the DS, by summing $P(I)$ for all the interpretations I where q is true.

In this case, given a query q, we are interested in the *lower and upper probabilities* of q defined as

$$\underline{P}(q) = \inf_{P \in \mathbf{P}} P(q)$$
$$\overline{P}(q) = \sup_{P \in \mathbf{P}} P(q)$$

---

[1] It was called *answer set semantics* in [Lukasiewicz, 2005, 2007], here we follow the terminology of [Cozman and Mauá, 2017].

If we are also given evidence e, we can define *lower and upper conditional probabilities* as

$$\underline{P}(q|e) = \inf_{P \in \mathbf{P}, P(e)>0} P(q \mid e)$$

$$\overline{P}(q|e) = \sup_{P \in \mathbf{P}, P(e)>0} P(q \mid e)$$

and leave them undefined when $P(e) = 0$ for all $P \in \mathbf{P}$.

Example 70 (Insomnia – continued – [Cozman and Mauá, 2017]). *Consider again the program of Example 69. A probability model that assigns the following probabilities to the models of the program*

$$P(I_1) = \alpha$$
$$P(I_2) = \gamma(1 - \alpha)$$
$$P(I_3) = (1 - \gamma)(1 - \alpha)$$

for $\gamma \in [0, 1]$, satisfies the two conditions of the semantics, and thus belongs to $\mathbf{P}$. *The elements of* $\mathbf{P}$ *are obtained by varying γ.*

Considering the query sleep, we can easily see that $\underline{P}(sleep = true) = 0$ and $\overline{P}(sleep = true) = 1 - \alpha$.

With the semantics of [Hadjichristodoulou and Warren, 2012] instead, we have

$$P(I_1) = \alpha$$
$$P(\mathcal{I}_2) = 1 - \alpha$$

so

$$P(sleep = true) = 0$$
$$P(sleep = false) = \alpha$$
$$P(sleep = undefined) = 1 - \alpha.$$

Example 71 (Barber paradox – [Cozman and Mauá, 2017]). *The barber paradox was introduced by Russell [1967]. If the village barber shaves all, and only, those in the village who don't shave themselves, does the barber shave himself?*

A probabilistic version of this paradox can be encoded with the program
    $shaves(X, Y) \leftarrow barber(X), villager(Y), {\sim}shaves(Y, Y).$
    $villager(a).$
    $barber(b).$
    $0.5 :: villager(b).$
and the query $shaves(b, b)$.

The program has two worlds, w_1 and w_2, the first not containing the fact $villager(b)$ and the latter containing it. The first world has a single stable model $I_1 = \{villager(a), barber(b), shaves(b, a)\}$ that is also the total WFM. In the latter world, the rule has an instance that can be simplified to $shaves(b, b) \leftarrow \sim shaves(b, b)$. Since it contains a loop through an odd number of negations, the world has no stable model and the three-valued WFM:

$$\mathcal{I}_2 = \{villager(a), villager(b), barber(b),$$
$$shaves(b, a), \sim shaves(a, a), \sim shaves(a, b)\}.$$

So the program is not consistent and the credal semantics is not defined for it, while the semantics of [Hadjichristodoulou and Warren, 2012] is still defined and would yield

$$P(shaves(b, b) = false) = 0.5$$
$$P(shaves(b, b) = undefined) = 0.5$$

The WFS for probabilistic logic programs assigns a semantics to more programs. However, it introduces the truth value *undefined* that expresses uncertainty and, since probability is used as well to deal with uncertainty, some confusion may arise. For example, one may ask what is the value of $(q = true | e = undefined)$. If $e = undefined$ means that we don't know anything about e, then $P(q = true | e = undefined)$ should be equal to $P(q = true)$ but this is not true in general. The credal semantics avoids these problems by considering only two truth values.

Cozman and Mauá [2017] show that the set **P** is the set of all probability measures that dominate an infinitely monotone Choquet capacity.

An *infinitely monotone Choquet capacity* is a function $\underline{P}$ from an algebra Ω on a set W to the real interval $[0, 1]$ such that

1. $\underline{P}(W) = 1 - \underline{P}(\varnothing) = 1$, and
2. for any $\omega_1, \ldots, \omega_n \subseteq \Omega$,

$$\underline{P}(\cup_i \omega_i) \geqslant \sum_{J \subseteq \{1, \ldots, n\}} (-1)^{|J|+1} \underline{P}(\cap_{j \in J} \omega_j) \qquad (6.1)$$

Infinitely monotone Choquet capacities are a generalization of finitely additive probability measures: the latter are special cases of the first where Equation (6.1) holds with equality. In fact, the right member of Equation (6.1) is an application of the inclusion–exclusion principle that gives the probability of the union of non-disjoint sets. Infinitely monotone Choquet capacities also appear as belief functions of Dempster–Shafer theory [Shafer, 1976].

Given an infinitely monotone Choquet capacity $\underline{P}$, we can construct the set of measures $D(\underline{P})$ that dominate $\underline{P}$ as

$$D(\underline{P}) = \{P | \forall \omega \in \Omega : P(\omega) \geqslant \underline{P}(\omega)\}$$

We say that $\underline{P}$ *generates* the credal set $D(\underline{P})$ and we call $D(\underline{P})$ an *infinitely monoton credal set*. It is possible to show that the lower probability of $D(\underline{P})$ is exactly the generating infinitely monotone Choquet capacity: $\underline{P}(\omega) = \inf_{P \in D(\underline{P})} P(\omega)$.

Infinitely monotone credal sets are closed and convex. Convexity here means that if P_1 and P_2 are in the credal set, then $\alpha P_1 + (1 - \alpha) P_2$ is also in the credal set for $\alpha \in [0, 1]$. Given a consistent program, its credal semantics is thus a closed and convex set of probability measures.

Moreover, given a query q, we have

$$\underline{P}(q) = \sum_{w \in W, AS(w) \subseteq J_q} P(\sigma) \qquad \overline{P}(q) = \sum_{w \in W, AS(w) \cap J_q \neq \emptyset} P(\sigma)$$

where J_q is the set of interpretations where q is true and $AS(w)$ is the set of stable models of world w.

The lower and upper conditional probabilities of a query q are given by [Augustin et al., 2014]:

$$\underline{P}(q \mid e) = \frac{\underline{P}(q, e)}{\underline{P}(q, e) + \overline{P}(\sim q, e)} \tag{6.2}$$

If $\underline{P}(q, e) + \overline{P}(\sim q, e) = 0$ and $\overline{P}(q, e) > 0$, $\underline{P}(q \mid e) = 1$. If both $\overline{P}(q, e)$ and $\overline{P}(\sim q, e)$ are 0, this value is undefined.

$$\overline{P}(q \mid e) = \frac{\overline{P}(q, e)}{\overline{P}(q, e) + \underline{P}(\sim q, e)} \tag{6.3}$$

If $\overline{P}(q, e) + \underline{P}(\sim q, e) = 0$ and $\overline{P}(\sim q, e) > 0$, $\overline{P}(q \mid e) = 0$. As before, if both $\overline{P}(q, e)$ and $\overline{P}(\sim q, e)$ are 0, this value is undefined.

Note that these formulas are the same as equations (4.6) and (4.7) of Section 4.5.1.

A world w contributes to the upper probability of a conjunction of ground literals q if q is true in at least one of its stable models and to the lower probability if q is true in all its stable models. Algorithm 3 shows this computation.

Algorithm 3 Function CREDAL: Computation of the probability of a query.

1: **function** CREDAL($\mathcal{P}, q$)
2:     $\underline{P}(q) \leftarrow 0, \overline{P}(q) \leftarrow 0$
3:     **for all** worlds w of $\mathcal{P}$ **do**
4:         **if** $\forall A \in AS(w), A \models q$ **then**
5:             $\underline{P}(q) \leftarrow \underline{P}(q) + P(w)$
6:         **end if**
7:         **if** $\exists A \in AS(w), A \models q$ **then**
8:             $\overline{P}(q) \leftarrow \overline{P}(q) + P(w)$
9:         **end if**
10:     **end for**
11:     **return** $[\underline{P}(q), \overline{P}(q)]$
12: **end function**

For computing the bounds of the conditional probability of conjunction of ground literals q given the conjunction of ground literals e, we must keep four values, as in Algorithm 4.

In the case in which the probabilistic program is sound, i.e., if every world has a total WFM, then, by Theorem 2, every world has a single stable model and the credal set contains a single probability distribution. In this case

$$\overline{P}(q) = \underline{P}(q) = P(q)$$

and

$$\overline{P}(q|e) = \underline{P}(q|e) = P(q|e)$$

and the probability is the same as that assigned by the distribution semantics, so the credal and the distribution semantics coincide.

6.2 Features of Answer Set Programming

Answer Set Programming allows syntactic features beyond normal logic programs (see Section 1.3). However, the definition of the semantics remains the same as that of Section 1.4.3.

An *ASP program* is a set of *rules* of the form

$$a_1 \vee \ldots \vee a_n \leftarrow b_1, \ldots, b_m.$$

where each a_i is an atom and each b_j is a literal. $a_1 \vee \ldots \vee a_n$ is called the *head* of the rule and $b_1, \ldots, b_m$ is called the *body* . If $n > 1$ the rule is called *disjunctive*. If $n = 1$ is called *normal* and if $n = 0$ is called a *constraint*.

Algorithm 4 Function CREDALCOND: Computation of the probability of a query given evidence.

1: **function** CREDALCOND($\mathcal{P}, q, e$)
2:    $up_{qe} \leftarrow 0,\ lp_{qe} \leftarrow 0,\ up_{nqe} \leftarrow 0,\ lp_{nqe} \leftarrow 0$
3:    **for all** worlds w of $\mathcal{P}$ **do**
4:       **if** $\forall A \in AS(w), A \models q, e$ **then**
5:          $lp_{qe} \leftarrow lp_{qe} + P(w)$
6:       **end if**
7:       **if** $\exists A \in AS(w), A \models q, e$ **then**
8:          $up_{qe} \leftarrow up_{qe} + P(w)$
9:       **end if**
10:       **if** $\forall A \in AS(w), A \models \sim q, e$ **then**
11:          $lp_{nqe} \leftarrow lp_{nqe} + P(w)$
12:       **end if**
13:       **if** $\exists A \in AS(w), A \models \sim q, e$ **then**
14:          $up_{nqe} \leftarrow up_{nqe} + P(w)$
15:       **end if**
16:    **end for**
17:    **if** $up_{qe} + up_{nqe} = 0$ **then**
18:       **return** failure
19:    **else**
20:       **if** $up_{qe} + lp_{nqe} = 0$ and $up_{nqe} > 0$ **then**
21:          **return** $[0, 0]$
22:       **else**
23:          **if** $lp_{qe} + up_{nqe} = 0$ and $up_{qe} > 0$ **then**
24:             **return** $[1, 1]$
25:          **else**
26:             **return** $\left[\frac{lp_{qe}}{lp_{qe} + up_{nqe}}, \frac{up_{qe}}{up_{qe} + lp_{nqe}}\right]$
27:          **end if**
28:       **end if**
29:    **end if**
30: **end function**

A *positive program* is a program that does not contain negative literals (but that can contain disjunctive rules).

A ground rule is *satisfied* in a two-valued interpretation if some literals in the body are false or if all the literals in the body are true and some literals in the head are true in the interpretation. If the rule is a constraint it is thus satisfied only if some literals in the body are false.

A *model* of a program is a two-valued interpretation that satisfies all grounding of all the rules of the program. A model I is minimal if there is no other model J such that $J \subseteq I$.

Using the notion of reduct given in Definition 5, an *answer set* of a program P is an interpretation I that is a minimal model of the reduct P^I of P relative to I.

This definition is the same as that of Definition 6 but note that, while for normal logic programs the reduct is a definite program and it has a single minimal model, the least Herbrand model, for ASP programs the reduct is a positive program that may have more than one minimal model.

Answer Set Programming is a paradigm in which the user writes rules and constraints describing a problem and the answer sets are solution to the problem. Usually, the strategy adopted is "Guess & Check", where disjunctive ruless are used to guess solutions nondeterministically and constraints serve to discard interpretations that are not solutions. Let us see an example.

Example 72 (Graph Three-Coloring). *Graph coloring is a way to assign colors to nodes of an undirected graph such that two adjacent nodes have different colors. The following Answer Set Program describes the problem when there are three colors:*

$red(X) \lor green(X) \lor blue(X) \leftarrow node(X).$
$\leftarrow edge(X,Y), red(X), red(Y).$
$\leftarrow edge(X,Y), green(X), green(Y).$
$\leftarrow edge(X,Y), blue(X), blue(Y).$

This program should be completed with facts for predicates $node/1$ and $edges/2$ describing a specific graph.

Each answer set for this program describes a three-coloring of the graph. The disjunctive rule serves to guess an assignment of color to nodes and the constraints check the assignments by ruling out interpretations where two nodes connected by an edge share the same color.

ASP also offers other features such as strong negation, see [Eiter et al., 2009], and aggregate literals, see [Faber et al., 2011a], that we won't discuss here.

6.3 Probabilistic Answer Set Programming

When we add probabilistic facts to ASP programs and we use the credal semantics of Section 6.1, we obtain Probabilistic answer set programming (PASP), which is an expressive probabilistic formalism. Let us see an example.

Example 73 (Probabilistic Graph Three-Coloring - [Cozman and Mauá, 2020].). *Consider the program from Example 72 but suppose that the graph is proba-*

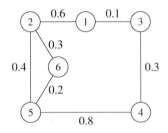

Figure 6.1 Example of a probabilistic graph.

bilistic, such as the graph shown in Figure 6.1 and described by the following
probabilistic facts:

$0.6 :: edge(1, 2).$
$0.1 :: edge(1, 3).$
$0.4 :: edge(2, 5).$
$0.3 :: edge(2, 6).$
$0.3 :: edge(3, 4).$
$0.8 :: edge(4, 5).$
$0.2 :: edge(5, 6).$

Suppose also that the program contains the following certain facts

$red(1).$
$green(4).$
$green(6).$

Each total choice identifies a graph. If a graph has multiple three-colorings,
the corresponding world has multiple answer sets and the probability of the
world can be spread over the answer sets. Consider for instance node 3. If
edges to 1 and 4 are both present, then its color will be blue in all answer
sets, as 1 is red and 4 is green. The probability that edges 1-3 and 3-4 are
present is $0.1 \cdot 0.3 = 0.03$, so the lower probability of $blue(3)$ will be at least
0.03. In fact, $\underline{P}(blue(3)) = 0.03$. Moreover, we also have $\overline{P}(blue(3)) = 1$,
$\underline{P}(red(3)) = 0.0$ and $\overline{P}(red(3)) = 0.9$.

7

Complexity of Inference

Inference includes a variety of tasks. In this chapter, we first provide a list of inference tasks and then, after introducing some background on complexity theory, we present the result on the complexity of the various tasks that are present in the literature.

7.1 Inference Tasks

We list here the various inference tasks. Let q and e be conjunctions of ground literals, the query and the evidence respectively.

The tasks of inference are:

- The EVID task is to compute an unconditional probability $P(e)$, the probability of evidence. This terminology is especially used when $P(e)$ is computed as part of a solution for the COND task. When there is no evidence, we will speak of $P(q)$, the probability of the query.
- In the COND task, we want to compute the conditional probability distribution of the query given the evidence, i.e., compute $P(q|e)$. A related task is CONDATOMS where we are given a set of ground atoms Q and we want to compute $P(q|e)$ for each $q \in Q$.
- The MPE task, or *most probable explanation*, is to find the most likely truth value of all non-evidence atoms given the evidence, i.e., solving the optimization problem

$$\arg\max_q P(q|e)$$

with q being the unobserved atoms, i.e., $Q = \mathcal{B} \backslash E$, where E is the set of atoms appearing in e and q is an assignment of truth values to the atoms in Q.

- The MAP task, or *maximum a posteriori*, is to find the most likely value of a set of non-evidence atoms given the evidence, i.e., finding

$$\arg \max_{q} P(q|e)$$

  where q is a set of ground atoms. MPE is a special case of MAP where $Q \cup E = \mathcal{B}$.
- The VIT task, or finding the *Viterbi proof* or *most probable proof*, is the task of finding the composite choice κ that is an explanation (in the sense of Section 3.1) and has maximum probability, i.e.

$$\arg \max_{\kappa \text{ is an explanation for } q} P(\kappa).$$

  It differs from both MPE and MAP because it aims to find an assignment to a small set of variables sufficient for explaining a query. It is called Viterbi proof because in a program that implements a Hidden Markov Model such as Example 74 it corresponds to the output of the Viterbi algorithm on the model, the sequence of states that most likely originated the output.
- The DISTR task involves computing the probability distribution or density of the non-ground arguments of a conjunction of literals q, e.g., computing the probability density of X in goal $mix(X)$ of the Gaussian mixture of Example 55. If the argument is a single one and is numeric (integer or real), then EXP is the task of computing the expected value of the argument (see Section 1.5).

7.2 Background on Complexity Theory

Here we provide a brief review of concepts from complexity theory following [Cozman and Mauá, 2020]. For a more in depth treatment see [Papadimitriou and Steiglitz, 1998].

A string is a sequence of 0 and 1. A language is a set of strings. A complexity class of languages is a set of languages. A language defines a *decision problem*; that is, the problem of deciding whether an input string is in the language.

A Turing machine is an abstract machine containing a tape and a head that can move over the tape and read/write symbols. The tape initially contains the input and the machine can accept or reject the input. It is formally represented by a tuple $(Q, \Sigma, q_0, q_a, q_r, \delta)$ where Q is a set of states, with $q_0/q_q/q_r$ the initial/accepting/rejecting states. Σ is the alphabet of symbols on the tape, including 0, 1, and blank, a symbol never present in the input. δ is a transition function that takes the current state and the symbol under the head in the tape (a pair from $Q \times \Sigma$) and returns a subset $\delta(q, s)$ of $Q \times \Sigma \times \{-1, 0, 1\}$ where each triple (q', s', m) in the subset indicates the next state q', the next symbol to write to the tape s' and the direction in which to move the head (-1: left, 0: no motion, 1: right). If the machine reaches q_a, the input is accepted, if the machine reaches q_r, the input is rejected.

If $\delta(q, s)$ is always a singleton, then the machine is deterministic, otherwise it is nondeterministic.

A language is decided by a Turing machine if the machine accepts all strings in the language and rejects all strings not in the language. If the number of steps to reach a decision is polynomial in the size of the input, the machine is said to be polynomial-time. The complexity class P is the set of languages that can be decided by a deterministic polynomial-time Turing machine, while NP is the set of languages that can be decided by a nondeterministic polynomial-time Turing machine. The complexity class EXP is the set of languages that can be decided by a deterministic Turing machine in time exponential in the input,

A probabilistic Turing machine differs from the above definition because it defines a uniform probability distribution over triples in $\delta(q, s)$. The complexity class PP consists of the languages that are decided by a probabilistic Turing machine in a number of steps polynomial in the input size, with an error probability strictly less than 1/2 for all input strings. Equivalently, the complexity class PP consists of those languages $\mathcal{L}$ that satisfy the following property: there is a polynomial time nondeterministic Turing machine such that $\ell \in \mathcal{L}$ if and only if more than half of the computations of the machine on input ℓ end up accepting.

The class PEXP consists of those languages $\mathcal{L}$ such that there is an exponential time nondeterministic Turing machine such that $\ell \in \mathcal{L}$ iff more than half of the computations of the machine on input ℓ end up accepting.

The *complement of a decision problem* is the decision problem resulting from reversing the YES and NO answers. The complement of a complexity class C is the set of complement of every problem in the class and is indicated by coC.

A Turing machine has an oracle for a language $\mathcal{L}$ if it has a second pair tape/head such that it can write strings to the secondary tape and then, in a single step, read whether the string is in the language $\mathcal{L}$.

The class of languages that can be decided by machines defining complexity class C, with each machine using an oracle for $\mathcal{L}$, is denoted by $C^{\mathcal{L}}$. If D is another complexity class, then C^D is defined a $\bigcup_{\mathcal{L} \in D} C^{\mathcal{L}}$.

Let us define classes $\Sigma_0^p = P$, $\Sigma_{k+1}^p = NP^{\Sigma_k^p}$, $\Pi_k^p = co\Sigma_k^p$, $\Delta_{k+1}^p = P^{\Sigma_k^p}$. These classes form the polynomial hierarchy PH.

Wagner counting hierarchy includes classes PP and $PP^{\Sigma_k^p}$ for $k > 0$.

A many-one reduction from language $\mathcal{L}$ to language $\mathcal{L}'$ is a polynomial time algorithm that transforms a string $\ell \in \mathcal{L}$ into a string $\ell' \in \mathcal{L}'$ such that $\ell \in \mathcal{L}$ if and only if $\ell' \in \mathcal{L}'$. For a complexity class C, a decision problem $\mathcal{L}$ is C-hard if each language in C can be reduced to $\mathcal{L}$ with a many-one reduction. A language is then C-complete if it is in C and it is C-hard.

Besides decision problems, we also consider *function problems*, where the output is not simply YES or NO as for decision problems but is more complex. Formally, a function problem is defined as a relation R between strings such that an algorithm solves the problem if, for every input x such that there is an y satisfying $(x, y) \in R$, the algorithm produces one such y.

The complexity class #P is the class of function problems where the relation R associates input with the number of accepting paths in a nondeterministic polynomial-time Turing machine. A #P problem is at least as hard as the corresponding NP problem: in fact to solve the NP problem, it is enough to count solutions with the #P problem and return YES if the number of solutions is greater than 0. #P is also at least as hard as PP that asks whether the majority of the computation paths accept. With a PP problem we can find the first bit of the solution of the corresponding #P problem.

7.3 Complexity for Nonprobabilistic Inference

In order to discuss the complexity of the probabilistic inference problems seen above, let us first consider the complexity of nonprobabilistic inference.

Recall the definitions of acyclic and locally stratified program from Definition 4. Here we extend them to the case of disjunctive rules. A program is *acyclic* if there exists a level mapping for ground atoms such that the level of each atom in the head of each ground rule is strictly greater that the level of each literal in the body. A program is *locally stratified* if there exists a level mapping for ground atoms such that the level of each atom in the head of each ground rule is strictly greater than the level of each negative literal in the body and greater or equal than the level of each positive literal.

We distinguish two restrictions on the class of programs

Table 7.1 Complexity of the WFS [Dantsin et al., 2001].

Language	Propositional	Unrestricted
{}	P	EXP
{not}	P	EXP

- *propositional programs* are finite ground programs
- *bounded-arity programs* are programs where the arity of predicates is bounded. So, when considering the inferential complexity, we want to know the computational cost as the size of the program increases but the arity of predicates is bounded. In this case, the Herbrand base contains a polynomial number of ground atoms but the grounded program may be exponentially large as there is no bound on the number of variables in each rule.

Consider first the decision problem

- **Input**: a logic program P without function symbols and a conjunction of ground literals q over atoms in $\mathcal{B}_P$
- **Output**: YES if $WFM(P) \models q$ and NO otherwise.

The complexity of this problem as a function of the encoding in binary of the program and the query is discussed in [Dantsin et al., 2001] and the results are shown in Table 7.1 for the case of positive ({}) and normal programs ({not}) and for the case of propositional or unrestricted programs. The cells report the complexity class for which the problem is complete. As you can see, negation doesn't add complexity to the problem.

For ASP we consider the problem of *cautious inference*:

- **Input**: a logic program P without function symbols and a conjunction of ground literals q over atoms in $\mathcal{B}_P$
- **Output**: YES if q is a cautious consequence of P under the answer set semantics and NO otherwise.

The complexity of this problem was studied in [Faber et al., 2011b] and the results are shown in Table 7.2. The rows are associated to the presence or not of various syntactic features: not_s indicates negation with local stratification; not non locally stratified negation; and $\vee$ disjunction in the head.

In the case of ASP, locally stratified negation, negation and disjunction all add complexity

Table 7.2   Complexity of ASP [Faber et al., 2011b].

Language	Propositional	Bounded-arity
$\{\}$	P	NP
$\{not_s\}$	P	Δ_2^p
$\{not\}$	coNP	Π_2^p
$\{\vee\}$	coNP	Π_2^p
$\{not_s, \vee\}$	Π_2^p	Π_3^p
$\{not, \vee\}$	Π_2^p	Π_3^p

7.4 Complexity for Probabilistic Programs

We consider probabilistic programs $\mathcal{P}$ in the form of ProbLog programs without function symbols, composed of a set of rules $\mathcal{R}$ and a set of probabilistic facts $\mathcal{F}$.

If the rules $\mathcal{R}$ of a program $\mathcal{P}$ are acyclic (locally stratified), then each world of $\mathcal{P}$ is acyclic (locally stratified), as probabilistic facts do not impose any constraint on the level mapping.

By Theorem 1, a locally stratified non-probabilistic program has a two-valued WFM, so a locally stratified probabilistic program has a two-valued WFM for each world, and thus a single answer set. Therefore, the distribution and the credal semantics for locally stratified probabilistic programs coincide. Since every acyclic program is also locally stratified, the same holds for acyclic programs.

We now present the complexity results for acyclic and locally stratified program from [Cozman and Mauá, 2017] and the the results for general programs from [Mauá and Cozman, 2020].

7.4.1 Complexity for acyclic and locally stratified programs

Since the distribution and the credal semantics coincide for acyclic and locally stratified programs, we can consider decision problems involving sharp probabilities.

The decision problem in this case is:

- **Input**: a probabilistic logic program $\mathcal{P}$ whose probabilities are rational numbers, a pair (q, e) where q and e are conjunction of ground literals over atoms in $\mathcal{B}_{\mathcal{P}}$ and a rational $\gamma \in [0, 1]$
- **Output**: YES if $P(q \mid e) > \gamma$ and NO otherwise. If $P(e) = 0$ the output is by convention NO (the input is rejected).

Table 7.3 Complexity of inference for acyclic and locally stratified programs, extracted from [Cozman and Mauá, 2017, Table 2].

Language	Propositional	Bounded Arity	Unrestricted	Query
$\{not_a\}$	PP	PP^{NP}	PEXP	PP
$\{not_s\}$	PP	PP^{NP}	PEXP	PP

The requirement of rationality of the numbers is imposed in order to be able to represent them as a pair of binary integers in the input. The complexity of this problem as a function of the encoding in binary of the program and the numbers is called the *inferential complexity*.

We also take into account the case where the program is fixed:

- **Fixed**: a probabilistic logic progam $\mathcal{P}$ whose probabilities are rational numbers
- **Input**: a pair (q, e) where q and e are conjunction of ground literals over atoms in $\mathcal{B}_\mathcal{P}$ and a rational $\gamma \in [0, 1]$
- **Output**: whether or not $P(q \mid e) > \gamma$. If $P(e) = 0$ the output is by convention NO (the input is rejected).

The complexity for this problem is the *query complexity*.

Cozman and Mauá [2017] provided various results regarding the complexity of the above problems for propositional, bounded-arity and unrestricted programs. These results are summarized in Table 7.3, where $\{not_a\}$ indicates acyclic programs and $\{not_s\}$ indicates locally stratified programs. The column are associated to propositional, bounded arity and unrestricted programs, while the last column refers to the query complexity. The cells contain a complexity class for which the inferential or query complexity is complete. As you can see, there is no advantage in restricting the program to be acyclic.

The function problem of computing $P(q|e)$ from an acyclic program is #P-complete. In fact it is #P-hard because a Bayesian network can be converted into an acyclic program (see Example 28) and inference in Bayesian network is #P-complete [Koller and Friedman, 2009, Theorem 9.2]. On the other hand the problem is in #P because an acyclic program can be converted to a Bayesian network (see Section 2.5).

7.4.2 Complexity results from [Mauá and Cozman, 2020]

Mauá and Cozman [2020] provided more complexity results, taking into account also positive programs, general programs and the problems of MPE and MAP.

Differently from the previous section, here the credal semantics does not assign sharp probability values to queries, so we must considerer lower and upper probabilities. The first problem is called *cautious reasoning* (CR) and is defined as

Input: a probabilistic logic program $\mathcal{P}$ whose probabilities are rational numbers, a pair (q, e) where q and e are conjunction of ground literals over atoms in $\mathcal{B}_\mathcal{P}$ and a rational $\gamma \in [0, 1]$

Output: YES if $\underline{P}(q \mid e) > \gamma$ and NO otherwise. If $\underline{P}(e) = 0$ the output is by convention NO (the input is rejected).

This problem corresponds to the inferential complexity problem of the previous section. It is called cautious reasoning as it involves checking the truth of queries in all answer sets so it is similar to the problem of computing cautious consequences in non probabilistic reasoning. Similarly, we can call the problem of checking whether $\overline{P}(q \mid e) > \gamma$ *brave reasoning*. Note that one problem reduces to the other as $\overline{P}(q \mid e) \leqslant \gamma$ if and only if $\underline{P}(\sim q \mid e) > 1 - \gamma$.

Consider the decision problem for MPE:

Input: a probabilistic logic program $\mathcal{P}$ whose probabilities are rational numbers, a conjunction of ground literals e over atoms in $\mathcal{B}_\mathcal{P}$ and a rational $\gamma \in [0, 1]$

Output: YES if $\max_q \underline{P}(q|e) > \gamma$ and NO otherwise, with $Q = \mathcal{B}_\mathcal{P} \backslash E$, where E is the set of atoms appearing in e, and q is an assignment of truth values to the atoms in Q.

and for MAP:

Input: a probabilistic logic program $\mathcal{P}$ whose probabilities are rational numbers, a conjunction of ground literals e over atoms in $\mathcal{B}_\mathcal{P}$, a set Q of atoms in $\mathcal{B}_\mathcal{P}$ and a rational $\gamma \in [0, 1]$

Output: YES if $\max_q \underline{P}(q|e) > \gamma$ and NO otherwise, with q an assignment of truth values to the atoms in Q.

The complexity for CR and MPE is given in Table 7.4, an extract from [Mauá and Cozman, 2020, Table 1]. The columns correspond to the distinction between propositional and bounded-arity programs and to CR and MPE.

Table 7.4 Complexity of the credal semantics, extracted from [Mauá and Cozman, 2020, Table 1].

Language	Propositional		Bounded Arity	
	CR	MPE	CR	MPE
$\{\}$	PP	NP	PP^{NP}	Σ_2^p
$\{not_s\}$	PP	NP	PP^{NP}	Σ_2^p
$\{not\}$	PP^{NP}	Σ_2^p	$PP^{\Sigma_2^p}$	Σ_3^p
$\{\vee\}$	PP^{NP}	Σ_3^p	$PP^{\Sigma_2^p}$	Σ_4^p
$\{not_s, \vee\}$	$PP^{\Sigma_2^p}$	Σ_3^p	$PP^{\Sigma_3^p}$	Σ_4^p
$\{not, \vee\}$	$PP^{\Sigma_2^p}$	Σ_3^p	$PP^{\Sigma_3^p}$	Σ_4^p

MAP is absent from the table as its complexity is always PP^{NP} for propositional programs and $PP^{NP^{NP}}$ for bounded-arity programs.

8

Exact Inference

Several approaches have been proposed for inference. Exact inference aims at solving the tasks listed in Chapter 7 in an exact way, modulo errors of computer floating point arithmetic. Exact inference can be performed in various ways: dedicated algorithms for special cases, knowledge compilation, conversion to graphical models, or lifted inference. This chapter discusses exact inference approaches except lifted inference which is presented in Chapter 9.

Exact inference is very expensive as shown in Chapter 7. Therefore, in some cases, it is necessary to perform approximate inference, i.e., finding an approximation of the answer that is cheaper to compute. The main approach for approximate inference is sampling, but there are others such as iterative deepening or bounding. Approximate inference is discussed in Chapter 10.

In Chapter 3, we saw that the semantics for programs with function symbols is given in terms of explanations, i.e., sets of choices that ensure that the query is true. The probability of a query (EVID task) is given as a function of a covering set of explanations, i.e., a set containing all possible explanations for a query.

This definition suggests an inference approach that consists in finding a covering set of explanations and then computing the probability of the query from it.

To compute the probability of the query, we need to make the explanations pairwise incompatible: once this is done, the probability is the result of a summation.

Early inference algorithms such as [Poole, 1993b] and PRISM [Sato, 1995] required the program to be such that it always had a pairwise incompatible covering set of explanations. In this case, once the set is found, the computation of the probability amounts to performing a sum of products. For programs to allow this kind of approach, they must satisfy the assumptions of independence of subgoals and exclusiveness of clauses, which mean that [Sato et al., 2017]:

1. the probability of a conjunction (A, B) is computed as the product of the probabilities of A and B (*independent-and assumption*),
2. the probability of a disjunction $(A; B)$ is computed as the sum of the probabilities of A and B (*exclusive-or assumption*).

See also Section 8.10.

8.1 PRISM

PRISM [Sato, 1995; Sato and Kameya, 2001, 2008] performs inference on programs respecting the assumptions of independent-and and exclusive-or by means of an algorithm for computing and encoding explanations in a factorized way instead of explicitly generating all explanations. In fact, the number of explanations may be exponential, even if they can be encoded compactly.

Example 74 (Hidden Markov model – PRISM [Sato and Kameya, 2008]). *An HMM [Rabiner, 1989] is a dynamical system that, at each integer time point t, is in a state S from a finite set and emits one symbol O according to a probability distribution $P(O|S)$ that is independent of time. Moreover, it transitions to a new state $NextS$ at time $t + 1$, with $NextS$ chosen according to $P(NextS|S)$, again independently of time. HMMs are so called because they respect the Markov condition: the state at time t depends only from the state at time $t - 1$ and is independent of previous states. Moreover, the states are usually hidden: the task is to obtain information on them from the sequence of output symbols, modeling systems that can be only observed from the outside. HMMs and Kalman filters (see Example 57) are similar, they differ because the first uses discrete states and output symbols and the latter continuous ones. HMMs have applications in many fields, such as speech recognition.*

The following program encodes an HMM with two states, $\{s1, s2\}$, of which $s1$ is the start state, and two output symbols, a and b:

$values(tr(s1), [s1, s2])$.
$values(tr(s2), [s1, s2])$.
$values(out(\_), [a, b])$.
$hmm(Os) \leftarrow hmm(s1, Os)$.
$hmm(\_S, [])$.
$hmm(S, [O|Os]) \leftarrow$

$$E_1 = m(out(s1), a), m(tr(s1), s1), m(out(s1), b), m(tr(s1), s1),$$
$$\quad m(out(s1), b), m(tr(s1), s1),$$
$$E_2 = m(out(s1), a), m(tr(s1), s1), m(out(s1), b), m(tr(s1), s1),$$
$$\quad m(out(s1), b), m(tr(s1), s2),$$
$$E_3 = m(out(s1), a), m(tr(s1), s1), m(out(s2), b), m(tr(s1), s2),$$
$$\quad m(out(s2), b), m(tr(s2), s1),$$
$$\ldots$$
$$E_8 = m(out(s1), a), m(tr(s1), s2), m(out(s2), b), m(tr(s2), s2),$$
$$\quad m(out(s2), b), m(tr(s2), s2)$$

Figure 8.1 Explanations for query $hmm([a, b, b])$ of Example 74.

$$msw(out(S), O), msw(tr(S), NextS), hmm(NextS, Os).$$
$$\leftarrow set\_sw(tr(s0), [0.2, 0.8]).$$
$$\leftarrow set\_sw(tr(s1), [0.8, 0.2]).$$
$$\leftarrow set\_sw(out(s0), [0.5, 0.5]).$$
$$\leftarrow set\_sw(out(s1), [0.6, 0.4]).$$

An example of EVID task on this program is computing $P(hmm(Os))$ where Os is a list of as and bs, that is the probability that the sequence of symbols Os is emitted.

Note that msw atoms have two arguments here, so each call to such atoms is intended to refer to a different random variable. This means that if the same msw is encountered again in a derivation, it is associated with a different random variable, differently from the other languages under the DS where a ground instance of a probabilistic clause is associated with only one random variable. The latter approach is also called memoing, *meaning that the associations between atoms and random variables are stored for reuse, while the approach of PRISM is often adopted by non-logic probabilistic programming languages.*

Consider the query $hmm([a, b, b])$ and the problem of computing the probability of output sequence $[a, b, b]$. Such a query has the eight explanations shown in Figure 8.1 where msw is abbreviated by m, repeated atoms correspond to different random variables, and each explanation is a conjunction of msw atoms. In general, the number of explanations is exponential in the length of the sequence.

If the query q has the explanations $E_1 \ldots, E_n$, we can build the formula

$$q \Leftrightarrow E_1 \vee \ldots \vee E_n$$

expressing the truth of q as a function of the msw atoms in the explanations. The probability of q (EVID task) is then given by $P(q) = \sum_{i=1}^{n} P(E_i)$

$$hmm([a, b, b]) \Leftrightarrow hmm(s1, [a, b, b])$$
$$hmm(s1, [a, b, b]) \Leftrightarrow m(out(s1), a), m(tr(s1), s1), hmm(s1, [b, b]) \vee$$
$$m(out(s1), a), m(tr(s1), s2), hmm(s2, [b, b])$$
$$hmm(s1, [b, b]) \Leftrightarrow m(out(s1), b), m(tr(s1), s1), hmm(s1, [b]) \vee$$
$$m(out(s1), b), m(tr(s1), s2), hmm(s2, [b])$$
$$hmm(s2, [b, b]) \Leftrightarrow m(out(s2), b), m(tr(s2), s1), hmm(s1, [b]) \vee$$
$$m(out(s2), b), m(tr(s2), s2), hmm(s2, [b])$$
$$hmm(s1, [b]) \Leftrightarrow m(out(s1), b), m(tr(s1), s1), hmm(s1, []) \vee$$
$$m(out(s1), b), m(tr(s1), s2), hmm(s2, [])$$
$$hmm(s2, [b]) \Leftrightarrow m(out(s2), b), m(tr(s2), s1), hmm(s1, []) \vee$$
$$m(out(s2), b), m(tr(s2), s2), hmm(s2, [])$$
$$hmm(s1, []) \Leftrightarrow true$$
$$hmm(s2, []) \Leftrightarrow true$$

Figure 8.2   PRISM formulas for query $hmm([a, b, b])$ of Example 74.

and the probability of each explanation is the product of the probability of each atom, because explanations are mutually exclusive, as each explanation differs from the others in the choice for at least one msw atom.

PRISM performs inference by deriving the query with tabling and storing, for each subgoal g, the switches and atoms on which g directly depends. In practice, for each subgoal g, PRISM builds a formula

$$g \Leftrightarrow S_1 \vee \ldots \vee S_n$$

where each S_i is a conjunction of msw atoms and subgoals. For the query $hmm([a, b, b])$ from the program of Example 74, PRISM builds the formulas shown in Figure 8.2.

Differently from explanations, the number of such formulas is linear rather than exponential in the length of the output sequence.

PRISM assumes that the subgoals in the derivation of q can be ordered $\{g_1, \ldots, g_m\}$ such that

$$g_i \Leftrightarrow S_{i1} \vee \ldots \vee S_{in_i}$$

where $q = g_1$ and each S_{ij} contains only msw atoms and subgoals from $\{g_{i+1}, \ldots, g_m\}$. This is called the *acyclic support condition* and is true if tabling succeeds in evaluating q, i.e., if it doesn't go into a loop.

From these formulas, the probability of each subgoal can be obtained by means of Algorithm 5 that computes the probability of each subgoal bottom up and reuses the computed values for subgoals higher up. This is a *dynamic programming* algorithm: the problem is solved by breaking it down into simpler sub-problems in a recursive manner.

Algorithm 5 Function PRISM-PROB: Computation of the probability of a query.

1: **function** PRISM-PROB(q)
2:     **for all** i, k **do**
3:         $P(msw(i, v_k)) \leftarrow \Pi_{ik}$
4:     **end for**
5:     **for** $i \leftarrow m \rightarrow 1$ **do**
6:         $P(g_i) \leftarrow 0$ $\triangleright$ $P(g_i)$ is the probability of goal g_i
7:         **for** $j \leftarrow 1 \rightarrow n_i$ **do**
8:             Let S_{ij} be $h_1, \dots, h_o$
9:             $R(g_i, S_{ij}) \leftarrow \prod_{l=1}^{o} P(h_l)$ $\triangleright$ $R(g_i, S_{ij})$ is the probability of explanation
10:             S_{ij} of goal g_i
11:             $P(g_i) \leftarrow P(g_i) + R(g_i, S_{ij})$
12:         **end for**
13:     **end for**
14:     **return** $P(q)$
15: **end function**

$$P(hmm(s1, [])) = 1$$
$$P(hmm(s2, [])) = 1$$
$$P(hmm(s1, [b]) =$$
$$P(m(out(s1), b)) \cdot P(m(tr(s1), s1)) \cdot P(hmm(s1, []))+$$
$$P(m(out(s1), b)) \cdot P(m(tr(s1), s2)) \cdot P(hmm(s2, []))$$
$$P(hmm(s2, [b]) =$$
$$P(m(out(s2), b)) \cdot P(m(tr(s2), s1)) \cdot P(hmm(s1, []))+$$
$$P(m(out(s2), b)) \cdot P(m(tr(s2), s2)) \cdot P(hmm(s2, []))$$

$\dots$

Figure 8.3   PRISM computations for query $hmm([a, b, b])$ of Example 74.

For the example above, the probabilities are computed as in Figure 8.3.

The cost of computing the probability of the query in this case is thus linear in the length of the output sequence, rather than exponential.

In the case of HMMs, computing the probability of an output sequence using PRISM has the same complexity $O(T)$ as the specialized forward algorithm [Rabiner, 1989], where T is the length of the sequence.

The MPE task can be performed by replacing summation in Algorithm 5 with max and arg max. In the case of HMM, this yields the most likely sequence of states that originated the output sequence, also called the Viterbi path. Such a path is computed for HMMs by the Viterbi algorithm [Rabiner, 1989] and PRISM has the same complexity $O(T)$.

Writing programs satisfying the assumptions of independence of subgoals and exclusiveness of clauses is not easy and significantly limits the modeling power of the language. Therefore, work was dedicated to lifting these limitations, leading to the AILog2 system Poole [2000] that used the splitting algorithm (Algorithm 1), and to the adoption of knowledge compilation.

8.2 Knowledge Compilation

Knowledge compilation [Darwiche and Marquis, 2002] is an approach for solving certain hard inference tasks on a Boolean formula by compiling it into a form on which the tasks are tractable. Clearly, the complexity is not eliminated but moved to the compilation process. The inference tasks of COND, MPE, and EVID can be solved using well-known techniques from the SAT community applied to weighted Boolean formulas, such as techniques for Weighted model counting (WMC) or weighted MAX-SAT. For example, EVID reduces to WMC, i.e., computing the sum of the weights of the worlds where the formula is true. WMC is a generalization of the problem of counting the number of worlds where the query is true, also known as *model counting*. Model counting and WMC are #P-complete in general but can be computed in polynomial time for Boolean formulas in certain forms.

The knowledge compilation approach to inference follows the two-step method where first the program, the query, and the evidence are converted into a Boolean formula encoding a covering set of explanations and then knowledge compilation is applied to the formula.

The formula is a function of Boolean variables, each encoding a choice, that takes value 1 exactly for assignments corresponding to worlds where the query is true. Therefore, to compute the probability of the query, we can compute the probability that the formula takes value 1 knowing the probability distribution of all the variables and that they are pairwise independent. This is done in the second step, which amounts to converting the formula into a form from which computing the probability is easy. The conversion step uses knowledge compilation because it compiles the formula into a special form with the property that the cost of solving the problem is polynomial. This second step is a well-known problem also called *disjoint-sum* and is an instance of WMC.

8.3 ProbLog1

The ProbLog1 system [De Raedt et al., 2007] compiles explanations for queries from ProbLog programs to BDDs. It uses a source to source transformation of the program [Kimmig et al., 2008] that replaces probabilistic facts with clauses that store information about the fact in the dynamic database of the Prolog interpreter. When a successful derivation for the query is found, the set of facts stored in the dynamic database is collected to form a new explanation that is stored away and backtracking is triggered to find other possible explanations.

If K is the set of explanations found for query q, the probability of q is given by the probability of the formula

$$f_K(\mathbf{X}) = \bigvee_{\kappa \in K} \bigwedge_{(F_i, \theta_j, 1) \in \kappa} X_{ij} \bigwedge_{(F_i, \theta_j, 0) \in \kappa} \neg X_{ij}$$

where X_{ij} is a Boolean random variable associated with grounding $F_i\theta_j$ of fact F_i and $P(X_{ij} = 1) = \Pi_i$.

Consider Example 14 that we repeat here for ease of reading

$$\begin{aligned}
& sneezing(X) \leftarrow flu(X), flu\_sneezing(X). \\
& sneezing(X) \leftarrow hay\_fever(X), hay\_fever\_sneezing(X). \\
& flu(bob). \\
& hay\_fever(bob). \\
F_1 \;=\; & 0.7 :: flu\_sneezing(X). \\
F_2 \;=\; & 0.8 :: hay\_fever\_sneezing(X),
\end{aligned}$$

A set of covering explanations for $sneezing(bob)$ is $K = \{\kappa_1, \kappa_2\}$ with

$$\kappa_1 = \{(F_1, \{X/bob\}, 1)\} \quad \kappa_2 = \{(F_2, \{X/bob\}, 1)\}$$

If we associate X_{11} with $F_1\{X/bob\}$ and X_{21} with $F_2\{X/bob\}$, the Boolean formula is

$$f_K(\mathbf{X}) = X_{11} \vee X_{21} \tag{8.1}$$

In this simple case, the probability that $f_K(\mathbf{X})$ takes value 1 can be computed by using the formula for the probability of a disjunction:

$$P(X_{11} \vee X_{21}) = P(X_{11}) + P(X_{21}) - P(X_{11} \wedge X_{21})$$

and, since X_{11} and X_{21} are independent, we get

$$P(f_K(\mathbf{X})) = P(X_{11} \vee X_{21}) = P(X_{11}) + P(X_{21}) - P(X_{11})P(X_{21}).$$

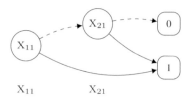

Figure 8.4   BDD representing Function 8.1.

In the general case, however, simple formulas like this can't be applied.

BDDs are a target language for knowledge compilation. A BDD for a function of Boolean variables is a rooted graph that has one level for each Boolean variable. A node n has two children: one corresponding to the 1 value of the variable associated with the level of n and one corresponding to the 0 value of the variable. When drawing BDDs, the 0-branch is distinguished from the 1-branch by drawing it with a dashed line. The leaves store either 0 or 1. For example, a BDD representing function (8.1) is shown in Figure 8.4.

Given values for all the variables, the computation of the value of the function can be performed by traversing the BDD starting from the root and returning the value associated with the leaf that is reached.

To compile a Boolean formula $f(\mathbf{X})$ into a BDD, software packages incrementally combine sub-diagram using Boolean operations.

BDDs can be built with various software packages that perform knowledge compilation by providing Boolean operations between diagrams. So the diagram for a formula is obtained by applying the Boolean operations in the formula bottom-up, combining diagrams representing X_{ij} or $\neg X_{ij}$ into progressively more complex diagrams.

After the application of an operation, isomorphic portions of the resulting diagram are merged and redundant nodes are deleted, possibly changing the order of variables if useful. This often allows the diagram to have a number of nodes much smaller than exponential in the number of variables that a naive representation of the function would require.

In the BDD of Figure 8.4, a node for variable X_{21} is absent from the path from the root to the 1 leaf. The node has been deleted because both arcs from the node would go to the 1 leaf, so the node is redundant.

Example 75 (Epidemic – ProbLog).   *The following ProbLog program* $\mathcal{P}$ *encodes a very simple model of the development of an epidemic:*

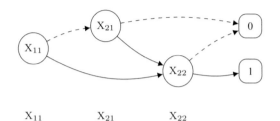

Figure 8.5 BDD for query *epidemic* of Example 75.

$$epidemic \leftarrow flu(X), ep(X), cold.$$
$$flu(david).$$
$$flu(robert).$$
$$F_1 \quad = \quad 0.7 :: cold.$$
$$F_2 \quad = \quad 0.6 :: ep(X).$$

This program models the fact that, if somebody has the flu and the climate is cold, there is the possibility that an epidemic arises. We are uncertain about whether the climate is cold but we know for sure that David and Robert have the flu. The atom $ep(X)$ models the fact that individual X enables the onset of the epidemic. Fact F_1 has one grounding, associated with variable X_{11}, while F_2 has two groundings, associated with variables X_{21} and X_{22}. The query epidemic is true if the Boolean formula

$$f(\mathbf{X}) = X_{11} \wedge (X_{21} \vee X_{22})$$

is true. The BDD representing this formula is shown in Figure 8.5. As you can see, the subtree rooted at X_{22} can be reached by more than one path. In this case, the BDD compilation system recognized the presence of two isomorphic subgraphs and merged them, besides deleting nodes for X_{21} from the path from X_{11} to X_{22} and for X_{22} from the path from X_{21} to the 0 leaf.

BDDs perform a Shannon expansion of the Boolean formula: they express the formula as

$$f_K(\mathbf{X}) = X_1 \wedge f_K^{X_1}(\mathbf{X}) \vee \neg X_1 \wedge f_K^{\neg X_1}(\mathbf{X})$$

where X_1 is the variable associated with the root node of the diagram, $f_K^{X_1}(\mathbf{X})$ is the Boolean formula where X_1 is set to 1, and $f_K^{\neg X_1}(\mathbf{X})$ is the Boolean formula where X_1 is set to 0. The expansion can be applied recursively to the functions $f_K^{X_1}(\mathbf{X})$ and $f_K^{\neg X_1}(\mathbf{X})$.

The formula is thus expressed as a disjunction of mutually exclusive terms, as one contains X_1 and the other $\neg X_1$. Moreover X_1 is independent from $f_K^{X_1}(\mathbf{X})$ and $f_K^{\neg X_1}(\mathbf{X})$ because it does not appear there, so the probability of the formula can be computed with

$$P(f_K(\mathbf{X})) = P(X_1)P(f_K^{X_1}(\mathbf{X})) + (1 - P(X_1))P(f_K^{\neg X_1}(\mathbf{X})).$$

For the BDD of Figure 8.5, this becomes

$$P(f_K(\mathbf{X})) = 0.7 \cdot P(f_K^{X_{11}}(\mathbf{X})) + 0.3 \cdot P(f_K^{\neg X_{11}}(\mathbf{X}))$$

This means that the probability of the formula, and so of the query, can be computed with Algorithm 6: the BDD is recursively traversed and the probability of a node is computed as a function of the probabilities of its children. Note that a table is updated to store the probability of nodes already visited: in fact, BDDs can have multiple paths to a node in case two sub-diagrams are merged and, if a node already visited is encountered again, we can simply retrieve its probability from the table. This ensures that each node is visited exactly once, so the cost of the algorithm is linear in the number of nodes. This is an instance of a dynamic programming algorithm.

Algorithm 6 Function PROB: Computation of the probability of a BDD.

```
 1: function PROB(node)
 2:     if node is a terminal then
 3:         return 1
 4:     else
 5:         if Table(node) ≠ null then
 6:             return Table(node)
 7:         else
 8:             p0 ←PROB(child₀(node))
 9:             p1 ←PROB(child₁(node))
10:             let π be the probability of being true of var(node)
11:             Res ← p1 · π + p0 · (1 − π)
12:             add node → Res to Table
13:             return Res
14:         end if
15:     end if
16: end function
```

8.4 cplint

The `cplint` system (CPLogic INTerpreter) [Riguzzi, 2007a] applies knowledge compilation to LPADs. Differently from ProbLog1, the random variables associated with clauses can have more than two values. Moreover, with cplint, programs may contain negation.

To handle multivalued random variables, we can use MDDs [Thayse et al., 1978], an extension of BDDs. Similarly to BDDs, an MDD represents a function $f(\mathbf{X})$ taking Boolean values on a set of multivalued variables $\mathbf{X}$ by means of a rooted graph that has one level for each variable. Each node has one child for each possible value of the multivalued variable associated with the level of the node. The leaves store either 0 or 1. Given values for all the variables $\mathbf{X}$, we can compute the value of $f(\mathbf{X})$ by traversing the graph starting from the root and returning the value associated with the leaf that is reached.

In order to represent sets of explanations with MDDs, each ground clause $C_i\theta_j$ appearing in the set of explanations is associated with a multivalued variable X_{ij} with as many values as atoms in the head of C_i. Each atomic choice (C_i, θ_j, k) is represented by the propositional equation $X_{ij} = k$. Equations for a single explanation are conjoined and the conjunctions for the different explanations are disjoined. The resulting function takes value 1 if the values taken by the multivalued variables correspond to an explanation for the goal.

Example 76 (Detailed medical symptoms – MDD). *Consider Example 20 that we repeat here for readability:*

$$C_1 = strong\_sneezing(X) : 0.3 \,; moderate\_sneezing(X) : 0.5 \leftarrow flu(X).$$

$$C_2 = strong\_sneezing(X) : 0.2 \,; moderate\_sneezing(X) : 0.6 \leftarrow hay\_fever(X).$$

$$flu(bob).$$

$$hay\_fever(bob).$$

A set of explanations for $strong\_sneezing(bob)$ *is* $K = \{\kappa_1, \kappa_2\}$ *with*

$$\kappa_1 = \{(C_1, \{X/bob\}, 1)\} \quad \kappa_2 = \{(C_2, \{X/bob\}, 1)\}$$

This set of explanations can be represented by the function

$$f_K(\mathbf{X}) = (X_{11} = 1) \vee (X_{21} = 1) \tag{8.2}$$

The corresponding MDD is shown in Figure 8.6.

The probability of the goal is given by the probability of $f_K(\mathbf{X})$ *taking value 1.*

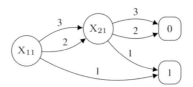

Figure 8.6 MDD for the diagnosis program of Example 20.

As BDDs, MDDs represent a Boolean function $f(\mathbf{X})$ by means of a generalization of the Shannon expansion:

$$f(\mathbf{X}) = (X_1 = 1) \wedge f^{X_1=1}(\mathbf{X}) \vee \ldots \vee (X_1 = n) \wedge f^{X_1=n}(\mathbf{X})$$

where X_1 is the variable associated with the root node of the diagram and $f^{X_1=k}(\mathbf{X})$ is the function associated with the k-th child of the root node. The expansion can be applied recursively to the functions $f^{X_1=k}(\mathbf{X})$. This expansion allows the probability of $f(\mathbf{X})$ to be expressed by means of the following recursive formula

$$P(f(\mathbf{X})) = P(X_1 = 1) \cdot P(f^{X_1=1}(\mathbf{X})) + \ldots + \\ P(X_1 = n) \cdot P(f^{X_1=n}(\mathbf{X}))$$

because the disjuncts are mutually exclusive due to the presence of the $X_1 = k$ equations and X_1 doesn't appear in $f^{X_1=k}(\mathbf{X})$. Thus, the probability of $f(\mathbf{X})$ can be computed by means of a dynamic programming algorithm similar to Algorithm 6 that traverses the MDD and sums up probabilities.

Knowledge compilation libraries for MDDs combine diagrams representing equations of the form $X_i = k$ into progressively more complex diagrams using Boolean operations. However, most libraries are restricted to work on BDD, i.e., decision diagrams where all the variables are Boolean. To work on MDDs with a BDD package, we must represent multivalued variables by means of binary variables. Various options are possible, in cplint [Riguzzi, 2007a], the choice was to use a binary encoding. A multivalued variable X with n values is encoded with $b = \lceil log_2 n \rceil$ Boolean variables $X_1, \ldots, X_b$: if $k = k_b \ldots k_1$ is the binary encoding of value k, then $X = k$ is encoded as $X_1 = k_1 \wedge \ldots \wedge X_b = k_b$.

When compiling the formula to a BDD, we need to ensure that Boolean variables encoding the same multivalued variable are kept together in the BDD. Then, the dynamic programming algorithm for computing the probability is adjusted to correctly retrieve the probability values Π_k by detecting the value k from the configuration of Boolean variables.

cplint finds explanations by using a meta-interpreter (see Section 1.3) that resolves the query and keeps a list of the choices encountered during the derivation. Negative goals of the form $\sim a$ are handled by finding a covering set K of explanations for a and then computing their complement, i.e., a set of explanations $\overline{K}$ that identifies all the worlds where a is false. This is done with an algorithm similar to function DUALS(K) of Algorithm 2 [Poole, 2000]: an explanation κ in $\overline{K}$ is generated by picking an atomic choice (C_i, θ_j, k) from each explanation of K and inserting in $\overline{K}$ an explanation containing (C_i, θ_j, k') with $k' \neq k$. By doing this in all possible ways, the complement $\overline{K}$ of K is obtained.

The system PICL [Riguzzi, 2009] applies this approach to ICL and, together with the cplint system, formed the initial core of the cplint suite of algorithms.

8.5 SLGAD

SLGAD [Riguzzi, 2008a, 2010] was an early system for performing inference from LPADs using a modification of SLG resolution [Chen and Warren, 1996], see Section 1.4.2. SLG resolution is the main inference procedure for normal programs under the WFS and uses tabling to ensure termination and correctness for a large class of programs.

SLGAD is of interest because it performs inference without using knowledge compilation, exploiting the feature of SLG resolution that answers are added to the table only once, the first time they are derived, while the following calls to the same subgoal retrieve the answers from the table. So the decision of considering an atom as true is an atomic operation. Since this happens when the body of the grounding of a clause with that atom in the head has been proved true, this corresponds to making a choice regarding the clause grounding. SLGAD modifies SLG by performing backtracking on such choices: when an answer can be added to the table, SLGAD checks whether this is consistent with previous choices and, if so, it adds the current choice to the set of choices of the derivation, adds the answer to the table and leaves a choice point, so that the other choices are explored in backtracking. SLGAD thus returns, for a ground goal, a set of explanations that are mutually exclusive because each backtracking choice is made among incompatible alternatives. Therefore, the probability of the goal can be computed by summing the probability of the explanations.

SLGAD was implemented by modifying the Prolog meta-interpreter of [Chen et al., 1995]. Its comparison with systems performing knowledge compilation, however, showed that SLGAD was slower, probably because it is not able to factor explanations as, for example, PRISM does.

8.6 PITA

The PITA system [Riguzzi and Swift, 2010, 2011, 2013] performs inference for LPADs using knowledge compilation to BDDs.

PITA applies a program transformation to an LPAD to create a normal program that contains calls for manipulating BDDs. In the implementation, these calls provide a Prolog interface to the CUDD [Somenzi, 2015] C library and use the following predicates[1]

- *init* and *end*: for allocation and deallocation of a BDD manager, a data structure used to keep track of the memory for storing BDD nodes;
- $zero(-BDD)$, $one(-BDD)$, $and(+BDD1, +BDD2, -BDDO)$, $or(+BDD1, +BDD2, -BDDO)$ and $not(+BDDI, -BDDO)$: Boolean operations between BDDs, where $+$ denotes input arguments and $-$ output arguments;
- $add\_var(+N\_Val, +Probs, -Var)$: addition of a new multivalued variable with N_Val values and parameters $Probs$ (a list). It returns an integer;
- $equality(+Var, +Value, -BDD)$: returns a BDD representing the equality $Var = Value$, i.e., that the random variable Var is assigned $Value$ in the BDD;
- $ret\_prob(+BDD, -P)$: returns the probability of the formula encoded by BDD.

$add\_var(+N\_Val, +Probs, -Var)$ adds a new random variable associated with a new instantiation of a rule with N_Val head atoms and parameters list $Probs$, and returns an integer indexing the new variable. The auxiliary predicate $get\_var\_n/4$ is used to wrap $add\_var/3$ and avoids adding a new variable when one already exists for an instantiation. As shown below, a new fact $var(R, S, Var)$ is asserted each time a new random variable is created, where R is an identifier for the LPAD clause, S is a list of constants, one for each variables of the clause, and Var is a integer that identifies the random variable associated with the specific grounding of clause R identified by S. The auxiliary predicate has the following definition:

---

[1] BDDs are represented in CUDD as pointers to their root node.

$get\_var\_n(R, S, Probs, Var) \leftarrow$
  $(var(R, S, Var) \rightarrow$
    $true$
  $;$
    $length(Probs, L),$
    $add\_var(L, Probs, Var),$
    $assert(var(R, S, Var))$
  $).$

where $Probs$ is a list of floats that stores the parameters in the head of rule R. R, S, and $Probs$ are input arguments while Var is an output argument. $assert/1$ is a builtin Prolog predicate that adds its argument to the program, allowing its dynamic extension.

The PITA transformation applies to atoms, literals, conjunction of literals, and clauses. The transformation for an atom a and a variable D, $PITA(a, D)$, is a with the variable D added as the last argument. The transformation for a negative literal $b = \sim a$, $PITA(b, D)$, is the expression

$$(PITA(a, DN) \rightarrow not(DN, D); one(D))$$

which is an if-then-else construct in Prolog: if $PITA(a, DN)$ evaluates to true, then $not(DN, D)$ is called, otherwise $one(D)$ is called.

A conjunction of literals $b_1, \ldots, b_m$ becomes:
$PITA(b_1, \ldots, b_m, D) = one(DD_0),$
  $PITA(b_1, D_1), and(DD_0, D_1, DD_1), \ldots,$
  $PITA(b_m, D_m), and(DD_{m-1}, D_m, D).$

The disjunctive clause $C_r = h_1 : \Pi_1 \vee \ldots \vee h_n : \Pi_n \leftarrow b_1, \ldots, b_m$, where the parameters sum to 1, is transformed into the set of clauses $PITA(C_r) = \{PITA(C_r, 1), \ldots PITA(C_r, n)\}$ with:

$$PITA(C_r, i) = PITA(h_i, D) \leftarrow PITA(b_1, \ldots, b_m, DD_b),$$
$$get\_var\_n(r, S, [\Pi_1, \ldots, \Pi_n], Var), equality(Var, i, DD), \qquad (8.3)$$
$$and(DD_b, DD, D).$$

for $i = 1, \ldots, n$, where S is a list containing all the variables appearing in C_r.

A non-disjunctive fact $C_r = h$ is transformed into the clause
$PITA(C_r) = PITA_h(h, D) \leftarrow one(D).$

A disjunctive fact $C_r = h_1 : \Pi_1 \vee \ldots \vee h_n : \Pi_n$, where the parameters sum to 1, is transformed into the set of clauses
$PITA(C_r) = \{PITA(C_r, 1), \ldots PITA(C_r, n)\}$

with:

$$PITA(C_r, i) = PITA(h_i, D) \leftarrow get\_var\_n(r, S, [\Pi_1, \ldots, \Pi_n], Var),$$
$$equality(Var, i, D).$$

for $i = 1, \ldots, n$.

In the case where the parameters do not sum to one, the clause is first transformed into $null : 1 - \sum_1^n \Pi_i \vee h_1 : \Pi_1 \vee \ldots \vee h_n : \Pi_n$. and then into the clauses above, where the list of parameters is $[1 - \sum_1^n \Pi_i, \Pi_1, \ldots, \Pi_n,]$ but the 0-th clause (the one for $null$) is not generated.

The definite clause $C_r = h \leftarrow b_1, b_2, \ldots, b_m$. is transformed into the clause

$$PITA(C_r) = PITA(h, D) \leftarrow PITA(b_1, \ldots, b_m, D).$$

Example 77 (Medical example – PITA).   *Clause C_1 from the LPAD of Example 76 is translated to*

$$strong\_sneezing(X, D) \leftarrow one(DD_0), flu(X, D_1),$$
$$and(DD_0, D_1, DD_1),$$
$$get\_var\_n(1, [X], [0.3, 0.5, 0.2], Var),$$
$$equality(Var, 1, DD), and(DD_1, DD, D).$$
$$moderate\_sneezing(X, D) \leftarrow one(DD_0), flu(X, D_1),$$
$$and(DD_0, D_1, DD_1),$$
$$get\_var\_n(1, [X], [0.3, 0.5, 0.2], Var),$$
$$equality(Var, 2, DD), and(DD_1, DD, D).$$

while clause C_3 is translated to

$$flu(david, D) \leftarrow one(D).$$

In order to answer queries, the goal *prob(Goal,P)* is used, which is defined by

$$prob(Goal, P) \leftarrow init, retractall(var(\_, \_, \_)),$$
$$add\_bdd\_arg(Goal, BDD, GoalBDD),$$
$$(call(GoalBDD) \rightarrow ret\_prob(BDD, P); P = 0.0),$$
$$end.$$

where $add\_bdd\_arg(Goal, BDD, GoalBDD)$ returns $PITA(Goal, BDD)$ in $GoalBDD$.

Since variables may by multivalued, an encoding with Boolean variables must be chosen. The encoding used by PITA is the same as that used to translate LPADs into ProbLog seen in Section 2.4 that was proposed in [De Raedt et al., 2008].

Consider a variable X_{ij} associated with grounding θ_j of clause C_i having n values. We encode it using $n - 1$ Boolean variables

$$X_{ij1}, \ldots, X_{ijn-1}.$$

We represent the equation $X_{ij} = k$ for $k = 1, \ldots n - 1$ by means of the conjunction $\overline{X_{ij1}} \wedge \ldots \wedge \overline{X_{ijk-1}} \wedge X_{ijk}$, and the equation $X_{ij} = n$ by means of the conjunction $\overline{X_{ij1}} \wedge \ldots \wedge \overline{X_{ijn-1}}$. The BDD representation of the function in Equation (8.2) is given in Figure 8.7. The Boolean variables are associated

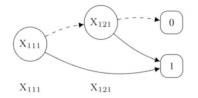

Figure 8.7 BDD representing the function in Equation (8.2).

with the following parameters:

$$P(X_{ij1}) = P(X_{ij1} = 1)$$

$$\ldots$$

$$P(X_{ijk}) = \frac{P(X_{ij} = k)}{\prod_{l=1}^{k-1}(1 - P(X_{ijl}))}$$

PITA uses tabling, see Section 1.4.2, that ensures that, when a goal is asked again, the answers for it already computed are retrieved rather than recomputed. This saves time because explanations for different goals are factored as in PRISM. Moreover, it also avoids non-termination in many cases.

PITA also exploits a feature of XSB Prolog called *answer subsumption* [Swift and Warren, 2012] that, when a new answer for a tabled subgoal is found, combines old answers with the new one according to a partial order or lattice. For example, if the lattice is on the second argument of a binary predicate p, answer subsumption may be specified by means of the declaration

```
:-table p(_, lattice(or/3)).
```

where or/3 is the join operation of the lattice. Thus, if a table has an answer p(a,d1) and a new answer p(a,d2) is derived, the answer p(a,d1) is replaced by p(a,d3), where d3 is obtained by calling or(d1,d2,d3).

In PITA, various predicates should be declared as tabled. For a predicate p/n, the declaration is

```
:-table p(_1,...,_n, lattice(or/3)).
```

which indicates that answer subsumption is used to form the disjunction of BDDs in the last argument, using the disjunction operation between BDDs.

At a minimum, the predicate of the goal and all the predicates appearing in negative literals should be tabled with answer subsumption.

Thanks to answer subsumption, a call to a goal $PITA(a, D)$, where b is ground, returns in D a BDD encoding the set of all of the explanations for a. Therefore, the transformation $PITA(b, D)$ for a negative literal $b =\sim a$ in the body of a rule, first calls $PITA(a, DN)$. If the call fails, a does not have any explanation, so the BDD for b should be the one Boolean function. Otherwise, the BDD DN is negated with $not/2$. So the transformation of the body of a clause makes sure that, to compute the BDD associated with the head atom, the BDDs of all literals are computed and conjoined with the BDD encoding the choice relative to the clause.

If predicates appearing in negative literals are not tabled with answer subsumption, PITA is not correct as a call to a subgoal doesn't collect all explanations. It is usually useful to table every predicate whose answers have multiple explanations and are going to be reused often since in this way repeated computations are avoided and explanations are factored.

PITA was originally available only for XSB because it was the only Prolog offering answer subsumption. Recently, answer subsumption was included in SWI-prolog and PITA is now available also for it in the `cplint` suite for SWI-prolog. In Prologs without answer subsumption, such as YAP, answer subsumption can be simulated using a slightly different PITA transformation with explicit *findall/3* calls. *findall(Template, Goal, Bag)* creates the list *Bag* of instantiations of *Template* for which *Goal* succeeds. For example, *findall(X, p(X), Bag)* returns in *Bag* the list of values of X for which $P(X)$ succeeds.

PITA was shown correct and terminating under mild conditions [Riguzzi and Swift, 2013] .

8.7 ProbLog2

The ProbLog2 system [Fierens et al., 2015] is a new version of ProbLog1 (Section 8.3) that performs knowledge compilation to d-DNNFs rather than to BDDs.

ProbLog2 can perform the tasks CONDATOMS, EVID, and MPE over ProbLog programs. It also allows probabilistic intensional facts of the form

$$\Pi :: f(X_1, X_2, \ldots, X_n) \leftarrow Body$$

with *Body* a conjunction of calls to non-probabilistic facts that define the domains of the variables $X_1, X_2, \ldots, X_n$. Moreover, ProbLog2 allows annotated disjunctions in LPAD style of the form

$$\Pi_{i1} :: h_{i1} ; \ldots ; \Pi_{in_i} :: h_{in_i} \leftarrow b_{i1}, \ldots, b_{im_i}$$

which are equivalent to an LPAD clauses of the form

$$h_{i1} : \Pi_{i1} ; \ldots ; h_{in_i} : \Pi_{in_i} \leftarrow b_{i1}, \ldots, b_{im_i}$$

and are handled by translating them into probabilistic facts using the technique of Section 2.4. Let us call ProbLog2 this extension of the language of ProbLog.

Example 78 (Alarm – ProbLog2 [Fierens et al., 2015]). *The following program is similar to the alarm BN of Examples 11 and 28:*

    $0.1 :: burglary.$
    $0.2 :: earthquake.$
    $0.7 :: hears\_alarm(X) \leftarrow person(X).$
    $alarm \leftarrow burglary.$
    $alarm \leftarrow earthquake.$
    $calls(X) \leftarrow alarm, hears\_alarm(X).$
    $person(mary).$
    $person(john).$
Differently from the alarm BN of Examples 11 and 28, two people can call in case they hear the alarm.

ProbLog2 converts the program into a weighted Boolean formula and then performs WMC. A *weighted Boolean formula* is a Boolean formula over a set of variables $V = \{V_1, \ldots, V_n\}$ associated with a weight function $w(\cdot)$ that assigns a real number to each literal (a variable or its negation) built on V. The weight function is extended to assign a real number to each assignment $\omega = \{V_1 = v_1, \ldots, V_n = v_n\}$ to the variables of V:

$$w(\omega) = \prod_{l \in \omega} w(l)$$

where each variable assignment in ω is interpreted as a literal. Given the weighted Boolean formula ϕ, the *weighted model count* of ϕ, $WMC_V(\phi)$, with respect to the set of variables V, is defined as

$$WMC_V(\phi) = \sum_{\omega \in SAT(\phi)} w(\omega).$$

where $SAT(\phi)$ is the set of assignments satisfying ϕ (the assignments for which ϕ is true).

ProbLog2 converts the program into a weighted formula in three steps:

1. Grounding $\mathcal{P}$ yielding a program $\mathcal{P}_g$, taking into account q and e in order to consider only the part of the program that is relevant to the query given the evidence.
2. Converting the ground rules in $\mathcal{P}_g$ to an equivalent Boolean formula ϕ_r.
3. Taking into account the evidence and defining a weight function. A Boolean formula ϕ_e representing the evidence is conjoined with ϕ_r obtaining formula ϕ and a weight function is defined for all literals built on variables in ϕ.

The grounding of the program can be restricted to the relevant rules only (see Section 1.3). SLD resolution is used to find relevant rules by proving all atoms in q, e. Tabling is used to avoid proving the same atom twice and to avoid going into infinite loops if the rules are cyclic. As programs are range restricted, all the atoms in the rules used during the SLD resolution will eventually become ground, and hence also the rules themselves.

Moreover, inactive rules encountered during SLD resolution are omitted. A ground rule is *inactive* if the body of the rule contains a literal l that is false in the evidence (l can be an atom that is false in e, or the negation of an atom that is true in e). Inactive rules do not contribute to the probability of the query, so they can be safely omitted.

The relevant ground program contains all the information necessary for solving the corresponding EVID, COND, or MPE task.

Example 79 (Alarm – grounding – ProbLog2 [Fierens et al., 2015]). *If $q = \{burglary\}$ and $e = calls(john)$ in Example 78, the relevant ground program is*

> $0.1 :: burglary.$
> $0.2 :: earthquake.$
> $0.7 :: hears\_alarm(john).$
> $alarm \leftarrow burglary.$
> $alarm \leftarrow earthquake.$
> $calls(john) \leftarrow alarm, hears\_alarm(john).$

The relevant ground program is now converted to an equivalent Boolean formula. The conversion is not merely syntactical as logic programming makes the Closed World Assumption while first-order logic doesn't.

If rules are acyclic, Clark's completion (see Section 1.4.1) can be used [Lloyd, 1987]. If rules are cyclic, i.e., they contain atoms that depend positively on each other, Clark's completion is not correct [Janhunen, 2004]. Two algorithms can then be used to perform the translation. The first [Janhunen, 2004] removes positive loops by introducing auxiliary atoms and rules and then applies Clark's completion. The second [Mantadelis and Janssens, 2010] first uses tabled SLD resolution to construct the proofs of all atoms in $atoms(q) \cup atoms(e)$, then collects the proofs in a data structure (a set of nested tries), and breaks the loops to build the Boolean formula.

Example 80 (Smokers – ProbLog [Fierens et al., 2015]). *The following program models causes for people to smoke: either they spontaneously start because of stress or they are influenced by one of their friends:*

$0.2 :: stress(P) \leftarrow person(P).$
$0.3 :: influences(P1, P2) \leftarrow friend(P1, P2).$
$person(p1).$
$person(p2).$
$person(p3).$
$friend(p1, p2).$
$friend(p2, p1).$
$friend(p1, p3).$
$smokes(X) \leftarrow stress(X).$
$smokes(X) \leftarrow smokes(Y), influences(Y, X).$

With the evidence smokes(p2) and the query smokes(p1), we obtain the following ground program:

$0.2 :: stress(p1).$
$0.2 :: stress(p2).$
$0.3 :: influences(p2, p1).$
$0.3 :: influences(p1, p2).$
$smokes(p1) \leftarrow stress(p1).$
$smokes(p1) \leftarrow smokes(p2), influences(p2, p1).$
$smokes(p2) \leftarrow stress(p2).$
$smokes(p2) \leftarrow smokes(p1), influences(p1, p2).$

Clark's completion would generate the Boolean formula

$smokes(p1) \leftrightarrow stress(p1) \vee smokes(p2), influences(p2, p1).$
$smokes(p2) \leftrightarrow stress(p2) \vee smokes(p1), influences(p1, p2).$

which has a model

$$\{smokes(p1), smokes(p2), \neg stress(p1), \neg stress(p2),$$
$$influences(p1, p2), influences(p2, p1), \ldots\}$$

which is not a model of any world of the ground ProbLog program: for total choice

$$\{\neg stress(p1), \neg stress(p2), influences(p1, p2), influences(p2, p1)\}$$

the model assigns false to both $smokes(p1)$ and $smokes(p2)$.

The conversion algorithm of [Mantadelis and Janssens, 2010] generates:
  $smokes(p1) \leftrightarrow aux1 \vee stress(p2)$
  $smokes(p2) \leftrightarrow aux2 \vee stress(p1)$
  $aux1 \leftrightarrow smokes(p2) \wedge influences(p2, p1)$
  $aux2 \leftrightarrow stress(p1) \wedge influences(p1, p2)$
Note that the loop in the original ProbLog program between $smokes(p1)$ and $smokes(p2)$ has been broken by using $stress(p1)$ instead of $smokes(p1)$ in the last formula.

Lemma 15 (Correctness of the ProbLog Program Transformation [Fierens et al., 2015]). *Let $\mathcal{P}_g$ be a ground ProbLog. $SAT(\phi_r) = MOD(\mathcal{P}_g)$ where $MOD(\mathcal{P}_g)$ is the set of models of instances of $\mathcal{P}_g$.*

The final Boolean formula ϕ is built from the one for the rules, ϕ_r, and that for the evidence ϕ_e obtained as

$$\phi_e = \bigwedge_{\sim a \in e} \neg a \wedge \bigwedge_{a \in e} a$$

Then $\phi = \phi_r \wedge \phi_e$. We illustrate this on the Alarm example, which is acyclic.

Example 81 (Alarm – Boolean formula – ProbLog2 [Fierens et al., 2015]). *For Example 79, the Boolean formula ϕ is*
  $alarm \leftrightarrow burglary \vee earthquake$
  $calls(john) \leftrightarrow alarm \wedge hears\_alarm(john)$
  $calls(john)$
where the three rows are meant to be conjoined.

Then the weight function $w(\cdot)$ is defined as: for each probabilistic fact $\Pi :: f$, f is assigned weight Π and $\neg f$ is assigned weight $1 - \Pi$. All the other literals are assigned weight 1. The weight of a world ω is given by the product of the weight of all literals in ω. The following theorem establishes the relationship between the relevant ground program and the weighted formula.

Theorem 17 (Model and weight equivalence [Fierens et al., 2015]). *Let $\mathcal{P}_g$ be the relevant ground program for some ProbLog program with respect to* *q and e. Let $MOD_e(\mathcal{P}_g)$ be those models in $MOD(\mathcal{P}_g)$ that are consistent with the evidence e. Let ϕ denote the formula and $w(\cdot)$ the weight function of the weighted formula derived from $\mathcal{P}_g$. Then:*

- *(model equivalence) $SAT(\phi) = MOD_e(\mathcal{P}_g)$,*
- *(weight equivalence) $\forall \omega \in SAT(\phi) : w(\omega) = P_{\mathcal{P}_g}(\omega)$, i.e., the weight of ω according to $w(\cdot)$ is equal to the probability of ω according to $\mathcal{P}_g$.*

If V is the set of the variables associated with $\mathcal{B}_\mathcal{P}$, then $WMC_V(\phi) = P(e)$. When V is clear from the context, it is omitted. So

$$P(e) = \sum_{\omega \in SAT(\phi)} \prod_{l \in \omega} w(l)$$

The inference tasks of COND, MPE, and EVID can be solved using state-of-the-art algorithms for WMC or weighted MAX-SAT.

By knowledge compilation, ProbLog2 translates ϕ to a smooth d-DNNF Boolean formula that allows WMC in polynomial time by in turn converting the d-DNNF into an arithmetic circuit. A Negation normal form (NNF) formula is a rooted directed acyclic graph in which each leaf node is labeled with a literal and each internal node is labeled with a conjunction or disjunction. Smooth d-DNNF formulas also satisfy

- Decomposability (D): for every conjunction node, no pair of children of the node have any variable in common.
- Determinism (d): for every disjunction node, every pair of children represent formulas that are logically inconsistent with each other.
- Smoothness: for every disjunction node, all children use exactly the same set of variables.

Compilers for d-DNNF usually start from formulas in Conjunctive normal form (CNF). A CNF is a Boolean formula that takes the form of a conjunction of disjunctions of literals, i.e., a formula of the form:

$$(l_{11} \vee \ldots \vee l_{1m_1}) \wedge \ldots \wedge (l_{n1} \vee \ldots \vee l_{nm_n})$$

where each l_{ij} is a literal. Examples of compilers from CNF to d-DNNF are c2d [Darwiche, 2004] and DSHARP [Muise et al., 2012]. The formula of Example 81 is translated to the d-DNNF of Figure 8.8.

The conversion of a d-DNNF formula into an arithmetic circuit is done in two steps [Darwiche, 2009, Chapter 12]: first conjunctions are replaced by multiplications and disjunctions by summations, and then each leaf node labeled with a literal l is replaced by a subtree consisting of a multiplication

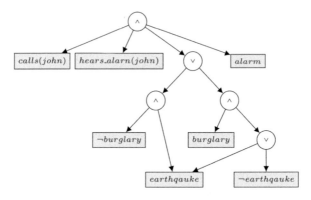

Figure 8.8   d-DNNF for the formula of Example 81. From [Fierens et al., 2015].

node with two children, a leaf node with a Boolean indicator variable $\lambda(l)$ for the literal l and a leaf node with the weight of l. The circuit for the Alarm example is shown in Figure 8.9. This transformation is equivalent to transforming the WMC formula into

$$AC(\phi) = \sum_{\omega \in SAT(\phi)} \prod_{l \in \omega} w(l)\lambda(l) = \sum_{\omega \in SAT(\phi)} \prod_{l \in \omega} w(l) \prod_{l \in \omega} \lambda(l)$$

Given the arithmetic circuit, the WMC can be computed by evaluating the circuit bottom-up after having assigned the value 1 to all the indicator variables. The value computed for the root, f, is the probability of evidence and so solves EVID. Figure 8.9 shows the values that are computed for each node: the value for the root, 0.196, is the probability of evidence.

With the arithmetic circuit, it is also possible to compute the probability of any evidence, provided that it extends the initial evidence. To compute $P(e, l_1 \ldots l_n)$ for any conjunction of literals $l_1, \ldots, l_n$, it is enough to set the indicator variables as $\lambda(l_i) = 1$, $\lambda(\neg l_i) = 0$ for $i = 1, \ldots, n$ (where $\neg\neg a = a$) and $\lambda(l) = 1$ for the other literals l, and evaluate the circuit. In fact, the value $f(l_1 \ldots l_n)$ of the root node will give:

$$f(l_1 \ldots l_n) = \sum_{\omega \in SAT(\phi)} \prod_{l \in \omega} w(l) \prod_{l \in \omega} \begin{cases} 1, & \text{if } \{l_1 \ldots l_n\} \subseteq \omega \\ 0, & \text{otherwise} \end{cases} =$$

$$\sum_{\omega \in SAT(\phi), \{l_1 \ldots l_n\} \subseteq \omega} \prod_{l \in \omega} w(l) =$$

$$P(e, l_1 \ldots l_n)$$

So in theory, one could build the circuit for formula ϕ_r only, since the probability of any set of evidence can then be computed. The formula for evidence however usually simplifies the compilation process and the resulting circuit.

Given the definition of conditional probability, $P(q|e) = \frac{P(q,e)}{P(e)}$, COND can solved by computing the probability of evidence q, e and dividing by $P(e)$.

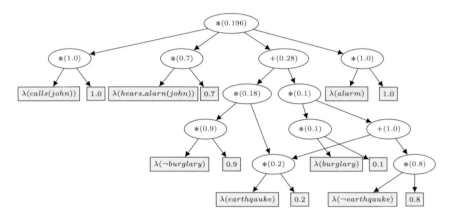

Figure 8.9 Arithmetic circuit for the d-DNNF of Figure 8.8. From [Fierens et al., 2015].

To compute CONDATOMS, we are given a set of ground atoms Q and evidence e and we want to compute $P(q|e)$ for all atoms $q \in Q$. One could solve COND for all atoms in Q. However, consider the partial derivative $\frac{\partial AC(\phi)}{\partial \lambda_q}$ for an atom q:

$$\frac{\partial AC(\phi)}{\partial \lambda_q} = \sum_{\omega \in SAT(\phi), q \in \omega} \prod_{l \in \omega} w(l) \prod_{l \in \omega, l \neq q} \lambda(l)$$

If we assign 1 to all indicator variables we obtain $\frac{\partial f}{\partial \lambda_q}$ that is given by

$$\frac{\partial f}{\partial \lambda_q} = \sum_{\omega \in SAT(\phi), q \in \omega} \prod_{l \in \omega} w(l) = P(e, q)$$

So if we compute the partial derivatives of f for all indicator variables $\lambda(q)$, we get $P(q, e)$ for all atoms q. We can solve this problem by traversing the circuit twice, once bottom-up and once top-down; see [Darwiche, 2009, Algorithms 34 and 35]. The algorithm computes the value $v(n)$ of each node

n and the derivative $d(n)$ of the value of the root node r with respect to n, i.e., $d(n) = \frac{\partial v(r)}{\partial v(n)}$. $v(n)$ is computed by traversing the circuit bottom-up and evaluating it at each node. $d(n)$ can be computed by observing that $d(r) = 1$ and, by the chain rule of calculus, for an arbitrary non-root node n with p indicating its parents

$$d(n) = \sum_p \frac{\partial v(r)}{\partial v(p)} \frac{\partial v(p)}{\partial v(n)} = \sum_p d(p) \frac{\partial v(p)}{\partial v(n)}.$$

If parent p is a multiplication node with n' indicating its children

$$\frac{\partial v(p)}{\partial v(n)} = \frac{\partial v(n) \prod_{n' \neq n} v(n')}{\partial v(n)} = \prod_{n' \neq n} v(n').$$

If parent p is an addition node with n' indicating its children

$$\frac{\partial v(p)}{\partial v(n)} = \frac{\partial v(n) + \sum_{n' \neq n} v(n')}{\partial v(n)} = 1.$$

So, if we indicate with $+p$ an addition parent of n and with $*p$ a multiplication parent of n, then

$$d(n) = \sum_{+p} d(+p) + \sum_{*p} d(*p) \prod_{n' \neq n} v(n').$$

Moreover, $\frac{\partial v(*p)}{\partial v(n)}$ can be computed as $\frac{\partial v(*p)}{\partial v(n)} = \frac{v(*p)}{v(n)}$ if $v(n) \neq 0$. If all indicator variables are set to 1, as required to compute f, and if no parameter is 0, which can be assumed as otherwise the formula could be simplified, then $v(n) \neq 0$ for all nodes and

$$d(n) = \sum_{+p} d(+p) + \sum_{*p} d(*p) v(*p) / v(n).$$

This leads to Procedure CIRCP shown in Algorithm 7 that is a simplified version of [Darwiche, 2009, Algorithm 35] for the case $v(n) \neq 0$ for all nodes. $v(n)$ may be 0 if f is evaluated at additional evidence (see $f(l_1 \ldots l_n)$ above), in that case, [Darwiche, 2009, Algorithm 35] must be used that takes into account this case and is slightly more complex.

ProbLog2 also offers compilation to BDDs. In this case, EVID and COND can be performed with Algorithm 6. In fact, Algorithm 6 performs WMC

Algorithm 7 Procedure CIRCP: Computation of value and derivatives of circuit nodes.

1: **procedure** CIRCP(*circuit*)
2:     assign values to leaves
3:     **for all** non-leaf node n with children c (visit children before parents) **do**
4:         **if** n is an addition node **then**
5:             $v(n) \leftarrow \sum_c v(c)$
6:         **else**
7:             $v(n) \leftarrow \prod_c v(c)$
8:         **end if**
9:     **end for**
10:    $d(r) \leftarrow 1, d(n) = 0$ for all non-root nodes
11:    **for all** non-root node n (visit parents before children) **do**
12:        **for all** parents p of n **do**
13:            **if** p is an addition parent **then**
14:                $d(n) = d(n) + d(p)$
15:            **else**
16:                $d(n) \leftarrow d(n) + d(p)v(p)/v(n)$
17:            **end if**
18:        **end for**
19:    **end for**
20: **end procedure**

---

over BDDs. This can be seen by observing that BDDs are d-DNNF that also satisfy the properties of decision and ordering [Darwiche, 2004]. A d-DNNF satisfies the property of *decision* iff the root node is a decision node, i.e., a node labeled with 0, 1 or the subtree

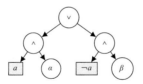

where a is a variable and α and β are decision nodes. a is called the *decision variable*. A d-DNNF satisfying the property of decision also satisfies the property of *ordering* if decision variables appear in the same order along any path from the root to any leaf. A d-DNNF satisfying decision and ordering is a BDD. d-DNNF satisfying decision and ordering may seem different from a BDD as we have seen it: however, if each decision node of the form above is replaced by

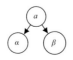

we obtain a BDD.

The d-DNNF of Figure 8.8, for example, does not satisfy decision and ordering. The same Boolean formula, however, can be encoded with the BDD of Figure 8.10 that can be converted to a d-DNNF using the above equivalence. Algorithm 6 for computing the probability of a BDD is equivalent to the evaluation of the arithmetic circuit that can be obtained from the BDD by seeing it as a d-DNNF.

More recently, ProbLog2 has also included the possibility of compiling the Boolean function to SDDs [Vlasselaer et al., 2014; Dries et al., 2015]. An SDD for the formula of Example 81 is shown in Figure 8.11.

An SDD [Darwiche, 2011] contains two types of nodes: *decision nodes*, represented as circles, and *elements*, represented as paired boxes. Elements are the children of decision nodes and each box in an element can contain a pointer to a decision node or a *terminal node*, either a literal or the constants 0 or 1. In an element (p, s), p is called a *prime* and s is called a *sub*. A decision node with children $(p_1, s_1), \ldots, (p_n, s_n)$ represents the function $(p_1 \wedge s_1) \vee$

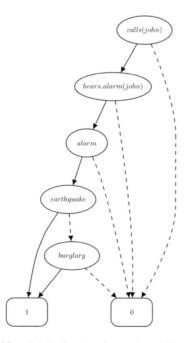

Figure 8.10   BDD for the formula of Example 81.

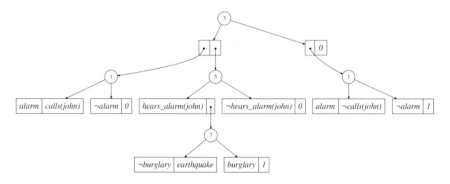

Figure 8.11   SDD for the formula of Example 81.

... $\vee\, (p_n \wedge s_n)$. Primes $p_1, \ldots, p_n$ must form a partition: $p_i \neq 0$, $p_i \wedge p_j = 0$ for $i \neq j$, and $p_1 \vee \ldots \vee p_n = 1$.

A *vtree* is a full binary tree whose leaves are in one-to-one correspondence with the formula variables. Each SDD is normalized for some vtree. Figure 8.12 shows the vtree for which the SDD of Figure 8.11 is normalized. Each SDD node is normalized for some vtree node. The root node of the SDD is normalized for the root vtree node. Terminal nodes are normalized for leaf vtree nodes. If a decision node is normalized for a vtree node v, then its primes are normalized for the left child of v, and its subs are normalized for the right child of v. As a result, primes and subs of same decision node do not share variables. The SDD of a Boolean formula is unique once a vtree is fixed. In Figure 8.11, decision nodes are labeled with the vtree nodes they are normalized for.

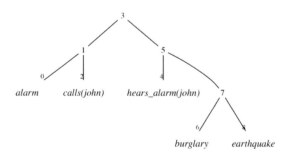

Figure 8.12   vtree for which the SDD of Figure 8.11 is normalized.

SDDs are special cases of d-DNNF: if one replaces circle-nodes with or-nodes, and paired-boxes with and-nodes, one obtains a d-DNNF. SDDs satisfy two additional properties with respect to d-DNNF: structured decomposability and strong determinism.

To define structured decomposability, consider a d-DNNF δ and assume, without loss of generality, that all conjunctions are binary. δ *respects* a vtree V if for every conjunction $\alpha \wedge \beta$ in δ, there is a node v in V such that $vars(\alpha) \subseteq vars(v_l)$ and $vars(\beta) \subseteq vars(v_r)$ where v_l and v_r are the left and right child of v and $vars(\alpha)$ and $vars(v)$ are the sets of variables appearing in the subdiagram rooted at α and the sub-vtree rooted at v respectively. δ enjoys *structured decomposability* if it satisfies some vtree.

Strong determinism requires not only that the children of or nodes are pairwise inconsistent but that they form a strongly deterministic decomposition. An $(\mathbf{X}, \mathbf{Y})$-*decomposition* of a function $f(\mathbf{X}, \mathbf{Y})$ over non-overlapping variables $\mathbf{X}$ and $\mathbf{Y}$ is a set $\{(p_1, s_1), \ldots, (p_n, s_n)\}$ such that

$$f = p_1(\mathbf{X}) \wedge s_1(\mathbf{Y}) \vee \ldots \vee p_n(\mathbf{X}) \wedge s_n(\mathbf{Y})$$

If $p_i \wedge p_j = 0$ for $i \neq j$, the decomposition is said to be *strongly deterministic*. A d-DNNF is *strongly deterministic* if each or node is a strongly deterministic decomposition.

BDDs are a special case of SDDs where decompositions are all Shannon: formula f is decomposed into $\{(X, f^X), (\neg X, f^{\neg X})\}$. SDDs generalize BDDs by considering non-binary decisions based on the value of primes and by considering vtrees instead of linear variable orders.

In ProbLog2, the user can choose whether to use d-DNNFs, BDDs or SDDs. The choice of the compilation language depends on the tradeoff between succinctness and tractability. Succinctness is defined by the size of a knowledge base once it is compiled. Tractability is determined by the set of operations that can be performed in polynomial time. The more tractable a representation is, the less succinct it is.

A language is *at least as succinct as* another if, for every sentence in the second language, there exists an equivalent sentence in the first with a polynomially smaller size. The succinctness order for BDD, SDD, and d-DNNF is

$$\text{d-DNNF} < \text{SDD} \leqslant \text{BDD}$$

meaning that d-DNNF is strictly more succinct than SDDs and that SDDs are at least as succinct as BDDs (whether SDD < BDD is an open problem). Since SDD $\nleqslant$ d-DNNF, there exist formulas whose smallest SDD representation is exponentially larger that its d-DNNF representation.

Table 8.1 Tractability of operations. ? means "unknown", ✓ means "tractable" and ○ means "not tractable unless P=NP". Operations are meant over a bounded number of operands and BDDs operands should have the same variable order and SDDs the same vtree. From [Vlasselaer et al., 2014]

Language	Negation	Conjunction	Disjunction	Model Counting
d-DNNF	?	○	○	✓
SDD	✓	✓	✓	✓
BDD	✓	✓	✓	✓

The operations for which we consider tractability are those that are useful for probabilistic inference, namely, negation, conjunction, disjunction, and model counting. The situation for the languages we consider is summarized in Table 8.1.

SDDs and BDDs support tractable Boolean combination operators. This means that they can be built bottom-up starting from the cycle-free ground program, similarly to what is done by ProbLog1 or PITA. d-DNNF compilers instead require the formula to be in CNF. Converting the Clark's completion of the rules into CNF introduces a new auxiliary variable for each rule which has a body with more than one literal. This adds cost to the compilation process.

Another advantage of BDDs and SDDs is that they support minimization: their size can be reduced by modifying the variable order or vtree. Minimization of d-DNNF is not supported, so circuits may be larger than necessary.

The disadvantage of BDDs with respect to d-DNNF and SDDs is that they have worse size upper bounds, while the upper bound for d-DNNF and SDD is the same [Razgon, 2014].

Experimental comparisons confirm this and show that d-DNNF leads to faster inference than BDDs [Fierens et al., 2015] and that SDDs lead to faster inference than d-DNNF [Vlasselaer et al., 2014].

The ProbLog2 system can be used in three ways. It can be used online at https://dtai.cs.kuleuven.be/problog/: the user can enter and solve ProbLog problems with just a web browser.

It can be used from the command line as a Python program. In this case, the user has full control over the system settings and can use all machine resources, in contrast with the online version that has resource limits. In this version, ProbLog programs may use external functions written in Python, such as those offered by the wide Python ecosystem.

ProbLog2 can also be used as a library that can be called from Python for building and querying probabilistic ProbLog models.

8.8 T_P Compilation

Previous inference algorithms work backward, by reasoning from the query toward the probabilistic choices. T_P compilation [Vlasselaer et al., 2015, 2016] is an approach for performing probabilistic inference in ProbLog using forward reasoning. In particular, it is based on the operator T_{cP}, a generalization of the T_P operator of logic programming that operates on parameterized interpretations. We have encountered a form of parameterized interpretations in Section 3.2 where each atom is associated with a set of composite choices. The parameterized interpretations of [Vlasselaer et al., 2016] associate ground atoms with Boolean formulas built on variables that represent probabilistic ground facts.

Definition 40 (Parameterized interpretation [Vlasselaer et al., 2015, 2016]). *A parameterized interpretation $\mathcal{I}$ of a ground probabilistic logic program $\mathcal{P}$ with probabilistic facts $\mathcal{F}$ and atoms $\mathcal{B}_\mathcal{P}$ is a set of tuples (a, λ_a) with $a \in \mathcal{B}_\mathcal{P}$ and λ_a a propositional formula over $\mathcal{F}$ expressing in which interpretations a is true.*

The T_{cP} operator takes as input a parameterized interpretation and returns another parameterized interpretation obtained by applying the rules once.

Definition 41 (T_{cP} operator [Vlasselaer et al., 2015, 2016]). *Let $\mathcal{P}$ be a ground probabilistic logic program with probabilistic facts $\mathcal{F}$, rules $\mathcal{R}$ and atoms $\mathcal{B}_\mathcal{P}$. Let $\mathcal{I}$ be a parameterized interpretation with pairs (a, λ_a). Then, the T_{cP} operator is $T_{cP}(\mathcal{I}) = \{(a, \lambda_a)|a \in \mathcal{B}_\mathcal{P}\}$ where*

$$
\lambda'_a = \begin{cases}
a & \text{if } a \in \mathcal{F} \\
\displaystyle\bigvee_{\substack{a \leftarrow b_1,\ldots,b_n,\sim c_1,\ldots,\sim c_m \in \mathcal{R}}} \left(\lambda_{b_1} \wedge \ldots \wedge \lambda_{b_n} \wedge \neg\lambda_{c_1} \wedge \ldots \wedge \neg\lambda_{c_m}\right) & \text{if } a \in \mathcal{B}_\mathcal{P} \backslash \mathcal{F}
\end{cases}
$$

The ordinal powers of T_{cP} start from $\{(a,0)|a \in \mathcal{B}_\mathcal{P}\}$. The concept of fixpoint must be defined in a semantic rather than syntactic way.

Definition 42 (Fixpoint of T_{cP} [Vlasselaer et al., 2015, 2016]). *A parameterized interpretation $\mathcal{I}$ is a fixpoint of the T_{cP} operator if and only if for all $a \in \mathcal{B}_\mathcal{P}$, $\lambda_a \equiv \lambda'_a$, where λ_a and λ'_a are the formulas for a in $\mathcal{I}$ and $T_{cP}(\mathcal{I})$, respectively.*

Vlasselaer et al. [2016] show that, for definite programs, Tcp has a least fixpoint $\mathrm{lfp}(Tcp) = \{(a, \lambda_a^\infty) | a \in B_P\}$ where the λ_a^∞s exactly describe the possible worlds where a is true and can be used to compute the probability for each atom by WMC, i.e., $P(a) = WMC(\lambda_a^\infty)$.

The probability of an atomic query q given evidence e can be computed as

$$P(q|e) = \frac{WMC(\lambda_q \wedge \lambda_e)}{WMC(\lambda_e)}$$

where $\lambda_e = \bigwedge_{e_i \in e} \lambda_{e_i}$.

The approach can also be applied to stratified normal logic programs by iterating the Tcp operator stratum by stratum: the fixpoint of Tc_p is computed by considering the rules for each stratum in turn.

So, to perform exact inference on a ProbLog program $\mathcal{P}$, the Tcp operator should be iterated stratum by stratum until the fixpoint is reached in each stratum. The parameterized interpretation that is obtained after the last stratum can then be used to perform COND and EVID.

The algorithm of [Vlasselaer et al., 2016] represents the formulas in the interpretations by means of SDDs. So the Boolean formulas λ_a in the definition of Tcp are replaced by SDD structures Λ_a. Since negation, conjunction, and disjunction are efficient for SDDs, then so is the application of Tcp.

Moreover, the Tcp operator can be applied in a granular way one atom at a time, which is useful for selecting more effective evaluation strategies in approximate inference, see Section 10.7. The operator $Tcp(a, \mathcal{I})$ considers only the rules with a in the head and updates only the formula λ_a. So an application of Tcp is modified in

1. select an atom $a \in B_P$,
2. compute $Tcp(a, \mathcal{I})$.

Vlasselaer et al. [2016] show that if each atom is selected frequently enough in step 1, then the same fixpoint $\mathrm{lfp}(Tcp)$ is reached as for the naive algorithm that considers all atoms at the same time, provided that the operator is still applied stratum by stratum in normal logic programs.

T_P compilation can also be used for performing inference in the case of updates of the program, where (ground) facts and rules can be added or removed. For definite programs, past compilation results can be reused to compute the new fixpoint. Moreover, T_P compilation can be used for dynamic models, where each atom has an argument that represents the time at which it is true. In this case, the rules express the dependency of an atom at a time step from atoms at the same or previous time step. An extension of T_P compilation can then be used for filtering, i.e., computing the probability of a query at a time t given evidence up to time t.

Experiments in [Vlasselaer et al., 2016] show that T_P compilation compares favorably with ProbLog2 with both d-DNNF and SDD.

8.9 MPE and MAP

In this section we discuss algorithms for performing the MPE and MAP tasks.

8.9.1 MAP and MPE in ProbLog

Shterionov et al. [2015] describe how MPE inference is performed in ProbLog. When the ProbLog program does not contain annotated disjunctions, the ProbLog2 algorithm for COND is initially followed: the relevant ground program is identified, it is translated into a CNF and the CNF is compiled to a d-DNNF. At this point the algorithms for COND and MPE differ in the way the formula is transformed into an arithmetic circuit: for MPE, the $\vee$ nodes are trasnformed into max nodes instead of $+$ nodes. The evaluation of the circuit gives the MPE probability of the query, see [Darwiche, 2004, Section 12.3.2]. To produce the explanation as well, the algorithms that visits the circuit has to keep track of which children of max nodes are selected.

When the ProbLog program contains annotated disjunctions, the translation of Section 2.4 using $n_i - 1$ Boolean variables for a clause with n_i heads does not work, as configurations of the variables exist that do not correspond to any value for the rule random variable. The problem is that the encoding is redundant and a value for the random variable associated with a rule may be encoded by multiple tuples of values for the Boolean variables besides the intended one. One of those unintended encodings may get chosen because it has a higher probability but this does not reflect on the correct choice of the multivalued variable. Shterionov et al. [2015] propose a different encoding, where n_i Boolean variables X_{ijk} for a clause $C_i\theta_j = head \leftarrow body$ with n_i heads are used and constraints are imposed, namely that one and only one X_{ijk} must be true. This is achieved by building the constraint formula

$$\left(\bigvee_{k=1}^{n_i} X_{ijk} \leftrightarrow body \right) \wedge \bigwedge_{k=1}^{n_i-1} \bigwedge_{m=k+1}^{n_i} \left(\neg X_{ijk} \vee \neg X_{ijm} \right)$$

for each multi-valued variable X_{ij}, translating it into a CNF and conjoining it with the CNF built for the query.

For MAP, ProbLog uses DTProbLog, an algorithm for maximizing an utility function by making decisions, see Section 11.2. In DTProbLog utility values are assigned to some ground literals, some ground atoms are probabilistic and some are decision. The aim is to find an assignment to decision variables that maximizes utility, given by the sum of the utility for the literals that are made true by the decisions. DTProbLog uses Algebraic decision diagrams (ADDs) as a target compilation language. ADDs are BDDs where leaves are associated with real numbers instead of Boolean values. ADDs built by DTProbLog contain only decision variables, probabilistic variables are compiled away.

Shterionov et al. [2015] also illustrate the difference between VIT and MPE.

Example 82 (VIT vs MPE [Shterionov et al., 2015]). *Consider the program:*

```
0.4::red.
0.9::green.
0.5::blue.
0.6::yellow.
win :- red, green.
win :- blue, yellow.
```

The query `win` *has two explanations (or proofs): the first uses facts* `red` *and* `green` *and has probability* $0.4 \times 0.9 = 0.36$, *the second uses facts* `blue` *and* `yellow` *and has probability* $0.5 \times 0.6 = 0.3$. *The Viterbi proof is the first. The MPE state for the query* `win`, *however, is*

```
[\+red, green, blue, yellow]
```

with probability $0.6 \times 0.9 \times 0.5 \times 0.6 = 0.162$. *This state doesn't extend the Viterbi proof.*

8.9.2 MAP and MPE in PITA

Bellodi et al. [2020] present an extension of PITA for performing MPE and MAP. They consider the following problem.

Definition 43 (PITA MAP Problem). *Given an LPAD $\mathcal{P}$, a conjunction of ground atoms e, the* evidence, *and a set of random variables $\mathbf{X}$ (query random variables), associated to some ground rules of $\mathcal{P}$, the MAP problem is to find an assignment $\mathbf{x}$ of values to $\mathbf{X}$ such that $P(\mathbf{x}|e)$ is maximized, i.e., solve*

$$\arg\max_{\mathbf{x}} P(\mathbf{x}|e)$$

The MPE problem is a MAP problem where **X** *includes all the random vari-ables associated with all ground clauses of* $\mathcal{P}$.

In PITA we indicate the query random variables in the program by prepending the functor `map_query` to the rules. Thus an MPE problem is one where `map_query` is in front of every probabilistic clause.

Example 83 (Bag of balls - MPE).   *Consider a game with a single bag containing red, green and blue balls, where the player randomly decides to pick a ball or not. This can be encoded with*

```
map_query red(b1):0.6; green(b1):0.3; blue(b1):0.1 :- pick(b1).
map_query pick(b1):0.6; no_pick(b1):0.4.
                    ev:- \+ blue(b1).
```

evidence `ev` *has the MPE assignment* **x***:*

```
[rule(0, red(b1), [red(b1):0.6, green(b1):0.3, blue(b1):0.1],
    pick(b1)),
 rule(1, pick(b1), [pick(b1):0.6, no_pick(b1):0.4], true),
```

where predicate `rule/4` *specifies clause number (zero-based), selected head, clause head, clause body, in that order. For this assignment,* $P(\mathbf{x}|ev) = 0.36$, *meaning that the most probable explanation* **x** *has a probability of 0.36.*

Example 84 (Bag of balls - MAP).   *Given the program*

```
            red(b1):0.6; green(b1):0.3; blue(b1):0.1 :- pick(b1).
map_query pick(b1):0.6; no_pick(b1):0.4.
            ev:- \+ blue(b1).
```

Evidence `ev` *has the MAP assignment:*

```
[rule(1, pick(b1), [pick(b1):0.6, no_pick(b1):0.4], true)].
```

For this assignment, $P(\mathbf{x}|ev) = 0.54$.

Example 85 (Disease - Difference between MPE and MAP).   *Consider the following LPAD:*

```
map_query disease:0.05.
map_query malfunction:0.05.
          positive :- malfunction.
map_query positive:0.999 :- disease.
map_query positive:0.0001 :- \+(malfunction), \+(disease).
```

The LPAD models the diagnosis of a disease by means of a lab test. The disease probability is 0.05, and, in case of disease, the test result will be positive with probability 0.999. However, there is a 5% chance of an equipment malfunction; in this case, the test will always be positive. Additionally, even in absence of disease or malfunction, the test result will be positive with probability 0.0001. The LPAD has 16 worlds, each corresponding to selecting, or not, the head of each annotated disjunctive clause.

Let us suppose for the test result to be positive: is the patient ill? Given evidence `ev = positive`, *the MPE assignment is*

```
[rule(0, disease, [disease:0.05, '' :0.95], true),
 rule(1, '', [malfunction:0.05, '' :0.95], true),
 rule(2, positive, [positive:0.999, '' :0.001], disease),
 rule(3, '', [positive:0.0001, '' :0.9999], (\+malfunction,
   \+disease))]
```

where `' '` *indicates the null head. The most probable world is the one where an actual disease caused the positive result, and its probability is* $P(\mathbf{x}|e) = 0.04702$.

Likewise, if we perform a MAP inference taking only the choice of the first clause as query variable, the result is

```
[rule(0, disease, [disease:0.05, '' : 0.95], true)]
```

so the patient is ill. However, if we take the choices for the first two clauses as query variables, i.e., if we look for the most likely combination of `disease` *and* `malfunction` *given* `positive`, *the MAP task produces*

```
[rule(0, '', [disease:0.05, '' : 0.95], true)]
 rule(1, malfunction, [malfunction:0.05, '' : 0.95], true),
```

meaning that the patient is not ill and the positive test is explained by an equipment malfunction. This examples shows that the value assigned to a query variable in a MAP task can be affected by the presence of other variables in the set of query variables; in particular, MPE and MAP inference over $\mathbf{X}$ *may assign different values to the same variable given the same evidence.*

PITA solves the MPE task [Bellodi et al., 2020] using BDDs. In particular, it exploits the CUDD library. In CUDD, BDD nodes are described by two fields: *pointer*, a pointer to the node, and *comp*, a Boolean indicating whether the node is complemented. In fact three types of edges are admitted:

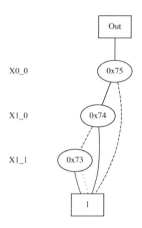

Figure 8.13　CUDD BDD for the query `ev` of Example 83. Labels Xi_j indicates the jth Boolean variable of ith ground clause and the label of each node is a part of its memory address.

an edge to a 1-child, an edge to a 0-child and a complemented edge to a 0-child, meaning that the function encoded by the child must be complemented. Moreover, the root node can be complemented. For these types of BDDs, only the 1 leaf is needed. For example, the CUDD BDD for the EVID query `ev` of Example 83 is shown in Figure 8.13. To compute the probability of the query (solving the EVID task), PITA uses Algorithm 8 which is the CUDD version of Algorithm 6.

PITA encodes random variables for query annotated disjunctive clauses as in [Shterionov et al., 2015]: n_i Boolean variables X_{ijk} for a clause with n_i heads are used and the following constraints are imposed

$$\left(\bigvee_{k=1}^{n_i} X_{ijk}\right) \wedge \bigwedge_{k=1}^{n_i-1} \bigwedge_{m=k+1}^{n_i} \left(\neg X_{ijk} \vee \neg X_{ijm}\right) \tag{8.4}$$

for each multi-valued variable X_{ij}. The constraints are translated into a BDD and conjoined it with the BDD built for the query with PITA. The BDDs built for examples 83 and 84 with this new encoding are shown in figures 8.14 and 8.15.

PITA solves MPE using the dynamic programming algorithm proposed by [Darwiche, 2004, Section 12.3.2] for computing MPE over d-DNNFs, which generalize BDDs. In fact, BDDs can be seen as d-DNNFs as shown in Section 8.7: a BDD node (Figure 8.16(a)) for variable a with children α

Algorithm 8 Function CUDDPROB: computation of the probability of a CUDD BDD.

1: **function** CUDDPROB(*node*)
2:    **if** *node* is a terminal **then**
3:       **return** 1
4:    **else**
5:       **if** $Table(node.pointer) \neq null$ **then**
6:          **return** $Table(node.pointer)$
7:       **else**
8:          $p0 \leftarrow$CUDDPROB($child_0(node)$)
9:          $p1 \leftarrow$CUDDPROB($child_1(node)$)
10:         **if** $child_0(node).comp$ **then**
11:            $p0 \leftarrow (1 - p0)$
12:         **end if**
13:         Let π be the probability of being true of $var(node)$
14:         $Res \leftarrow p1 \cdot \pi + p0 \cdot (1 - \pi)$
15:         Add $node.pointer \rightarrow Res$ to $Table$
16:         **return** Res
17:       **end if**
18:    **end if**
19: **end function**

---

and β is translated into the d-DNNF portion shown in Figure 8.16(b), where α' and β' are the translations of the BDDs α and β respectively. The algorithm proposed by [Darwiche, 2004] computes the probability of the MPE by replacing $\wedge$-nodes with product nodes and $\vee$-nodes with max-nodes: the result is an arithmetic circuit (Figure 8.16(c)) that, when evaluated bottom-up, gives the probability of the MPE and can be used to identify the MPE assignment. The equivalent algorithm operating on BDDs - Function MAP-INT in Algorithm 9 - modifies Algorithm 8 and returns both a probability and a set of assignments to random variables. At each node, instead of computing $Res \leftarrow p1 \cdot \pi + p0 \cdot (1 - \pi)$ as in Algorithm 8 line 14, it returns the assignment of the children having the maximum probability. This is computed in lines 41-45 in Algorithm 9. In MPE there are no non-query variables, so the test in line 26 succeeds only for the BDD leaf. MAPINT in practice computes the probability of paths from the root to the 1 leaf and returns the probability and the assignment corresponding to the most probable path.

Function MAP in Algorithm 9 takes as input the BDD representing the evidence *root*, builds the BDD representing Equation (8.4) for all i, j, conjoins it with *root* and calls MAPINT on the result.

Algorithm 9 Function MAP: computation of the maximum a posterior state of a set of query variables and of its probability

---

1: **function** MAP($root$)
2:      **for all** query variables var **do**
3:          $AtLeastOne \leftarrow$ BDD_ZERO
4:          $AtMostOne \leftarrow$ BDD_ONE
5:          **for** $i \leftarrow 1$ to $values(var) - 1$ **do**
6:              $AtLeastOne \leftarrow$ BDD_OR($AtLeastOne, bVar(var, i)$)
7:              **for** $j \leftarrow i + 1$ to $values(var)$ **do**
8:                  $Both \leftarrow$ BDD_AND($bVar(var, i), bVar(var, j)$)
9:                  $NotBoth \leftarrow$ BDD_NOT($Both$)
10:                 $AtMostOne \leftarrow$ BDD_AND($AtMostOne, NotBoth$)
11:             **end for**
12:             $AtLeastOne \leftarrow$ BDD_OR($AtLeastOne, bVar(var, values(var))$)
13:         **end for**
14:         $const \leftarrow$ BDD_AND($AtLeastOne, AtMostOne$)
15:         $root \leftarrow$ BDD_AND($root, const$)
16:     **end for**
17:     Reorder BDD $root$ so that variables associated to query variables come first in the order
18:     Let $root'$ be the new root
19:     $TableMAP \leftarrow \emptyset$
20:     $Table \leftarrow \emptyset$
21:     $(Prob, MAP) \leftarrow$ MAPINT($root'$, false)   ▷ MAP: assignment to Boolean random variables
22:     **return** $(Prob, MAP)$
23: **end function**
24: **function** MAPINT($node, comp$)   ▷ Internal function implementing the dynamic programming algorithm
25:     $comp \leftarrow node.comp \oplus comp$ ▷ $\oplus$ is exor
26:     **if** $var(node)$ is not associated to a query var **then**
27:         $p \leftarrow$ CUDDPROB($node$)   ▷ Algorithm 8
28:         **if** $comp$ **then**
29:             **return** $(1 - p, [])$
30:         **else**
31:             **return** $(p, [])$
32:         **end if**
33:     **else**
34:         **if** $TableMAP(node.pointer) \neq null$ **then**
35:             **return** $TableMAP(node.pointer)$
36:         **else**
37:             $(p0, MAP0) \leftarrow$ MAPINT($child_0(node), comp$)
38:             $(p1, MAP1) \leftarrow$ MAPINT($child_1(node), comp$)
39:             Let π be the probability of being true of the variable associated to $node$
40:             $p1 \leftarrow p1 \cdot \pi$
41:             **if** $p1 > p0$ **then**
42:                 $Res \leftarrow (p1, [var(node) = 1 | MAP1])$
43:             **else**
44:                 $Res \leftarrow (p0, MAP0)$
45:             **end if**
46:             Add $(node.pointer) \rightarrow Res$ to $TableMAP$
47:             **return** Res
48:         **end if**
49:     **end if**
50: **end function**

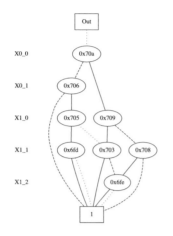

Figure 8.14   BDD for the MPE problem of Example 83. The variables X0_k and X1_k are associated with the second and first clause respectively.

Figure 8.15   BDD for the MAP problem of Example 84. The variables X0_k and X1_k are associated with the second and first clause respectively.

In a MAP task, i.e., when we have non-query variables, function MAP-INT cannot be used because when a node for a non-query variable is reached, it must be summed out instead of maximized out, and maximization and summation operations are not commutative. However, if its children are nodes for query variables, which of the two assignments for the children should be propagated towards the root? In case the non-query variables appear last in the ordering, when MAPINT reaches a node for a non-query variable, it can

(a) Node for variable   (b) d-DNNF equivalent por-   (c) Arithmetic circuit.
a in a BDD.   tion.

Figure 8.16   Translation from BDDs to d-DNNF.

sum out all non-query variables using function CUDDPROB from Algorithm 8. This assigns a probability to the node that can be used by MAPINT to identify the most probable path from the root. So PITA solves MAP by reordering variables in the BDD (line 17 in Algorithm 9), putting first the query variables.

With CUDD we can either create BDDs from scratch with a given variable order or modify BDDs according to a new variable order. Changing the position of a variable is made by successive swapping of adjacent variables [Somenzi, 2001]: the swap can be performed in a time proportional to the number of nodes associated with the two swapped variables. Changing the order of two adjacent variables does not affect the other levels of the BDD, so changes can be applied directly to the current BDD saving memory. To further reduce the cost of the swapping, the CUDD library keeps in memory an interaction matrix specifying which variables directly interact with others. This matrix is updated only when a new variable is inserted into the BDD, is symmetric and can be stored by using a single bit for each pair, making it very small. Moreover, the cost of building it is negligible compared to the cost of manipulating the BDD without checking it. Jiang et al. [2017]. empirically demonstrated that changing the order of variables by means of sequential swapping is usually much more time efficient than rebuilding the BDD following a fixed variable order.

8.10 Modeling Assumptions in PITA

Let us recall here PRISM modeling assumptions:

1. The probability of a conjunction (A, B) is computed as the product of the probabilities of A and B (*independent-and assumption*).

2. The probability of a disjunction $(A; B)$ is computed as the sum of the probabilities of A and B (*exclusive-or assumption*).

These assumptions can be stated more formally by referring to explanations. Given an explanation κ, let $RV(\kappa) = \{C_i\theta_j|(C_i, \theta_j, k) \in \kappa\}$. Given a set of explanations K, let $RV(K) = \bigcup_{\kappa \in K} RV(\kappa)$. Two sets of explanations, K_1 and K_2, are *independent* if $RV(K_1) \cap RV(K_2) = \varnothing$ and *exclusive* if, $\forall \kappa_1 \in K_1, \kappa_2 \in K_2$, κ_1 and κ_2 are incompatible.

The independent-and assumption means that, when deriving a covering set of explanations for a goal, the covering sets of explanations K_i and K_j for two ground subgoals in the body of a clause are independent.

The exclusive-or assumption means that, when deriving a covering set of explanations for a goal, two sets of explanations K_i and K_j obtained for a ground subgoal h from two different ground clauses are exclusive. This implies that the atom h is derived using clauses that have mutually exclusive bodies, i.e., that their bodies are not true at the same time in any world.

The systems PRISM [Sato and Kameya, 1997] and PITA(IND, EXC) [Riguzzi and Swift, 2011] exploit these assumptions to speed up the computation. In fact, these assumptions make the computation of probabilities "truth-functional" [Gerla, 2001] (the probability of conjunction/disjunction of two propositions depends only on the probabilities of those propositions), while, in the general case, this is false. PITA(IND, EXC) differs from PITA in the definition of the $one/1$, $zero/1$, $not/2$, $and/3$ and $or/3$ predicates that now work on probabilities P rather than on BDDs. Their definitions are

$zero(0)$.
$one(1)$.
$not(A, B) \leftarrow B \text{ is } 1 - A$.
$and(A, B, C) \leftarrow C \text{ is } A * B$.
$or(A, B, C) \leftarrow C \text{ is } A + B$.

Moreover, in the PITA transformation $PITA(C_r, i)$ for a clause C_r (Equation (8.3)), the conjunction

$get\_var\_n(r, S, [\Pi_1, \dots, \Pi_n], Var), equality(Var, i, DD)$

is replaced by

$nth(i, [\Pi_1, \dots, \Pi_n], DD)$

where $nth(I, List, Element)$ is a predicate that returns the Ith element of $List$ in $Element$.

Instead of the *exclusive-or assumption*, a program may satisfy the following assumption:

3. The probability of a disjunction $(A; B)$ is computed as if A and B were independent (*independent-or assumption*).

This means that, when deriving a covering set of explanations for a goal, two sets of explanations K_i and K_j obtained for a ground subgoal h from two different ground clauses are independent. If A and B are independent, the probability of their disjunction is

$$P(A \vee B) = P(A) + P(B) - P(A \wedge B) = \\ P(A) + P(B) - P(A)P(B)$$

by the laws of probability theory. PITA(IND, EXC) can be used for programs respecting this assumption by changing the $or/3$ predicate in this way
$$or(A, B, P) \leftarrow P \ is \ A + B - A * B.$$
PITA(IND,IND) is the resulting system.

The exclusiveness assumption for conjunctions of literals means that the conjunction is true in 0 worlds and thus has probability 0, so it does not make sense to consider a PITA(EXC,_) system.

The following program
$$path(Node, Node).$$
$$path(Source, Target) : 0.3 \leftarrow edge(Source, Node),$$
$$\quad path(Node, Target).$$
$$edge(0, 1) : 0.3.$$
$$\dots$$

satisfies the independent-and and independent-or assumptions depending on the structure of the graph. For example, the graphs in Figures 8.17(a) and 8.17(b) respect these assumptions for the query $path(0, 1)$. Similar graphs of increasing sizes can be obtained [Bragaglia and Riguzzi, 2011]. We call the first graph type a "lanes" graph and the second a "branches" graph. The graphs of the type of Figure 8.17(c), called "parachutes" graphs, instead, satisfy only the independent-and assumption for the query $path(0, 1)$.

All three types of graphs respect the independent-and assumption because, when deriving the goal $path(0, 1)$, paths are built incrementally starting from node 0 and adding one edge at a time with the second clause of the definition of $path/2$. Since the edge that is added does not appear in the rest of the path, the assumption is respected.

Lanes and branches graphs respect the independent-or assumption because, when deriving the goal $path(0, 1)$, ground instantiations of the second path clause have $path(i, 1)$ in the head and originate atomic choices of the form $(C_2, \{Source/i, Target/1, Node/j\}, 1)$.

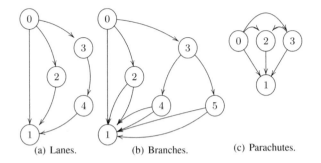

(a) Lanes.   (b) Branches.   (c) Parachutes.

Figure 8.17   Examples of graphs satisfying some of the assumptions. From [Bragaglia and Riguzzi, 2011].

Explanations for $path(i, 1)$ also contain atomic choices $(e_{ij}, \emptyset, 1)$ for every fact $edge(i, j) : 0.3.$ in the path. Each explanation corresponds to a path. In the lanes graph, each node except 0 and 1 lies on a single path, so the explanations for $path(i, 1)$ do not share random variables. In the branches graphs, each explanation for $path(i, 1)$ depends on a disjoint set of edges. In the parachutes graph, instead this is not true: for example, the path from 2 to 1 shares the edge from 2 to 1 with the path 3, 2, 1.

Another program satisfying the independent-and and independent-or assumptions is the following

> $sametitle(A, B) : 0.3 \leftarrow$
> $\quad haswordtitle(A, word\_10),$
> $\quad haswordtitle(B, word\_10).$
> $sametitle(A, B) : 0.3 \leftarrow$
> $\quad haswordtitle(A, word\_1321),$
> $\quad haswordtitle(B, word\_1321).$
> . . .

which computes the probability that the titles of two different citations are the same on the basis of the words that are present in the titles. The dots stand for clauses differing from the ones above only for the words considered. The $haswordtitle/2$ predicate is defined by a set of certain facts. This is part of a program to disambiguate citations in the Cora database [Singla and Domingos, 2005]. The program satisfies the independent-and assumption for the query

$$sametitle(tit1, tit2)$$

because

$$haswordtitle/2$$

has no uncertainty. It satisfies the independent-or assumption because each clause for $sametitle/2$ defines a different random variable.

8.10.1 PITA(OPT)

PITA(OPT) [Riguzzi, 2014] differs from PITA because it checks for the truth of the assumptions before applying BDD logical operations. If the assumptions hold, then the simplified probability computations are used.

The data structures used to store probabilistic information in PITA(OPT) are pairs (P, T) where P is a real number representing a probability and T is a term formed with the functors $zero/0, one/0, c/2, or/2, and/2, not/1$, and the integers. If T is an integer, it represents a pointer to the root node of a BDD. If T is not an integer, it represents a Boolean expression of which the terms of the form $zero, one, c(var, val)$ and the integers represent the base case: $c(var, val)$ indicates the equation $var = val$ while an integer indicates a BDD. In this way, we are able to represent Boolean formulas by means of either a BDD, a Prolog term, or a combination thereof.

For example, $or(\mathit{0x94ba008}, and(c(1, 1), not(c(2, 3))))$ represents the expression: $B \vee (X_1 = 1 \wedge \neg(X_2 = 3))$ where B is the Boolean function represented by the BDD whose root node address in memory is the integer $\mathit{0x94ba008}$ in Prolog hexadecimal notation.

PITA(OPT) differs from PITA also in the definition of $zero/1, one/1, not/2, and/3$ and $or/3$ that now work on pairs (P, T) rather than on BDDs.

Moreover, the PITA transformation $PITA(C_r, i)$ (Equation (8.3)) for a clause C_r, is modified by replacing the conjunction

$get\_var\_n(r, S, [\Pi_1, \ldots, \Pi_n], Var), equality(Var, i, DD)$

with

$get\_var\_n(r, S, [\Pi_1, \ldots, \Pi_n], Var), nth(i, [\Pi_1, \ldots, \Pi_n], \Pi_i),$
$DD = (\Pi_i, c(Var, i)$

The $one/1$ and $zero/1$ predicates are defined as

$zero((0, zero))$.
$one((1, one))$.

The $or/3$ and $and/3$ predicates first check whether one of their input argument is (an integer pointing to) a BDD. If so, they also convert the other input argument to a BDD and test for independence using the library function $bdd\_ind(B1, B2, I)$. Such a function is implemented in C and uses the CUDD function `Cudd_SupportIndex` that returns an array indicating which variables appear in a BDD (the support variables). $bdd\_ind(B1, B2, I)$ checks whether there is an intersection between the set of support variables of $B1$ and $B2$ and returns $I = 1$ if the intersection is empty. If the two BDDs are independent, then the value of the resulting probability is computed using a formula and a compound term is returned.

If none of the input arguments of *or*/3 and *and*/3 are BDDs, then these predicates test whether the independent-and or the exclusive-or assumptions hold. If so, they update the value of the probability using a formula and return a compound term. If not, they convert the terms to BDDs, apply the corresponding operation, and return the resulting BDD together with the probability it represents. The code for *or*/3 and *and*/3 is shown in Figures 8.18 and 8.19, respectively, where Boolean operation between BDDs are prefixed with *bdd_*.

In these predicate definitions, *ev*/2 evaluates a term returning a BDD. In *and*/3, after the first *bdd_and*/3 operation, a test is made to check whether the resulting BDD represent the 0 constant. If so, the derivation fails as this branch contributes with a 0 probability. These predicates make sure that,

$$
\begin{aligned}
&or((PA, TA), (PB, TB), (PC, TC)) \leftarrow \\
&\quad ((integer(TA); integer(TB)) \rightarrow \\
&\qquad ev(TA, BA), ev(TB, BB), \\
&\qquad bdd\_ind(BA, BB, I), \\
&\qquad (I = 1 \rightarrow \\
&\qquad\quad PC \text{ is } PA + PB - PA * PB, \\
&\qquad\quad TC = or(BA, BB) \\
&\qquad ; \\
&\qquad\quad bdd\_or(BA, BB, TC), ret\_prob(TC, PC) \\
&\qquad) \\
&\quad ; \\
&\quad (ind(TA, TB) \rightarrow \\
&\qquad PC \text{ is } PA + PB - PA * PB, \\
&\qquad TC = or(BA, BB) \\
&\quad ; \\
&\quad (exc(TA, TB) \rightarrow \\
&\qquad PC \text{ is } PA + PB, \\
&\qquad TC = or(BA, BB) \\
&\quad ; \\
&\qquad ev(TA, BA), ev(TB, BB), \\
&\qquad bdd\_or(BA, BB, TC), ret\_prob(TC, PC) \\
&\qquad) \\
&\quad) \\
&\quad).
\end{aligned}
$$

Figure 8.18 Code for the *or*/3 predicate of PITA(OPT).

$$and((PA, TA), (PB, TB), (PC, TC)) \leftarrow$$
$$((integer(TA); integer(TB)) \rightarrow$$
$$ev(TA, BA), ev(TB, BB),$$
$$bdd\_ind(A, BB, I),$$
$$(I = 1 \rightarrow$$
$$PC \ is \ PA * PB,$$
$$TC = and(BA, BB)$$
$$;$$
$$bdd\_and(BA, BB, TC), ret\_prob(TC, PC)$$
$$(bdd\_zero(TC) \rightarrow$$
$$fail$$
$$;$$
$$true$$
$$)$$
$$)$$
$$;$$
$$(ind(TA, TB) \rightarrow$$
$$PC \ is \ PA * PB,$$
$$TC = and(BA, BB)$$
$$;$$
$$(exc(TA, TB) \rightarrow$$
$$fail$$
$$;$$
$$ev(TA, BA), ev(TB, BB),$$
$$bdd\_and(BA, BB, TC), ret\_prob(TC, PC)$$
$$)$$
$$)$$
$$).$$

Figure 8.19   Code for the $and/3$ predicate of PITA(OPT).

once a BDD has been built, it is used in the following operations, avoiding the manipulation of terms and exploiting the work performed as much as possible.

The $not/2$ predicate is very simple: it complements the probability and returns a new term:

$$not((P, B), (P1, not(B))) \leftarrow P1 \ is \ 1 - P.$$

The predicate $exc/2$ checks for the exclusiveness between two terms with a recursion through the structure of the terms, see Figure 8.20.

For example, the goal

$$exc(or(c(1, 1), c(2, 1)), and(c(1, 2), c(2, 2)))$$

$exc(zero, \_) \leftarrow !.$
$exc(\_, zero) \leftarrow !.$
$exc(c(V, N), c(V, N1)) \leftarrow !, N \backslash = N1.$
$exc(c(V, N), or(X, Y)) \leftarrow !, exc(c(V, N), X),$
  $exc(c(V, N), Y).$
$exc(c(V, N), and(X, Y)) \leftarrow !, (exc(c(V, N), X);$
  $exc(c(V, N), Y)).$
$exc(or(A, B), or(X, Y)) \leftarrow !, exc(A, X), exc(A, Y),$
  $exc(B, X), exc(B, Y).$
$exc(or(A, B), and(X, Y)) \leftarrow !, (exc(A, X); exc(A, Y)),$
  $(exc(B, X); exc(B, Y)).$
$exc(and(A, B), and(X, Y)) \leftarrow !, exc(A, X); exc(A, Y);$
  $exc(B, X); exc(B, Y).$
$exc(and(A, B), or(X, Y)) \leftarrow !, (exc(A, X); exc(B, X)),$
  $(exc(A, Y); exc(B, Y)).$
$exc(not(A), A) \leftarrow !.$
$exc(not(A), and(X, Y)) \leftarrow !, exc(not(A), X);$
  $exc(not(A), Y).$
$exc(not(A), or(X, Y)) \leftarrow !, exc(not(A), X),$
  $exc(not(A), Y).$
$exc(A, or(X, Y)) \leftarrow !, exc(A, X), exc(A, Y).$
$exc(A, and(X, Y)) \leftarrow exc(A, X); exc(A, Y).$

Figure 8.20   Code for the $exc/2$ predicate of PITA(OPT).

matches the 7th clause and calls the subgoals

$$exc(c(1, 1), c(1, 2)), exc(c(1, 1), c(2, 2)), exc(c(2, 1), c(1, 2)),$$
$$exc(c(2, 1), c(2, 2)).$$

Of the first two calls, $exc(c(1, 1), c(1, 2))$ succeeds, thus satisfying the first conjunct in the body. Of the latter two calls, $exc(c(2, 1), c(2, 2))$ succeeds, thus satisfying the second conjunct in the body and proving the goal.

The $ind/2$ predicate checks for independence between two terms. It visits the structure of the first term until it reaches an atomic choice. Then it checks for the absence of the variable in the second term with the predicate $absent/2$. The code for $ind/2$ and $absent/2$ is shown in Figure 8.21. For example, the goal

$$ind(or(c(1, 1), c(2, 1)), and(c(3, 2), c(4, 2)))$$

matches the 6th clause and calls

$$ind(c(1, 1), and(c(3, 2), c(4, 2))), ind(c(2, 1), and(c(3, 2), c(4, 2))).$$

The first call matches the 5th clause and calls

$$absent(1, and(c(3, 2), c(4, 2)))$$

```
ind(one, _) ←!.
ind(zero, _) ←!.
ind(_, one) ←!.
ind(_, zero) ←!.
ind(c(V, _N), B) ←!, absent(V, B).
ind(or(X, Y), B) ←!, ind(X, B), ind(Y, B).
ind(and(X, Y), B) ←!, ind(X, B), ind(Y, B).
ind(not(A), B) ← ind(A, B).
absent(V, c(V1, _N1)) ←!, V\ = V1.
absent(V, or(X, Y)) ←!, absent(V, X), absent(V, Y).
absent(V, and(X, Y)) ←!, absent(V, X), absent(V, Y).
absent(V, not(A)) ← absent(V, A).
```

Figure 8.21   Code for the $ind/2$ predicate of PITA(OPT).

which, in turn, calls $absent(1, c(3, 2))$ and $absent(1, c(4, 2))$. Since they both succeed, $ind(c(1, 1), and(c(3, 2), c(4, 2)))$ succeeds as well. The second call matches the 5th clause and calls $absent(2, and(c(3, 2), c(4, 2)))$ which, in turn, calls $absent(2, c(3, 2))$ and $absent(2, c(4, 2))$. They both succeed so $ind(c(2, 1), and(c(3, 2), c(4, 2)))$ and the original goal is proved.

The predicates $exc/2$ and $ind/2$ define sufficient conditions for exclusion and independence, respectively. If the arguments of $exc/2$ and $ind/2$ do not contain integer terms representing BDDs, then the conditions are also necessary. The code for predicate $ev/2$ for the evaluation of a term is shown in Figure 8.22.

When the program satisfies the (IND,EXC) or (IND,IND) assumptions, the PITA(OPT) algorithm answers the query without building BDDs: terms are combined in progressively larger terms that are used to check the assump-

```
ev(B, B) ← integer(B), !.
ev(zero, B) ←!, bdd_zero(B).
ev(one, B) ←!, bdd_one(B).
ev(c(V, N), B) ←!, bdd_equality(V, N, B).
ev(and(A, B), C) ←!, ev(A, BA), ev(B, BB),
    bdd_and(BA, BB, C).
ev(or(A, B), C) ←!, ev(A, BA), ev(B, BB),
    bdd_or(BA, BB, C).
ev(not(A), C) ← ev(A, B), bdd_not(B, C).
```

Figure 8.22   Code for the $ev/2$ predicate of PITA(OPT).

tions, while the probabilities of the combinations are computed only from the probabilities of the operands without considering their structure.

When the program satisfies neither assumption, PITA(OPT) can still be beneficial since it delays the construction of BDDs as much as possible and may lead to the construction of less intermediate BDDs than PITA. While in PITA the BDD for each intermediate subgoal must be kept in memory because it is stored in the table and has to be available for future use, in PITA(OPT), BDDs are built only when necessary, leading to a smaller memory footprint and a leaner memory management.

8.10.2 VIT with PITA

VIT inference when the IND assumption holds can be computed by modifying PITA(IND,EXC) so that the probability data structure includes the most probable explanation for the subgoal besides the highest probability of the subgoal. In this case, the support predicates are modified as follows:

$$or(e(E1, P1), e(\_E2, P2), e(E1, P1)) \leftarrow P1 >= P2, !.$$
$$or(e(\_E1, \_P1), e(E2, P2), e(E2, P2)).$$
$$and(e(E1, P1), e(E2, P2), e(E3, P3)) \leftarrow P3 \ is \ P1 * P2,$$
$$\quad append(E1, E2, E3).$$
$$zero(e(null, 0)).$$
$$one(e([], 1)).$$
$$ret\_prob(B, B).$$

Moreover, in the PITA transformation $PITA(C_r, i)$ for a clause C_r (Equation (8.3)), the conjunction

$$get\_var\_n(r, S, [\Pi_1, \ldots, \Pi_n], Var), equality(Var, i, DD)$$

is replaced by

$$nth(i, [\Pi_1, \ldots, \Pi_n], \Pi_i), DD = e([(R, S, i)], \Pi_i)$$

In this way, we obtain PITAVIT(IND) that does not require the exclusiveness assumption.

8.11 Inference for Queries with an Infinite Number of Explanations

When a discrete program contains function symbols, the number of explanations may be infinite and the probability of the query may be the sum of a convergent series. In this case, the inference algorithm has to recognize the presence of an infinite number of explanations and identify the terms of the series. Sato and Meyer [2012, 2014] extend PRISM by considering programs under the *generative exclusiveness condition*: at any choice point in any execution path of the top-goal, the choice is done according to a value sampled from a PRISM probabilistic switch. The generative exclusiveness condition implies the exclusive-or condition and that every disjunction originates from a probabilistic choice made by some switch.

In this case, a *cyclic explanation graph* can be computed that encodes the dependency of atoms on probabilistic switches. From this, a system of equations can be obtained defining the probability of ground atoms. Sato and Meyer [2012, 2014] show that first assigning all atoms probability 0 and then repeatedly applying the equations to compute updated values result in a process that converges to a solution of the system of equations. For some program, such as those computing the probability of prefixes of strings from Probabilistic context-free grammars (PCFGs), the system is linear, so solving it is even simpler. In general, this provides an approach for performing inference when the number of explanations is infinite but the generative exclusiveness condition holds.

Gorlin et al. [2012] present the algorithm PIP (for Probabilistic Inference Plus), which is able to perform inference even when explanations are not necessarily mutually exclusive and the number of explanations is infinite. They require the programs to be *temporally well-formed*, i.e., that one of the arguments of predicates can be interpreted as a time that grows from head to body. In this case, the explanations for an atom can be represented succinctly by Definite clause grammars (DCGs). Such DCGs are called *explanation generators* and are used to build Factored explanation diagrams (FEDs) that have a structure that closely follows that of BDDs. From FEDs, one can obtain a system of polynomial equations that is monotonic and thus convergent as in [Sato and Meyer, 2012, 2014]. So, even when the system is non-linear, a least solution can be computed to within an arbitrary approximation bound by an iterative procedure.

9

Lifted Inference

Reasoning with real-world models is often very expensive due to their complexity. However, sometimes the cost can be reduced by exploiting symmetries in the model. This is the task of *lifted* inference, that answers queries by reasoning on populations of individuals as a whole instead of considering each entity individually. The exploitation of the symmetries in the model can significantly speed up inference.

Lifted inference was initially proposed by Poole [2003]. Since then, many techniques have appeared such as lifted versions of variable elimination and belief propagation, using approximations and dealing with models such as parfactor graphs and MLNs [de Salvo Braz et al., 2005; Milch et al., 2008; Van den Broeck et al., 2011].

9.1 Preliminaries on Lifted Inference

Applying lifted inference to PLP languages under the DS is problematic because the conclusions of different rules are combined with noisy-OR that requires aggregations at the lifted level when existential variables are present. For example, consider the following ProbLog program from [De Raedt and Kimmig, 2015]:

```
p :: famous(Y).
popular(X) :- friends(X, Y), famous(Y).
```

In this case, $P(\text{popular(john)}) = 1 - (1 - p)^m$ where m is the number of friends of john. This is because the body contains a logical variable not appearing in the head, which is thus existentially quantified. A grounding of the atom in the head of this clause represents the disjunction of a number of ground bodies. In this case, we don't need to know the identities of these friends, we just need to know how many there are. Hence, we don't need to ground the clauses.

Example 86 (Running example for lifted inference – ProbLog).   *We consider a ProbLog program representing the workshop attributes problem of [Milch et al., 2008]. It models the organization of a workshop where a number of people have been invited. The predicate* `series` *indicates whether the workshop is successful enough to start a series of related meetings while* `attends(P)` *indicates whether person* `P` *will attend the workshop. We can model this problem with the ProbLog program:*

```
series :- self.
series :- attends(P).
attends(P) :- at(P,A).
0.1::self.
0.3::at(P,A) :- person(P), attribute(A).
```

Note that all rules are range restricted, i.e., all variables in the head also appear in a positive literal in the body. A workshop becomes a series either because of its own merits with a 10% probability (represented by the probabilistic fact `self`*) or because people attend. People attend the workshop depending on the workshop's attributes such as location, date, fame of the organizers, etc. (modeled by the probabilistic fact* `at(P,A)`*). The probabilistic fact* `at(P,A)` *represents whether person* `P` *attends because of attribute* `A`*. Note that the last statement corresponds to a set of ground probabilistic facts, one for each person* `P` *and attribute* `A` *as in ProbLog2 (Section 8.7). For the sake of brevity, we omit the (non-probabilistic) facts describing the* `person/1` *and* `attribute/1` *predicates.*

Parameterized Random Variables (PRVs) and *parfactors* have been defined in Section 2.9.3. We briefly recall here their definition. PRVs represent sets of random variables, one for each possible ground substitution to all of its logical variables. Parfactors are triples

$$\langle \mathcal{C}, \mathbf{V}, F \rangle$$

where $\mathcal{C}$ is a set of inequality constraints on logical variables, $\mathbf{V}$ is a set of PRVs and F is a factor that is a function from the Cartesian product of ranges of PRVs of $\mathbf{V}$ to real values. A parfactor is also represented as $F(\mathbf{V})|\mathcal{C}$ or $F(\mathbf{V})$ if there are no constraints. A *constrained PRV* V is of the form V$|\mathcal{C}$, where V $= p(X_1, \ldots, X_n)$ is a non-ground atom and $\mathcal{C}$ is a set of constraints on logical variables $\boldsymbol{X} = \{X_1, \ldots, X_n\}$. Each constrained PRV represents the set of random variables $\{p(\boldsymbol{x})|\boldsymbol{x} \in \mathcal{C}\}$, where $\boldsymbol{x}$ is the tuple of constants $(x_1, \ldots, x_n)$. Given a (constrained) PRV V, we use $RV(\mathsf{V})$ to denote the set of random variables it represents. Each ground atom is associated with one random variable, which can take any value in $range(V)$.

PFL [Gomes and Costa, 2012] described in Section 2.9.3 extends Prolog to support probabilistic reasoning with parametric factors. We repeat below Example 34 for ease of reading.

Example 87 (Running example – PFL program). *A version of the workshop attributes problem can be modeled by a PFL program such as*

```
bayes series, attends(P); [0.51, 0.49, 0.49, 0.51];
   [person(P)].
bayes attends(P), at(P,A); [0.7, 0.3, 0.3, 0.7];
   [person(P),attribute(A)].
```

The first PFL factor has `series` *and* `attends(P)` *as Boolean random variable arguments,* `[0.51,0.49,0.49,0.51]` *as table and* `[person(P)]` *as constraint.*

This model is not equivalent to the one of Example 86, but it corresponds to a ProbLog program that has only the second and the third clause of Example 86. Models equivalent to Example 86 will be given in Examples 89 and 90.

9.1.1 Variable elimination

Variable Elimination (VE) [Zhang and Poole, 1994, 1996] is an algorithm for probabilistic inference on graphical models. VE takes as input a set of factors $\mathcal{F}$, an elimination order ρ, a query variable X, and a list **y** of observed values. After setting the observed variables in all factors to their corresponding observed values, VE eliminates the random variables from the factors one by one until only the query variable X remains. This is done by selecting the first variable Z from the elimination order ρ and then calling SUM-OUT that eliminates Z by first multiplying all the factors that include Z into a single factor and summing out Z from the newly constructed factor. This procedure is repeated until ρ becomes empty. In the final step, VE multiplies together the factors of $\mathcal{F}$ obtaining a new factor γ that is normalized as $\gamma(x)/\sum_{x'} \gamma(x')$ to give the posterior probability.

In many cases, we need to represent factors where a Boolean variable X with parents **Y** is true if any of the Y_i is true, i.e., the case where X is the disjunction of the variables in **Y**. This may, for example, represent the situation where the Y_is are causes of X, each capable of making X true independently

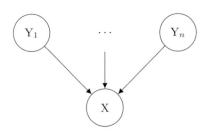

Figure 9.1   BN representing an OR dependency between X and **Y**.

of the values of the others. This is represented by the BN of Figure 9.1 where the CPT for X is deterministic and is given by

	At least one Y_i equal to 1	Remaining columns
X = 1	1.0	0.0
X = 0	0.0	1.0

In practice, however, each parent Y_i may have a noisy inhibitor variable I_i that independently blocks or activates Y_i, so X is true if either *any* of the causes Y_i holds true *and* is not inhibited. This can be represented with the BN of Figure 9.2 where the Y_i' are given by the Boolean formula $Y_i' = Y_i \land \neg I_i$, i.e., Y_i' is true if Y_i is true and is not inhibited. So the CPT for the Y_i' is deterministic. The I_i variables have no parents and their CPT is $P(I_i = 0) = \Pi_i$, where Π_i is the probability that Y_i is not inhibited.

This represents the fact that X is not simply the disjunction of **Y** but depends probabilistically from **Y** with a factor that encodes the probability that the Y_i variables are inhibited.

If we marginalize over the I_i variables, we obtain a BN like the one of Figure 9.1 where, however, the CPT for X is not anymore that of a disjunction but takes into account the probabilities that the parents are inhibited. This is called a *noisy-OR gate*. Handling this kind of factor is a non-trivial problem. Noisy-OR gates are also called *causal independent* models. An example of an entry in a noisy-OR factor is

$$P(X = 1 | Y_1 = 1, \ldots, Y_n = 1) = 1 - \prod_{i=1}^{n}(1 - \Pi_i)$$

In fact, X is true iff none of its causes is inhibited.

The factor for a noisy-OR can be expressed as a combination of factors by using the intermediate Y_i' variables that represent the effect of each cause taking into account the inhibitor.

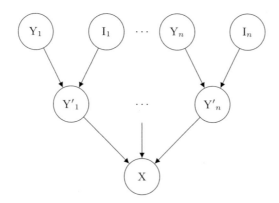

Figure 9.2 BN representing a noisy-OR dependency between X and **Y**.

For example, suppose X has two causes Y_1 and Y_2 and let $\phi(y_1, y_2, x)$ be the noisy-OR factor. Let the variables Y'_1 and Y'_2 be defined as in Figure 9.2 and consider the factors $\psi_1(y_1, y'_1)$ and $\psi_2(y_2, y'_2)$ modeling the dependency of Y'_i from Y_i. These factors are obtained by marginalizing the I_i variables, so, if $P(I_i = 0) = \Pi_i$, they are given by

$\psi(y_1, y'_1)$	$Y_i = 1$	$Y_i = 0$
$Y'_i = 1$	Π_i	0.0
$Y'_i = 0$	$1 - \Pi_i$	1.0

Then the factor $\phi(y_1, y_2, x)$ can be expressed as

$$\phi(y_1, y_2, x) = \sum_{y'_1 \vee y'_2 = x} \psi_1(y_1, y'_1)\psi_2(y_2, y'_2) \qquad (9.1)$$

where the summation is over all values y'_1 and y'_2 of Y'_1 and Y'_2 whose disjunction is equal to x. The X variable is called *convergent* as it is where independent contributions from different sources are collected and combined. Non-convergent variables are called *regular variables*.

Representing factors such as ϕ with ψ_1 and ψ_2 is advantageous when the number of parents grows large, as the combined size of the component factors grows linearly, instead of exponentially.

Unfortunately, a straightforward use of VE for inference would lead to construct $O(2^n)$ tables where n is the number of parents and the summation in Equation (9.1) will have an exponential number of terms. A modified algorithm, VE1 [Zhang and Poole, 1996], combines factors through a new operator $\otimes$:

$$\phi \otimes \psi(E_1 = \alpha_1, \ldots, E_k = \alpha_k, \mathbf{A}, \mathbf{B}_1, \mathbf{B}_2) =$$

$$\sum_{\alpha_{11} \vee \alpha_{12} = \alpha_1} \cdots \sum_{\alpha_{k1} \vee \alpha_{k2} = \alpha_k}$$

$$\phi(E_1 = \alpha_{11}, \ldots, E_k = \alpha_{k1}, \mathbf{A}, \mathbf{B}_1)\psi(E_1 = \alpha_{12}, \ldots, E_k = \alpha_{k2}, \mathbf{A}, \mathbf{B}_2) \quad (9.2)$$

Here, ϕ and ψ are two factors that share convergent variables $E_1 \ldots E_k$, $\mathbf{A}$ is the list of regular variables that appear in both ϕ and ψ, while $\mathbf{B}_1$ and $\mathbf{B}_2$ are the lists of variables appearing only in ϕ and ψ, respectively. By using the $\otimes$ operator, factors encoding the effect of parents can be combined in pairs, without the need to apply Equation (9.1) on all factors at once.

Factors containing convergent variables are called *heterogeneous* while the remaining factors are called *homogeneous*. Heterogeneous factors sharing convergent variables must be combined with the operator $\otimes$, called *heterogeneous multiplication*.

Algorithm VE1 exploits causal independence by keeping two lists of factors: a list of homogeneous factors $\mathcal{F}_1$ and a list of heterogeneous factors $\mathcal{F}_2$. Procedure SUM-OUT is replaced by SUM-OUT1 that takes as input $\mathcal{F}_1$ and $\mathcal{F}_2$ and a variable Z to be eliminated. First, all the factors containing Z are removed from $\mathcal{F}_1$ and combined with multiplication to obtain factor ϕ. Then all the factors containing Z are removed from $\mathcal{F}_2$ and combined with heterogeneous multiplication obtaining ψ. If there are no such factors $\psi = nil$. In the latter case, SUM-OUT1 adds the new (homogeneous) factor $\sum_z \phi$ to $\mathcal{F}_1$; otherwise, it adds the new (heterogeneous) factor $\sum_z \phi\psi$ to $\mathcal{F}_2$. Procedure VE1 is the same as VE with SUM-OUT replaced by SUM-OUT1 and with the difference that two sets of factors are maintained instead of one.

However, VE1 is not correct for any elimination order. Correctness can be ensured by *deputizing* the convergent variables: every such variable X is replaced by a new convergent variable X' (called a *deputy variable*) in the heterogeneous factors containing it, so that X becomes a regular variable. Finally, a new factor $\iota(X, X')$ is introduced, called *deputy factor*, that represents the identity function between X and X', i.e., it is defined by

$\iota(X, X')$	00	01	10	11
	1.0	0.0	0.0	1.0

The network on which VE1 works thus takes the form shown in Figure 9.3. Deputizing ensures that VE1 is correct as long as the elimination order is such that $\rho(X') < \rho(X)$.

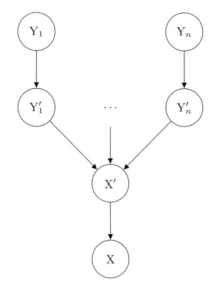

Figure 9.3 BN of Figure 9.1 after deputation.

9.1.2 GC-FOVE

Work on lifting VE started with FOVE [Poole, 2003] and led to the definition of C-FOVE [Milch et al., 2008]. C-FOVE was refined in GC-FOVE [Taghipour et al., 2013], which represents the state of the art. Then, Gomes and Costa [Gomes and Costa, 2012] adapted GC-FOVE to PFL.

First-order variable elimination (FOVE) [Poole, 2003; de Salvo Braz et al., 2005] computes the marginal probability distribution for a query random variable by repeatedly applying operators that are lifted counterparts of VE's operators. Models are in the form of a set of parfactors that are essentially the same as in PFL.

GC-FOVE tries to eliminate all (non-query) PRVs in a particular order by applying the following operations:

1. *Lifted Sum-Out* that excludes a PRV from a parfactor ϕ if the PRVs only occurs in ϕ;
2. *Lifted Multiplication* that multiplies two aligned parfactors. Matching variables must be properly aligned and the new coefficients must be computed taking into account the number of groundings in the constraints $\mathcal{C}$;

3. *Lifted Absorption* that eliminates n PRVs that have the same observed value.

If these operations cannot be applied, an enabling operation must be chosen such as *splitting* a parfactor so that some of its PRVs match another parfactor. If no operation can be executed, GC-FOVE completely grounds the PRVs and parfactors and performs inference on the ground level.

GC-FOVE also considers PRVs with counting formulas, introduced in C-FOVE [Milch et al., 2008]. A counting formula takes advantage of symmetries existing in factors that are products of independent variables. It allows the representation of a factor of the form $\phi(p(x_1), p(x_2), \ldots, p(x_n))$, where all PRVs have the same domain, as $\phi(\#_X[p(X)])$, where $\#_X[p(X)]$ is the *counting formula*. The factor implements a multinomial distribution, such that its values depend on the number of variables n and the domain size. Counting formulas may result from summing-out, when we obtain parfactors with a single PRV, or through *Counting Conversion* that searches for factors of the form

$$\phi(\prod_i (s(X_j)p(X_j, Y_i)))$$

and counts on the occurrences of Y_i.

GC-FOVE employs a constraint-tree to represent arbitrary constraints $\mathcal{C}$, whereas PFL simply uses sets of tuples. Arbitrary constraints can capture more symmetries in the data, which potentially offers the ability to perform more operations at a lifted level.

9.2 LP²

LP^2 [Bellodi et al., 2014] is an algorithm for performing lifted inference in ProbLog that translates the program into PFL and uses an extended GC-FOVE version for managing noisy-OR nodes.

9.2.1 Translating ProbLog into PFL

In order to translate ProbLog into PFL, the program must be acyclic (Definition 4, see Section 9.5 for the case of cyclic programs). If this condition if fulfilled, the ProbLog program can be converted first into a BN with noisy-OR nodes. Here we specialize the conversion for LPADs presented in Section 2.5 to the case of ProbLog.

For each atom a in the Herbrand base of the program, the BN contains a Boolean random variable with the same name. Each probabilistic fact $p :: a$ is represented by a parentless node with the CPT:

a	0	1
	$1 - p$	p

For each ground rule $R_i = h \leftarrow b_1, \ldots, b_n, \sim c_1, \ldots, \sim c_m$, we add to the network a random variable called h_i that has as parents the random variables representing the atoms $b_1, \ldots, b_n, c_1, \ldots, c_m$ and the following CPT:

h_i	$b_1 = 1, \ldots, b_n = 1, c_1 = 0, \ldots, c_m = 0$	All other columns
0	0.0	1.0
1	1.0	0.0

In practice, h_i is the result of the conjunction of the random variables representing the atoms in the body. Then, for each ground atom h in the Herbrand base not appearing in a probabilistic fact, we add random variable h to the network, with all the h_is of the ground rules with h in the head as parents and with CPT:

h	At least one $h_i = 1$	All other columns
0	0.0	1.0
1	1.0	0.0

representing the result of the disjunction of the random variables h_i. These families of random variables can be directly represented in PFL without the need to first ground the program, thus staying at the lifted level.

Example 88 (Translation of a ProbLog program into PFL). *The translation of the ProbLog program of Example 86 into PFL is*

```
bayes series1, self; [1, 0, 0, 1] ; [].
bayes series2, attends(P); [1, 0, 0, 1];
       [person(P)].
bayes series, series1, series2 ; [1, 0, 0, 0, 0,
       1, 1, 1]; [].
bayes attends1(P), at(P,A); [1, 0, 0, 1];
       [person(P),attribute(A)].
bayes attends(P), attends1(P); [1, 0, 0, 1];
       [person(P)].
```

```
bayes self; [0.9, 0.1]; [].
bayes at(P,A); [0.7, 0.3] ; [person(P),
     attribute(A)].
```

Notice that `series2` and `attends1(P)` can be seen as or-nodes, since they are in fact convergent variables. Thus, after grounding, factors derived from the second and the fourth parfactor should not be multiplied together but should be combined with heterogeneous multiplication.

To do so, we need to identify heterogeneous factors and add deputy variables and parfactors. We thus introduce two new types of parfactors to PFL, `het` and `deputy`. As mentioned before, the type of a parfactor refers to the type of the network over which that parfactor is defined. These two new types are used in order to define a noisy-OR (Bayesian) network. The first parfactor is such that its ground instantiations are heterogeneous factors. The convergent variables are assumed to be represented by the first atom in the parfactor list of atoms. Lifting identity is straightforward: it corresponds to two atoms with an identity factor between their ground instantiations. Since the factor is fixed, it is not indicated.

Example 89 (ProbLog program to PFL – LP^2). *The translation of the Prolog program of Example 86, shown in Example 88, is modified with the two new factors* het *and* deputy *as shown below:*

```
bayes series1p, self; [1, 0, 0, 1] ; [].
het series2p, attends(P); [1, 0, 0, 1];
     [person(P)].
deputy series2, series2p; [].
deputy series1, series1p; [].
bayes series, series1, series2; [1, 0, 0, 0, 0, 1,
     1, 1] ; [].
het attends1p(P), at(P,A); [1, 0, 0, 1];
     [person(P),attribute(A)].
deputy attends1(P), attends1p(P); [person(P)].
bayes attends(P), attends1(P); [1, 0, 0, 1];
     [person(P)].
bayes self; [0.9, 0.1]; [].
bayes at(P,A); [0.7, 0.3] ; [person(P),
     attribute(A)].
```

Here, series1p, series2p, *and* attends1p(P) *are the new convergent deputy random variables, and* series1, series2, *and* `attends1(P)` *are their corresponding regular variables. The fifth factor represents the OR combination of* `series1` *and* `series2` *to variable* `series`.

GC-FOVE must be modified in order to take into account heterogeneous parfactors and convergent PRVs. The VE algorithm must be replaced by VE1, i.e., two lists of factors must be maintained, one with homogeneous and the other with heterogeneous factors. When eliminating variables, homogeneous factors have higher priority and are combined with homogeneous factors only. Then heterogeneous factors are taken into account and combined before starting to mix factors from both types, to produce a final factor from which the selected random variable is eliminated.

Lifted heterogeneous multiplication considers the case in which the two factors share convergent random variables. The SUM-OUT operator must be modified as well to take into account the case that random variables must be summed out from a heterogeneous factor. The formal definition of these two operators is rather technical and we refer to [Bellodi et al., 2014] for the details.

9.3 Lifted Inference with Aggregation Parfactors

Kisynski and Poole [Kisynski and Poole, 2009a] proposed an approach based on *aggregation parfactors* instead of parfactors. Aggregation parfactors are very expressive and can represent different kinds of causal independence models, where noisy-OR and noisy-MAX are special cases. They are of the form $\langle \mathcal{C}, \mathsf{P}, \mathsf{C}, F_\mathsf{P}, \boxtimes, \mathcal{C}_A \rangle$, where P and C are PRVs which share all the parameters except one – let's say A which is in P but not in C – and the range of P (possibly non-Boolean) is a subset of that of C; $\mathcal{C}$ and $\mathcal{C}_A$ are sets of inequality constraints respectively not involving and involving A; F_P is a factor from the range of P to real values; and $\boxtimes$ is a commutative and associative deterministic binary operator over the range of C.

When $\boxtimes$ is the MAX operator, of which the OR operator is a special case, a total ordering $\prec$ on the range of C can be defined. An aggregation parfactor can be replaced with two parfactors of the form $\langle \mathcal{C} \cup \mathcal{C}_A, \{\mathsf{P}, \mathsf{C}'\}, F_\mathsf{C} \rangle$ and $\langle \mathcal{C}, \{\mathsf{C}, \mathsf{C}'\}, F_\Delta \rangle$, where C' is an auxiliary PRV that has the same parameterization and range as C. Let $\mathbf{v}$ be an assignment of values to random variables, then $F_\mathsf{C}(\mathbf{v}(\mathsf{P}), \mathbf{v}(\mathsf{C}')) = F_\mathsf{P}(\mathbf{v}(\mathsf{P}))$ when $\mathbf{v}(\mathsf{P}) \preceq \mathbf{v}(\mathsf{C}')$, $F_\mathsf{C}(\mathbf{v}(\mathsf{P}), \mathbf{v}(\mathsf{C}')) = 0$ otherwise, while $F_\Delta(\mathbf{v}(\mathsf{C}), \mathbf{v}(\mathsf{C}')) = 1$ if $\mathbf{v}(\mathsf{C}) = \mathbf{v}(\mathsf{C}')$, -1 if $\mathbf{v}(\mathsf{C})$ is equal to a successor of $\mathbf{v}(\mathsf{C}')$ and 0 otherwise.

In ProbLog, we can use aggregation parfactors to model the dependency between the head of a rule and the body, when the body contains a single literal with an extra variable. In this case in fact, given a grounding of the head, the contribution of all the ground clauses with that head must be combined by means of an OR. Since aggregation parfactors are replaced by regular parfactors, the technique can be used to reason with ProbLog by converting the program into PFL with these additional parfactors. The conversion is possible only if the ProbLog program is acyclic.

In the case of ProbLog, the range of PRVs is binary and $\boxtimes$ is OR. For example, the clause `series2 :- attends(P)` can be represented with the aggregation parfactor

$$\langle \emptyset, \texttt{attends(P)}, \texttt{series2}, F_P, \vee, \emptyset \rangle,$$

where $F_P(0) = 1$ and $F_P(1) = 1$. This is replaced by the parfactors

$$\langle \emptyset, \{\texttt{attends(P)}, \texttt{series2p}\}, F_C \rangle$$

$$\langle \emptyset, \{\texttt{series2}, \texttt{series2p}\}, F_\Delta \rangle$$

with $F_C(0,0) = 1$, $F_C(0,1) = 1$, $F_C(1,0) = 0$, $F_C(1,1) = 1$, $F_\Delta(0,0) = 1$, $F_\Delta(0,1) = 0$, $F_\Delta(1,0) = -1$, and $F_\Delta(1,1) = 1$.

When the body of a rule contains more than one literal and/or more than one extra variable with respect to the head, the rule must be first split into multiple rules (adding auxiliary predicate names) satisfying the constraint.

Example 90 (ProbLog program to PFL – aggregation parfactors). *The program of Example 86 using the above encoding for aggregation parfactors is*

```
bayes series1p, self; [1, 0, 0, 1] ; [].
bayes series2p, attends(P) [1, 0, 1, 1];
      [person(P)].
bayes series2, series2p; [1, 0, -1, 1]; [].
bayes series1, series1p; [1, 0, -1, 1]; [].
bayes series, series1, series2; [1, 0, 0, 0, 0, 1,
      1, 1] ; [].
bayes attends1p(P), at(P,A); [1, 0, 1, 1];
      [person(P),attribute(A)].
bayes attends1(P), attends1p(P); [1, 0, -1, 1];
      [person(P)].
bayes attends(P), attends1(P); [1, 0, 0, 1];
```

```
        [person(P)].
bayes self; [0.9, 0.1]; [].
bayes at(P,A); [0.7, 0.3] ;
        [person(P),attribute(A)].
```

Thus, by using the technique of [Kisynski and Poole, 2009a], we can perform lifted inference in ProbLog by a simple conversion to PFL, without the need to modify PFL algorithms.

9.4 Weighted First-order Model Counting

A different approach to lifted inference for PLP uses Weighted first order model counting (WFOMC). WFOMC takes as input a triple $(\Delta, w, \overline{w})$, where Δ is a sentence in first-order logic and w and $\overline{w}$ are weight functions which associate a real number to positive and negative literals, respectively, depending on their predicate. Given a triple $(\Delta, w, \overline{w})$ and a query ϕ, its probability $P(\phi)$ is given by

$$P(\phi) = \frac{WFOMC(\Delta \wedge \phi, w, \overline{w})}{WFOMC(\Delta, w, \overline{w})}$$

Here, $WFOMC(\Delta, w, \overline{w})$ corresponds to the sum of the weights of all Herbrand models of Δ, where the weight of a model is the product of its literal weights. Hence

$$WFOMC(\Delta, w, \overline{w}) = \sum_{\omega \models \Delta} \prod_{l \in \omega_0} \overline{w}(pred(l)) \prod_{l \in \omega_1} w(pred(l))$$

where ω_0 and ω_1 are, respectively, false and true literals in the interpretation ω and $pred$ maps literals l to their predicate. Two lifted algorithms exist for exact WFOMC, one based on first-order knowledge compilation [Van den Broeck et al., 2011; Van den Broeck, 2011; Van den Broeck, 2013] and the other based on first-order DPLL search [Gogate and Domingos, 2011]. They both require the input theory to be in *first-order CNF*. A first-order CNF is a theory consisting of a conjunction of sentences of the form

$$\forall X_1 \ldots, \forall X_n \, l_1 \vee \ldots \vee l_m.$$

A ProbLog program can be encoded as a first-order CNF using Clark's completion, see Section 1.4.1. For acyclic logic programs, Clark's completion is correct, in the sense that every model of the logic program is a model of the completion, and vice versa. The result is a set of rules in which each predicate is encoded by a single sentence. Consider ProbLog rules of the form $p(\boldsymbol{X}) \leftarrow b_i(\boldsymbol{X}, Y_i)$ where Y_i is a variable that appears in the body b_i but not in the head $p(\boldsymbol{X})$. The corresponding sentence in the completion is $\forall \boldsymbol{X}\ p(\boldsymbol{X}) \leftrightarrow \bigvee_i \exists Y_i\ b_i(\boldsymbol{X}, Y_i)$. For cyclic programs, see Section 9.5 below.

Since WFOMC requires an input where existential quantifiers are absent, Van den Broeck et al. [2014] presented a sound and modular Skolemization procedure to translate ProbLog programs into first-order CNF. Regular Skolemization cannot be used because it introduces function symbols, that are problematic for model counters. Therefore, existential quantifiers in expressions of the form $\exists X\ \phi(X, \boldsymbol{Y})$ are replaced by the following formulas [Van den Broeck et al., 2014]:

$$\forall \boldsymbol{Y}\ \forall X\ z(\boldsymbol{Y}) \vee \neg\phi(X, \boldsymbol{Y})$$

$$\forall \boldsymbol{Y}\ s(\boldsymbol{Y}) \vee z(\boldsymbol{Y})$$

$$\forall \boldsymbol{Y}\ \forall X\ s(\boldsymbol{Y}) \vee \neg\phi(X, \boldsymbol{Y})$$

Here z is the Tseitin predicate ($w(z) = \overline{w}(z) = 1$) and s is the Skolem predicate ($w(s) = 1$, $\overline{w}(s) = -1$). This substitution can also be used for eliminating universal quantifiers since

$$\forall X\ \phi(X, \boldsymbol{Y})$$

can be seen as

$$\neg\exists X\ \neg\phi(X\boldsymbol{Y}).$$

Existential quantifiers are removed until no more substitutions can be applied. The resulting program can then be encoded as a first-order CNF with standard transformations.

This replacement introduces a relaxation of the theory, thus the theory admits more models besides the regular, wanted ones. However, for every additional, unwanted model with weight W, there is exactly one additional model with weight $-W$, and thus the WFOMC does not change. The interaction between the three relaxed formulas and the model weights follows the behavior:

1. When $z(\boldsymbol{Y})$ is false, then $\exists X\ \phi(X, \boldsymbol{Y})$ is false while $s(\boldsymbol{Y})$ is true, this is a regular model whose weight is multiplied by 1.
2. When $z(\boldsymbol{Y})$ is true, then either:

    (a) $\exists X\ \phi(X, \boldsymbol{Y})$ is true and $s(\boldsymbol{Y})$ is true, this is a regular model whose weight is multiplied by 1; or

(b) $\exists X\ \phi(X, Y)$ is false and $s(Y)$ is true, this is an additional model with a positive weight W, or

(c) $\exists X\ \phi(X, Y)$ is true and $s(Y)$ is false, this is an additional model with weight $-W$.

The last two cases cancel out.

The WFOMC encoding for a ProbLog program exploits two mapping functions which associate the probability Π_i and $1 - \Pi_i$ of a probabilistic fact with the positive and negative literals of the predicate, respectively. After the application of Clark's completion, the result may not be in Skolem normal form; thus, the techniques described above must be applied before executing WFOMC. The system WFOMC[1] solves the WFOMC problem by compiling the input theory into first-order d-DNNF diagrams [Darwiche, 2002; Chavira and Darwiche, 2008].

Example 91 (ProbLog program to Skolem normal form). *The translation of the ProbLog program of Example 86 into the WMC input format of the WFOMC system is*

```
predicate series1 1 1
predicate series2 1 1
predicate self 0.1 0.9
predicate at(P,A) 0.3 0.7
predicate z1 1 1
predicate s1 1 -1
predicate z2(P) 1 1
predicate s2(P) 1 -1


series v ! z1
!series v z1
z1 v !self
z1 v !attends(P)
z1 v s1
s1 v !self
s1 v !attends(P)

attends(P) v ! z2(P)
!attends(P) v   z2(P)
```

---

[1] https://dtai.cs.kuleuven.be/software/wfomc

```
z2(P)  v  !at(P,A)
z2(P)  v  s2(P)
s2(P)  v  !at(P,A)
```

Here, `predicate` *is the mapping function for the probability values while* `z1` *and* `z2` *are Tseitin predicates and* `s1` *and* `s2` *are Skolem predicates.*

9.5 Cyclic Logic Programs

LP^2 and aggregation parfactors, described in Sections 9.2 and 9.3, respectively, require a conversion from ProbLog to PFL for performing inference. The first step of this translation is the transformation of a ProbLog program into a BN with noisy-OR nodes. However, since BNs cannot have cycles, this conversion is not correct if the program is cyclic or *non-tight*, i.e., if the program contains positive cycles. A similar problem occurs with WFOMC: Clark's completion [Clark, 1978] is correct only for acyclic logic programs.

Fages [1994] proved that if an LP program is acyclic, then the Herbrand models of its Clark's completion [Clark, 1978] are minimal and coincide with the stable models of the original LP program. The consequence of this theoretical result is that, if the ProbLog program is acylic, we can correctly convert it into a first-order theory by means of Clark's completion.

To apply these techniques to cyclic programs, we need to remove positive loops. We could first apply the conversion proposed by Janhunen [2004] (also see Section 8.7) that converts normal logic programs to *atomic normal programs* then to clauses. An atomic normal program contains only rules of the form

$$a \leftarrow \sim c_1, \dots, \sim c_m.$$

where a and c_i are atoms. Such programs are tight and, as a consequence, it is possible to translate them into PFL programs and use Clark's completion.

However, this conversion was proposed only for the case of ground LPs. Proposing a conversion for non-ground programs is an interesting direction for future work, especially if function symbols are allowed.

9.6 Comparison of the Approaches

Riguzzi et al. [2017a] experimentally compared LP^2, C-FOVE with aggregation parfactors (C-FOVE-AP), and WFOMC on five problems:

- *workshops attributes* Milch et al. [2008];
- two different versions of *competing workshops* Milch et al. [2008];
- two different versions of Example 7 in Poole [2008], that we call *plates*.

According to Jaeger and Van den Broeck [2012] nad Van den Broeck [2011], function-free first-order logic with equality and two variables per formula (2-FFFOL(=)) is domain-liftable, i.e., the complexity of reasoning is polynomial in the domain size. All these problems fall in 2-FFFOL(=) and the experiments confirm that systems take polynomial time. However, WFOMC performs much better that the other systems, while LP^2 and C-FOVE-AP show approximately the same performance on all problems.

10

Approximate Inference

Approximate inference aims at computing the results of inference in an approximate way so that the process is cheaper than the exact computation of the results.

We can divide approaches for approximate inference into two groups: those that modify an exact inference algorithm and those based on sampling.

10.1 ProbLog1

ProbLog1 includes three approaches for approximately solving the EVID task. The first is based on iterative deepening and computes a lower and an upper bound for the probability of the query. The second instead approximates the probability of the query only from below using a fixed number of proofs. The third uses Monte Carlo sampling.

10.1.1 Iterative deepening

In iterative deepening, the SLD tree is built only up to a certain depth [De Raedt et al., 2007; Kimmig et al., 2008]. Then two sets of explanations are built: K_l, encoding the successful proofs present in the tree, and K_u, encoding the successful and still open proofs present in the tree. The probability of K_l is a lower bound on the probability of the query, as some of the open derivations may succeed, while the probability of K_u is an upper bound on the probability of the query, as some of the open derivations may fail.

Example 92 (Path – ProbLog – iterative deepening). *Consider the program of Figure 10.1 which is a probabilistic version of the program of Example 1 and represents connectivity in the probabilistic graph of Figure 10.2.*

The query $path(c, d)$ has the covering set of explanations

$$K = \{\{ce, ef, fd\}, \{cd\}\}$$

255

$$
\begin{aligned}
&path(X,X). \\
&path(X,Y) \leftarrow edge(X,Z), path(Z,Y). \\
&0.8 :: edge(a,c). \\
&0.7 :: edge(a,b). \\
&0.8 :: edge(c,e). \\
&0.6 :: edge(b,c). \\
&0.9 :: edge(c,d). \\
&0.625 :: edge(e,f). \\
&0.8 :: edge(f,d).
\end{aligned}
$$

Figure 10.1   Program of Example 92.

Figure 10.2   Probabilistic graph of Example 92.

where atomic choices $(f, \varnothing, 1)$ *for facts of the form* $f = \Pi :: edge(x,y)$ *are represented as* xy. K *can be made pairwise incompatible as*

$$
K' = \{\{ce, ef, fd, \neg cd\}, \{cd\}\}
$$

where $\neg cd$ *indicates choice* $(f, \varnothing, 0)$ *for* $f = 0.9 :: edge(c,d)$. *The probability of the query is* $P(path(c,d)) = 0.8 \cdot 0.625 \cdot 0.8 \cdot 0.1 + 0.9 = 0.94$.

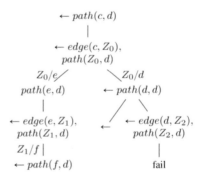

Figure 10.3   SLD tree up to depth 4 for the query $path(c,d)$ from the program of Example 92.

For a depth limit of 4, we get the tree of Figure 10.3. This tree has one successful derivation, associated with the explanation $\kappa_1 = \{cd\}$, one failed derivation, and one derivation that is still open, the one ending with $path(f, d)$, that is associated with composite choice $\kappa_1 = \{ce, ef\}$, so $K_l = \{\kappa_1\}$ and $K_u = \{\kappa_1, \kappa_2\}$. We have $P(K_l) = 0.9$ and $P(K_u) = 0.95$ and $P(K_l) \leqslant P(path(c, d)) \leqslant P(K_u)$.

The iterative deepening algorithm of ProbLog1 takes as input an error bound ϵ, a depth bound d, and a query q. It constructs an SLD tree for q up to depth d. Then it builds sets of composite choices K_l and K_u and computes their probabilities. If the difference $P(K_u) - P(K_l)$ is smaller than the error bound ϵ, this means that a solution with a satisfying accuracy has been found and the interval $[P(K_l), P(K_u)]$ is returned. Otherwise, the depth bound is increased and a new SLD tree is built up to the new depth bound. This process is iterated until the difference $P(K_u) - P(K_l)$ becomes smaller than the error bound.

Instead of a depth bound, ProbLog1 can use a bound on the probability of the proof: when the probability of the explanation associated with a proof drops below a threshold, the proof is stopped. The threshold is reduced in the following iterations by multiplying it with a constant smaller than one.

10.1.2 k-best

The second approach for approximate inference in ProbLog1 uses a fixed number of proofs to obtain a lower bound of the probability of the query [Kimmig et al., 2008, 2011a]. Given an integer k, the best k proofs are found, corresponding to the set of best k explanations K_k, and the probability of K_k is used as an estimate of the probability of the query.

Best is here intended in terms of probability: an explanation is better than another if its probability is higher.

Example 93 (Path – ProbLog – k-best). *Consider the program of Example 92 with the query $path(a, d)$. This query has four explanations that are listed below together with their probabilities:*

$$\begin{aligned}
\kappa_1 &= \{ac, cd\} & P(\kappa_1) &= 0.72 \\
\kappa_2 &= \{ab, bc, cd\} & P(\kappa_1) &= 0.378 \\
\kappa_3 &= \{ac, ce, ef, fd\} & P(\kappa_1) &= 0.32 \\
\kappa_4 &= \{ab, bc, ce, ef, fd\} & P(\kappa_1) &= 0.168
\end{aligned}$$

If $k = 1$, ProbLog1 considers only the best proof and $P(K_1) = 0.72$. For $k = 2$, ProbLog1 takes into account the best two explanations, $K_2 =$

$\{\kappa_1, \kappa_2\}$. *By making them pairwise incompatible, we get*

$$K'_2 = \{\kappa_1, \{ab, bc, cd, \neg ac\}\}$$

and $P(K'_2) = 0.72 + 0.378 \cdot 0.2 = 0.7956$. *For* $k = 3$, $K_3 = \{\kappa_1, \kappa_2, \kappa_3\}$ *and* $P(K_3) = 0.8276$. *For* $k = 4$, $K_4 = \{\kappa_1, \ldots, \kappa_4\}$ *and* $P(K_4) = P(path(a, d)) = 0.83096$, *the same for* $k > 4$.

To perform k-best inference, ProbLog uses a branch-and-bound approach: the current best k explanations are kept and, when the probability of a derivation drops below the probability of the k-th best explanation, the derivation is cut. When a new explanation is found, it is inserted in the list of k-best explanations in order of probability, possibly removing the last one if the list already contains k explanations.

The algorithm returns a lower bound on the probability of the query, the larger the k the better the bound.

10.1.3 Monte Carlo

The Monte Carlo approach for approximate inference is based on the following procedure, to be repeated until convergence

1. Sample a world, by sampling each ground probabilistic fact in turn.
2. Check whether the query is true in the world.
3. Compute the probability $\hat{p}$ of the query as the fraction of samples where the query is true.

Convergence is reached when the size of the confidence interval of $\hat{p}$ drops below a user-defined threshold δ. In order to compute the confidence interval of $\hat{p}$, ProbLog1 uses the central limit theorem to approximate the binomial distribution with a normal distribution. Then the binomial proportion confidence interval is calculated as

$$\hat{p} \pm z_{1-\alpha/2} \sqrt{\frac{\hat{p}(1 - \hat{p})}{n}}$$

where n is the number of samples and $z_{1-\alpha/2}$ is the $1 - \alpha/2$ percentile of a standard normal distribution with $\alpha = 0.05$ usually. If the width of the interval is below the user-defined threshold δ, ProbLog1 stops and returns $\hat{p}$.

This estimate of the confidence interval is good for a sample size larger than 30 and if $\hat{p}$ is not too close to 0 or 1. The normal approximation fails totally when the sample proportion is exactly zero or exactly one.

The above approach for generating samples, however, is not efficient on large programs, as proofs are often short while the generation of a world requires sampling many probabilistic facts. So ProbLog1 generates samples lazily by sampling probabilistic facts only when required by a proof. In fact, it is not necessary to sample facts not needed by a proof, as any value for them would do.

ProbLog1 performs a so-called *source-to-source transformation* of the program where probabilistic facts are transformed using the `term_expansion` mechanism of Prolog. For example, facts of the form

$0.8 :: edge(a, c)$.
$0.7 :: edge(a, b)$.

are transformed into

$edge(A, B) \leftarrow problog\_edge(ID, A, B, LogProb)$,
$\quad grounding\_id(edge(A, B), ID, GroundID)$,
$\quad add\_to\_proof(GroundID, LogProb)$.

$problog\_edge(0, a, c, -0.09691)$.
$problog\_edge(1, a, b, -0.15490)$.

where $problog\_edge$ is a new predicate for the internal representation of facts for the predicate $edge/2$, $grounding\_id/3$ is used in the case in which the probabilistic facts are not ground for obtaining a different identifier for each grounding, and $add\_to\_proof/2$ adds the fact to the current proof, stored in a global storage area. This approach is shared by all inference algorithms of ProbLog1.

The computation of $\hat{p}$ is usually done after taking a user defined small number of samples n instead of after every sample, see Algorithm 10. The algorithm converges because the *Samples* variables is always increasing, and thus the condition $2z_{1-\alpha/2}\sqrt{\frac{\hat{p}(1-\hat{p})}{Samples}} < \delta$ in line 13 of Algorithm 10 will eventually become true, unless the query has probability 0 or 1.

The function SAMPLE(q) is implemented by asking the query over the transformed program. ProbLog1 uses an array with an element for each ground probabilistic fact that stores one of three values: sampled true, sampled false, or not yet sampled. When a literal matching a probabilistic fact is called, ProbLog1 first checks whether the fact was already sampled by looking at the array. If it wasn't sampled, ProbLog1 samples it and stores the result in the array. Probabilistic facts that are non-ground in the program are treated differently: samples for groundings of these facts are stored in the internal database of the Prolog interpreter (YAP in the ProbLog1 case) and the sampled value is retrieved when they are called. If no sample has been taken for

---

Algorithm 10 Function MONTECARLO: Monte Carlo algorithm of ProbLog1.

1: **function** MONTECARLO($\mathcal{P}, q, n, \delta$)
2:      transform $\mathcal{P}$
3:      $Samples \leftarrow 0$
4:      $TrueSamples \leftarrow 0$
5:      **repeat**
6:          **for** $i = 1 \rightarrow n$ **do**
7:              $Samples \leftarrow Samples + 1$
8:              **if** SAMPLE(q) succeeds **then**
9:                  $TrueSamples \leftarrow TrueSamples + 1$
10:             **end if**
11:         **end for**
12:         $\hat{p} \leftarrow \frac{TrueSamples}{Samples}$
13:     **until** $2z_{1-\alpha/2}\sqrt{\frac{\hat{p}(1-\hat{p})}{Samples}} < \delta$
14:     **return** $\hat{p}$
15: **end function**

---

a grounding, a sample is taken and recorded in the database. No position in the array is reserved for them since their grounding is not known at the start.

Approximate inference by sampling is also available in the ProbLog2 system.

10.2 MCINTYRE

MCINTYRE (Monte Carlo INference wiTh Yap REcord) [Riguzzi, 2013] applies the Monte Carlo approach of ProbLog1 to LPADs using the YAP internal database for storing all samples and using tabling for speeding up inference.

MCINTYRE first transforms the program and then queries the transformed program. The disjunctive clause

$$C_i = h_{i1} : \Pi_{i1} \vee \ldots \vee h_{in} : \Pi_{in_i} : -b_{i1}, \ldots, b_{im_i},$$

where the parameters sum to 1, is transformed into the set of clauses $MC(C_i) = \{MC(C_i, 1), \ldots, MC(C_i, n_i)\}$:

$$MC(C_i, 1) = \quad h_{i1} : -b_{i1}, \ldots, b_{im_i},$$
$$sample\_head(ParList, i, VC, NH), NH = 1.$$

. . .

$$MC(C_i, n_i) = \quad h_{in_i} : -b_{i1}, \ldots, b_{im_i},$$
$$sample\_head(ParList, i, VC, NH), NH = n_i.$$

where VC is a list containing each variable appearing in C_i and $ParList$ is $[\Pi_{i1}, \ldots, \Pi_{in_i}]$. If the parameters do not sum up to 1, the last clause (the one for *null*) is omitted. MCINTYRE creates a clause for each head and samples a head index at the end of the body with `sample_head/4`. If this index coincides with the head index, the derivation succeeds; otherwise, it fails. Thus, failure can occur either because one of the body literals fails or because the current clause is not part of the sample.

Example 94 (Epidemic – LPAD). *The following LPAD models the development of an epidemic or a pandemic and is similar to the ProbLog program of Example 75:*

$$C_1 = \quad epidemic : 0.6 \; ; \; pandemic : 0.3 \leftarrow flu(X), cold.$$
$$C_2 = \quad cold : 0.7.$$
$$C_3 = \quad flu(david).$$
$$C_4 = \quad flu(robert).$$

Clause C_1 has two groundings, both with three atoms in the head, while clause C_2 has a single grounding with two atoms in the head, so overall there are $3 \times 3 \times 2 = 18$ worlds. The query $epidemic$ is true in five of them and its probability is

$$P(epidemic) = \quad 0.6 \cdot 0.6 \cdot 0.7 + 0.6 \cdot 0.3 \cdot 0.7 + 0.6 \cdot 0.1 \cdot 0.7 +$$
$$0.3 \cdot 0.6 \cdot 0.7 + 0.1 \cdot 0.6 \cdot 0.7$$
$$= \quad 0.588$$

Clause C_1 is transformed as

$$MC(C_1, 1) = \quad epidemic : -flu(X), cold,$$
$$sample\_head([0.6, 0.3, 0.1], 1, [X], NH), NH = 1.$$
$$MC(C_1, 2) = \quad pandemic : -flu(X), cold,$$
$$sample\_head([0.6, 0.3, 0.1], 1, [X], NH), NH = 2.$$

The predicate `sample_head/4` samples an index from the head of a clause and uses the built-in YAP predicates `recorded/3` and `recorda/3` for, respectively, retrieving or adding an entry to the internal database.

Since `sample_head/4` is at the end of the body and since we assume the program to be range restricted, all the variables of the clause have been grounded when `sample_head/4` is called.

If the rule instantiation was already sampled, `sample_head/4` retrieves the head index with `recorded/3`; otherwise, it samples a head index with `sample/2`:

```
sample_head(_ParList,R,VC,NH):-
   recorded(exp,(R,VC,NH),_),!.
sample_head(ParList,R,VC,NH):-
   sample(ParList,NH),
   recorda(exp,(R,VC,NH),_).

sample(ParList, HeadId) :-
   random(Prob),
   sample(ParList, 0, 0, Prob, HeadId).
sample([HeadProb|Tail], Index, Prev, Prob,
                         HeadId) :-
   Succ is Index + 1,
   Next is Prev + HeadProb,
   (Prob =< Next ->
      HeadId = Index
   ;
      sample(Tail, Succ, Next, Prob, HeadId)
   ).
```

Tabling can be effectively used to avoid re-sampling the same atom. To take a sample from the program, MCINTYRE uses the following predicate

```
sample(Goal):-
   abolish_all_tables,
   eraseall(exp),
   call(Goal).
```

For example, if the query is *epidemic*, resolution matches the goal with the head of clause $MC(C_1, 1)$. Suppose $flu(X)$ succeeds with $X/david$ and *cold* succeeds as well. Then

$$sample\_head([0.6, 0.3, 0.1], 1, [david], NH)$$

is called. Since clause 1 with X replaced by $david$ was not yet sampled, a number between 1 and 3 is sampled according to the distribution $[0.6, 0.3, 0.1]$ and stored in NH. If $NH = 1$, the derivation succeeds and the goal is true in the sample, if $NH = 2$ or $NH = 3$, then the derivation fails and backtracking is performed. This involves finding the solution $X/robert$ for $flu(X)$. $cold$ was sampled as true before, so it succeeds again. The

$$sample\_head([0.6, 0.3, 0.1], 1, [robert], NH)$$

is called to take another sample.

Differently from ProbLog1, MCINTYRE takes into account the validity of the binomial proportion confidence interval. The normal approximation is good for a sample size larger than 30 and if $\hat{p}$ is not too close to 0 or 1. Empirically, it has been observed that the normal approximation works well as long as $Sample \cdot \hat{p} > 5$ and $Sample \cdot (1 - \hat{p}) > 5$ [Ryan, 2007]. Thus, MCINTYRE changes the condition in line 13 of Algorithm 10 to

$$2z_{1-\alpha/2}\sqrt{\frac{\hat{p}(1-\hat{p})}{Samples}} < \delta \wedge Samples \cdot \hat{p} > 5 \wedge Samples \cdot (1 - \hat{p}) > 5$$

Recent versions of MCINTYRE for SWI-prolog (included in the `cplint` suite) use dynamic clauses for storing samples, as in SWI-prolog these are faster. $sample\_head/4$ is then defined as:

```
sample_head(R,VC,_HeadList,N):-
  sampled(R,VC,N),!.

sample_head(R,VC,HeadList,N):-
  sample(HeadList,N),
  assertz(sampled(R,VC,N)).
```

Monte Carlo sampling is attractive for the simplicity of its implementation and because the estimate can be improved as more time is available, making it an *anytime algorithm*.

10.3 Approximate Inference for Queries with an Infinite Number of Explanations

Monte Carlo inference can also be used for programs with function symbols, in which goals may have an infinite number of possibly infinite explanations and exact inference may loop. In fact, a sample of a query corresponds naturally to an explanation. The probability of taking that sample is the same as the probability of the corresponding explanation. The risk is that of incurring in an infinite explanation. But infinite explanations have probability zero, so the probability that the computation goes down such a path and does not terminate is zero as well. As a consequence, Monte Carlo inference can be used on programs with an infinite number of possibly infinite explanations.

Similarly, iterative deepening can also avoid infinite loops as the proof tree is built only up to a certain point. If the bound is on the depth, computation will eventually stop because the depth bound will be exceeded. If the bound is on the probability, it will eventually be exceeded as well, as the probability of an explanation goes to zero as more choices are added.

For an example of Monte Carlo inference on a program with an infinite set of explanations, see Section 15.11.

10.4 Conditional Approximate Inference

Monte Carlo inference also provides smart algorithms for computing the probability of a query given evidence (COND task): rejection sampling or Metropolis-Hastings Markov chain monte carlo (MCMC).

In rejection sampling [Von Neumann, 1951], the evidence is first queried and, if it is successful, the query is asked in the same sample; otherwise, the sample is discarded. Rejection sampling is available both in `cplint` and in ProbLog2.

In Metropolis-hastings MCMC, a Markov chain is built by taking an initial sample and by generating successor samples, see [Koller and Friedman, 2009] for a description of the general algorithm.

Nampally and Ramakrishnan [2014] developed a version of MCMC specific to PLP. In their algorithm, the initial sample is built by randomly sampling choices so that the evidence is true. A successor sample is obtained by deleting a fixed number (lag) of sampled probabilistic choices. Then the evidence is queried again by sampling starting with the undeleted choices. If the evidence succeeds, the query is then also asked by sampling. The query sample is accepted with a probability of

$$\min\left\{1, \frac{N_{i-1}}{N_i}\right\}$$

where N_{i-1} is the number of choices sampled in the previous sample and N_i is the number of choices sampled in the current sample. The number of successes of the query is increased by 1 if the query succeeded in the last accepted sample. The final probability is given by the number of successes over the total number of samples. Nampally and Ramakrishnan [2014] prove that this is a valid Metropolis-hastings MCMC algorithm if *lag* is equal to 1.

Metropolis-hastings MCMC is also implemented in `cplint` [Alberti et al., 2017]. Since the proof of the validity of the algorithm in [Nampally and Ramakrishnan, 2014] also holds when forgetting more than one sampled choice, *lag* is user-defined in `cplint`.

Algorithm 11 shows the procedure. Function INITIALSAMPLE returns a composite choice containing the choices sampled for proving the evidence. Function SAMPLE takes a goal and a composite choice as input and samples the goal returning a pair formed by the result of sampling (true or false) and the set of sampled choices extending the input composite choice. Function RESAMPLE(κ, lag) deletes *lag* choices from κ. In [Nampally and Ramakrishnan, 2014], *lag* is always 1. Function ACCEPT(κ_{i-1}, κ_i) decides whether to accept sample κ_i.

Algorithm 11 Function MCMC: Metropolis-hastings MCMC algorithm.

1: **function** MCMC($\mathcal{P}, q, Samples, lag$)
2:     $TrueSamples \leftarrow 0$
3:     $\kappa_0 \leftarrow$ INITIALSAMPLE(e)
4:     $(r_q, \kappa) \leftarrow$SAMPLE(q, κ_0)
5:     **for** $i = 1 \rightarrow Samples$ **do**
6:         $\kappa' \leftarrow$ RESAMPLE(κ, lag)
7:         $(r_e, \kappa_e) \leftarrow$SAMPLE($e, \kappa'$)
8:         **if** r_e=true **then**
9:             $(r_q', \kappa_q) \leftarrow$SAMPLE($q, \kappa_e$)
10:            **if** ACCEPT(κ, κ_q) **then**
11:                $\kappa \leftarrow \kappa_q$
12:                $r_q \leftarrow r_q'$
13:            **end if**
14:         **end if**
15:         **if** r_q=true **then**
16:            $TrueSamples \leftarrow TrueSamples + 1$
17:         **end if**
18:     **end for**
19:     $\hat{p} \leftarrow \frac{TrueSamples}{Samples}$
20:     **return** $\hat{p}$
21: **end function**

Function INITIALSAMPLE builds the initial sample with a meta-interpreter (see Section 1.3) that starts with the goal and randomizes the order in which clauses are used for resolution during the search so that the initial sample is unbiased. This is achieved by collecting all the clauses that match a subgoal and trying them in random order. Then the goal is queried using regular sampling.

10.5 k-optimal

In k-best, the set of proofs can be highly redundant with respect to each other. k-optimal [Renkens et al., 2012] improves on k-best for definite clauses by trying to find the set of k explanations $K = \{\kappa_1, \ldots, \kappa_k\}$ of the query q that lead to the largest probability $P(q)$, in order to obtain the best possible lower bound given the limit on the number of explanations.

k-optimal follows a greedy procedure shown in Algorithm 12. The optimization in line 4 is performed with an algorithm similar to 1-best: a branch-and-bound search is performed where, instead of evaluating the current partial explanation κ using its probability, the value $P(K \cup \{\kappa\}) - P(K)$ is used.

Algorithm 12 Function K-OPTIMAL: k-optimal algorithm.

1: **function** K-OPTIMAL($\phi_r, \phi_q, maxTime$)
2:      $K \leftarrow \emptyset$
3:      **for** $i = 1 \rightarrow k$ **do**
4:          $K \leftarrow K \cup \arg\max_{\kappa \text{ is an explanation}} P(K \cup \{\kappa\})$
5:      **end for**
6:      **return** K
7: **end function**

In order to efficiently compute $P(K \cup \{\kappa\})$, k-optimal uses compilation to BDDs. Instead of building the BDD for $K \cup \{\kappa\}$ from scratch, k-optimal uses a smarter approach. Let dnf represent the DNF formula for K and let $f_1 \wedge \ldots \wedge f_n$ represent the Boolean formula for κ, where the f_is are Boolean variables for ground probabilistic facts. Then

$$
\begin{aligned}
P(f_1 \wedge \ldots \wedge f_n \vee dnf) = {} & P(f_1 \wedge \ldots \wedge f_n) + \\
& P(\neg f_1 \wedge dnf) + \\
& P(f_1 \wedge \neg f_2 \wedge dnf) + \ldots \\
& P(f_1 \wedge \ldots \wedge f_{n-1} \wedge \neg f_n \wedge dnf)
\end{aligned}
$$

Since probabilistic facts are independent, $P(f_1 \wedge \ldots \wedge f_n)$ can be easily computed as $P(f_1) \cdot \ldots \cdot P(f_n)$. The other terms become

$$
\begin{aligned}
P(f_1 \wedge \ldots \wedge f_{i-1} \wedge \neg f_i \wedge dnf) = {} & P(f_1) \cdot \ldots \cdot P(f_{i-1}) \cdot (1 - P(f_i)) \cdot \\
& P(dnf | f_1 \wedge \ldots \wedge f_{i-1} \wedge \neg f_i)
\end{aligned}
$$

The factor $P(dnf|f_1 \wedge \ldots \wedge f_{i-1} \wedge \neg f_i)$ can be computed cheaply if the BDD for dnf is available: we can apply function PROB of Algorithm 6 by assuming that $P(f_j) = 1$ for the conditional facts $j < i$ and $P(f_i) = 0$.

So, at the beginning of a search iteration, K is compiled to a BDD and $P(K \cup \{\kappa\})$ is computed for each node of the SLD tree for the query q, where κ is the composite choice corresponding to the node, representing a possibly partial explanation. If κ has n elements, n conditional probabilities must be computed.

However, when the probability $P(f_1 \wedge \ldots \wedge f_n \wedge f_{n+1} \vee dnf)$ for the partial proof $f_1 \wedge \ldots \wedge f_n \wedge f_{n+1}$ must be computed, the probability $P(f_1 \wedge \ldots \wedge f_n \vee dnf)$ was computed in the parent of the current node. Since

$$P(f_1 \wedge \ldots \wedge f_n \wedge f_{n+1} \vee dnf) = P(f_1 \wedge \ldots \wedge f_n \vee dnf) + \\ P(f_1 \wedge \ldots \wedge f_n \wedge \neg f_{n+1} \wedge dnf)$$

then only $P(f_1 \wedge \ldots \wedge f_n \wedge \neg f_{n+1} \wedge dnf)$ must be computed.

In practice, Renkens et al. [2012] observe that computing $P(K \cup \{\kappa\})$ for each node of the SLD tree is still too costly because partial proofs have also to be considered and these may lead to dead ends. They found experimentally that using the bound $P(\kappa)$ of k-best for pruning incomplete proofs and computing $P(K \cup \{\kappa\})$ only when a complete proof is found provides better performance. This works because $P(\kappa)$ is an upper bound on $P(K \cup \{\kappa\}) - P(K)$, so cutting a branch because $P(\kappa)$ has become smaller than $P(K \cup \{\kappa'\}) - P(K)$ for the best explanation κ' found so far does not prune good solutions.

However, this approach performs less pruning, as it is based on an upper bound, and the computation of $P(K \cup \{\kappa\})$ at the parent of an SLD node of a complete proof is no longer available.

k-optimal, as k-best, still suffers from the problem that k is set beforehand and fixed, so it may happen that, of the k proofs, many provide only very small contributions and a lower value of k could have been used. $k-\theta$-optimal puts a threshold θ on the added proof probability: k-optimal is stopped before k proofs are found if no more proof has an added probability $P(K \cup \{\kappa\}) - P(K)$ larger than θ. This is achieved by setting the bound to θ at the beginning of each iteration of k-optimal.

Renkens et al. [2012] prove that the k-optimal optimization problem is NP-hard. They also show that the proposed greedy algorithm achieves an approximation which is not worse than $1 - \frac{1}{e}$ times the probability of the optimal solution.

The experiments in [Renkens et al., 2012] performed on biological graphs show that k-best is about an order of magnitude faster that k-optimal but that k-optimal obtains better bounds especially when k is low compared to the number of available proofs.

10.6 Explanation-based Approximate Weighted Model Counting

Renkens et al. [2014] solve EVID approximately by computing lower and upper bounds of the probability of evidence from ProbLog programs. The approach is based on computing explanations for evidence e one by one, where an explanation here is represented as a conjunction of Boolean variables representing ground probabilistic facts. So an explanation

$$\kappa = \{(f_1, \theta, k_1), \ldots, (f_n, \emptyset, k_n)\}$$

for ground probabilistic facts $\{f_1, \ldots, f_n\}$ is represented as

$$exp_\kappa = \bigwedge_{(f,\emptyset,1)\in\kappa} \lambda_f \wedge \bigwedge_{(f,\emptyset,0)\in\kappa} \neg\lambda_f$$

where λ_f is the Boolean variable associated with fact f.

An explanation exp is such that $\phi_r \wedge exp \models \phi_e$, where ϕ_r and ϕ_e are the propositional formulas representing the rules and the evidence, respectively, computed as in ProbLog2 (see Section 8.7).

Renkens et al. [2014] show that, given any set of explanations

$$\{exp_1, \ldots, exp_m\},$$

it holds that

$$WMC_V(\phi \wedge (exp_1 \vee \ldots \vee exp_m)) = WMC_E(exp_1 \vee \ldots \vee exp_m)$$

where $\phi = \phi_r \wedge \phi_e$ and V is the set of all variables of the programs, i.e., those for probabilistic facts and those of the head of clauses in the grounding of the program, while E is the set of variables of the program for probabilistic facts only.

Given two weighted formulas ψ and ξ over the same set of variables V, we have that $WMC_V(\psi) \geqslant WMC_V(\psi \wedge \xi)$ as the models of $\psi \wedge \xi$ are a subset of those of ψ. So $WMC_V(\phi \wedge (exp_1 \vee \ldots \vee exp_m))$ is a lower bound for $WMC_V(\phi)$ and tends toward it as the number explanations increases, as each explanation encodes a set of worlds. Since the number of explanations is finite, when considering all explanations, the two counts will be equal.

Moreover, we can compute $WMC_V(\phi \wedge (exp_1 \vee \ldots \vee exp_m))$ more quickly by computing $WMC_E(exp_1 \vee \ldots \vee exp_m)$ because it has fewer variables. This leads to Algorithm 13 for computing a lower bound of the evidence, where function NEXTEXPL returns a new explanation. The algorithm is anytime, we can stop it at any time still obtaining a lower bound of $P(e)$.

Algorithm 13 Function AWMC: Approximate WMC for computing a lower bound of $P(e)$.

1: **function** AWMC($\phi_r, \phi_e, maxTime$)
2:    $\psi \leftarrow 0$
3:    **while** $time < maxTime$ **do**
4:       $exp \leftarrow$ NEXTEXPL($\phi_r \wedge \phi_e$)
5:       $\psi \leftarrow \psi \vee exp$
6:    **end while**
7:    **return** $WMC_{V(\psi)}(\psi)$
8: **end function**

NEXTEXPL looks for the next best explanation, i.e., the one with maximal probability (or WMC). This is done by solving a weighted MAX-SAT problem: given a CNF formula with non-negative weights assigned to clauses, find assignments for the variables that minimize the sum of the weights of the violated clauses. An appropriate weighted CNF formula built over an extended set of variables is passed to a weighted MAX-SAT solver that returns an assignment for all the variables. An explanation is built from the assignment. To ensure that the same explanation is not found every time, a new clause excluding it is added to the CNF formula for every found explanation.

An upper bound of $P(e)$ can be computed by observing that, for ProbLog, $WMC(\phi_r) = 1$, because the variables for probabilistic facts can take any combination of values, the weights for their literals sum to 1 (represent a probability distribution) and the weight for derived literals (those of atoms appearing in the head of clauses) are all 1, so they don't influence the weight of worlds. Therefore

$$WMC(\phi_r \wedge \phi_e) = WMC(\phi_r) - WMC(\phi_r \wedge \neg\phi_e) = 1 - WMC(\phi_r \wedge \neg\phi_e)$$

As a consequence, if we compute a lower bound on $WMC(\phi_r \wedge \neg\phi_e)$, we can derive an upper bound on $WMC(\phi_r \wedge \phi_e)$. The lower bound on $WMC(\phi_r \wedge \neg\phi_e)$ is computed as for $WMC(\phi_r \wedge \phi_e)$, by looking for explanations for $\phi_r \wedge \neg\phi_e$.

This leads to Algorithm 14 that, at each iteration, updates the bound that at the previous iteration had the largest change in value. The algorithm is anytime: at any time point, low and up are the lower and upper bounds of $P(e)$, respectively.

Algorithm 14 Function AWMC: Approximate WMC for computing lower and upper bounds of $P(e)$.

1: **function** AWMC($\phi_r, \phi_e, maxTime$)
2:     $improveTop \leftarrow 0.5$
3:     $improveBot \leftarrow 0.5$
4:     $top \leftarrow 1$
5:     $bot \leftarrow 0$
6:     $up \leftarrow 1.0$
7:     $low \leftarrow 0.0$
8:     **while** $time < maxTime$ **do**
9:         **if** $improveTop > improveBot$ **then**
10:             $exp \leftarrow$ NEXTEXPL($\phi_r \wedge \neg\phi_e$)
11:             $next \leftarrow$ WMC($top \wedge \neg exp$)
12:             $improveTop \leftarrow up - next$
13:             $top \leftarrow top \wedge \neg exp$
14:             $up \leftarrow next$
15:         **else**
16:             $exp \leftarrow$ NEXTEXPL($\phi_r \wedge \phi_e$)
17:             $next \leftarrow$ WMC($bot \vee exp$)
18:             $improveBot \leftarrow next - low$
19:             $bot \leftarrow bot \vee exp$
20:             $low \leftarrow next$
21:         **end if**
22:     **end while**
23:     **return** $[low, up]$
24: **end function**

10.7 Approximate Inference with T_P-compilation

T_P compilation [Vlasselaer et al., 2015, 2016] discussed in Section 8.8 can be used to perform approximate CONDATOMS inference by computing a lower and an upper bound of the probabilities of query atoms, similarly to iterative deepening of Section 10.1.1.

Vlasselaer et al. [2016] show that, for each iteration i of application of Tc_P, if λ_a^i is the formula associated with atom a in the result of $Tc_P \uparrow i$, then $WMC(\lambda_a^i)$ is a lower bound on $P(a)$. So T_P compilation is an anytime algorithm for approximate inference: at any time, the algorithm provides a lower bound of the probability of each atom.

Moreover, T_{CP} is applied using the one atom at a time approach where the atom to evaluate is selected using a heuristic that is

- proportional to the increase in the probability of the atom;
- inversely proportional to the complexity increase of the SDD for the atom;
- proportional to the importance of the atom for the query, computed as the inverse of the minimal depth of the atom in the SLD trees for each of the queries of interest.

An upper bound for definite programs is instead computed by selecting a subset $\mathcal{F}'$ of the facts $\mathcal{F}$ of the program and by assigning them the value true, which is achieved by conjoining each λ_a with $\lambda_{\mathcal{F}'} = \bigwedge_{f \in \mathcal{F}'} \lambda_f$. If we then compute the fixpoint, we obtain an upper bound: $WMC(\lambda_a^\infty) \geqslant P(a)$. Moreover, conjoining with $\lambda_{\mathcal{F}'}$ simplifies formulas and so also compilation.

The subset $\mathcal{F}'$ is selected by considering the minimal depth of each fact in the SLD trees for each of the queries and by inserting into $\mathcal{F}'$ only the facts with a minimal depth smaller than a constant d. This is done to make sure that the query depends on at least one probabilistic fact and the upper bound is smaller than 1.

While the lower bound is also valid for normal programs, the upper bound can be used only for definite programs.

11

Non-standard Inference

This chapter discusses inference problems for languages that are related to PLP, such as Possibilistic Logic Programming, or are generalizations of PLP, such as Algebraic ProbLog. Moreover, the chapter illustrates how decision-theoretic problems can be solved by exploiting PLP techniques.

11.1 Possibilistic Logic Programming

Possibilistic Logic [Dubois et al., 1994] is a logic of uncertainty for reasoning under incomplete evidence. In this logic, the degree of *necessity* of a formula expresses to what extent the available evidence entails the truth of the formula and the degree of *possibility* expresses to what extent the truth of the formula is not incompatible with the available evidence.

Given a formula ϕ, we indicate with $\Pi(\phi)$ the degree of possibility assigned by *possibility measure* Π to it, and with $N(\phi)$ the degree of necessity assigned by *necessity measure* N to it. Possibility and necessity measures must satisfy the constraint $N(\phi) = 1 - \Pi(\neg\phi)$ for all formulas ϕ.

A *possibilistic clause* is a first-order logic clause C associated with a number that is a lower bound on its necessity or possibility degree. We consider here the possibilistic logic CPL1 [Dubois et al., 1991] in which only lower bounds on necessity are considered. Thus, (C, α) means that $N(C) \geqslant \alpha$. A *possibilistic theory* is a set of possibilistic clauses.

A possibility measure *satisfies a possibilistic clause* (C, α) if $N(C) \geqslant \alpha$ or, equivalently, if $\Pi(\neg C) \leqslant 1 - \alpha$. A possibility measure *satisfies a possibilistic theory* if it satisfies every clause in it. A possibilistic clause (C, α) is a *consequence* of a possibilistic theory F if every possibility measure satisfying F also satisfies (C, α).

Inference rules of classical logic have been extended to rules in possibilistic logic. Here we report two sound inference rules [Dubois and Prade, 2004]:

- $(\phi, \alpha), (\psi, \beta) \vdash (R(\phi, \psi), \min(\alpha, \beta))$ where $R(\phi, \psi)$ is the resolvent of ϕ and ψ (extension of resolution);
- $(\phi, \alpha), (\phi, \beta) \vdash (\phi, \max(\alpha, \beta))$ (weight fusion).

Dubois et al. [1991] proposed a Possibilistic Logic Programming language. A program in such a language is a set of formulas of the form (C, α) where C is a definite clause

$$h \leftarrow b_1, \ldots, b_n.$$

and α is a possibility or necessity degree. We consider the subset of this language that is included in CPL1, i.e., α is a real number in (0,1] that is a lower bound on the necessity degree of C. The problem of inference in this language consists in computing the maximum value of α such that $N(q) \geqslant \alpha$ holds for a query q. The above inference rules are complete for this language.

Example 95 (Possibilistic logic program).   *The following possibilistic program computes the least unsure path in a graph, i.e., the path with maximal weight, the weight of a path being the weight of its weakest edge [Dubois et al., 1991].*

$$
\begin{array}{ll}
(path(X, X), & 1) \\
(path(X, Y) \leftarrow path(X, Z), edge(Z, Y), & 1) \\
(edge(a, b), & 0.3) \\
\ldots &
\end{array}
$$

We restricted our discussion here to positive programs. However, approaches for normal Possibilistic Logic programs have been proposed in [Nieves et al., 2007; Nicolas et al., 2006; Osorio and Nieves, 2009], and [Bauters et al., 2010].

PITA(IND,IND), see Section 8.10, can also be used to perform inference in Possibilistic Logic Programming where a program is composed only of clauses of the form $h : \alpha \leftarrow b_1, \ldots, b_n$ which are interpreted as possibilistic clauses of the form $(h \leftarrow b_1, \ldots, b_n, \alpha)$.

The PITA transformation of PITA(IND,IND) can be used unchanged provided that the support predicates are defined as

$$or(A, B, C) \leftarrow C \ is \ max(A, B).$$
$$and(A, B, C) \leftarrow C \ is \ min(A, B).$$
$$zero(0.0).$$
$$one(1.0).$$
$$ret\_prob(P, P).$$

We obtain in this way PITA(POSS).

Computing the possibility is much easier than computing the general probability, which must solve the disjoint sum problem to obtain answers.

11.2 Decision-theoretic ProbLog

Decision-Theoretic ProbLog [Van den Broeck et al., 2010] or DTPROBLOG tackles *decision problems*: the selection of actions from a set of alternatives so that a utility function is maximized. In other words, the problem is to choose the actions that bring the most expected reward (or the least expected cost) to the acting agent. DTPROBLOG supports decision problems where the domain is described using ProbLog so that probabilistic effects of actions can be taken into account.

DTPROBLOG extends ProbLog by adding decision facts $\mathcal{D}$ and utility facts $\mathcal{U}$. *Decision facts* model decision variables, i.e., variables on which we can act by setting their truth value. They are represented as

$$? :: d.$$

where d is an atom, possibly non-ground.

A *utility fact* is of the form

$$u \rightarrow r$$

where u is a literal and $r \in \mathbb{R}$ is a reward or utility for achieving u. It may be interpreted as a query that, when succeeding, gives a reward of r. u may be non-ground; in this case, the reward is given once if any grounding succeeds.

A *strategy* σ is a function $\mathcal{D} \rightarrow [0, 1]$ that assigns a decision fact to a probability. All grounding of the same decision fact are assigned the same probability. We call Σ the set of all possible strategies. We indicate with $\sigma(\mathcal{D})$ the set of probabilistic facts obtained by assigning probability $\sigma(d)$ to each decision fact $? :: d.$ of $\mathcal{D}$, i.e., $\sigma(\mathcal{D}) = \{\sigma(d) :: d | ? :: d \in \mathcal{D}\}$. A deterministic strategy is a strategy that only assigns probabilities 0 and 1 to decision facts. It is thus equivalent to a Boolean assignments to the decision atoms.

Given a DTPROBLOG program $\mathcal{DT} = \mathcal{BK} \cup \mathcal{D}$ program and a strategy σ, the probability to a query q is the probability $P_\sigma(q)$ assigned by the ProbLog program $\mathcal{BK} \cup \sigma(\mathcal{D})$.

The *utility* of a logic program P given a set of utility facts $\mathcal{U}$ is defined as

$$\text{Util}(P) = \sum_{u \to r \in \mathcal{U}, P \models u} r$$

The *expected utility* of a ProbLog program $\mathcal{P}$ given a set of utility facts $\mathcal{U}$ can thus be defined as

$$\text{Util}(\mathcal{P}) = \sum_{w \in W_\mathcal{P}} P(w) \sum_{u \to r \in \mathcal{U}, w \models u} r.$$

By exchanging the sum, we get

$$\text{Util}(\mathcal{P}) = \sum_{u \to r \in \mathcal{U}} \sum_{w \in W_\mathcal{P}, w \models u} r \cdot P(w) = \sum_{u \to r \in \mathcal{U}} r P(u)$$

The *expected utility* of a DTPROBLOG program $\mathcal{DT} = \mathcal{BK} \cup \mathcal{D} \cup \mathcal{U}$ and a strategy σ is the expected utility of $\mathcal{BK} \cup \sigma(\mathcal{D})$ given $\mathcal{U}$

$$\text{Util}(\sigma(\mathcal{DT})) = \text{Util}(\mathcal{BK} \cup \sigma(\mathcal{D})).$$

If we call $\text{Util}(u, \sigma(\mathcal{DT})) = r \cdot P(u)$ the expected utility due to atom u for a strategy σ, we have

$$\text{Util}(\sigma(\mathcal{DT})) = \sum_{u \to r \in \mathcal{U}} \text{Util}(u, \sigma(\mathcal{DT})).$$

Example 96 (Remaining dry [Van den Broeck et al., 2010]). *Consider the problem of remaining dry even when the weather is unpredictable. The possible actions are wearing a raincoat and carrying an umbrella:*

$? :: umbrella.$
$? :: raincoat.$
$0.3 :: rainy.$
$0.5 :: windy.$
$broken\_umbrella \leftarrow umbrella, rainy, windy.$
$dry \leftarrow rainy, umbrella, {\sim}broken\_umbrella.$
$dry \leftarrow rainy, raincoat.$
$dry \leftarrow {\sim}rainy.$
Utility facts associate real numbers to atoms
$\quad umbrella \to -2 \quad dry \to 60$
$\quad raincoat \to -20 \quad broken\_umbrella \to -40$

The *inference problem* in DTPROBLOG is to compute $\text{Util}(\sigma(\mathcal{DT}))$ for a particular strategy σ.

The *decision problem* instead consists of finding the optimal strategy, i.e., the one that provides the maximum expected utility. Formally, it means solving

$$\arg\max_{\sigma} \text{Util}(\sigma(\mathcal{DT})).$$

Since all the decisions are independent, we can consider only deterministic strategies. In fact, if the derivative of the total utility with respect to the probability assigned to a decision variable is positive (negative), the best result is obtained by assigning probability 1 (0). If the derivative is 0, it does not matter.

The inference problem is solved in DTPROBLOG by computing $P(u)$ with probabilistic inference for all decision facts $u \to r$ in $\mathcal{U}$. DTPROBLOG uses compilation of the query to BDDs as ProbLog1.

Example 97 (Continuation of Example 96). *For the utility fact dry, ProbLog1 builds the BDD of Figure 11.1. For the strategy*

$$\sigma = \{umbrella \to 1, raincoat \to 0\},$$

the probability of dry is $0.7 + 0.3 \cdot 0.5 = 0.85$, *so* $\text{Util}(dry, \sigma(\mathcal{DT})) = 60 \cdot 0.85 = 51$.

For the utility fact broken_umbrella, ProbLog1 builds the BDD of Figure 11.2. For the strategy $\{umbrella \to 1, raincoat \to 0\}$, *the probability of broken_umbrella is* $0.3 \cdot 0.5 = 0.15$ *and*

$$\text{Util}(broken\_umbrella, \sigma(\mathcal{DT})) = -40 \cdot 0.15 = -6.$$

Overall, we get

$$\text{Util}(\sigma(\mathcal{DT})) = 51 + (-6) + (-2) = 43.$$

To solve decision problems, DTPROBLOG uses ADDs [Bahar et al., 1997] that are a generalization of BDDs where the leaves store a value in $\mathbb{R}$ instead of 0 or 1. An ADD thus represents a function from Boolean variables to the real numbers $f : \{0,1\}^n \to \mathbb{R}$ using a form of Shannon expansion:

$$f(x_1, x_2, \ldots, x_n) = x_1 \cdot f(1, x_2, \ldots, x_n) + (1 - x_1) \cdot f(0, x_2, \ldots, x_n).$$

As BDDs, ADDs can be combined with operations. We consider here scalar multiplication $c \cdot g$ of an ADD g with the constant c, addition $f \oplus g$ of two

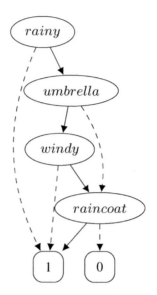

Figure 11.1 $\mathrm{BDD}_{dry}(\sigma)$ for Example 96. From [Van den Broeck et al., 2010]. © [2010] Association for the Advancement of Artificial Intelligence. All rights reserved. Reprinted with permission.

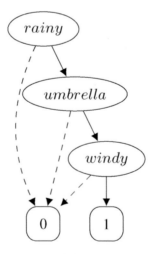

Figure 11.2 $\mathrm{BDD}_{broken\_umbrella}(\sigma)$ for Example 96. From [Van den Broeck et al., 2010]. © [2010] Association for the Advancement of Artificial Intelligence. All rights reserved. Reprinted with permission.

ADDs, and if-then-else ITE(b, f, g) where b is a Boolean variable.

In scalar multiplication, $h = c \cdot g$ with $c \in \mathbb{R}$ and $g : \{0, 1\}^n \to \mathbb{R}$, the output $h : \{0, 1\}^n \to \mathbb{R}$ is defined as: $\forall \mathbf{x} : h(\mathbf{x}) = c \cdot g(\mathbf{x})$.

In addition, $h = f \oplus g$ with $f, g : \{0, 1\}^n \to \mathbb{R}$, the output $h : \{0, 1\}^n \to \mathbb{R}$ is defined as $\forall \mathbf{x} : h(\mathbf{x}) = f(\mathbf{x}) + g(\mathbf{x})$.

The version of if-then-else of interest here, ITE(b, f, g) with $b \in \{0, 1\}$ and $f, g : \{0, 1\}^n \to \mathbb{R}$, returns $h : \{0, 1\}^{n+1} \to \mathbb{R}$ computed as

$$\forall b, \mathbf{x} : h(b, \mathbf{x}) = \begin{cases} f(\mathbf{x}) & \text{if } b = 1 \\ g(\mathbf{x}) & \text{if } b = 0 \end{cases}.$$

The CUDD [Somenzi, 2015] package, for example, offers these operations.

DTPROBLOG stores three functions:

- $P_\sigma(u)$, the probability of literal u as a function of the strategy;
- Util$(u, \sigma(\mathcal{DT}))$, the expected utility of literal u as a function of the strategy;
- Util(σ), the total expected utility as a function of the strategy.

Since we can consider only deterministic strategies, one of them can be represented with a Boolean vector $\mathbf{d}$ with an entry for each decision variable d_i. Therefore, all these functions are Boolean functions and can be represented with the ADDs ADD(u), ADD$^{util}(u)$, and ADD$^{util}_{tot}$, respectively.

Given ADD$^{util}_{tot}$, finding the best strategy is easy: we just have to identify the leaf with the highest value and return a path from the root to the leaf, represented as a Boolean vector $\mathbf{d}$.

To build ADD(u), DTPROBLOG builds the BDD BDD(u) representing the truth of the query u as a function of the probabilistic and decision facts: given an assignment $\mathbf{f}, \mathbf{d}$ for those, BDD(u) returns either 0 or 1. BDD(u) represents the probability $P(u|\mathbf{f}, \mathbf{d})$ for all values of $\mathbf{f}, \mathbf{d}$.

Function $P_\sigma(u)$ requires $P(u|\mathbf{d})$ that can be obtained from $P(u|\mathbf{f}, \mathbf{d})$ by summing out the $\mathbf{f}$ variables, i.e., computing

$$P(u|\mathbf{d}) = \sum_{\mathbf{f}} P(u, \mathbf{f}|\mathbf{d}) = \sum_{\mathbf{f}} P(u|\mathbf{f}, \mathbf{d}) P(\mathbf{f}|\mathbf{d}) =$$

$$\sum_{\mathbf{f}} P(u|\mathbf{f}, \mathbf{d}) P(\mathbf{f}) = \sum_{\mathbf{f}} P(u|\mathbf{f}, \mathbf{d}) \prod_{f \in \mathbf{f}} \Pi_f =$$

$$\sum_{f_1} \Pi_{f_1} \sum_{f_2} \Pi_{f_2} \cdots \sum_{f_n} \Pi_{f_n} P(u|f_1, \ldots, f_n, \mathbf{d})$$

We can obtain $\text{ADD}(u)$ from $\text{BDD}(u)$ by traversing $\text{BDD}(u)$ from the leaves to the root and, for each sub-BDD with root in node n, building a corresponding sub-ADD with root node m. If n is the 0-terminal (1-terminal), we return a 0-terminal (1-terminal). If n is associated with a probabilistic variable f, we have already built the ADDs ADD_l and ADD_h for its 0- and 1-child. They represent $P(u|f = 0, \mathbf{d}')$ and $P(u|f = 1, \mathbf{d}')$, respectively, for all values $\mathbf{d}'$ where $\mathbf{D}'$ is the set of Boolean decision variables of ADD_l and ADD_h. We must sum out variable f, so

$$P(u|\mathbf{d}') = \Pi_f \cdot P(u|f = 0, \mathbf{d}') + (1 - \Pi_f) \cdot P(u|f = 1, \mathbf{d}')$$

The ADD

$$\Pi_f \cdot \text{ADD}_l \oplus (1 - \Pi_f) \cdot \text{ADD}_h$$

represents $P(u|\mathbf{d}')$ and is the ADD we are looking for.

If n is associated with decision variable d with ADDs ADD_l and ADD_h for its 0- and 1-child, the ADD for representing $P(u|d, \mathbf{d}')$ is

$$\text{ITE}(d, \text{ADD}_h, \text{ADD}_l).$$

The conversion from $\text{BDD}(u)$ to $\text{ADD}(u)$ is computed by function PROBABILITYDD of Algorithm 15.

Once we have $\text{ADD}(u)$, $\text{ADD}^{util}(u)$ is simply given by $r \cdot \text{ADD}(u)$ if $u \to r \in \mathcal{U}$. Finally, $\text{ADD}^{util}_{tot} = \bigoplus_{u \to r \in \mathcal{U}} \text{ADD}^{util}(u)$. This gives Algorithm 15 that solves the decision problem exactly. The function EXACTSOLUTION initializes ADD^{util}_{tot} to the zero function and then cycles over each utility fact in turn, building $\text{BDD}(u)$, $\text{ADD}(u)$, and $\text{ADD}^{util}(u)$. Then ADD^{util}_{tot} is updated by summing $\text{ADD}^{util}(u)$ to the current value.

Example 98 (Continuation of Example 96). *For the utility fact dry, DT-PROBLOG builds* $\text{ADD}(dry)$ *and* $\text{ADD}^{util}(dry)$ *of Figure 11.3. For the strategy*

$$\sigma = \{umbrella \to 1, raincoat \to 0\},$$

the figure confirms that $\text{Util}(dry, \sigma(\mathcal{DT})) = 60 \cdot 0.85 = 51.$

For broken_umbrella, DTPROBLOG builds $\text{ADD}(broken\_umbrella)$ *and* $\text{ADD}^{util}(broken\_umbrella)$ *of Figure 11.4. For the strategy* σ*, the figure confirms that*

$$\text{Util}(broken\_umbrella, \sigma(\mathcal{DT})) = -40 \cdot 0.15 = -6.$$

Figure 11.5 shows ADD^{util}_{tot} *that confirms that, for strategy* σ,

$$\text{Util}(\sigma(\mathcal{DT})) = 43.$$

Algorithm 15 Function EXACTSOLUTION: solving the DTPROBLOG decision problem exactly.

1: **function** EXACTSOLUTION($\mathcal{DT}$)
2:     $\text{ADD}_{tot}^{util} \leftarrow 0$
3:     **for all** $(u \rightarrow r) \in \mathcal{U}$ **do**
4:         Build $\text{BDD}(u)$, the BDD for u
5:         $\text{ADD}(u) \leftarrow \text{PROBABILITYDD}(\text{BDD}(u))$
6:         $\text{ADD}^{util}(u) \leftarrow r \cdot \text{ADD}(u)$
7:         $\text{ADD}_{tot}^{util} \leftarrow \text{ADD}_{tot}^{util} \oplus \text{ADD}^{util}(u)$
8:     **end for**
9:     let t_{max} be the terminal node of ADD_{tot}^{util} with the highest utility
10:     let p be a path from t_{max} to the root of ADD_{tot}^{util}
11:     **return** the Boolean decisions made on p
12: **end function**
13: **function** PROBABILITYDD(n)
14:     **if** n is the 1-terminal **then**
15:         **return** a 1-terminal
16:     **end if**
17:     **if** n is the 0-terminal **then**
18:         **return** a 0-terminal
19:     **end if**
20:     let h and l be the high and low children of n
21:     $\text{ADD}_h \leftarrow \text{PROBABILITYDD}(h)$
22:     $\text{ADD}_l \leftarrow \text{PROBABILITYDD}(h)$
23:     **if** n represents a decision d **then**
24:         **return** $\text{ITE}(d, \text{ADD}_h, \text{ADD}_l)$
25:     **end if**
26:     **if** n represents a fact with probability p **then**
27:         **return** $(p \cdot \text{ADD}_h) \oplus ((1 - p) \cdot \text{ADD}_l)$
28:     **end if**
29: **end function**

Moreover, this is also the optimal strategy.

Algorithm 15 can be optimized by pruning ADD_{tot}^{util} to remove the portions that may never lead to an optimal strategy. Denote by $\max \text{ADD}$ and $\min \text{ADD}$ the maximum and minimum value, respectively, that ADD assigns to any combination of its variables, i.e., the maximum and minimum values that appear in its leaves.

When $\text{ADD}^{util}(u_i)$ is summed to ADD_{tot}^{util}, a leaf of ADD_{tot}^{util} with value v before the sum belongs to $[v + \min \text{ADD}^{util}(u_i), v + \max \text{ADD}^{util}(u_i)]$ after the sum. Thus, if m is $\max \text{ADD}_{tot}^{util}$ before the sum, any leaf with value v such that $v + \max \text{ADD}^{util}(u_i) < m + \min \text{ADD}^{util}(u_i)$ will never lead

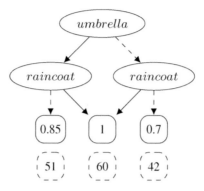

Figure 11.3   ADD(dry) for Example 96. The dashed terminals indicate ADD^{util}(dry). From [Van den Broeck et al., 2010]. © [2010] Association for the Advancement of Artificial Intelligence. All rights reserved. Reprinted with permission.

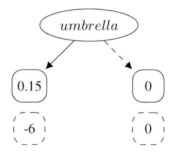

Figure 11.4   ADD($broken\_umbrella$) for Example 96. The dashed terminals indicate ADD^{util}($broken\_umbrella$). From [Van den Broeck et al., 2010]. © [2010] Association for the Advancement of Artificial Intelligence. All rights reserved. Reprinted with permission.

to an optimal strategy. All such leaves can be pruned by merging them and assigning them the value $-\infty$.

If we compute the impact of utility attribute u_i as

$$\mathrm{Im}(u_i) = \max \mathrm{ADD}^{util}(u_i) - \min \mathrm{ADD}^{util}(u_i)$$

we can prune all the leaves of ADD$^{util}_{tot}$ that, before the sum, have a value below

$$\max \mathrm{ADD}^{util}_{tot} - \mathrm{Im}(u_i)$$

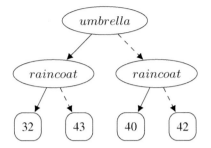

Figure 11.5 ADD$_{tot}^{util}$ for Example 96. From [Van den Broeck et al., 2010]. © [2010] Association for the Advancement of Artificial Intelligence. All rights reserved. Reprinted with permission.

We then perform the summation with the simplified ADD$_{tot}^{util}$ which is cheaper than the summation with the original ADD.

Moreover, we can also consider the utility attributes still to be added and prune all the leaves of ADD$_{tot}^{util}$ that have a value below

$$\max \text{ADD}_{tot}^{util} - \sum_{j \geq i} \text{Im}(u_j)$$

Finally, we can sort the utility attributes in order of decreasing $\text{Im}(u_i)$ and add them in this order, so that the maximum pruning is achieved.

The decision problem can also be solved approximately by adopting two techniques that can be used individually or in combination.

The first technique uses local search: a random strategy σ is initially selected by randomly assigning values to the decision variables and then a cycle is entered in which a single decision is flipped obtaining strategy σ'. If $\text{Util}(\sigma'(\mathcal{DT}))$ is larger than $\text{Util}(\sigma(\mathcal{DT}))$, the modification is retained and σ' becomes the current best strategy. $\text{Util}(\sigma(\mathcal{DT}))$ can be computed using the BDD $\text{BDD}(u)$ for each utility attribute using function PROB of Algorithm 6 for computing $P(u)$.

The second technique involves computing an approximation of the utility by using k-best (see Section 10.1.2) for building the BDDs for utility attributes.

Example 99 (Viral marketing [Van den Broeck et al., 2010]). *A firm is interested in marketing a new product to its customers. These are connected in a social network that is known to the firm: the network represents the trust relationships between customers. The firm wants to choose the customers on* *which to perform marketing actions. Each action has a cost, and a reward is given for each person that buys the product.*

We can model this domain with the DTPROBLOG *program*

```
? :: market(P) :- person(P).
0.4 :: viral(P,Q).
0.3 :: from_marketing(P).
market(P) -> -2 :- person(P).
buys(P) -> 5 :- person(P).
buys(P) :- market(P), from_marketing(P).
buys(P) :- trusts(P,Q), buys(Q), viral(P,Q).
```

Here the notation `:- person(P).` *after decision and utility facts means that there is a fact for each grounding of* `person(P)`, *i.e., a fact for each person. The program states that a person* P *buys the product if he is the target of a marketing action and the action causes the person to buy the product (*`from_marketing(P)`*), or if he trusts a person* Q *that buys the product and there is a viral effect (*`viral(P,Q)`*). The decisions are* `market(P)` *for each person* P. *A reward of 5 is assigned for each person that buys the product and each marketing action costs 2.*

Solving the decision problem for this program means deciding on which person to perform a marketing action so that the expected utility is maximized.

11.3 Algebraic ProbLog

Algebraic ProbLog (aProbLog) [Kimmig, 2010; Kimmig et al., 2011b] generalizes ProbLog to deal with labels of facts that are more general than probabilities. In particular, the labels are required to belong to a *semiring*, an algebraic structure.

Definition 44 (Semiring). *A semiring is a tuple* $(\mathcal{A}, \oplus, \otimes, e^{\oplus}, e^{\otimes})$ *such that*

- $\mathcal{A}$ *is a set;*
- $\oplus$ *is a binary operations over* $\mathcal{A}$ *called* addition *that is commutative and associative and has* neutral element $e^{\oplus}$, *i.e.,* $\forall a, b, c \in \mathcal{A}$,

$$a \oplus b = b \oplus a$$
$$(a \oplus b) \oplus c = a \oplus (b \oplus c)$$
$$a \oplus e^{\oplus} = a.$$

- $\otimes$ *is a binary operations over* $\mathcal{A}$ *called* multiplication *that left and right distributes over addition and has* neutral element $e^{\otimes}$*, i.e.,* $\forall a, b, c \in \mathcal{A}$,

$$(a \oplus b) \otimes c = (a \otimes c) \oplus (b \otimes c)$$
$$a \otimes (b \oplus c)c = (a \otimes b) \oplus (a \otimes b)$$
$$a \otimes e^{\otimes} = e^{\otimes} \otimes a = a.$$

- $e^{\oplus}$ *annihilates* $\mathcal{A}$*, i.e.,* $\forall a \in \mathcal{A}$

$$a \otimes e^{\oplus} = e^{\oplus} \otimes a = e^{\oplus}.$$

A commutative semiring *is a semiring* $(\mathcal{A}, \oplus, \otimes, e^{\oplus}, e^{\otimes})$ *such that multiplication is commutative, i.e.,* $\forall a, b \in \mathcal{A}$,

$$a \otimes b = b \otimes a$$

An example of a commutative semiring is $([0, 1], +, \times, 0, 1)$ where $[0, 1] \subseteq \mathbb{R}$ and $+$ and $\times$ are addition and multiplication over the reals. ProbLog associates each probabilistic fact with an element of $[0, 1]$ and computes the probability of queries by using addition and multiplication, so it can be seen as operating on the semiring $([0, 1], +, \times, 0, 1)$ that we call *probabilistic semiring*.

Another example of a commutative semiring is $([0, 1], \max, \min, 0, 1)$ where $\max$ and $\min$ are maximum and minimum operations over the reals. PITA(POSS) can be seen as operating on the semiring $([0, 1], \max, \min, 0, 1)$ that we call *possibilistic semiring*.

ProbLog can be generalized to operate on a semiring. For a set of ground atoms A, let $L(A)$ be the set of literals that can be built on atoms from A, i.e., $L(A) = A \cup \{\sim a | a \in A\}$. For a two-valued interpretation J over a set of ground atoms A, define the *complete interpretation* $c(J) = J \cup \{\sim a | a \in A \backslash J\}$ and the set of all possible complete interpretations $\mathcal{I}(A) = \{c(J) | J \subseteq A\}$. Consistent sets of literals built on atoms A form the set $\mathcal{C}(A) = \{H | H \subseteq I, I \in \mathcal{I}(A)\}$.

Definition 45 (aProbLog [Kimmig et al., 2011b]). *An* aProbLog *program consists of*

- *a commutative semiring* $(\mathcal{A}, \oplus, \otimes, e^{\oplus}, e^{\otimes})$;
- *a finite set of ground atoms* $\mathcal{F} = \{f_1, \ldots, f_n\}$ *called* algebraic facts;
- *a finite set of rules* $\mathcal{R}$;
- *a labeling function* $\alpha : L(\mathcal{F}) \rightarrow \mathcal{A}$.

The possible complete interpretations for $\mathcal{F}$ are also called *worlds* and $\mathcal{I}(\mathcal{F})$ is the set of all worlds. aProbLog assigns labels to worlds and sets of worlds as follows. The label of a world $I \in \mathcal{I}(\mathcal{F})$ is the product of the labels of its literals

$$\mathbf{A}(I) = \bigotimes_{l \in I} \alpha(l)$$

The label of a set of complete interpretations $S \subseteq \mathcal{I}(F)$ is the sum of the labels of each interpretation

$$\mathbf{A}(S) = \bigoplus_{I \in S} \bigotimes_{l \in I} \alpha(l).$$

A query is a set of ground literals. Given a query q, we denote the set of complete interpretations where the query is true as $\mathcal{I}(q)$ defined as

$$\mathcal{I}(q) = \{I | I \in \mathcal{I}(F) \wedge I \cup \mathcal{R} \models q\}$$

The label of the query q is then defined as the label of $\mathcal{I}(q)$:

$$\mathbf{A}(q) = \mathbf{A}(\mathcal{I}(q)) = \bigoplus_{I \in \mathcal{I}(q)} \bigotimes_{l \in I} \alpha(l).$$

Since both operations are commutative and associative, the label of a query does not depends on the order of literals and of interpretations.

The inference problem in aProbLog consists of computing the labels of queries. Depending on the choice of commutative semiring, an inference task may correspond to a certain known problem or new problems. Table 11.1 lists some known inference tasks with their corresponding commutative semirings.

Table 11.1 Inference tasks and corresponding semirings for aProbLog. Adapted from [Kimmig et al., 2011b] © [2011] Association for the Advancement of Artificial Intelligence. All rights reserved. Reprinted with permission.

task	$\mathcal{A}$	$e^{\oplus}$	$e^{\otimes}$	$a \oplus b$	$a \otimes b$	$\alpha(f)$	$\alpha(\sim f)$
PROB	$[0,1]$	0	1	$a+b$	$a \cdot b$	$\alpha(f)$	$1 - \alpha(f)$
POSS	$[0,1]$	0	1	$\max(a,b)$	$\min(a,b)$	$\alpha(f)$	1
MPE	$[0,1]$	0	1	$\max(a,b)$	$a \cdot b$	$\alpha(f)$	$1 - \alpha(f)$
MPE State	$[0,1] \times \mathbb{P}(\mathcal{C}(\mathcal{F}))$	$(0,\varnothing)$	$(1,\{\varnothing\})$	Eq. 11.2	Eq. 11.1	$(p,\{\{f\}\})$	$(1-p, \{\{\sim f\}\})$
SAT	$\{0,1\}$	0	1	$a \vee b$	$a \wedge b$	1	1
#SAT	$\mathbb{N}$	0	1	$a+b$	$a \cdot b$	1	1
BDD	$BDD(\mathcal{V})$	$bdd(0)$	$bdd(1)$	$a \vee_{bdd} b$	$a \wedge_{bdd} b$	$bdd(f)$	$\neg_{bdd}bdd(f)$
Sensitivity	$\mathbb{R}[\boldsymbol{X}]$	0	1	$a+b$	$a \cdot b$	x or in $[0,1]$	$1 - \alpha(f)$
Gradient	$[0,1] \times \mathbb{R}$	$(0,0)$	$(1,0)$	Eq. 11.3	Eq. 11.4	Eq. 11.5	Eq. 11.6

Example 100 (Alarm – aProbLog [Kimmig et al., 2011b]). *Consider the following aProbLog program similar to the ProbLog program of Example 78:*

$calls(X) \leftarrow alarm, hears\_alarm(X).$
$alarm \leftarrow burglary.$
$alarm \leftarrow earthquake.$
$0.7 :: hears\_alarm(john).$
$0.7 :: hears\_alarm(mary).$
$0.05 :: burglary.$
$0.01 :: earthquake.$

where the labels of positive literals are attached to each fact f. This program is a variation of the alarm BN of Example 11. The program has 16 worlds and the query $calls(mary)$ is true in six of them, those shown in Figure 11.6. For the PROB task, we consider the probability semiring and the label of negative literals are defined as $\alpha(\sim f) = 1 - \alpha(f)$. Then the

{	$hears\_alarm(john),$	$hears\_alarm(mary),$	$burglary,$	$earthquake$	}
{	$hears\_alarm(john),$	$hears\_alarm(mary),$	$burglary,$	$\sim earthquake$	}
{	$hears\_alarm(john),$	$hears\_alarm(mary),$	$\sim burglary,$	$earthquake$	}
{	$\sim hears\_alarm(john),$	$hears\_alarm(mary),$	$burglary,$	$earthquake$	}
{	$\sim hears\_alarm(john),$	$hears\_alarm(mary),$	$burglary,$	$\sim earthquake$	}
{	$\sim hears\_alarm(john),$	$hears\_alarm(mary),$	$\sim burglary,$	$earthquake$	}

Figure 11.6 Worlds where the query $calls(mary)$ from Example 100 is true.

label of $calls(mary)$ *is*

$$
\begin{aligned}
\mathbf{A}(calls(mary)) \;=\; & 0.7 \cdot 0.7 \cdot 0.05 \cdot 0.01 + \\
& 0.7 \cdot 0.7 \cdot 0.05 \cdot 0.99 + \\
& 0.7 \cdot 0.7 \cdot 0.95 \cdot 0.01 + \\
& 0.3 \cdot 0.7 \cdot 0.05 \cdot 0.01 + \\
& 0.3 \cdot 0.7 \cdot 0.05 \cdot 0.99 + \\
& 0.3 \cdot 0.7 \cdot 0.95 \cdot 0.01 = \\
& 0.04165
\end{aligned}
$$

For the MPE task, the semiring is $([0,1], \max, \times, 0, 1)$, *the label of negative literals are defined as* $\alpha(\sim f) = 1 - \alpha(f)$, *and the label of* $calls(mary)$ *is*

$$
\begin{aligned}
\mathbf{A}(calls(mary)) \;=\; & 0.7 \cdot 0.7 \cdot 0.05 \cdot 0.99 = \\
& 0.001995
\end{aligned}
$$

For the SAT task, the semiring is $(\{0,1\}, \vee, \wedge, 0, 1)$, *the label of literals is always 1, and the label of* $calls(mary)$ *is 1 as there are six worlds where the query is true.*

The MPE State task is an extension of the MPE task that also returns the world with the highest label. The set $\mathcal{A}$ is $[0,1] \times \mathbb{P}(\mathcal{CF})$ where $\mathbb{P}(\mathcal{C}(\mathcal{F}))$ is the powerset of $\mathcal{C}(\mathcal{F})$, so the second element of the labels is a set of consistent sets of literals built on algebraic facts. The aim is for the label of queries to have as first argument the maximum of the probability of the worlds and as second argument the set of worlds with that probability (there can be more than one if they share the same probability). The operations are defined as

$$
(p, S) \otimes (q, T) \;=\; (p \cdot q, \{I \cup J \mid I \in S, J \in T\} \tag{11.1}
$$

$$
(p, S) \oplus (q, T) \;=\;
\begin{cases}
(p, S) & \text{if } p > q \\
(q, T) & \text{if } p < q \\
(p, S \cup T) & \text{if } p = q
\end{cases}
\tag{11.2}
$$

The label for the query $mary(calls)$ of Example 100 is

$$
\begin{aligned}
&\mathbf{A}(calls(mary)) = (0.7 \cdot 0.7 \cdot 0.05 \cdot 0.99, I) = (0.001995, I) \\
&I = \{hears\_alarm(john), hears\_alarm(mary), burglary, \\
&\qquad \sim\!earthquake\}
\end{aligned}
$$

We can count the number of satisfying assignment with the #SAT task with semiring $(\mathbb{N}, +, \times, 0, 1)$ and labels $\alpha(f_i) = \alpha(\sim f_i) = 1$. We can also have labels encoding functions or data structures. For example, labels may encode Boolean functions represented as BDDs and algebraic facts may be Boolean variables from a set $\mathcal{V}$. In this case, we can use the semiring

$$(\text{BDD}(\mathcal{V}), \vee_{bdd}, \wedge_{bdd}, bdd(0), bdd(1))$$

and assign labels as $\alpha(f_i) = bdd(f_i)$ and $\alpha(\sim f_i) = \neg_{bdd} bdd(f_i)$ where $\text{BDD}(\mathcal{V})$ is the set of BDDs over variables $\mathcal{V}$, $\vee_{bdd}, \wedge_{bdd}, \neg_{bdd}$ are Boolean operations over BDDs, and $bdd(\cdot)$ can be applied to the values 0, 1, $f \in F$ returning the BDD representing the 0, 1, or f Boolean functions.

aProbLog can also be used for sensitivity analysis, i.e., estimating how a change in the probability of the facts changes the probability of the query. In this case, the labels are polynomials over a set of variables (indicated with $\mathbb{R}[\boldsymbol{X}]$) in Table 11.1. In Example 100, if we use variables x and y to label the facts $burglary$ and $hears\_alarm(mary)$, respectively, the label of $calls(mary)$ becomes $0.99 \cdot x \cdot y + 0.01 \cdot y$ that is also the probability of $calls(mary)$.

Another task is gradient computation where we want to compute the gradient of the probability of the query, as, for example, is done by LeProbLog, see Section 13.3. We consider here the case where we want to compute the derivative with respect to the parameter p_k of the k-th fact. The labels are pairs where the first element stores the probability and the second its derivative with respect to p_k. Using the rule for the derivative of a product, it is easy to see that the operations can be defined as

$$(a_1, a_2) \oplus (b_1, b_2) = (a_1 + b_1, a_2 + b_2) \tag{11.3}$$
$$(a_1, a_2) \otimes (b_1, b_2) = (a_1 \cdot b_1, a_1 \cdot b_2 + a_2 \cdot b_1) \tag{11.4}$$

and the labels of the algebraic facts as

$$\alpha(f_i) = \begin{cases} (p_i, 1) & \text{if } i = k \\ (p_i, 0) & \text{if } i \neq k \end{cases} \tag{11.5}$$

$$\alpha(\sim f_i) = \begin{cases} (1 - p_i, -1) & \text{if } i = k \\ (1 - p_i, 0) & \text{if } i \neq k \end{cases} \tag{11.6}$$

To perform inference, aProbLog avoids the generation of all possible worlds and computes a covering set of explanations for the query, as defined in Section 3.1, similarly to what ProbLog1 does for PROB. We represent here an explanation E as a set of literals built on $\mathcal{F}$ that are sufficient for entailing the query, i.e., $\mathcal{R} \cup E \models q$, and a covering set of explanations $\mathcal{E}(q)$ as a set such that

$$\forall I \in \mathcal{I}(q), \exists J \in \mathcal{E}(q) : J \subseteq I$$

We define the label of an explanation E as

$$\mathbf{A}(E) = \mathbf{A}(\mathcal{I}(E)) = \bigoplus_{I \in \mathcal{I}(E)} \bigotimes_{l \in I} \alpha(l)$$

We call $\mathbf{A}(E)$ a *neutral sum* if

$$\mathbf{A}(E) = \bigotimes_{l \in E} \alpha(l)$$

If $\forall f \in F : \alpha(f) \oplus \alpha(\sim f) = e^\otimes$, then $\mathbf{A}(E)$ is a neutral sum.

We call $\bigoplus_{E \in \mathcal{E}(q)} \mathbf{A}(E)$ a *disjoint sum* if

$$\bigoplus_{E \in \mathcal{E}(q)} \mathbf{A}(E) = \bigoplus_{I \in \mathcal{I}(q)} \mathbf{A}(I)$$

$\oplus$ is *idempotent* if $\forall a \in \mathcal{A} : a \oplus a = a$. If $\oplus$ is idempotent, then $\bigoplus_{E \in \mathcal{E}(q)} \mathbf{A}(E)$ is a disjoint sum.

Given a covering set of explanations $\mathcal{E}(q)$, we define the *explanation sum* as

$$\mathbf{S}(\mathcal{E}(q)) = \bigoplus_{E \in \mathcal{E}(q)} \bigotimes_{l \in E} \alpha(l)$$

If $\mathbf{A}(E)$ is a neutral sum for all $E \in \mathcal{E}(q)$ and $\bigoplus_{E \in \mathcal{E}(q)} \mathbf{A}(E)$ is a disjoint sum, then the explanation sum is equal to the label of the query, i.e.,

$$\mathbf{S}(\mathcal{E}(q)) = \mathbf{A}(q).$$

In this case, inference can be performed by computing $\mathbf{S}(\mathcal{E}(q))$. Otherwise, the *neutral sum* and/or *disjoint sum problems* must be solved.

To tackle the neutral-sum problem, let $free(E)$ denote the variables not occurring in an explanations E:

$$free(E) = \{f \mid f \in \mathcal{F}, f \notin E, \sim f \notin E\}$$

We can thus express $\mathbf{A}(E)$ as

$$\mathbf{A}(E) = \bigotimes_{l \in E} \alpha(l) \otimes \bigotimes_{l \in free(E)} (\alpha(l) \oplus \alpha(\sim l))$$

given the properties of commutative semirings.

The sum $\mathbf{A}(E_0) \oplus \mathbf{A}(E_1)$ of two explanations can be computed by exploiting the following property. Let $V_i = \{f | f \in E_i \vee \sim f \in E_i\}$ be the variables appearing in explanation E_i, then

$$\mathbf{A}(E_0) \oplus \mathbf{A}(E_1) = (\mathbf{P}_1(E_0) \oplus \mathbf{P_0}(E_1)) \otimes \bigotimes_{f \in \mathcal{F} \backslash (V_0 \cup V_1)} (\alpha(f) \oplus \alpha(\sim f))$$

(11.7)

with

$$\mathbf{P}_j(E_i) = \bigotimes_{l \in E_i} \alpha(l) \otimes \bigotimes_{f \in V_j \backslash V_i} (\alpha(f) \oplus \alpha(\sim f))$$

So we can evaluate $\mathbf{A}(E_0) \oplus \mathbf{A}(E_1)$ by taking into account the set of variables on which the two explanations depend.

To solve the disjoint-sum problem, aProbLog builds a BDD representing the truth of the query as a function of the algebraic facts. If sums are neutral, aProbLog assigns a label to each node n as

$$\mathbf{label}(1) = e^{\otimes}$$
$$\mathbf{label}(0) = e^{\oplus}$$
$$\mathbf{label}(n) = (\alpha(n) \otimes \mathbf{label}(h)) \oplus (\alpha(\sim n) \otimes \mathbf{label}(l))$$

where h and l denote the high and low child of n. In fact, a full Boolean decision tree expresses $\mathcal{E}(q)$ as an expression of the form

$$\bigvee_{l_1} l_1 \wedge \ldots \wedge \bigvee_{l_n} l_n \wedge \mathbf{1}(\{l_1, \ldots, l_n\} \in \mathcal{E}(q))$$

where l_i is a literal built on variable f_i and $\mathbf{1}(\{l_1, \ldots, l_n\} \in \mathcal{E}(q))$ is 1 if $\{l_1, \ldots, l_n\} \in \mathcal{E}(q)$ and 0 otherwise. By the properties of semirings,

$$\mathbf{A}(q) = \bigoplus_{l_1} l_1 \otimes \ldots \otimes \bigoplus_{l_n} l_n \otimes \mathbf{e}(\{l_1, \ldots, l_n\} \in \mathcal{E}(q))$$

(11.8)

where $\mathbf{e}(\{l_1, \ldots, l_n\} \in \mathcal{E}(q))$ is $e^{\otimes}$ if $\{l_1, \ldots, l_n\} \in \mathcal{E}(q)$ and $e^{\oplus}$ otherwise. So given a full Boolean decision tree, the label of the query can be computed by traversing the tree bottom-up, as for the computation of the probability of the query with Algorithm 6.

BDDs are obtained from full Boolean decision trees by repeatedly merging isomorphic subgraphs and deleting nodes whose children are the same until no more operations are possible. The merging operation does not affect

Equation (11.8), as it simply identifies identical sub-expressions. The deletion operation deletes a node n when its high and low children are the same node s. In this case, the label of node n would be

$$\mathbf{label}(n) = (\alpha(n) \otimes \mathbf{label}(s)) \oplus (\alpha(\sim n) \otimes \mathbf{label}(s))$$

that is equal to $\mathbf{label}(s)$ if sums are neutral. If not, Algorithm 16 is used that uses Equation (11.7) to take into account deleted nodes. Function LABEL is called after initializing $Table(n)$ to $null$ for all nodes n. $Table(n)$ stores intermediate results similarly to Algorithm 6 to keep the complexity linear in the number of nodes.

Algorithm 16 Function LABEL: aProbLog inference algorithm.

1:   **function** LABEL(n)
2:       **if** $Table(n) \neq null$ **then**
3:          **return** $Table(n)$
4:       **else**
5:          **if** n is the 1-terminal **then**
6:             **return** $(e^{\otimes}, \varnothing)$
7:          **end if**
8:          **if** n is the 0-terminal **then**
9:             **return** $(e^{\oplus}, \varnothing)$
10:          **end if**
11:          let h and l be the high and low children of n
12:          $(H, V_h) \leftarrow$ LABEL(h)
13:          $(L, V_l) \leftarrow$ LABEL(l)
14:          $\mathbf{P}_l(h) \leftarrow H \otimes \bigotimes_{x \in V_l \setminus V_h} (\alpha(x) \oplus \alpha(\sim x))$
15:          $\mathbf{P}_h(l) \leftarrow L \otimes \bigotimes_{x \in V_h \setminus V_l} (\alpha(x) \oplus \alpha(\sim x))$
16:          $\mathbf{label}(n) \leftarrow (\alpha(n) \otimes \mathbf{P}_l(h)) \oplus (\alpha(\sim n) \otimes \mathbf{P}_h(l))$
17:          $Table(n) \leftarrow (\mathbf{label}(n), \{n\} \cup V_h \cup V_l)$
18:          **return** $Table(n)$
19:       **end if**
20: **end function**

12

Inference for Hybrid Programs

In this chapter we present approaches for performing various inference tasks on hybrid programs. We start from the DISTR task in Extended PRISM, then we consider COND by Weighted Model Integration. We describe approximate inference: first for the EVID and COND tasks, also with bounds on error, and then for the DISTR and EXP tasks.

12.1 Inference for Extended PRISM

Islam et al. [2012b]; Islam [2012] propose an algorithm for performing the DISTR task for Extended PRISM, see Section 4.3. Since it is impossible to enumerate all explanations for the query because there is an uncountable number of them, the idea is to represent derivations symbolically.

In the following, we use *Constr* to denote a set (conjunction) of linear equality constraints. We also denote by X a vector of variables and/or values, explicitly specifying the size only when it is not clear from the context. This allows us to write linear equality constraints compactly (e.g., $Y = a \cdot X + b$).

Definition 46 (Symbolic derivation [Islam et al., 2012b]). *A goal g directly derives goal g′, denoted g $\rightarrow$ g′, if one of the following conditions holds*

PCR *if $g = q_1(X_1), g_1$, and there exists a clause in the program, $q_1(Y) \leftarrow r_1(Y_1), r_2(Y_2), \ldots, r_m(Y_m)$ such that $\theta = mgu(q_1(X_1), q_1(Y))$ then $g′ = (r_1(Y_1), r_2(Y_2), \ldots, r_m(Y_m), g_1)\theta$*

MSW *if $g = msw(rv(X), Y), g_1$ then $g′ = g_1$*

CONSTR *if $g = Constr, g_1$ and Constr is satisfiable: then $g′ = g_1$.*

*where **PCR** stands for* program clause resolution. *A symbolic derivation of g is a sequence of goals $g_0, g_1, \ldots$ such that $g = g_0$ and, for all $i \geqslant 0$, $g_i \rightarrow g_{i+1}$.*

Example 101 (Symbolic derivation).   *Consider Example 54 that we repeat here for ease of reading.*

$widget(X) \leftarrow$
   $msw(m, M), msw(st(M), Z), msw(pt, Y), X = Y + Z.$
$values(m, [a, b]).$
$values(st(\_), real).$
$values(pt, real).$
$\leftarrow set\_sw(m, [0.3, 0.7]).$
$\leftarrow set\_sw(st(a), norm(2.0, 1.0)).$
$\leftarrow set\_sw(st(b), norm(3.0, 1.0)).$
$\leftarrow set\_sw(pt, norm(0.5, 0.1)).$

The symbolic derivation for goal $widget(X)$ is

$$g_1 : widget(X)$$
$$\downarrow$$
$$g_2 : msw(m, M), msw(st(M), Z), msw(pt, Y), X = Y + Z$$
$$\downarrow$$
$$g_3 : msw(st(M), Z), msw(pt, Y), X = Y + Z$$
$$\downarrow$$
$$g_4 : msw(pt, Y), X = Y + Z$$
$$\downarrow$$
$$g_5 : X = Y + Z$$
$$\downarrow$$
$$true$$

Given a goal, the aim of inference is to return a probability density function over the variables of the goal. To do so, all successful symbolic derivations are collected. Then a representation of the probability density associated with the variables of each goal is built bottom-up starting from the leaves. This representation is called a *success function*.

First, we need to identify, for each goal g_i in a symbolic derivation, the set of its *derivation variables* $V(g_i)$, the set of variables appearing as parameters or outcomes of msws in some subsequent goal g_j, $j > i$. V is further partitioned into two disjoint sets, V_c and V_d, representing continuous and discrete variables, respectively.

Definition 47 (Derivation variables [Islam et al., 2012b]).   *Let $g \rightarrow g'$ such that g' is derived from g using*

PCR *Let θ be the mgu in this step. Then $V_c(g)$ and $V_d(g)$ are the largest set of variables in g such that $V_c(g)\theta \subseteq V_c(g')$ and $V_d(g)\theta \subseteq V_d(g')$*

MSW *Let $g = msw(rv(\mathbf{X}), Y), g_1$. Then $V_c(g)$ and $V_d(g)$ are the largest set of variables in g such that $V_c(g)\theta \subseteq V_c(g') \cup \{Y\}$ and $V_d(g)\theta \subseteq V_d(g') \cup \mathbf{X}$ if Y is continuous, otherwise $V_c(g)\theta \subseteq V_c(g')$ and $V_d(g)\theta \subseteq V_d(g') \cup \mathbf{X} \cup \{Y\}$*

CONSTR *Let $g = Constr, g_1$. Then $V_c(g)$ and $V_d(g)$ are the largest set of variables in g such that $V_c(g)\theta \subseteq V_c(g') \cup vars(Constr)$ and $V_d(g)\theta \subseteq V_d(g')$*

So $V(g)$ is built from $V(g')$ and it can be computed for all goals in a symbolic derivation bottom-up.

Let $\mathbf{C}$ denote the set of all linear equality constraints using set of variables $\mathbf{V}$ and let $\mathbf{L}$ be the set of all linear functions over $\mathbf{V}$. Let $\mathcal{N}_X(\mu, \sigma^2)$ be the PDF of a univariate Gaussian distribution with mean μ and variance σ^2, and $\delta_x(X)$ be the Dirac delta function which is zero everywhere except at x and integration of the delta function over its entire range is 1. A *Product probability density function (PPDF)* ϕ over $\mathbf{V}$ is an expression of the form

$$\phi = k \cdot \prod_l \delta_v(V_l) \prod_i \mathcal{N}_{f_i}(\mu_i, \delta_i^2)$$

where k is a non-negative real number, $V_l \in \mathbf{V}$ $f_i \in \mathbf{L}$. A pair (ϕ, C) where $C \subseteq \mathbf{C}$ is called a *constrained PPDF*. A sum of a finite number of constrained PPDFs is called a *success function*, represented as

$$\psi = \sum_i (\phi_i, C_i)$$

We use $C_i(\psi)$ to denote the constraints (i.e., C_i) in the i-th constrained PPDF of success function ψ and $D_i(\psi)$ to denote the i-th PPDF ϕ_i of ψ.

The success function of the query is built bottom-up from the set of derivations for it. The success function of a constraint C is $(1, C)$. The success function of $true$ is $(1, true)$. The success function of $msw(rv(\mathbf{X}), Y)$ is $(\psi, true)$ where ψ is the probability density function of rv's distribution if rv is continuous, and its probability mass function if rv is discrete.

Example 102 (Success functions of msw atoms). *The success function of $msw(m, M)$ for the program in Example 101 is*

$$\psi_{msw(m,M)}(M) = 0.3\delta_a(M) + 0.7\delta_b(M)$$

We can represent success functions using tables, where each table row denotes discrete random variable valuations. For example, the above success function can be represented as

M	$\psi_{msw(m,M)}(M)$
a	0.3
b	0.7

For a $g \rightarrow g'$ derivation step, the success function of g is computed from the success function of g' using the join and marginalization operations, the first for **MSW** and **CONSTR** steps and the latter for **PCR** steps.

Definition 48 (Join operation). *Let $\psi_1 = \sum_i(D_i, C_i)$ and $\psi_2 = \sum_j(D_j, C_j)$ be two success functions, then the* join *$\psi_1 * \psi_2$ of ψ_1 and ψ_2 is the success function*

$$\sum_{i,j}(D_i D_j, C_i \wedge C_j)$$

Example 103 (Join operation). *Let $\psi_{msw(m,M)}(M)$ and $\psi_g(X, Y, Z, M)$ be defined as follows:*

M	$\psi_{msw(m,M)}(M)$		M	$\psi_G(X, Y, Z, M)$
a	0.3		a	$(\mathcal{N}_Z(2.0, 1.0)\mathcal{N}_Y(0.5, 0.1), X = Y + Z)$
b	0.7		b	$(\mathcal{N}_Z(3.0, 1.0)\mathcal{N}_Y(0.5, 0.1), X = Y + Z)$

The join of $\psi_{msw(m,M)}(M)$ and $\psi_G(X, Y, Z, M)$ is:

M	$\psi_{msw(m,M)}(M) * \psi_G(X, Y, Z, M)$
a	$(0.3\mathcal{N}_Z(2.0, 1.0)\mathcal{N}_Y(0.5, 0.1), X = Y + Z)$
b	$(0.7\mathcal{N}_Z(3.0, 1.0)\mathcal{N}_Y(0.5, 0.1), X = Y + Z)$

Since $\delta_a(M)\delta_b(M) = 0$ because M cannot be both a and b at the same time, we simplified the result by eliminating any such inconsistent PPDF term in ψ.

In the case of a **PCR** derivation step $g \rightarrow g'$, g may contain a subset of the variables of g'. To compute the success function for g, we thus must marginalize over the eliminated variables. If an eliminated variable is discrete, marginalization is done by summation in the obvious way. If an eliminated variable V is continuous, marginalization is done in two steps: projection and integration. The goal of projection is to eliminate any linear constraint on V. The projection operation finds a linear constraint $V = \boldsymbol{a}\boldsymbol{X} + b$ on V and replaces all occurrences of V in the success function by $\boldsymbol{a}\boldsymbol{X} + b$.

Definition 49 (Projection of a success function). *The* projection *of a success function ψ w.r.t. a continuous variable V, denoted by $\psi{\downarrow}_V$, is a success* *function ψ' such that $\forall i$:*

$$D_i(\psi') = D_i(\psi)[V/\boldsymbol{a}\boldsymbol{X} + b]$$

and

$$C_i(\psi') = (C_i(\psi) - C_{ip})[V/\boldsymbol{a}\boldsymbol{X} + b]$$

where C_{ip} is a linear constraint $V = \boldsymbol{a}\boldsymbol{X} + b$ on V in $C_i(\psi)$ and $t[x/s]$ denotes the replacement of all occurrences of x in t by s.

If ψ does not contain any linear constraint on V, then the projected form remains the same.

Example 104 (Projection operation).   *Let ψ_1 be the success function*

$$\psi_1 = (0.3\mathcal{N}_Z(2.0, 1.0)\mathcal{N}_Y(0.5, 0.1), X = Y + Z)$$

The projection of ψ_1 w.r.t. Y is

$$\psi_1\!\downarrow_Y = 0.3\mathcal{N}_Z(2.0, 1.0)\mathcal{N}_{X-Z}(0.5, 0.1), true)$$

We can now define the integration operation.

Definition 50 (Integration of a success function).   *Let ψ be a success function that does not contain any linear constraints on V. Then the* integration of ψ *w.r.t. to V, denoted by $\oint_V \psi$, is the success function ψ' such that*

$$\forall i : D_i(\psi') = \int D_i(\psi)dV$$

Islam et al. [2012b]; Islam [2012] prove that the integration of a PPDF with respect to a variable V is a PPDF, i.e., that

$$\alpha \int_{-\infty}^{+\infty} \prod_{k=1}^{m} \mathcal{N}_{\boldsymbol{a}_k \boldsymbol{X}_k + b_k}(\mu_k, \sigma_k^2)dV = \alpha' \prod_{l=1}^{m'} \mathcal{N}_{\boldsymbol{a}_l' \boldsymbol{X}_l' + b_l'}(\mu_l', \sigma_l'^2)$$

where $V \in \boldsymbol{X}_k$ and $V \notin \boldsymbol{X}_l'$.

For example, the integration of $\mathcal{N}_{a_1 V - X_1}(\mu_1, \sigma_1^2)\mathcal{N}_{a_2 V - X_2}(\mu_2, \sigma_2^2)$ w.r.t. variable V is

$$\begin{array}{r} \int_{-\infty}^{+\infty} \mathcal{N}_{a_1 V - X_1}(\mu_1, \sigma_1^2)\mathcal{N}_{a_2 V - X_2}(\mu_2, \sigma_2^2)dV = \\ \mathcal{N}_{a_2 X_1 - a_1 X_2}(a_1\mu_1 - a_2\mu_1, a_2^2\sigma_1^2 + a_1^2\sigma_2^2) \end{array} \quad (12.1)$$

where X_1 and X_2 are linear combinations of variables except V.

Example 105 (Integration of a success function). *Let ψ_2 represent the following success function*

$$\psi_2 = (0.3\mathcal{N}_Z(2.0, 1.0)\mathcal{N}_{X-Z}(0.5, 0.1), true)$$

Then integration of ψ_2 w.r.t. Z yields

$$\oint_Z \psi_2 = \left(\int 0.3\mathcal{N}_Z(2.0, 1.0)\mathcal{N}_{X-Z}(0.5, 0.1)dZ, true \right) =$$

$$(0.3\mathcal{N}_X(2.5, 1.1), true)$$

by Equation (12.1).

The marginalization operation is the composition of the join and integration operations.

Definition 51 (Marginalization of a success function). *The* marginalization *of a success function ψ with respect to a variable V, denoted by $\mathbb{M}(\psi, V)$, is a success function ψ' such that*

$$\psi' = \oint_V \psi \downarrow_V$$

The marginalization over a set of variables is defined as $\mathbb{M}(\psi, \{V\} \cup \mathbf{X}) = \mathbb{M}(\mathbb{M}(\psi, V), \mathbf{X})$ and $\mathbb{M}(\psi, \varnothing) = \psi$.

The set of all success functions is closed under join and marginalization operations. The success function for a derivation can now be defined as follows.

Definition 52 (Success function of a goal). *The success function of a goal g, denoted by ψ_g, is computed based on the derivation $g \to g'$:*

$$\psi_g = \begin{cases} \sum_{g'} \mathbb{M}(\psi_{g'}, V(g') - V(g)) & \text{for all } \textbf{PCR } g \to g' \\ \psi_{msw(rv(\mathbf{X}),Y)} * \psi_{g'} & \text{if } g = msw(rv(\mathbf{X}), Y), g_1 \\ \psi_{Constr} * \psi_{g'} & \text{if } g = Constr, g_1 \end{cases}$$

Example 106 (Success function of a goal). *Consider the symbolic derivation of Example 101. The success function of goal g_5 is $\psi_{g_5}(X, Y, Z) = (1, X = Y + Z)$. To obtain ψ_{g_4}, we must perform a join operation:*

$$\psi_{g_4}(X, Y, Z) = \psi_{msw(pt,Y)}(Y) * \psi_{g_5}(X, Y, Z) = (\mathcal{N}_Y(0.5, 0.1), X = Y + Z)$$

The success function of goal g_3 is $\psi_{msw(st(M),Z)}(Z) * \psi_{g_4}(X, Y, Z)$:

M	$\psi_{g_3}(X, Y, Z, M)$
a	$(\mathcal{N}_Z(2.0, 1.0)\mathcal{N}_Y(0.5, 0.1), X = Y + Z)$
b	$(\mathcal{N}_Z(3.0, 1.0)\mathcal{N}_Y(0.5, 0.1), X = Y + Z)$

Then we join $\psi_{msw(m,M)}(M)$ *and* $\psi_{g_3}(X, Y, Z, M)$:

M	$\psi_{g_2}(X, Y, Z, M)$
a	$(0.3\mathcal{N}_Z(2.0, 1.0)\mathcal{N}_Y(0.5, 0.1), X = Y + Z)$
b	$(0.7\mathcal{N}_Z(3.0, 1.0)\mathcal{N}_Y(0.5, 0.1), X = Y + Z)$

The success function of g_1 *is* $\psi_{g_1}(X) = \mathbb{M}(\psi_{g_2}(X, Y, Z, M), \{M, Y, Z\})$. *We marginalize* $\psi_{g_2}(X, Y, Z, M)$ *first w.r.t.* M:

$$\psi'_{g_2} = \mathbb{M}(\psi_{g_2}, M) = \oint_M \psi_{g_2} \downarrow_M =$$
$$= (0.3\mathcal{N}_Z(2.0, 1.0)\mathcal{N}_Y(0.5, 0.1), X = Y + Z) +$$
$$(0.7\mathcal{N}_Z(3.0, 1.0)\mathcal{N}_Y(0.5, 0.1), X = Y + Z)$$

Then we marginalize $\psi'_{g_2}(X, Y, Z)$ *w.r.t.* Y:

$$\psi''_{g_2} = \mathbb{M}(\psi'_{g_2}, Y) = \oint_Y \psi'_{g_2} \downarrow_Y =$$
$$= 0.3\mathcal{N}_Z(2.0, 1.0)\mathcal{N}_{X-Z}(0.5, 0.1) +$$
$$0.7\mathcal{N}_Z(3.0, 1.0)\mathcal{N}_{X-Z}(0.5, 0.1)$$

Finally, we get $\psi_{g_1}(X)$ *by marginalizing* $\psi''_{g_2}(X, Z)$ *w.r.t.* Z:

$$\psi_{g_1}(X) = \mathbb{M}(\psi''_{g_2}, Z) = \oint_Z \psi''_{g_2} \downarrow_Z =$$
$$= 0.3\mathcal{N}_X(2.5, 1.1) + 0.7\mathcal{N}_X(3.5, 1.1)$$

So the algorithm returns the probability density of the continuous random variables in the query.

This algorithm is correct if the program satisfies PRISM's assumptions: independent-and and exclusive-or. The first is equivalent to requiring that an instance of a random variable occurs at most once in any derivation. In fact, the join operation used in a $g \to g'$ **MSW** step is correct only if the random variable defined by the msw atom does not appear in g'. Moreover, the sum over all **PCR** steps in Definition 52 is correct only if the terms are mutually exclusive.

A subgoal may appear more than once in the derivation tree for a goal, so tabling can be effectively used to avoid redundant computation.

12.2 Inference with Weighted Model Integration

Weighted model integration (WMI) [Belle et al., 2015b,a, 2016; Morettin et al., 2017] is a recent approach that generalizes WMC to formulas with continuous variables.

12.2.1 Weighted model integration

Satisfiability (SAT) is the problem of deciding whether there is a satisfying assignment to a propositional formula or not. Satisfiability modulo theory (SMT) generalizes SAT by allowing expressions from a background theory.

Definition 53 (Satisfiability Modulo Theory). *Let $\mathbb{R}$ denote the set of real numbers and $\mathbb{B} = \{0, 1\}$ the set of Boolean values, let $\mathbf{B}$ be a set of m Boolean variables and $\mathbf{X}$ a set of n real variables. SMT($\mathcal{RA}$) (real arithmetics) theories are combinations by means of the standard Boolean operators $\{\neg, \wedge, \vee, \rightarrow, \leftrightarrow\}$ of atomic propositions from $\mathbf{B}$ and of atomic formulas in the form $g(\mathbf{X}) \bowtie c$ where $c \in \mathbb{R}$, $\bowtie \in \{=, \neq, \leqslant, \geqslant, <>\}$ and $g : \mathbb{R}^n \rightarrow \mathbb{R}$.*

SMT($\mathcal{NRA}$) (non-linear real arithmetics) is SMT($\mathcal{RA}$) where atomic formulas are restricted to use functions $g : \mathbb{R}^n \rightarrow \mathbb{R}$ of the form $\sum_i c_i \cdot X_i^{p_i}$ with $X_i \in \mathbf{X}$ and $c_i, p_i \in \mathbb{Q}$.

SMT($\mathcal{LRA}$) (linear real arithmetics) is SMT($\mathcal{NRA}$) where atomic formulas are restricted to use functions $g : \mathbb{R}^n \rightarrow \mathbb{R}$ of the form $\sum_i c_i \cdot X_i$ with $X_i \in \mathbf{X}$ and $c_i \in \mathbb{Q}$.

The SMT($\mathcal{RA}$) (SMT($\mathcal{NRA}$), SMT($\mathcal{LRA}$)) problem consists in deciding whether there is an assignment of the Boolean and real variables that satisfy an SMT($\mathcal{RA}$) (SMT($\mathcal{NRA}$), SMT($\mathcal{LRA}$)) theory.

Example 107 (Broken - SMT($\mathcal{LRA}$) [Zuidberg Dos Martires et al., 2019, 2018]). *Consider the following SMT($\mathcal{LRA}$) theory broken:*

$$(\text{no\_cool} \wedge (t > 20)) \vee (t > 30) \tag{12.2}$$

where no_cool *is a Boolean variable and* t *a real variable. SMT($\mathcal{LRA}$) means deciding whether there is an assignment to* no_cool *and* t *that satisfy the formula.*

Definition 54 (Interpretation and Model).   *Given an SMT formula ϕ built on Boolean variables $\mathbf{B}$ and real variables $\mathbf{X}$, an* interpretation *is an assignment $(\mathbf{b}, \mathbf{x})$ to $(\mathbf{B}, \mathbf{X})$. A interpretation $(\mathbf{b}, \mathbf{x})$ is a* model *of ϕ if ϕ evaluates to 1 when $(\mathbf{B}, \mathbf{X})$ are assigned to $(\mathbf{b}, \mathbf{x})$. The set of all the models of a formula ϕ is denoted by $M(\phi) = \{(\mathbf{b}, \mathbf{x}) \mid \phi(\mathbf{b}, \mathbf{x}) = 1\}$. The projection $M_{\mathbf{B}}(\phi)$ of $M(\phi)$ over $\mathbf{B}$ is*

$$M_{\mathbf{B}}(\phi) = \{\mathbf{b} \mid \exists \mathbf{x} : (\mathbf{b}, \mathbf{x}) \in M(\phi)\}$$

and contains partial models. *Given a set of Boolean values $\mathbf{b}$, we define the formula $\phi^{\mathbf{b}}$ as the formula ϕ where the Boolean variables $\mathbf{B}$ are replaced by $\mathbf{b}$. Then $M(\phi^{\mathbf{b}})$ is the set*

$$M(\phi^{\mathbf{b}}) = \{\mathbf{x} \mid (\mathbf{b}, \mathbf{x}) \in M(\phi)\}$$

of elements $\mathbf{x}$ that can extend a partial model from $M_{\mathbf{B}}(\phi)$ to a model.

We are now ready to define WMI.

Definition 55 (Weighted Model Integration).   *Given a set $\mathbf{B}$ of m Boolean variables, a set $\mathbf{X}$ of n real variables, a weight function $w(\mathbf{X}, \mathbf{B}) : \mathbb{B}^m \times \mathbb{R}^n \rightarrow \mathbb{R}^{+}$[1], and an SMT formula $\phi(\mathbf{X}, \mathbf{B})$, the* **weighted model integral (WMI)** *is*

$$WMI(\phi, w \mid \mathbf{X}, \mathbf{B}) = \sum_{\mathbf{b} \in M_{\mathbf{B}}(\phi)} \int_{\mathbf{x} \in M(\phi^{\mathbf{b}})} w(\mathbf{x}, \mathbf{b}) d\mathbf{x} \qquad (12.3)$$

The weight function is used to map a set of variable assignments to their weight. The weight function usually *factorizes* as the product of the weights over the different variables, i.e.,

$$w(\mathbf{x}, \mathbf{b}) = w_x(\mathbf{x}) w_b(\mathbf{b}) = w_x(\mathbf{x}) \prod_{b_i \in \mathbf{b}} w_{b_i}(b_i) \qquad (12.4)$$

where $w_x : \mathbb{R}^n \rightarrow \mathbb{R}^{+}$, $w_b : \mathbb{B}^m \rightarrow \mathbb{R}^{+}$ and $w_{b_i} : \mathbb{B} \rightarrow \mathbb{R}^{+}$. This does not limit the generality as a weight function that does not factorize in this way can be rewritten as a sum of weight functions over mutually exclusive partial assignments to the Boolean variables, with each individual term factorizing as Equation (12.4).

Example 108 (Broken - WMI [Zuidberg Dos Martires et al., 2019, 2018]). *Consider again the theory broken of Example 107. Assume that $w_x(\mathsf{t}) =$*

---

[1] $\mathbb{R}^{+} = \{x \in \mathbb{R} \mid x \geqslant 0\}$.

$\mathcal{N}_t(20, 5)$ *and* $w_b(\text{no\_cool} = 1) = 0.01$. *Then we have*

$$
\begin{aligned}
WMI(broken, w \mid \text{t}, \text{no\_cool}) &= 0.01 \int_{20 < \text{t} \leqslant 30} \mathcal{N}_t(20, 5) dt + \\
&\quad \int_{\text{t} > 30} \mathcal{N}_t(20, 5) dt.
\end{aligned}
$$

WMI can be used to perform inference over hybrid probabilistic logic programs. Consider PCLPs. We can collect a set of explanation with an algorithm such as PRISM, ProbLog or PITA and then build an SMT formula whose WMI is the probability of the query.

Example 109 (Broken machine - PCLP [Zuidberg Dos Martires et al., 2018]). *The following PCLP models a machine that breaks down if the temperature is above 30 degrees or if it is above 20 degrees in case there is no cooling*
> 0.01 :: no_cool.
> t ∼ *gaussian*(20, 5).
> *broken* ← no_cool, ⟨T > 20⟩.
> *broken* ← ⟨T > 30⟩.

The query broken has the set of explanations: $\omega = \omega_1 \cup \omega_2$ *with*
> $\omega_1 = \{(\text{t}, \text{no\_cool}) | t > 20, \text{no\_cool} = 1\}$
> $\omega_2 = \{(\text{t}, \text{no\_cool}) | t > 30\}$

These two explanations can be easily found from the above program using inference techniques for discrete programs. They can be immediately translated into the SMT formula of Example 107. Computing the WMI of that formula produces the probability of the query broken.

There are various techniques for performing WMI: [Belle et al., 2015b,a, 2016; Morettin et al., 2017], see [Morettin et al., 2021] for a survey. Here we present the approach of [Zuidberg Dos Martires et al., 2018, 2019] that is based on Algebraic model counting (AMC).

12.2.2 Algebraic model counting

AMC [Kimmig et al., 2017] generalizes WMC to commutative semirings, see Section 11.3.

Definition 56 (Algebraic Model Counting (AMC) [Kimmig et al., 2017]). *Given:*

- *a propositional logic formula* ϕ *over a set of Boolean variables* **B**
- *a commutative semiring* $(\mathcal{A}, \oplus, \otimes, e^{\oplus}, e^{\otimes})$

- a labeling function $\alpha : \mathcal{L} \to \mathcal{A}$, mapping literals built from the variables in $\mathbf{B}$ to values of the semiring $\mathcal{A}$

The algebraic model count of ϕ is:

$$AMC(\phi, \alpha \mid \mathbf{B}) = \bigoplus_{\mathbf{b} \in M(\phi)} \bigotimes_{b_i \in \mathbf{b}} \alpha(b_i)$$

where $M(\phi)$ are the models of ϕ

AMC can be performed using knowledge compilation. Once the formula is translated to a d-DNNF, Algorithm 17 can be applied

---

Algorithm 17 Function EVAL: Evaluating an NNF circuit.

1: **function** EVAL($n, \oplus, \otimes, e^{\oplus}, e^{\otimes}$)
2:      **if** n is a true node **then**
3:          **return** $e^{\otimes}$
4:      **end if**
5:      **if** n is a false node **then**
6:          **return** $e^{\oplus}$
7:      **end if**
8:      **if** n is a literal node l **then**
9:          **return** $\alpha(l)$
10:     **end if**
11:     **if** n is a disjunction $\bigvee_{i=1}^{m} n_i$ **then**
12:         **return** $\bigoplus_{i=1}^{n} \text{EVAL}(n_i, \oplus, \otimes, e^{\oplus}, e^{\otimes})$
13:     **end if**
14:     **if** n is a conjunction $\bigwedge_{i=1}^{m} n_i$ **then**
15:         **return** $\bigotimes_{i=1}^{n} \text{EVAL}(n_i, \oplus, \otimes, e^{\oplus}, e^{\otimes})$
16:     **end if**
17: **end function**

We first define a useful property of semiring addition and then present a theorem on the correctness of Algorithm 17.

Definition 57 (Neutral-sum property). *A semiring addition and labeling function pair $(\oplus, \alpha)$ is neutral if and only if $\forall b \in \mathbf{B} : \alpha(b) \oplus \alpha(\neg b) = e^{\otimes}$*

Theorem 18 (Correctness of Algorithm 17 [Kimmig et al., 2017]). *Evaluating a d-DNNF representation of the propositional theory using Algorithm 17 for a semiring and labeling function with neutral tuple $(\oplus, \alpha)$, is a correct computation of the algebraic model count.*

12.2.2.1 The probability density semiring and WMI

In order to cast WMI as AMC, we define a *probability density semiring* [Zuidberg Dos Martires et al., 2018, 2019].

Let $c(\mathbf{X})$ be an atomic formula from Definition 53, then $abs_{c(\mathbf{X})}$ is a Boolean variable called the *atomic formula abstraction*, or simply *abstraction*, of $c(\mathbf{X})$.

Definition 58 (Labeling function α). *If the literal l represents either a Boolean variable b or its negation $\neg b$ then its label is*

$$\alpha(b) = (w_b(b), \varnothing) \tag{12.5}$$
$$\alpha(\neg b) = (1 - w_b(b), \varnothing) \tag{12.6}$$

where we assume that the weights of the individual Boolean variables are probabilities (they sum up to one). If this is not true, they must be normalized. Otherwise if the literal l corresponds to an atomic formula abstraction $abs_{c(\mathbf{X})}$ or its negation, then the label of l is given by:

$$\alpha(abs_{c(\mathbf{X})}) = ([c(\mathbf{X})], \mathbf{X}) \tag{12.7}$$
$$\alpha(\neg abs_{c(\mathbf{X})}) = ([\neg c(\mathbf{X})], \mathbf{X}) \tag{12.8}$$

where $\mathbf{X}$ is the set of variables appearing in $c(\mathbf{X})$ and square brackets denote the so-called Iverson brackets [Knuth, 1992]: $[a]$ evaluate to 1 if formula a evaluates to true and to 0 otherwise.

We can now define the set of elements of the semiring:

Definition 59 (Probability density semiring $\mathcal{S}$). *The semring $\mathcal{S}$ is defined by*

$$\mathcal{A} = \{(a, \mathcal{V}(a))\} \tag{12.9}$$

where a denotes any algebraic expression over $\mathcal{RA}$ plus Iverson brackets and $\mathcal{V}(a)$ denotes the set of real variables occurring in a. The neutral elements $\oplus$ and $\otimes$ are:

$$e^{\oplus} := (0, \varnothing) \qquad\qquad e^{\otimes} := (1, \varnothing) \tag{12.10}$$

Addition and multiplication are defined as:

$$(a_1, \mathcal{V}(a_1)) \oplus (a_2, \mathcal{V}(a_2)) = (a_1 + a_2, \mathcal{V}(a_1 + a_2)) \tag{12.11}$$
$$(a_1, \mathcal{V}(a_1)) \otimes (a_2, \mathcal{V}(a_2)) = (a_1 \times a_2, \mathcal{V}(a_1 \times a_2)) \tag{12.12}$$

For instance, for $a = 0.01[20 < t \leqslant 30] + [t > 30]$, $\mathcal{V}(a) = \{t\}$ we have that $(a, \mathcal{V}(a)) \in \mathcal{S}$.

Lemma 16 (The probability density semiring is commutative [Zuidberg Dos Martires et al., 2018, 2019]). *The structure* $\mathcal{S} = (\mathcal{A}, \oplus, \otimes, e^{\oplus}, e^{\otimes})$ *is a commutative semiring.*

Lemma 17 (The probability density semiring has neutral addition and labeling function). *The pair* $(\oplus, \alpha)$ *is neutral.*

The following theorem shows how to exploit AMC to perform WMI: since there is no integration in AMC, we need to perform it last, yielding $WMI = \int AMC$. Moreover, AMC has to be performed on the abstracted formula, as it is defined on propositional formulas.

Theorem 19 (AMC to perform WMI [Zuidberg Dos Martires et al., 2018, 2019]). *Let ϕ be an SMT($\mathcal{RA}$) theory, w a factorized weight function over the Boolean variables $\mathbf{B}$ and continuous variables $\mathbf{X}$. Let ϕ_a be the propositional logic formulas over the set of Boolean variables $\mathbf{B}$ and $\mathbf{B_X}$, where $\mathbf{B_X}$ is the set of abstraction of atomic formulas. Furthermore, assume that $AMC(\phi_a, \alpha | \mathbf{B_X} \cup \mathbf{B})$ evaluates to $(\Psi, \mathcal{V}(\Psi))$ in the semiring $\mathcal{S}$. Then*

$$WMI(\phi, w | \mathbf{X}, \mathbf{B}) = \int_{\mathbf{x} \in \mathbf{X}} \Psi w_x(\mathbf{x}) dx$$

where $\mathbf{X}$ is the set of all possible assignments to the variables in $\mathcal{V}(\Psi)$.

12.2.2.2 Symbo

Symbo is an algorithm that produces the weighted model integral of an SMT($\mathcal{NRA}$) formula ϕ via knowledge compilation. Using theorems 18 and 19 we obtain Algorithm 18.

Symbo actually uses SDDs instead of d-DNNFs. Since SDDs are d-DNNFs, Theorem 18 continues to hold. For symbolic integration Symbo uses the PSI-Solver [Gehr et al., 2016].

Example 110 (WMI of the *broken* theory [Zuidberg Dos Martires et al., 2018, 2019].). *Consider the SMT formula of Example 107. The first two steps of Symbo produce the compiled logic formula that is shown in Figure 12.1. The following two step yield the arithmetic circuit in Figure 12.2.*

Algorithm 18 Function SYMBO: symbolic evaluation of WMI [Zuidberg Dos Martires et al., 2018, 2019].

1: **function** SYMBO(ϕ)
2:      Abstract of all the atomica formulas in ϕ in order to obtain ϕ_a
3:      Compile ϕ_a into a d-DNNF representation $\phi_{compiled}$
4:      Transform the logic formula $\phi_{compiled}$ into an arithmetic circuit AC_ϕ
5:      Label the literals in AC_ϕ according to the labeling function given in Definition 58
6:      Symbolically evaluate AC_ϕ obtaining $(\Psi, \mathcal{V}(\Psi))$
7:      Symbolically multiply Ψ, which is a sum-product of weighted indicator functions (Iverson brackets) by the weights of the continuous variables in $\mathcal{V}(\Psi)$
8:      Symbolically integrate the formula by calling a symbolic inference engine
9: **end function**

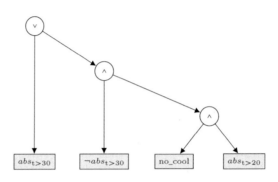

Figure 12.1   d-DNNF circuit for Example 107.

Then the arithmetic circuit is evaluated (line 6), the resulting expression is multiplied by the weight for t *(line 7) and the integral is solved symbolically*

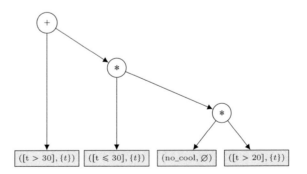

Figure 12.2   Arithmetic circuit for Example 107.

using PSI-Solver (line 8):

$$WMI(broken, w \mid t, no\_cool) = \qquad\qquad (12.13)$$

$$= \int (0.01[t{>}20][t{\leqslant}30] + [t{>}30]) \, \mathcal{N}_t(20, 5) dt$$

$$= 0.01 \int_{20<t\leqslant30} \mathcal{N}_t(20, 5) dt + \int_{t>30} \mathcal{N}_t(20, 5) dt$$

$$= 1 - 0.01 \int_{-\infty}^{-\frac{5}{2}\sqrt{8}+\frac{20}{\sqrt{8}}} e^{-x^2} dx - 0.99 \int_{-\infty}^{-\frac{5\sqrt{8}}{2}+\frac{30}{\sqrt{8}}} e^{-x^2} dx$$

The formula obtained includes integrals $\int_{-\infty}^{x} e^{-t^2} dt$ that are not solvable symbolically and must be integrated numerically.

WMI(broken, w $\mid$ t, no_cool) is also equal to P(broken) in the PCLP of Example 109.

12.2.2.3 Sampo

The system Sampo [Zuidberg Dos Martires et al., 2019] replaces symbolic integration with Monte Carlo sampling. This is useful when the symbolic manipulation of the formula is too expensive or when it is not possible because the resulting integral needs numeric integration, as in Example 110. In these cases Monte Carlo methods serve to approximate integrals with summations, as the next theorem shows.

Theorem 20 (Monte Carlo approximation of WMI [Zuidberg Dos Martires et al., 2019]). *Let ϕ be an $SMT(\mathcal{RA})$ theory, w a factorizable weight function over the Boolean variables $\mathbf{B}$ and continuous variables $\mathbf{X}$. Furthermore, let $AMC(\phi, \alpha | \mathbf{X_B} \cup \mathbf{B})$, where $\mathbf{B_X}$ is the set of abstraction of atomic formulas, evaluate to $(\Psi, \mathcal{V}(\Psi))$. Then the Monte Carlo approximation of $WMI(\phi, w | \mathbf{X}, \mathbf{B})$ is given by:*

$$WMI_{MC}(\phi, w | \mathbf{X}, \mathbf{B}) = \frac{1}{N} \sum_{i=1}^{N} \Psi(\mathbf{x}_i)$$

where the $\mathbf{x}_i$'s are N independent and identically distributed values for the continuous random variables drawn from the density w.

The formula obtain by knowledge compilation must thus be evaluated N times, each time with different values for the real variables. This shows an advantage of knowledge compilation: the formula is complied once with an expensive process and then it is evaluated often with a cheap computation.

Moreover, the arithmetic circuit resulting from knowledge compilation can be transformed into a computation graph to be handled by TensorFlow [Abadi et al., 2015], a numerical computation library specialized for manipulating computation graphs over tensors. In this case the labels of literals in the compiled formula must be expressed as tensors.

Sampo implements Algorithm 19. Sampo uses TensorFlow for numerical computation and the Edward library [Tran et al., 2016] for sampling variables.

Algorithm 19 Function SAMPO: Monte Carlo computation of WMI [Zuidberg Dos Martires et al., 2019]

1: **function** SAMPO(ϕ)
2:      Abstract all the atomica formulas in ϕ in order to obtain ϕ_a
3:      Compile ϕ_a into a d-DNNF representation $\phi_{compiled}$
4:      Transform the logic formula $\phi_{compiled}$ into an arithmetic circuit AC_ϕ
5:      Label the literals in AC_ϕ according to the labeling function given in Definition 58 with corresponding tensors
6:      Symbolically evaluate AC_ϕ obtaining $(\Psi, \mathcal{V}(\Psi))$ represented as a computation graph CG
7:      Run the CG N times, where N is the number of samples
8:      Take the mean of the values of the N samples
9: **end function**

Example 111 (Sampo [Zuidberg Dos Martires et al., 2019]). *Consider the formula in Example 107. We sample N values for the random variable* t. *Suppose $N = 5$ and the values are:*

$$\{12.8, 35.1, 17.6, 22.2, 21.4\}$$

The Boolean variable no_cool *is mapped to a 1D tensor whose entries are all 0.01. The arithmetic circuit of Figure 12.2 results in the following computation:*

$$\Psi_{MC} =$$

$$= \begin{bmatrix} 0.01 \\ 0.01 \\ 0.01 \\ 0.01 \\ 0.01 \end{bmatrix} \circ \begin{bmatrix} [12.8 > 20] \\ [35.1 > 20] \\ [17.6 > 20] \\ [22.2 > 20] \\ [21.4 > 20] \end{bmatrix} \circ \begin{bmatrix} [12.8 \leqslant 30] \\ [35.1 \leqslant 30] \\ [17.6 \leqslant 30] \\ [22.2 \leqslant 30] \\ [21.4 \leqslant 30] \end{bmatrix} + \begin{bmatrix} [12.8 > 30] \\ [35.1 > 30] \\ [17.6 > 30] \\ [22.2 > 30] \\ [21.4 > 30] \end{bmatrix}$$

$$= \begin{bmatrix} 0.01 \\ 0.01 \\ 0.01 \\ 0.01 \\ 0.01 \end{bmatrix} \circ \begin{bmatrix} 0 \\ 1 \\ 0 \\ 1 \\ 1 \end{bmatrix} \circ \begin{bmatrix} 1 \\ 0 \\ 1 \\ 1 \\ 1 \end{bmatrix} + \begin{bmatrix} 0 \\ 1 \\ 0 \\ 0 \\ 0 \end{bmatrix} = \begin{bmatrix} 0 \\ 1 \\ 0 \\ 0.01 \\ 0.01 \end{bmatrix}$$

where $\circ$ is elementwise multiplication of tensors. Thus the estimate of the WMI is

$$WMI_{MC} = \frac{1}{5} \sum_{i=1}^{5} \Psi_{MC,i} = 1.02/5 = 0.204$$

The example shows that sampling is embarrassingly parallelizable, thus allowing Sampo to exploit modern GPUs.

12.3 Approximate Inference by Sampling for Hybrid Programs

Monte Carlo inference for programs with only discrete variables has the attractive feature that it can be used almost directly for approximate inference for hybrid programs. For example, to handle a hybrid clause of the form
$\quad C_i = g(X,Y) : gaussian(Y,0,1) \leftarrow object(X).$
MCINTYRE transforms it into [Riguzzi et al., 2016a; Alberti et al., 2017]:
$\quad g(X,Y) \leftarrow object(X), sample\_gauss(i, [X], 0, 1, Y).$
Samples for continuous random variables are stored using asserts as for discrete variables. In fact, predicate $sample\_gauss/4$ is defined by

```
sample_gauss(R,VC,_Mean,_Variance,S):-
  sampled(R,VC,S),!.

sample_gauss(R,VC,Mean,Variance,S):-
  gauss(Mean,Variance,S),
  assertz(sampled(R,VC,S)).
```

where $gauss(Mean, Variance, S)$ returns in S a value sampled from a Gaussian distribution with parameters $Mean$ and $Variance$.

Monte Carlo inference for hybrid programs derives his correctness from the stochastic T_P operator: a clause that is ground except for the continuous random variable defined in the head defines a sampling process that extracts a sample of the continuous variables according to the distribution and parameters specified in the head. Since programs are range restricted, when the sampling predicate is called, all variables in the clause are ground except for the one defined by the head, so the T_P operator can be applied to the clause to sample a value for the defined variable.

Monte Carlo inference is the most common inference approach also for imperative or functional probabilistic programming languages, where a sample of the output of a program is taken by executing the program and generating samples when a probabilistic primitive is called. In probabilistic programming usually memoing is not used, so new samples are taken each time a probabilistic primitive is encountered.

Conditional inference can be performed in a similar way by using rejection sampling or Metropolis-hastings MCMC, unless the evidence is on ground atoms that have continuous values as arguments. In this case, rejection sampling or Metropolis-hastings cannot be used, as the probability of the evidence is 0. However, the conditional probability of the query given the evidence may still be defined, see Section 1.5. In this case, *likelihood weighting* [Nitti et al., 2016] can be used.

For each sample to be taken, likelihood weighting samples the query and then assigns a weight to the sample on the basis of evidence. The weight is computed by deriving the evidence backward in the same sample of the query starting with a weight of one: each time a choice should be taken or a continuous variable sampled, if the choice/variable has already been sampled, the current weight is multiplied by the probability of the choice/by the density value of the continuous variable.

Then the probability of the query is computed as the sum of the weights of the samples where the query is true divided by the total sum of the weights of the samples. This technique is useful also for non-hybrid programs as samples are never rejected, so sampling can be faster.

Likelihood weighting in `cplint` [Alberti et al., 2017; Nguembang Fadja and Riguzzi, 2017] uses a meta-interpreter that randomizes the choice of clauses when more than one resolves with the goal, in order to obtain an unbiased sample of the query. This meta-interpreter is similar to the one used to generate the first sample in Metropolis-hastings.

Then a different meta-interpreter is used to evaluate the weight of the sample. This meta-interpreter starts with the evidence as the query and a weight of 1. Each time the meta-interpreter encounters a probabilistic choice, it first checks whether a value has already been sampled. If so, it computes the probability/density of the sampled value and multiplies the weight by it. If the value has not been sampled, it takes a sample and records it, leaving the weight unchanged. In this way, each sample of the query is associated with a weight that reflects the influence of evidence.

In some cases, likelihood weighting encounters numerical problems, as the weights of samples may go rapidly to very small numbers that can be rounded to 0 by floating point arithmetic. This happens, for example, for dynamic models, where predicates depend on time and we have evidence for many time points. In these cases, *particle filtering* can be used [Nitti et al., 2016], which periodically resamples the individual samples/particles so that their weight is reset to 1.

In particle filtering, the evidence is a list of literals. A number n of samples of the query are taken that are weighted by the likelihood of the first element of the evidence list. Each sample constitutes a particle and the sampled random variables are stored away.

After weighting, n particles are resampled with replacement with a probability proportional to their weight. Specifically, the weights of the previous n particles are normalized. Let w_i be the normalized weight of particle s_i. Each of the new n particles is sampled from the set of previous particles with particle s_i selected with probability w_i. After each sample, the sampled particle is replaced back into the set so that the same particle can be sampled repeatedly.

After resampling, the next element of the evidence is considered. A new weight for each particle is computed on the basis of the new evidence element and the process is repeated until the last evidence element is reached.

12.4 Approximate Inference with Bounded Error for Hybrid Programs

Michels et al. [2016] present the Iterative hybrid probabilistic model counting (IHPMC) algorithm for computing bounds on queries to hybrid programs. They consider both the EVID and COND tasks for the PCLP language (see Section 4.5). IHPMC builds trees that split the variables domains and builds them to an increasing depth in order to achieve the desired accuracy.

A HPT is a binary tree where each node n is associated with a propositional formula φ_n and a range denoted by $range(n, X)$ for each random variable X. For the root node r, the range of each variable is its whole range: $range(r, X) = Range_X$. Each non-leaf node n splits the range of a random variable into two parts and the propositional formula of each child is obtained from that for the node by conditioning on the split made. Since the variables may be continuous, the range of a random variable can be split several times along the same tree branch. If the children of n are $\{c_1, c_2\}$, each edge $n \rightarrow c_i, i \in \{1, 2\}$, is associated with a range τ_{ni} for a random variable Y such that $\tau_{n1} \cup \tau_{n2} = range(n, Y)$ and $\tau_{n1} \cap \tau_{n2} = \emptyset$. Moreover, $range(c_i, Y) = \tau_{ni}$ and $range(c_i, Z) = range(n, Z)$ if $Y \neq Z$.

Then the formula φ_{c_i} associated to c_i is obtained from φ_n by imposing a restriction on the range on Y and the formula is simplified if some primitive constraints can be replaced by $\top$ or $\bot$. Each edge $n \rightarrow c_i$ is associated with a probability p_{ni} such that $p_{ni} = P(Y \in \tau_{ni} | Y \in range(n, Y))$. Leaf nodes l are those where $\varphi_l = \top$ or $\varphi_l = \bot$.

Given an HPT, the probability of the event represented by the formula associated with the root can be computed using Algorithm 6 for computing the probability of a BDD.

Example 112 (Machine diagnosis problem [Michels et al., 2016]). *Consider a diagnosis problem very similar to the one of Example 109 where a machine fails if the temperature is above a threshold. If cooling fails ($noc = true$), then the threshold is lower. This problem can be modeled with the PCLP program:*

$$fail \leftarrow \langle t > 30.0 \rangle$$
$$fail \leftarrow \langle t > 20.0 \rangle, \langle noc = true \rangle$$
$$t \sim gaussian(20.0, 50.0)$$
$$noc \sim \{0.01 : true, 0.99 : false\}$$

The event that the machine fails is then represented by the formula

$$(noc = true \wedge t > 20.0) \vee t > 30.0$$

The HPT for this formula is shown in Figure 12.3.

The probability of fails is then

$$P(fails) = 0.9772 \cdot 0.01 \cdot 0.4884 + 0.0228 \approx 0.0276$$

In Example 112, we were able to compute the probability of the query exactly. In general, this may not be possible because the query event may not be representable using hyperrectangles over the random variables. In this case,

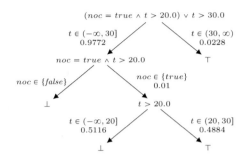

Figure 12.3 HPT for Example 112. From [Michels et al., 2016].. ©
[2016] Association for the Advancement of Artificial Intelligence. All rights
reserved. Reprinted with permission.

the propositional formulas may never simplify to ⊥ or ⊤. However, we can
consider PHPTs, HPTs where not all leaves are ⊥ or ⊤. From a PHPT, we
can obtain a lower and an upper bound on the probability of the query: the ⊤
leaves in the tree contribute to the lower bound $\underline{P}(q)$ and all the leaves of the
tree except the ⊥ ones contribute to the upper bound $\overline{P}(q)$.

Example 113 (Machine diagnosis problem – approximate inference – [Michels
et al., 2016]). *Consider the program:*
$$fail \leftarrow \langle t > l \rangle$$
$$t \sim gaussian(20.0, 50.0)$$
$$l \sim gaussian(30.0, 50.0)$$
*The event that the machine fails is then represented by the formula $t > l$ and
the PHPT for this formula is shown in Figure 12.4.*
The lower bound of the probability of fails is then

$$\underline{P}(fails) = 0.9772 \cdot 0.5$$

Since the only ⊥ leaf has probability $0.0228 \cdot 0.5$, then

$$\overline{P}(fails) = 1 - 0.0228 \cdot 0.5$$

Given a precision ϵ, IHPMC builds a PHPT such that $\overline{P}(q) - \underline{P}(q) \leq$
ϵ and $\overline{P}(q) - \underline{P}(q) \leq \epsilon$. To do so, the tree must be built to a sufficient
depth.

To compute bounds on conditional probabilities, IHPMC needs to com-
pute bounds for $q \wedge e$ and $\neg q \wedge e$ where q is the query and e the evidence.
IHPMC computes the bounds using two PHPTs. The bounds on the condi-
tional probability are those given by equations (4.6) and (4.7) of Section 4.5.1.

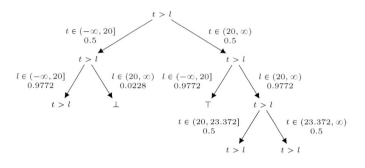

Figure 12.4 PHPT for Example 113. From [Michels et al., 2016]. © [2016] Association for the Advancement of Artificial Intelligence. All rights reserved. Reprinted with permission.

Arbitrary precision can still be achieved by building the trees to a sufficient depth.

When building trees, IHPMC uses heuristics for selecting the next node to expand, the variable to be used for splitting, and the partitioning of the range of the variable. IHPMC expands the leaf node with the highest probability mass. Variables occurring more frequently in the formula are preferred for splitting, unless a different choice may eliminate a primitive constraint. For partitioning continuous variables, split points that can lead to a simplification of the formula are selected. If there are no such points, a partitioning is chosen that splits evenly the probability of the node.

12.5 Approximate Inference for the DISTR and EXP Tasks

Monte Carlo inference can also be used to solve DISTR and EXP tasks, i.e., computing probability distributions or expectations over arguments of queries. In this case, the query contains one or more variables. In the DISTR task, we record the values of these arguments in successful samples of the query. If the program is range restricted, queries succeed with all arguments instantiated, so these values are guaranteed to exist. For unconditional inference or conditional inference with rejection sampling or Metropolis-hastings, the result is a list of terms, one for each sample. For likelihood weighting, the results is a list of weighted terms, where the weight of each term is the sample weight.

From these lists, approximations of probability distributions or probability densities can be built, depending on the type of values, discrete or continuous, respectively. For an unweighted list of discrete values, the probability of each value is the number of occurrences of that value in the list, divided by the total number of values. For a weighted list of discrete values, the probability of each value is the sum of the weights of each occurrence of the value in the list, divided by the sum of all the weights.

For an unweighted list of continuous values, a line plot of the probability density function can be drawn by dividing the domain of the variable in a number of intervals or bins. The function then has a point for each interval, whose y value is the number of values in the list that fall in the interval, divided by the total number of values. For a weighted list of continuous values, the y value is the sum of the weights of each value in the list that falls in the interval, divided by the sum of all the weights. A bar plot can be drawn similarly.

Note that, if likelihood weighting is used, the set of samples without the weight can be interpreted as the density of the variable prior to the observation of the evidence. So we can draw a plot of the density before and after observing the evidence.

The EXP task can be solved by first solving the DISTR task, where we collect a list of numerical values, possibly weighted. Then the required value can be computed as a (weighted) mean. For unweighted samples, this is given by

$$\mathbf{E}(q|e) = \frac{\sum_{i=1}^{n} v_i}{n}$$

where $[v_1, \ldots, v_n]$ is the list of values. For weighted samples, it is given by

$$\mathbf{E}(q|e) = \frac{\sum_{i=1}^{n} w_i \cdot v_i}{\sum_{i=1}^{n} w_i}$$

where $[(v_1, w_1), \ldots, (v_n, w_n)]$ is the list of weighted values, with w_i the weights.

`cplint` [Alberti et al., 2017; Nguembang Fadja and Riguzzi, 2017] offers functions for performing both DISTR and EXP using sampling, rejection sampling, Metropolis-hastings, likelihood weighting, and particle filtering, see Section 15.1.

Notice that a query may return more than one value for an output argument in a given world. The query returns a single value for each sample only if the query predicate is determinate in each world. A predicate is *determinate* if, given values for input arguments of a query over that predicate, there is a single value for output arguments that makes the query true. The user should be aware of this and write the program so that predicates are determinate, or otherwise consider only the first value for a sample. Or he may be interested in all possible values for the output argument in a sample, in which case a call to *findall*/3 should be wrapped around the query and the resulting list of sampled values will be a list of lists of values.

If the program is not determinate, the user may be interested in a sampling process where first the world is sampled, and then the value of the output argument is sampled uniformly from the set of values that make the query true. In this case, to ensure uniformity without computing first all values, a meta-interpreter should be used that randomizes the choice of clauses for resolution, such as the one used by `cplint` in likelihood weighting.

Programs satisfying the exclusive-or assumption, see Chapter 8, are determinate, because, in program satisfying this assumption, clauses sharing an atom in the head are mutually exclusive, i.e., in each world, the body of at most one clause is true. In fact, the semantics of PRISM, where this assumption is made, can also be seen as defining a probability distribution over the values of output arguments.

Some probabilistic logic languages, such as SLPs (see Section 2.10.1), directly define probability distributions over arguments rather than probability distributions over truth values of ground atoms. Inference in such programs can be simulated with programs under the DS by solving the DISTR task.

Example 114 (Generative model). *The following program*[2] *encodes the model from [Goodman and Tenenbaum, 2018] for generating random functions:*

```
eval(X,Y) :- random_fn(X,0,F), Y is F.
op(+):0.5; op(-):0.5.
random_fn(X,L,F) :- comb(L), random_fn(X,l(L),F1),
    random_fn(X,r(L),F2), op(Op), F=..[Op,F1,F2].
random_fn(X,L,F) :- \+comb(L),base_random_fn(X,L,F).
comb(_):0.3.
base_random_fn(X,L,X) :- identity(L).
base_random_fn(_,L,C) :- \+identity(L),
                         random_const(L,C).
identity(_):0.5.
random_const(_,C):discrete(C,[0:0.1,1:0.1,2:0.1,
    3:0.1,4:0.1,5:0.1,6:0.1,7:0.1,8:0.1,9:0.1]).
```

---

[2] https://cplint.eu/e/arithm.pl

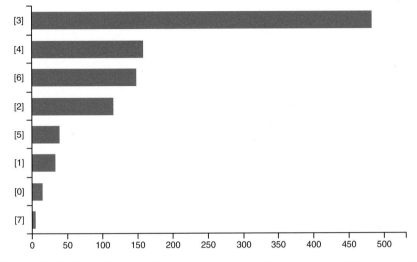

Figure 12.5 Distribution of sampled values in the Program of Example 114.

A random function is either an operator ("+" or "−") applied to two random functions or a base random function. A base random function is either an identity or a constant drawn uniformly from the integers $0, \ldots, 9$.

You may be interested in the distribution of all possible output values of the random function with input 2 given that the function outputs 3 for input 1.

If we take 1000 samples with Metropolis-hastings, we may get the bar plot of the frequencies of the sampled values shown in Figure 12.5. Since each world of the program is determinate, there is a single value of Y *that makes* eval(2,Y) *true in each world and the list of values in each sampled world contains a single element.*

Example 115 (Gaussian mixture – sampling arguments – cplint). *Example 55 encodes a mixture of two Gaussians with the program[3] that we report below*

```
heads:0.6;tails:0.4.
g(X): gaussian(X,0, 1).
h(X): gaussian(X,5, 2).
```

---

[3] https://cplint.eu/e/gauss_mean_est.pl

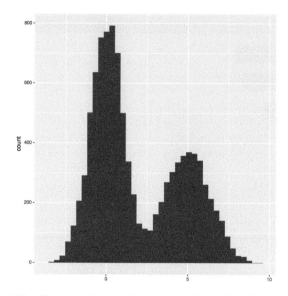

Figure 12.6   Distribution of sampled values from the Gaussian mixture of Example 115.

```
mix(X)  :- heads, g(X).
mix(X)  :- tails, h(X).
```

If we take 10000 samples of argument X of mix(X), we may get the distribution of values that is shown in Figure 12.6.

13

Parameter Learning

This chapter discusses the problem of learning the parameters of probabilistic logic programs with a given structure. We are given data, in the form of ground atoms or interpretations, and a probabilistic logic program, and we want to find the parameters of the program that assign maximum probability to the examples.

13.1 PRISM Parameter Learning

The PRISM system included a parameter learning algorithm since the original article [Sato, 1995]. The learning task considered there is given in the following definition.

Definition 60 (PRISM parameter learning problem). *Given a PRISM program* $\mathcal{P}$ *and a set of examples* $E = \{e_1, \ldots, e_T\}$ *which are ground atoms, find the parameters of* msw *facts so that the* likelihood *of the atoms* $L = \prod_{t=1}^{T} P(e_t)$ *is maximized. Equivalently, find the parameters of* msw *facts so that the Log likelihood (LL) of the atoms* $LL = \sum_{t=1}^{T} \log P(e_t)$ *is maximized.*

Example 116 (Bloodtype – PRISM [Sato et al., 2017]). *The following program*

```
values(gene,[a,b,o]).
bloodtype(P) :-
  genotype(X,Y),
  ( X=Y -> P=X
  ; X=o -> P=Y
  ; Y=o -> P=X
  ; P=ab
  ).
genotype(X,Y) :- msw(gene,X),msw(gene,Y).
```

319

*encodes how a person's blood type is determined by his genotype, formed by a pair of two genes (*a, b *or* o*).*

Learning in PRISM can be performed using predicate learn/1 *that takes a list of ground atoms (the examples) as argument, as in*

```
?- learn([
     count(bloodtype(a),40),
     count(bloodtype(b),20),
     count(bloodtype(o),30),
     count(bloodtype(ab),10)
     ]).
```

where count(At,N) *denotes the repetition of atom* At N *times. After parameter learning, the parameters can be obtained with predicate* show_sw/0, *e.g.,*

```
?- show_sw.
Switch gene: unfixed: a (0.292329558535712)
b (0.163020241540856)
o (0.544650199923432)
```

These values represents the probability distribution over the values a, b, *and* o *of switch* gene.

PRISM looks for the maximum likelihood parameters of the msw atoms. However, these are not observed in the dataset, which contains only derived atoms. Therefore, relative frequency cannot be used for computing the parameters and an algorithm for learning from incomplete data must be used. One such algorithm is Expectation maximization (EM) [Dempster et al., 1977].

To perform EM, we can associate a random variable X_{ijl} with values $D = \{x_{i1}, \ldots, x_{in_i}\}$ to each occurrence l of the ground switch name $i\theta_j$ of $msw(i, x)$ with domain D, with θ_j being a grounding substitution for i. Since PRISM learning algorithm uses $msw/2$ instead of $msw/3$ (the trial identifier is omitted), each occurrence of $msw(i\theta_k, x)$ represents a distinct random variable. PRISM will learn different parameters for each ground switch name $i\theta_j$.

The EM algorithm alternates between the two phases:

- Expectation: compute $\mathbf{E}[c_{ijk}|e]$ for all examples e, switches $msw(i\theta_j, x)$ and $k \in \{1, \ldots, n_i\}$, where c_{ijk} is the number of times the switch $msw(i\theta_j, x)$ takes value x_{ik}. $\mathbf{E}[c_{ijk}|e]$ is given by $\sum_l P(X_{ijl} = x_{ik}|e)$.

- Maximization: compute Π_{ijk} for all $msw(i\theta_j, x)$ and $k = 1, \ldots, n_i$ as

$$\Pi_{ijk} = \frac{\sum_{e \in E} \mathbf{E}[c_{ijk}|e]}{\sum_{e \in E} \sum_{k=1}^{n_i} \mathbf{E}[c_{ijk}|e]}$$

For each e, X_{ijl}, and x_{ik}, we compute $P(X_{ijl} = x_{ik}|e)$, the probability distribution of X_{ijl} given the example, with $k \in \{1, \ldots, n_i\}$. In this way we complete the dataset and we can compute the parameters by relative frequency. If c_{ijk} is number of times a variable X_{ijl} takes value x_{ik} for all l, $\mathbf{E}[c_{ijk}|e]$ is its expected value given example e. If $\mathbf{E}[c_{ijk}]$ is its expected value given all the examples, then

$$\mathbf{E}[c_{ijk}] = \sum_{t=1}^{T} \mathbf{E}[c_{ijk}|e_t]$$

and

$$\Pi_{ijk} = \frac{\mathbf{E}[c_{ijk}]}{\sum_{k=1}^{n_i} \mathbf{E}[c_{ijk}]}.$$

If the program satisfies the exclusive-or assumption, $P(X_{ijl} = x_{ik}|e)$ can be computed as

$$P(X_{ijl} = x_{ik}|e) = \frac{P(X_{ijl} = x_{ik}, e)}{P(e)} = \frac{\sum_{\kappa \in K_e, msw(i\theta_j, x_{ik}) \in \kappa} P(\kappa)}{P(e)}$$

where K_e is the set of explanations of e and each explanation κ is a multiset of ground msw atoms of the form $msw(i\theta_j, x_{ik})$. Then

$$\mathbf{E}[c_{ijk}|e] = \sum_{l} P(X_{ijl} = x_{ik}|e) = \frac{\sum_{\kappa \in K_e} n_{ijk\kappa} P(\kappa)}{P(e)}$$

where $n_{ijk\kappa}$ is the number of times $msw(i\theta_j, x_{ik})$ appears in mulltiset κ. This leads to the naive learning function of Algorithm 20 [Sato, 1995] that iterates the expectation and maximization steps until the LL converges.

This algorithm is naive because there can be exponential numbers of explanations for the examples, as in the case of the HMM of Example 74. As for inference, a more efficient dynamic programming algorithm can be devised that does not require the computation of all the explanations in case the program also satisfies the independent-and assumption [Sato and Kameya, 2001]. Tabling is used to find formulas of the form

$$g_i \Leftrightarrow S_{i1} \vee \ldots \vee S_{is_i}$$

Algorithm 20 Function PRISM-EM-NAIVE: Naive EM learning in PRISM.

1: **function** PRISM-EM-NAIVE($E, \mathcal{P}, \epsilon$)
2:      $LL = -inf$
3:      **repeat**
4:          $LL_0 = LL$
5:          **for all** i, j, k **do**   ▷ Expectation step
6:              $\mathbf{E}[c_{ijk}] \leftarrow \sum_{e \in E} \frac{\sum_{\kappa \in K_e} n_{ijk\kappa} P(\kappa)}{P(e)}$
7:          **end for**
8:          **for all** i, j, k **do**   ▷ Maximization step
9:              $\Pi_{ijk} \leftarrow \frac{\mathbf{E}[c_{ijk}]}{\sum_{k'=1}^{n_i} \mathbf{E}[c_{ijk'}]}$
10:         **end for**
11:         $LL \leftarrow \sum_{e \in E} \log P(e)$
12:     **until** $LL - LL_0 < \epsilon$
13:     **return** LL, Π_{ijk} for all i, j, k
14: **end function**

---

where the g_is are subgoals in the derivation of an example e that can be ordered as $\{g_1, \ldots, g_m\}$ such that $e = g_1$ and each S_{ij} contains only msw atoms and subgoals from $\{g_{i+1}, \ldots, g_m\}$.

The dynamic programming algorithm computes, for each example, the probability $P(g_i)$ of the subgoals $\{g_1, \ldots, g_m\}$, also called the *inside prob-ability*, and the value $Q(g_i)$, which is called the *outside probability*. These names derive from the fact that the algorithm generalizes the Inside–Outside algorithm for Probabilistic context-free grammar [Baker, 1979]. It also gener-alizes the forward-backward algorithm used for parameter learning in HMMs by the Baum–Welch algorithm [Rabiner, 1989].

The inside probabilities are computed by procedure GET-INSIDE-PROBS shown in Algorithm 21 that is the same as function PRISM-PROB of Algo-rithm 5.

Outside probabilities instead are defined as

$$Q(g_i) = \frac{\partial P(e)}{\partial P(g_i)}$$

and are computed recursively from $i = 1$ to $i = m$ using an algorithm sim-ilar to Procedure CIRCP of Algorithm 7 for d-DNNF. The derivation of the recursive formulas is also similar. Suppose g_i appears in the ground program as

$$b_1 \leftarrow g_i^{n_{11}}, W_{11} \quad \ldots \quad b_1 \leftarrow g_i^{n_{1i_1}}, W_{1i_1}$$
$$\ldots$$
$$b_K \leftarrow g_i^{n_{K1}}, W_{K1} \quad \ldots \quad b_K \leftarrow g_i^{n_{Ki_K}}, W_{Ki_K}$$

Algorithm 21 Procedure GET-INSIDE-PROBS: Computation of inside probabilities.

```
1: procedure GET-INSIDE-PROBS(e)
2:     for all i, j, k do
3:         P(msw(iθⱼ, vₖ)) ← Πᵢⱼₖ
4:     end for
5:     for i ← m → 1 do
6:         P(gᵢ) ← 0
7:         for j ← 1 → sᵢ do
8:             Let Sᵢⱼ be h₁, . . . , hₒ
9:             P(gᵢ, Sᵢⱼ) ← ∏ᵒₗ₌₁ P(hₗ)
10:            P(gᵢ) ← P(gᵢ) + P(gᵢ, Sᵢⱼ)
11:        end for
12:    end for
13: end procedure
```

where $g_i^{n_{jk}}$ indicates atom g_i repeated n_{jk} times. In case g_i is not an msw atom, then n_{jk} is always 1. Then

$$P(b_1) = P(g_i^{n_{11}}, W_{11}) + \ldots + P(g_i^{n_{1i_1}}, W_{1i_1})$$
$$\ldots$$
$$P(b_K) = P(g_i^{n_{K1}}, W_{K1}) + \ldots + P(g_i^{n_{Ki_K}}, W_{Ki_K})$$

and

$$P(b_1) = P(g_i)^{n_{11}} P(W_{11}) + \ldots + P(g_i)^{n_{1i_1}} P(W_{1i_1})$$
$$\ldots$$
$$P(b_K) = P(g_i)^{n_{K1}} P(W_{K1}) + \ldots + P(g_i)^{n_{Ki_K}} PW_{Ki_K})$$

because $P(g_i, W_{jk}) = P(g_i)P(W_{jk})$ for the independent and-assumption. We have that $Q(g_1) = 1$ as $e = g_1$. For $i = 2, \ldots, m$, we can derive $Q(g_i)$ by the chain rule of the derivative knowing that $P(e)$ is a function of $P(b_1), \ldots, P(b_K)$:

$$Q(g_i) = \frac{\partial P(e)}{\partial P(b_1)} \frac{\partial P(g_i^{n_{11}}, W_{11})}{\partial P(g_1)} + \ldots + \frac{\partial P(e)}{\partial P(b_K)} \frac{\partial P(g_i^{n_{Ki_K}}, W_{Ki_K})}{\partial P(g_1)} =$$

$$Q(b_1) \frac{\partial P(g_i)^{n_{11}} P(W_{11})}{\partial P(g_i)} + \ldots +$$

$$Q(b_K) \frac{\partial P(g_i)^{n_{Ki_K}} P(W_{Ki_K})}{\partial P(g_i)} =$$

$$Q(b_1) n_{11} P(g_i)^{n_{11}-1} P(W_{11}) + \ldots +$$

$$Q(b_K) n_{Ki_K} P(g_i)^{n_{Ki_K}-1} P(W_{Ki_K}) =$$

$$Q(b_1) n_{11} \frac{P(g_i^{n_{11}}, W_{11})}{P(g_i)} + \ldots +$$

$$Q(b_K) n_{Ki_K} \frac{P(g_i^{n_{Ki_K}}, W_{Ki_K})}{P(g_i)} =$$

$$Q(b_1) \sum_{s=1}^{i_1} \frac{n_{1s} P(g_i^{n_{1s}}, W_{1s})}{P(g_i)} + \ldots +$$

$$Q(b_K) \sum_{s=1}^{i_K} \frac{n_{Ks} P(g_i^{n_{Ks}}, W_{Ks})}{P(g_i)}$$

If we consider each repeated occurrence of g_i independently, we can obtain the following recursive formula

$$Q(g_1) = 1$$

$$Q(g_i) = Q(b_1) \sum_{s=1}^{i_1} \frac{P(g_i, W_{1s})}{P(g_i)} + \ldots + Q(b_K) \sum_{s=1}^{i_K} \frac{P(g_i, W_{Ks})}{P(g_i)}$$

that can be evaluated top-down from $q = g_1$ down to g_m.

In fact, in case g_i is a msw atom that is repeated n_{jk} times in the body of clause $b_j \leftarrow g_i^{n_{jk}}, W_{jk}$ and if we apply the algorithm to each occurrence independently, we obtain the following contribution from that clause to $Q(g_i)$:

$$Q(b_j) \frac{P(g_i^{n_{jk}}, W_{jk})}{P(g_i)} + \ldots + Q(b_j) \frac{P(g_i^{n_{jk}}, W_{jk})}{P(g_i)} = Q(b_j) n_{jk} \frac{P(g_i^{n_{jk}}, W_{jk})}{P(g_i)}$$

because the term $Q(b_j) \frac{P(g_i^{n_{jk}}, W_{jk})}{P(g_i)}$ is repeated n_{jk} times.

Procedure GET-OUTSIDE-PROBS of Algorithm 22 does this: for each subgoal b_k and each of its explanations g_i, W_{ks}, it updates the outside probability $Q(g_i)$ for the subgoal g_i.

If $g_i = msw(i\theta_j, x_k)$, we can divide the explanations for e into two sets, K_{e1}, that includes the explanations containing $msw(i\theta_j, x_k)$, and K_{e2}, that includes the other explanations. Then $P(e) = P(K_{e1}) + P(K_{e2})$ and $\mathbf{E}[c_{ijk}|e] = \sum_{\kappa \in K_{e1}} \frac{n_{ijk\kappa} P(\kappa)}{P(e)}$. Since each explanation in K_{e1} contains $g_i = msw(i\theta_j, x_k)$, K_{e1} takes the form $\{\{g_i^{n_1}, W_1\}, \ldots, \{g_i^{n_s}, W_s\}\}$ where n_j is the multiplicity of g_i in the various explanations. So we obtain

$$
\begin{aligned}
\mathbf{E}[c_{ijk}|e] &= \frac{1}{P(e)} \sum_{\{g_i^n, W\} \in K_{e1}} nP(g_i)^n P(W) = \\
&\frac{P(g_i)}{P(e)} \sum_{\{g_i^n, W\} \in K_{e1}} nP(g_i)^{n-1} P(W) = \\
&\frac{P(g_i)}{P(e)} \sum_{\kappa \in K_{e1}} \frac{\partial P(\kappa)}{\partial P(g_i)} = \\
&\frac{P(g_i)}{P(e)} \frac{\partial P(K_{e1})}{\partial P(g_i)} = \\
&\frac{P(g_i)}{P(e)} \frac{\partial P(K_e)}{\partial P(g_i)} = \\
&\frac{P(g_i)}{P(e)} \frac{\partial P(e)}{\partial P(g_i)} = \\
&\frac{Q(g_i) P(g_i)}{P(e)}
\end{aligned}
\tag{13.1}
$$

where equality (13.1) holds because $\frac{\partial P(K_{e2})}{\partial P(g_i)} = 0$.

Procedure PRISM-EXPECTATION of Algorithm 23 updates the expected values of the counters. Function PRISM-EM of Algorithm 24 implements the overall EM algorithm [Sato and Kameya, 2001]. The algorithm stops when the difference between the LL of the current and previous iteration drops below a threshold ϵ.

Sato and Kameya [2001] show that the combination of tabling with Algorithm 24 yields a procedure that has the same time complexity for programs encoding HMMs and PCFGs as the specific parameter learning algorithms: the Baum–Welch algorithm for HMMs [Rabiner, 1989] and the Inside–Outside algorithm for PCFGs [Baker, 1979].

Algorithm 22 Procedure GET-OUTSIDE-PROBS: Computation of outside probabilities.

1: **procedure** GET-OUTSIDE-PROBS(e)
2:     $Q(g_1) \leftarrow 1.0$
3:     **for** $i \leftarrow 2 \rightarrow m$ **do**
4:         $Q(g_i) \leftarrow 0.0$
5:         **for** $j \leftarrow 1 \rightarrow s_i$ **do**
6:             Let S_{ij} be $h_1, \ldots, h_o$
7:             **for** $l \leftarrow 1 \rightarrow o$ **do**
8:                 $Q(h_l) \leftarrow Q(h_l) + Q(g_i)P(g_i, S_{ij})/P(h_l)$
9:             **end for**
10:         **end for**
11:     **end for**
12: **end procedure**

Algorithm 23 Procedure PRISM-EXPECTATION.

1: **function** PRISM-EXPECTATION(E)
2:     $LL = 0$
3:     **for all** $e \in E$ **do**
4:         GET-INSIDE-PROBS(e)
5:         GET-OUTSIDE-PROBS(e)
6:         **for all** i, j **do**
7:             **for** $k = 1$ to n_i **do**
8:                 $\mathbf{E}[c_{ijk}] = \mathbf{E}[c_{ijk}] + Q(msw(i\theta_j, x_k))\Pi_{ijk}/P(e)$
9:             **end for**
10:         **end for**
11:         $LL = LL + \log P(e)$
12:     **end for**
13:     **return** LL
14: **end function**

13.2 LLPAD and ALLPAD Parameter Learning

The systems LLPAD [Riguzzi, 2004] and ALLPAD [Riguzzi, 2007b, 2008b] consider the problem of learning both the parameters and the structure of LPADs from interpretations. We consider here parameter learning; we will discuss structure learning in Section 14.2.

Definition 61 (LLPAD Parameter learning problem). *Given a set*

$$E = \{(I, p_I) | I \in Int2, p_I \in [0, 1]\}$$

Algorithm 24 Function PRISM-EM.

1: **function** PRISM-EM($E, \mathcal{P}, \epsilon$)
2:     $LL = -inf$
3:     **repeat**
4:         $LL_0 = LL$
5:         $LL = $ PRISM-EXPECTATION(E)
6:         **for all** i, j **do**
7:             $Sum \leftarrow \sum_{k=1}^{n_i} \mathbf{E}[c_{ijk}]$
8:             **for** $k = 1$ **to** n_i **do**
9:                 $\Pi_{ijk} = \frac{\mathbf{E}[c_{ijk}]}{Sum}$
10:             **end for**
11:         **end for**
12:     **until** $LL - LL_0 < \epsilon$
13:     **return** LL, Π_{ijk} for all i, j, k
14: **end function**

---

such that $\sum_{(I,p_I) \in E} p_I = 1$, *find the value of the parameters of a ground LPAD $\mathcal{P}$, if they exist, such that*

$$\forall (I, p_I) \in E : P(I) = p_I.$$

E may also be given as a multiset E' of interpretations. From this case, we can obtain a learning problem of the form above by computing a probability for each distinct interpretation in E' by relative frequency.

Notice that, if $\forall (I, p_I) \in E : P(I) = p_I$, then $\forall I \in Int2 : P(I) = p_I$ if we define $p_I = 0$ for those I not appearing in E, as $P(I)$ is a probability distribution over $Int2$ and $\sum_{(I,p_I) \in E} p_I = 1$.

Riguzzi [2004] presents a theorem that shows that, if all the pairs of clauses of $\mathcal{P}$ that share an atom in the head have mutually exclusive bodies, then the parameters can be computed by relative frequency.

Definition 62 (Mutually exclusive bodies). *Ground clauses $h_1 \leftarrow B_1$ and $h_2 \leftarrow B_2$ have mutually exclusive bodies over a set of interpretations J if, $\forall I \in J$, B_1 and B_2 are not both true in I.*

Mutual exclusivity of bodies is equivalent to the exclusive-or assumption.

Theorem 21 (Parameters as relative frequency). *Consider a ground locally stratified LPAD $\mathcal{P}$ and a clause $C \in \mathcal{P}$ of the form*

$$C = h_1 : \Pi_1 ; h_2 : \Pi_2 ; \dots ; h_m : \Pi_m \leftarrow B.$$

Suppose all the clauses of $\mathcal{P}$ that share an atom in the head with C have mutually exclusive bodies with C over the set of interpretations $\mathcal{J} = \{I|P(I) > 0\}$. In this case:

$$P(h_i|B) = \Pi_i$$

This theorem means that, under certain conditions, the probabilities in a clause's head can be interpreted as conditional probabilities of the head atoms given the body. Since $P(h_i|B) = P(h_i, B)/P(B)$, the probabilities of the head disjuncts of a ground rule can be computed from the probability distribution $P(I)$ defined by the program over the interpretations: for a set of literals S, $P(S) = \sum_{S \subseteq I} P(I)$. Moreover, since $\forall I \in Int2 : P(I) = p_I$, then $P(S) = \sum_{S \subseteq I} p_I$.

In fact, if the clauses have mutually exclusive bodies, there is no more uncertainty on the values of the hidden variables: for an atom in the head of a clause to be true, it must be selected by the only clause whose body is true. Therefore, there is no need of an EM algorithm and relative frequency can be used.

13.3 LeProbLog

LeProbLog [Gutmann et al., 2008] is a parameter learning system that starts from a set of examples annotated with a probability. The aim of LeProbLog is then to find the value of the parameters of a ProbLog program so that the probability assigned by the program to the examples is as close as possible to the one given.

Definition 63 (LeProbLog parameter learning problem). *Given a ProbLog program $\mathcal{P}$ and a set of training examples $E = \{(e_1, p_i), \ldots, (e_T, p_T)\}$ where e_t is a ground atom and $p_t \in [0, 1]$ for $t = 1, \ldots, T$, find the parameter of the program so that the mean squared error*

$$MSE = \frac{1}{T} \sum_{t=1}^{T} (P(e_t) - p_t)^2$$

is minimized.

To perform learning, LeProbLog uses gradient descent, i.e., it iteratively updates the parameters in the opposite direction of the gradient of MSE. This requires the computation of the gradient which is

$$\frac{\partial MSE}{\partial \Pi_j} = \frac{2}{T} \sum_{t=1}^{T} (P(e_t) - p_t) \cdot \frac{\partial P(e_t)}{\partial \Pi_j}$$

LeProbLog compiles queries to BDDs; therefore, $P(e_t)$ can be computed with Algorithm 6. To compute $\frac{\partial P(e_t)}{\partial \Pi_j}$, it uses a dynamic programming algorithm that traverses the BDD bottom up. In fact

$$\frac{\partial P(e_t)}{\partial \Pi_j} = \frac{\partial P(f(\mathbf{X}))}{\partial \Pi_j}$$

where $f(\mathbf{X})$ is the Boolean function represented by the BDD. $f(\mathbf{X})$ is

$$f(\mathbf{X}) = X_k \cdot f^{X_k}(\mathbf{X}) + \neg X_k \cdot f^{\neg X_k}(\mathbf{X})$$

where X_k is the random Boolean variable associated with the root and to ground fact $\Pi_k :: f_k$, so

$$P(f(\mathbf{X})) = \Pi_k \cdot P(f^{X_k}(\mathbf{X})) + (1 - \Pi_k) \cdot P(f^{\neg X_k}(\mathbf{X}))$$

and

$$\frac{\partial P(f(\mathbf{X}))}{\partial \Pi_j} = P(f^{X_k}(\mathbf{X})) - P(f^{\neg X_k}(\mathbf{X}))$$

if $k = j$, or

$$\frac{\partial P(f(\mathbf{X}))}{\partial \Pi_j} = \Pi_k \cdot \frac{\partial P(f^{X_k}(\mathbf{X}))}{\partial \Pi_j} + (1 - \Pi_k) \cdot \frac{\partial P(f^{\neg X_k}(\mathbf{X}))}{\partial \Pi_j}$$

if $k \neq j$. Moreover

$$\frac{\partial P(f(\mathbf{X}))}{\partial \Pi_j} = 0$$

if X_j does not appear in $\mathbf{X}$.

When performing gradient descent, we have to ensure that the parameters remain in the $[0, 1]$ interval. However, updating the parameters using the gradient does not guarantee that. Therefore, a reparameterization is used by means of the sigmoid function $\sigma(x) = \frac{1}{1+e^{-x}}$ that takes a real value $x \in (-\infty, +\infty)$ and returns a real value in $(0, 1)$. So each parameter is expressed as $\Pi_j = \sigma(a_j)$ and the a_js are used as the parameters to update. Since $a_j \in (-\infty, +\infty)$, we do not risk to get values outside the domain.

Algorithm 25 Function GRADIENT.

1: **function** GRADIENT(BDD, j)
2:    $(val, seen) \leftarrow$ GRADIENTEVAL(BDD, j)
3:    **if** $seen = 1$ **then**
4:       **return** $val \cdot \sigma(a_j) \cdot (1 - \sigma(a_j))$
5:    **else**
6:       **return** 0
7:    **end if**
8: **end function**
9: **function** GRADIENTEVAL(n, j)
10:    **if** n is the 1-terminal **then**
11:       **return** $(1, 0)$
12:    **end if**
13:    **if** n is the 0-terminal **then**
14:       **return** $(0, 0)$
15:    **end if**
16:    $(val(child_1(n)), seen(child_1(n))) \leftarrow$ GRADIENTEVAL($child_1(n), j$)
17:    $(val(child_0(n)), seen(child_0(n))) \leftarrow$ GRADIENTEVAL($child_0(n), j$)
18:    **if** $varindex(n) = j$ **then**
19:       **return** $(val(child_1(n)) - val(child_0(n)), 1)$
20:    **else if** $seen(child_1(n)) = seen(child_0(n))$ **then**
21:       **return** $(\sigma(a_n) \cdot val(child_1(n)) + (1 - \sigma(a_n)) \cdot val(child_0(n)), seen(child_1(n)))$
22:    **else if** $seen(child_1(n)) = 1$ **then**
23:       **return** $(\sigma(a_n) \cdot val(child_1(n)), 1)$
24:    **else if** $seen(child_0(n)) = 1$ **then**
25:       **return** $((1 - \sigma(a_n)) \cdot val(child_0(n)), 1)$
26:    **end if**
27: **end function**

Given that $\frac{d\sigma(x)}{dx} = \sigma(x) \cdot (1 - \sigma(x))$, using the chain rule of derivatives, we get

$$\frac{\partial P(e_t)}{\partial a_j} = \sigma(a_j) \cdot (1 - \sigma(a_j)) \frac{\partial P(f(\mathbf{X}))}{\partial \Pi_j}$$

LeProbLog dynamic programming function for computing $\frac{\partial P(f(\mathbf{X}))}{\partial a_j}$ is shown in Algorithm 25. GRADIENTEVAL(n, j) traverses the BDD n and returns two values: a real number and a Boolean variable $seen$ which is 1 if the variable X_j was seen in n. We consider three cases:

1. If the variable of node n is below X_j in the BDD order, then GRADIEN-TEVAL returns the probability of node n and $seen = 0$.

2. If the variable of node n is X_j, then GRADIENTEVAL returns $seen = 1$ and the gradient given by the difference of the values of its two children $val(child_1(n)) - val(child_0(n))$.

3. If the variable of node n is above X_j in the BDD order, then GRADIEN-TEVAL returns $\sigma(a_n) \cdot val(child_1(n)) + (1 - \sigma(a_n)) \cdot val(child_0(n))$ unless X_j does not appear in one of the sub-BDD, in which case the corresponding term is 0.

GRADIENTEVAL determines which of the cases applies by using function $varindex(n)$ that returns the index of the variable of node n and by considering the values $seen(child_1(n))$ and $seen(child_0(n))$ of the children: if one of them is 1 and the other is 0, then X_j is below the variable of node n and we fall in the third case above. If they are both 1, we are in the third case again. If they are both 0, we are either in the first case or in third case but X_j does not appear in the BDD. We deal with the latter situation by returning 0 in the outer function GRADIENT.

The overall LeProbLog function is shown in Algorithm 26. Given a ProbLog program $\mathcal{P}$ with n probabilistic ground facts, it returns the values of their parameters. It initializes the vector of parameters $\mathbf{a} = (a_1, \ldots, a_n)$ randomly and then computes an update $\Delta\mathbf{a}$ by computing the gradient. $\mathbf{a}$ is then updated by substracting $\Delta\mathbf{a}$ multiplied by a learning rate η.

Algorithm 26 Function LEPROBLOG: LeProbLog algorithm.

1: **function** LEPROBLOG($E, \mathcal{P}, k, \eta$)
2:     initialize all a_j randomly
3:     **while** not converged **do**
4:         $\Delta\mathbf{a} \leftarrow 0$
5:         **for** $t \leftarrow 1 \rightarrow T$ **do**
6:             find k best proofs and generate BDD_t for e_t
7:             $y \leftarrow \frac{2}{T}(P(e_t) - p_t)$
8:             **for** $j \leftarrow 1 \rightarrow n$ **do**
9:                 $deriv_j \leftarrow$ GRADIENT(BDD_t, j)
10:                 $\Delta a_j \leftarrow \Delta a_j + y \cdot deriv_j$
11:             **end for**
12:         **end for**
13:         $\mathbf{a} \leftarrow \mathbf{a} - \eta \cdot \Delta\mathbf{a}$
14:     **end while**
15:     **return** $\{\sigma(a_1), \ldots, \sigma(a_n)\}$
16: **end function**

The BDDs for examples are built by computing the k best explanations for each example, as in the k-best inference algorithm, see Section 10.1.2. As the set of the k best explanations may change when the parameters change, the BDDs are recomputed at each iteration.

13.4 EMBLEM

EMBLEM [Bellodi and Riguzzi, 2013, 2012] applies the algorithm for performing EM over BDDs proposed in [Thon et al., 2008; Ishihata et al., 2008a,b; Inoue et al., 2009] to the problem of learning the parameters of an LPAD.

Definition 64 (EMBLEM parameter learning problem). *Given an LPAD $\mathcal{P}$ with unknown parameters and two sets $E^+ = \{e_1, \dots, e_T\}$ and $E^- = \{e_{T+1}, \dots, e_Q\}$ of ground atoms (positive and negative examples), find the value of the parameters Π of $\mathcal{P}$ that maximize the likelihood of the examples, i.e., solve*

$$\arg\max_{\Pi} P(E^+, \sim E^-) = \arg\max_{\Pi} \prod_{t=1}^{T} P(e_t) \prod_{t=T+1}^{Q} P(\sim e_t).$$

The predicates for the atoms in E^+ and E^- are called target *because the objective is to be able to better predict the truth value of atoms for them.*

Typically, the LPAD $\mathcal{P}$ has two components: a set of rules, annotated with parameters and representing general knowledge, and a set of certain ground facts, representing background knowledge on individual cases of a specific world, from which consequences can be drawn with the rules, including the examples. Sometimes, it is useful to provide information on more than one world. For each world, a background knowledge and sets of positive and negative examples are provided. The description of one world is also called a *mega-interpretation* or *mega-example*. In this case, it is useful to encode the positive examples as ground facts of the mega-interpretation and the negative examples as suitably annotated ground facts (such as $neg(a)$ for negative example a) for one or more target predicates. The task then is maximizing the product of the likelihood of the examples for all mega-interpretations.

EMBLEM generates a BDD for each example in $E = \{e_1, \dots, e_T, \sim e_{T+1}, \dots, \sim e_Q\}$ using PITA. The BDD for an example e encodes its explanations in the mega-example to which it belongs. Then EMBLEM enters the EM cycle, in which the steps of expectation and maximization are repeated until the log likelihood of the examples reaches a local maximum.

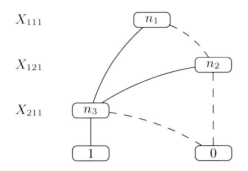

Figure 13.1 BDD for query *epidemic* for Example 117. From [Bellodi and Riguzzi, 2013].

Let us now present the formulas for the expectation and maximization phases. EMBLEM adopts the encoding of multivalued random variable with Boolean random variables used in PITA, see Section 8.6. Let $g(i)$ be the set of indexes od such substitutions:

$$g(i) = \{j|\theta_j \text{ is a grounding substitution for clause } C_i \}.$$

Let X_{ijk} for $k = 1, \ldots, n_i - 1$ and $j \in g(i)$ be the Boolean random variables associated with grounding $C_i\theta_j$ of clause C_i of $\mathcal{P}$ where n_i is the number of head atoms of C_i and $j \in g(i)$.

Example 117 (Epidemic – LPAD – EM). *Let us recall Example 94 about the development of an epidemic*

$$\begin{aligned}
C_1 &= \quad epidemic : 0.6 \; ; \; pandemic : 0.3 \leftarrow flu(X), cold. \\
C_2 &= \quad cold : 0.7. \\
C_3 &= \quad flu(david). \\
C_4 &= \quad flu(robert).
\end{aligned}$$

Clause C_1 has two groundings, both with three atoms in the head, the first associated with Boolean random variables X_{111} and X_{112} and the latter with X_{121} and X_{122}. C_2 has a single grounding with two atoms in the head and is associated with variable X_{211}. The probabilities are $\pi_{11} = 0.6$, $\pi_{12} = \frac{0.3}{1-\pi_{11}} = \frac{0.3}{0.4} = 0.75$ and $\pi_{21} = 0.7$. The BDD for query epidemic is shown in Figure 13.1.

The EM algorithm alternates between the two phases:

- Expectation: compute $\mathbf{E}[c_{ik0}|e]$ and $\mathbf{E}[c_{ik1}|e]$ for all examples e, rules C_i in $\mathcal{P}$ and $k = 1, \ldots, n_i - 1$, where c_{ikx} is the number of times a

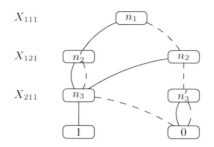

Figure 13.2 BDD after applying the merge rule only for Example 117. From [Bellodi and Riguzzi, 2013].

variable X_{ijk} takes value x for $x \in \{0,1\}$, with $j \in g(i)$. $\mathbf{E}[c_{ikx}|e]$ is given by $\sum_{j \in g(i)} P(X_{ijk} = x|e)$.

- Maximization: compute π_{ik} for all rules C_i and $k = 1, \ldots, n_i - 1$ as

$$\pi_{ik} = \frac{\sum_{e \in E} \mathbf{E}[c_{ik1}|e]}{\sum_{e \in E} \mathbf{E}[c_{ik0}|e] + \mathbf{E}[c_{ik1}|e]}.$$

$P(X_{ijk} = x|e)$ is given by $\frac{P(X_{ijk}=x,e)}{P(e)}$.

Now consider a BDD for an example e built by applying only the merge rule, fusing together identical sub-diagrams but not deleting nodes. For example, by applying only the merge rule in Example 117, the diagram in Figure 13.2 is obtained. The resulting diagram, that we call Complete binary decision diagram (CBDD), is such that every path contains a node for every level.

$P(e)$ is given by the sum of the probabilities of all the paths in the CBDD from the root to a 1 leaf, where the probability of a path is defined as the product of the probabilities of the individual choices along the path. Variable X_{ijk} is associated with a level l in the sense that all nodes at that level test variable X_{ijk}. All paths from the root to a leaf pass through a node of level l. We can express $P(e)$ as

$$P(e) = \sum_{\rho \in R(e)} \prod_{d \in \rho} \pi(d)$$

where $R(e)$ is the set of paths for query e that lead to a 1 leaf, d is an edge of path ρ, and $\pi(d)$ is the probability associated with the edge: if d is the 1–branch from a node associated with a variable X_{ijk}, then $\pi(d) = \pi_{ik}$; if

d is the 0–branch from a node associated with a variable X_{ijk}, then $\pi(d) = 1 - \pi_{ik}$.

We can further expand $P(e)$ as

$$P(e) = \sum_{n \in N(X_{ijk}), \rho \in R(e), x \in \{0,1\}} \pi_{ikx} \prod_{d \in \rho^{n,x}} \pi(d) \prod_{d \in \rho_n} \pi(d)$$

where $N(X_{ijk})$ is the set of nodes associated with variable X_{ijk}, ρ_n is the portion of path ρ up to node n, $\rho^{n,x}$ is the portion of path ρ from $child_x(n)$ to the 1 leaf, and π_{ikx} is π_{ik} if $x = 1$ and $1 - \pi_{ik}$ otherwise. Then

$$P(e) = \sum_{n \in N(X_{ijk}), \rho_n \in R_n(q), x \in \{0,1\} \rho^{n,x} \in R^n(q,x)} \pi_{ikx} \prod_{d \in \rho^{n,x}} \pi(d) \prod_{d \in \rho_n} \pi(d)$$

where $R_n(q)$ is the set containing the paths from the root to n and $R^n(q, x)$ is the set of paths from $child_x(n)$ to the 1 leaf.

To compute $P(X_{ijk} = x, e)$, we can observe that we need to consider only the paths passing through the x-child of a node n associated with variable X_{ijk}, so

$$P(X_{ijk} = x, e) = \sum_{n \in N(X_{ijk}), \rho_n \in R_n(q), \rho^n \in R^n(q,x)} \pi_{ikx} \prod_{d \in \rho^n} \pi(d) \prod_{d \in \rho_n} \pi(d)$$

We can rearrange the terms in the summation as

$$P(X_{ijk} = x, e) = \sum_{n \in N(X_{ijk})} \sum_{\rho_n \in R_n(q)} \sum_{\rho^n \in R^n(q,x)} \pi_{ikx} \prod_{d \in \rho^n} \pi(d) \prod_{d \in \rho_n} \pi(d)$$

$$= \sum_{n \in N(X_{ijk})} \pi_{ikx} \sum_{\rho_n \in R_n(q)} \prod_{d \in \rho_n} \pi(d) \sum_{\rho^n \in R^n(q,x)} \prod_{d \in \rho^n} \pi(d)$$

$$= \sum_{n \in N(X_{ijk})} \pi_{ikx} F(n) B(child_x(n))$$

where $F(n)$ is the *forward probability* [Ishihata et al., 2008b], the probability mass of the paths from the root to n, while $B(n)$ is the *backward probability* [Ishihata et al., 2008b], the probability mass of paths from n to the 1 leaf. If *root* is the root of a tree for a query e, then $B(root) = P(e)$.

The expression $\pi_{ikx} F(n) B(child_x(n))$ represents the sum of the probability of all the paths passing through the x-edge of node n. We indicate with $e^x(n)$ such an expression. Thus

$$P(X_{ijk} = x, e) = \sum_{n \in N(X_{ijk})} e^x(n) \tag{13.2}$$

For the case of a BDD, i.e., a diagram obtained by also applying the deletion rule, Equation (13.2) is no longer valid since paths where there is no node associated with X_{ijk} can also contribute to $P(X_{ijk} = x, e)$. In fact, it is necessary to also consider the deleted paths: suppose a node n associated with variable Y has a level higher than variable X_{ijk} and suppose that $child_0(n)$ is associated with variable W that has a level lower than variable X_{ijk}. The nodes associated with variable X_{ijk} have been deleted from the paths from n to $child_0(n)$. One can imagine that the current BDD has been obtained from a BDD having a node m associated with variable X_{ijk} that is a descendant of n along the 0-branch and whose outgoing edges both point to $child_0(n)$. The probability mass of the two paths that were merged was $e^0(n)(1 - \pi_{ik})$ and $e^0(n)\pi_{ik}$ for the paths passing through the 0-child and 1-child of m respectively. The first quantity contributes to $P(X_{ijk} = 0, e)$ and the latter to $P(X_{ijk} = 1, e)$.

Formally, let $Del^x(X)$ be the set of nodes n such that the level of X is below that of n and is above that of $child_x(n)$, i.e., X is deleted between n and $child_x(n)$. For the BDD in Figure 13.1, for example, $Del^1(X_{121}) = \{n_1\}$, $Del^0(X_{121}) = \varnothing$, $Del^1(X_{221}) = \varnothing$, and $Del^0(X_{221}) = \{n_3\}$. Then

$$P(X_{ijk} = 0, e) = \sum_{n \in N(X_{ijk})} e^0(n) +$$

$$(1 - \pi_{ik}) \left(\sum_{n \in Del^0(X_{ijk})} e^0(n) + \sum_{n \in Del^1(X_{ijk})} e^1(n) \right)$$

$$P(X_{ijk} = 1, e) = \sum_{n \in N(X_{ijk})} e^1(n) +$$

$$\pi_{ik} \left(\sum_{n \in Del^0(X_{ijk})} e^0(n) + \sum_{n \in Del^1(X_{ijk})} e^1(n) \right)$$

Having shown how to compute the probabilities, we now describe EMBLEM in detail. The typical input for EMBLEM will be a set of mega-interpretations, i.e., sets of ground facts, each describing a portion of the domain of interest. Among the predicates for the input facts, the user has to indicate which are target predicates: the facts for these predicates will then form the examples, i.e., the queries for which the BDDs are built. The predicates can be treated as closed-world or open-world. In the first case, a closed-world assumption is made, so the body of clauses with a target predicate in the head is resolved only with facts in the interpretation. In the second case, the body of clauses with a target predicate in the head is resolved both with facts in the interpretation and with clauses in the theory. If the last option is set and the theory is cyclic, EMBLEM uses a depth bound on the derivations to avoid going into infinite loops, as proposed by [Gutmann et al., 2010].

EMBLEM, shown in Algorithm 27, consists of a cycle in which the procedures EXPECTATION and MAXIMIZATION are repeatedly called. Procedure EXPECTATION returns the LL of the data that is used in the stopping criterion: EMBLEM stops when the difference between the LL of the current and previous iteration drops below a threshold ϵ or when this difference is below a fraction δ of the current LL.

Procedure EXPECTATION, shown in Algorithm 28, takes as input a list of BDDs, one for each example, and computes the expectation for each one, i.e., $P(e, X_{ijk} = x)$ for all variables X_{ijk} in the BDD. In the procedure, we use $\eta^x(i, k)$ to indicate $\sum_{j \in g(i)} P(e, X_{ijk} = x)$. EXPECTATION first calls GETFORWARD and GETBACKWARD that compute the forward, the backward probability of nodes and $\eta^x(i, k)$ for non-deleted paths only. Then it updates $\eta^x(i, k)$ to take into account deleted paths.

Algorithm 27 Function EMBLEM.

1: **function** EMBLEM($E, \mathcal{P}, \epsilon, \delta$)
2:     build $BDDs$
3:     $LL = -inf$
4:     **repeat**
5:         $LL_0 = LL$
6:         $LL = $ EXPECTATION($BDDs$)
7:         MAXIMIZATION
8:     **until** $LL - LL_0 < \epsilon \vee LL - LL_0 < -LL \cdot \delta$
9:     return LL, π_{ik} for all i, k
10: **end function**

Procedure MAXIMIZATION (Algorithm 29) computes the parameters values for the next EM iteration.

Procedure GETFORWARD, shown in Algorithm 30, computes the value of the forward probabilities. It traverses the diagram one level at a time starting from the root level. For each level, it considers each node n and computes its contribution to the forward probabilities of its children. Then the forward probabilities of its children, stored in table F, are updated.

Function GETBACKWARD, shown in Algorithm 31, computes the backward probability of nodes by traversing recursively the tree from the root to

---

Algorithm 28 Function EXPECTATION.

1: **function** EXPECTATION($BDDs$)
2:      $LL = 0$
3:      **for all** $BDD \in BDDs$ **do**
4:          **for all** i **do**
5:              **for** $k = 1$ to $n_i - 1$ **do**
6:                  $\eta^0(i, k) = 0$; $\eta^1(i, k) = 0$
7:              **end for**
8:          **end for**
9:          **for all** variables X **do**
10:             $\varsigma(X) = 0$
11:         **end for**
12:         GETFORWARD($root(BDD)$)
13:         $Prob$=GETBACKWARD($root(BDD)$)
14:         $T = 0$
15:         **for** $l = 1$ to $levels(BDD)$ **do**
16:             Let X_{ijk} be the variable associated with level l
17:             $T = T + \varsigma(X_{ijk})$
18:             $\eta^0(i, k) = \eta^0(i, k) + T \times (1 - \pi_{ik})$
19:             $\eta^1(i, k) = \eta^1(i, k) + T \times \pi_{ik}$
20:         **end for**
21:         **for all** i **do**
22:             **for** $k = 1$ to $n_i - 1$ **do**
23:                 $\mathbf{E}[c_{ik0}] = \mathbf{E}[c_{ik0}] + \eta^0(i, k)/Prob$
24:                 $\mathbf{E}[c_{ik1}] = \mathbf{E}[c_{ik1}] + \eta^1(i, k)/Prob$
25:             **end for**
26:         **end for**
27:         $LL = LL + \log(Prob)$
28:     **end for**
29:     **return** LL
30: **end function**

Algorithm 29 Procedure MAXIMIZATION.

1: **procedure** MAXIMIZATION
2:      **for all** i **do**
3:          **for** $k = 1$ to $n_i - 1$ **do**
4:              $\pi_{ik} = \frac{\mathbf{E}[c_{ik1}]}{\mathbf{E}[c_{ik0}] + \mathbf{E}[c_{ik1}]}$
5:          **end for**
6:      **end for**
7: **end procedure**

---

the leaves. When the calls of GETBACKWARD for both children of a node n return, we have all the information that is needed to compute the e^x values and the value of $\eta^x(i, k)$ for non-deleted paths.

The array ς stores, for every variable X_{ijk}, an algebraic sum of $e^x(n)$: those for nodes in upper levels that do not have a descendant in the level l of X_{ijk} minus those for nodes in upper levels that have a descendant in level

---

Algorithm 30 Procedure GETFORWARD: Computation of the forward probability.

1: **procedure** GETFORWARD(*root*)
2:     $F(root) = 1$
3:     $F(n) = 0$ for all nodes
4:     **for** $l = 1$ to *levels* **do**   ▷ *levels* is the number of levels of the BDD rooted at *root*
5:         $Nodes(l) = \varnothing$
6:     **end for**
7:     $Nodes(1) = \{root\}$
8:     **for** $l = 1$ to *levels* **do**
9:         **for all** $node \in Nodes(l)$ **do**
10:            let X_{ijk} be $v(node)$, the variable associated with *node*
11:            **if** $child_0(node)$ is not terminal **then**
12:                $F(child_0(node)) = F(child_0(node)) + F(node) \cdot (1 - \pi_{ik})$
13:                add $child_0(node)$ to $Nodes(level(child_0(node)))$ ▷ *level(node)* returns the
        level of *node*
14:            **end if**
15:            **if** $child_1(node)$ is not terminal **then**
16:                $F(child_1(node)) = F(child_1(node)) + F(node) \cdot \pi_{ik}$
17:                add $child_1(node)$ to $Nodes(level(child_1(node)))$
18:            **end if**
19:        **end for**
20:    **end for**
21: **end procedure**

---

l. In this way, it is possible to add the contributions of the deleted paths by starting from the root level and accumulating $\varsigma(X_{ijk})$ for the various levels in a variable T (see lines 15–20 of Algorithm 28): an $e^x(n)$ value that is added to the accumulator T for the level of X_{ijk} means that n is an ancestor for nodes in that level. When the x-branch from n reaches a node in a level $l' \leqslant l$, $e^x(n)$ is subtracted from the accumulator, as it is not relative to a deleted node on the path anymore, see lines 14 and 15 of Algorithm 31.

Let us see an example of execution. Consider the program of Example 117 and the single example *epidemic*. The BDD of Figure 13.1 (also shown in Figure 13.3) is built and passed to EXPECTATION in the form of a pointer to its root node n_1. After initializing the η counters to 0, GETFORWARD is called with argument n_1. The F table for n_1 is set to 1 since this is the root. Then F is computed for the 0-child, n_2, as $0 + 1 \cdot 0.4 = 0.4$ and n_2 is added to $Nodes(2)$, the set of nodes for the second level. Then F is computed for the 1-child, n_3, as $0 + 1 \cdot 0.6 = 0.6$, and n_3 is added to $Nodes(3)$. At the next iteration of the cycle, level 2 is considered and node n_2 is fetched from $Nodes(2)$. The 0-child is a terminal, so it is skipped, while the 1-child is n_3 and its F value is updated as $0.6 + 0.4 \cdot 0.6 = 0.84$. In the third iteration, node

---

Algorithm 31 Procedure GETBACKWARD: Computation of the backward probability, updating of η and of ς.

1: **function** GETBACKWARD(*node*)
2:     **if** *node* is a terminal **then**
3:         **return** $value(node)$
4:     **else**
5:         let X_{ijk} be $v(node)$
6:         $B(child_0(node)) =$GETBACKWARD$(child_0(node))$
7:         $B(child_1(node)) =$GETBACKWARD$(child_1(node))$
8:         $e^0(node) = F(node) \cdot B(child_0(node)) \cdot (1 - \pi_{ik})$
9:         $e^1(node) = F(node) \cdot B(child_1(node)) \cdot \pi_{ik}$
10:        $\eta^0(i,k) = \eta^0(i,k) + e^0(node)$
11:        $\eta^1(i,k) = \eta^1(i,k) + e^1(node)$
12:        $VSucc = succ(v(node))$ ▷ $succ(X)$ returns the variable following X in the order
13:        $\varsigma(VSucc) = \varsigma(VSucc) + e^0(node) + e^1(node)$
14:        $\varsigma(v(child_0(node))) = \varsigma(v(child_0(node))) - e^0(node)$
15:        $\varsigma(v(child_1(node))) = \varsigma(v(child_1(node))) - e^1(node)$
16:        **return** $B(child_0(node)) \cdot (1 - \pi_{ik}) + B(child_1(node)) \cdot \pi_{ik}$
17:     **end if**
18: **end function**

---

n_3 is fetched but, since its children are leaves, F is not updated. The resulting forward probabilities are shown in Figure 13.3.

Then GETBACKWARD is called on n_1. The function calls GETBACKWARD(n_2) that in turn calls GETBACKWARD(0). This call returns 0 because it is a terminal node. Then GETBACKWARD(n_2) calls GETBACKWARD(n_3) that in turn calls GETBACKWARD(1) and GETBACKWARD(0), returning respectively 1 and 0. Then GETBACKWARD(n_3) computes $e^0(n_3)$ and $e^1(n_3)$ in the following way:

$e^0(n_3) = F(n_3) \cdot B(0) \cdot (1 - \pi_{21}) = 0.84 \cdot 0 \cdot 0.3 = 0$
$e^1(n_3) = F(n_3) \cdot B(1) \cdot \pi_{21} = 0.84 \cdot 1 \cdot 0.7 = 0.588$. Now the counters for clause C_2 are updated:

$\eta^0(2,1) = 0$
$\eta^1(2,1) = 0.588$

while we do not show the update of ς since its value for the level of the leaves is not used afterward. GETBACKWARD(n_3) now returns the backward probability of n_3 $B(n_3) = 1 \cdot 0.7 + 0 \cdot 0.3 = 0.7$. GETBACKWARD$(n_2)$ can proceed to compute

$e^0(n_2) = F(n_2) \cdot B(0) \cdot (1 - \pi_{11}) = 0.4 \cdot 0.0 \cdot 0.4 = 0$
$e^1(n_2) = F(n_2) \cdot B(n_3) \cdot \pi_{11} = 0.4 \cdot 0.7 \cdot 0.6 = 0.168$,

and $\eta^0(1,1) = 0$, $\eta^1(1,1) = 0.168$. The variable following X_{121} is X_{211}, so $\varsigma(X_{211}) = e^0(n_2) + e^1(n_2) = 0 + 0.168 = 0.168$. Since X_{121} is also

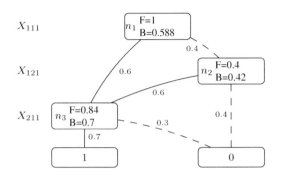

Figure 13.3 Forward and backward probabilities. F indicates the forward probability and B the backward probability of each node. From [Bellodi and Riguzzi, 2013].

associated with the 1-child n_2, then $\varsigma(X_{211}) = \varsigma(X_{211}) - e^1(n_2) = 0$. The 0-child is a leaf so ς is not updated.

GETBACKWARD(n_2) then returns $B(n_2) = 0.7 \cdot 0.6 + 0 \cdot 0.4 = 0.42$ to GETBACKWARD(n_1) that computes $e^0(n_1)$ and $e^1(n_1)$ as

$$e^0(n_1) = F(n_1) \cdot B(n_2) \cdot (1 - \pi_{11}) = 1 \cdot 0.42 \cdot 0.4 = 0.168$$
$$e^1(n_1) = F(n_1) \cdot B(n_3) \cdot \pi_{11} = 1 \cdot 0.7 \cdot 0.6 = 0.42$$

and updates the η counters as $\eta^0(1,1) = 0.168$, $\eta^1(1,1) = 0.168 + 0.42 = 0.588$.

Finally, ς is updated:

$$\varsigma(X_{121}) = e^0(n_1) + e^1(n_1) = 0.168 + 0.42 = 0.588$$
$$\varsigma(X_{121}) = \varsigma(X_{121}) - e^0(n_1) = 0.42$$
$$\varsigma(X_{211}) = \varsigma(X_{211}) - e^1(n_1) = -0.42$$

GETBACKWARD(n_1) returns $B(n_1) = 0.7 \cdot 0.6 + 0.42 \cdot 0.4 = 0.588$ to EXPECTATION, that adds the contribution of deleted nodes by cycling over the BDD levels and updating T. Initially, T is set to 0, and then, for variable X_{111}, T is updated to $T = \varsigma(X_{111}) = 0$ which implies no modification of $\eta^0(1,1)$ and $\eta^1(1,1)$. For variable X_{121}, T is updated to $T = 0 + \varsigma(X_{121}) = 0.42$ and the η table is modified as

$$\eta^0(1,1) = 0.168 + 0.42 \cdot 0.4 = 0.336$$
$$\eta^1(1,1) = 0.588 + 0.42 \cdot 0.6 = 0.84$$

For variable X_{211}, T becomes $0.42 + \varsigma(X_{211}) = 0$, so $\eta^0(2,1)$ and $\eta^1(2,1)$ are not updated. At this point, the expected counts for the two rules can be computed

$$\mathbf{E}[c_{110}] = 0 + 0.336/0.588 = 0.5714285714$$

$$\mathbf{E}[c_{111}] = 0 + 0.84/0.588 = 1.4285714286$$
$$\mathbf{E}[c_{210}] = 0 + 0/0.588 = 0$$
$$\mathbf{E}[c_{211}] = 0 + 0.588/0.588 = 1$$

13.5 ProbLog2 Parameter Learning

ProbLog2 [Fierens et al., 2015] includes the algorithm LFI-ProbLog [Gutmann et al., 2011b] that learns the parameters of ProbLog programs from partial interpretations.

Partial interpretations are three valued interpretations: they specify the truth value of some but not necessarily all ground atoms. A partial interpretation $\mathcal{I} = \langle I_T, I_F \rangle$ states that the atoms in I_T are true and those in I_F are false. A partial interpretation $\mathcal{I} = \langle I_T, I_F \rangle$ can be associated with a conjunction $q(\mathcal{I}) = \bigwedge_{a \in I_T} \wedge \bigwedge_{a \in I_F} \sim a$.

Definition 65 (LFI-ProbLog learning problem). *Given a ProbLog program $\mathcal{P}$ with unknown parameters and a set $E = \{\mathcal{I}_1, \ldots, \mathcal{I}_T\}$ of partial interpretations (the examples), find the value of the parameters $\mathbf{\Pi}$ of $\mathcal{P}$ that maximize the likelihood of the examples, i.e., solve*

$$\arg\max_{\mathbf{\Pi}} P(E) = \arg\max_{\mathbf{\Pi}} \prod_{t=1}^{T} P(q(\mathcal{I}_t))$$

If all interpretations in E are total and the clauses that share an atom in the head have mutually exclusive bodies, then Theorem 21 can be applied and the parameters can be computed by relative frequency, see Section 13.2. If some interpretations in E are partial or bodies are not mutually exclusive, instead, an EM algorithm must be used that is similar to the one used by PRISM and EMBLEM.

LFI-ProbLog generates a d-DNNF circuit for each partial interpretation $\mathcal{I} = \langle I_T, I_F \rangle$ by using the ProbLog2 algorithm of Section 8.7 with the evidence $q(\mathcal{I})$.

Then it associates a Boolean random variable X_{ij} with each ground probabilistic fact $f_i\theta_j$. For each example $\mathcal{I}$, variable X_{ij}, and $x \in \{0, 1\}$, LFI-ProbLog computes $P(X_{ij} = x|\mathcal{I})$. Then it uses this to compute $\mathbf{E}[c_{ix}|\mathcal{I}]$, the expected value given example $\mathcal{I}$ of the number of times variable X_{ij} takes value x for any j in $g(i)$, the set of grounding substitutions of f_i. $\mathbf{E}[c_{ix}]$ is the expected value given all the examples. As in PRISM and EMBLEM, these are given by:

$$\mathbf{E}[c_{ix}] = \sum_{t=1}^{T} \mathbf{E}[c_{ix}|\mathcal{I}_t]$$

and

$$\mathbf{E}[c_{ix}|\mathcal{I}_t] = \sum_{j \in g(i)} P(X_{ij} = x|\mathcal{I}_t).$$

In the maximization phase, the parameter π_i of probabilistic fact f_i can be computed as

$$\pi_i = \frac{\mathbf{E}[c_{i1}]}{\mathbf{E}[c_{i0}] + \mathbf{E}[c_{i1}]}$$

LFI-ProbLog computes $P(X_{ij} = x|\mathcal{I})$ by computing $P(X_{ij} = x, \mathcal{I})$ using Procedure CIRCP shown in Algorithm 7: the d-DNNF circuit is visited twice, once bottom up to compute $P(q(\mathcal{I}))$ and once top down to compute $P(X_{ij} = x, \mathcal{I})$ for all the variables X_{ij} and values x. Then $P(X_{ij} = x|\mathcal{I})$ is given by $\frac{P(X_{ij} = x, \mathcal{I})}{P(\mathcal{I})}$.

Nishino et al. [2014] extended LFI-ProbLog in order to perform sparse parameter learning, i.e., parameter learning while trying to reduce the number of parameters different from 0 or 1, in order to obtain a simpler program. To do so, they add a penalty term to the objective function and use gradient descent to optimize the parameters.

13.6 Parameter Learning for Hybrid Programs

Gutmann [2011] proposes an approach for learning the parameters of hybrid ProbLog programs that is based on the LeProbLog algorithm described in Section 13.3. In particular, Gutmann [2011] shows how the gradient of the objective function can also be computed for hybrid ProbLog programs.

Islam [2012]; Islam et al. [2012a] present a parameter learning algorithm for Extended PRISM. The algorithm is based on PRISM's EM procedure and involves the computation of the Expected sufficient statistics (ESS) of the random variables. The ESS for discrete random variables are represented by a tuple of the expected counts of each values of the variable.

The ESS of a Gaussian random variable X are the triple

$$(ESS^X, ESS^{X^2}, ESS^{count})$$

where the components denote the expected sum, expected sum of squares, and the expected number of uses of random variable X, respectively.

ESS can be computed by deriving examples individually. A quicker approach consists in building a symbolic derivation, computing ESS functions instead of plain ESS, and then applying them to each example. The derivation of ESS functions is similar to the one of success functions for Extended PRISM discussed in Section 12.1.

13.7 DeepProbLog

DeepProbLog [Manhaeve et al., 2018, 2021] combines ProbLog with Neural networks (NNs) and is an instance of neuro-symbolic integration, a recent approach that aims to combine the advantages of symbolic reasoning with those of connectionist methods [d'Avila Garcez et al., 2019].

In fact, NNs, and Deep Learning [Goodfellow et al., 2016] in particular, excel at low-level perception, being able to deal with images, text and speech with high accuracy, while systems employing logic and probability perform complex symbol manipulation and high-level reasoning. Combining the two approaches would thus allow the exploitation of the benefits of both.

The approach taken by DeepProbLog for such an integration is to minimally modify ProbLog in order accomodate NNs that return a probability distribution over a finite set: the output of NNs is used to assign probability values to atoms. DeepProbLog has the interesting feature that it retains the three reasoning mechanisms, NNs, graphical models and logic programming, as special cases. Let us illustrate the idea with an example.

Example 118 (Sum of handwritten digits). *Consider the problem of predicting the sum of two handwritten digits: we are given two images, each containing a handwritten digit, and we want to infer their sum. For example, the images of handwritten digits could be taken from the famous MNIST dataset [LeCun, 1998].*

Using machine learning, we can solve this problem by giving to the machine learning system a dataset composed by pairs of digit images and a label which is an integer between 0 and 18. The system will then extract a model for classifying pairs of digits into one of 19 classes.

Deep Learning can be applied to this problem by using a network that takes as input the two images and classifies them into 19 classes. However, a Deep Learning system cannot incorporate background information regarding the addition operation, that can be used to guide learning.

In DeepProbLog you could have a predicate $addition(X, Y, Z)$, where X and Y are representation of images of digits and Z is an integer between 0 *and 18 corresponding to the sum of these digits. Examples then take the form of atoms like* $addition(\boxed{3}, \boxed{5}, 8)$. *The background knowledge on addition is expressed by a rule of the form*

$addition(I_X, I_Y, N_Z) \leftarrow digit(I_X, N_X), digit(I_Y, N_Y), N_Z$ *is* $N_X + N_Y$.

where $digit/2$ *is a predicate to be learned based on a NN (a neural predicate) that maps the image of a digit* I_D *to the corresponding natural number* N_D.

This approach improves over a NN classifier in terms of speed of convergence and of accuracy of the model because the NN needs to learn making a decision for the pair of input digits (and there are 100 different possible pairs), whereas the DeepProbLog's neural predicate only needs to recognize individual digits (with only 10 possibilities).

Moreover, the $digit/2$ *neural single digit classifier can be reused for further tasks such as addition of multi-digit numbers without further training.*

Let us now illustrate the DeepProbLog language that is based on neural annotated disjunctions.

Definition 66 (Neural annotated disjunction). *A* Neural annotated disjunction (NAD) *has the form*

$nn(m_r, \boldsymbol{I}, O, \boldsymbol{d}) :: r(\boldsymbol{I}, O).$

where nn *is a reserved predicate,* m_r *identifies a NN with* k *inputs and* n *outputs defining a probability distribution over* n *classes,* $\boldsymbol{I} = I_1, ..., I_k$ *is a sequence of input variables for the NN, O is the output variable,* $\boldsymbol{d} = d_1, ..., d_n$ *is a sequence of ground terms (the classes of the NN) and* r *is a predicate, the* neural predicate.

A ground NAD *has the form*

$nn(m_r, \boldsymbol{i}, d_1) :: r(\boldsymbol{i}, d_1) \; ; \; ... \; ; \; nn(m_r, \boldsymbol{i}, d_n) :: r(\boldsymbol{i}, d_n).$

where $\boldsymbol{i} = i_1, ..., i_k$ *is a sequence of ground terms (the input to the NN) and* $d_1, ..., d_n$ *are ground terms (the classes of this NN).*

The $nn(m_r, \boldsymbol{i}, d_j)$ term in a ground NAD can be seen as a function that returns the probability of class d_j when evaluating the network m_r on input $\boldsymbol{i}$. Therefore, from a ground NAD, a normal AD can be obtained by evaluating the NN and replacing the term with the computed probability. This normal AD is called the *instantiated NAD* of the ground NAD. For example, in the digit addition case, we could have the NAD

$nn(m\_digit, [X], Y, [0, \dots, 9]) :: digit(X, Y).$

where m_digit is a network that classifies single digits. To generate the grounding we consider input image $\boxed{3}$ and obtain the ground NAD:

$nn(m\_digit, [\boxed{3}], 0) :: digit(\boxed{3}, 0) ; \ldots ;$
$nn(m\_digit, [\boxed{3}], 9) :: digit(\boxed{3}, 9).$

Evaluating this would result in the instantiated NAD:

$p_0 :: digit(\boxed{3}, 0) ; \ldots ; p_9 :: digit(\boxed{3}, 9).$

where $[p_0, \ldots, p_9]$ is the output vector of the m_digit network when evaluated on $\boxed{3}$.

There is no constraint on the type of NN except that its output layer returns a probability distribution. So the NN could be convolutional, recurrent, ...

Definition 67 (DeepProbLog program). *A DeepProbLog program is composed of a set of probabilistic facts $\mathcal{F}$, a set of NADs and a set of rules $\mathcal{R}$.*

From a DeepProbLog program, a ground DeepProbLog program can be obtained by grounding probabilistic and NADs. By instantiating the ground NADs we get a regular ProbLog program. The semantics of the DeepProgLog program is the one of this ProbLog program,

13.7.1 DeepProbLog inference

A strategy similar to the one of ProbLog2 is used to perform inference in DeepProbLog: the program is first grounded with respect to the query. Then the ground NADs are obtained from NADs and ground NADs are instantiated by making a forward pass on the NNs with the ground input. At this point, a ground ProbLog programs is obtained and inference can proceed as in ProbLog2: the program is rewritten into a propositional formula, the formula is compiled and transformed into an arithmetic circuit and the circuit is evaluated to compute the probability.

Example 119 (DeepProbLog program for the sum of handwritten digits [Manhaeve et al., 2021]). *Consider the MNIST addition problem of Example 118. The DeepProbLog program for the problem is*

```
nn(m_digit, [X], Y, [0...9]) :: digit(X,Y).
addition(X,Y,Z) :- digit(X,N1), digit(Y,N2), Z is N1+N2.
```

that includes a NAD and the background rule regarding addition.
Consider the query `addition(`$\boxed{0}$`, `$\boxed{1}$`, 1)`*. Grounding with respect to the query produces the ground DeepProbLog program:*

```
nn(m_digit, [0],0)::digit(0,0);
  nn(m_digit, [0], 1)::digit(0,1).
nn(m_digit, [1],0)::digit(1,0);
```

```
nn(m_digit, [1], 1)::digit(1,1).
addition(0,1,1) :- digit(0,0), digit(1,1).
addition(0,1,1) :- digit(0,1), digit(1,0).
```

As in ProbLog2, only the relevant part of the program is grounded, so in this case only digits 0 and 1 are kept as the larger digits cannot sum to 1. Thus the irrelevant terms (digit(0, 2), ...,digit(0, 9) *and* digit(1, 2), ..., digit(1, 9)) *are removed from the ground NAD.*
   Instantiating the ground NADs into regular ADs could give:

```
0.8 :: digit(0,0); 0.1 :: digit(0,1).
0.2 :: digit(1,0); 0.6 :: digit(1,1).
addition(0,1,1) :- digit(0,0), digit(1,1).
addition(0,1,1) :- digit(0,1), digit(1,0).
```

where the probabilities of the ADs do not sum up to one because of the removal of irrelevant terms, even if the NNs still assigns probability mass to them.

   At this point inference continues as in ProbLog to compute the probability of the query.

13.7.2 Learning in DeepProbLog

Learning in DeepProbLog means finding values for the parameters of the NNs (which we will call neural parameters) and the parameters in the logic program (which we call probabilistic parameters). The same approach of LeProbLog of Section 13.3 is followed: the definition of the learning problem is the one given in Definition 63, where we are given a set E of atoms each annotated with a probability and we want to minimize a loss function such as the mean squared error, where the error is the difference between the probability assigned by the DeepProbLog program to an atom and its probability label.

   Often in DeepProbLog only atoms labeled with probability 1 are given, in this case the aim is to maximize the probability assigned to the atoms, which can be expressed by by minimizing the average negative log likelihood of the atoms

$$\arg\min_{\theta} \mathcal{L} = \arg\min_{\theta} \frac{1}{|E|} \sum_{(q,1)\in E} -\log P_{\theta}(q)$$

where $\mathcal{L}$ is the loss, θ is the vector of all parameters and $P_{\theta}(q)$ is the probability assigned by the DeepProbLog program to the query q.

   Similarly to LeProbLog, gradient descent is used to solve the learning problem, so that the neural and probabilistic parameters can be tuned in an integrated way. The gradient is computed by resorting to aProbLog (see Section 11.3) and AMC (see Section 12.2.2) With respect to probabilistic parameters, the aProbLog approach is basically unchanged.

To tune the neural parameters, we must propagate the gradient to the NNs. We can use the chain rule of derivatives to compute the partial derivative of the loss with respect to a neural parameter θ_k:

$$\frac{d\mathcal{L}}{d\theta_k} = \frac{\partial\mathcal{L}}{\partial P(q)} \sum_i \frac{\partial P(q)}{\partial\hat{p}_i} \frac{\partial\hat{p}_i}{\partial\theta_k}$$

where $P(q)$ is the probability of the output and $\hat{p}$ is the vector of probabilities of an instantiated NAD whose neural network contains θ_k. The terms $\partial\hat{p}_i/\partial\theta_k$ are thus the derivatives of the ith component of the neural network's output with respect to θ_k and can be computed by backpropagation in the network. The terms $\frac{\partial P(q)}{\partial\hat{p}_i}$ instead can be computed by using aProbLog and the gradient semiring.

In Section 11.3 we saw the gradient semiring but there it was restricted to the case of a single parameter to be tuned. We now present the gradient semiring for several parameters. Its elements are tuples $(p, \nabla p)$, where p is a probability and ∇p is the gradient of that probability with respect to $\boldsymbol{\theta}$, the vector composed of all the probabilistic parameters and the concatenations of the vectors of probabilities (outputs of the NN) for the instantiated NADs.

The $\oplus$ and $\otimes$ operations with their neutral elements are a simple generalization of those for the single parameter case:

$$(a_1, \boldsymbol{a_2}) \oplus (b_1, \boldsymbol{b_2}) = (a_1 + b_1, \boldsymbol{a_2} + \boldsymbol{b_2}) \tag{13.3}$$

$$(a_1, \boldsymbol{a_2}) \otimes (b_1, \boldsymbol{b_2}) = (a_1 b_1, b_1 \boldsymbol{a_2} + a_1 \boldsymbol{b_2}) \tag{13.4}$$

$$e^\oplus = (0, \boldsymbol{0}) \tag{13.5}$$

$$e^\otimes = (1, \boldsymbol{0}) \tag{13.6}$$

The labeling function α for probabilistic facts $(p_i) :: f_i$ is

$$\alpha(f_i) = (p_i, \mathbf{e}_i) \tag{13.7}$$

$$\alpha(\sim f_i) = (1 - p_i, -\mathbf{e}_i) \tag{13.8}$$

where the vector $\mathbf{e}_i$ has a 1 in the position corresponding to the ith probabilistic parameter and 0 in all others.

The label for an NAD is:

$$\alpha(f_j) = (\hat{p}_j, \mathbf{e}_j) \tag{13.9}$$

where f_j is $r(\boldsymbol{i}, d_j)$ in a ground NAD $\quad \ldots \quad ; \quad nn(m, \boldsymbol{i}, d_j) :: r(\boldsymbol{i}, d_j) \; ; \; \ldots$ and the vector $\mathbf{e}_j$ has a 1 in the position corresponding to the jth output of the NN of the parameter and 0 in all others.

In the case where different ground NAD correspond to the same neural network, the contributions to the gradient of the different ground NAD are summed.

DeepProbLog has been successfully applied also to the following problems, besides the MNIST addition problem of Example 118 [Manhaeve et al., 2021]:

- addition of lists of MNIST digit images, where we are given two lists of digits and we want to compute the sum of the numbers represented by the lists in base 10;
- program induction, in particular it was used to infer programs in differentiable Forth for addition, sorting and word algebra problems;
- probabilistic programming, where the aim is to recognize when two coins show the same face or to predict the probability of winning in a simplified poker game from images of cards;
- training embeddings, where DeepProbLog is used to indirectly tune embeddings for images using soft unification;
- compositional language understanding, where the aim is to extract logical facts from natural language sentences.

14

Structure Learning

The techniques presented in this chapter aim at inducing whole programs from data, including both their structure and parameters.

We first briefly review some concepts from Inductive logic programming and then discuss systems for Probabilistic inductive logic programming (PILP) [De Raedt et al., 2008; Riguzzi et al., 2014].

14.1 Inductive Logic Programming

The ILP field is concerned with learning logic programs from data. One of the learning problems that is considered is *learning from entailment*.

Definition 68 (Inductive Logic Programming – learning from entailment). *Given two sets $E^+ = \{e_1, \dots, e_T\}$ and $E^- = \{e_{T+1}, \dots, e_Q\}$ of ground atoms (positive and negative examples), a logic program B (background knowledge), and a space of possible programs $\mathcal{H}$ (language bias), find a program $P \in \mathcal{H}$ such that*

- $\forall e \in E^+$, $P \cup B \models e$ *(completeness)*,
- $\forall e \in E^-$, $P \cup B \not\models e$ *(consistency)*,

An example e such that $P \cup B \models e$ is said to be covered. *We also define the following functions*

- $covers(P, e) = true$ *if $B \cup P \models e$,*
- $covers(P, E) = \{e | e \in E, covers(P, e) = true\}$.

The predicates for which we are given examples are called target predicates. *There is often a single target predicate.*

351

Example 120 (ILP problem).   *Suppose we have*

$$E^+ = \{\ father(john, mary), father(david, steve)\ \}$$
$$E^- = \{\ father(kathy, mary), father(john, steve)\ \}$$
$$\begin{aligned} B\ =\ & parent(john, mary), \\ & parent(david, steve), \\ & parent(kathy, mary), \\ & female(kathy), \\ & male(john), \\ & male(david)\ \} \end{aligned}$$

then a solution of the learning from entailment problem is

$$father(X, Y) \leftarrow parent(X, Y), male(X).$$

ILP systems that solve the learning form entailment problem differ in the way they search the program space. They are usually based on two nested loops, an external *covering loop* which adds a clause to the current theory and removes the covered positive examples, and an internal *clause search loop* that searches the space of clause. Examples of ILP systems are FOIL [Quinlan, 1990], mFOIL [Džeroski, 1993], Aleph [Srinivasan, 2007], and Progol [Muggleton, 1995].

The space of clauses is organized in terms of a generality relation that directs the search. A clause C is *more general* than D if $covers(\{C\}, U) \supseteq covers(\{D\}, U)$ where U is the set of all ground atoms built over target predicates. If $B, \{C\} \models D$, then C is more general than D because $B, \{D\} \models e$ implies $B, \{C\} \models e$. However, entailment is semi-decidable, so simpler generality relations are used in practice. The one most used is θ-subsumption: C θ-*subsumes* D ($C \geqslant D$) if there exists a substitution θ such that $C\theta \subseteq D$ [Plotkin, 1970], where the clauses are intended as sets of literals. If $C \geqslant D$, then $C \models D$, so C is more general than D. However, the opposite is not true in general, i.e., $C \geqslant D \nRightarrow C \models D$. While θ-subsumption is not equivalent to entailment, it is decidable (even if NP-complete), so it is chosen as the generality relation in practice.

Example 121 (Examples of theta subsumption).   *Let*

$$\begin{aligned} C_1\ &=\ father(X, Y) \leftarrow parent(X, Y) \\ C_2\ &=\ father(X, Y) \leftarrow parent(X, Y), male(X) \\ C_3\ &=\ father(john, steve) \leftarrow parent(john, steve), male(john) \end{aligned}$$

Then

- $C_1 \geqslant C_2$ with $\theta = \varnothing$;
- $C_1 \geqslant C_3$ with $\theta = \{X/john, Y/steve\}$;
- $C_2 \geqslant C_3$ with $\theta = \{X/john, Y/steve\}$.

ILP systems differ in the direction of search in the space of clauses ordered by generality: top-down systems search the space from more general clauses to less general ones and bottom-up systems do the opposite. Aleph and Progol are examples of top-down systems. In top-down systems, the clause search loop consists of gradually specializing clauses using heuristics to guide the search, for example, by using *beam search*. Clause specializations are obtained by applying a *refinement operator* ρ that, given a clause C, returns a set of its specializations, i.e., $\rho(C) \subseteq \{D|D \in \mathcal{L}, C \geqslant D\}$ where $\mathcal{L}$ is the space of possible clauses that is described by the *language bias*. A refinement operator usually generates only minimal specializations and typically applies two syntactic operations:

- a substitution, or
- the addition of a literal to the body.

In Progol, for example, the refinement operator adds a literal from the *bottom clause* $\perp$ after having replaced some of the constants with variables. $\perp$ is the most specific clause covering an example e, i.e., $\perp = e \leftarrow B_e$, where B_e is set of ground literals that are true regarding example e that are allowed by the language bias. In this way, we are sure that, at all times during the search, the refinements at least cover example e, that can be selected at random from the set of positive examples.

In turn, the language bias is expressed in Progol by means of *mode* declarations. Following [Muggleton, 1995], a mode declaration m is either a head declaration $modeh(r, s)$ or a body declaration $modeb(r, s)$, where s, the *schema*, is a ground literal and r is an integer called the *recall*. A schema is a template for literals in the head or body of a clause and can contain special placemarker terms of the form $\#type$, $+type$, and $-type$, which stand, respectively, for ground terms, input variables, and output variables of a type. An input variable in a body literal of a clause must be either an input variable in the head or an output variable in a preceding body literal in the clause. If M is a set of mode declarations, $\mathcal{L}(M)$ is the *language of* M, i.e., the set of clauses $\{C = h \leftarrow b_1, \ldots, b_m\}$ such that the head atom h (resp. body literals b_i) is obtained from some head (resp. body) declaration in M by replacing all $\#$ placemarkers with ground terms and all $+$ (resp. $-$) placemarkers with input (resp. output) variables.

The bottom clause is built with a procedure called *saturation*, shown in Algorithm 32. This method is a deductive procedure used to find atoms related to e.

Suppose $modeh(r, s)$ is a head declaration such that e is an answer for the goal $schema(s)$, where $schema(s)$ denotes the literal obtained from s by replacing all placemarkers with distinct variables $X_1, \ldots, X_n$. The terms in e are used to initialize a growing set of input terms *InTerms*: these are the terms corresponding to $+$ placemarkers in s. Then each body declaration m is considered in turn. The terms from *InTerms* are substituted into the $+$ placemarkers of m to generate a set Q of goals. Each goal is then executed against the database and up to r (the recall) successful ground instances (or all if $r = \star$) are added to the body of the clause. Any term corresponding to a $-$ placemarker in m is inserted in *InTerms* if it is not already present. This cycle is repeated for an user-defined number NS of times.

The resulting ground clause $\perp = e \leftarrow b_1, \ldots, b_m$ is then processed to obtain a program clause by replacing each term in a $+$ or $-$ placemarker with a variable, using the same variable for identical terms. Terms corresponding to $\#$ placemarkers are instead kept in the clause.

Example 122 (Bottom clause example). *Consider the learning problem of Example 120 and the language bias*

$\quad modeh(father(+person, +person)).$
$\quad modeb(parent(+person, -person)).$
$\quad modeb(parent(\#person, +person)).$
$\quad modeb(male(+person)).$
$\quad modeb(female(\#person)).$

then the bottom clause for $father(john, mary)$ is

$\quad father(john, mary) \leftarrow parent(john, mary), male(john),$
$\quad\quad parent(kathy, mary), female(kathy).$

After replacing constants with variables we get

$\quad father(X, Y) \leftarrow parent(X, Y), male(X), parent(kathy, Y),$
$\quad\quad female(kathy).$

14.2 LLPAD and ALLPAD Structure Learning

LLPAD [Riguzzi, 2004] and ALLPAD [Riguzzi, 2007b, 2008b] were two early systems for performing structure learning. They learned ground LPADs

---

Algorithm 32 Function SATURATION.

```
1:  function SATURATION(e, NS)
2:      for all types t do
3:          InTerms(t) = ∅
4:      end for
5:      ⊥ = ∅                                                    ▷ ⊥: bottom clause
6:      let modeh(r, s) be a mode declaration where schema(s) unifies with e
7:      for all arguments t of e do
8:          if t corresponds to a +type in modeh(r, s) then
9:              add t to InTerms(type)
10:         end if
11:     end for
12:     let ⊥'s head be e
13:     repeat
14:         Steps ← 1
15:         for all modeb declarations modeb(r, s) do
16:             for all possible subs. σ of variables corresponding to +type in schema(s) by terms from
            InTerms(type) do
17:                 for j = 1 → r do
18:                     if goal b = schema(s)σ succeeds with answer substitution σ' then
19:                         for all V/t ∈ σ' do
20:                             if V corresponds to a −type then
21:                                 add t to the set InTerms(type) if not already present
22:                             end if
23:                         end for
24:                         Add b to ⊥'s body
25:                     end if
26:                 end for
27:             end for
28:         end for
29:         Steps ← Steps + 1
30:     until Steps > NS
31:     replace constants with variables in ⊥, using the same variable for identical terms
32:     return ⊥
33: end function
```

---

from interpretations. We discussed parameter learning in Section 13.2; we consider here the problem of learning the structure.

Definition 69 (ALLPAD Structure learning problem). *Given a set*

$$E = \{(I, p_I)|I \in Int2, p_I \in [0, 1]\}$$

such that $\sum_{(I,p_I)\in E} p_I = 1$, *and a space of possible programs* $\mathcal{S}$, *find an LPAD* $\mathcal{P} \in \mathcal{S}$ *such that*

$$Err = \sum_{(I,p_I)\in E} |P(I) - p_I|$$

is minimized, where $P(I)$ *is the probability assigned by* $\mathcal{P}$ *to* I.

As for parameter learning, E may also be given as a multiset E' of interpretations.

LLPAD and ALLPAD learn ground programs satisfying the exclusive-or assumption, so each pair of clauses that share an atom in the head have mutually exclusive bodies, i.e., not both true in the same interpretation from $\mathcal{I}$.

The systems perform learning in three phases: they first find a set of clause structures satisfying some constraints, then compute the annotations of head atoms of such clauses using Theorem 21, and finally solve a constraint optimization problem for selecting a subset of clauses to include in the solution.

The first phase can be cast in the framework proposed by [Stolle et al., 2005] in which the problem of descriptive ILP is seen as the problem of finding all the clauses in the language bias that satisfy a number of constraints. Exploiting the properties of constraints, the search in the space of clauses can be usefully pruned.

A constraint is *monotonic* if it is the case that when a clause does not satisfy it, none of its generalizations (in the θ-subsumption generalization order) satisfy it. A constraint is *anti-monotonic* if it is the case that when a clause does not satisfy it, none of its specializations satisfy it.

The first phase can be formulated in this way: find all the disjunctive clauses that satisfy the following constraints:

C1 have their body true in at least one interpretation;
C2 are satisfied in all the interpretations;
C3 their atoms in the head are mutually exclusive over the set of interpretations where the body is true (i.e., no two head atoms are both true in an interpretation where the body is true);
C4 they have no redundant head atom, i.e., no head atom that is false in all the interpretations where the body is true.

The systems search the space of disjunctive clauses by first searching depth-first and top-down for bodies true in at least one interpretation and then, for each such body, searching for a head satisfying the remaining constraints. When a body is found that is true in zero interpretations, the search along that branch is stopped (constraint C1 is anti-monotonic).

The systems employ bottom-up search in the space of heads, exploiting the monotonic constraint C2 that requires the clause to be true in all the interpretations for pruning the search.

The second phase is performed using Theorem 21: given a ground clause generated by the second phase, the probabilities of head atoms are given by the conditional probability of the head atoms given the body according to the distribution p_I.

In the third phase, the systems associate a Boolean decision variable with each of the clauses found in the first phase. Thanks to the exclusive-or assumption, the probability of each interpretation can be expressed as a function of the decision variables, so we set Err as the objective function of an optimization problem. The exclusive-or assumption is enforced by imposing constraints among pairs of decisions.

Both the constraints and the objective function are linear, so we can use mixed-integer programming techniques.

The restriction to ground programs satisfying the exclusive-or assumption limits the applicability of LLPAD and ALLPAD in practice.

14.3 ProbLog Theory Compression

De Raedt et al. [2008] consider the problem of compressing a ProbLog theory given a set of positive and negative examples. The problem can be defined as follows.

Definition 70 (Theory compression). *Given a ProbLog program $\mathcal{P}$ containing the set of probabilistic facts $\mathcal{F} = \{\Pi_1 :: f_1, \ldots, \Pi_n :: f_n\}$, two sets $E^+ = \{e_1, \ldots, e_T\}$ and $E^- = \{e_{T+1}, \ldots, e_Q\}$ of ground atoms (positive and negative examples), and a constant $k \in \mathbb{N}$, find a subset of the probabilistic facts $\mathcal{G} \subseteq \mathcal{F}$ of size at most k (i.e., $|\mathcal{G}| \leq k$) that maximizes the likelihood of the examples, i.e., solve*

$$\underset{\mathcal{G} \subseteq \mathcal{F}, |\mathcal{G}| \leq k}{\arg\max} \prod_{i=1}^{T} P(e_i) \prod_{i=T+1}^{Q} P(\sim e_i)$$

The aim is to modify the theory by removing clauses in order to maximize the likelihood of the examples. This is an instance of a *theory revision* process. However, in case an example has probability 0, the whole likelihood would be 0. To be able to consider also this case, $P(e)$ is replaced by $\hat{P}(e) = \min(\epsilon, P(e))$ for a small user-defined constant ϵ.

The ProbLog compression algorithm of [De Raedt et al., 2008] proceeds by greedily removing one probabilistic fact at a time from the theory. The fact is chosen as the one whose removal results in the largest likelihood increase. The algorithm continues removing facts if there are more than k of them and there is a fact whose removal can improve the likelihood.

The algorithm first builds the BDDs for all the examples. Then it enters the removal cycle. Computing the effect of the removal of a probabilistic fact f_i on the probability of an example is easy: it is enough to set Π_i to 0 and re-evaluate the BDD using function PROB of Algorithm 6. The value of the root will be the updated probability of the example. Computing the likelihood after the removal of a probabilistic fact is thus quick, as the expensive construction of the BDDs does not have to be redone.

14.4 ProbFOIL and ProbFOIL+

ProbFOIL [De Raedt and Thon, 2011] and ProbFOIL+ [Raedt et al., 2015] learn rules from probabilistic examples. The learning problem they consider is defined as follows.

Definition 71 (ProbFOIL/ProbFoil+ learning problem [Raedt et al., 2015]). *Given*

1. *a set of training examples $E = \{(e_1, p_1), \ldots, (e_T, p_T)\}$ where each e_i is a ground fact for a target predicate;*
2. *a background theory $\mathcal{B}$ containing information about the examples in the form of a ProbLog program;*
3. *a space of possible clauses $\mathcal{L}$.*

find a hypothesis $H \subseteq \mathcal{L}$ so that the absolute error $AE = \sum_{i=1}^{T} |P(e_i) - p_i|$ is minimized, i.e.,

$$\underset{H \subseteq \mathcal{L}}{\arg\min} \sum_{i=1}^{T} |P(e_i) - p_i|$$

The difference between ProbFOIL and ProbFOIL+ is that in ProbFOIL the clauses in H are definite, i.e., of the form $h \leftarrow B$, while in ProbFOIL+ they are probabilistic, i.e., of the form $x :: h \leftarrow B$, with $x \in [0, 1]$. Such rules are to be interpreted as the combination of

$$h \leftarrow B, prob(id).$$
$$x :: prob(id).$$

where id is an identifier of the rule and $x :: prob(id)$ is a ground probabilistic fact associated with the rule. Note that this is different from an LPAD rule of the form $h : x \leftarrow B$, as this stands for the union of ground rules $h' : x \leftarrow B'$. obtained by grounding $h : x \leftarrow B$. So LPAD rules generate an independent random variable for each of their groundings, while the above

ProbFOIL+ rule generates a single random variable independently on the number of groundings.

ProbFOIL+ generalizes the mFOIL system [Džeroski, 1993], itself a generalization of FOIL [Quinlan, 1990]. It adopts the standard technique for learning sets of rules consisting of a covering loop in which one rule is added to the theory at each iteration. A nested clause search loop builds the rule by iteratively adding literals to the body of the rule. The covering loop ends when a condition based on a global scoring function is satisfied. The construction of single rules is performed by means of beam search as in mFOIL and uses a local scoring function as the heuristic. Algorithm 33 shows the overall approach[1].

Algorithm 33 Function PROBFOIL+.

```
 1:  function PROBFOIL+(target)
 2:      H ← ∅
 3:      while true do
 4:          clause ← LEARNRULE(H, target)
 5:          if GSCORE(H) < GSCORE(H ∪ {clause}) ∧ SIGNIFICANT(H, clause) then
 6:              H ← H ∪ {clause}
 7:          else
 8:              return H
 9:          end if
10:      end while
11:  end function
12:  function LEARNRULE(H, target)
13:      candidates ← {x :: target ← true}
14:      best ← (x :: target ← true)
15:      while candidates ≠ ∅ do
16:          next_cand ← ∅
17:          for all x :: target ← body ∈ candidates do
18:              for all (target ← body, refinement) ∈ ρ(target ← body) do
19:                  if not REJECT(H, best, (x :: target ← body, refinement)) then
20:                      next_cand ← next_cand ∪ {(x :: target ← body, refinement)}
21:                      if LSCORE(H, (x :: target ← body, refinement)) > LSCORE(H, best) then
22:                          best ← (x :: target ← body, refinement)
23:                      end if
24:                  end if
25:              end for
26:          end for
27:          candidates ← next_cand
28:      end while
29:      return best
30:  end function
```

---

[1] The description of ProbFOIL+ is based on [Raedt et al., 2015] and the code at https: //bitbucket.org/antondries/prob2foil

The global scoring function is the accuracy over the dataset, given by

$$accuracy_H = \frac{TP_H + TN_H}{T}$$

where T is the number of examples and TP_H and TN_H are, respectively, the number of *true positives* and of *true negatives*, i.e., the number of positive (negative) examples correctly classified as positive (negative).

The local scoring function is an *m-estimate* [Mitchell, 1997] of the *precision*, or the probability that an example is positive given that it is covered by the rule:

$$m\text{-}estimate_H = \frac{TP_H + m\frac{P}{P+N}}{TP_H + FP_H + m}$$

where m is a parameter of the algorithm, FP_H is the number of *false positives* (negative examples classified as positive), and P and N indicate the number of positive and negative examples in the dataset, respectively.

These measures are based on usual metrics for rule learning that assume that the training set is composed of positive and negative examples and that classification is sharp. ProbFOIL+ generalizes this settings as each example e_i is associated with a probability p_i. The deterministic setting is obtained by having $p_i = 1$ for positive examples and $p_i = 0$ for negative examples. In the probabilistic setting, we can see an example (e_i, p_i) as contributing a part p_i to the positive part of training set and $1 - p_i$ to the negative part. So in this case, $P = \sum_{i=1}^{T} p_i$ and $N = \sum_{i=1}^{T}(1 - p_i)$. Similarly, prediction is generalized: the hypothesis H assigns a probability $p_{H,i}$ to each example e_i, instead of simply saying that the example is positive ($p_{H,i} = 1$) or negative ($p_{H,i} = 0$). The number of true positive and true negatives can be generalized as well. The contribution $tp_{H,i}$ of example e_i to TP_H will be $p_{H,i}$ if $p_i > p_{H,i}$ and p_i otherwise, because if $p_i < p_{H,i}$, the hypothesis is overestimating e_i. The contribution $fp_{H,i}$ of example e_i to FP_H will be $p_{H,i} - p_i$ if $p_i < p_{H,i}$ and 0 otherwise, because if $p_i > p_{H,i}$ the hypothesis is underestimating e_i. Then $TP_H = \sum_{i=1}^{T} tp_{H,i}$, $FP_H = \sum_{i=1}^{T} fp_{H,i}$, $TN_H = N - FP_H$, and $FN_H = P - TP_H$ as for the deterministic case, where FN_H is the number of *false negatives*, or positive examples classified as negatives.

The function LSCORE($H, x :: C$) computes the local scoring function for the addition of clause $C(x) = x :: C$ to H using the m-estimate. However, the heuristic depends on the value of $x \in [0, 1]$. Thus, the function has to find the value of x that maximizes the score

$$M(x) = \frac{TP_{H \cup C(x)} + mP/T}{TP_{H \cup C(x)} + FP_{H \cup C(x)} + m}.$$

To do so, we need to compute $TP_{H \cup C(x)}$ and $FP_{H \cup C(x)}$ as a function of x. In turn, this requires the computation of $tp_{H \cup C(x),i}$ and $fp_{H \cup C(x),i}$, the contributions of each example.

Note that $p_{H \cup C(x),i}$ is monotonically increasing in x, so the minimum and maximum values are obtained for $x = 0$ and $x = 1$, respectively. Let us call them l_i and u_i, so $l_i = p_{H \cup C(0),i} = p_{H,i}$ and $u_i = p_{H \cup C(1),i}$. Since ProbFOIL differs from ProbFOIL+ only for the use of deterministic clauses instead of probabilistic ones, u_i is the value that is used by ProbFOIL for the computation of $\text{LSCORE}(H, C)$ which thus returns $M(1)$.

In ProbFOIL+, we need to study the dependency of $p_{H \cup C(x),i}$ on x. If the clause is deterministic, it adds probability mass $u_i - l_i$ to $p_{H,i}$. We can imagine the u_i as being the probability that the Boolean formula $F = X_H \lor \neg X_H \land X_B$ takes value 1, with X_H a Boolean variable that is true if H covers the example, $P(X_H) = p_{H,i}$, X_B a Boolean variable that is true if the body of clause C covers the example and $P(\neg X_H \land X_B) = u_i - l_i$. In fact, since the two Boolean terms are mutually exclusive, $P(F) = P(X_H) + P(\neg X_H \land X_B) = p_{H,i} + u_i - p_{H,i} = u_i$. If the clause is probabilistic, its random variable X_C is independent from all the other random variables, so the probability of the example can be computed as the probability that the Boolean function $F' = X_H \lor X_C \land \neg X_H \land X_B$ takes value 1, with $P(X_C) = x$. So $p_{H \cup C(x),i} = P(F') = p_{H,i} + x(u_i - l_i)$ and $p_{H \cup C(x),i}$ is a linear function of x.

We can isolate the contribution of $C(x)$ to $tp_{H \cup C(x),i}$ and $fp_{H \cup C(x),i}$ as follows:

$$tp_{H \cup C(x),i} = tp_{H,i} + tp_{C(x),i} \quad fp_{H \cup C(x),i} = fp_{H,i} + fp_{C(x),i}$$

Then the examples can be grouped into three sets:

$E_1 : p_i \leqslant l_i$, the clause overestimates the example independently of the value of x, so $tp_{C(x),i} = 0$ and $fp_{C(x),i} = x(u_i - l_i)$

$E_2 : p_i \geqslant u_i$, the clause underestimates the example independently of the value of x, so $tp_{C(x),i} = x(u_i - l_i)$ and $fp_{C(x),i} = 0$

$E_3 : l_i \leqslant p_i \leqslant u_i$, there is a value of x for which the clause predicts the correct probability for the example. This value is obtained by solving $x(u_i - l_i) = p_i - l_i$ for x, so

$$x_i = \frac{p_i - l_i}{u_i - l_i}$$

For $x \leqslant x_i$, $tp_{C(x),i} = x(u_i - l_i)$ and $fp_{C(x),i} = 0$. For $x > x_i$, $tp_{C(x),i} = p_i - l_i$ and $fp_{C(x),i} = x(u_i - l_i) - (p_i - l_i)$.

We can express $TP_{H \cup C(x)}$ and $FP_{H \cup C(x)}$ as

$$TP_{H \cup C(x)} = TP_H + TP_1(x) + TP_2(x) + TP_3(x)$$

$$FP_{H \cup C(x)} = FP_H + FP_1(x) + FP_2(x) + FP_3(x)$$

where $TP_l(x)$ and $FP_l(x)$ are the contribution of the set of examples E_l. These can be computed as

$$TP_1(x) = 0$$

$$FP_1(x) = x \sum_{i \in E_1} (u_i - l_i) = xU_1$$

$$TP_2(x) = x \sum_{i \in E_2} (u_i - l_i) = xU_2$$

$$FP_2(x) = 0$$

$$TP_3(x) = x \sum_{i : i \in E_3, x \leqslant x_i} (u_i - l_i) + \sum_{i : i \in E_3, x > x_i} (p_i - l_i) = xU_3^{\leqslant x_i} + P_3^{> x_i}$$

$$FP_3(x) = x \sum_{i : i \in E_3, x > x_i} (u_i - l_i) - \sum_{i : i \in E_3, x > x_i} (p_i - l_i) = xU_3^{> x_i} - P_3^{> x_i}$$

By replacing these formulas into $M(x)$, we get

$$M(x) = \frac{(U_2 + U_3^{\leqslant x_i})x + TP_H + P_3^{> x_i} + mP/T}{(U_1 + U_2 + U_3)x + TP_H + FP_H + m}$$

where $U_3 = x \sum_{i \in E_3} (u_i - l_i) = (TP_3(x) + FP_3(x))/x$.

Since $U_3^{\leqslant x_i}$ and $P_3^{> x_i}$ are constant in the interval between two consecutive values of x_i, $M(x)$ is a piecewise function where each piece is of the form

$$\frac{Ax + B}{Cx + D}$$

with $A, B, C,$ and D constants. The derivative of a piece is

$$\frac{dM(x)}{dx} = \frac{AD - BC}{(Cx + D)^2}$$

which is either 0 or different from 0 everywhere in each interval, so the maximum of $M(x)$ can occur only at the x_is values that are the endpoints of the intervals. Therefore, we can compute the value of $M(x)$ for each x_i and pick the maximum. This can be done efficiently by ordering the x_i values and computing $U_3^{\leq x_i} = \sum_{i:i \in E_3, x \leq x_i} (u_i - l_i)$ and $P_3^{> x_i} = \sum_{i:i \in E_3, x > x_i} (p_i - l_i)$ for increasing values of x_i, incrementally updating $U_3^{\leq x_i}$ and $P_3^{> x_i}$.

ProbFOIL+ prunes refinements (line 19 of Algorithm 33) when they cannot lead to a local score higher than the current best, when they cannot lead to a global score higher than the current best or when they are not significant, i.e., when they provide only a limited contribution.

By adding a literal to a clause, the true positives and false positives can only decrease, so we can obtain an upper bound of the local score that any refinement can achieve by setting the false positives to 0 and computing the m-estimate. If this value is smaller than the current best, the refinement is discarded.

By adding a clause to a theory, the true positives and false positives can only increase, so if the number of true positives of $H \cup C(x)$ is not larger than the true positives of H, the refinement $C(x)$ can be discarded.

ProbFOIL+ performs a *significance test* borrowed from mFOIL that is based on the *likelihood ratio statistics*.

ProbFOIL+ computes a statistics $LhR(H, C)$ that takes into account the effect of the addition of C to H on TP and FP so that a clause is discarded if it has limited effect. $LhR(H, C)$ is distributed according to χ^2 with one degree of freedom, so the clause can be discarded if $LhR(H, C)$ is outside the interval for the confidence chosen by the user.

Another system that solves the ProbFOIL learning problem is SkILL [Côrte-Real et al., 2015]. Differently from ProbFOIL, it is based on the ILP system TopLog [Muggleton et al., 2008]. In order to prune the universe of candidate theories and speed up learning, SkILL uses estimates of the predictions of theories [Côrte-Real et al., 2017].

14.5 SLIPCOVER

SLIPCOVER [Bellodi and Riguzzi, 2015] learns LPADs by first identifying good candidate clauses and then by searching for a theory guided by the LL of the data. As EMBLEM (see Section 13.4), it takes as input a set of mega-examples and an indication of which predicates are target, i.e., those for which we want to optimize the predictions of the final theory. The mega-examples must contain positive and negative examples for all predicates that may appear in the head of clauses, either target or non-target (background predicates).

14.5.1 The language bias

The language bias for clauses is expressed by means of *mode* declarations. as in Progol [Muggleton, 1995], see Section 14.1. SLIPCOVER extends this type of mode declarations with placemarker terms of the form $-\#$ which are treated as $\#$ when variabilizing the clause and as $-$ when performing saturation, see Algorithm 32.

SLIPCOVER also allows head declarations of the form

$$modeh(r, [s_1, \ldots, s_n], [a_1, \ldots, a_n], [P_1/Ar_1, \ldots, P_k/Ar_k]).$$

These are used to generate clauses with more than two head atoms: $s_1, \ldots, s_n$ are schemas, $a_1, \ldots, a_n$ are atoms such that a_i is obtained from s_i by replacing placemarkers with variables, and P_i/Ar_i are the predicates admitted in the body. $a_1, \ldots, a_n$ are used to indicate which variables should be shared by the atoms in the head.

Examples of mode declarations can be found in Section 14.5.3.

14.5.2 Description of the algorithm

The main function is shown by Algorithm 34: after the search in the space of clauses, encoded in lines 2–27, SLIPCOVER performs a greedy search in the space of theories, described in lines 28–38.

The first phase aims at finding a set of promising ones (in terms of LL of the data), that will be used in the following greedy search phase. By starting from promising clauses, the greedy search is able to generate good final theories. The search in the space of clauses is split in turn in two steps: (1) the construction of a set of beams containing bottom clauses (function INITIALBEAMS at line 2 of Algorithm 34) and (2) a beam search over each of these beams to refine the bottom clauses (function CLAUSEREFINEMENTS at line 11). The overall output of this search phase is represented by two lists of promising clauses: TC for target predicates and BC for background predicates. The clauses found are inserted either in TC, if a target predicate appears in their head, or in BC. These lists are sorted by decreasing LL.

Algorithm 34 Function SLIPCOVER.

1: **function** SLIPCOVER($NInt, NS, NA, NI, NV, NB, NTC, NBC, D, NEM, \epsilon, \delta$)
2:    $IB =$ INITIALBEAMS($NInt, NS, NA$)   ▷ Clause search
3:    $TC \leftarrow []$
4:    $BC \leftarrow []$
5:    **for all** $(PredSpec, Beam) \in IB$ **do**
6:       $Steps \leftarrow 1$
7:       $NewBeam \leftarrow []$
8:       **repeat**
9:          **while** $Beam$ is not empty **do**
10:            remove the first triple $(Cl, Literals, LL)$ from $Beam$ ▷ Remove the first clause
11:            $Refs \leftarrow$ CLAUSEREFINEMENTS($(Cl, Literals), NV$) ▷ Find all refinements $Refs$
     of $(Cl, Literals)$ with at most NV variables
12:            **for all** $(Cl', Literals') \in Refs$ **do**
13:               $(LL'', \{Cl''\}) \leftarrow$ EMBLEM($\{Cl'\}, D, NEM, \epsilon, \delta$)
14:               $NewBeam \leftarrow$ INSERT($(Cl'', Literals', LL''), NewBeam, NB$)
15:               **if** Cl'' is range-restricted **then**
16:                  **if** Cl'' has a target predicate in the head **then**
17:                     $TC \leftarrow$ INSERT($(Cl'', LL''), TC, NTC$)
18:                  **else**
19:                     $BC \leftarrow$ INSERT($(Cl'', LL''), BC, NBC$)
20:                  **end if**
21:               **end if**
22:            **end for**
23:          **end while**
24:          $Beam \leftarrow NewBeam$
25:          $Steps \leftarrow Steps + 1$
26:       **until** $Steps > NI$
27:    **end for**
28:    $Th \leftarrow \emptyset, ThLL \leftarrow -\infty$ ▷ Theory search
29:    **repeat**
30:       remove the first pair (Cl, LL) from TC
31:       $(LL', Th') \leftarrow$ EMBLEM($Th \cup \{Cl\}, D, NEM, \epsilon, \delta$)
32:       **if** $LL' > ThLL$ **then**
33:          $Th \leftarrow Th', ThLL \leftarrow LL'$
34:       **end if**
35:    **until** TC is empty
36:    $Th \leftarrow Th \bigcup_{(Cl,LL) \in BC} \{Cl\}$
37:    $(LL, Th) \leftarrow$ EMBLEM($Th, D, NEM, \epsilon, \delta$)
38:    **return** Th
39: **end function**

The second phase starts with an empty theory Th which is assigned the lowest value of LL (line 28 of Algorithm 34). Then one target clause Cl at a time is added from the list TC. After each addition, parameter learning with EMBLEM is run on the extended theory $Th \cup \{Cl\}$ and the LL LL' of the data is used as the score of the resulting theory Th'. If LL' is better than the current best, the clause is kept in the theory; otherwise, it is discarded (lines 31–34). This is done for each clause in TC.

Finally, SLIPCOVER adds all the (background) clauses from the list BC to the theory composed of target clauses only (line 36) and performs parameter learning on the resulting theory (line 37). The clauses that are never used to derive the examples will get a value of 0 for the parameters of the atoms in their head and will be removed in a post-processing phase.

In the following, we provide a detailed description of the two support functions for the first phase, the search in the space of clauses.

14.5.2.1 Function INITIALBEAMS

Algorithm 35 shows how the initial set of beams IB, one for each predicate P (with arity Ar) appearing in a modeh declaration, is generated by building a set of bottom clauses as in Progol, see Section 14.1. The algorithm outputs the initial clauses that will be then refined by Function CLAUSEREFINEMENTS.

In order to generate a bottom clause for a mode declaration $modeh(r, s)$ specified in the language bias, an input mega-example I is selected and an answer h for the goal $schema(s)$ is selected (lines 5–9 of Algorithm 35). The mega-example and the atom h are both randomly sampled with replacement, the former from the available set of training mega-examples and the latter from the set of all answers found for the goal $schema(s)$ in the mega-example. Each of these answers represents a positive example.

Then h is saturated using Algorithm 32 modified so that, when a term in an answer substitution (line 20) corresponds to a $-\#type$ argument, it is added to $InTerms$ as for $-type$ arguments. Moreover, when replacing constants with variables, terms corresponding to $-\#$ placemarkers are kept in the clause as for $\#$ placemarker. This is useful when we want to test the equality of the value of an argument with a constant but we also want to retrieve other atoms related to that constant.

The initial beam $Beam$ associated with predicate P/Ar of h contains the clause with empty body $h : 0.5 \leftarrow true$ for each bottom clause of the form $h :- b_1, \ldots, b_m$ (lines 10 and 11 of Algorithm 35). This process is repeated for a number $NInt$ of input mega-examples and a number NA of answers, thus obtaining $NInt \cdot NA$ bottom clauses.

The generation of a bottom clause for a mode declaration
$$m = modeh(r, [s_1, \ldots, s_n], [a_1, \ldots, a_n], [P_1/Ar_1, \ldots, P_k/Ar_k])$$

is the same except for the fact that the goal to call is composed of more than one atom. In order to build the head, the goal $a_1, \ldots, a_n$ is called and NA answers that ground all a_is are kept (lines 15–19). From these, the set of input terms $InTerms$ is built and body literals are found by Function SATURATION (line 20 of Algorithm 35) as above. The resulting bottom clauses then have the form

$$a_1 \; ; \; \ldots \; ; a_n \leftarrow b_1, \ldots, b_m$$

and the initial beam $Beam$ will contain clauses with an empty body of the form

$$a_1 : \frac{1}{n+1} \; ; \; \ldots \; ; a_n : \frac{1}{n+1} \leftarrow true.$$

Finally, the set of the beams for each predicate P is returned to Function SLIPCOVER.

Algorithm 35 Function INITIALBEAMS.

1: **function** INITIALBEAMS($NInt, NS, NA$)
2:     $IB \leftarrow \varnothing$
3:     **for all** predicates P/Ar **do**
4:         $Beam \leftarrow []$
5:         **for all** modeh declarations $modeh(r, s)$ with P/Ar predicate of s **do**
6:             **for** $i = 1 \to NInt$ **do**
7:                 select randomly a mega-example I
8:                 **for** $j = 1 \to NA$ **do**
9:                     select randomly an atom h from I matching $schema(s)$
10:                     bottom clause $BC \leftarrow$ SATURATION(h, NS), let BC be $Head :- Body$
11:                     $Beam \leftarrow [(h : 0.5 \leftarrow true, Body, -\infty)|Beam]$
12:                 **end for**
13:             **end for**
14:         **end for**
15:         **for all** modeh declarations $modeh(r, [s_1, \ldots, s_n], [a_1, \ldots, a_n], PL)$ with P/Ar in PL appearing in $s_1, \ldots, s_n$ **do**
16:             **for** $i = 1 \to NInt$ **do**
17:                 select randomly a mega-example I
18:                 **for** $j = 1 \to NA$ **do**
19:                     select randomly a set of atoms $h_1, \ldots, h_n$ from I matching $a_1, \ldots, a_n$
20:                     bottom clause $BC \leftarrow$ SATURATION($(h_1, \ldots, h_n), NS$), let BC be $Head :- Body$
21:                     $Beam \leftarrow [(a_1 : \frac{1}{n+1} \; ; \; \ldots \; ; a_n : \frac{1}{n+1} \leftarrow true, Body, -\infty)|Beam]$
22:                 **end for**
23:             **end for**
24:         **end for**
25:         $IB \leftarrow IB \cup \{(P/Ar, Beam)\}$
26:     **end for**
27:     **return** IB
28: **end function**

14.5.2.2 Beam search with clause refinements

SLIPCOVER then performs a cycle over each predicate, either target or background (line 5 of Algorithm 34): in each iteration, it runs a beam search in the space of clauses for the predicate (line 9).

For each clause Cl in the beam, with $Literals$ admissible in the body, Function CLAUSEREFINEMENTS, shown in Algorithm 36, computes refinements by adding a literal from $Literals$ to the body or by deleting an atom from the head in the case of multiple-head clauses with a number of disjuncts (including the *null* atom) greater than 2. Furthermore, the refinements must respect the input–output modes of the bias declarations, must be connected (i.e., each body literal must share a variable with the head or a previous body literal), and their number of variables must not exceed a user-defined number NV. The pair $(Cl', Literals')$ indicates a refined clause Cl' together with the new set $Literals'$ of literals allowed in the body of Cl'; the pair $(Cl'_h, Literals)$ indicates a specialized clause Cl' where one disjunct in its head has been removed.

At line 13 of Algorithm 34, parameter learning is performed using EMBLEM, see Section 13.4, on a theory composed of the single refined clause.

This clause is then inserted into a list of promising clauses: either into TC, if a target predicate appears in its head, or into BC. The insertion is in order of decreasing LL. If the clause is not range-restricted, i.e., if some of the variables in the head do not appear in a positive literal in the body, then it is not inserted in TC nor in BC. These lists have a maximum size: if an insertion increases the size over the maximum, the last element is removed. In Algorithm 34, Function INSERT($I, Score, List, N$) is used to insert in order a clause I with score $Score$ in a $List$ with at most N elements. Beam search is repeated until the beam becomes empty or a maximum number NI of iterations is reached.

The separate search for clauses has similarity with the covering loop of ILP systems such as Aleph and Progol. Differently from ILP, however, the test of an example requires the computation of all its explanations, while, in ILP, the search stops at the first successful derivation. The only interaction among clauses in PLP happens if the clauses are recursive. If not, then adding clauses to a theory only adds explanations for the example – increasing its probability – so clauses can be added individually to the theory. If the clauses are recursive, the examples for the head predicates are used to resolve literals in the body; thus, the test of examples on individual clauses approximates the test on a complete theory.

Algorithm 36 Function CLAUSEREFINEMENTS.

```
1:  function CLAUSEREFINEMENTS((Cl, Literals), NV)
2:      Refs = ∅, Nvar = 0;                    ▷ Nvar: number of different variables in a clause
3:      for all b ∈ Literals do
4:          Literals' ← Literals\{b}
5:          add b to Cl body obtaining Cl'
6:          Nvar ← number of Cl' variables
7:          if Cl' is connected ∧ Nvar < NV then
8:              Refs ← Refs ∪ {(Cl', Literals')}
9:          end if
10:     end for
11:     if Cl is a multiple-head clause then      ▷ It has 3 or more disjuncts including the null atom
12:         remove one atom from Cl head obtaining Cl'_h      ▷ Not the null atom
13:         adjust the probabilities on the remaining head atoms
14:         Refs ← Refs ∪ {(Cl'_h, Literals')}
15:     end if
16:     return Refs
17: end function
```

14.5.3 Execution example

We now show an example of execution on the UW-CSE dataset [Kok and Domingos, 2005a] that describes the Computer Science Department of the University of Washington with 22 different predicates, such as advisedby/2, yearsinprogram/2, and taughtby/3. The aim is to predict the predicate advisedby/2, namely, the fact that a person (student) is advised by another person (professor).

The language bias contains *modeh* declarations for two-head clauses such as

```
modeh(*,advisedby(+person,+person)).
```

and *modeh* declarations for multi-head clauses such as

```
modeh(*,[advisedby(+person,+person),
  tempadvisedby(+person,+person)],
  [advisedby(A,B),tempadvisedby(A,B)],
  [professor/1,student/1,hasposition/2,inphase/2,
   publication/2,
  taughtby/3,ta/3,courselevel/2,yearsinprogram/2]).

modeh(*,[student(+person),professor(+person)],
  [student(P),professor(P)],
  [hasposition/2,inphase/2,taughtby/3,ta/3,
   courselevel/2,
```

```
yearsinprogram/2,advisedby/2,tempadvisedby/2]).
```

```
modeh(*,[inphase(+person,pre_quals),inphase
        (+person,post_quals),
    inphase(+person,post_generals)],
    [inphase(P,pre_quals),inphase(P,post_quals),
    inphase(P,post_generals)],
    [professor/1,student/1,taughtby/3,ta/3,courselevel/2,
    yearsinprogram/2,advisedby/2,tempadvisedby/2,
    hasposition/2]).
```

Moreover, the bias contains *modeb* declarations such as

```
modeb(*,courselevel(+course, -level)).
modeb(*,courselevel(+course, #level)).
```

An example of a two-head bottom clause that is generated from the first *modeh* declaration and the example advisedby(person155, person101) is

```
advisedby(A,B):0.5 :- professor(B),student(A),
        hasposition(B,C),
    hasposition(B,faculty),inphase(A,D),
        inphase(A,pre_quals),
    yearsinprogram(A,E),taughtby(F,B,G),taughtby(F,B,H),
    taughtby(I,B,J), taughtby(I,B,J),taughtby(F,B,G),
    taughtby(F,B,H),
    ta(I,K,L),ta(F,M,H),ta(F,M,H),ta(I,K,L),ta(N,K,O),
        ta(N,A,P),
    ta(Q,A,P),ta(R,A,L),ta(S,A,T),ta(U,A,O),ta(U,A,O),
        ta(S,A,T),
    ta(R,A,L),ta(Q,A,P),ta(N,K,O),ta(N,A,P),ta(I,K,L),
        ta(F,M,H).
```

An example of a multi-head bottom clause generated from the second *modeh* declaration and the examples

```
student(person218).
professor(person218).
```

is

```
student(A):0.33; professor(A):0.33 :-
    inphase(A,B),
    inphase(A,post_generals),
    yearsinprogram(A,C).
```

When searching the space of clauses for the `advisedby/2` predicate, an example of a refinement from the first bottom clause is

```
advisedby(A,B):0.5 :- professor(B).
```

EMBLEM is then applied to the theory composed of this single clause, using the positive and negative facts for `advisedby/2` as queries for which to build the BDDs. The single parameter is updated obtaining:

```
advisedby(A,B):0.108939 :- professor(B).
```

The clause is further refined to

```
advisedby(A,B):0.108939 :- professor(B),
                hasposition(B,C).
```

An example of a refinement that is generated from the second bottom clause is

```
student(A):0.33; professor(A):0.33 :-
          inphase(A,B).
```

The updated refinement after EMBLEM is

```
student(A):0.5869;professor(A):0.09832 :-
          inphase(A,B).
```

When searching the *space of theories* for the target predicate `advisedby`, SLIPCOVER generates the program:

```
advisedby(A,B):0.1198 :- professor(B),
                inphase(A,C).
```

with an LL of -350.01. Then a clause is added

```
advisedby(A,B):0.1198 :- professor(B),
                inphase(A,C).
advisedby(A,B):0.1198 :- professor(B),student(A).
```

and EMBLEM is run obtaining

```
advisedby(A,B):0.05465 :- professor(B),
                inphase(A,C).
advisedby(A,B):0.06893 :- professor(B),
                student(A).
```

client		
cliId	*age*	*creditScore*
ann	33	—
bob	40	500
carl	—	450
john	55	700

hasAcc	
cliId	*accId*
ann	a_11
bob	a_11
ann	a_20
john	a_10

hasLoan	
accId	*loanId*
a_11	l_20
a_10	l_20
a_20	l_31
a_20	l_41

loan		
loanId	*loanAmt*	*status*
l_20	20050	appr
l_21	—	pend
l_31	25000	decl
l_41	10000	—

account		
accId	*savings*	*freq*
a_10	3050	high
a_11	—	low
a_19	3010	?
a_20	?	?

Table 14.1   An example of a database. From [Kumar et al., 2022].

with an LL of -318.17. Since the LL decreased, the last clause is retained and at the next iteration, a new clause is added:

```
advisedby(A,B):0.12032  :- hasposition(B,C),
                           inphase(A,D).
advisedby(A,B):0.05465  :- professor(B),
                           inphase(A,C).
advisedby(A,B):0.06893  :- professor(B),student(A).
```

14.6 Learning the Structure of Hybrid Programs

DiceML [Kumar et al., 2022] is a system for learning the structure and the parameters of DC programs, see Section 4.2. In particular, it tackles the problem of *relational autocompletion*, where the goal is to automatically fill out some entries in multiple related tables.

For example, consider the relational database shown in Table 14.1 about a banking domain: clients are described by their age and credit score, they have accounts that are described by savings and frequency and in turn accounts are connected to loans described by amount and status

In this database, some entries are unknown, marked by -, and some are missing, marked by "?". The task is to predict the missing cells, that are those identified by the user as being of interest. Some of these cells regard discrete attributes, such as freq in the account table, some regard continuous attributes, such savings in the account table.

DiceML learns a hybrid program that is able to predict the missing cells. To do so, it assumes that the database is divided into entity tables and associative tables. The entity tables contain no foreign keys and describe entities, while associative tables contain only foreign keys and describe associations among entities. A database $\mathcal{DB}$ is transformed into a set $\mathcal{A}_{\mathcal{DB}} \cup \mathcal{R}_{\mathcal{DB}}$ of facts that will be used as training data:

- For every primary key t in an entity table e, we add the fact $e(t)$ to $\mathcal{R}_{\mathcal{DB}}$. For example, client (ann).
- For each tuple (t_1, t_2) in an associative table r, we add a fact $r(t_1, t_2)$ to $\mathcal{R}_{\mathcal{DB}}$. For example, hasAcc(ann, a_11).
- For each primary key t of an entity table with an attribute a of value v, we add a deterministic fact $a(t) \sim val(v)$ to $\mathcal{A}_{\mathcal{DB}}$. For example, age(ann) $\sim$ val(33). This notation extends DCs and means that the variable age(ann) gets value 33.

The DC program models all the attributes of the database as random variables. Two extensions are used with respect to the usual DC syntax: aggregate atoms and statistical models.

Aggregate atoms express the dependency of a random variable from a set of values for other random variables. Remember that there must be a unique ground $h \sim \mathcal{D}$ in the least fixpoint of the ST_P operator for each ground random variable h. This means that if there are two rules defining h, their bodies must be mutually exclusive. Now suppose that the credit score of a client depends on the frequency of operations on their bank accounts. We could write a rule such as

```
creditScore(C) ~ gaussian(300,10.1) := client(C),
  hasAcc(C,A), freq(A)~=low.
creditScore(C) ~ gaussian(400,10.1) := client(C),
  hasAcc(C,A), freq(A)~=high.
```

where := is concrete syntax for ←. However, if a client has two accounts, one with frequency low and one with frequency high, we would have two different definitions for the density of their credit score. In order to solve this problem, we can use an aggregate function $agg(T, Q, R)$ where agg is an aggregation function, Q is a query, T is a variable in Q and R is the result of the aggregation. As aggregation functions we consider the mode, mean, maximum, minimum, cardinality, etc. For example, we could have the credit score depend on the mode of the frequency on the accounts of a client with the clause

```
creditScore(C) ~ gaussian(300,10.1) := client(C),
   mod(X,(hasAcc(C,A), freq(A)~=X),Z), Z==low.
```

The second extension, statistical models, are used to specify the dependence of the distribution of the variable in the head from continuous variables in the body. A DC with statistical model takes the form

$$h \sim \mathcal{D}_\phi \leftarrow b_1, \ldots, b_n, \mathcal{M}_\phi$$

where $\mathcal{M}_\phi$ is an atom encoding a function that computes the values of the parameters ϕ of $\mathcal{D}_\phi$ from the values of continuous random variables in the body $b_1 \ldots, b_n$. For example, the clause

```
creditScore(C) ~ gaussian(M,0.1) := age(C)~=Y,
   linear([Y],[10.1,200],M).
```

uses a linear model with coefficients 10.1 and 200 to compute the mean of the Gaussian distribution of the credit score of a client given their age.

Table 14.2 lists the available statistical models, which include, besides the linear one, also the logistic and softmax models.

Inference in these programs is performed by likelihood weighting, see Section 12.3: sampling is performed by backward reasoning from the query and each sample is assigned a weight. The probability of the query is then the fraction of the weights of the samples of the evidence where the query is also true.

DiceML learns DC programs for the relational autocompletion problem that are called Joint model programs (JMPs) and are composed of 1. the facts in the transformed $\mathcal{R}_{\mathcal{DB}}$; 2. a set of learned DCs $\mathcal{H}$ that define all the attributes in the database.

Example 123 (JMP for the banking domain [Kumar et al., 2022]). *Form the database in Table 14.1 the following JMP could be learned:*

```
client(ann).  client(john).  ...
hasAcc(ann,a_11).  hasAcc(ann,a_20).  ...
freq(A) ~ discrete([0.2:low,0.8:high]) := account(A).
savings(A) ~ gaussian(2002,10.2) := account(A), freq(A)~=X,
   X==low.
savings(A) ~ gaussian(3030,11.3) := account(A), freq(A)~=X,
   X==high.
age(C) ~ gaussian(Mean,3) := client(C),
```

type of random variable (X)	statistical model atom $(\mathcal{M}_\psi)$ in the body	function implemented by $\mathcal{M}_\psi$	the head
continuous	$linear([Y_1, \ldots, Y_n],$ $[W_1, \ldots, W_{n+1}], M)$	$M = Z$	$X \sim gaussian(M, \sigma^2)$
boolean	$logistic([Y_1, \ldots, Y_n],$ $[W_1, \ldots, W_{n+1}],$ $[P_1, P_2])$	$P_1 = \dfrac{1}{1 + e^{-Z}}$ $P_2 = 1 - P_1$	$X \sim discrete([P_1 :$ $true, P_2 : false])$
discrete	$softmax([Y_1, \ldots, Y_n],$ $[[W_{1_1}, \ldots, W_{n+1_1}], \ldots,$ $[W_{1_d}, \ldots, W_{n+1_d}]],$ $[P_1, \ldots, P_d])$	$P_1 = \dfrac{e^{Z_1}}{N}$ $\vdots$ $P_d = \dfrac{e^{Z_d}}{N}$	$X \sim discrete([P_1 :$ $l_1, \ldots, P_d : l_d])$
where Z is $Y_1.W_1 + \ldots + Y_n.W_n + W_{n+1}$, Z_i is $Y_1.W_{1_i} + \ldots + Y_n.W_{n_i} + W_{n+1_i}$, N is $\sum_{i=1}^{d} e^{Z_i}$, d is the size of domain of X $(dom(X))$ and $l_i \in dom(X)$			

Table 14.2 Available statistical model atoms ($\mathcal{M}_\psi$). From [Kumar et al., 2022].

```
  avg(X,(hasAcc(C,A), savings(A)~=X), Y), creditScore(C)~=Z,
  linear([Y,Z],[30,0.2,-0.4],Mean).
loanAmt(L) ~ gaussian(Mean,10) := loan(L),
  avg(X,(hasLoan(A,L), savings(A)~=X),Y),
  linear([Y],[100.1, 10],Mean).
loanAmt(L) ~ gaussian(25472.3,10.2) := loan(L),
  \+avg(X,(hasLoan(A,L),savings(A)~=X),Y).
status(L) ~ discrete([P1:appr, P2:pend, P3:decl]) := loan(L),
  avg(X, (hasLoan(A,L),hasAcc(C,A),creditScore(C)~=X),Y),
  loanAmt(L)~=Z, softmax([Y,Z],[[0.1,-0.3,-2.4],[0.3,0.4,0.2],
  [0.8,1.9,-2.9]],[P1,P2,P3]).
creditScore(C) ~ gaussian(300,10.1) := client(C),
  mod(X,(hasAcc(C,A), freq(A)~=X),Z), Z==low.
creditScore(C) ~ gaussian(Mean,15.3) := client(C),
  mod(X,(hasAcc(C,A), freq(A)~=X),Z), Z==high,
  max(X,(hasAcc(C,A), savings(A)~=X), Y),
  linear([Y],[600,0.2],Mean).
creditScore(C) ~ gaussian(Mean,12.3) := client(C),
  \+mod(X,(hasAcc(C,A), freq(A)~=X),Z),
  max(X,(hasAcc(C,A), savings(A)~=X), Y),
  linear([Y],[500,0.8],Mean).
```

Here negated aggregate atoms succeed if they query does not have any answer.

For example, the clause for status expresses that its distribution depends on the average credit score of the clients with an account on which the loan is requested and on the amount of the loan. The distribution for status is discrete with three values and the probabilities are obtained from a softmax model with the coefficients specified in the statistical model atom.

DiceML learns a JMP $\mathcal{H}$ from the data $\mathcal{A}_{DB}$ using the relational structure $\mathcal{R}_{BD}$ and possibly a background knowledge $\mathcal{BK}$.

Since DCs defining the same random variable must have mutually exclusive bodies, DiceML learns Distributional logic trees (DLTs), a kind of first-order decision trees [Blockeel and Raedt, 1998], so that mutual exclusion is enforced by construction.

A DLT for an attribute, $a(T)$, is a rooted tree, where the root is an entity atom $e(T)$, each leaf is labeled by a probability distribution $\mathcal{D}_\phi$ and/or a statistical model $\mathcal{M}_\psi$, and each internal node is labeled with an atom b_i. Internal nodes b_i can be of two types:

- a binary atom of the form $a_j(T)\sim=V$ that unifies the outcome of an attribute $a_j(T)$ with a variable V.
- an aggregation atom of the form $aggr(X, Q, V)$, where Q is of the form $(r(T, T_1), a_j(T_1)\sim=X)$ in which r is a link relation and $a_j(T_1)$ is an attribute.

The children of nodes depend on the value V can take:

- if V takes discrete values $\{v_1, ..., v_n\}$ then there is one child for each value v_i.
- if V takes numeric values then its value is used to estimate the parameters of the distribution $\mathcal{D}_\phi$ and/or it is used in the statistical model $\mathcal{M}_\psi$ in the leaves.

Moreover, the binary and the aggregation atom b_i can fail, the first in case the attribute is not defined. Therefore there is also an extra child that captures that V is undefined.

A DLT can be converted to a set of distributional clauses by translating every path from the root to a leaf node in the DLT to a distributional clause of the form $h \sim \mathcal{D}_\phi \leftarrow b_1, ..., b_n, \mathcal{M}_\psi$. Figure 14.1 shows a set of DLTs that together encode the JMP of Example 123.

Learning then consists in building a DLT for each attribute using $\mathcal{A}_{DB}$ as training data. The algorithm follows the structure of decision tree learning

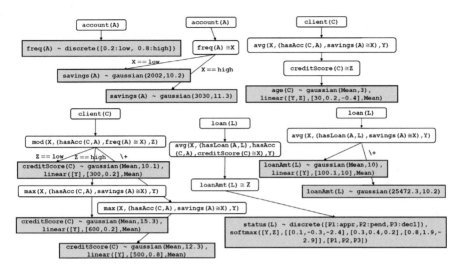

Figure 14.1   A collection of DLTs corresponding to the JMP in Example 123.

algorithms such as [Blockeel and Raedt, 1998]: the set of examples is recursively partitioned into smaller sets by choosing a test for the node. The test is selected on the basis of a refinement operator, that generates literals to be added to the current path according to the language bias, and on the basis of a scoring function, that evaluates the test. Once the test is chosen, the children of the nodes are generated and the algorithm is called recursively on the children. The process terminates when examples are sufficiently homogeneous or when there are no more literals to test. In this case, a leaf is generated and the parameters of the distribution and/or the parameters for the statistical model must be estimated. This is done by means of inference and log-likelihood maximization.

In order to score refinements, DiceML uses the Bayesian Information Criterions (BIC [Schwarz, 1978]). The score of a clause $h \sim \mathcal{D}_\phi \leftarrow \mathcal{Q}, \mathcal{M}_\psi$, corresponding to a path from the root to a leaf, is

$$s(h \sim \mathcal{D}_\phi \leftarrow \mathcal{Q}, \mathcal{M}_\psi) = 2E(\hat{\varphi}) - k \ln |\mathcal{E}| \qquad (14.1)$$

where $E(\hat{\varphi})$ is the expected log-likelihood of the examples $\mathcal{E}$ in the leaf for the maximum likelihood parameters $\hat{\varphi}$ and k is the number of parameters. The score trades off model complexity with model accuracy, preventing overfitting.

To determine the score of the refinement $(\mathcal{Q}, l(V))$ of the clause, the score of the children are summed, where each child is considered as a leaf, completed with a distribution and/or a statistical model, and the parameters estimated.

In order to induce a JMP, an order among the attributes is decided and a DLT for each attribute is learned following the order, with the constraint that only previous attributes can be used in the DLT. in this way, circular definitions are avoided.

To handle missing attributes, two approaches are possible: one can either exploit the extra child corresponding to the absence of a value, or resort to an EM algorithm.

The learned JMP can then be used for the relational autocompletion task: given a set of cells, predict the values of the others. This can be done using inference.

DiceML has been experimented on a synthetic university data set, on a financial dataset [Berka, 2000] and on a dataset about the NBA [Schulte and Routley, 2014].

14.7 Scaling PILP

PLP usually requires expensive learning procedures due to the high cost of inference. SLIPCOVER (see Section 14.5) for example performs structure learning of probabilistic logic programs using knowledge compilation for parameter learning: the expectations needed for the EM parameter learning algorithm are computed using the BDDs that are built for inference. Compiling explanations for queries into BDDs has a #P cost in the number of random variables.

Two systems that try to remedy this are LIFTCOVER [Nguembang Fadja and Riguzzi, 2019] and SLEAHP [Nguembang Fadja et al., 2021]

14.7.1 LIFTCOVER

Lifted inference, see Chapter 9 was proposed for improving the performance of reasoning in probabilistic relational models by reasoning on whole populations of individuals instead of considering each individual separately.

Here we propose a simple PLP language (called *liftable PLP*) where programs contain clauses with a single annotated atom in the head and the predicate of this atom is the same for all clauses. In this case, all the approaches for lifted inference coincide and reduce to a simple computation.

14.7.1.1 Liftable PLP

We restrict the language of LPADs by allowing only clauses of the form

$$C_i = h_i : \Pi_i \leftarrow b_{i1}, \ldots, b_{iu_i}$$

in the program where all the clauses share the same predicate for the single atom in the head, let us call this predicate $target/a$ with a the arity. The literals in the body have predicates other than $target/a$ and are defined by facts and rules that are certain, i.e., they have a single atom in the head with probability 1. The predicate $target/a$ is called *target* and the others *input predicates*. Suppose there are n probabilistic clauses of the form above in the program. We call this language *liftable PLP*.

The problem is to compute the probability of a ground instantiation q of $target/a$. This can be done at the lifted level. We should first find the number of ground instantiations of clauses for $target/a$ such that the body is true and the head is equal to q. Suppose there are m_i such instantiations $\{\theta_{i1}, \ldots, \theta_{im_i}\}$, for rule C_i for $i = 1, \ldots, n$. Each instantiation θ_{ij} corresponds to a random variable X_{ij} taking values 1 with probability Π_i and 0 with probability $1 - \Pi_i$. The query q is true if at least one of the random variables for a rule takes value 1: $q = true \Leftrightarrow \bigvee_{i=1}^{n} \bigvee_{j=1}^{m_i} (X_{ij} = 1)$. In other words q is false only if no random variable takes value 1. All the random variables are mutually independent so the probability that none takes value 1 is $\prod_{i=1}^{n} \prod_{j=1}^{m_i} (1 - \Pi_i) = \prod_{i=1}^{n} (1 - \Pi_i)^{m_i}$ and the probability of q being true is $P(q) = 1 - \prod_{i=1}^{n} (1 - \Pi_i)^{m_i}$. So once the number of clause instantiations with the body true is known, the probability of the query can be computed in logarithmic time. Note that finding an assignment of a set of logical variables that makes a conjunction true is an NP-complete problem [Kietz and Lübbe, 1994], therefore computing the probability of the query may be prohibitive.

However, when using knowledge compilation, to the cost of finding the assignment, we must sum the cost of performing the compilation, that is #P in the number of satisfying logical variables assignments (clause instantiations with the body true). Therefore inference in liftable PLP is significantly cheaper than in the general case. Moreover, in machine learning the conjunctions are usually short and the knowledge compilation cost dominates.

The general language of PLP is necessary when the user wants to induce a knowledge base or an ontology regarding the domain. In that case, the possibility of having more than one head, possibly involving more than one predicate, and the possibility of learning probabilistic rules for subgoals is useful because the resulting program can thus represent and organize general knowledge about the domain. Moreover, the resulting program can then be used for answering different types of queries instead of being restricted to answering queries about a single predicate. This is similar to the problem of learning multiple predicates in Inductive Logic Programming. While this problem has received considerable attention, most work concentrated on learning a single predicate, for example systems such as FOIL [Quinlan, 1990], Progol [Muggleton, 1995] and Aleph [Srinivasan, 2007] learn a single predicate at a time. Furthermore, most benchmark datasets are focused on predicting the truth value of atoms for a single predicate.

We can picture the dependence of the random variable q associated with the query from the random variables of clause groundings with the body true as in Figure 14.2. Here the conditional probability table of q is that of an or: $P(q) = 1$ if at least one of its parents is equal to 1 and 0 otherwise. The variables from clause groundings are

$$\{X_{11}, \ldots, X_{1m_1}, X_{21}, \ldots, X_{2m_2}, \ldots, X_{n1}, \ldots, X_{nm_n}\}.$$

These are parentless variables, with X_{ij} having the conditional probability table (CPT) $P(X_{ij} = 1) = \Pi_i$ and $P(X_{ij} = 0) = 1 - \Pi_i$.

This is an example of a *noisy-OR* model [Good, 1961; Pearl, 1988]: (see also Section 9.1.1) an event is associated to a number of conditions each of which alone can cause the event to happen. The conditions/causes are noisy, i.e., they have a probability of being active, and they are mutually unconditionally independent. A liftable PLP program encodes a noisy-OR model where the event is the query q being true and causes are the ground instantiations of the clauses that have the body true: each can cause the query to be true with the probability given by the clause annotation.

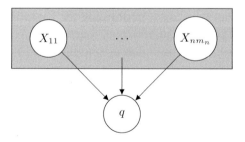

Figure 14.2 Bayesian Network representing the dependency between the query q and the random variables associated with groundings of the clauses with the body true.

Example 124 (Liftable PLP for the UW-CSE domain). *Let us consider the UW-CSE domain [Kok and Domingos, 2005b] where the objective is to predict the "advised by" relation between students and professors. In this case the target predicate is $advisedby/2$ and a program for predicting such predicate may be*

$advisedby(A, B) : 0.4 \leftarrow$
   $student(A), professor(B), publication(C, A), publication(C, B).$
$advisedby(A, B) : 0.5 \leftarrow$
   $student(A), professor(B), ta(C, A), taughtby(C, B).$

where $publication(A, B)$ means that A is a publication with author B, $ta(C, A)$ means that A is a teaching assistant for course C and $taughtby(C, B)$ means that course C is taught by B. The probability that a student is advised by a professor depends on the number of joint publications and the number of courses the professor teaches where the student is a TA, the higher these numbers the higher the probability.

Suppose we want to compute the probability of $q = advisedby(harry, ben)$ where $harry$ is a student, ben is a professor, they have 4 joint publications and ben teaches 2 courses where $harry$ is a TA. Then the first clause has 4 groundings with head q where the body is true, the second clause has 2 groundings with head q where the body is true and $P(advisedby(harry, ben)) = 1 - (1 - 0.4)^4(1 - 0.5)^2 = 0.9676$.

14.7.1.2 Parameter learning

We consider discriminative learning because we want to predict only atoms for the target predicate, while the atoms for the input predicates are assumed as given.

The problem of discriminative learning of the parameters of a liftable PLP $\mathcal{P} = \{C_1, \ldots, C_n\}$ can be expressed as follows: given a liftable PLP $\mathcal{P}$, a set

$$E^+ = \{e_1, \ldots, e_Q\}$$

of positive examples (ground atoms for the target predicate) and a set

$$E^- = \{e_{Q+1}, \ldots, e_R\}$$

of negative examples (ground atoms for the target predicate) and background knowledge B, find the parameters of $\mathcal{P}$ such that the likelihood

$$L = \prod_{q=1}^{Q} P(e_q) \prod_{r=Q+1}^{R} P(\sim e_r)$$

is maximized.

The background knowledge B is a normal logic program defining the input predicates with certainty. In the simplest case it is a set of ground facts, i.e., an interpretation I, describing the domain by means of the observed facts for the input predicates. It can also be a mega-example because we can consider the case where we have a set of interpretations $\mathcal{I} = \{I_1, \ldots, I_U\}$ each describing a different sub-domain from the universe considered. In that case, each mega-example I_u will be associated with its set of positive and negative examples E_u^+ and E_u^- that are to be evaluated against I_u.

The likelihood can be unfolded to

$$
L = \prod_{q=1}^{Q} \left(1 - \prod_{l=1}^{n} (1 - \Pi_l)^{m_{lq}} \right) \prod_{r=Q+1}^{R} \prod_{l=1}^{n} (1 - \Pi_l)^{m_{lr}} \tag{14.2}
$$

where m_{iq} (m_{ir}) is the number of instantiations of C_i whose head is e_q (e_r) and whose body is true. We can aggregate the negative examples

$$
L = \prod_{l=1}^{n} (1 - \Pi_l)^{m_{l-}} \prod_{q=1}^{Q} \left(1 - \prod_{l=1}^{n} (1 - \Pi_l)^{m_{lq}} \right) \tag{14.3}
$$

where $m_{l-} = \sum_{r=Q+1}^{R} m_{lr}$.

We can maximize L using an Expectation Maximization (EM) algorithm [Dempster et al., 1977] since the X_{ij} variables are hidden. To perform EM, we need to compute the conditional probabilities $P(X_{ij} = 1|e)$ and $P(X_{ij} = 1|\neg e)$ where e is an example (a ground atom) and X_{ij} are its parents.

Alternatively, we can use gradient descent to optimize L. In this case, we need to compute the gradient of the likelihood with respect to the parameters. In the following subsections we consider each method in turn.

14.7.1.2.1 EM Algorithm

To perform EM, we need to compute the distribution of the hidden variables given the observed ones, in our case $P(X_{ij} = 1|e)$ and $P(X_{ij} = 1| \sim e)$. e is a single example that is a ground atom for the target predicate. The X_{ij} variables are relative to the ground instantiations of the probabilistic clauses whose body is true when the head is unified with e. Different examples don't share clause groundings, as the constants in them are different. Therefore the X_{ij} variables are not shared among examples.

Let us now compute $P(X_{ij} = 1, e)$:

$$
P(X_{ij} = 1, e) = P(e|X_{ij} = 1)P(X_{ij} = 1) = P(X_{ij} = 1) = \Pi_i
$$

since $P(e|X_{ij} = 1) = 1$, so

$$P(X_{ij} = 1|e) = \frac{P(X_{ij} = 1, e)}{P(e)} = \frac{\Pi_i}{1 - \prod_{i=1}^{n}(1 - \Pi_i)^{m_i}} \quad (14.4)$$

$$P(X_{ij} = 0|e) = 1 - \frac{\Pi_i}{1 - \prod_{i=1}^{n}(1 - \Pi_i)^{m_i}} \quad (14.5)$$

$P(X_{ij} = 1| \sim e)$ is given by

$$P(X_{ij} = 1, \sim e) = P(\sim e|X_{ij} = 1)P(X_{ij} = 1) = 0$$

since $P(\sim e|X_{ij} = 1) = 0$, so

$$P(X_{ij} = 1| \sim e) = 0 \quad (14.6)$$
$$P(X_{ij} = 0| \sim e) = 1. \quad (14.7)$$

This leads to the EM algorithm of Algorithm 37, with the EXPECTATION and MAXIMIZATION functions shown in Algorithms 38 and 39.

Function EM stops when the difference between the current value of the LL and the previous one is below a given threshold or when such a difference relative to the absolute value of the current one is below a given threshold.

Function EXPECTATION updates, for each clause C_i, two counters, c_{i0} and c_{i1}, one for each value of the random variables X_{ij} associated with clause C_i. These counters accumulate the values of the conditional probability of the values of the hidden variables. The counters are updated taking into account first the negative examples and then the positive ones. Negative examples can be considered in bulk because their contribution is the same for all groundings of all examples, while positive examples must be considered one by one, for each one updating the counters of all the clauses.

Function Maximization then simply computes the new values of the parameters by dividing c_{i1} by the sum of c_{i0} and c_{i1}.

14.7.1.2.2 Gradient-Based Optimization

Gradient-based methods include gradient descent and its derivatives, such as second-order methods like Limited-memory BFGS (LBFGS) [Nocedal, 1980], an optimization algorithm in the family of quasi-Newton methods that approximates the Broyden–Fletcher–Goldfarb–Shanno (BFGS) algorithm using a limited amount of computer memory.

To perform gradient-based optimization we need to compute the partial derivatives of the likelihood with respect to the parameters. Let us recall the

---

Algorithm 37 Function LIFTCOVER-EM

1: **function** LIFTCOVER-EM$(restarts, max\_iter, \epsilon, \delta)$
2:      $BestLL \leftarrow -inf$
3:      $BestPar \leftarrow []$
4:      **for** $j \leftarrow 1 \rightarrow restarts$ **do**
5:          **for** $i \leftarrow 1 \rightarrow n$ **do**   ▷ n: number of rules
6:              $\Pi_i \leftarrow random$
7:          **end for**
8:          $LL = -inf$
9:          $iter \leftarrow 0$
10:          **repeat**
11:              $iter \leftarrow iter + 1$
12:              $LL_0 = LL$
13:              $LL = \text{EXPECTATION}$
14:              MAXIMIZATION
15:          **until** $LL - LL_0 < \epsilon \vee LL - LL_0 < -LL \cdot \delta \vee iter > max\_iter$
16:          **if** $LL > BestLL$ **then**
17:              $BestLL \leftarrow LL$
18:              $BestPar \leftarrow [\Pi_1, \ldots, \Pi_n]$
19:          **end if**
20:      **end for**
21:      return $BestLL, BestPar$
22: **end function**

---

likelihood

$$L = \prod_{l=1}^{n}(1 - \Pi_l)^{m_{l-}} \prod_{q=1}^{Q}\left(1 - \prod_{l=1}^{n}(1 - \Pi_l)^{m_{lq}}\right) \tag{14.8}$$

where $m_{l-} = \sum_{r=Q+1}^{R} m_{lr}$. Its partial derivative with respect to Π_i is

$$\frac{\partial L}{\partial \Pi_i} = \frac{\partial \prod_{l=1}^{n}(1 - \Pi_l)^{m_{l-}}}{\partial \Pi_i} \prod_{q=1}^{Q}\left(1 - \prod_{l=1}^{n}(1 - \Pi_l)^{m_{lq}}\right)$$

$$+ \prod_{l=1}^{n}(1 - \Pi_l)^{m_{l-}} \frac{\partial \prod_{q=1}^{Q}(1 - \prod_{l=1}^{n}(1 - \Pi_l)^{m_{lq}})}{\partial \Pi_i}$$

$$= -m_{i-}(1 - \Pi_i)^{m_{i-}-1} \prod_{l=1,l\neq i}^{n}(1 - \Pi_l)^{m_{l-}} \prod_{q=1}^{Q}\left(1 - \prod_{l=1}^{n}(1 - \Pi_l)^{m_{lq}}\right)$$

$$+ \prod_{l=1}^{n}(1 - \Pi_l)^{m_{l-}} \sum_{q=1}^{Q} m_{iq}(1 - \Pi_i)^{m_{iq}-1} \prod_{l=1,l\neq i}^{n}(1 - \Pi_l)^{m_{lq}}$$

$$\cdot \prod_{q'=1,q'\neq q}^{Q}\left(1 - \prod_{l=1}^{n}(1 - \Pi_l)^{m_{lq'}}\right) \tag{14.9}$$

Algorithm 38 Function Expectation

1: **function** EXPECTATION
2:     $LL \leftarrow \sum_{i \in Rules} m_{i-} \log(1 - \Pi_i)$
3:             $\triangleright$ m_{i-}: total number of groundings of rule i with the body true in a negative example
4:     **for** $i \leftarrow 1 \rightarrow n$ **do**
5:         $c_{i1} \leftarrow 0$
6:         $c_{i0} \leftarrow m_{i-}$
7:     **end for**
8:     **for** $r \leftarrow 1 \rightarrow P$ **do** $\triangleright$ P: number of positive examples
9:         $probex \leftarrow 1 - \prod_{i \in Rules}(1 - \Pi_i)^{m_{ir}}$
10:             $\triangleright$ m_{ir}: number of groundings of rule i with the body true in example r
11:         $LL \leftarrow LL + \log probex$
12:         **for** $i \leftarrow 1 \rightarrow n$ **do**
13:             $condp \leftarrow \frac{\Pi_i}{probex}$
14:             $c_{i1} \leftarrow c_{i1} + m_{ir} condp$
15:             $c_{i0} \leftarrow c_{i0} + m_{ir}(1 - condp)$
16:         **end for**
17:     **end for**
18:     **return** LL
19: **end function**

Algorithm 39 Function Maximization

1: **procedure** MAXIMIZATION
2:     **for** $i \leftarrow 1 \rightarrow n$ **do**
3:         $\Pi_i = \frac{c_{i1}}{c_{i1} + c_{i0}}$
4:     **end for**
5: **end procedure**

---

for the differentiation product rule, and

$$
\frac{\partial L}{\partial \Pi_i} = -m_{i-}(1 - \Pi_i)^{m_{i-}-1} \prod_{l=1, l \neq i}^{n} (1 - \Pi_l)^{m_{l-}} \frac{(1 - \Pi_i)^{m_{i-}}}{(1 - \Pi_i)^{m_{i-}}}
$$

$$
\prod_{q=1}^{Q} \left(1 - \prod_{l=1}^{n}(1 - \Pi_l)^{m_{lq}} \right) +
$$

$$
\prod_{l=1}^{n}(1 - \Pi_l)^{m_{l-}} \sum_{q=1}^{Q} m_{iq} \frac{\prod_{l=1}^{n}(1 - \Pi_l)^{m_{lq}}}{1 - \Pi_i}
$$

$$
\prod_{q'=1, q' \neq q}^{Q} \left(1 - \prod_{l=1}^{n}(1 - \Pi_l)^{m_{lq'}} \right) \cdot \frac{1 - \prod_{l=1}^{n}(1 - \Pi_l)^{m_{lq}}}{1 - \prod_{l=1}^{n}(1 - \Pi_l)^{m_{lq}}} \quad (14.10)
$$

by dividing and multiplying for $(1 - \Pi_i)^{m_{i-}}$, $(1 - \Pi_i)$ and $1 - \prod_{l=1}^{n}(1 - \Pi_l)^{m_{lq}}$ various factors. Then

$$
\begin{aligned}
\frac{\partial L}{\partial \Pi_i} &= -\frac{m_{i-}(1 - \Pi_i)^{m_{i-}-1}L}{(1 - \Pi_i)^{m_{i-}}} + \sum_{q=1}^{Q} \frac{m_{iq}\prod_{l=1}^{n}(1 - \Pi_l)^{m_{lq}}L}{(1 - \Pi_i)(1 - \prod_{l=1}^{n}(1 - \Pi_l)^{m_{lq}})} \\
&= -\frac{m_{i-}L}{1 - \Pi_i} + \sum_{q=1}^{Q} \frac{m_{iq}\prod_{l=1}^{n}(1 - \Pi_l)^{m_{lq}}L}{(1 - \Pi_i)(1 - \prod_{l=1}^{n}(1 - \Pi_l)^{m_{lq}})} \\
&= \frac{L}{1 - \Pi_i}\left(\sum_{q=1}^{Q} \frac{m_{iq}\prod_{l=1}^{n}(1 - \Pi_l)^{m_{lq}}}{1 - \prod_{l=1}^{n}(1 - \Pi_l)^{m_{lq}}} - m_{i-}\right) \\
&= \frac{L}{1 - \Pi_i}\left(\sum_{q=1}^{Q} m_{iq}\frac{1 - P(e_q)}{P(e_q)} - m_{i-}\right) \\
&= \frac{L}{1 - \Pi_i}\left(\sum_{q=1}^{Q} m_{iq}\left(\frac{1}{P(e_q)} - 1\right) - m_{i-}\right)
\end{aligned}
\tag{14.11}
$$

by simple algebra.

The equation $\frac{\partial L}{\partial \Pi_i} = 0$ does not admit a closed form solution, not even where there is a single clause, so we must use optimization to find the maximum of L.

14.7.1.3 Structure learning

The discriminative structure learning problem can be expressed as: given a set $E^+ = \{e_1, \ldots, e_Q\}$ of positive examples, a set $E^- = \{e_{Q+1}, \ldots, e_R\}$ of negative examples and a background knowledge B, find a liftable PLP $\mathcal{P}$ such that the likelihood is maximized. The background knowledge B may be a normal logic program defining all the predicates except the target (the input predicates).

We solve this problem by first identifying good clauses guided by the log likelihood (LL) of the data. Clauses are found by a top-down beam search. The refinement operator adds a literal to the body of the current clause, the literal is taken from a *bottom clause* built as in Progol [Muggleton, 1995]. The set of clauses found in this phase is then considered as a single theory and parameter learning is performed on it. Then the clauses with a parameter below a user define threshold *WMin* are discarded and the theory is returned. The resulting algorithm, LIFTCOVER, is very similar to SLIPCOVER, see Section 14.5. The difference between the two is that LIFTCOVER uses lifted parameter learning instead of the EM algorithm over BDDs of [Bellodi and

Riguzzi, 2013]. Moreover they use a different approach for performing the selection of the rules to be included in the final model: while SLIPCOVER does a hill-climbing search in which it adds one clause at a time to the theory, learns the parameters and keeps the clause if the LL is smaller than before, LIFTCOVER learns the parameters for the whole set of clauses found during the search in the space of clauses. This is allowed by the fact that parameter learning in LIFTCOVER is much faster so it can be applied to large theories. Then rules with a small parameter can be discarded as they provide small contributions to the predictions. In practice structure search is thus performed in LIFTCOVER by parameter learning, as is done for example in [Nishino et al., 2014; Wang et al., 2014].

Algorithm 40 Function LIFTCOVER

1: **function** LIFTCOVER(NB, NI, $NInt$, NS, NA, NV)
2:      $Beam$ =INITIALBEAM($NInt$, NS, NA)   ▷ Bottom clauses building
3:      $CC \leftarrow \varnothing$
4:      $Steps \leftarrow 1$
5:      $NewBeam \leftarrow []$
6:      **repeat**
7:          Remove the first pair $((Cl, Literals), LL)$ from $Beam$ ▷ Remove the first clause
8:          $Refs \leftarrow$ CLAUSEREFINEMENTS$((Cl, Literals, NV))$ ▷ Find all refinements $Refs$ of
     $(Cl, Literals)$
9:          **for all** $(Cl', Literals') \in Refs$ **do**
10:             $(LL'', \{Cl''\}) \leftarrow$ LEARNWEIGHTS$(\{Cl'\})$
11:             $NewBeam \leftarrow$ INSERT$((Cl'', Literals'), LL'', NewBeam, NB)$ ▷ The
     refinement is inserted in the beam in order of likelihood, possibly removing the last clause if the size
     of the beam NB is exceeded
12:             $CC \leftarrow CC \cup \{Cl'\}$
13:          **end for**
14:          $Beam \leftarrow NewBeam$
15:          $Steps \leftarrow Steps + 1$
16:      **until** $Steps > NI$ or $Beam$ is empty
17:      $(LL, Th) \leftarrow$ LEARNWEIGHTS(CC)
18:      Remove from Th the clauses with a weight smaller than $WMin$
19:      **return** Th
20: **end function**

Algorithm 40 shows the main LIFTCOVER function. Line 2 calls INI-TIALBEAM that builds an initial beam $Beam$ consisting of bottom clauses and is very similar to Algorithm 35

As in SLIPCOVER, a beam is a set of tuples $((Cl, Literals), LL)$ with Cl a clause, $Literals$ the set of literals admissible in the body of Cl and LL the log-likelihood of Cl. Function INITIALBEAM returns returns an initial beam containing tuples $((h : 0.5 :- true, Literals), -\infty)$ for each bottom clause $h : 0.5 :- Literals$. The likelihood is initialized to $-\infty$.

Then LIFTCOVER runs a beam search in the space of clauses for the target predicate.

In each beam search iteration, the first clause of the beam is removed and all its refinements are computed. Each refinement Cl' is scored by performing parameter learning with $\mathcal{P} = \{Cl'\}$ and using the resulting LL as the heuristic. The scored refinements are inserted back into the beam in order of heuristic. If the beam exceeds a maximum user-defined size, the bottom elements are removed. Moreover, the refinements are added to a set of clauses CC.

For each clause Cl with $Literals$ admissible in the body, Function CLAUSEREFINEMENTS, the same as that of SLIPCOVER in Algorithm 36, computes refinements by adding a literal from $Literals$ to the body. Furthermore, the refinements must respect the input-output modes of the bias declarations, must be connected (i.e., each body literal must share a variable with the head or a previous body literal) and their number of variables must not exceed a user-defined number NV. Refinements are of the form (Cl', L') where Cl' is the refined clause Cl' and L' is the new set of literals allowed in the body of Cl'.

Beam search is iterated a user-defined number of times or until the beam becomes empty. The output of this search phase is represented by the set CC of clauses. Then parameter learning is applied to the whole set CC, i.e., $\mathcal{P} = CC$. Finally clauses with a weight smaller than $WMin$ are removed.

The separate search for clauses has similarity with the covering loop of ILP systems such as Aleph [Srinivasan, 2007] and Progol [Muggleton, 1995]. Differently from the ILP case, however, the positive examples covered are not removed from the training set because coverage is probabilistic, so an example that is assigned nonzero probability by a clause may have its probability increased by further clauses. A selection of clauses is performed by parameter learning: clauses with very small weights are removed.

LIFTCOVER has been tested on 12 datasets in its two versions LIFTCOVER-EM and LIFTCOVER-LBFGS. Overall we see that both lifted algorithms are usually faster, sometimes by a large margin, with respect to SLIPCOVER, especially LIFTCOVER-EM. Moreover, this system often finds better quality solutions, showing that structure search by parameter learning is effective.

14.7.2 SLEAHP

SLEAHP [Nguembang Fadja et al., 2021] tries to achieve scalability by restricting the language to Hierarchical Probabilistic Logic Programs (HPLPs) which, by construction, satisfy the independent-or assumption. This makes the computation of probabilities in such programs "truth-functional" [Gerla, 2001]. With the independent-or assumption we can collect the contribution of multiple groundings of a clause. Therefore it is suitable for domains where entities may be related to a varying number of other entities. The differences in numbers are taken into account by the semantics. The assumption is not weaker or stronger than the exclusive-or one. It is probably less easy for users to write HPLP programs than PRISM programs but our aim is to devise an algorithm for automatically learning them.

14.7.2.1 Hierarchical probabilistic logic programs

Suppose we want to compute the probability of atoms for a single predicate r using a PLP. In particular, we want to compute the probability of a ground atom $r(t)$, where t is a vector of terms. Let us call r the target predicate. This is a common situation in relational learning.

We consider a specific form of LPADs defining r in terms of *input predicates* (their definition is given as input and is certain) and *hidden predicates*, defined by clauses of the program. We discriminate between input predicates, which encapsulate the input data and the background knowledge, and target predicates, which are predicates we are interested in predicting. Hidden predicates are disjoint from input and target predicates. Each clause in the program has a single head atom annotated with a probability. Furthermore, the program is hierarchically defined so that it can be divided into layers. Each layer defines a set of hidden predicates in terms of predicates of the layer immediately below or in terms of input predicates. A generic clause C is of the form

$$C = p(\boldsymbol{X}) : \pi \leftarrow \phi(\boldsymbol{X}, \boldsymbol{Y}), b_1(\boldsymbol{X}, \boldsymbol{Y}), \ldots, b_m(\boldsymbol{X}, \boldsymbol{Y})$$

where $\phi(\boldsymbol{X}, \boldsymbol{Y})$ is a conjunction of literals for the input predicates. The vector $\boldsymbol{X}$ represents variables appearing in the head of C and $\boldsymbol{Y}$ represents the variables introduced by input predicates. $b_i(\boldsymbol{X}, \boldsymbol{Y})$ for $i = 1, \ldots, m$ is a literal built on a hidden predicate. Variables in $\boldsymbol{Y}$ are existentially quantified with scope the body. Only literals for input predicates can introduce new variables into the clause. Moreover, all literals for hidden predicates must use the whole set of variables of the predicate in the head $\boldsymbol{X}$ and input predicates $\boldsymbol{Y}$, see predicate $r_{1\_1}(A, B, C)$ of Example 125. This restriction is imposed to allow independence among ground clauses associated to target/hidden predicates, see Section 14.7.2.1.1. Moreover, we require that the predicate of each $b_i(\boldsymbol{X}, \boldsymbol{Y})$ does not appear elsewhere in the body of C or in the body of any other clause, i.e each hidden predicate literal is unique in the program. We call hierarchical PLP (HPLP) the language that admits only programs of this form Nguembang Fadja et al. [2017]. A generic hierarchical program is defined as follows:

$$
\begin{aligned}
C_1 = r(\boldsymbol{X}) : \pi_1 &\leftarrow \phi_1, b_{1\_1}, \ldots, b_{1\_m_1} \\
&\cdots \\
C_n = r(\boldsymbol{X}) : \pi_n &\leftarrow \phi_n, b_{n\_1}, \ldots, b_{n\_m_n} \\
C_{1\_1\_1} = r_{1\_1}(\boldsymbol{X}) : \pi_{1\_1\_1} &\leftarrow \phi_{1\_1\_1}, b_{1\_1\_1\_1}, \ldots, b_{1\_1\_1\_m_{111}} \\
&\cdots \\
C_{1\_1\_n_{11}} = r_{1\_1}(\boldsymbol{X}) : \pi_{1\_1\_n_{11}} &\leftarrow \phi_{1\_1\_n_{11}}, b_{1\_1\_n_{11}\_1}, \ldots, b_{1\_1\_n_{11}\_m_{11n_{11}}} \\
&\cdots \\
C_{n\_1\_1} = r_{n\_1}(\boldsymbol{X}) : \pi_{n\_1\_1} &\leftarrow \phi_{n\_1\_1}, b_{n\_1\_1\_1}, \ldots, b_{n\_1\_1\_m_{n11}} \\
&\cdots \\
C_{n\_1\_n_{n1}} = r_{n\_1}(\boldsymbol{X}) : \pi_{n\_1\_n_{n1}} &\leftarrow \phi_{n\_1\_n_{n1}}, b_{n\_1\_n_{n1}\_1}, \ldots, b_{n\_1\_n_{n1}\_m_{n1n_{n1}}} \\
&\cdots
\end{aligned}
$$

where r is the target predicate and $r_{1\_1\ldots\_n}$ is the predicate of $b_{1\_1\ldots\_n}$, e.g. r_{1_1} and r_{n_1} are the predicates of b_{1_1} and b_{n_1} respectively. The bodies of the lowest layer of clauses are composed only of input predicates and do not contain hidden predicates, e.g C_2 and $C_{1\_1\_1}$ in Example 125. Note that here the variables were omitted except for rule heads.

A generic program can be represented by a tree, see Figure 14.3, with a node for each clause and literal for hidden predicates. Each clause (literal) node is indicated with $C_{\boldsymbol{p}}$ ($b_{\boldsymbol{p}}$) where $\boldsymbol{p}$ is a sequence of integers encoding the path from the root to the node. The predicate of literal $b_{\boldsymbol{p}}$ is $r_{\boldsymbol{p}}$ which is different for every value of $\boldsymbol{p}$.

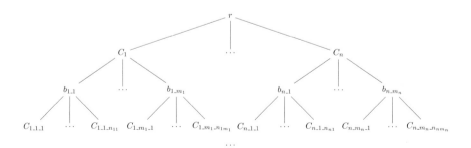

Figure 14.3   Probabilistic program tree.

Example 125 (HPLP for the UW-CSE domain). *Let us consider a modified version of the program of Example 124:*

$C_1 = advised\_by(A, B) : 0.3 \leftarrow$
$\quad student(A), professor(B), project(C, A), project(C, B),$
$\quad r_{1\_1}(A, B, C).$
$C_2 = advised\_by(A, B) : 0.6 \leftarrow$
$\quad student(A), professor(B), ta(C, A), taughtby(C, B).$
$C_{1\_1\_1} = r_{1\_1}(A, B, C) : 0.2 \leftarrow$
$\quad publication(P, A, C), publication(P, B, C).$

where $publication(P, A, C)$ means that P is a publication with author A produced in project C and $student/1, professor/1, project/2, ta/2, taughtby/2$ and $publication/3$ are input predicates.

In this case, the probability of $q = advised\_by(harry, ben)$ depends not only on the number of joint courses and projects but also on the number of joint publications from projects. Note that the set of variables of the hidden predicate $r_{1\_1}(A, B, C)$ is the union of the variables $\mathbf{X} = \{A, B\}$ of the predicate $advised\_by(A, B)$ in the head of the clause and $\mathbf{Y} = \{C\}$ which is the variable introduced by the input predicate $project(C, A)$ in the body. The clause for $r_{1\_1}(A, B, C)$ ($C_{1\_1\_1}$) computes an aggregation over publications of a project and the clause in the level above (C_1) aggregates over projects.

This program can be represented with the tree of Figure 14.4.

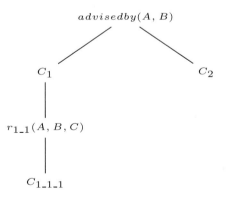

Figure 14.4 Probabilistic program tree for Example 125.

14.7.2.1.1 Inference in HPLP HPLPs satisfy the independent-or assumption as every hidden predicate appears just once in the body of a single clause and has all the variables of the clause as arguments. If we consider the grounding of the program, each ground atom for a hidden predicate appears in the body of a single ground clause. A ground atom for a hidden predicate may appear in the head of more than one ground clauses and each ground clause can provide a set of explanations for it but these sets do not share random variables. Moreover, HPLPs also satisfy the independent-and assumptions as every ground atom for a hidden predicate in the body of a ground clause has explanations that depend on disjoint sets of random variables.

Remember that atoms for input predicates are not random, they are either true or false in the data and they play a role in determining which groundings of clauses contribute to the probability of the goal: the groundings whose atoms for input predicates are false do not contribute to the computation of the probability.

Given a ground clause $G_{pi} = a_p : \pi_{pi} \leftarrow b_{pi1}, \ldots, b_{pim_{p_l}}$. where p is a path, we can compute the probability that the body is true by multiplying the probability of being true of each individual literals. If the literal is positive, its probability is equal to the probability of the corresponding atom. Otherwise it is one minus the probability of the corresponding atom. Therefore the probability of the body of G_{pi} is $P(b_{pi1}, \ldots, b_{pim_{p_l}}) = \prod_{i=k}^{m_p} P(b_{pik})$ and $P(b_{pik}) = 1 - P(a_{pik})$ if $b_{pik} = \sim a_{pik}$. If $P(b_{pik})$ is a literal for an input predicate, $P(b_{pik}) = 1$ if it is true and $P(b_{pik}) = 0$ otherwise. We can use this formula because HPLPs satisfy the independent-and assumption.

Given a ground atom a_p for a hidden predicate, to compute $P(a_p)$ we need to take into account the contribution of every ground clause for the predicate of a_p. Suppose these clauses are $\{G_{p1}, \ldots, G_{po_p}\}$. If we have a single ground clause $G_{p1} = a_p : \pi_{p1} \leftarrow b_{p11}, \ldots, b_{p1m_{p1}}$, then

$$P(a_p) = \pi_{p1} \cdot P(body(G_{p1})).$$

If we have two clauses, the contribution of each clause is computed as above. Note that, random variables associated with these contributions are independent since we allow hidden predicates in the body of each clause to use the whole set of variables appearing in the head and those introduced by input predicates. It is also worth noting that the probability of a disjunction of two independent random variables is

$$P(a \vee b) = P(a) + P(b) - P(a) \cdot P(b) = 1 - (1 - P(a)) \cdot (1 - P(b)).$$

Therefore, if we have two clauses their contributions are combined as follows:

$$P(a_{\boldsymbol{p}}) = 1 - (1 - \pi_{\boldsymbol{p}1} \cdot P(body(G_{\boldsymbol{p}1})) \cdot (1 - \pi_{\boldsymbol{p}2} \cdot P(body(G_{\boldsymbol{p}2})))$$
$$= (\pi_{\boldsymbol{p}1} \cdot P(body(G_{\boldsymbol{p}1}))) \oplus (\pi_{\boldsymbol{p}2} \cdot P(body(G_{\boldsymbol{p}2}))).$$

where we used the operator $\oplus$ that combines two probabilities as follows $p \oplus q = 1 - (1 - p) \cdot (1 - q)$. This operator is commutative and associative and we can compute sequences of applications as

$$\bigoplus_i p_i = 1 - \prod_i (1 - p_i) \tag{14.12}$$

The operator is called probabilistic sum and is the t-norm of the product fuzzy logic Hájek [1998]. Therefore, if the probabilistic program is ground, the probability of the example atom can be computed with the Arithmetic Circuit (AC) of Figure 14.5, where nodes are labeled with the operation they perform and edges from $\oplus$ nodes are labeled with a probabilistic parameter that must be multiplied by the child output before combining it with $\oplus$. We can thus compute the output p in time linear in the number of ground clauses. Note that the AC can also be interpreted as a deep neural network with nodes (or neurons) whose (non linear) activation functions are $\times$ and $\oplus$. When the program is not ground, we can build its grounding obtaining a circuit/neural network of the type of Figure 14.5, where however some of the parameters can be the same for different edges. In this case the circuit will exhibit parameter sharing.

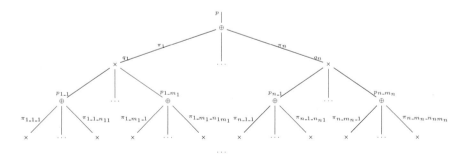

Figure 14.5 Arithmetic circuit/neural net.

Example 126 (Complete HPLP for the UW-CSE domain). *Consider the completed version of Example 125: An online implementation can be found at https://cplint.eu/e/phil/uwcse.pl*

$C_1 = advised\_by(A, B) : 0.3 \leftarrow$
   $student(A), professor(B), project(C, A), project(C, B),$
   $r_{1\_1}(A, B, C).$

$C_2 = advised\_by(A, B) : 0.6 \leftarrow$
   $student(A), professor(B), ta(C, A), taughtby(C, B).$

$C_{1\_1\_1} = r_{1\_1}(A, B, C) : 0.2 \leftarrow$
   $publication(P, A, C), publication(P, B, C).$

$student(harry).$

$professor(ben).$

$project(pr_1, harry). \ project(pr_2, harry).$

$project(pr_1, ben). \ project(pr_2, ben).$

$taught\_by(c_1, ben). \ taught\_by(c_2, ben).$

$ta(c_1, harry). \ ta(c_2, harry).$

$publication(p_1, harry, pr_1). \ publication(p_2, harry, pr_1).$

$publication(p_3, harry, pr_2). \ publication(p_4, harry, pr_2).$

$publication(p_1, ben, pr_1). \ publication(p_2, ben, pr_1).$

$publication(p_3, ben, pr_2). \ publication(p_4, ben, pr_2).$

where we suppose that harry and ben have two joint courses c_1 and c_2, two joint projects pr_1 and pr_2, two joint publications p_1 and p_2 from project pr_1 and two joint publications p_3 and p_4 from project pr_2. The resulting ground program is

$G_1 \ = \ advisedby(harry, ben) : 0.3 \leftarrow$
     $student(harry), professor(ben), project(pr_1, harry),$
     $project(pr_1, ben), r_{1\_1}(harry, ben, pr_1).$

$$G_2 = advisedby(harry, ben) : 0.3 \leftarrow$$
$$student(harry), professor(ben), project(pr_2, harry),$$
$$project(pr_2, ben), r_{1\_1}(harry, ben, pr_2).$$

$$G_3 = advisedby(harry, ben) : 0.6 \leftarrow$$
$$student(harry), professor(ben), ta(c_1, harry),$$
$$taughtby(c_1, ben).$$

$$G_4 = advisedby(harry, ben) : 0.6 \leftarrow$$
$$student(harry), professor(ben), ta(c_2, harry),$$
$$taughtby(c_2, ben).$$

$$G_{1\_1\_1} = r_{1\_1}(harry, ben, pr_1) : 0.2 \leftarrow$$
$$publication(p_1, harry, pr_1), publication(p_1, ben, pr_1).$$

$$G_{1\_1\_2} = r_{1\_1}(harry, ben, pr_1) : 0.2 \leftarrow$$
$$publication(p_2, harry, pr_1), publication(p_2, ben, pr_1).$$

$$G_{2\_1\_1} = r_{1\_1}(harry, ben, pr_2) : 0.2 \leftarrow$$
$$publication(p_3, harry, pr_2), publication(p_3, ben, pr_2).$$

$$G_{2\_1\_2} = r_{1\_1}(harry, ben, pr_2) : 0.2 \leftarrow$$
$$publication(p_4, harry, pr_2), publication(p_4, ben, pr_2).$$

The program tree is shown in Figure 14.6 and the corresponding arithmetic circuit in Figure 14.7 together with the values computed by the nodes. Inference in the AC of Figure 14.7 can be computed at https://cplint.eu/e/phil/ uwcse.pl by running the query

$$inference\_hplp(advisedby(harry, ben), ai, Prob).$$

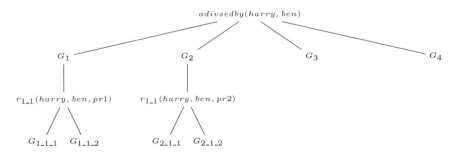

Figure 14.6 Ground probabilistic program tree for Example 126.

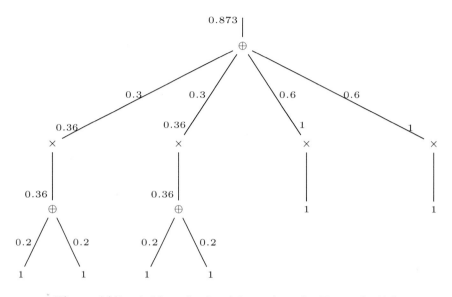

Figure 14.7   Arithmetic circuit/neural net for Example 126.

14.7.2.1.2 Building the Arithmetic Circuit   The network can be built by performing inference using tabling and answer subsumption using PITA (IND, IND) [Riguzzi, 2014; Riguzzi and Swift, 2010], see Section 8.10. Computation by PITA(IND, IND) is thus equivalent to the evaluation of the program arithmetic circuit.

We use an algorithm similar to PITA(IND,IND) to build the Arithmetic circuit or the neural network instead of just computing the probability. To build the arithmetic circuit, it is enough to use the extra argument for storing a term representing the circuit instead of the probability and changing the implementation of the predicates for combining the values of the extra arguments in the body and for combining the values from different clause groundings. The result of inference would thus be a term representing the arithmetic circuit.

There is a one to one correspondence between the data structure built by PITA(IND,IND) and the circuit so there is no need of an expensive compilation step. The term representing the AC in Figure 14.7 is[2]

---

[2] Obtaining by running the query $inference\_hplp(advisedby(harry, ben), ai, Prob, Circuit)$. at https://cplint.eu/e/phil/uwcse.pl

or([and([0, or([and([2])])]), and([0, or([and([2])])]),
and([0, or([and([2])])]), and([0, or([and([2])])]), and([1]), and([1])])

where the operators *and* and *or* represent the product × and the probabilistic sum ⊕ respectively. Once the ACs are built, parameter learning can
be performed over them by applying gradient descent/back-propagation or
Expectation Maximization. The following section presents these algorithms
and their regularized versions. Because of the constraints imposed on HPLPs,
writing these programs may be unintuitive for human so we also propose, in
Section 14.7.2.3, an algorithm for learning both the structure and the parameters from data.

14.7.2.2 Parameter learning

Here we present the algorithm Parameter learning for HIerarchical probabilistic Logic programs (PHIL), which learns HPLP's parameters from data. We
present two versions of PHIL. The first, Deep PHIL (DPHIL), learns HPLP's
parameters by applying a gradient-based method and the second, Expectation
Maximization PHIL (EMPHIL), applies Expectation Maximization (EM).
Different regularized versions of each algorithm will also be presented. The
parameter learning problem can be defined as follows:

Definition 72 (Parameter Learning Problem). *Given a HPLP H with parameters* $\Pi = \{\pi_1 \cdots \pi_n\}$, *an interpretation I defining input predicates and a
training set* $E = \{e_1, \ldots, e_Q, \sim e_{Q+1}, \ldots, \sim e_R\}$ *where each* e_i *is a ground
atom for the target predicate* r, *find the values of* Π *that maximize the log
likelihood (LL)*

$$LL = \arg\max_{\Pi}(\sum_{i=1}^{Q} \log P(e_i) + \sum_{i=Q+1}^{R} \log(1 - P(e_i))) \qquad (14.13)$$

where $P(e_i)$ *is the probability assigned to* e_i *by* $H \cup I$.

Maximizing the LL can be equivalently seen as minimizing the sum of
cross entropy errors err_i for all the examples

$$err = \sum_{i=1}^{R} (-y_i \log P(e_i) - (1 - y_i) \log(1 - P(e_i))) \qquad (14.14)$$

where e_i is an example with y_i indicating its sign ($y_i = 1$ if the example is positive and $y_i = 0$ otherwise) and $P(e_i)$ indicating the probability that atom e_i is true.

DPHIL and EMPHIL minimize the cross entropy error or equivalently maximize the log-likelihood of the data. These algorithms (and their regularized variants) are presented in subsections 14.7.2.2.1 and 14.7.2.2.3 respectively.

14.7.2.2.1 Gradient Descent: DPHIL   DPHIL computes the gradient of the error *err* (14.14) with respect to each parameter and updates the parameters. We do this by building an AC for each example and by running a dynamic programming algorithm for computing the gradient. To simplify gradient computation, we transformed the AC of Figure 14.5 as follows: weight, π_i, labeling arcs from $\oplus$ to $\times$ nodes, are set as children leaves of $\times$ nodes and shared weights are considered as individual leaves with many $\times$ parents. Moreover, negative literals are represented by nodes of the form $not(a)$ with the single child a. The AC in Figure 14.7 is converted into the one shown in Figure 14.8. Note that, the ACs in figures 14.7 and 14.8 are equivalent but the one in Figure 14.8 highlights parameters sharing which is more convenient for illustrating the algorithm.

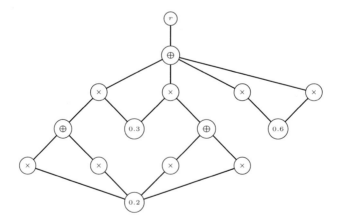

Figure 14.8   Converted arithmetic circuit of Figure 14.7.

The standard gradient descent algorithm computes gradients at each iteration using all examples in the training set. If the training set is large, the algorithm can converge very slowly. To avoid slow convergence, gradients can be computed using a single example, randomly selected in the training set. Even if in this case the algorithm can converge quickly, it is generally hard to reach high training set accuracy. A compromise often used is mini batch stochastic gradient descent (SGD): at each iteration a mini batch of examples is randomly sampled to compute the gradient. This method usually provides fast converge and high accuracy. DPHIL, shown in Algorithm 41, implements SGD.

After building the ACs and initializing the weights, the gradients and the moments, line 2–6, DPHIL performs two passes over each AC in the current batch, line 8–15. In the first, the circuit is evaluated so that each node is assigned a real value representing its probability. This step is bottom-up or forward (line 12) from the leaves to the root. The second step is backward (line 13) or top-down, from the root to the leaves, and computes the derivatives of the loss function with respect to each node. At the end of the backward step, G contains the vector of the derivatives of the error with respect to each parameter. Line 16 updates the weights.

The parameters are repeatedly updated until a maximum number of steps, $MaxIter$, is reached, or until the difference between the LL of the current and the previous iteration drops below a threshold, ϵ, or the difference is below a fraction δ of the current LL. Finally, function UPDATETHEORY (line 18) updates the parameters of the theory. We reparametrized the program using weights between $-\infty$ and $+\infty$ and expressing the parameters using the sigma function $\pi_i = \sigma(W_i) = \frac{1}{1+e^{-W_i}}$ (14.15). In this way we do not have to impose the constraint that the parameters are in [0,1].

Function FORWARD of Algorithm 42 is a recursive function that takes as input an AC $node$ (root node) and evaluates each node from the leaves to the root, assigning value $v(n)$ to each node n. If $node = not(n)$, $p = $ FORWARD(n) is computed and $1 - p$ is assigned to $v(node)$, lines 2–5. If $node = \oplus(n_1, \ldots n_m)$, function $v(n_i) = $ FORWARD(n_i) is recursively called on each child node, and the node value is given by $v(node) = v(n_1) \oplus \ldots \oplus v(n_i)$, lines 7–13. If $node = \times(\pi_i, n_1, \ldots n_m)$, function $v(n_i) = $ FORWARD(n_i) is recursively called on each child node, and the node value is given by $v(n) = \pi_i \cdot v(n_1) \cdot \ldots \cdot v(n_n)$, lines 14–20.

Procedure BACKWARD takes an evaluated AC $node$ and computes the derivative of the contribution of the AC to the cost function, $err = -y \log(p) - (1 - y) \log(1 - p)$ where p is the probability of the atom representing the

---

Algorithm 41 Function DPHIL.

1: **function** PHIL($Theory, \epsilon, \delta, MaxIter, \beta_1, \beta_2, \eta, \hat{\epsilon}, Strategy$)
2: 　　$Examples \leftarrow$ BUILDACS($Theory$) ▷ Build the set of ACs
3: 　　**for** $i \leftarrow 1 \rightarrow |Theory|$ **do** ▷ Initialize weights,gradient and moments vector
4: 　　　　$W[i] \leftarrow random(Min, Max)$ ▷ initially $W[i] \in [Min, Max]$.
5: 　　　　$G[i] \leftarrow 0.0, M_0[i] \leftarrow 0.0, M_1[i] \leftarrow 0.0$
6: 　　**end for**
7: 　　$Iter \leftarrow 1$
8: 　　**repeat**
9: 　　　　$LL \leftarrow 0$
10: 　　　　$Batch \leftarrow$ NEXTBATCH($Examples$) ▷ Select the batch according to the strategy
11: 　　　　**for all** $node \in Batch$ **do**
12: 　　　　　　$P \leftarrow$ FORWARD($node$)
13: 　　　　　　BACKWARD($G, -\frac{1}{P}, node$)
14: 　　　　　　$LL \leftarrow LL + \log P$
15: 　　　　**end for**
16: 　　　　UPDATEWEIGHTSADAM($W, G, M_0, M_1, \beta_1, \beta_2, \eta, \hat{\epsilon}, Iter$)
17: 　　**until** $LL - LL_0 < \epsilon \vee LL - LL_0 < -LL.\delta \vee Iter > MaxIter$
18: 　　$FinalTheory \leftarrow$ UPDATETHEORY($Theory, W$)
19: 　　**return** $FinalTheory$
20: **end function**

---

example. This derivative is given in Equation 14.16

$$\frac{\partial err}{\partial v(n)} = -d(n)\frac{1}{v(r)} \tag{14.16}$$

with

$$d(n) = \begin{cases} d(pa_n)\frac{v(pa_n)}{v(n)} & \text{if } n \text{ is a } \oplus \text{ node,} \\ d(pa_n)\frac{1-v(pa_n)}{1-v(n)} & \text{if } n \text{ is a } \times \text{ node} \\ \sum_{pa_n} d(pa_n).v(pa_n).(1 - \pi_i) & \text{if } n = \sigma(W_i) \\ -d(pa_n) & \text{if } pa_n = not(n) \end{cases} \tag{14.17}$$

where pa_n indicates the parents of n.

This leads to Procedure BACKWARD shown in Algorithm 43 which is a simplified version for the case $v(n) \neq 0$ for all $\oplus$ nodes. To compute $d(n)$, BACKWARD proceeds by recursively propagating the derivative of the parent node to the children. Initially, the derivative of the error with respect to the root node, $-\frac{1}{v(r)}$, is computed. If the current node is $not(n)$, with derivative $AccGrad$, the derivative of its unique child, n, is $-AccGrad$, line 2-3. If the

---

Algorithm 42 FUNCTION FORWARD

1: **function** FORWARD(*node*)   ▷ node is an AC
2:      **if** $node = not(n)$ **then**
3:          $v(node) \leftarrow 1 - $ FORWARD(n)
4:          **return** $v(node)$
5:      **else**
6:                    ▷ Compute the output example by recursively call Forward on its sub AC
7:          **if** $node = \oplus(n_1, \dots n_m)$ **then**   ▷ $\oplus$ node
8:              **for all** n_j **do**
9:                  $v(n_j) \leftarrow$ FORWARD(n_j)
10:             **end for**
11:             $v(node) \leftarrow v(n_1) \oplus \dots \oplus v(n_m)$
12:             **return** $v(node)$
13:          **else**   ▷ and Node
14:             **if** $node = \times(\pi_i, n_1, \dots n_m)$ **then**
15:                **for all** n_j **do**
16:                    $v(n_j) \leftarrow$ FORWARD(n_j)
17:                **end for**
18:                $v(node) \leftarrow \pi_i \cdot v(n_1) \cdot \dots \cdot v(n_m)$
19:                **return** $v(node)$
20:             **end if**
21:          **end if**
22:      **end if**
23: **end function**

---

current node is a $\oplus$ node, with derivative $AccGrad$, the derivative of each child, n, is computed as follows:

$$AccGrad' = AccGrad \cdot \frac{1 - v(node)}{1 - v(n)}$$

and back-propagated, line 5-9. If the current node is a $\times$ node, the derivative of a non leaf child node n is computed as follows:

$$AccGrad'_1 = AccGrad \cdot \frac{v(node)}{v(n)}$$

The derivative for a leaf child node $n = \pi_i$ is

$$AccGrad'_2 = AccGrad \cdot v(node) \cdot (1 - \sigma(W_i))$$

and back-propagated, line 11-15. For leaf node, i.e a π_i node, the derivative is accumulated, line 20.

Algorithm 43 PROCEDURE BACKWARD

1: **procedure** BACKWARD(G, $AccGrad$, $node$)
2:      **if** $node = not(n)$ **then**
3:          BACKWARD(G, $-AccGrad$, n)
4:      **else**
5:          **if** $node = \bigoplus(n_1, \ldots n_m)$ **then**   ▷ $\bigoplus$ node
6:              **for all** n_j **do**
7:                  $AccGrad'_1 \leftarrow AccGrad \cdot \frac{v(node)}{v(n_i)}$
8:                  BACKWARD(G, $AccGrad'$, n_i)
9:              **end for**
10:         **else**
11:             **if** $node = \times(\pi_i \cdot n_1, \ldots n_m)$ **then**   ▷ $\times$ node
12:                 **for all** n_j **do**   ▷ non leaf child
13:                     $AccGrad' \leftarrow AccGrad \cdot \frac{1-v(node)}{1-v(n_j)}$
14:                     BACKWARD(G, $AccGrad'_1$, n_j)
15:                 **end for**
16:                 $AccGrad'_2 \leftarrow AccGrad \cdot v(node).(1 - \sigma(W_i))$ ▷ leaf child
17:                 BACKWARD(G, $AccGrad'_2$, π_i)
18:             **else**   ▷ leaf node
19:                 let $node = \pi_i$
20:                 $G[i] \leftarrow G[i] + AccGrad$
21:             **end if**
22:         **end if**
23:     **end if**
24: **end procedure**

After the computation of the gradients, weights are updated. Standard gradient descent adds a fraction η, called learning rate, of the gradient to the current weights. η is a value between 0 and 1 that is used to control the parameter update. Small η can slow down the algorithm and find local minimum. High η avoids local minima but can swing around global minima. A good compromise updates the learning rate at each iteration combining the advantages of both strategies. We use the update method *Adam*, adaptive moment estimation [Kingma and Ba, 2014], that uses the first order gradient to compute the exponential moving averages of the gradient and the squared gradient. Hyper-parameters $\beta_1, \beta_2 \in [0, 1)$ control the exponential decay rates of these moving averages. These quantities are estimations of the *first moment* (the mean M_0) and the *second moment* (the uncentered variance M_1) of the gradient. The weights are updated with a fraction, current learning rate, of the combination of these moments, see Procedure UPDATEWEIGHTSADAM in Algorithm 44.

Algorithm 44 PROCEDURE UPDATEWEIGHTSADAM

1: **procedure** UPDATEWEIGHTSADAM$(W, G, M_0, M_1, \beta_1, \beta_2, \eta, \hat{\epsilon}, iter)$
2:      $\eta_{iter} \leftarrow \eta \frac{\sqrt{1-\beta_2^{iter}}}{1-\beta_1^{iter}}$
3:      **for** $i \leftarrow 1 \rightarrow |W|$ **do**
4:          $M_0[i] \leftarrow \beta_1 \cdot M_0[i] + (1 - \beta_1) \cdot G[i]$
5:          $M_1[i] \leftarrow \beta_2 \cdot M_1[i] + (1 - \beta_2) \cdot G[i] \cdot G[i]$
6:          $W[i] \leftarrow W[i] - \eta_{iter} \cdot \frac{M_0[i]}{(\sqrt{M_1[i]})+\hat{\epsilon}}$
7:      **end for**
8: **end procedure**

14.7.2.2.2 DPHIL regularization: DPHIL$_1$ and DPHIL$_2$ In deep learning and machine learning in general, a technique called **regularization** is often used to avoid over-fitting. Regularization penalizes the loss function by adding a *regularization* term for favoring small parameters. In the literature, there exist two main regularization techniques called L_1 and L_2 regularization that differ on the way they penalize the loss function. While L_1 adds to the loss function the sum of the absolute values of the parameters, L_2 adds the sum of their squares. Given the loss function defined in Equation 14.14, the corresponding regularized loss function are given by equations 14.18 and 14.19.

$$err_1 = \sum_{i=1}^{R} -y_i \log P(e_i) - (1 - y_i) \log(1 - P(e_i)) + \gamma \sum_{i=1}^{k} |\pi_i| \quad (14.18)$$

$$err_2 = \sum_{i=1}^{R} -y_i \log P(e_i) - (1 - y_i) \log(1 - P(e_i)) + \frac{\gamma}{2} \sum_{i=1}^{k} \pi_i^2 \quad (14.19)$$

where the regularization hyper-parameter γ determines how much to penalize the parameters and k is the number of parameters. When γ is zero, the regularization term becomes zero and we are back to the original loss function. When γ is large, we penalize the parameters and they tend to become small. Note also that we add the regularization term to the initial loss function because we are performing minimization. The main difference between these techniques is that, while L_1 favor sparse parameters (many parameters equal to zero), L_2 brings parameters to be close to 0, not necessarily equal to 0. Moreover in general, L_1 (resp. L_2) is computationally inefficient (resp. efficient due to having analytical solutions).

Now let us compute the derivative of the regularized error with respect to each node in the AC. The regularized term depends only on the leaves (the parameters π_i) of the AC. So the gradients of the parameters can be calculated by adding the derivative of the regularization term with respect to π_i to the one obtained in Equation 14.17. The regularized errors are given by:

$$E_{reg} = \begin{cases} \gamma \sum_{i=1}^{k} \pi_i & \text{for } L_1 \\ \frac{\gamma}{2} \sum_{i=1}^{k} \pi_i^2 & \text{for } L_2 \end{cases} \tag{14.20}$$

where $\pi_i = \sigma(W_i)$. Note that since $0 \leqslant \pi_i \leqslant 1$ we can consider π_i rather than $|\pi_i|$ in L_1. So

$$\frac{\partial E_{reg}}{\partial W_i} = \begin{cases} \gamma \frac{\partial \sigma(W_i)}{\partial W_i} = \gamma \cdot \sigma(W_i) \cdot (1 - \sigma(W_i)) = \gamma \cdot \pi_i \cdot (1 - \pi_i) \\ \frac{\gamma}{2} \frac{\partial \sigma(W_i)^2}{\partial W_i} = \gamma \cdot \sigma(W_i) \cdot \sigma(W_i) \cdot (1 - \sigma(W_i)) = \gamma \cdot \pi_i^2 \cdot (1 - \pi_i) \end{cases}$$
$$\tag{14.21}$$

So Equation 14.17 becomes

$$d(n) = \begin{cases} d(pa_n) \frac{v(pa_n)}{v(n)} & \text{if } n \text{ is a } \oplus \text{ node,} \\ d(pa_n) \frac{1 - v(pa_n)}{1 - v(n)} & \text{if } n \text{ is a } \times \text{ node} \\ \sum_{pa_n} d(pa_n).v(pa_n).(1 - \pi_i) + \frac{\partial E_{reg}}{\partial W_i} & \text{if } n = \sigma(W_i) \\ -d(pa_n) & \text{if } pa_n = not(n) \end{cases}$$
$$\tag{14.22}$$

In order to implement the regularized version of DPHIL (DPHIL$_1$ and DPHIL$_2$), the forward and the backward passes described in algorithms 42 and 43 remain unchanged. The unique change occurs while updating the parameters in Algorithm 44. *UpdateWeightsAdam* line 6 becomes

$$W[i] \leftarrow W[i] - \eta_{iter} * \frac{M_0[i]}{(\sqrt{M_1[i]}) + \hat{\epsilon}} + \frac{\partial E_{reg}}{\partial W_i} \tag{14.23}$$

14.7.2.2.3 Expectation Maximization: EMPHIL   EMPHIL learns the parameters of HPLP by applying Expectation Maximization (EM). The algorithm maximizes the log-likelihood LL defined in Equation 14.13 by alternating between an Expectation (E) and a Maximization (M) step. E-step computes the expected values of the incomplete data given the complete data and the current parameters and the M-step determines the new values of the parameters that maximize the likelihood. Each iteration is guaranteed to increase the log-likelihood. Given a *hierarchical* PLP $H = \{C_i | i = 1, \cdots, n\}$ (each C_i annotated with the parameter π_i) and a training set of positive and negative examples $E = \{e_1, \ldots, e_Q, \sim e_{Q+1}, \ldots, \sim e_R\}$, EMPHIL proceeds as follows:

Let C_i be a generic rule and $g(i) = \{j | \theta_j$ is a substitution grounding $C_i\}$. For a single example e, the E-step computes $\mathbf{E}[c_{i0}|e]$ and $\mathbf{E}[c_{i1}|e]$ for all rules C_i. c_{ix} is the number of times a variable X_{ij} takes value x for $x \in \{0,1\}$, for all $j \in g(i)$. So $\mathbf{E}[c_{ix}|e] = \sum_{j \in g(i)} P(X_{ij} = x|e)$. These values are aggregated over all examples obtaining

$$N_0[i] = \mathbf{E}[c_{i0}] = \sum_{e \in E} \sum_{j \in g(i)} P(X_{ij} = 0|e) \tag{14.24}$$

$$N_1[i] = \mathbf{E}[c_{i1}] = \sum_{e \in E} \sum_{j \in g(i)} P(X_{ij} = 1|e) \tag{14.25}$$

Then the M-step computes π_i by maximum likelihood, i.e. $\pi_i = \frac{N_1[i]}{N_0[i]+N_1[i]}$. Note that for a single substitution θ_j of clause C_i we have $P(X_{ij} = 0|e) + P(X_{ij} = 1|e) = 1$. So $E[c_{i0}] + E[c_{i1}] = \sum_{e \in E} |g(i)|$. So the M-step computes

$$\pi_i = \frac{N_1[i]}{\sum_{e \in E} |g(i)|} \tag{14.26}$$

Therefore to perform EMPHIL, we have to compute $P(X_{ij} = 1|e)$ for each example e by performing the belief propagation algorithm over the factor graph associated with the AC. Message passing is then applied over the AC. The messages in the bottom-up, c_N, and top-down, t_N, directions are respectively given as

$$c_N = v(N) \tag{14.27}$$

$$t_N = \begin{cases} \frac{t_P}{t_P + v(P) \ominus v(N) \cdot t_P + (1 - v(P) \ominus v(N)) \cdot (1 - t_p)} & \text{if } P \text{ is a } \oplus \text{ node} \\ \frac{t_P \cdot \frac{v(P)}{v(N)} + (1 - t_P) \cdot (1 - \frac{v(P)}{v(N)})}{t_P \cdot \frac{v(P)}{v(N)} + (1 - t_P) \cdot (1 - \frac{v(P)}{v(N)}) + (1 - t_P)} & \text{if } P \text{ is a } \times \text{ node} \\ 1 - t_P & \text{if } P \text{ is a } \textit{not} \text{ node} \end{cases} \tag{14.28}$$

where $v(N)$ is the value of node N, P is its parent and the operator $\ominus$ is defined as

$$v(p) \ominus v(n) = 1 - \frac{1 - v(p)}{1 - v(n)} \qquad (14.29)$$

c_N is computed by applying the forward pass described in Algorithm 42.

Since the belief propagation algorithm (for ACs) converges after two passes, we can compute the unnormalized belief of each parameter during the backward pass by multiplying t_N by $v(N)$ (that is all incoming messages). Algorithm 45 performs the backward pass of belief propagation algorithm and computes the normalized belief of each parameter, i.e., t_N. It also computes the expectations $N_0[i]$ and $N_1[i]$ for each parameter, lines 17–19.

Algorithm 45 PROCEDURE BACKWARD IN EMPHIL

1:   **procedure** BACKWARDEM($t_p, node, N_0, N_1$)
2:     **if** $node = not(n)$ **then**
3:         BACKWARD($1 - t_p, n, B, Count$)
4:     **else**
5:         **if** $node = \oplus(n_1, \ldots n_m)$ **then** $\triangleright \oplus$ node
6:             **for all** child n_i **do**
7:                  $t_{n_i} \leftarrow \dfrac{t_p}{t_p + v(node) \ominus v(n_i) \cdot t_p + (1 - v(node) \ominus v(n_i)) \cdot (1 - t_p)}$
8:                 BACKWARDEM($t_{n_i}, n_i, B, Count$)
9:             **end for**
10:         **else**
11:             **if** $node = \times(n_1, \ldots n_m)$ **then** $\triangleright \times$ node
12:                 **for all** child n_i **do**
13:                      $t_{n_i} \leftarrow \dfrac{t_p \cdot \frac{v(node)}{v(n_i)} + (1 - t_p) \cdot (1 - \frac{v(node)}{v(n_i)})}{t_p \cdot \frac{v(node)}{v(n_i)} + (1 - t_p) \cdot (1 - \frac{v(node)}{v(n_i)}) + (1 - t_p)}$
14:                   BACKWARDEM($t_{n_i}, n_i, B, Count$)
15:                 **end for**
16:             **else** $\triangleright$ leaf node π_i
17:                 **let** $E = \dfrac{\pi_i t_p}{\pi_i t_p + (1 - \pi_i)(1 - t_p)}$
18:                  $N_1[i] \leftarrow N_1[i] + E$
19:                  $N_0[i] \leftarrow N_0[i] + 1 - E$
20:             **end if**
21:         **end if**
22:     **end if**
23:   **end procedure**

EMPHIL is then presented in Algorithm 46. After building the ACs (sharing parameters) for positive and negative examples and initializing the parameters, the expectations and the counters, lines 2–5, EMPHIL proceeds by alternating between expectation step 8–13 and maximization step 13–24. The algorithm stops when the LL converges. The theory is then updated and returned (lines 26–27).

Algorithm 46 Function EMPHIL.

1: **function** EMPHIL($Theory, \epsilon, \delta, MaxIter, \gamma, a, b, Type$)
2:     $Examples \leftarrow$ BUILDACS($Theory$)   ▷ Build the set of ACs
3:     **for** $i \leftarrow 1 \rightarrow |Theory|$ **do**
4:         $\Pi[i] \leftarrow random; B[i], Count[i] \leftarrow 0$ ▷ Initialize the parameters
5:     **end for**
6:     $LL \leftarrow -inf; Iter \leftarrow 0$
7:     **repeat**
8:         $LL_0 \leftarrow LL, LL \leftarrow 0$ ▷ Expectation step
9:         **for all** $node \in Examples$ **do**
10:             $P \leftarrow$ FORWARD($node$)
11:             BACKWARDEM($1, node, N_0, N_1$)
12:             $LL \leftarrow LL + \log P$
13:         **end for**   ▷ Maximization step
14:         **for** $i \leftarrow 1 \rightarrow |Theory|$ **do**
15:             **switch** $Type$
16:                 **case 0:** $\Pi[i] \leftarrow \frac{N_1[i]}{N_0[i]+N_1[i]}$
17:                 **case 1:** $\Pi[i] \leftarrow \frac{4N_1[i]}{2(\gamma+N_0[i]+N_1[i]+\sqrt{(N_0[i]+N_1[i])^2+\gamma^2+2\gamma(N_0[i]-N_1[i]))}}$
18:                 **case 2:**
19:                     let $V = 2\sqrt{\frac{3N_0+3N_1+\gamma}{\gamma}} \cos\left(\frac{\arccos\left(\frac{\sqrt{\frac{\gamma}{3N_0+3N_1+\gamma}}\left(\frac{9N_0}{2}-9N_1+\gamma\right)}{3N_0+3N_1+\gamma} \right)}{3} - \frac{2\pi}{3} \right)$
20:                   $\Pi[i] \leftarrow \frac{V}{3} + \frac{1}{3}$
21:                 **case 3:** $\Pi[i] \leftarrow \frac{N_1+a}{N_0+N_1+a+b}$
22:             **end switch**
23:             $B[i], Count[i] \leftarrow 0$
24:         **end for**
25:     **until** $LL - LL_0 < \epsilon \vee LL - LL_0 < -LL.\delta \vee Iter > MaxIter$
26:     $FinalTheory \leftarrow$ UPDATETHEORY($Theory, \Pi$)
27:     **return** $FinalTheory$
28: **end function**

14.7.2.2.4 EMPHIL regularization: EMPHIL$_1$, EMPHIL$_2$ and EMPHIL$_B$

In this section, we propose three regularized versions of EMPHIL. As described in [Li et al., 2005], EM can be regularized for two reasons: first, for highlighting the strong relationship existing between the incomplete and the missing data, and second for favoring smaller parameters. We regularize

EMPHIL mainly for the latter reason. As in gradient descent regularization, we define the following regularization objective functions for L_1 and L_2 respectively.

$$J(\theta) = \begin{cases} N_1 \log \theta + N_0 \log(1 - \theta) - \gamma\theta & \text{for } L_1 \\ N_1 \log \theta + N_0 \log(1 - \theta) - \frac{\gamma}{2}\theta^2 & \text{for } L_2 \end{cases} \tag{14.30}$$

where $\theta = \pi_i$, N_0 and N_1 are the expectations computed in the E-step (see equations 14.24 and 14.25). The M-step aims at computing the value of θ that maximizes $J(\theta)$. This is done by solving the equation $\frac{\partial J(\theta)}{\partial \theta} = 0$. The following theorems give the optimal value of θ in each case.

Theorem 22 (Maximum of the L_1 regularized objective function). *The L_1 regularized objective function:*

$$J_1(\theta) = N_1 \log \theta + N_0 \log(1 - \theta) - \gamma\theta \tag{14.31}$$

is maximum in

$$\theta_1 = \frac{4N_1}{2(\gamma + N_0 + N_1 + \sqrt{(N_0 + N_1)^2 + \gamma^2 + 2\gamma(N_0 - N_1)})}$$

Theorem 23 (Maximum of the L_2 regularized objective function). *The L_2 regularized objective function:*

$$J_2(\theta) = N_1 \log \theta + N_0 \log(1 - \theta) - \frac{\gamma}{2}\theta^2 \tag{14.32}$$

is maximum in

$$\theta_2 = \frac{2\sqrt{\frac{3N_0 + 3N_1 + \gamma}{\gamma}} \cos\left(\frac{\arccos\left(\frac{\sqrt{\frac{\gamma}{3N_0 + 3N_1 + \gamma}}\left(\frac{9N_0}{2} - 9N_1 + \gamma\right)}{3N_0 + 3N_1 + \gamma}\right)}{3} - \frac{2\pi}{3}\right)}{3} + \frac{1}{3}$$

We consider another regularization method for EMPHIL (called EMPHIL$_B$) which is based on a Bayesian update of the parameters assuming a prior that takes the form of a Dirichlet distribution with parameters $[a, b]$. In the M-step, instead of computing $\pi_i = \frac{N_1}{N_0 + N_1}$, EMPHIL$_B$ computes

$$\pi_i = \frac{N_1 + a}{N_0 + N_1 + a + b} \tag{14.33}$$

as described in Bishop [2016]. a and b are hyper-parameters. We choose $a = 0$ and b as a fraction of the training set size, since we want small parameters.

So algorithms EMPHIL (the standard EM), $EMPHIL_1$, $EMPHIL_2$ and $EMPHIL_B$ differ in the way they update the parameters in the M-step, Algorithm 46 lines 15-22.

14.7.2.3 Structure learning

In the previous section, the structure of an HPLP was given and the task was to learn its parameters from data. Since hidden predicates could be difficult to interprete for humans in many domains of interest, providing the structure of an HPLP may be unintuitive and tedious even for experts of the domain. In this section, we propose an algorithm for learning both the structure and the parameters from data. The structure is learned by mean of predicate invention. The structure learning problem is defined as follows:

Definition 73 (Structure Learning Problem). *Given a set of mega-examples (interpretations), each containing positive and negative examples for a target predicate and facts for input predicates, $I = \{e_1, \ldots, e_Q, \sim e_{Q+1}, \ldots, \sim e_R\}$, find the HPLP with parameters Π that maximizes the (log) likelihood*

$$LL = \arg\max_{\Pi} \sum_{I} (\sum_{i=1}^{Q} \log P(e_i) + \sum_{i=Q+1}^{R} \log(1 - P(e_i))) \qquad (14.34)$$

where $P(e_i)$ is the probability assigned to e_i (an example from the interpretation I).

SLEAHP learns HPLPs by generating an initial set of bottom clauses (from a language bias) from which a large HPLP is derived. Then SLEAHP performs structure learning by using parameter learning. Regularization is used to bring as many parameters as possible close to 0 so that their clauses can be removed, thus pruning the initial large program and keeping only useful clauses.

14.7.2.3.1 Description of the algorithm In order to learn an HPLP, SLEAHP (Algorithm 47) initially generates a set of bottom clauses, line 2. Then an n-ary tree, whose nodes are literals appearing in the head or in the body of bottom clauses is constructed, line 3. An initial HPLP is generated from the tree, line 4 and a regularized version of PHIL is performed on the initial program. Finally clauses with very small probabilities are removed, line 5. The components of this algorithm are described in the following subsections.

Algorithm 47 Function STRUCTURE LEARNING

1: **function** SLEAHP($NInt, NS, NA, MaxProb, NumLayer, MaxIter, \epsilon, \delta, MinProb$)
2:      $Clauses \leftarrow$ GENCLAUSES($NInt, NS, NA$)   ▷ Generate clauses
3:      $Tree \leftarrow$ GENTREE(Clauses)   ▷ Build the tree
4:      $init\_HPLP \leftarrow$ GENHPLP(Clauses,MaxProb,NumLayer)   ▷ Generate the initial HPLP
5:      $(LL, final\_HPLP) \leftarrow$ PHIL_REG($init\_HPLP, MaxIter, \epsilon, \delta$) ▷ Learns the parameters
6:      **return** $final\_HPLP$
7: **end function**

14.7.2.3.2 Clause generation   Algorithm 48 generates a set of bottom clauses as in Progol, [Muggleton, 1995]. These bottom clauses are then used for creating a tree of literals, Algorithm 49.

Each ground bottom clause $BC = h :- b_1, \ldots, b_m$ is then processed to obtain a probabilistic program clause by replacing each term in a + or − place-marker with a variable, using the same variable for identical terms. Terms corresponding to # or −# place-markers are instead kept in the clause. This process is repeated for a number $NInt$ of input mega-examples and a number NA of answers, thus obtaining $NInt \cdot NA$ bottom clauses.

Algorithm 48 Function GENERATECLAUSES

1: **function** GENCLAUSES($NInt, NS, NA$)
2:      **for all** predicates P/Ar **do**
3:          $Clauses \leftarrow []$
4:          **for all** modeh declarations $modeh(rec, s)$ with P/Ar predicate of s **do**
5:              **for** $i = 1 \rightarrow NInt$ **do**
6:                  Select randomly a mega-example I
7:                  **for** $j = 1 \rightarrow NA$ **do**
8:                      Select randomly an atom h from I matching $schema(s)$
9:                      Bottom clause $BC \leftarrow$ SATURATION(h, rec, NS), let BC be $Head :- Body$
10:                     $Clauses \leftarrow [Head : 0.5 :- Body | Clauses]$
11:                 **end for**
12:             **end for**
13:         **end for**
14:     **end for**
15:     **return** $Clauses$
16: **end function**

14.7.2.3.3 Tree generation   Since an HPLP can be mapped into a tree as described in Section 14.7.2.1, we create a tree whose nodes are literals appearing in the head or in the body of bottom clauses generated in the previous section. Every node in the tree shares at least one variable with its parent. The tree is then converted into the initial HPLP, see Section 14.7.2.3.4.

To create the tree, Algorithm 49 starts by considering each bottom clause in turn, line 3. Each bottom clause creates a tree, lines 4 - 11. Consider the following bottom clause

$$BC = r(\boldsymbol{Arg}) :- b_1(\boldsymbol{Arg}_1), \ldots, b_m(\boldsymbol{Arg}_m)$$

where $\boldsymbol{Arg}$ and $\boldsymbol{Arg}_i$ are tuples of arguments and the $b_i(\boldsymbol{Arg}_i)$ for $i = 1, \ldots, m$ are literals. Initially $r(\boldsymbol{Arg})$ is set as the root of the tree, lines 5. Literals in the body are considered in turn from left to right. When a literal $b_i(\boldsymbol{Arg}_i)$ is chosen, the algorithm tries to insert the literal in the tree, see Algorithm 50. If $b_i(\boldsymbol{Arg}_i)$ cannot be inserted, it is set as the right-most child of the root. This proceeds until all the $b_i(\boldsymbol{Arg}_i)$ are inserted into a tree, lines 6–10. Then the resulting tree is appended into a list of trees (initially empty), line 11, and the list is merged obtaining a unique tree, line 13. The trees in L are merged by unifying the arguments of the roots.

Algorithm 49 GENERATE TREE

1:   **function** GENTREE(*Bottoms*)
2:      $L \leftarrow []$
3:      **for all** Bottom in Bottoms **do**
4:          let *Bottom* be $r(\boldsymbol{Arg}) :- b_1(\boldsymbol{Arg}_1), \ldots, b_m(\boldsymbol{Arg}_m)$
5:          $Tree \leftarrow r(\boldsymbol{Arg})$ $\triangleright r(\boldsymbol{Arg})$ is the root of the tree
6:          **for all** $b_i(\boldsymbol{Arg}_i)$ **do**
7:             **if** $not(\text{INSERTTREE}(Tree, b_i(\boldsymbol{Arg}_i)))$ **then**
8:                addChild($r(\boldsymbol{Arg})$,$b_i(\boldsymbol{Arg}_i)$)
9:             **end if**
10:        **end for**
11:        $L \leftarrow L \cdot append(Tree)$
12:     **end for**
13:     $final\_Tree \leftarrow mergeTrees(L)$
14:     **return** $final\_Tree$
15: **end function**

To insert the literal $b_i(\boldsymbol{Arg}_i)$ into the tree, Algorithm 50, nodes in the tree are visited depth-first. When a node $b(\boldsymbol{Arg})$ is visited, if $\boldsymbol{Arg}$ and $\boldsymbol{Arg}_i$ share at least one variable, $b_i(\boldsymbol{Arg}_i)$ is set as the right-most child of $b(\boldsymbol{Arg})$ and the algorithm stops and returns $True$. Otherwise $InsertTree$ is recursively called on each child of $b(\boldsymbol{Arg})$, lines 6 - 12. The algorithm returns $False$ if the literal cannot be inserted after visiting all the nodes, line 3.

Algorithm 50 INSERT A LITERAL INTO A TREE

1: **function** INSERTTREE($Tree$,$b_i(\boldsymbol{Arg_i})$)
2:      **if** Tree=NULL **then**   ▷ All nodes are visited
3:          return $False$
4:      **else**
5:          let $Tree$ be $b(\boldsymbol{Arg})$
6:          **if** $shareArgument(\boldsymbol{Arg}, \boldsymbol{Arg_i})$ **then**
7:              addChild($Tree$,$b_i(\boldsymbol{Arg_i})$)
8:              return $True$
9:          **else**
10:             **for all** $Child$ of $Tree$ **do**
11:                 return INSERTTREE($Child, b_i(\boldsymbol{Arg_i})$)
12:             **end for**
13:         **end if**
14:     **end if**
15: **end function**

Example 127 (Bottom clause for the UW-CSE dataset).   *Consider the following bottom clause from the UW-CSE dataset:*

$advised\_by(A, B) \leftarrow$
$\quad student(A), professor(B), has\_position(B, C),$
$\quad publication(D, B), publication(D, E), in\_phase(A, F),$
$\quad taught\_by(G, E, H), ta(I, J, H).$

In order to build the tree, $advised\_by(A, B)$ is initially set as the root of the tree. Then predicates in the body are considered in turn. The predicates $student(A)$ (resp. $professor(B)$, $hasposition(B, C)$ and $publication(D, B)$) are set as the children of $advised\_by(A, B)$ because their arguments share variable A (resp. B). Then the predicate $publication(D, E)$ is set as a child of $publication(D, B)$ because their arguments share variable D, $in\_phase(A, F)$ as a child of $advised\_by(A, B)$ (they share variable A), $taughtby(G, E, H)$ as a child of $publication(D, E)$ (they share variable E) and finally $ta(I, J, H)$ as a child of $taughtby(G, E, H)$ (they share variable H). The corresponding tree is shown in Figure 14.9.

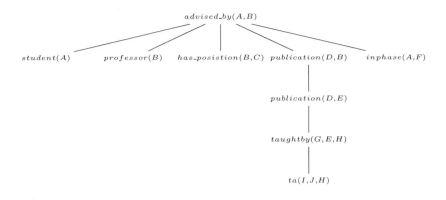

Figure 14.9   Tree created from the bottom clause of Example 127.

14.7.2.3.4 HPLP generation   Once the tree is built, an initial HPLP is generated at random from the tree. Before describing how the program is created, note that for computation purposes, we consider clauses with at most two literals in the body. This can be extended to any number of literals. Algorithm 51 takes as input the tree, $Tree$, an initial probability, $0 \leqslant MaxProb \leqslant 1$, a rate, $0 \leqslant rate \leqslant 1$, and the number of layers $1 \leqslant NumLayer \leqslant height(Tree)$ of the HPLP we are about to generate. Let $\boldsymbol{X}$, $\boldsymbol{Y}$, $\boldsymbol{Z}$ and $\boldsymbol{W}$ be tuples of variables.

In order to generate the initial HPLP, the tree is visited breadth-first, starting from level 1. For each node n_i at level $Level$ ($1 \leqslant Level \leqslant NumLayer$), n_i is visited with probability $Prob$. Otherwise n_i and the subtree rooted at n_i are not visited. $Prob$ is initialized to $MaxProb$, 1.0 by default. The new value of $Prob$ at each level is $Prob \times rate$ where $rate \in [0, 1]$ is a constant value, 0.95 by default. Thus the deeper the level, the lower the probability value. Supposing that n_i is visited, two cases can occur: n_i is a leaf or an internal node.

If $n_i = b_i(\boldsymbol{Y})$ is a leaf node with parent $Parent_i$, we consider two cases. If $Parent_i = r(\boldsymbol{X})$ (the root of the tree), then the clause

$$C = r(\boldsymbol{X}) : 0.5 :- b_i(\boldsymbol{Y}).$$

is generated, lines 9-11. Otherwise let $path$ is the path from the root to $Parent_i$, $Parent_i$ be $b_{path}(\boldsymbol{X})$ and n_i be $b_{path\_i}(\boldsymbol{Y})$. Then clause

$$C = hidden_{path}(\boldsymbol{Z}) : 0.5 :- b_{path\_i}(\boldsymbol{Y}).$$

is generated, lines 13-15.

If $n_i = b_i(\boldsymbol{Y})$ is an internal node having parent $Parent_i$, we consider two cases. If $Parent_i$ is the root, the clause

$$C = r(\boldsymbol{X}) : 0.5 :- b_i(\boldsymbol{Y}), hidden\_i(\boldsymbol{Z}).$$

is generated, where $\boldsymbol{Z} = \boldsymbol{X} \cup \boldsymbol{Y}$, lines 19-20. If $Parent_i$ is an internal node, let $path$ is the path from the root to $Parent_i$ and n_i be $b_{path\_i}(\boldsymbol{Y})$. Then the clause

$$C = hidden_{path}(\boldsymbol{Z}) : 0.5 :- b_{path\_i}(\boldsymbol{Y}), hidden_{path\_i}(\boldsymbol{W}).$$

is generated where $\boldsymbol{W} = \boldsymbol{Z} \cup \boldsymbol{Y}$, lines 23-24.

The generated clause C is added to a list (initially empty), line 27, and the algorithm proceeds for every node at each level until layer $NumLayer$ is reached or all nodes in the tree are visited, line 5. Then hidden predicates appearing in the body of clauses without associated clauses (in the next layer) are removed, line 33, and the program is reduced, line 34. To reduce the program, a set of clauses (without hidden predicates in the body) that are renaming of each other are reduced to a single representative of the set. Note that atoms in the head of the generated clauses are all annotated with probability 0.5 for exposition purposes. These values are replaced by random values between 0 and 1 at the beginning the parameter learning process, see Algorithm 47 line 5.

Example 128 (HPLP generated by SLEAHP for the UW-CSE domain). *The HPLP generated from the tree of Figure 14.9 is:*
> $advised\_by(A, B) : 0.5 \leftarrow student(A).$
> $advised\_by(A, B) : 0.5 \leftarrow professor(B).$
> $advised\_by(A, B) : 0.5 \leftarrow has\_position(B, C).$
> $advised\_by(A, B) : 0.5 \leftarrow publication(D, B), hidden_1(A, B, D).$
> $advised\_by(A, B) : 0.5 \leftarrow in\_phase(A, E).$
> $hidden_1(A, B, D) : 0.5 \leftarrow publication(D, F), hidden_{1\_1}(A, B, D, F).$
> $hidden_{1\_1}(A, B, D, F) : 0.5 \leftarrow taught\_by(G, F, H),$
> $\quad hidden_{1\_1\_1}(A, B, D, F, G, H).$
> $hidden_{1\_1\_1}(A, B, D, F, G, H) : 0.5 \leftarrow ta(I, J, H).$

SLEAHP was compared with PLP systems such as SLIPCOVER and PROB-FOIL+ and with with Statistical Relational Learning methods such as MLN-BC and MLN-BT [Khot et al., 2011] for learning Markov Logic Networks (MLNs) and with RDN-B [Natarajan et al., 2012] for learning Relational Dependency Networks. The comparison was performed on five datasets.

Algorithm 51 FUNCTION GENERATEHPLP

1: **function** GENERATEHPLP($Tree, MaxProb, Rate, NumLayer$)
2:     $HPLP \leftarrow []$
3:     $Level \leftarrow 1$
4:     $Prob \leftarrow MaxProb$
5:     **while** $Level < NumLayer$ *and* all nodes in $Tree$ are not visited **do**
6:         **for all** node n_i at level $Level$ having parent $Parent_i$ **do**
7:             **if** maybe(Prob) **then**
8:                 **if** n_i is a leaf node **then**   ▷ n_i is a leaf node
9:                     **if** $Parent_i$ is the root node **then**
10:                         let n_i be $b_i(\boldsymbol{Y})$ and $Parent_i$ be $r(\boldsymbol{X})$
11:                         $C \leftarrow r(\boldsymbol{X}) : 0.5 :- b_i(\boldsymbol{Y}).$
12:                     **else**
13:                         let $Parent_i$ be $b_{path}(\boldsymbol{X})$
14:                         let n_i be $b_{path\_i}(\boldsymbol{Y})$
15:                         $C \leftarrow hidden_{path}(\boldsymbol{Z}) : 0.5 :- b_{path\_i}(\boldsymbol{Y}).$
16:                     **end if**
17:                 **else**   ▷ n_i is an internal node
18:                     **if** $Parent_i$ is the root node **then**
19:                         let n_i be $b_i(\boldsymbol{Y})$ and $\boldsymbol{Z}$ be $\boldsymbol{X} \cup \boldsymbol{Y}$
20:                         $C \leftarrow r(\boldsymbol{X}) : 0.5 :- b_i(\boldsymbol{Y}), hidden\_i(\boldsymbol{Z}).$
21:                     **else**
22:                         let $Parent_i$ be $b_{path}(\boldsymbol{X})$
23:                         n_i be $b_{path\_i}(\boldsymbol{Y})$ and $\boldsymbol{W}$ be $\boldsymbol{Z} \cup \boldsymbol{Y}$
24:                         $C \leftarrow hidden_{path}(\boldsymbol{Z}) : 0.5 :- b_{path\_i}(\boldsymbol{Y}), hidden_{path\_i}(\boldsymbol{W}).$
25:                     **end if**
26:                 **end if**
27:                 $HPLP \leftarrow [C|HPLP]$
28:             **end if**
29:         **end for**
30:         $Prob \leftarrow Prob * Rate$
31:         $level \leftarrow level + 1$
32:     **end while**
33:     $HPLP \leftarrow removeHidden(HPLP)$
34:     $initial\_HPLP \leftarrow reduce(HPLP)$
35:     Return initial_HPLP
36: **end function**

SLEAHP beats the other systems in terms of computation time in almost all datasets and achieves a similar quality of the solution. Thus SLEAHP achieves a good compromise between accuracy and learning time.

14.8 Examples of Datasets

PILP systems have been applied to many datasets. Some of them are:

- UW-CSE [Kok and Domingos, 2005a]: see Section 14.5.3.
- Mutagenesis [Srinivasan et al., 1996]: a classic ILP benchmark dataset for Quantitative structure-activity relationship (QSAR), i.e., predicting the biological activity of chemicals from their physicochemical properties or molecular structure. In this case, the goal is to predict the mutagenicity (a property correlated with cancerogenicity) of compounds from their chemical structure.
- Carcinogenesis [Srinivasan et al., 1997]: another classic ILP benchmark dataset for QSAR where the goal is to predict the cancerogenicity of compounds from their chemical structure.
- Mondial [Schulte and Khosravi, 2012]: a dataset containing information regarding geographical regions of the world, including population size, political system, and the country border relationship.
- Hepatitis [Khosravi et al., 2012]: a dataset derived from the Discovery Challenge Workshop of ECML/PKDD 2002 containing information on laboratory examinations of hepatitis B and C infected patients. The goal is to predict the type of hepatitis of a patient.
- Bupa [McDermott and Forsyth, 2016]: diagnosing patients with liver disorders.
- NBA [Schulte and Routley, 2014]: predicting the results of basketball matches from NBA.
- Pyrimidine, Triazine [Layne and Qiu, 2005]: QSAR datasets for predicting the inhibition of dihydrofolate reductase by pyrimidines and triazines, respectively.
- Financial [Berka, 2000]: predicting the success of loan applications by clients of a bank.
- Sisyphus [Blockeel and Struyf, 2001]: a dataset regarding clients of an insurance business, the aim is to classify households and persons in relation to private life insurance.
- Yeast [Davis et al., 2005]: predicting whether a yeast gene codes for a protein involved in metabolism.
- Event Calculus [Schwitter, 2018]: learning effect axioms for the Event Calculus [Kowalski and Sergot, 1986].

15

---

cplint Examples

This chapter shows some examples of programs and how the `cplint` system can be used to reason on them.

15.1 cplint Commands

`cplint` uses two Prolog modules for performing inference, `pita` for exact inference with PITA (see Section 8.6) and `mcintyre` for approximate inference with MCINTYRE (see Section 10.2). We present here the predicates provided by these two modules.

The unconditional probability of an atom can be asked using `pita` with the predicate

```
prob(+Query:atom,-Probability:float).
```

where + and − mean that the argument is input or output, respectively, and the annotation of arguments after the colon indicates their type.

The conditional probability of a query atom given an evidence atom can be asked with the predicate

```
prob(+Query:atom,+Evidence:atom,-Probability:float).
```

The BDD representing the explanations for the query atom can be obtained with the predicate

```
bdd_dot_string(+Query:atom,-BDD:string,-Var:list).
```

that returns a string encoding the BDD in the dot format of Graphviz [Koutsofios et al., 1991]. See Section 15.3 for an example of use.

With `mcintyre`, the unconditional probability of a goal can be computed by taking a given number of samples using the predicate

```
mc_sample(+Query:atom,+Samples:int,-Probability:float).
```

417

Moreover, the following predicate samples arguments of queries:

```
mc_sample_arg(+Query:atom,+Samples:int,?Arg:var,-Values:list).
```

where ? means that the argument must be a variable. The predicate samples Query Samples times. Arg must be a variable in Query. The predicate returns a list of pairs L-N in Values where L is the list of all values of Arg for which Query succeeds in a world sampled at random and N is the number of samples returning that list of values. If L is the empty list, it means that for that sample, the query failed. If L is a list with a single element, it means that for that sample, the query is determinate. If, in all pairs L-N, L is a list with a single element, it means that the program satisfies the exclusive-or assumption.

The version

```
mc_sample_arg_first(+Query:atom,+Samples:int,?Arg:var,
                    -Values:list).
```

also samples arguments of queries but just returns the first answer of the query for each sampled world.

Conditional queries can be asked with rejection sampling or Metropolis-hastings MCMC. In the first case, the predicate is:

```
mc_rejection_sample(+Query:atom,+Evidence:atom,
  +Samples:int,-Successes:int,-Failures:int,
  -Probability:float).
```

In the latter case, the predicate is

```
mc_mh_sample(+Query:atom,+Evidence:atom,Samples:int,
  +Lag:int,-Successes:int,-Failures:int,-Probability:float).
```

Moreover, the arguments of the queries can be sampled with rejection sampling and Metropolis-hastings MCMC using

```
mc_rejection_sample_arg(+Query:atom,+Evidence:atom,
  +Samples:int,?Arg:var,-Values:list).
mc_mh_sample_arg(+Query:atom,+Evidence:atom,
  +Samples:int,+Lag:int,?Arg:var,-Values:list).
```

Expectations can be computed with

```
mc_expectation(+Query:atom,+Samples:int,?Arg:var,-Exp:float).
```

that returns the expected value of the argument Arg in Query computed by sampling.

The predicate

```
mc_mh_expectation(+Query:atom,+Evidence:atom,+Samples:int,
  +Lag:int,?Arg:var,-Exp:float).
```

computes conditional expectations using Metropolis-hastings MCMC.

The `cplint` on SWISH web application (https://cplint.eu/) [Riguzzi et al., 2016a; Alberti et al., 2017] allows the user to write and run probabilistic programs online. It is based on the SWISH [Wielemaker et al., 2015, 2019] web front-end for SWI-prolog. `cplint` on SWISH also adds graphics capabilities to `cplint`: the results of sampling arguments can be rendered as bar charts. All the predicates shown above have a form with an extra last argument `+Options` that accepts a list of terms specifying options. If the option `bar(-Chart:dict)` is used, the predicate returns in `Chart` an SWI-prolog dictionary to be rendered with C3.js[1] as a bar chart. For example, the query https://cplint.eu/e/markov_chain.pl returns a chart with a bar for each possible sampled value whose size is the number of samples returning that value.

When the program has continuous random variables, the user can build a probability density of the sampled argument. When the evidence is on ground atoms with continuous values as arguments, the user needs to use likelihood weighting or particle filtering (see Section 10.4).

The predicate

```
mc_lw_sample_arg(+Query:atom,+Evidence:atom,+Samples:int,
     ?Arg:var,-ValList:list).
```

returns in `ValList` a list of pairs `V-W` where `V` is a value of `Arg` for which `Query` succeeds and `W` is the weight computed by likelihood weighting according to `Evidence`.

In particle filtering, the evidence is a list of atoms. The predicate

```
mc_particle_sample_arg(+Query:atom,+Evidence+term,
  +Samples:int,?Arg:var,-Values:list).
```

samples the argument `Arg` of `Query` using particle filtering given `Evidence`. `Evidence` is a list of goals and `Query` can be either a single goal or a list of goals.

---

[1] http://c3js.org/

The samples obtained can be used to draw the probability density function of the argument. The predicate

```
histogram(+List:list,-Chart:dict,+Options:list)
```

takes a list of weighted samples and draws a histogram of the samples using C3.js in `cplint` on SWISH.

The predicate

```
density(+List:list,-Chart:dict,+Options:list)
```

draws a line chart of the density of the weighted samples in `List`.

In `histogram/3` and `density/3`, the options can be used to specify the bounds and the number of bins on the X-axis.

The predicate

```
densities(+PriorList:list,+PostList:list,-Chart:dict,+Options:
          list)
```

draws a line chart of the density of two sets of samples, usually prior to and post observations. The same options as for `histogram/3` and `density/3` are recognized.

For example, the query

```
?-  mc_sample_arg(val(0,X),1000,X,L0,[]),histogram(L0,Chart,[]).
```

from https://cplint.eu/e/gauss_mean_est.pl takes 1000 samples of argument `X` of `val(0,X)` and draws the density of the samples using an histogram.

For discrete arguments, the predicate

```
argbar(+Values:list,-Chart:dict)
```

returns a bar chart with a bar for each value, where `Values` is a list of pairs `V-N` with `V` the value and `N` the number of samples returning that value.

The predicates `density_r/1`, `densities_r/2`, `histogram_r/2`, and `argbar_r/1` are the counterparts of those above for drawing graphs in `cplint` on SWISH using the R language for statistical computing[2].

EMBLEM (see Section 13.4) can be run with the predicate

```
induce_par(+ListOfFolds:list,-Program:list)
```

that induces the parameters of a program starting from the examples contained in the indicated *folds* (groups of examples). The predicate

```
induce(+ListOfFolds:list,-Program:list)
```

instead induces a program using SLIPCOVER (see Section 14.5).

---

[2] https://www.r-project.org/

The induced programs can be tested on a set of folds with

```
test(+Program:list,+ListOfFolds:list,-LL:float,
  -AUCROC:float,-ROC:list,-AUCPR:float,-PR:list)
```

that returns the log likelihood of the test examples (`LL`), the ROC and precision recall curves (`ROC` and `PR`) for rendering with C3.js, and the areas under the curves (`AUCROC` and `AUCPR`) that are standard metrics for the evaluation of machine learning algorithms [Davis and Goadrich, 2006].

Predicate `test_r/5` is similar to `test/7` but plots the graphs using R.

15.2 Natural Language Processing

In Natural language processing (NLP), a common task is checking whether a sentence respects a grammar. Another common task is tagging each word of a sentence with a Part-of-speech (POS) tag. For NLP, the grammars that are used in the theory of formal languages such as context-free grammars or left corner grammars don't work well because the rules are too strict. Natural language is more flexible and is characterized by many exceptions to rules. To model natural language, probabilistic versions of the grammars above have been developed, such as Probabilistic context-free grammar or Probabilistic left corner grammar (PLCG). Similarly, for POS tagging, statistical tools such as HMMs give good results. These models can all be encoded with PLP [Riguzzi et al., 2017b].

15.2.1 Probabilistic context-free grammars

A PCFG consists of:

1. A context-free grammar $G = (N, \Sigma, I, R)$ where N is a finite set of non-terminal symbols, Σ is a finite set of terminal symbols, $I \in N$ is a distinguished start symbol, and R is a finite set of rules of the form $X \to Y_1, \ldots, Y_n$, where $X \in N$ and $Y_i \in (N \cup \Sigma)$.
2. A parameter θ for each rule $\alpha \to \beta \in R$. Therefore, we have probabilistic rules of the form $\theta : \alpha \to \beta$

This kind of model can be represented by PLP. For instance, consider the PCFG

$$0.2 : S \to aS$$
$$0.2 : S \to bS$$
$$0.3 : S \to a$$
$$0.3 : S \to b,$$

where N is $\{S\}$ and Σ is $\{a, b\}$.

The program https://cplint.eu/e/pcfg.pl (adapted from [Sato and Kubota, 2015]) computes the probability of strings using top-down parsing:

```
pcfg(L):- pcfg(['S'],[],_Der,L,[]).
pcfg([A|R],Der0,Der,L0,L2):-
  rule(A,Der0,RHS),
  pcfg(RHS,[rule(A,RHS)|Der0],Der1,L0,L1),
  pcfg(R,Der1,Der,L1,L2).
pcfg([A|R],Der0,Der,[A|L1],L2):-
  \+ rule(A,_,_),
  pcfg(R,Der0,Der,L1,L2).
pcfg([],Der,Der,L,L).
rule('S',Der,[a,'S']):0.2; rule('S',Der,[b,'S']):0.2;
rule('S',Der,[a]):0.3; rule('S',Der,[b]):0.3.
```

In this example, if we want to ask the probability of the string `abaa` using exact inference, we can use the query `?- prob(pcfg([a,b,a,a]), Prob)`. We obtain the value 0.0024. In this case, the grammar is not ambiguous so there exists only one derivation with probability $0.2 \cdot 0.2 \cdot 0.2 \cdot 0.3 = 0.0024$.

15.2.2 Probabilistic left corner grammars

A PLCG is a probabilistic version of a *left-corner grammar* which uses the same set of rules as a PCFG. Whereas PCFGs assume top-down parsing, PLCGs are based on bottom-up parsing. PLCGs set probabilities to three elementary operations in bottom-up parsing, i.e., shift, attach and project, rather than to expansion of non-terminals. As a result, they define a class of distributions different from that of PCFGs.

Programs for PLCGs look very different from those for PCFGs. Consider the PLCG with the rules

$$S \rightarrow SS$$
$$S \rightarrow a$$
$$S \rightarrow b$$

The program https://cplint.eu/e/plcg.pl (adapted from Sato et al. [2008]) below encodes such a grammar:

```
plc(Ws) :- g_call(['S'],Ws,[],[],_Der).
g_call([],L,L,Der,Der).
g_call([G|R], [G|L],L2,Der0,Der) :- % shift
  terminal(G),
  g_call(R,L,L2,Der0,Der).
```

```
g_call([G|R], [Wd|L],L2,Der0,Der) :-
  \+ terminal(G), first(G,Der0,Wd),
  lc_call(G,Wd,L,L1,[first(G,Wd)|Der0],Der1),
  g_call(R,L1,L2,Der1,Der).
lc_call(G,B,L,L1,Der0,Der) :- % attach
  lc(G,B,Der0,rule(G, [B|RHS2])),
  attach_or_project(G,Der0,attach),
  g_call(RHS2,L,L1,[lc(G,B,rule(G, [B|RHS2])),
        attach|Der0],Der).
lc_call(G,B,L,L2,Der0,Der) :- % project
  lc(G,B,Der0,rule(A, [B|RHS2])),
  attach_or_project(G,Der0,project),
  g_call(RHS2,L,L1,[lc(G,B,rule(A, [B|RHS2])),
        project|Der0],Der1),
  lc_call(G,A,L1,L2,Der1,Der).
lc_call(G,B,L,L2,Der0,Der) :-
  \+ lc(G,B,Der0,rule(G,[B|_])),
  lc(G,B,Der0,rule(A, [B|RHS2])),
  g_call(RHS2,L,L1,[lc(G,B,rule(A, [B|RHS2]))|Der0],
        Der1),
  lc_call(G,A,L1,L2,Der1,Der).
attach_or_project(A,Der,Op) :-
  lc(A,A,Der,_), attach(A,Der,Op).
attach_or_project(A,Der,attach) :-
  \+ lc(A,A,Der,_).
lc('S','S',_Der,rule('S',['S','S'])).
lc('S',a,_Der,rule('S',[a])).
lc('S',b,_Der,rule('S',[b])).
first('S',Der,a):0.5; first('S',Der,b):0.5.
attach('S',Der,attach):0.5; attach('S',Der,project):0.5.
terminal(a). terminal(b).
```

If we want to know the probability that the string ab is generated by the grammar, we can use the query ?- mc_prob(plc([a,b]),P). and obtain ≈ 0.031.

15.2.3 Hidden Markov models

HMMs (see Example 74) can be used for POS tagging: words can be considered as output symbols and a sentence as the sequence of output symbols emitted by an HMM. In this case, the states are POS tags and the sequence of states that most probably originated the sequence of output symbols is the POS tagging of the sentence. So we can perform POS tagging by solving an MPE task.

Program https://cplint.eu/e/hmmpos.pl (adapted from [Lager, 2018; Nivre, 2000; Sato and Kameya, 2001]) encodes a simple HMM where the output probabilities are set to 1 (for every state, there is only one possible output). The assumption is that a POS of a word depends only on the POS of the preceding word (or on the start state in case there is no preceding word). The program is:

```
hmm(O):-hmm(_,O).
hmm(S,O):-
  trans(start,Q0,[]),hmm(Q0,[],S0,O),reverse(S0,S).
hmm(Q,S0,S,[L|O]):-
  trans(Q,Q1,S0),
  out(L,Q,S0),
  hmm(Q1,[Q|S0],S,O).
hmm(_,S,S,[]).
trans(start,det,_):0.30; trans(start,aux,_):0.20;
  trans(start,v,_):0.10; trans(start,n,_):0.10;
  trans(start,pron,_):0.30.
trans(det,det,_):0.20; trans(det,aux,_):0.01;
  trans(det,v,_):0.01; trans(det,n,_):0.77;
  trans(det,pron,_):0.01.
trans(aux,det,_):0.18; trans(aux,aux,_):0.10;
  trans(aux,v,_):0.50; trans(aux,n,_):0.01;
  trans(aux,pron,_):0.21.
trans(v,det,_):0.36; trans(v,aux,_):0.01;
  trans(v,v,_):0.01; trans(v,n,_):0.26; trans(v,pron,_)
                                                  :0.36.
trans(n,det,_):0.01; trans(n,aux,_):0.25; trans(n,v,_)
                                                  :0.39;
  trans(n,n,_):0.34; trans(n,pron,_):0.01.
trans(pron,det,_):0.01; trans(pron,aux,_):0.45;
  trans(pron,v,_):0.52; trans(pron,n,_):0.01;
  trans(pron,pron,_):0.01.
out(a,det,_).
out(can,aux,_).
out(can,v,_).
out(can,n,_).
out(he,pron,_).
```

For instance, we may want to know the most probable POS sequence for the sentence "he can can a can." By using the query

```
?- mc_sample_arg( hmm(S,[he,can,can,a,can]),100,S,O).
```

we obtain that the sequence [pron, aux, v, det, n] appears most frequently in O.

15.3 Drawing Binary Decision Diagrams

Example 94 models the development of an epidemic or a pandemic and is https://cplint.eu/e/epidemic.pl:

```
epidemic:0.6; pandemic:0.3 :- flu(_), cold.
cold : 0.7.
flu(david).
flu(robert).
```

In order to compute the probability that a pandemic arises, we can call the query:

```
?- prob(pandemic,Prob).
```

The corresponding BDD can be obtained with:

```
?- bdd_dot_string(pandemic,BDD,Var).
```

The call returns the BDD in the form of a graph in the dot format of Graphviz that the `cplint` on SWISH system renders and visualizes as shown in Figure 15.1. Moreover, the call returns a data structure in `Var` encoding Table 15.1 that associates multivalued variable indexes with ground instantiations of rules.

The BDD built by CUDD are discussed in Section 43: they differ from those introduced in Section 8.3 because edges to 0-children can be negated, i.e., the function encoded by the 0-child is negated before being used in the parent node. Negated edges to 0-children are represented in the graph by dotted arcs, while edges to 1-children and regular edges to 0-children with solid and dashed arcs, respectively. Moreover, the output of the BDD can be negated as well, indicated by a dotted arc connecting an Out node to the root of the diagram, as in Figure 15.1. CUDD uses this form of BDDs for computational reasons, for example, negation is very cheap, as it just requires changing the type of an edge.

Each level of the BDD is associated with a variable of the form Xi_k indicated on the left: i indicates the multivalued variable index and k the index of the Boolean variable. The association between the multivalued variables and the clause groundings is encoded in the `Var` argument. For example, multivalued variable with index 1 is associated with the rule with index 0 (the first rule of the program) with grounding $\_/david$ and is encoded with two Boolean variables, X1_0 and X1_1, since it can take three values. The hexadecimal numbers in the nodes are part of their memory address and are used to uniquely identify nodes.

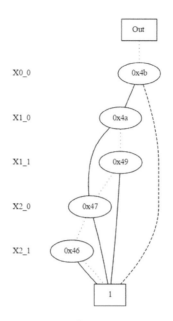

Figure 15.1 BDD for query *pandemic* in the `epidemic.pl` example, drawn using the CUDD function for exporting the BDD to the dot format of Graphviz.

Table 15.1 Associations between variable indexes and ground rules

Multivalued Variable Index	Rule Index	Grounding Substitution
0	1	[]
1	0	[david]
2	0	[robert]

15.4 Gaussian Processes

A Gaussian process (GP) defines a probability distribution over functions [Bishop, 2016, Section 6.4]. This distribution has the property that, given N values, their image through a function sampled from the Gaussian process follows a multivariate normal with N dimensions, mean 0, and covariance matrix K. In other words, if function $f(\mathbf{x})$ is sampled from a Gaussian process, then, for any finite selection of points $\mathbf{X} = \{\mathbf{x}^1, \ldots, \mathbf{x}^N\}$, the density is

$$p(f(\mathbf{x}^1), \ldots, f(\mathbf{x}^N)) = \mathcal{N}(\mathbf{0}, \mathbf{K}),$$

i.e., it is a Gaussian with mean 0 and covariance matrix $\mathbf{K}$. A GP is defined by a kernel function k that determines $\mathbf{K}$ as $\mathbf{K}_{ij} = k(\mathbf{x}^i, \mathbf{x}^j)$.

GPs can be used for regression: the random functions predict the y value corresponding to a x value using the model

$$y = f(x) + \epsilon$$

where ϵ is a random noise variable with variance s^2.

Given sets (columns vectors) $\mathbf{X} = (x^1, \dots, x^N)^T$ and $\mathbf{Y} = (y^1, \dots, y^N)^T$ of observed values, the task is to predict the y value for a new point x. It can be proved [Bishop, 2016, Equations (6.66) and (6.67)] that y is Gaussian distributed with mean and variance

$$\mu = \mathbf{k}^T \mathbf{C}^{-1} \mathbf{Y} \tag{15.1}$$
$$\sigma^2 = k(x, x) - \mathbf{k}^T \mathbf{C}^{-1} \mathbf{k} \tag{15.2}$$

where $\mathbf{k}$ is the column vector with elements $k(x^i, x)$ and $\mathbf{C}$ has elements $\mathbf{C}_{ij} = k(x^i, x^j) + s^2 \delta_{ij}$, with s^2 user defined (the variance that is assumed for the random noise in the linear regression model) and δ_{ij} the Kronecker function ($\delta_{ij} = 1$ if $i = j$ and 0 otherwise). So $\mathbf{C} = \mathbf{K} + s^2 \mathbf{I}$ and $\mathbf{C} = \mathbf{K}$ if $s^2 = 0$.

A popular choice of kernel is the squared exponential

$$k(x, x') = \sigma^2 \exp\left[\frac{-(x - x')^2}{2l^2} \right]$$

with parameters σ and l. The user can define a prior distribution over the parameters instead of choosing particular values. In this case, the kernel itself is a random function and the predictions of regression will be random as well.

The program below (https://cplint.eu/e/gpr.pl) can sample kernels (and thus functions) and compute the expected value of the predictions for a squared exponential kernel (defined by predicate `sq_exp_p/3`) with parameter l uniformly distributed in $1, 2, 3$ and σ uniformly distributed in $[-2, 2]$.

Goal `gp(X, Kernel, Y)`, given a list of values X and a kernel name, returns in Y the list of values $f(x)$ where x belongs to X and f is a function sampled from the Gaussian process.

Goal `compute_cov(X, Kernel, Var, C)` returns in C the matrix $\mathbf{C}$ defined above with Var=s^2. It is called by `gp/3` with Var=0 in order to return $\mathbf{K}$

```
gp(X,Kernel,Y) :-
    compute_cov(X,Kernel,0,C),
```

```
    gp(C,Y).
gp(Cov,Y):gaussian(Y,Mean,Cov):-
    length(Cov,N),
    list0(N,Mean).

compute_cov(X,Kernel,Var,C)  :-
    length(X,N),
    cov(X,N,Kernel,Var,CT,CND),
    transpose(CND,CNDT),
    matrix_sum(CT,CNDT,C).

cov([],_,_,_,[],[]).
cov([XH|XT],N,Ker,Var,[KH|KY],[KHND|KYND])  :-
    length(XT,LX),
    N1 is N-LX-1,
    list0(N1,KH0),
    cov_row(XT,XH,Ker,KH1),
    call(Ker,XH,XH,KXH0),
    KXH is KXH0+Var,
    append([KH0,[KXH],KH1],KH),
    append([KH0,[0],KH1],KHND),
    cov(XT,N,Ker,Var,KY,KYND).

cov_row([],_,_,[]).
cov_row([H|T],XH,Ker,[KH|KT])  :-
    call(Ker,H,XH,KH),
    cov_row(T,XH,Ker,KT).

sq_exp_p(X,XP,K)  :-
    sigma(Sigma),
    l(L),
    K is Sigma^2*exp(-((X-XP)^2)/2/(L^2)).

l(L):uniform(L,[1,2,3]).

sigma(Sigma):uniform(Sigma,-2,2).
```

Here `list0(N,L)` is true if `L` is a list with `N` elements all 0. This program exploits the possibility offered by `cplint` of defining multivariate Gaussian distributions.

`gp_predict(XP,Kernel,Var,XT,YT,YP)`, given the points described by the lists `XT` and `YT`, a kernel, and a list of points `XP`, predicts y values of points with x values in `XP` and returns them in `YP`. The predictions are the mean of y given by Equation (15.1), with `Var` being the s^2 parameter:

```
gp_predict(XP,Kernel,Var,XT,YT,YP) :-
  compute_cov(XT,Kernel,Var,C),
  matrix_inversion(C,C_1),
  transpose([YT],YST),
  matrix_multiply(C_1,YST,C_1T),
  gp_predict_single(XP,Kernel,XT,C_1T,YP).

gp_predict_single([],_,_,_,[]).
gp_predict_single([XH|XT],Kernel,X,C_1T,[YH|YT]) :-
  compute_k(X,XH,Kernel,K),
  matrix_multiply([K],C_1T,[[YH]]),
  gp_predict_single(XT,Kernel,X,C_1T,YT).

compute_k([],_,_,[]).
compute_k([XH|XT],X,Ker,[HK|TK]) :-
  call(Ker,XH,X,HK),
  compute_k(XT,X,Ker,TK).
```

Since the kernel here is random, the predictions of `gp_predict/6` will be random as well.

By calling the query

```
?- numlist(0,10,X),
   mc_sample_arg_first(gp(X,sq_exp_p,Y),5,Y,L).
```

we get five functions sampled from the Gaussian process with a squared exponential kernel at points $X = [0, ..., 10]$. An example of output is shown in Figure 15.2.

The query

```
?- numlist(0,10,X),
   XT=[2.5,6.5,8.5],
   YT=[1,-0.8,0.6],
   mc_lw_sample_arg(gp_predict(X,sq_exp_p,
     0.3,XT,YT,Y),gp(XT,Kernel,YT),5,Y,L).
```

draws five functions with a squared exponential kernel predicting points with X values in $[0, . . . , 10]$ given the three pairs of points $XT = [2.5, 6.5, 8.5]$, $YT = [1, -0.8, 0.6]$. The graph of Figure 15.3 shows three of the functions together with the given points.

Figure 15.2 Functions sampled from a Gaussian process with a squared exponential kernel in `gpr.pl`.

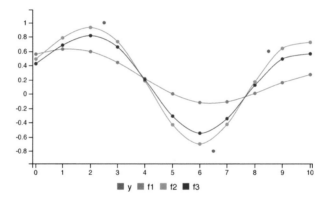

Figure 15.3 Functions from a Gaussian process predicting points with $X = [0, \ldots, 10]$ with a squared exponential kernel in `gpr.pl`.

15.5 Dirichlet Processes

A Dirichlet process (DP) [Teh, 2011] is a probability distribution whose range is itself a set of probability distributions. The DP is specified by a base distribution, which represents the expected value of the process. When sampling from a distribution in turn sampled from a DP, new samples have a non-zero probability of being equal to already sampled values. The process depends on a parameter α, called *concentration parameter*: with $\alpha \to 0$, a single value is sampled; with $\alpha \to \infty$, the distribution is equal to the base distribution. A DP with base distribution H and concentration parameter α is indicated with

$\mathrm{DP}(H, \alpha)$. A sample from $\mathrm{DP}(H, \alpha)$ is a distribution P. We are interested in sampling values from P. With abuse of terminology, we say that these values are sampled from the DP. There are several equivalent views of the DP, we present two of them in the following.

15.5.1 The stick-breaking process

Example https://cplint.eu/e/dirichlet_process.pl encodes a view of DPs called *stick-breaking process*.

In this view, the procedure for sampling values from $\mathrm{DP}(H, \alpha)$ can be described as follows. To sample the first value, a sample β_1 is taken from the beta distribution $Beta(1, \alpha)$ and a coin with heads probability equal to β_1 is flipped. If the coin lands on heads, a sample x_1 from the base distribution is taken and returned. Otherwise, a sample β_2 is taken again from $Beta(1, \alpha)$ and a coin is flipped. This procedure is repeated until heads are obtained, the index i of β_i being the index of the value x_i to be returned. The following values are sampled in a similar way, with the difference that, if for an index i, values x_i and β_i were already sampled, that value is returned.

This view is called stick-breaking because we can see the process as starting with a stick of length 1 which is progressively broken: first a piece β_1 long is broken off, then a piece β_2 long is broken off from the remaining piece, and so on. The length of the i-th piece is therefore

$$\prod_{k=1}^{i-1}(1 - \beta_k)\beta_i$$

and indicates the probability that the i-th sample x_i from the base distribution is returned. The smaller α is, the more probable high values of β_i are and the more often already sampled values are returned, yielding a more concentrated distribution.

In the example below, the base distribution is a Gaussian with mean 0 and variance 1, $\mathcal{N}(0, 1)$. The distribution of values is handled by predicates `dp_value(NV,Alpha,V)`, which returns (in V) the NV-th sample from the DP with concentration parameter `Alpha`, and

, which returns in L a list of N-N0 samples from the DP with concentration parameter `Alpha`.

The distribution of indexes is handled by predicate `dp_stick_index/4`.

```
dp_value(NV,Alpha,V):-
  dp_stick_index(NV,Alpha,I),
```

```
dp_pick_value(I,V).

dp_pick_value(_,V):gaussian(V,0,1).

dp_stick_index(NV,Alpha,I) :-
  dp_stick_index(1,NV,Alpha,I).
dp_stick_index(N,NV,Alpha,V) :-
  stick_proportion(N,Alpha,P),
  choose_prop(N,NV,Alpha,P,V).

choose_prop(N,NV,_Alpha,P,N) :-
  pick_portion(N,NV,P).
choose_prop(N,NV,Alpha,P,V) :-
  neg_pick_portion(N,NV,P),
  N1 is N+1,
  dp_stick_index(N1,NV,Alpha,V).

stick_proportion(_,Alpha,P):beta(P,1,Alpha).

pick_portion(_,_,P):P;neg_pick_portion(_,_,P):1-P.

dp_n_values(N,N,_Alpha,[]) :- !.

dp_n_values(N0,N,Alpha,[[V]-1|Vs]) :-
  N0<N,
  dp_value(N0,Alpha,V),
  N1 is N0+1,
  dp_n_values(N1,N,Alpha,Vs).
```

The query

```
?- mc_sample_arg(dp_stick_index(1,10.0,V),2000,V,L),
   histogram(L,Chart,[nbins(100)]).
```

draws the density of indexes with concentration parameter 10 using 2000 samples (see Figure 15.4).

The query

```
?- mc_sample_arg_first(dp_n_values(0,2000,10.0,V),1,V,L),
   L=[Vs-_],
   histogram(Vs,Chart,[nbins(100)]).
```

draws the density of values over 2000 samples from a DP with concentration parameter 10 (see Figure 15.5).

The query

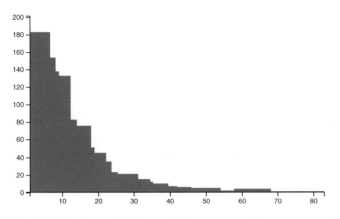

Figure 15.4 Distribution of indexes with concentration parameter 10 for the stick-breaking example `dirichlet_process.pl`.

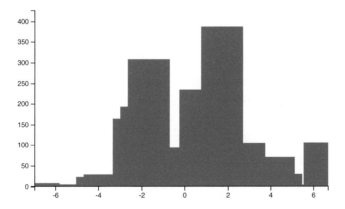

Figure 15.5 Distribution of values with concentration parameter 10 for the stick-breaking example `dirichlet_process.pl`.

```
?- hist_repeated_indexes(1000,100,G).
```

called over the program:

```
hist_repeated_indexes(Samples,NBins,Chart) :-
  repeat_sample(0,Samples,L),
  histogram(L,Chart,[nbins(NBins)]).

repeat_sample(S,S,[]) :- !.
repeat_sample(S0,S,[[N]-1|LS]) :-
  mc_sample_arg_first(dp_stick_index(1,1,10.0,V),10,V,L),
```

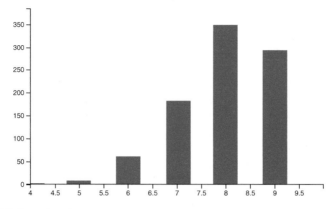

Figure 15.6 Distribution of unique indexes with concentration parameter 10 for the stick-breaking example `dirichlet_process.pl`.

```
length(L,N),
S1 is S0+1,
repeat_sample(S1,S,LS).
```

shows the distribution of the number of unique indexes over 10 samples from a DP with concentration parameter 10 (see Figure 15.6).

15.5.2 The Chinese restaurant process

According to the Chinese restaurant view, a DP is a discrete-time stochastic process, analogous to seating customers at tables in a Chinese restaurant. When a new customer arrives at the restaurant, it is seated to a random table. It can be an existing table, chosen with a probability proportional to the number of clients already sitting at the table, or a new table, chosen with a probability proportional to α.

Formally, a sequence of samples $x_1, x_2, \ldots$ is drawn as follows. x_1 is drawn from the base distribution (corresponding to a new table as no customer is present). For $n > 1$, let $X^n = \{x^1, \ldots, x^m\}$ be the set of distinct values previously sampled. x_n is set to a value $x^i \in X^n$ with probability $\frac{n_i}{\alpha + n - 1}$, where n_i is the number of previous observations $x_j, j < n$, such that $x_j = x^i$ (seating at an existing table), and is drawn from the base distribution with probability $\frac{\alpha}{\alpha + n - 1}$ (seating at a new table). Since

$$\sum_{i=1}^{m} \frac{n_i}{\alpha + n - 1} + \frac{\alpha}{\alpha + n - 1} = \frac{n - 1}{\alpha + n - 1} + \frac{\alpha}{\alpha + n - 1} = 1$$

this is a valid sampling process.

In example https://cplint.eu/e/dp_chinese.pl, the base distribution is a Gaussian with mean 0 and variance 1. Counts are kept and updated by predicate `update_counts/5`.

```
dp_n_values(N0,N,Alpha,[[V]-1|Vs],Counts0,Counts) :-
  N0<N,
  dp_value(N0,Alpha,Counts0,V,Counts1),
  N1 is N0+1,
  dp_n_values(N1,N,Alpha,Vs,Counts1,Counts).

dp_value(NV,Alpha,Counts,V,Counts1) :-
  draw_sample(Counts,NV,Alpha,I),
  update_counts(0,I,Alpha,Counts,Counts1),
  dp_pick_value(I,V).

update_counts(_I0,_I,Alpha,[_C],[1,Alpha]) :- !.
update_counts(I,I,_Alpha,[C|Rest],[C1|Rest]) :-
  C1 is C+1.
update_counts(I0,I,Alpha,[C|Rest],[C|Rest1]) :-
  I1 is I0+1,
  update_counts(I1,I,Alpha,Rest,Rest1).

draw_sample(Counts,NV,Alpha,I) :-
  NS is NV+Alpha,
  maplist(div(NS),Counts,Probs),
  length(Counts,LC),
  numlist(1,LC,Values),
  maplist(pair,Values,Probs,Discrete),
  take_sample(NV,Discrete,I).

take_sample(_,D,V):discrete(V,D).

dp_pick_value(_,V):gaussian(V,0,1).

div(Den,V,P) :- P is V/Den.

pair(A,B,A:B).
```

Here `maplist/3` is a library predicate encoding the `maplist` primitive of functional programming: `maplist(Goal,List1,List2)` is true if `Goal` can be successfully applied to all pairs of elements in the same position in the two lists.

The query
```
?- mc_sample_arg_first(dp_n_values(0,2000,10.0,V,[10.0],_),
     1,V,L),
```

```
    L=[Vs-_],
    histogram(Vs,100,Chart).
```

draws the density of values over 2000 samples from a DP with concentration parameter 10. The resulting graph is similar to the one of Figure 15.5.

15.5.3 Mixture model

DPs can be used as a prior probability distribution in infinite mixture models. The objective is to build a mixture model without specifying in advance the number k of components. In example https://cplint.eu/e/dp_mix.pl, samples are drawn from a mixture of normal distributions whose parameters are defined by means of a DP. For each component, the variance is sampled from a gamma distribution and the mean is sampled from a Gaussian with mean 0 and variance 30 times the variance of the component. The program in this case is equivalent to the one encoding the stick-breaking example, except for the dp_pick_value/3 predicate that is shown below:

```
dp_pick_value(I,NV,V) :-
    ivar(I,IV),
    Var is 1.0/IV,
    mean(I,Var,M),
    value(NV,M,Var,V).

ivar(_,IV):gamma(IV,1,0.1).

mean(_,V0,M):gaussian(M,0,V) :- V is V0*30.

value(_,M,V,Val):gaussian(Val,M,V).
```

Given a vector of observations obs([-1,7,3]), the queries

```
?- prior(1000,100,G).
?- post(1000,30,G).
```

called over the program

```
prior(Samples,NBins,Chart) :-
    mc_sample_arg_first(dp_n_values(0,Samples,10.0,V),1,V,L),
    L=[Vs-_],
    histogram(Vs,Chart,[nbins(NBins)]).

post(Samples,NBins,Chart) :-
    obs(O),
    maplist(to_val,O,O1),
    length(O1,N),
```

```
mc_lw_sample_arg_log(dp_value(0,10.0,T),
    dp_n_values(0,N,10.0,O1),Samples,T,L),
maplist(keys,L,LW),
min_list(LW,Min),
maplist(exp(Min),L,L1),
histogram(L1,Chart,[nbins(NBins),min(-8),max(15)]).

keys(_-W,W).

exp(Min,L-W,L-W1) :- W1 is exp(W-Min).

to_val(V,[V]-1).
```

draw the prior and the posterior densities, respectively, using 200 samples (Figures 15.7 and 15.8). Likelihood weighting is used because the evidence involves values for continuous random variables. `mc_lw_sample_arg_log/5` differs from `mc_lw_sample_arg/5` because it returns the natural logarithm of the weights, useful when the evidence is very unlikely.

15.6 Bayesian Estimation

Let us consider a problem proposed for the Anglican system for probabilistic programming [Wood et al., 2014][3]. We are trying to estimate the true value of a Gaussian-distributed random variable, given some observed data.

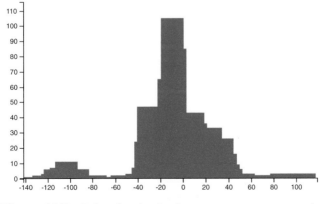

Figure 15.7   Prior density in the `dp_mix.pl` example.

---

[3]   https://bitbucket.org/probprog/anglican-examples/src/master/worksheets/gaussian-posteriors.clj

The variance is known (its value is 2) and we suppose that the mean has itself a Gaussian distribution with mean 1 and variance 5. We take different measurements (e.g., at different times), indexed by an integer.

The program https://cplint.eu/e/gauss_mean_est.pl

```
val(I,X) :- mean(M), val(I,M,X).
mean(M):gaussian(M,1.0,5.0).
val(_,M,X):gaussian(X,M,2.0).
```

models this problem.

Given that we observe 9 and 8 at indexes 1 and 2, how does the distribution of the random variable (value at index 0) change with respect to the case of no observations? This example shows that the parameters of the distribution atoms can be taken from the probabilistic atoms (`gaussian(X,M,2.0)` and `value(_,M,X)` respectively). The query

```
?- mc_sample_arg(val(0,Y),1000,Y,L0),
   mc_lw_sample_arg(val(0,X),(val(1,9),val(2,8)),1000,X,L),
   densities(L0,L,Chart,[nbins(40)]).
```

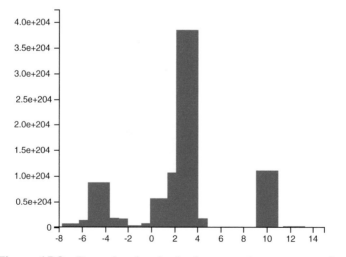

Figure 15.8   Posterior density in the `dp_mix.pl` example.

takes 1000 samples of argument X of `val(0,X)` before and after the observation of `val(1,9),val(2,8)` and draws the prior and posterior densities of the samples using a line chart. Figure 15.9 shows the resulting graph where the posterior is clearly peaked at around 8.

15.7 Kalman Filter

Example 57 represents a Kalman filter, i.e., a hidden Markov model with a real value as state and a real value as output. Program https://cplint.eu/e/ kalman_filter.pl (adapted from [Nampally and Ramakrishnan, 2014]) encodes the example:

```
kf_fin(N,O,T) :-
  init(S),
  kf_part(0,N,S,O,T).

kf_part(I,N,S,[V|RO],T) :-
  I < N,
  NextI is I+1,
  trans(S,I,NextS),
  emit(NextS,I,V),
  kf_part(NextI,N,NextS,RO,T).
kf_part(N,N,S,[],S).

trans(S,I,NextS) :-
  {NextS =:= E+S},
  trans_err(I,E).
```

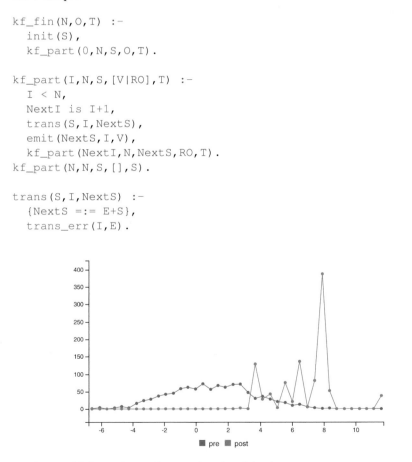

Figure 15.9 Prior and posterior densities in `gauss_mean_est.pl`.

```
emit(NextS,I,V) :-
  {V =:= NextS+X},
  obs_err(I,X).

init(S):gaussian(S,0,1).

trans_err(_,E):gaussian(E,0,2).

obs_err(_,E):gaussian(E,0,1).
```

The next state is given by the current state plus Gaussian noise (with mean 0 and variance 2 in this example) and the output is given by the current state plus Gaussian noise (with mean 0 and variance 1 in this example). A Kalman filter can be considered as modeling a random walk of a single continuous state variable with noisy observations.

The goals {NextS =:= E+S} and {V =:= NextS+X} are CLP(R) constraints.

Given that, at time 0, the value 2.5 was observed, what is the distribution of the state at time 1 (filtering problem)? Likelihood weighting can be used to condition the distribution on evidence on a continuous random variable (evidence with probability 0). With CLP(R) constraints, it is possible to sample and to weight samples with the same program: when sampling, the constraint {V=:=NextS+X} is used to compute V from X and NextS. When weighting, the constraint is used to compute X from V and NextS. The above query can be expressed with

```
?- mc_sample_arg(kf_fin(1,_O1,Y),1000,Y,L0),
   mc_lw_sample_arg(kf_fin(1,_O2,T),kf_fin(1,[2.5],_T),1000,
   T,L),densities(L0,L,Chart,[nbins(40)]).
```

that returns the graph of Figure 15.10, showing that the posterior distribution is peaked around 2.5.

Given a Kalman filter with four observations, the value of the state at those time points can be sampled by running particle filtering:

```
?- [O1,O2,O3,O4]=[-0.133, -1.183, -3.212, -4.586],
   mc_particle_sample_arg([kf_fin(1,T1),kf_fin(2,T2),
     kf_fin(3,T3),kf_fin(4,T4)],[kf_o(1,O1),kf_o(2,O2),
     kf_o(3,O3),kf_o(4,O4)],100,[T1,T2,T3,T4],
     [F1,F2,F3,F4]).
```

where kf_o/2 is defined as

```
kf_o(N,ON):-
  init(S),
```

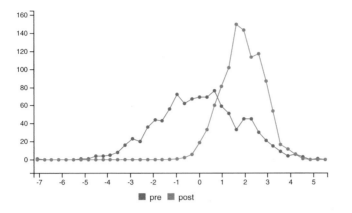

Figure 15.10 Prior and posterior densities in `kalman.pl`.

```
N1 is N-1,
kf_part(0,N1,S,_O,_LS,T),
emit(T,N,ON).
```

The list of samples is returned in `[F1,F2,F3,F4]`, with each element being the samples for a time point.

Given the true states from which the observations were obtained, Figure 15.11 shows a graph with the distributions of the state variable at time 1, 2, 3, and 4 (S1, S2, S3, S4, density on the left Y-axis) and with the points for the observations and the states with respect to time (time on the right Y-axis).

A two-dimensional Kalman filter can be used to track the movements of an object over a plane. For example,[4] the object may perform a noisy circular motion. We receive noisy observations of the position and the objective is to estimate its position at the next time point. A Kalman filter may produce a 2-dimensional distribution of the next position of the object such as that shown in Figure 15.12, where the true and observed trajectories are shown in the upper part as red and green lines, respectively.

---

[4] Inspired by https://bitbucket.org/probprog/anglican-examples/src/master/worksheets/kalman.clj.

15.8 Stochastic Logic Programs

SLPs (see Section 2.10.1) are used most commonly for defining a distribution over the values of arguments of a query. SLPs are a direct generalization of PCFGs and are particularly suitable for representing them. For example, the grammar

```
0.2:S->aS
0.2:S->bS
0.3:S->a
0.3:S->b
```

can be represented with the SLP

```
0.2::s([a|R]):-
  s(R).

0.2::s([b|R]):-
  s(R).

0.3::s([a]).

0.3::s([b]).
```

This SLP is encoded in `cplint` as program https://cplint.eu/e/slp_pcfg.pl:

```
s_as(N):0.2;s_bs(N):0.2;s_a(N):0.3;s_b(N):0.3.

s([a|R],N0):-
  s_as(N0),
```

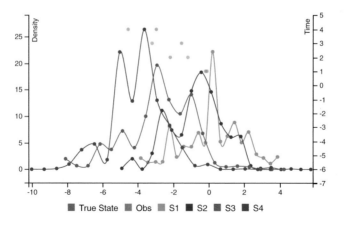

Figure 15.11   Example of particle filtering in `kalman.pl`.

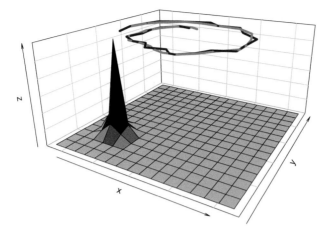

Figure 15.12   Particle filtering for a 2D Kalman filter.

```
  N1 is N0+1,
  s(R,N1).

s([b|R],N0):-
  s_bs(N0),
  N1 is N0+1,
  s(R,N1).

s([a],N0):-
  s_a(N0).

s([b],N0):-
  s_b(N0).

s(L):-
  s(L,0).
```

where the predicate `s/2` has one more argument with respect to the SLP, which is used for passing a counter to ensure that different calls to `s/2` are associated with independent random variables.

Inference with `cplint` can then simulate the behavior of SLPs. For example, the query

```
?- mc_sample_arg_bar(s(S),100,S,P),
  argbar(P,C).
```

samples 100 sentences from the language and draws the bar chart of Figure 15.13.

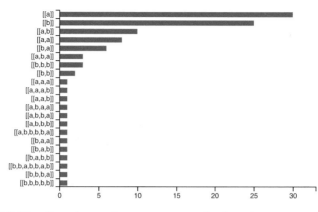

Figure 15.13 Samples of sentences of the language defined in `slp_pcfg.pl`.

15.9 Tile Map Generation

PLP can be used to generate random complex structures. For example, we can write programs for randomly generating maps of video games. Suppose that we are given a fixed set of tiles and we want to combine them to obtain a 2D map that is random but satisfies some soft constraints on the placement of tiles.

Suppose we want to draw a 10x10 map with a tendency to have a lake in the center. The tiles are randomly placed such that, in the central area, water is more probable. The problem can be modeled with the example https://cplint.eu/e/tile_map.swinb, where `map(H,W,M)` instantiates `M` to a map of height `H` and width `W`:

```
map(H,W,M):-
  tiles(Tiles),
  length(Rows,H),
  M=..[map,Tiles|Rows],
  foldl(select(H,W),Rows,1,_).

select(H,W,Row,N0,N):-
  length(RowL,W),
  N is N0+1,
  Row=..[row|RowL],
  foldl(pick_row(H,W,N0),RowL,1,_).

pick_row(H,W,N,T,M0,M):-
```

```
M is M0+1,
pick_tile(N,M0,H,W,T).
```

Here `foldl/4` is an SWI-prolog [Wielemaker et al., 2012] library predicate that implements the `foldl` meta-primitive from functional programming: it aggregates the results of the application of a predicate to one or more lists. `foldl/4` is defined as:

```
foldl(P, [X11,...,X1n], [Xm1,...,Xmn], V0, Vn) :-
  P(X11, Xm1, V0, V1),
  ...
  P(X1n, Xmn, Vn-1, Vn).
```

`pick_tile(Y,X,H,W,T)` returns a tile for position `(X,Y)` of a map of size `W*H`. The center tile is water:

```
pick_tile(HC,WC,H,W,water):-
  HC is H//2,
  WC is W//2,!.
```

In the central area, water is more probable:

```
pick_tile(Y,X,H,W,T):
  discrete(T,[grass:0.05,water:0.9,tree:0.025,rock:0.025]):-
  central_area(Y,X,H,W),!.
```

`central_area(Y,X,H,W)` is true if `(X,Y)` is adjacent to the center of the `W*H` map (definition omitted for brevity). In other places, tiles are chosen at random with distribution
   `grass:0.5,water:0.3,tree:0.1,rock:0.1`:

```
pick_tile(_,_,_,_,T):
  discrete(T,[grass:0.5,water:0.3,tree:0.1,rock:0.1]).
```

We can generate a map by taking a sample of the query `map(10,10,M)` and collecting the value of `M`. For example, the map of Figure 15.14 can be obtained[5].

---

[5] Tiles from https://github.com/silveira/openpixels

Figure 15.14 A random tile map.

15.10 Markov Logic Networks

We have seen in Section 2.11.2.1 that the MLN

```
1.5 Intelligent(x) => GoodMarks(x)
1.1 Friends(x, y) => (Intelligent(x) <=> Intelligent(y))
```

can be translated to the program below (https://cplint.eu/e/inference/mln.
swinb):

```
clause1(X): 0.8175744762:- \+intelligent(X).
clause1(X): 0.1824255238:- intelligent(X), \+good_marks(X).
clause1(X): 0.8175744762:- intelligent(X), good_marks(X).

clause2(X,Y): 0.7502601056:-
  \+friends(X,Y).
clause2(X,Y): 0.7502601056:-
  friends(X,Y), intelligent(X),intelligent(Y).
clause2(X,Y): 0.7502601056:-
  friends(X,Y), \+intelligent(X),\+intelligent(Y).
clause2(X,Y): 0.2497398944:-
  friends(X,Y), intelligent(X),\+intelligent(Y).
```

```
clause2(X,Y): 0.2497398944:-
   friends(X,Y), \+intelligent(X),intelligent(Y).

intelligent(_):0.5.
good_marks(_):0.5.
friends(_,_):0.5.

student(anna).
student(bob).
```

The evidence must include the truth of all groundings of the `clausei` predicates:

```
evidence_mln:- clause1(anna),clause1(bob),clause2(anna,anna),
     clause2(anna,bob),clause2(bob,anna),clause2(bob,bob).
```

We have also evidence that Anna is friend with Bob and Bob is intelligent:

```
ev_intelligent_bob_friends_anna_bob :-
     intelligent(bob),friends(anna,bob),
     evidence_mln.
```

If we want to query the probability that Anna gets good marks given the evidence, we can ask:

```
?- prob(good_marks(anna),
   ev_intelligent_bob_friends_anna_bob,P).
```

while the prior probability of Anna getting good marks is given by:

```
?- prob(good_marks(anna),evidence_mln,P).
```

We obtain `P` = 0.733 from the first query and `P` = 0.607 from the second: given that Bob is intelligent and Anna is her friend, it is more probable that Anna gets good marks.

15.11 Truel

A truel [Kilgour and Brams, 1997] is a duel among three opponents. There are three truelists, a, b, and c, that take turns in shooting with a gun. The firing order is a, b, and c. Each truelist can shoot at another truelist or at the sky (deliberate miss). The truelists have these probabilities of hitting the target (if they are not aiming at the sky): 1/3, 2/3, and 1 for a, b, and c, respectively. The aim for each truelist is to kill all the other truelists. The question is: what should a do to maximize his probability of winning? Aim at b, c or the sky?

Let us see first the strategy for the other truelists and situations, following [Nguembang Fadja and Riguzzi, 2017]. When only two players are left, the best strategy is to shoot at the other player.

When all three players remain, the best strategy for b is to shoot at c, since if c shoots at him he his dead and if c shoots at a, b remains with c which is the best shooter. Similarly, when all three players remain, the best strategy for c is to shoot at b, since in this way, he remains with a, the worst shooter.

For a, it is more complex. Let us first compute the probability of a to win a duel with a single opponent. When a and c remain, a wins if it shoots c, with probability 1/3. If he misses c, c will surely kill him. When a and b remain, the probability p of a winning can be computed with

$$p = P(a \text{ hits } b) + P(a \text{ misses } b)P(b \text{ misses } a)p$$
$$p = \frac{1}{3} + \frac{2}{3} \times \frac{1}{3} \times p$$
$$p = \frac{3}{7}$$

The probability can also be computed by building the probability tree of Figure 15.15. The probability that a survives is thus

$$p = \frac{1}{3} + \frac{2}{3} \cdot \frac{1}{3} \cdot \frac{1}{3} + \frac{2}{3} \cdot \frac{1}{3} \cdot \frac{2}{3} \cdot \frac{1}{3} \cdot \frac{1}{3} + \dots =$$
$$= \frac{1}{3} + \frac{2}{3^3} + \frac{2^2}{3^5} + \dots = \frac{1}{3} + \sum_{i=0}^{\infty} \frac{2}{3^3} \left(\frac{2}{9}\right)^i = \frac{1}{3} + \frac{\frac{2}{3^3}}{1 - \frac{2}{9}} =$$
$$= \frac{1}{3} + \frac{\frac{2}{3^3}}{\frac{7}{9}} = \frac{1}{3} + \frac{\frac{2}{3}}{7} = \frac{1}{3} + \frac{2}{21} = \frac{9}{21} = \frac{3}{7}$$

When all three players remain, if a shoots at b, b is dead with probability 1/3 but then c will kill a. If b is not dead (probability 2/3), b shoots at c and kills him with probability 2/3. In this case, a is left in a duel with b, with a probability of surviving of 3/7. If b doesn't kill c (probability 1/3), c surely kills b and a is left in a duel with c, with a probability of surviving of 1/3. So overall, if a shoots at b, his probability of winning is

$$\frac{2}{3} \cdot \frac{2}{3} \cdot \frac{3}{7} + \frac{2}{3} \cdot \frac{1}{3} \cdot \frac{1}{3} = \frac{4}{21} + \frac{2}{27} = \frac{36 + 15}{189} = \frac{50}{189} \approx 0.2645$$

When all three players remain, if a shoots at c, c is dead with probability 1/3. b then shoots at a and a survives with probability 1/3 and a is then in a duel

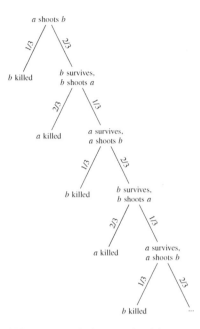

Figure 15.15 Probability tree of the truel with opponents a and b. From [Nguembang Fadja and Riguzzi, 2017].

with b and surviving with probability 3/7. If c survives (probability 2/3), b shoots at c and kills him with probability 2/3, so a remains in a duel with b and wins with probability 3/7. If c survives again, he surely kills b and a is left in a duel with c, with a probability 1/3 of winning. So overall, if a shoots at c, his probability of winning is

$$\frac{1}{3} \cdot \frac{1}{3} \cdot \frac{3}{7} + \frac{2}{3} \cdot \frac{2}{3} \cdot \frac{3}{7} + \frac{2}{3} \cdot \frac{1}{3} \cdot \frac{1}{3} = \frac{1}{21} + \frac{4}{21} + \frac{2}{27} = \frac{59}{189} \approx 0.3122$$

When all three players remain, if a shoots at the sky, b shoots at c and kills him with probability 2/3, with a remaining in a duel with b. If b doesn't kill c, c surely kills b and a remains in a duel with c. So overall, if a shoots at the sky, his probability of winning is

$$\frac{2}{3} \cdot \frac{3}{7} + \frac{1}{3} \cdot \frac{1}{3} = \frac{2}{7} + \frac{1}{9} = \frac{25}{63} \approx 0.3968.$$

So the best strategy for a at the beginning of the game is to aim at the sky, contrary to intuition that would suggest trying to immediately eliminate one of the adversaries.

This problem can be modeled with an LPAD [Nguembang Fadja and Riguzzi, 2017]. However, as can be seen from Figure 15.15, the number of explanations may be infinite, so we need to use an appropriate exact inference algorithm, such as those discussed in Section 8.11, or a Monte Carlo inference algorithm. We discuss below the program https://cplint.eu/e/truel.pl. that uses MCINTYRE.

`survives_action(A,L0,T,S)` is true if A survives the truel performing action S with L0 still alive in turn T:

```
survives_action(A,L0,T,S):-
  shoot(A,S,L0,T,L1),
  remaining(L1,A,Rest),
  survives_round(Rest,L1,A,T).
```

`shoot(H,S,L0,T,L)` is true when H shoots at S in round T with L0 and L the list of truelists still alive before and after the shot:

```
shoot(H,S,L0,T,L):-
    (S=sky -> L=L0
  ;   (hit(T,H) ->   delete(L0,S,L)
    ;   L=L0
      )
    ).
```

The probabilities of each truelist to hit the chosen target are

```
hit(_,a):1/3.
hit(_,b):2/3.
hit(_,c):1.
```

`survives(L,A,T)` is true if individual A survives the truel with truelists L at round T:

```
survives([A],A,_):-!.
```

```
survives(L,A,T):-
  survives_round(L,L,A,T).
```

`survives_round(Rest,L0,A,T)` is true if individual A survives the truel at round T with Rest still to shoot and L0 still alive:

```
survives_round([],L,A,T):-
  survives(L,A,s(T)).
```

```
survives_round([H|_Rest],L0,A,T):-
  base_best_strategy(H,L0,S),
  shoot(H,S,L0,T,L1),
  remaining(L1,H,Rest1),
  member(A,L1),
  survives_round(Rest1,L1,A,T).
```

The following strategies are easy to find:

```
base_best_strategy(b,[b,c],c).
base_best_strategy(c,[b,c],b).
base_best_strategy(a,[a,c],c).
base_best_strategy(c,[a,c],a).
base_best_strategy(a,[a,b],b).
base_best_strategy(b,[a,b],a).
base_best_strategy(b,[a,b,c],c).
base_best_strategy(c,[a,b,c],b).
```

Auxiliary predicate `remaining/3` is defined as

```
remaining([A|Rest],A,Rest):-!.
remaining([_|Rest0],A,Rest):-
  remaining(Rest0,A,Rest).
```

We can decide the best strategy for `a` by asking the probability of the queries

```
?- survives_action(a,[a,b,c],0,b)
?- survives_action(a,[a,b,c],0,c)
?- survives_action(a,[a,b,c],0,sky)
```

By taking 1000 samples, we may get 0.256, 0.316, and 0.389, respectively, showing that *a* should aim at the sky.

15.12 Coupon Collector Problem

In the coupon collector problem [Kaminski et al., 2016], a company sells boxes of cereals each containing a coupon belonging to N different types. The probability of a coupon type in a box is uniform over the set of coupon types. The customers buying the boxes collect the coupons and, one they have one coupon of each type, they can obtain a prize. The problem is: if there are N different coupons, how many boxes, T, do I have to buy to get the prize?

This problem is modeled by program https://cplint.eu/e/coupon.swinb defining predicate `coupons/2` such that goal `coupons(N,T)` is true if we need `T` boxes to get `N` coupons. The coupons are represented with a term for functor `cp/N` with the number of coupons as arity. The i-th argument of the term is 1 if the i-th coupon has been collected and is a variable otherwise. The term thus represents an array:

```
coupons(N,T):-
  length(CP,N),
  CPTerm=..[cp|CP],
  new_coupon(N,CPTerm,0,N,T).
```

If 0 coupons remain to be collected, the collection ends:

```
new_coupon(0,_CP,T,_N,T).
```

If `N0` coupons remain to be collected, we collect one and recurse:

```
new_coupon(N0,CP,T0,N,T):-
  N0>0,
  collect(CP,N,T0,T1),
  N1 is N0-1,
  new_coupon(N1,CP,T1,N,T).
```

`collect/4` collects one new coupon and updates the number of boxes bought:

```
collect(CP,N,T0,T):-
  pick_a_box(T0,N,I),
  T1 is T0+1,
  arg(I,CP,CPI),
  (var(CPI)->
    CPI=1, T=T1
  ;
    collect(CP,N,T1,T)
  ).
```

`pick_a_box/3` randomly picks a box and so a coupon type, an element from the list $[1 \ldots N]$:

```
pick_a_box(_,N,I):uniform(I,L):- numlist(1, N, L).
```

If there are five different coupons, we may ask:

- How many boxes do I have to buy to get the prize?
- What is the distribution of the number of boxes I have to buy to get the prize?
- What is the expected number of boxes I have to buy to get the prize?

To answer the first query, we can take a single sample for `coupons(5,T)`: in the sample, the query will succeed as `coupons/2` is a determinate predicate and the result will instantiate `T` to a specific value. For example, we may get `T=15`. Note that the maximum number of boxes to buy is unbounded but the case where we have to buy an infinite number of boxes has probability 0, so sampling will surely finish.

To compute the distribution on the number of boxes, we can take a number of samples, say 1000, and plot the number of times a value is obtained as a function of the value. By doing so, we may get the graph in Figure 15.16.

To compute the expected number of boxes, we can take a number of samples, say 100, of `coupons(5,T)`. Each sample will instantiate `T`. By summing all these values and dividing by 100, the number of samples, we can get an estimate of the expectation. This computation is performed by the query

```
?- mc_expectation(coupons(5,T),100,T,Exp).
```

For example, we may get a value of 11.47.

We can also plot the dependency of the expected number of boxes from the number of coupons, obtaining Figure 15.17. As observed in [Kaminski et al., 2016], the number of boxes grows as $O(N \log N)$ where N is the number of coupons. The graph also includes the curve $1 + 1.2N \log N$ that is close to the first.

The coupon collector problem is similar to the sticker collector problem, where we have an album with a space for every different sticker, we can buy stickers in packs and our objective is to complete the album. A program for the coupon collector problem can be applied to solve the sticker collector problem: if you have N different stickers and packs contain P stickers, we can solve the coupon collector problem for N coupons and get the number of boxes T. Then the number of packs you have to buy to complete the collection is $\lceil T/P \rceil$. So we can write:

```
stickers(N,P,T):- coupons(N,T0),  T is ceiling(T0/P).
```

If there are 50 different stickers and packs contain four stickers, by sampling the query `stickers(50,4,T)`, we can get `T=47`, i.e., we have to buy 47 packs to complete the entire album.

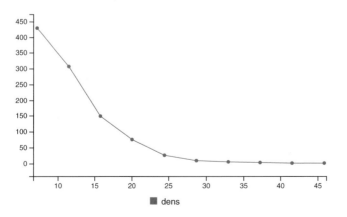

Figure 15.16 Distribution of the number of boxes.

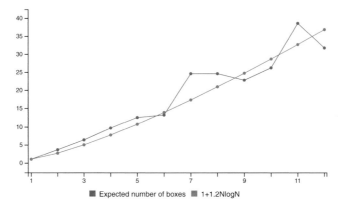

Figure 15.17   Expected number of boxes as a function of the number of coupons.

15.13 One-dimensional Random Walk

Let us consider the version of a random walk described in [Kaminski et al., 2016]: a particle starts at position $x = 10$ and moves with equal probability one unit to the left or one unit to the right in each turn. The random walk stops if the particle reaches position $x = 0$.

The walk terminates with probability 1 [Hurd, 2002] but requires, on average, an infinite time, i.e., the expected number of turns is infinite [Kaminski et al., 2016].

We can compute the number of turns with program https://cplint.eu/e/ random_walk.swinb. The walk starts at time 0 and $x = 10$:

```
walk(T):- walk(10,0,T).
```

If x is 0, the walk ends; otherwise, the particle makes a move:

```
walk(0,T,T).
```

```
walk(X,T0,T):-
  X>0,
  move(T0,Move),
  T1 is T0+1,
  X1 is X+Move,
  walk(X1,T1,T).
```

The move is either one step to the left or to the right with equal probability.

```
move(T,1):0.5; move(T,-1):0.5.
```

By sampling the query `walk(T)`, we obtain a success as `walk/1` is determinate. The value for T represents the number of turns. For example, we may get T = 3692.

15.14 Latent Dirichlet Allocation

Text mining [Holzinger et al., 2014] aims at extracting knowledge from texts. LDA [Blei et al., 2003] is a text mining technique which assigns topics to words in documents. Topics are taken from a finite set $\{1, \ldots, K\}$. The model describes a generative process where documents are represented as random mixtures over latent topics and each topic defines a distribution over words. LDA assumes the following generative process for a corpus D consisting of M documents each of length N_i:

1. Sample $\boldsymbol{\theta}_i$ from $\mathrm{Dir}(\boldsymbol{\alpha})$, where $i \in \{1, \ldots, M\}$ and $\mathrm{Dir}(\boldsymbol{\alpha})$ is the Dirichlet distribution with parameter $\boldsymbol{\alpha}$.
2. Sample $\boldsymbol{\varphi}_k$ from $\mathrm{Dir}(\boldsymbol{\beta})$, where $k \in \{1, \ldots, K\}$.
3. For each of the word positions i, j, where $i \in \{1, \ldots, M\}$ and $j \in \{1, \ldots, N_i\}$:
   (a) Sample a topic $z_{i,j}$ from $\mathrm{Discrete}(\boldsymbol{\theta}_i)$.
   (b) Sample a word $w_{i,j}$ from $\mathrm{Discrete}(\boldsymbol{\varphi}_{z_{i,j}})$.

This is a smoothed LDA model to be precise. Subscripts are often dropped, as in the plate diagrams in Figure 15.18.

The Dirichlet distribution is a continuous multivariate distribution whose parameter $\boldsymbol{\alpha}$ is a vector $(\alpha_1, \ldots, \alpha_K)$ and a value $\mathbf{x} = (x_1, \ldots, x_K)$ sampled from $\mathrm{Dir}(\boldsymbol{\alpha})$ is such that $x_j \in (0, 1)$ for $j = 1, \ldots, K$ and $\sum_{j=1}^{K} x_i = 1$. A sample $\mathbf{x}$ from a Dirichlet distribution can thus be the parameter for a discrete distribution $\mathrm{Discrete}(\mathbf{x})$ with as many values as the components of $\mathbf{x}$: the distribution has $P(v_j) = x_j$ with v_j a value. Therefore, Dirichlet distributions are often used as priors for discrete distributions. The $\boldsymbol{\beta}$ vector above has V components where V is the number of distinct words.

The aim is to compute the probability distributions of words for each topic, of topics for each word, and the particular topic mixture of each document. This can be done with inference: the documents in the dataset represent the observations (evidence) and we want to compute the posterior distribution of the above quantities.

This problem can modeled by the MCINTYRE program https://cplint.eu/e/lda.swinb, where predicate

```
word(Doc,Position,Word)
```

indicates that document `Doc` in position `Position` (from 1 to the number of words of the document) has word `Word` and predicate

```
topic(Doc,Position,Topic)
```

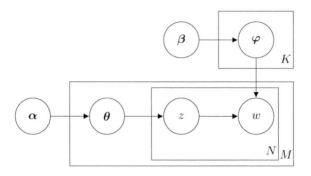

Figure 15.18 Smoothed LDA. From [Nguembang Fadja and Riguzzi, 2017].

indicates that document `Doc` associates topic `Topic` to the word in position `Position`. We also assume that the distributions for both θ_i and φ_k are symmetric Dirichlet distributions with scalar concentration parameter η set using a fact for the predicate `eta/1`, i.e., $\boldsymbol{\alpha} = [\eta, \ldots, \eta]$ and $\boldsymbol{\beta} = [\eta, \ldots, \eta]$. The program is then:

```
theta(_,Theta):dirichlet(Theta,Alpha):-
  alpha(Alpha).

topic(DocumentID,_,Topic):discrete(Topic,Dist):-
  theta(DocumentID,Theta),
  topic_list(Topics),
  maplist(pair,Topics,Theta,Dist).

word(DocumentID,WordID,Word):discrete(Word,Dist):-
  topic(DocumentID,WordID,Topic),
  beta(Topic,Beta),
  word_list(Words),
  maplist(pair,Words,Beta,Dist).

beta(_,Beta):dirichlet(Beta,Parameters):-
  n_words(N),
  eta(Eta),
  findall(Eta,between(1,N,_),Parameters).

alpha(Alpha):-
  eta(Eta),
  n_topics(N),
  findall(Eta,between(1,N,_),Alpha).
```

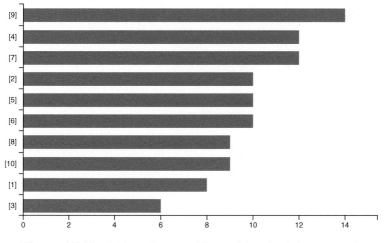

Figure 15.19 Values for word in position 1 of document 1.

```
eta(2).
```

```
pair(V,P,V:P).
```

Suppose we have two topics, indicated with integers 1 and 2, and 10 words, indicated with integers $1, \ldots, 10$:

```
topic_list(L):-
  n_topics(N),
  numlist(1,N,L).
```

```
word_list(L):-
  n_words(N),
  numlist(1,N,L).
```

```
n_topics(2).
```

```
n_words(10).
```

We can, for example, use the model generatively and sample values for the word in position 1 of document 1. The histogram of the frequency of word values when taking 100 samples is shown in Figure 15.19.

We can also sample values for pairs (word, topic) in position 1 of document 1. The histogram of the frequency of the pairs when taking 100 samples is shown in Figure 15.20.

We can use the model to classify the words into topics. Here we use conditional inference with Metropolis-hastings. A priori both topics are about

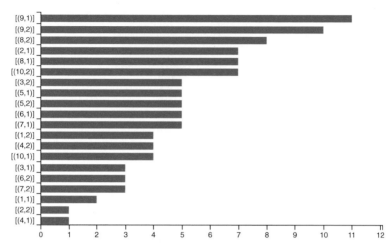

Figure 15.20   Values for couples (word,topic) in position 1 of document 1.

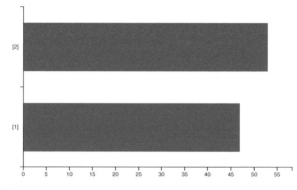

Figure 15.21   Prior distribution of topics for word in position 1 of document 1.

equally probable for word 1 of document, so if we take 100 samples of `topic(1,1,T)`, we get the histogram in Figure 15.21. If we observe that words 1 and 2 of document 1 are equal (`word(1,1,1)`, `word(1,2,1)` as evidence) and take again 100 samples, one of the topics gets more probable, as the histogram of Figure 15.22 shows. You can also see this if you look at the density of the probability of topic 1 before and after observing that words 1 and 2 of document 1 are equal: the observation makes the distribution less uniform, see Figure 15.23. `piercebayes` [Turliuc et al., 2016] is a

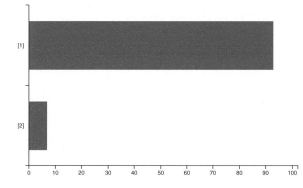

Figure 15.22 Posterior distribution of topics for word in position 1 of document 1.

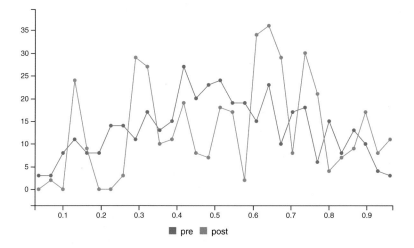

Figure 15.23 Density of the probability of topic 1 before and after observing that words 1 and 2 of document 1 are equal.

PLP language that allows the specification of Dirichlet priors over discrete distribution. Writing LDA models with it is particularly simple.

15.15 The Indian GPA Problem

In the Indian GPA problem proposed by Stuart Russel [Perov et al., 2017; Nitti et al., 2016], the question is: if you observe that a student GPA is exactly 4.0, what is the probability that the student is from India, given that the American GPA score is from 0.0 to 4.0 and the Indian GPA score is from 0.0 to 10.0? Stuart Russel observed that most probabilistic programming systems are not able to deal with this query because it requires combining continuous and discrete distributions. This problem can be modeled by building a mixture of a continuous and a discrete distribution for each nation to account for grade inflation (extreme values have a non-zero probability). Then the probability of the student's GPA is a mixture of the nation mixtures. Given this model and the fact that the student's GPA is exactly 4.0, the probability that the student is American is thus 1.0.

This problem can be modeled in MCINTYRE with program https://cplint. eu/e/indian_gpa.pl. The probability distribution of GPA scores for American students is continuous with probability 0.95 and discrete with probability 0.05:

```
is_density_A:0.95;is_discrete_A:0.05.
```

The GPA of an American student follows a beta distribution if the distribution is continuous:

```
agpa(A): beta(A,8,2) :- is_density_A.
```

The GPA of an American student is 4.0 with probability 0.85 and 0.0 with probability 0.15 if the distribution is discrete:

```
american_gpa(G) : discrete(G,[4.0:0.85,0.0:0.15]) :-
                  is_discrete_A.
```

or is obtained by rescaling the value of returned by `agpa/1` to the (0.0,4.0) interval:

```
american_gpa(A):- agpa(A0), A is A0*4.0.
```

The probability distribution of GPA scores for Indian students is continuous with probability 0.99 and discrete with probability 0.01.

```
is_density_I : 0.99; is_discrete_I:0.01.
```

The GPA of an Indian student follows a beta distribution if the distribution is continuous:

```
igpa(I): beta(I,5,5) :- is_density_I.
```

The GPA of an Indian student is 10.0 with probability 0.9 and 0.0 with probability 0.1 if the distribution is discrete:

```
indian_gpa(I): discrete(I,[0.0:0.1,10.0:0.9]):- is_discrete_I.
```

or is obtained by rescaling the value returned by `igpa/1` to the (0.0,10.0) interval:

```
indian_gpa(I) :- igpa(I0), I is I0*10.0.
```

The nation is America with probability 0.25 and India with probability 0.75.

```
nation(N) : discrete(N,[a:0.25,i:0.75]).
```

The GPA of the student is computed depending on the nation:

```
student_gpa(G) :- nation(a),american_gpa(G).
student_gpa(G) :- nation(i),indian_gpa(G).
```

If we query the probability that the nation is America given that the student got 4.0 in his GPA, we obtain 1.0, while the prior probability that the nation is America is 0.25.

15.16 Bongard Problems

The Bongard Problems Bongard [1970] were used in [De Raedt and Van Laer, 1995] as a testbed for ILP. Each problem consists of a number of pictures divided into two classes, positive and negative. The goal is to discriminate between the two classes.

The pictures contain geometric figures such as squares, triangles, and circles, with different properties, such as small, large, and pointing down, and different relationships between them, such as inside and above. Figure 15.24 shows some of these pictures.

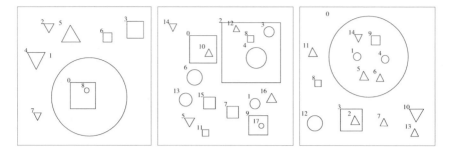

Figure 15.24   Bongard pictures.

A Bongard problem is encoded by https://cplint.eu/e/bongard_R.pl. Each picture is described by a mega-interpretation, in this case, contains a single example, either positive or negative. One such mega-interpretation can be

```
begin(model(2)).
pos.
triangle(o5).
config(o5,up).
square(o4).
in(o4,o5).
circle(o3).
triangle(o2).
config(o2,up).
in(o2,o3).
triangle(o1).
config(o1,up).
end(model(2)).
```

where `begin(model(2))` and `end(model(2))` denote the beginning and end of the mega-interpretation with identifier 2. The target predicate is `pos/0` that indicates the positive class. The mega-interpretation above includes one positive example.

Consider the input LPAD

```
pos:0.5 :-
  circle(A),
  in(B,A).
pos:0.5 :-
  circle(A),
  triangle(B).
```

and definitions for folds (sets of examples) such as

```
fold(train,[2,3,...]).
fold(test,[490,491,...]).
```

We can learn the parameters of the input program with EMBLEM using the query

```
?- induce_par([train],P).
```

The result is a program with updated values for the parameters:

```
pos:0.0841358 :-
  circle(A),
  in(B,A).
pos:0.412669 :-
  circle(A),
  triangle(B).
```

We can perform structure learning using SLIPCOVER by specifying a language bias:

```
modeh(*,pos).
modeb(*,triangle(-obj)).
modeb(*,square(-obj)).
modeb(*,circle(-obj)).
modeb(*,in(+obj,-obj)).
modeb(*,in(-obj,+obj)).
modeb(*,config(+obj,-#dir)).
```

Then the query

```
?- induce([train],P).
```

performs structure learning and returns a program:

```
pos:0.220015 :-
  triangle(A),
  config(A,down).
pos:0.12513 :-
  triangle(A),
  in(B,A).
pos:0.315854 :-
  triangle(A).
```

16

Conclusions

We have come to the end of our journey through probabilistic logic programming. I sincerely hope that I was able to communicate my enthusiasm for this field which combines the powerful results obtained in two previously separated fields: uncertainty in artificial intelligence and logic programming. PLP is growing fast but there is still much to do. An important open problem is how to scale the systems to large data, ideally of the size of Web, in order to exploit the data available on the Web, the Semantic Web, the so-called "knowledge graphs," big databases such as Wikidata, and semantically annotated Web pages. Another important problem is how to deal with unstructured data such as natural language text, images, videos, and multimedia data in general.

For facing the scalability challenge, faster systems can be designed by exploiting symmetries in model using, for example, lifted inference, or restrictions can be imposed in order to obtain more tractable sublanguages. Another approach consists in exploiting modern computing infrastructures such as clusters and clouds and developing parallel algorithms, for example, using MapReduce [Riguzzi et al., 2016b].

For unstructured and multimedia data, handling continuous distributions effectively is fundamental. Inference for hybrid programs is relatively new but is already offered by various systems. The problem of learning hybrid programs, instead, is less explored, especially as regards structure learning. In domains with continuous random variables, neural networks and deep learning [Goodfellow et al., 2016] achieved impressive results. An interesting avenue for future work is how to exploit the techniques of deep learning for learning hybrid probabilistic logic programs.

Some works have already started to appear on the topic, see sections 13.7 and 14.6, but an encompassing framework dealing with different levels of certainty, complex relationships among entities, mixed discrete and continuous unstructured data, and extremely large size is still missing.

Bibliography

M. Abadi, A. Agarwal, P. Barham, E. Brevdo, Z. Chen, C. Citro, G. S. Corrado, A. Davis, J. Dean, M. Devin, S. Ghemawat, I. Goodfellow, A. Harp, G. Irving, M. Isard, Y. Jia, R. Jozefowicz, L. Kaiser, M. Kudlur, J. Levenberg, D. Mané, R. Monga, S. Moore, D. Murray, C. Olah, M. Schuster, J. Shlens, B. Steiner, I. Sutskever, K. Talwar, P. Tucker, V. Vanhoucke, V. Vasudevan, F. Viégas, O. Vinyals, P. Warden, M. Wattenberg, M. Wicke, Y. Yu, and X. Zheng. TensorFlow: Large-scale machine learning on heterogeneous systems, 2015. URL https://www.tensorflow.org/. Software available from tensorflow.org.

M. Alberti, E. Bellodi, G. Cota, F. Riguzzi, and R. Zese. cplint on SWISH: Probabilistic logical inference with a web browser. *Intelligenza Artificiale*, 11(1):47–64, 2017. doi:10.3233/IA-170105.

M. Alviano, F. Calimeri, C. Dodaro, D. Fuscà, N. Leone, S. Perri, F. Ricca, P. Veltri, and J. Zangari. The ASP system DLV2. In M. Balduccini and T. Janhunen, editors, *14th International Conference on Logic Programming and Non-monotonic Reasoning (LPNMR 2017)*, volume 10377 of *LNCS*. Springer, 2017. doi:10.1007/978-3-319-61660-5_19.

N. Angelopoulos. clp(pdf(y)): Constraints for probabilistic reasoning in logic programming. In F. Rossi, editor, *9th International Conference on Principles and Practice of Constraint Programming (CP 2003)*, volume 2833 of *LNCS*, pages 784–788. Springer, 2003. doi:10.1007/978-3-540-45193-8_53.

N. Angelopoulos. Probabilistic space partitioning in constraint logic programming. In M. J. Maher, editor, *9th Asian Computing Science Conference (ASIAN 2004)*, volume 3321 of *LNCS*, pages 48–62. Springer, 2004. doi:10.1007/978-3-540-30502-6_4.

N. Angelopoulos. Notes on the implementation of FAM. In A. Hommersom and S. A. Abdallah, editors, *3rd International Workshop on Probabilistic Logic Programming (PLP 2016)*, volume 1661 of *CEUR Workshop Proceedings*, pages 46–58. CEUR-WS.org, 2016.

K. R. Apt and M. Bezem. Acyclic programs. *New Generation Computing*, 9 (3/4):335–364, 1991.

K. R. Apt and R. N. Bol. Logic programming and negation: A survey. *Journal of Logic Programming*, 19:9–71, 1994.

R. Ash and C. Doléans-Dade. *Probability and Measure Theory*. Harcourt/Academic Press, 2000. ISBN 9780120652020.

T. Augustin, F. P. Coolen, G. De Cooman, and M. C. Troffaes. *Introduction to imprecise probabilities*. John Wiley & Sons, Ltd., 2014.

D. Azzolini, F. Riguzzi, and E. Lamma. A semantics for hybrid probabilistic logic programs with function symbols. *Artificial Intelligence*, 294:103452, 2021. ISSN 0004-3702. doi:10.1016/j.artint.2021.103452.

F. Bacchus. Using first-order probability logic for the construction of bayesian networks. In *9th Conference Conference on Uncertainty in Artificial Intelligence (UAI 1993)*, pages 219–226, 1993.

R. I. Bahar, E. A. Frohm, C. M. Gaona, G. D. Hachtel, E. Macii, A. Pardo, and F. Somenzi. Algebraic decision diagrams and their applications. *Formal Methods in System Design*, 10(2/3):171–206, 1997. doi:10.1023/A:1008699807402.

J. K. Baker. Trainable grammars for speech recognition. In D. H. Klatt and J. J. Wolf, editors, *Speech Communication Papers for the 97th Meeting of the Acoustical Society of America*, pages 547–550, 1979.

C. Baral, M. Gelfond, and N. Rushton. Probabilistic reasoning with answer sets. *Theory and Practice of Logic Programming*, 9(1):57–144, 2009. doi:10.1017/S1471068408003645.

L. Bauters, S. Schockaert, M. De Cock, and D. Vermeir. Possibilistic answer set programming revisited. In *26th International Conference on Uncertainty in Artificial Intelligence (UAI 2010)*. AUAI Press, 2010.

V. Belle, G. V. den Broeck, and A. Passerini. Hashing-based approximate probabilistic inference in hybrid domains. In M. Meila and T. Heskes, editors, *31st International Conference on Uncertainty in Artificial Intelligence (UAI 2015)*, pages 141–150. AUAI Press, 2015a.

V. Belle, A. Passerini, and G. V. den Broeck. Probabilistic inference in hybrid domains by weighted model integration. In Q. Yang and M. Wooldridge, editors, *24th International Joint Conference on Artificial Intelligence (IJCAI 2015)*, pages 2770–2776. AAAI Press, 2015b.

V. Belle, G. V. den Broeck, and A. Passerini. Component caching in hybrid domains with piecewise polynomial densities. In D. Schuurmans and M. P. Wellman, editors, *30th National Conference on Artificial Intelligence (AAAI 2015)*, pages 3369–3375. AAAI Press, 2016.

E. Bellodi and F. Riguzzi. Experimentation of an expectation maximization algorithm for probabilistic logic programs. *Intelligenza Artificiale*, 8(1): 3–18, 2012. doi:10.3233/IA-2012-0027.

E. Bellodi and F. Riguzzi. Expectation maximization over binary decision diagrams for probabilistic logic programs. *Intelligent Data Analysis*, 17 (2):343–363, 2013.

E. Bellodi and F. Riguzzi. Structure learning of probabilistic logic programs by searching the clause space. *Theory and Practice of Logic Programming*, 15(2):169–212, 2015. doi:10.1017/S1471068413000689.

E. Bellodi, E. Lamma, F. Riguzzi, V. S. Costa, and R. Zese. Lifted variable elimination for probabilistic logic programming. *Theory and Practice of Logic Programming*, 14(4-5):681–695, 2014. doi:10.1017/S1471068414000283.

E. Bellodi, M. Alberti, F. Riguzzi, and R. Zese. MAP inference for probabilistic logic programming. *Theory and Practice of Logic Programming*, 20(5):641–655, 2020. doi:10.1017/S1471068420000174.

P. Berka. Guide to the financial data set. In *ECML/PKDD 2000 Discovery Challenge*, 2000.

C. Bishop. *Pattern Recognition and Machine Learning*. Information Science and Statistics. Springer, 2016. ISBN 9781493938438.

D. M. Blei, A. Y. Ng, and M. I. Jordan. Latent Dirichlet allocation. *Journal of Machine Learning Research*, 3:993–1022, 2003.

H. Blockeel. Probabilistic logical models for Mendel's experiments: An exercise. In *Inductive Logic Programming (ILP 2004), Work in Progress Track*, pages 1–5, 2004.

H. Blockeel and L. D. Raedt. Top-down induction of first-order logical decision trees. *Artificial Intelligence*, 101(1-2):285–297, 1998. doi:10.1016/S0004-3702(98)00034-4.

H. Blockeel and J. Struyf. Frankenstein classifiers: Some experiments on the Sisyphus data set. In *Workshop on Integration of Data Mining, Decision Support, and Meta-Learning (IDDM 2001)*, 2001.

M. M. Bongard. *Pattern Recognition*. Hayden Book Co., Spartan Books, 1970.

S. Bragaglia and F. Riguzzi. Approximate inference for logic programs with annotated disjunctions. In *21st International Conference on Inductive Logic Programming (ILP 2011)*, volume 6489 of *LNAI*, pages 30–37, Florence, Italy, 27-30 June 2011. Springer.

D. Brannan. *A First Course in Mathematical Analysis*. Cambridge University Press, 2006. ISBN 9781139458955.

R. Carnap. *Logical Foundations of Probability*. University of Chicago Press, 1950.

M. Chavira and A. Darwiche. On probabilistic inference by weighted model counting. *Artificial Intelligence*, 172(6-7):772–799, 2008.

W. Chen and D. S. Warren. Tabled evaluation with delaying for general logic programs. *Journal of the ACM*, 43(1):20–74, 1996. doi:10.1145/227595.227597.

W. Chen, T. Swift, and D. S. Warren. Efficient top-down computation of queries under the well-founded semantics. *Journal of Logic Programming*, 24(3):161–199, 1995.

Y. S. Chow and H. Teicher. *Probability Theory: Independence, Interchangeability, Martingales*. Springer Texts in Statistics. Springer, 2012.

K. L. Clark. Negation as failure. In *Logic and data bases*, pages 293–322. Springer, 1978.

P. Cohn. *Basic Algebra: Groups, Rings, and Fields*. Springer, 2003.

A. Colmerauer, H. Kanoui, R. Pasero, and P. Roussel. Un systeme de communication homme-machine en français. Technical report, Groupe de Recherche en Intelligence Artificielle, Université d'Aix-Marseille, 1973.

J. Côrte-Real, T. Mantadelis, I. de Castro Dutra, R. Rocha, and E. S. Burnside. SkILL - A stochastic inductive logic learner. In T. Li, L. A. Kurgan, V. Palade, R. Goebel, A. Holzinger, K. Verspoor, and M. A. Wani, editors, *14th IEEE International Conference on Machine Learning and Applications (ICMLA 2015)*, pages 555–558. IEEE Press, 2015. doi:10.1109/ICMLA.2015.159.

J. Côrte-Real, I. de Castro Dutra, and R. Rocha. Estimation-based search space traversal in PILP environments. In J. Cussens and A. Russo, editors, *26th International Conference on Inductive Logic Programming (ILP 2016)*, volume 10326 of *LNCS*, pages 1–13. Springer, 2017. doi:10.1007/978-3-319-63342-8_1.

V. S. Costa, D. Page, M. Qazi, and J. Cussens. CLP(BN): Constraint logic programming for probabilistic knowledge. In *19th International Conference on Uncertainty in Artificial Intelligence (UAI 2003)*, pages 517–524. Morgan Kaufmann Publishers, 2003.

F. G. Cozman and D. D. Mauá. On the semantics and complexity of probabilistic logic programs. *Journal of Artificial Intelligence Research*, 60: 221–262, 2017. doi:10.1613/jair.5482.

F. G. Cozman and D. D. Mauá. The joy of probabilistic answer set programming: Semantics, complexity, expressivity, inference. *International*

Journal of Approximate Reasoning, 125:218–239, 2020. ISSN 0888-613X. doi:10.1016/j.ijar.2020.07.004.

J. Cussens. Parameter estimation in stochastic logic programs. *Machine Learning*, 44(3):245–271, 2001. doi:10.1023/A:1010924021315.

E. Dantsin. Probabilistic logic programs and their semantics. In *Russian Conference on Logic Programming*, volume 592 of *LNCS*, pages 152–164. Springer, 1991.

E. Dantsin, T. Eiter, G. Gottlob, and A. Voronkov. Complexity and expressive power of logic programming. *ACM Computing Surveys*, 33(3):374–425, 2001. doi:10.1145/502807.502810.

A. Darwiche. A logical approach to factoring belief networks. In D. Fensel, F. Giunchiglia, D. L. McGuinness, and M. Williams, editors, *8th International Conference on Principles and Knowledge Representation and Reasoning*, pages 409–420. Morgan Kaufmann, 2002.

A. Darwiche. New advances in compiling CNF into decomposable negation normal form. In R. L. de Mántaras and L. Saitta, editors, *16th European Conference on Artificial Intelligence (ECAI 20014)*, pages 328–332. IOS Press, 2004.

A. Darwiche. *Modeling and Reasoning with Bayesian Networks*. Cambridge University Press, 2009.

A. Darwiche. SDD: A new canonical representation of propositional knowledge bases. In T. Walsh, editor, *22nd International Joint Conference on Artificial Intelligence (IJCAI 2011)*, pages 819–826. AAAI Press/IJCAI, 2011. doi:10.5591/978-1-57735-516-8/IJCAI11-143.

A. Darwiche and P. Marquis. A knowledge compilation map. *Journal of Artificial Intelligence Research*, 17:229–264, 2002. doi:10.1613/jair.989.

A. S. d'Avila Garcez, M. Gori, L. C. Lamb, L. Serafini, M. Spranger, and S. N. Tran. Neural-symbolic computing: An effective methodology for principled integration of machine learning and reasoning. *Journal of Applied Logics - IfCoLog Journal of Logics and their Applications*, 6(4):611–632, 2019.

J. Davis and M. Goadrich. The relationship between precision-recall and ROC curves. In *European Conference on Machine Learning (ECML 2006)*, pages 233–240. ACM, 2006.

J. Davis, E. S. Burnside, I. de Castro Dutra, D. Page, and V. S. Costa. An integrated approach to learning bayesian networks of rules. In J. Gama, R. Camacho, P. Brazdil, A. Jorge, and L. Torgo, editors, *European Conference on Machine Learning (ECML 2005)*, volume 3720 of *LNCS*, pages 84–95. Springer, 2005. doi:10.1007/11564096_13.

L. De Raedt and A. Kimmig. Probabilistic (logic) programming concepts. *Machine Learning*, 100(1):5–47, 2015. doi:10.1007/s10994-015-5494-z.

L. De Raedt and I. Thon. Probabilistic rule learning. In P. Frasconi and F. A. Lisi, editors, *20th International Conference on Inductive Logic Programming (ILP 2010)*, volume 6489 of *LNCS*, pages 47–58. Springer, 2011. doi:10.1007/978-3-642-21295-6_9.

L. De Raedt and W. Van Laer. Inductive constraint logic. In *5th Conference on Algorithmic Learning Theory*, volume 997 of *LNAI*, pages 80–94. Springer, 1995.

L. De Raedt, A. Kimmig, and H. Toivonen. ProbLog: A probabilistic Prolog and its application in link discovery. In M. M. Veloso, editor, *20th International Joint Conference on Artificial Intelligence (IJCAI 2007)*, volume 7, pages 2462–2467. AAAI Press/IJCAI, 2007.

L. De Raedt, B. Demoen, D. Fierens, B. Gutmann, G. Janssens, A. Kimmig, N. Landwehr, T. Mantadelis, W. Meert, R. Rocha, V. Santos Costa, I. Thon, and J. Vennekens. Towards digesting the alphabet-soup of statistical relational learning. In *NIPS 2008 Workshop on Probabilistic Programming*, 2008.

L. De Raedt, P. Frasconi, K. Kersting, and S. Muggleton, editors. *Probabilistic Inductive Logic Programming*, volume 4911 of *LNCS*, 2008. Springer. ISBN 978-3-540-78651-1.

L. De Raedt, K. Kersting, A. Kimmig, K. Revoredo, and H. Toivonen. Compressing probabilistic Prolog programs. *Machine Learning*, 70(2-3): 151–168, 2008. doi:10.1007/s10994-007-5030-x.

R. de Salvo Braz, E. Amir, and D. Roth. Lifted first-order probabilistic inference. In L. P. Kaelbling and A. Saffiotti, editors, *19th International Joint Conference on Artificial Intelligence (IJCAI 2005)*, pages 1319–1325. Professional Book Center, 2005.

A. Dekhtyar and V. Subrahmanian. Hybrid probabilistic programs. *Journal of Logic Programming*, 43(2):187–250, 2000.

A. P. Dempster, N. M. Laird, and D. B. Rubin. Maximum likelihood from incomplete data via the EM algorithm. *Journal of the Royal Statistical Society. Series B (methodological)*, 39(1):1–38, 1977.

A. Dries, A. Kimmig, W. Meert, J. Renkens, G. Van den Broeck, J. Vlasselaer, and L. De Raedt. ProbLog2: Probabilistic logic programming. In *European Conference on Machine Learning and Principles and Practice of Knowledge Discovery in Databases (ECMLPKDD 2015)*, volume 9286 of *LNCS*, pages 312–315. Springer, 2015. doi:10.1007/978-3-319-23461-8_37.

D. Dubois and H. Prade. Possibilistic logic: a retrospective and prospective view. *Fuzzy Sets and Systems*, 144(1):3–23, 2004.

D. Dubois, J. Lang, and H. Prade. Towards possibilistic logic programming. In *8th International Conference on Logic Programming (ICLP 1991)*, pages 581–595, 1991.

D. Dubois, J. Lang, and H. Prade. Possibilistic logic. In D. M. Gabbay, C. J. Hogger, and J. A. Robinson, editors, *Handbook of logic in artificial intelligence and logic programming, vol. 3*, pages 439–514. Oxford University Press, 1994.

S. Džeroski. Handling imperfect data in inductive logic programming. In *4th Scandinavian Conference on Artificial Intelligence (SCAI 1993)*, pages 111–125, 1993.

T. Eiter, G. Ianni, and T. Krennwallner. Answer set programming: A primer. In S. Tessaris, E. Franconi, T. Eiter, C. Gutiérrez, S. Handschuh, M. Rousset, and R. A. Schmidt, editors, *Reasoning Web. Semantic Technologies for Information Systems, 5th International Summer School*, volume 5689 of *LNCS*, pages 40–110. Springer, 2009. doi:10.1007/978-3-642-03754-2_2.

W. Faber, G. Pfeifer, and N. Leone. Semantics and complexity of recursive aggregates in answer set programming. *Artificial Intelligence*, 175(1):278–298, 2011a. doi:10.1016/j.artint.2010.04.002.

W. Faber, G. Pfeifer, and N. Leone. Semantics and complexity of recursive aggregates in answer set programming. *Artificial Intelligence*, 175(1):278–298, 2011b.

F. Fages. Consistency of Clark's completion and existence of stable models. *Journal of Methods of Logic in Computer Science*, 1(1):51–60, 1994.

R. Fagin and J. Y. Halpern. Reasoning about knowledge and probability. *Journal of the ACM*, 41(2):340–367, 1994. doi:10.1145/174652.174658.

D. Fierens, G. Van den Broeck, J. Renkens, D. S. Shterionov, B. Gutmann, I. Thon, G. Janssens, and L. De Raedt. Inference and learning in probabilistic logic programs using weighted Boolean formulas. *Theory and Practice of Logic Programming*, 15(3):358–401, 2015.

N. Fuhr. Probabilistic datalog: Implementing logical information retrieval for advanced applications. *Journal of the American Society for Information Science*, 51:95–110, 2000.

H. Gaifman. Concerning measures in first order calculi. *Israel Journal of Mathematics*, 2:1–18, 1964.

M. Gebser, B. Kaufmann, R. Kaminski, M. Ostrowski, T. Schaub, and M. T. Schneider. Potassco: The Potsdam answer set solving collection. *AI Commununications*, 24(2):107–124, 2011. doi:10.3233/AIC-2011-0491.

T. Gehr, S. Misailovic, and M. Vechev. PSI: exact symbolic inference for probabilistic programs. In S. Chaudhuri and A. Farzan, editors, *28th International Conference on Computer Aided Verification (CAV 2016), Part I*, volume 9779 of *LNCS*, pages 62–83. Springer, 2016. doi:10.1007/978-3-319-41528-4_4.

M. Gelfond and V. Lifschitz. The stable model semantics for logic programming. In *5th International Conference and Symposium on Logic Programming (ICLP/SLP 1988)*, volume 88, pages 1070–1080. MIT Press, 1988.

G. Gerla. *Fuzzy Logic*, volume 11 of *Trends in Logic*. Springer, 2001. doi:10.1007/978-94-015-9660-2_8.

V. Gogate and P. M. Domingos. Probabilistic theorem proving. In F. G. Cozman and A. Pfeffer, editors, *27th International Conference on Uncertainty in Artificial Intelligence (UAI 2011)*, pages 256–265. AUAI Press, 2011.

T. Gomes and V. S. Costa. Evaluating inference algorithms for the Prolog factor language. In F. Riguzzi and F. Železný, editors, *21st International Conference on Inductive Logic Programming (ILP 2012)*, volume 7842 of *LNCS*, pages 74–85. Springer, 2012.

I. J. Good. A causal calculus (i). *The British journal for the philosophy of science*, 11(44):305–318, 1961.

I. Goodfellow, Y. Bengio, and A. Courville. *Deep learning*, volume 1. MIT Press, 2016.

N. D. Goodman and J. B. Tenenbaum. Inducing arithmetic functions, 2018. http://forestdb.org/models/arithmetic.html, accessed January 5, 2018.

A. Gorlin, C. R. Ramakrishnan, and S. A. Smolka. Model checking with probabilistic tabled logic programming. *Theory and Practice of Logic Programming*, 12(4-5):681–700, 2012.

P. Grünwald and J. Y. Halpern. Updating probabilities. *Journal of Artificial Intelligence Research*, 19:243–278, 2003. doi:10.1613/jair.1164.

B. Gutmann. *On continuous distributions and parameter estimation in probabilistic logic programs*. PhD thesis, Katholieke Universiteit Leuven, Belgium, 2011.

B. Gutmann, A. Kimmig, K. Kersting, and L. D. Raedt. Parameter learning in probabilistic databases: A least squares approach. In *European Conference on Machine Learning and Principles and Practice of Knowledge Discovery in Databases (ECMLPKDD 2008)*, volume 5211 of *LNCS*, pages 473–488. Springer, 2008.

B. Gutmann, A. Kimmig, K. Kersting, and L. De Raedt. Parameter estimation in ProbLog from annotated queries. Technical Report CW 583, KU Leuven, 2010.

B. Gutmann, M. Jaeger, and L. De Raedt. Extending problog with continuous distributions. In P. Frasconi and F. A. Lisi, editors, *20th International Conference on Inductive Logic Programming (ILP 2010)*, volume 6489 of *LNCS*, pages 76–91. Springer, 2011a. doi:10.1007/978-3-642-21295-6_12.

B. Gutmann, I. Thon, and L. De Raedt. Learning the parameters of probabilistic logic programs from interpretations. In D. Gunopulos, T. Hofmann, D. Malerba, and M. Vazirgiannis, editors, *European Conference on Machine Learning and Principles and Practice of Knowledge Discovery in Databases (ECMLPKDD 2011)*, volume 6911 of *LNCS*, pages 581–596. Springer, 2011b.

B. Gutmann, I. Thon, A. Kimmig, M. Bruynooghe, and L. De Raedt. The magic of logical inference in probabilistic programming. *Theory and Practice of Logic Programming*, 11(4-5):663–680, 2011c.

Z. Gyenis, G. Hofer-Szabo, and M. Rédei. Conditioning using conditional expectations: the Borel–Kolmogorov paradox. *Synthese*, 194(7):2595–2630, 2017.

S. Hadjichristodoulou and D. S. Warren. Probabilistic logic programming with well-founded negation. In D. M. Miller and V. C. Gaudet, editors, *42nd IEEE International Symposium on Multiple-Valued Logic, (ISMVL 2012)*, pages 232–237. IEEE Computer Society, 2012. doi:10.1109/ISMVL.2012.26.

P. Hájek. *Metamathematics of fuzzy logic*, volume 4. Springer, 1998.

J. Halpern. *Reasoning About Uncertainty*. MIT Press, 2003.

J. Y. Halpern. An analysis of first-order logics of probability. *Artificial Intelligence*, 46(3):311–350, 1990.

A. C. Harvey. *Forecasting, structural time series models and the Kalman filter*. Cambridge University Press, 1990.

J. Herbrand. *Recherches sur la théorie de la démonstration*. PhD thesis, Université de Paris, 1930.

P. Hitzler and A. Seda. *Mathematical Aspects of Logic Programming Semantics*. Chapman & Hall/CRC Studies in Informatics Series. CRC Press, 2016.

A. Holzinger, J. Schantl, M. Schroettner, C. Seifert, and K. Verspoor. Biomedical text mining: State-of-the-art, open problems and future challenges. In A. Holzinger and I. Jurisica, editors, *Interactive Knowledge Discovery and Data Mining in Biomedical Informatics*, volume 8401 of *LNCS*, pages 271–300. Springer, 2014. doi:10.1007/978-3-662-43968-5_16.

J. Hurd. A formal approach to probabilistic termination. In V. Carreño, C. A. Muñoz, and S. Tahar, editors, *15th International Conference on Theorem Proving in Higher Order Logics (TPHOLs 2002)*, volume 2410 of *LNCS*, pages 230–245. Springer, 2002. doi:10.1007/3-540-45685-6_16.

K. Inoue, T. Sato, M. Ishihata, Y. Kameya, and H. Nabeshima. Evaluating abductive hypotheses using an EM algorithm on BDDs. In *21st International Joint Conference on Artificial Intelligence (IJCAI 2009)*, pages 810–815. Morgan Kaufmann Publishers Inc., 2009.

M. Ishihata, Y. Kameya, T. Sato, and S. Minato. Propositionalizing the EM algorithm by BDDs. In *Late Breaking Papers of the 18th International Conference on Inductive Logic Programming (ILP 2008)*, pages 44–49, 2008a.

M. Ishihata, Y. Kameya, T. Sato, and S. Minato. Propositionalizing the EM algorithm by BDDs. Technical Report TR08-0004, Dep. of Computer Science, Tokyo Institute of Technology, 2008b.

M. A. Islam. *Inference and learning in probabilistic logic programs with continuous random variables*. PhD thesis, State University of New York at Stony Brook, 2012.

M. A. Islam, C. Ramakrishnan, and I. Ramakrishnan. Parameter learning in PRISM programs with continuous random variables. *CoRR*, abs/1203.4287, 2012a.

M. A. Islam, C. Ramakrishnan, and I. Ramakrishnan. Inference in probabilistic logic programs with continuous random variables. *Theory and Practice of Logic Programming*, 12:505–523, 2012b. ISSN 1475-3081. doi:10.1017/S1471068412000154.

M. Jaeger. Reasoning about infinite random structures with relational bayesian networks. In A. G. Cohn, L. K. Schubert, and S. C. Shapiro, editors, *4th International Conference on Principles of Knowledge Representation and Reasoning*, pages 570–581. Morgan Kaufmann, 1998.

M. Jaeger and G. Van den Broeck. Liftability of probabilistic inference: Upper and lower bounds. In *2nd International Workshop on Statistical Relational AI (StarAI 2012)*, pages 1–8, 2012.

J. Jaffar, M. J. Maher, K. Marriott, and P. J. Stuckey. The semantics of constraint logic programs. *Journal of Logic Programming*, 37(1-3):1–46, 1998. doi:10.1016/S0743-1066(98)10002-X.

T. Janhunen. Representing normal programs with clauses. In R. L. de Mántaras and L. Saitta, editors, *16th European Conference on Artificial*

Intelligence (ECAI 20014), pages 358–362. IOS Press, 2004.

C. Jiang, J. Babar, G. Ciardo, A. S. Miner, and B. Smith. Variable reordering in binary decision diagrams. In *26th International Workshop on Logic and Synthesis*, pages 1–8, 2017.

B. L. Kaminski, J.-P. Katoen, C. Matheja, and F. Olmedo. Weakest precondition reasoning for expected run-times of probabilistic programs. In P. Thiemann, editor, *25th European Symposium on Programming, on Programming Languages and Systems (ESOP 2016)*, volume 9632 of *LNCS*, pages 364–389. Springer, 2016. doi:10.1007/978-3-662-49498-1_15.

K. Kersting and L. De Raedt. Towards combining inductive logic programming with Bayesian networks. In *11th International Conference on Inductive Logic Programming (ILP 2001)*, volume 2157 of *LNCS*, pages 118–131, 2001.

K. Kersting and L. De Raedt. Basic principles of learning Bayesian logic programs. In *Probabilistic Inductive Logic Programming*, volume 4911 of *LNCS*, pages 189–221. Springer, 2008.

H. Khosravi, O. Schulte, J. Hu, and T. Gao. Learning compact Markov logic networks with decision trees. *Machine Learning*, 89(3):257–277, 2012.

T. Khot, S. Natarajan, K. Kersting, and J. W. Shavlik. Learning Markov Logic Networks via functional gradient boosting. In *Proceedings of the 11th IEEE International Conference on Data Mining*, pages 320–329. IEEE, 2011.

J. Kietz and M. Lübbe. An efficient subsumption algorithm for inductive logic programming. In W. W. Cohen and H. Hirsh, editors, *11th International Conference on Machine Learning*, pages 130–138. Morgan Kaufmann, 1994. ISBN 1-55860-335-2.

D. M. Kilgour and S. J. Brams. The truel. *Mathematics Magazine*, 70(5): 315–326, 1997.

A. Kimmig. *A Probabilistic Prolog and its Applications*. PhD thesis, Katholieke Universiteit Leuven, Belgium, 2010.

A. Kimmig, V. Santos Costa, R. Rocha, B. Demoen, and L. De Raedt. On the efficient execution of ProbLog programs. In *24th International Conference on Logic Programming (ICLP 2008)*, volume 5366 of *LNCS*, pages 175–189. Springer, December 2008. doi:10.1007/978-3-540-89982-2_22.

A. Kimmig, B. Demoen, L. De Raedt, V. S. Costa, and R. Rocha. On the implementation of the probabilistic logic programming language ProbLog. *Theory and Practice of Logic Programming*, 11(2-3):235–262, 2011a.

A. Kimmig, G. V. den Broeck, and L. D. Raedt. An algebraic Prolog for reasoning about possible worlds. In W. Burgard and D. Roth, editors, *Pro-*

ceedings of the Twenty-Fifth AAAI Conference on Artificial Intelligence (AAAI 2011). AAAI Press, 2011b.

A. Kimmig, G. Van den Broeck, and L. De Raedt. Algebraic model counting. *J. of Applied Logic*, 22(C):46–62, July 2017. ISSN 1570-8683. doi:10.1016/j.jal.2016.11.031.

D. Kingma and J. Ba. Adam: A method for stochastic optimization. *arXiv preprint arXiv:1412.6980*, 2014.

J. Kisynski and D. Poole. Lifted aggregation in directed first-order probabilistic models. In C. Boutilier, editor, *21st International Joint Conference on Artificial Intelligence (IJCAI 2009)*, pages 1922–1929, 2009a.

J. Kisynski and D. Poole. Constraint processing in lifted probabilistic inference. In J. Bilmes and A. Y. Ng, editors, *25th International Conference on Uncertainty in Artificial Intelligence (UAI 2009)*, pages 293–302. AUAI Press, 2009b.

B. Knaster and A. Tarski. Un théorème sur les fonctions d'ensembles. *Annales de la Société Polonaise de Mathématique*, 6:133–134, 1928.

K. Knopp. *Theory and Application of Infinite Series*. Dover Books on Mathematics. Dover Publications, 1951.

D. E. Knuth. Two notes on notation. *The American Mathematical Monthly*, 99(5):403–422, 1992.

S. Kok and P. Domingos. Learning the structure of Markov logic networks. In L. De Raedt and S. Wrobel, editors, *22nd International Conference on Machine learning*, pages 441–448. ACM Press, 2005a.

S. Kok and P. Domingos. Learning the structure of Markov Logic Networks. In *22nd International Conference on Machine learning*, pages 441–448. ACM, 2005b.

D. Koller and N. Friedman. *Probabilistic Graphical Models: Principles and Techniques*. Adaptive computation and machine learning. MIT Press, Cambridge, MA, 2009.

E. Koutsofios, S. North, et al. Drawing graphs with dot. Technical Report 910904-59113-08TM, AT&T Bell Laboratories, 1991.

R. A. Kowalski. Predicate logic as programming language. In *IFIP Congress*, pages 569–574, 1974.

R. A. Kowalski and M. J. Sergot. A logic-based calculus of events. *New Generation Computing*, 4(1):67–95, 1986. doi:10.1007/BF03037383.

N. Kumar, O. Kuzelka, and L. De Raedt. Learning distributional programs for relational autocompletion. *Theory and Practice of Logic Programming*, 22 (1):81–114, 2022. doi:10.1017/S1471068421000144.

T. Lager. Spaghetti and HMMeatballs, 2018. https://web.archive.org/web/20150619013510/http://www.ling.gu.se/~lager/Spaghetti/spaghetti.html, accessed June 14, 2018, snapshot at the Internet Archive from June 6, 2015 of http://www.ling.gu.se/~lager/Spaghetti/spaghetti.html, no more accessible.

L. J. Layne and S. Qiu. Prediction for compound activity in large drug datasets using efficient machine learning approaches. In M. Khosrow-Pour, editor, *International Conference of the Information Resources Management Association*, pages 57–61. Idea Group Publishing, 2005. doi:10.4018/978-1-59140-822-2.ch014.

Y. LeCun. The mnist database of handwritten digits. *http://yann. lecun. com/exdb/mnist/*, 1998.

N. Leone, G. Pfeifer, W. Faber, T. Eiter, G. Gottlob, S. Perri, and F. Scarcello. The DLV system for knowledge representation and reasoning. *ACM Transactions on Computational Logic*, 7(3):499–562, 2006. doi:10.1145/1149114.1149117.

H. Li, K. Zhang, and T. Jiang. The regularized em algorithm. In *AAAI*, pages 807–812, 2005.

J. W. Lloyd. *Foundations of Logic Programming, 2nd Edition*. Springer, 1987. ISBN 3-540-18199-7.

T. Lukasiewicz. Probabilistic description logic programs. In L. Godo, editor, *Symbolic and Quantitative Approaches to Reasoning with Uncertainty, 8th European Conference, ECSQARU 2005, Barcelona, Spain, July 6-8, 2005, Proceedings*, volume 3571 of *LNCS*, pages 737–749. Springer, 2005. doi:10.1007/11518655_62.

T. Lukasiewicz. Probabilistic description logic programs. *International Journal of Approximate Reasoning*, 45(2):288–307, 2007. doi:10.1016/j.ijar.2006.06.012.

R. Manhaeve, S. Dumancic, A. Kimmig, T. Demeester, and L. De Raedt. DeepProbLog: Neural probabilistic logic programming. In S. Bengio, H. M. Wallach, H. Larochelle, K. Grauman, N. Cesa-Bianchi, and R. Garnett, editors, *Advances in Neural Information Processing Systems 31 (NeurIPS 2018)*, pages 3753–3763, 2018. URL https://proceedings.neurips.cc/paper/2018/hash/dc5d637ed5e62c36ecb73b654b05ba2a-Abstract.html.

R. Manhaeve, S. Dumancic, A. Kimmig, T. Demeester, and L. De Raedt. Neural probabilistic logic programming in DeepProbLog. *Artificial Intelligence*, 298:103504, 2021. doi:10.1016/j.artint.2021.103504.

T. Mantadelis and G. Janssens. Dedicated tabling for a probabilistic setting. In M. V. Hermenegildo and T. Schaub, editors, *Technical Communications of the 26th International Conference on Logic Programming (ICLP 2010)*, volume 7 of *LIPIcs*, pages 124–133. Schloss Dagstuhl - Leibniz-Zentrum fuer Informatik, 2010. doi:10.4230/LIPIcs.ICLP.2010.124.

D. D. Mauá and F. G. Cozman. Complexity results for probabilistic answer set programming. *International Journal of Approximate Reasoning*, 118: 133–154, 2020. doi:10.1016/j.ijar.2019.12.003.

J. McDermott and R. S. Forsyth. Diagnosing a disorder in a classification benchmark. *Pattern Recognition Letters*, 73:41–43, 2016. doi:10.1016/j.patrec.2016.01.004.

S. Michels. *Hybrid Probabilistic Logics: Theoretical Aspects, Algorithms and Experiments*. PhD thesis, Radboud University Nijmegen, 2016.

S. Michels, A. Hommersom, P. J. F. Lucas, M. Velikova, and P. W. M. Koopman. Inference for a new probabilistic constraint logic. In F. Rossi, editor, *IJCAI 2013, Proceedings of the 23rd International Joint Conference on Artificial Intelligence, Beijing, China, August 3-9, 2013*, pages 2540–2546. AAAI Press/IJCAI, 2013.

S. Michels, A. Hommersom, P. J. F. Lucas, and M. Velikova. A new probabilistic constraint logic programming language based on a generalised distribution semantics. *Artificial Intelligence*, 228:1–44, 2015. doi:10.1016/j.artint.2015.06.008.

S. Michels, A. Hommersom, and P. J. F. Lucas. Approximate probabilistic inference with bounded error for hybrid probabilistic logic programming. In S. Kambhampati, editor, *25th International Joint Conference on Artificial Intelligence (IJCAI 2016)*, pages 3616–3622. AAAI Press/IJCAI, 2016.

B. Milch, L. S. Zettlemoyer, K. Kersting, M. Haimes, and L. P. Kaelbling. Lifted probabilistic inference with counting formulas. In D. Fox and C. P. Gomes, editors, *23rd AAAI Conference on Artificial Intelligence (AAAI 2008)*, pages 1062–1068. AAAI Press, 2008.

T. M. Mitchell. *Machine learning*. McGraw Hill series in computer science. McGraw-Hill, 1997. ISBN 978-0-07-042807-2.

P. Morettin, A. Passerini, and R. Sebastiani. Efficient weighted model integration via SMT-based predicate abstraction. In C. Sierra, editor, *26th International Joint Conference on Artificial Intelligence (IJCAI 2017)*, pages 720–728. IJCAI, 2017. doi:10.24963/ijcai.2017/100.

P. Morettin, P. Zuidberg Dos Martires, S. Kolb, and A. Passerini. Hybrid probabilistic inference with logical and algebraic constraints: a survey. In Z. Zhou, editor, *30th International Joint Conference on Artificial Intelligence (IJCAI 2021)*, pages 4533–4542. IJCAI, 2021. doi:10.24963/ijcai.2021/617.

S. Muggleton. Inverse entailment and Progol. *New Generation Computing*, 13:245–286, 1995.

S. Muggleton. Learning stochastic logic programs. *Electronic Transaction on Artificial Intelligence*, 4(B):141–153, 2000a.

S. Muggleton. Learning stochastic logic programs. In L. Getoor and D. Jensen, editors, *Learning Statistical Models from Relational Data, Papers from the 2000 AAAI Workshop*, volume WS-00-06 of *AAAI Workshops*, pages 36–41. AAAI Press, 2000b.

S. Muggleton. Learning structure and parameters of stochastic logic programs. In S. Matwin and C. Sammut, editors, *12th International Conference on Inductive Logic Programming (ILP 2002)*, volume 2583 of *LNCS*, pages 198–206. Springer, 2003. doi:10.1007/3-540-36468-4_13.

S. Muggleton, J. C. A. Santos, and A. Tamaddoni-Nezhad. Toplog: ILP using a logic program declarative bias. In M. G. de la Banda and E. Pontelli, editors, *24th International Conference on Logic Programming (ICLP 2008)*, volume 5366 of *LNCS*, pages 687–692. Springer, 2008. doi:10.1007/978-3-540-89982-2_58.

S. Muggleton et al. Stochastic logic programs. *Advances in inductive logic programming*, 32:254–264, 1996.

C. J. Muise, S. A. McIlraith, J. C. Beck, and E. I. Hsu. Dsharp: Fast d-DNNF compilation with sharpSAT. In L. Kosseim and D. Inkpen, editors, *25th Canadian Conference on Artificial Intelligence, Canadian AI 2012*, volume 7310 of *LNCS*, pages 356–361. Springer, 2012. doi:10.1007/978-3-642-30353-1_36.

K. P. Murphy. *Machine learning: a probabilistic perspective*. The MIT Press, 2012.

A. Nampally and C. Ramakrishnan. Adaptive MCMC-based inference in probabilistic logic programs. *arXiv preprint arXiv:1403.6036*, 2014.

S. Natarajan, T. Khot, K. Kersting, B. Gutmann, and J. Shavlik. Gradient-based boosting for statistical relational learning: The relational dependency network case. *Machine Learning*, 86(1):25–56, 2012.

R. T. Ng and V. S. Subrahmanian. Probabilistic logic programming. *Information and Computation*, 101(2):150–201, 1992.

A. Nguembang Fadja and F. Riguzzi. Probabilistic logic programming in action. In A. Holzinger, R. Goebel, M. Ferri, and V. Palade, editors, *Towards Integrative Machine Learning and Knowledge Extraction*, volume 10344 of *LNCS*, pages 89–116. Springer, 2017. doi:10.1007/978-3-319-69775-8_5.

A. Nguembang Fadja and F. Riguzzi. Lifted discriminative learning of probabilistic logic programs. *Machine Learning*, 108(7):1111–1135, 2019. doi:10.1007/s10994-018-5750-0.

A. Nguembang Fadja, E. Lamma, and F. Riguzzi. Deep probabilistic logic programming. In C. Theil Have and R. Zese, editors, *4th International Workshop on Probabilistic Logic Programming (PLP 2017)*, volume 1916 of *CEUR-WS*, pages 3–14. Sun SITE Central Europe, 2017.

A. Nguembang Fadja, F. Riguzzi, and E. Lamma. Learning hierarchical probabilistic logic programs. *Machine Learning*, 110(7):1637–1693, 2021. doi:10.1007/s10994-021-06016-4.

P. Nicolas, L. Garcia, I. Stéphan, and C. Lefèvre. Possibilistic uncertainty handling for answer set programming. *Annals of Mathematics and Artificial Intelligence*, 47(1-2):139–181, 2006.

J. C. Nieves, M. Osorio, and U. Cortés. Semantics for possibilistic disjunctive programs. In *9th International Conference on Logic Programming and Non-monotonic Reasoning (LPNMR 2007)*, volume 4483 of *LNCS*, pages 315–320. Springer, 2007.

N. J. Nilsson. Probabilistic logic. *Artificial Intelligence*, 28(1):71–87, 1986.

M. Nishino, A. Yamamoto, and M. Nagata. A sparse parameter learning method for probabilistic logic programs. In *Statistical Relational Artificial Intelligence, Papers from the 2014 AAAI Workshop*, volume WS-14-13 of *AAAI Workshops*. AAAI Press, 2014.

D. Nitti, T. De Laet, and L. De Raedt. Probabilistic logic programming for hybrid relational domains. *Machine Learning*, 103(3):407–449, 2016. ISSN 1573-0565. doi:10.1007/s10994-016-5558-8.

J. Nivre. Logic programming tools for probabilistic part-of-speech tagging. Master thesis, School of Mathematics and Systems Engineering, Växjö University, October 2000.

J. Nocedal. Updating Quasi-Newton matrices with limited storage. *Mathematics of Computation*, 35(151):773–782, 1980.

M. Osorio and J. C. Nieves. Possibilistic well-founded semantics. In *8th Mexican International International Conference on Artificial Intelligence (MICAI 2009)*, volume 5845 of *LNCS*, pages 15–26. Springer, 2009.

A. Paes, K. Revoredo, G. Zaverucha, and V. S. Costa. Probabilistic first-order theory revision from examples. In S. Kramer and B. Pfahringer, editors, *15th International Conference on Inductive Logic Programming (ILP 2005)*, volume 3625 of *LNCS*, pages 295–311. Springer, 2005. doi:10.1007/11536314_18.

A. Paes, K. Revoredo, G. Zaverucha, and V. S. Costa. PFORTE: revising probabilistic FOL theories. In J. S. Sichman, H. Coelho, and S. O. Rezende, editors, *2nd International Joint Conference, 10th Ibero-American Conference on AI, 18th Brazilian AI Symposium, IBERAMIA-SBIA 2006*, volume 4140 of *LNCS*, pages 441–450. Springer, 2006. doi:10.1007/11874850_48.

L. Page, S. Brin, R. Motwani, and T. Winograd. The PageRank citation ranking: Bringing order to the web. Technical report, Stanford InfoLab, 1999.

C. Papadimitriou and K. Steiglitz. *Combinatorial Optimization: Algorithms and Complexity*. Dover Books on Computer Science. Dover Publications, 1998. ISBN 9780486402581.

J. Pearl. *Probabilistic Reasoning in Intelligent Systems: Networks of Plausible Inference*. Morgan Kaufmann, 1988.

Y. Perov, B. Paige, and F. Wood. The Indian GPA problem, 2017. https://bitbucket.org/probprog/anglican-examples/src/master/worksheets/indian-gpa.clj, accessed June 1, 2018.

A. Pfeffer. *Practical Probabilistic Programming*. Manning Publications, 2016. ISBN 9781617292330.

G. D. Plotkin. A note on inductive generalization. In *Machine Intelligence*, volume 5, pages 153–163. Edinburgh University Press, 1970.

D. Poole. Probabilistic Horn abduction and Bayesian networks. *Artificial Intelligence*, 64(1):81–129, 1993a.

D. Poole. Logic programming, abduction and probability - a top-down anytime algorithm for estimating prior and posterior probabilities. *New Generation Computing*, 11(3):377–400, 1993b.

D. Poole. The Independent Choice Logic for modelling multiple agents under uncertainty. *Artificial Intelligence*, 94:7–56, 1997.

D. Poole. Abducing through negation as failure: Stable models within the independent choice logic. *Journal of Logic Programming*, 44(1–3):5–35, 2000. doi:10.1016/S0743-1066(99)00071-0.

D. Poole. First-order probabilistic inference. In G. Gottlob and T. Walsh, editors, *IJCAI-03, Proceedings of the Eighteenth International Joint*

Conference on Artificial Intelligence, Acapulco, Mexico, August 9-15, 2003, pages 985–991. Morgan Kaufmann Publishers, 2003.

D. Poole. The independent choice logic and beyond. In L. De Raedt, P. Frasconi, K. Kersting, and S. Muggleton, editors, *Probabilistic Inductive Logic Programming*, volume 4911 of *LNCS*, pages 222–243. Springer, 2008.

T. C. Przymusinski. Perfect model semantics. In R. A. Kowalski and K. A. Bowen, editors, *5th International Conference and Symposium on Logic Programming (ICLP/SLP 1988)*, pages 1081–1096. MIT Press, 1988.

T. C. Przymusinski. Every logic program has a natural stratification and an iterated least fixed point model. In *Proceedings of the 8th ACM SIGACT-SIGMOD-SIGART Symposium on Principles of Database Systems (PODS-1989)*, pages 11–21. ACM Press, 1989.

J. R. Quinlan. Learning logical definitions from relations. *Machine Learning*, 5:239–266, 1990. doi:10.1007/BF00117105.

L. R. Rabiner. A tutorial on hidden Markov models and selected applications in speech recognition. *Proceedings of the IEEE*, 77(2):257–286, 1989.

L. D. Raedt, A. Dries, I. Thon, G. V. den Broeck, and M. Verbeke. Inducing probabilistic relational rules from probabilistic examples. In Q. Yang and M. Wooldridge, editors, *24th International Joint Conference on Artificial Intelligence (IJCAI 2015)*, pages 1835–1843. AAAI Press, 2015.

I. Razgon. On OBDDs for CNFs of bounded treewidth. In C. Baral, G. D. Giacomo, and T. Eiter, editors, *14th International Conference on Principles of Knowledge Representation and Reasoning (KR 2014)*. AAAI Press, 2014.

J. Renkens, G. Van den Broeck, and S. Nijssen. k-optimal: a novel approximate inference algorithm for ProbLog. *Machine Learning*, 89(3):215–231, 2012. doi:10.1007/s10994-012-5304-9.

J. Renkens, A. Kimmig, G. Van den Broeck, and L. De Raedt. Explanation-based approximate weighted model counting for probabilistic logics. In *Proceedings of the Twenty-Eighth AAAI Conference on Artificial Intelligence, July 27 -31, 2014, Québec City, Québec, Canada*, pages 2490–2496. AAAI Press, 2014.

K. Revoredo and G. Zaverucha. Revision of first-order Bayesian classifiers. In S. Matwin and C. Sammut, editors, *12th International Conference on Inductive Logic Programming (ILP 2002)*, volume 2583 of *LNCS*, pages 223–237. Springer, 2002. doi:10.1007/3-540-36468-4_15.

F. Riguzzi. Learning logic programs with annotated disjunctions. In A. Srinivasan and R. King, editors, *14th International Conference on Inductive*

Logic Programming (ILP 2004), volume 3194 of *LNCS*, pages 270–287. Springer, Sept. 2004. doi:10.1007/978-3-540-30109-7_21.

F. Riguzzi. A top down interpreter for LPAD and CP-logic. In *10th Congress of the Italian Association for Artificial Intelligence, (AI*IA 2007)*, volume 4733 of *LNAI*, pages 109–120. Springer, 2007a. doi:10.1007/978-3-540-74782-6_11.

F. Riguzzi. ALLPAD: Approximate learning of logic programs with annotated disjunctions. In S. Muggleton and R. Otero, editors, *16th International Conference on Inductive Logic Programming (ILP 2006)*, volume 4455 of *LNAI*, pages 43–45. Springer, 2007b. doi:10.1007/978-3-540-73847-3_11.

F. Riguzzi. Inference with logic programs with annotated disjunctions under the well founded semantics. In *24th International Conference on Logic Programming (ICLP 2008)*, volume 5366 of *LNCS*, pages 667–771. Springer, 2008a. doi:10.1007/978-3-540-89982-2_54.

F. Riguzzi. ALLPAD: Approximate learning of logic programs with annotated disjunctions. *Machine Learning*, 70(2-3):207–223, 2008b. doi:10.1007/s10994-007-5032-8.

F. Riguzzi. Extended semantics and inference for the independent choice logic. *Logic Journal of the IGPL*, 17(6):589–629, 2009. doi:10.1093/jigpal/jzp025.

F. Riguzzi. SLGAD resolution for inference on logic programs with annotated disjunctions. *Fundamenta Informaticae*, 102(3-4):429–466, Oct. 2010. doi:10.3233/FI-2010-392.

F. Riguzzi. MCINTYRE: A Monte Carlo system for probabilistic logic programming. *Fundamenta Informaticae*, 124(4):521–541, 2013. doi:10.3233/FI-2013-847.

F. Riguzzi. Speeding up inference for probabilistic logic programs. *The Computer Journal*, 57(3):347–363, 2014. doi:10.1093/comjnl/bxt096.

F. Riguzzi. The distribution semantics for normal programs with function symbols. *International Journal of Approximate Reasoning*, 77:1–19, 2016. doi:10.1016/j.ijar.2016.05.005.

F. Riguzzi and N. Di Mauro. Applying the information bottleneck to statistical relational learning. *Machine Learning*, 86(1):89–114, 2012. doi:10.1007/s10994-011-5247-6.

F. Riguzzi and T. Swift. Tabling and answer subsumption for reasoning on logic programs with annotated disjunctions. In *Technical Communications of the 26th International Conference on Logic Programming (ICLP 2010)*, volume 7 of *LIPIcs*, pages 162–171. Schloss Dagstuhl - Leibniz-Zentrum fuer Informatik, 2010. doi:10.4230/LIPIcs.ICLP.2010.162.

F. Riguzzi and T. Swift. The PITA system: Tabling and answer subsumption for reasoning under uncertainty. *Theory and Practice of Logic Programming*, 11(4–5):433–449, 2011. doi:10.1017/S147106841100010X.

F. Riguzzi and T. Swift. Well-definedness and efficient inference for probabilistic logic programming under the distribution semantics. *Theory and Practice of Logic Programming*, 13(2):279–302, 2013. doi:10.1017/S1471068411000664.

F. Riguzzi and T. Swift. Terminating evaluation of logic programs with finite three-valued models. *ACM Transactions on Computational Logic*, 15(4): 32:1–32:38, 2014. ISSN 1529-3785. doi:10.1145/2629337.

F. Riguzzi and T. Swift. Probabilistic logic programming under the distribution semantics. In M. Kifer and Y. A. Liu, editors, *Declarative Logic Programming: Theory, Systems, and Applications*. Association for Computing Machinery and Morgan & Claypool, 2018.

F. Riguzzi, E. Bellodi, and R. Zese. A history of probabilistic inductive logic programming. *Frontiers in Robotics and AI*, 1(6), 2014. ISSN 2296-9144. doi:10.3389/frobt.2014.00006.

F. Riguzzi, E. Bellodi, E. Lamma, R. Zese, and G. Cota. Probabilistic logic programming on the web. *Software: Practice and Experience*, 46(10): 1381–1396, 10 2016a. doi:10.1002/spe.2386.

F. Riguzzi, E. Bellodi, R. Zese, G. Cota, and E. Lamma. Scaling structure learning of probabilistic logic programs by MapReduce. In M. Fox and G. Kaminka, editors, *22nd European Conference on Artificial Intelligence (ECAI 2016)*, volume 285 of *Frontiers in Artificial Intelligence and Applications*, pages 1602–1603. IOS Press, 2016b. doi:10.3233/978-1-61499-672-9-1602.

F. Riguzzi, E. Bellodi, R. Zese, G. Cota, and E. Lamma. A survey of lifted inference approaches for probabilistic logic programming under the distribution semantics. *International Journal of Approximate Reasoning*, 80: 313–333, 1 2017a. doi:10.1016/j.ijar.2016.10.002.

F. Riguzzi, E. Lamma, M. Alberti, E. Bellodi, R. Zese, and G. Cota. Probabilistic logic programming for natural language processing. In F. Chesani, P. Mello, and M. Milano, editors, *Workshop on Deep Understanding and Reasoning, URANIA 2016*, volume 1802 of *CEUR Workshop Proceedings*, pages 30–37. Sun SITE Central Europe, 2017b.

J. A. Robinson. A machine-oriented logic based on the resolution principle. *Journal of the ACM*, 12(1):23–41, 1965. doi:10.1145/321250.321253.

B. Russell. Mathematical logic as based on the theory of types. In J. van Heikenoort, editor, *From Frege to Godel*, pages 150–182. Harvard Univ. Press, 1967.

T. P. Ryan. *Modern Engineering Statistics*. John Wiley & Sons, 2007.

V. Santos Costa, R. Rocha, and L. Damas. The YAP Prolog system. *Theory and Practice of Logic Programming*, 12(1-2):5–34, 2012.

T. Sato. A statistical learning method for logic programs with distribution semantics. In L. Sterling, editor, *Logic Programming, Proceedings of the Twelfth International Conference on Logic Programming, Tokyo, Japan, June 13-16, 1995*, pages 715–729. MIT Press, 1995.

T. Sato and Y. Kameya. PRISM: a language for symbolic-statistical modeling. In *15th International Joint Conference on Artificial Intelligence (IJCAI 1997)*, volume 97, pages 1330–1339, 1997.

T. Sato and Y. Kameya. Parameter learning of logic programs for symbolic-statistical modeling. *Journal of Artificial Intelligence Research*, 15:391–454, 2001.

T. Sato and Y. Kameya. New advances in logic-based probabilistic modeling by PRISM. In L. De Raedt, P. Frasconi, K. Kersting, and S. Muggleton, editors, *Probabilistic Inductive Logic Programming - Theory and Applications*, volume 4911 of *LNCS*, pages 118–155. Springer, 2008. doi:10.1007/978-3-540-78652-8_5.

T. Sato and K. Kubota. Viterbi training in PRISM. *Theory and Practice of Logic Programming*, 15(02):147–168, 2015.

T. Sato and P. Meyer. Tabling for infinite probability computation. In A. Dovier and V. S. Costa, editors, *Technical Communications of the 28th International Conference on Logic Programming (ICLP 2012)*, volume 17 of *LIPIcs*, pages 348–358. Schloss Dagstuhl - Leibniz-Zentrum fuer Informatik, 2012.

T. Sato and P. Meyer. Infinite probability computation by cyclic explanation graphs. *Theory and Practice of Logic Programming*, 14:909–937, 11 2014. ISSN 1475-3081. doi:10.1017/S1471068413000562.

T. Sato, Y. Kameya, and K. Kurihara. Variational Bayes via propositionalized probability computation in PRISM. *Annals of Mathematics and Artificial Intelligence*, 54(1-3):135–158, 2008.

T. Sato, N.-F. Zhou, Y. Kameya, Y. Izumi, K. Kubota, and R. Kojima. PRISM User's Manual (Version 2.3), 2017. http://rjida.meijo-u.ac.jp/prism/download/prism23.pdf, accessed June 8, 2018.

O. Schulte and H. Khosravi. Learning graphical models for relational data via lattice search. *Machine Learning*, 88(3):331–368, 2012.

O. Schulte and K. Routley. Aggregating predictions vs. aggregating features for relational classification. In *IEEE Symposium on Computational Intelligence and Data Mining (CIDM 2014)*, pages 121–128. IEEE, 2014.

G. Schwarz. Estimating the dimension of a model. *The Annals of Statistics*, 6 (2):461–464, 1978.

R. Schwitter. Learning effect axioms via probabilistic logic programming. In R. Rocha, T. C. Son, C. Mears, and N. Saeedloei, editors, *Technical Communications of the 33rd International Conference on Logic Programming (ICLP 2017)*, volume 58 of *OASICS*, pages 8:1–8:15. Schloss Dagstuhl - Leibniz-Zentrum fuer Informatik, 2018. doi:10.4230/OASIcs.ICLP.2017.8.

P. Sevon, L. Eronen, P. Hintsanen, K. Kulovesi, and H. Toivonen. Link discovery in graphs derived from biological databases. In *International Workshop on Data Integration in the Life Sciences*, volume 4075 of *LNCS*, pages 35–49. Springer, 2006.

G. Shafer. *A Mathematical Theory of Evidence*. Princeton University Press, 1976.

D. S. Shterionov, J. Renkens, J. Vlasselaer, A. Kimmig, W. Meert, and G. Janssens. The most probable explanation for probabilistic logic programs with annotated disjunctions. In J. Davis and J. Ramon, editors, *24th International Conference on Inductive Logic Programming (ILP 2014)*, volume 9046 of *LNCS*, pages 139–153, Berlin, Heidelberg, 2015. Springer. doi:10.1007/978-3-319-23708-4_10.

P. Singla and P. Domingos. Discriminative training of Markov logic networks. In *20th National Conference on Artificial Intelligence (AAAI 2005)*, pages 868–873. AAAI Press/The MIT Press, 2005.

F. Somenzi. Efficient manipulation of decision diagrams. *International Journal on Software Tools for Technology Transfer*, 3(2):171–181, 2001. doi:10.1007/s100090100042. URL https://doi.org/10.1007/s100090100042.

F. Somenzi. *CUDD: CU Decision Diagram Package Release 3.0.0*. University of Colorado, 2015. URL http://vlsi.colorado.edu/~fabio/CUDD/cudd.pdf.

A. Srinivasan. The aleph manual, 2007. http://www.cs.ox.ac.uk/activities/machlearn/Aleph/aleph.html, accessed April 3, 2018.

A. Srinivasan, S. Muggleton, M. J. E. Sternberg, and R. D. King. Theories for mutagenicity: A study in first-order and feature-based induction. *Artificial Intelligence*, 85(1-2):277–299, 1996.

A. Srinivasan, R. D. King, S. Muggleton, and M. J. E. Sternberg. Carcinogenesis predictions using ILP. In N. Lavrac and S. Džeroski, editors, *7th International Workshop on Inductive Logic Programming*, volume 1297 of *LNCS*, pages 273–287. Springer Berlin Heidelberg, 1997.

S. Srivastava. *A Course on Borel Sets*. Graduate Texts in Mathematics. Springer, 2013.

L. Steen and J. Seebach. *Counterexamples in Topology*. Dover Books on Mathematics. Dover Publications, 2013.

L. Sterling and E. Shapiro. *The Art of Prolog: Advanced Programming Techniques*. Logic programming. MIT Press, 1994. ISBN 9780262193382.

C. Stolle, A. Karwath, and L. De Raedt. *Cassic'cl*: An integrated ILP system. In A. Hoffmann, H. Motoda, and T. Scheffer, editors, *8th International Conference on Discovery Science (DS 2005)*, volume 3735 of *LNCS*, pages 354–362. Springer, 2005.

T. Swift and D. S. Warren. XSB: Extending prolog with tabled logic programming. *Theory and Practice of Logic Programming*, 12(1-2):157–187, 2012. doi:10.1017/S1471068411000500.

T. Syrjänen and I. Niemelä. The Smodels system. In T. Eiter, W. Faber, and M. Truszczynski, editors, *6th International Conference on Logic Programming and Non-Monotonic Reasoning (LPNMR 2001)*, volume 2173 of *LNCS*. Springer, 2001. doi:10.1007/3-540-45402-0_38.

N. Taghipour, D. Fierens, J. Davis, and H. Blockeel. Lifted variable elimination: Decoupling the operators from the constraint language. *Journal of Artificial Intelligence Research*, 47:393–439, 2013.

A. Tarski. A lattice-theoretical fixpoint theorem and its applications. *Pacific Journal of Mathematics*, 5(2):285–309, 1955.

Y. W. Teh. Dirichlet process. In *Encyclopedia of machine learning*, pages 280–287. Springer, 2011.

A. Thayse, M. Davio, and J. P. Deschamps. Optimization of multivalued decision algorithms. In *8th International Symposium on Multiple-Valued Logic*, pages 171–178. IEEE Computer Society Press, 1978.

I. Thon, N. Landwehr, and L. D. Raedt. A simple model for sequences of relational state descriptions. In *European conference on Machine Learning and Knowledge Discovery in Databases*, volume 5212 of *LNCS*, pages 506–521. Springer, 2008. ISBN 978-3-540-87480-5.

D. Tran, A. Kucukelbir, A. B. Dieng, M. Rudolph, D. Liang, and D. M. Blei. Edward: A library for probabilistic modeling, inference, and criticism. *arXiv preprint arXiv:1610.09787*, 2016.

C. Turliuc, L. Dickens, A. Russo, and K. Broda. Probabilistic abductive logic programming using Dirichlet priors. *International Journal of Approximate Reasoning*, 78:223–240, 2016. doi:10.1016/j.ijar.2016.07.001.

G. Van den Broeck. On the completeness of first-order knowledge compilation for lifted probabilistic inference. In J. Shawe-Taylor, R. S. Zemel, P. L. Bartlett, F. C. N. Pereira, and K. Q. Weinberger, editors, *Advances in Neural Information Processing Systems 24 (NIPS 2011)*, pages 1386–1394, 2011.

G. Van den Broeck. *Lifted Inference and Learning in Statistical Relational Models*. PhD thesis, Ph. D. Dissertation, KU Leuven, 2013.

G. Van den Broeck, I. Thon, M. van Otterlo, and L. De Raedt. DTProbLog: A decision-theoretic probabilistic Prolog. In M. Fox and D. Poole, editors, *Proceedings of the Twenty-Fourth AAAI Conference on Artificial Intelligence*, pages 1217–1222. AAAI Press, 2010.

G. Van den Broeck, N. Taghipour, W. Meert, J. Davis, and L. De Raedt. Lifted probabilistic inference by first-order knowledge compilation. In T. Walsh, editor, *22nd International Joint Conference on Artificial Intelligence (IJCAI 2011)*, pages 2178–2185. IJCAI/AAAI, 2011.

G. Van den Broeck, W. Meert, and A. Darwiche. Skolemization for weighted first-order model counting. In C. Baral, G. D. Giacomo, and T. Eiter, editors, *14th International Conference on Principles of Knowledge Representation and Reasoning (KR 2014)*, pages 111–120. AAAI Press, 2014.

A. Van Gelder, K. A. Ross, and J. S. Schlipf. The well-founded semantics for general logic programs. *Journal of the ACM*, 38(3):620–650, 1991.

J. Vennekens and S. Verbaeten. Logic programs with annotated disjunctions. Technical Report CW386, KU Leuven, 2003.

J. Vennekens, S. Verbaeten, and M. Bruynooghe. Logic programs with annotated disjunctions. In B. Demoen and V. Lifschitz, editors, *20th International Conference on Logic Programming (ICLP 2004)*, volume 3131 of *LNCS*, pages 431–445. Springer, 2004. doi:10.1007/978-3-540-27775-0_30.

J. Vennekens, M. Denecker, and M. Bruynooghe. CP-logic: A language of causal probabilistic events and its relation to logic programming. *Theory and Practice of Logic Programming*, 9(3):245–308, 2009. doi:10.1017/S1471068409003767.

J. Vlasselaer, J. Renkens, G. Van den Broeck, and L. De Raedt. Compiling probabilistic logic programs into sentential decision diagrams. In *1st*

International Workshop on Probabilistic Logic Programming (PLP 2014), pages 1–10, 2014.

J. Vlasselaer, G. Van den Broeck, A. Kimmig, W. Meert, and L. De Raedt. Anytime inference in probabilistic logic programs with Tp-compilation. In *24th International Joint Conference on Artificial Intelligence (IJCAI 2015)*, pages 1852–1858, 2015.

J. Vlasselaer, G. Van den Broeck, A. Kimmig, W. Meert, and L. De Raedt. Tp-compilation for inference in probabilistic logic programs. *International Journal of Approximate Reasoning*, 78:15–32, 2016. doi:10.1016/j.ijar.2016.06.009.

J. Von Neumann. Various techniques used in connection with random digits. *Nattional Bureau of Standard (U.S.), Applied Mathematics Series*, 12:36–38, 1951.

W. Y. Wang, K. Mazaitis, and W. W. Cohen. Structure learning via parameter learning. In J. Li, X. S. Wang, M. N. Garofalakis, I. Soboroff, T. Suel, and M. Wang, editors, *23rd ACM International Conference on Conference on Information and Knowledge Management, CIKM 2014*, pages 1199–1208. ACM Press, 2014. doi:10.1145/2661829.2662022.

W. Y. Wang, K. Mazaitis, N. Lao, and W. W. Cohen. Efficient inference and learning in a large knowledge base. *Machine Learning*, 100(1):101–126, Jul 2015. doi:10.1007/s10994-015-5488-x.

M. P. Wellman, J. S. Breese, and R. P. Goldman. From knowledge bases to decision models. *The Knowledge Engineering Review*, 7(1):35–53, 1992.

J. Wielemaker, T. Schrijvers, M. Triska, and T. Lager. SWI-Prolog. *Theory and Practice of Logic Programming*, 12(1-2):67–96, 2012. doi:10.1017/S1471068411000494.

J. Wielemaker, T. Lager, and F. Riguzzi. SWISH: SWI-Prolog for sharing. In S. Ellmauthaler and C. Schulz, editors, *International Workshop on User-Oriented Logic Programming (IULP 2015)*, 2015.

J. Wielemaker, F. Riguzzi, B. Kowalski, T. Lager, F. Sadri, and M. Calejo. Using SWISH to realise interactive web based tutorials for logic based languages. *Theory and Practice of Logic Programming*, 19(2):229–261, 2019. doi:10.1017/S1471068418000522.

S. Willard. *General Topology*. Addison-Wesley series in mathematics. Dover Publications, 1970.

F. Wood, J. W. van de Meent, and V. Mansinghka. A new approach to probabilistic programming inference. In *17th International conference on Artificial Intelligence and Statistics (AISTAT 2014)*, pages 1024–1032, 2014.

N. L. Zhang and D. Poole. A simple approach to bayesian network computations. In *10th Canadian Conference on Artificial Intelligence, Canadian AI 1994*, pages 171–178, 1994.

N. L. Zhang and D. L. Poole. Exploiting causal independence in Bayesian network inference. *Journal of Artificial Intelligence Research*, 5:301–328, 1996.

P. Zuidberg Dos Martires, A. Dries, and L. De Raedt. Knowledge compilation with continuous random variables and its application in hybrid probabilistic logic programming. In *8th International Workshop on Statistical Relational AI, (StarAI 2018)*, 2018.

P. Zuidberg Dos Martires, A. Dries, and L. De Raedt. Exact and approximate weighted model integration with probability density functions using knowledge compilation. In *Proceedings of the Thirty-Third AAAI Conference on Artificial Intelligence (AAAI-19)*, pages 7825–7833. AAAI Press, 2019. doi:10.1609/aaai.v33i01.33017825.

Wielemaker2019general

Index

About the Author

Fabrizio Riguzzi is Full Professor of Computer Science at the Department of Mathematics and Computer Science of the University of Ferrara. He was previously Associate Professor and Assistant Professor at the same university. He got his Master and PhD in Computer Engineering from the University of Bologna. Fabrizio Riguzzi is Editor in Chief of Intelligenza Artificiale, the official journal of the Italian Association for Artificial Intelligence. He is the author of more than 200 peer reviewed papers in the areas of Machine Learning, Inductive Logic Programming and Statistical Relational Learning. His aim is to develop intelligent systems by combining in novel ways techniques from artificial intelligence, logic and statistics.